A NATURAL HISTORY
OF
NETTLES

Frontispiece. Nettle variety which has remained constant for five years. At the beginning of the year the foliage is green but later with spring growth this colour variant develops.

i

Dedication
To my father George and my mother Daisy

For their interest in my natural history pursuits, for letting me go out very late at night catching moths, for letting me keep tadpoles and frogs in the copper, for letting me keep tortoiseshell caterpillars on nettles in my bedroom, however, they drew the line at allowing me to keep goat moth larvae in the house!

'It is good to have some worthy object before you, as a prevalent pursuit and purpose in life; particularly while you are young. It gives steadiness and determination to the character; makes every morrow a point of interest and hope'.

Philip Henry Gosse (1810-1888) writing to his son Edmund

A
NATURAL HISTORY
OF
NETTLES

KEITH G R WHEELER

Order this book online at www.trafford.com
or email orders@trafford.com

Most Trafford titles are also available at major online book retailers.

Print information available on the last page.

ISBN: 978-1-4120-2694-9 (sc)
ISBN: 978-1-4669-8102-7 (e)

Trafford rev. 04/10/2019

 www.trafford.com

North America & international
toll-free: 1 888 232 4444 (USA & Canada)
fax: 812 355 4082

CONTENTS

CHAPTER 1 - INTRODUCTION (1-19)

How are nettles recognised? - Boyhood memories of stinging nettles - Contrasting views on the stinging nettle - 1 The nettle subclass Hamamelidae - Nettle relations – A lesson in pollination - The classification of the subclass Hamamelidae - Floral structure in the Urticales - 3 The nettle order Urticales - Memories of the British elm and plant studies - 3 Nettle family Urticaceae - The British species belonging to the Urticaceae - When is a "nettle" a nettle? -The unique exploding stamens - The beautiful inflictor of pain - Insects.www.co.nettles - A follower of man and his animals - Prehistory of the nettle (*Urtica dioica*) - Nettles as indicators of past human settlements - Nettle medicine, food and fodder - Nettle ecology.

CHAPTER 2 - IT NEEDS SOME DESCRIPTION (20-26)

Nettle clump or clone - The structure/morphology of the vegetative parts of the nettle - The shoot - The underground parts of a nettle clone - The reproductive parts of the nettle shoot - Brief note on anatomy.

CHAPTER 3 - OTHER BRITISH NETTLES (27-41)

Distinguishing features of the British nettles - The roman nettle (*Urtica pilulifera*) - The names - The structure and reproduction - Dodart's nettle – Historical - European distribution - Recent history of the Roman nettle in Britain - As an unsuccessful colonist of Britain - For Roman use as a herbal plant - The Elizabethian pleasure gardens, Herbalists and their connection with the roman nettle - The small nettle (*Urtica urens*) - Introduction – Names – Distribution - Structure and reproduction – Habitats - as a weed and a ruderal – Germination - Insects associated with the small nettle - Ecology of the small nettle - The survival of Urtica urens on a coastal headland - Variation and genetics - Herbal medicinal and other uses.

CHAPTER 4 – FOLKLORE AND LITERATURE (42-55)

Common names - Place names - Legends and fairy stories stings, saying and chants - Oak apple day - Literature throughout history.

CHAPTER 5 – A PURIFIER OF THE BLOOD AND A PANACEA (56-65)

Introduction - Past and present uses- As a medicinal plant - Antibacterial and antifungal properties - Blood diseases - Alimentary dear Watson - Problems related to the kidneys - Chesty problems – Rheumatism - The male disease - Benign prostatic hyperplasia - Tumours and - Neoplastic diseases – Miscellaneous - Other diseases - Milk and deer - As an anti-venom - Bees and frogs - Chicks and capons - Purifier of the blood - Dosage and use.

CHAPTER 6 – THE TALE IN THE STING 1 – THE MARVELLOUS MICRO-PIPETTE (66-79)

The structure and mechanism of the stinging trichome – Introduction - Hooke, Leeuwenhoek and stinging hairs of the common nettle - The structure of stinging trichomes - Introduction - The development and structure of the stinging trichome - Structure - A much closer look - The origin of the toxin secretion - Stinging hairs of other genera of the Urticeae - The mechanism of the nettle sting – Historical - Active of passive injection - Gently grasp or boldly grasp? - Old stinging hairs.

CHAPTER 7 – THE TALE IN THE STING 2 – STINGING SYMPTOMS AND POISONOUS PRINCIPLES (80-97)

Stinging symptoms - Tropical and temperate tormentors - New Zealand - Timor and Java – India - Australian nettle trees - Australian stinging tree symptoms - Symptoms of the gympie nettle bush - Subjective effects - Objective reactions – Antidotes – Alleviation - Temperate tormentors - The identity of the toxic substances - Acid or alkali? - Pharmacological bio-assay techniques – Introduction - Formic acid - Emmelin and Feldburg - Acetylcholine – Histamine - Serotonin - The triple response - Physiological effects of stinging substances on animals – Leucotrienes - Evolutionary implications - Nettle tree toxins.

CHAPTER 8 – THE TALE IN THE STING 3 – HERBIVORE INTERACTIONS AND OTHER FAMILIES OF STINGING PLANTS (98-113)

Introduction - Functions of trichomes - Vertebrate   herbivores - The stinging plants of the Urticaceae - Do stinging hairs of U.dioica deter larger herbivores? – Rabbits – Sheep - Field experiments - More grazing studies - Long term grazing pressure - Effect of simulated herbivore damage on stinging trichome density - Effect of cutting and nutrient level on stinging trichome density - Other groups of stinging plants - Stinging plants of the Euphorbiaceae – Introduction - The bull nettle and herbivores - Stinging trichomes of *Cnidoscolus* - Development and structure - Chemical constituents - The unique stinging plants of the Euphorbiaceae. – Introduction - Stinging symptoms of *Cnidoscolus urens* – Structure. - The mechanism of the sting - Evolutionary relationships - Stinging trichomes of the Loasaceae – Introduction – Historical - The stinging Loasaceae - – Plant collectors in the Andes - The stinging plants of the Hydrophyllaceae. - The Hydrophyllaceae - Historical - Structure of the stinging trichome of *Wigandia caracasana* - Do stinging trichomes deter invertebrate herbivores? - Urticaceae and insects - The 'evil woman': the ultimate defensive plant - Insects herbivores choose the stinging plant *Wigandia urens* - Molluscs – gastropods- -Slugs, snails and stinging trichomes.

CHAPTER 9 – FOOD, FODDER, FAMINE AND WAR (114-127)

Historical - As a pot herb and famine food - On the continent - As a food - Little, often and essential - Vitamin E - Scurvy, the seaman's scourge - Vitamin A - Minerals matters - Bones and teeth - Calcium, phosphorus and magnesium - Blood vascular - Nuts over nettles - Recipes for food dishes - Sources of nettles – Junkets – Fodder – Roughage - Chemistry of *Urtica* species.

CHAPTER 10 – AS A FIBRE PLANT IN PEACE AND WAR (128-149)

Introduction - Introduction to fibre extraction in nettles – Historical - Structure of the stem and fibre extraction in nettle - 16th and 17th century Scotland - 16th and 17th century in Europe and Russia - 18th century England - Nettles and the first world war 1914-1918 - German prelude - Extraction of fibre from the nettle during the first world war - Fibre properties and spinning - No such thing as waste - Fibre uses - Suitable areas for nettle cultivation - Danish experiments on nettle fibre.- Nettle fibre studies in Germany leading up to the World War 11 - Cultivation of the nettle as a fibre plant - Other uses - The Second World War (1939-1945) - On the German front - On the British home front - For food - Paper making - Returning to natural fibre crops in Europe.

CHAPTER 11 – PARASITES AND SAPROPHYTES – NETTLE DODDER, NETTLE RUST AND MICRO-FUNGI (150-169)

Parasitic flowering plants- -Dodders: Cuscutaceae - The greater dodder (*Cuscuta europaea*) - Distribution – Habitat - The host plant - General ecology - Life cycle - flowers and pollination - Seeds and seed dispersal - Germination and establishment - Field studies on *Cuscuta europaea* - The nettle and sedge rust (*Puccinia carcina*) – Micro-fungi found on the dead stems of *Urtica dioica* - Nettle lectins and genetic-engineering - *Urtica dioica* agglutinin and its role in nettle defense.

CHAPTER 12 – INSECTS ON NETTLES 1 - BUTTERFLIES AND MOTHS (LEPIDOPTERA)
(170-189)

Butterflies - Introduction - The stinging nettle and insects - British butterflies and nettles - The life-cycles and food preferences of British vanessids - The small tortoiseshell (*Aglais urticae*) - Life cycle - Egg layiing - Larval stage – Pupation - Peacock (*Inachis io*) - The red admiral (*Vanessa atlanta*) – Comma - (*Polygonia c-album*) - Painted lady (*Cynthia cardui*) - European map (*Arashnia levana*) - Vanessid butterflies and farming practices - Tidiness - The butterfly/wildlife garden area - Moths - The autumnal nettle tap (*Anthophilia fabriciana*) -. Birds and nettles - Cuckoos and caterpillars.

CHAPTER 13 – INSECTS ON NETTLES 2 – FLIES, BUGS AND BEETLES
(190-205)

Flies, bugs and beetles – Introduction - Flies (Diptera) - Plant galls (cecidia) - Cecidomyiidae (gall midges) - The nettle gall midge (*Dasineura urticae*) - Leaf miners (Agromyzidae) - Other flies - Beetles (Coleoptera) – Flower beetles (Nitidulidae) - Weevils (Curculionidae) - Other beetles - Bugs (Hemiptera) - Heteroptera (bugs) - Homoptera (frog and leaf hoppers, plant lice, aphids and psyllids) - Nettles and crop pests.

CHAPTER 14 – IS THE COMMON NETTLE UBIQUITOUS? (206-215)

Worldwide and altitudinal distribution – habitats - Herbals and local floras - Throughout the British isles - On farms - Biological flora of the British Isles - Flora of Wiltshire - European plant communities which include Urtica dioica - Natural communities - Broad-leaved woodlands- Flood plains - Sub- alpine – Man-made habitats - Autecological accounts of the commoner British plant species.

CHAPTER 15 – THE COMPETITOR PLANT (216-241)

The growth requirements of the common nettle - Nutritional requirements - Is the nettle a nitrophyte/nitrophile? - Nettle water and strawberries - Mineral requirements - Phosphate indicator - Light requirements - Growth of nettles in pastures and woodlands - Moisture/water requirements - Asexual reproduction - Regulation of clonal density - Density-dependent shoot self-thinning - Mosaics and their effect on self-thinning - Age of nettle clones - Re-growth - Resource allocation strategy - Responses to herbivory - Modification by competition and fertilization - Seedling strategy - Seed characteristics - Germination and establishment in woodland and pastureland clones - Field germination of Urtica dioica in relation to temperature and light - Seed banks - The common nettle as a competitor plant - Relative growth rate - The relationship between litter, standing crop and competitive/dominance in plants - Mosses and nettle litter - Floristic diversity of stinging nettle stands - Competition between Urtica dioica and other dominant competitors such as Himalayan balsam (*Impatiens glandulifera*) - The growth strategies of the common nettle - Is the nettle increasing in abundance? - Circumstantial evidence - Inorganic fertilizers: nitrogen and phosphorus – Soil disturbance by mankind – Roadsides - Evidence for the increase in abundance of Urtica dioica in Wiltshire over the last 50 years – Woodlands - Commonest and rarity in the British flora.

CHAPTER 16 – NETTLE SEX LIFE (242-253)

Introduction - Phenology - The male flowers - The explosive/catapult mechanism for pollen liberation in the flowers of the nettles and other members of the Urticaceae. – Historical - Pollen - Pollen structure - Nettle pollinosis - Female inflorescence and flowers - Adaptation of *Urtica dioica* and the Urticales to wind-pollination. Sexual types - Monoecious clones - Hermaphrodite/bisexual clones - Factors affecting the reproductive effort in *Urtica dioica* - Seed production, dispersal and spread - Explosive fruit dispersal in the Urticaceae .

CHAPTER 17 – NETTLE BREEDING SYSTEMS, VARIATION AND EVOLUTION (254-269)

Introduction - Breeding systems in the Urticales/Urticaceae - Dioecy in the Urticales and other plants – Distribution – Origin - Advantages and disadvantages of dioecy. - Dioecy in relation to tropical forest trees - Sex determination in plants and in the Urticales - Secondary sexual characteristics in *Urtica dioica* – Vegetative sexual differences - Gender ratios in *Urtica dioica* - Ecotypes/physiological races/genecological differentiation - Do different ecotypes of *Urtica dioica* exist in relation to woodland and pastureland habitats? – The 'stingless' ecotype of Wicken fen - Variation in *Urtica dioica* - European varieties - The fen or stingless nettle, *Urtica dioica var. galeopsifolia,* - Plant freaks/teratology – Pathogenic – Stipules - Stem spiraling/torsion - Stem fasciation - Three-leaved and variable-leaved shoots - Terminal injury variants.

APPENDIX (270-287)

CHAPTER 18 – BRITISH NETTLEWORTS: – PELLITORY-OF-THE-WALL (*PARIETARIA JUDAICA* L.) MIND-YOUR-OWN-BUSINESS (*SOLEIROLIA SOLEIROLII*)

British nettleworts – Introduction - Pellitory-of-the-wall (*Parietaria judaica* l.) – Introduction -General Morphology - Reproduction and life cycle - Plant relationships - Animal relationships - Variation, classification and genetics - Herbal medicinal properties - Pellitory and pollinosis - Mind-your-own-business (*Soleirolia soleirolii* ([rew] dandy}) - Introduction - Distribution - General morphology - Reproduction and life cycle - Variation, classification and genetics - As a garden plant.

NETTLE TREES AND HOUSE PLANTS

BIBLIOGRAPHY/AUTHOR PAGE INDEX (288-297)

SUBJECT INDEX (298-304)

Nettle Place Names, such as Nettlecombe in Somerset, England. (Chapter 4 Folklore).

PREFACE

The idea of the book was conceived during my middle-age crisis in the mid-1970. Natural history had always been my passion, I was a biology teacher and I had a degree in Botany. What to do? Suddenly my mind came up with a study on the common stinging nettle. It fitted in perfectly with my interest in butterflies, moths, insects, fungi, photography and microscopy. The first thing I looked at was a stinging hair and then I was hooked. Next I got the Science Advisor to look at a stinging hair under the microscope and he got hooked getting me a one year secondment (1975-76) to do an M. Sc. thesis (title: 'Are there nettle ecotypes in relation to woodland and pastureland habitats?') at Exeter University under the ecologist Dr M. C. F. Proctor. With a further two years' field work my examiner from Leeds University, Dr J. P Grime, recommended me for a Ph. D. (1982).

I was surprised at the amount of previous research that had been carried out on the common nettle, over one hundred major papers, with a large proportion by French and German authors. The annual total of papers involving the common nettle today is approximately eighty. The first British study of the autecology of Urtica dioica was that of Grieg-Smith (1948) in the series of 'Biological Floras of the British Isles' under the wing of the 'Journal of Ecology'. These autecological studies were continued by the National Environment Research Council's Unit of Comparative Plant Ecology during its 25 years of its existence and involved a survey of plants within an area of 3000km² in Sheffield area and the results were finally published as 'Comparative Plant Ecology: A functional approach to common British species' Grime J. P. et al (1988). Despite the accumulating amount of information on British plants, there have only been a few monographs published: one on 'Lords and Ladies' (Arum maculatum) by Cecil T. Prime in the New Naturalist's Series, one scientific study on 'The British Oak' from a number of specialists and edited by Morris M.G., and F. H. Perring, and two studies on the elm of a more general nature, 'Elm' by R. H. Richens and the 'Epitaph for the Elm' by Wilkinson G. which was a beautifully produced book.

I have tried to produce a book for naturalists, scientists and a lot of general studies on the nettle (folklore, literature, herbal use, as a food and fiber plant during wars and famine, as well as the structure of the stinging hair and its effects upon the body and herbivore animals) which together with a large number of photographs and illustrations would appeal to many of the general public. The aim is to consider the nettle as a plant and consider it in relation to the plants and animals that rely on it from the point of view of their interactions with the nettle. In a broader context the study includes other nettles from the nettle family (Urticaceae) such as the nettle trees in Australia, as well as, the 36 nettle trees distributed in Continental Asia through to western Malesia, to as far as Moluccas. I have also included nettles that belong to completely different families (Euphorbiaceae [spurge family], Loasaceae and Hydrophyllaceae), many with attractive flowers but with stinging hairs remarkably like those of the common nettle.

The nettle clump/clone is like a miniature forest and contains small denizens which are often bizarre and I hope my book enables the reader to enter this world to appreciate what goes on in this micro-ecosystem. The photographs have been taken mainly with an Olympus OM4 Ti together with macro-lenses and twin-macro flash. The microscope was a Gillett and Sibert Conference Projection Microscope. Line drawings were made on tracing paper from photographs or projected images and then tinted with water colors. Latterly scanners and Photoshop have made all this much easier! I have thoroughly enjoyed my retirement since 1994, discovering the parasitic flowering plant the greater dodder that lives principally on the nettle, the joy of seeing for myself the complete courtship of the small tortoiseshell butterfly and actually seeing them *walking* into the nettle patch, the unique explosion of the stamens of nettle flowers, the beauty of the stinging hair and the anatomy of the nettle, the world of parasitoids and the incredible beauty of the jewelled parasitic wasps, the transformations of our vanessid butterflies, the nettle's amazing under-ground rhizome system resulting in its power of re-growth, and much more.

It has been mainly a personal crusade but I would like to thank nettle characters such as: Jack Oliver for his work on the distribution of nettles in Wiltshire with his band of junior botanists, Martin Crag-Barber for his information on colour varieties of the nettle, Ewa Prokop for her enthusiastic study of the possible control of big N (=nettles) problem in the Little Wittenham Nature Reserve, Cambridgeshire, Harry Gilbertson for his help regarding the extraction of nettle fiber (using his new machine for decortication of nettle stems) now that the stinging nettle is a crop plant in the European Fiber Crop Project. My thanks to Kew Gardens for supplying me with nettle references, translations, seeds and material from tropical nettle groups, Oxford Botanic Gardens for seeds of the varieties of the Roman nettle, to the Natural History Museum for the use of the Botany library and examination of the British nettle material, to mention a few. Thanks also to Mr. J. Pollock who actually enjoyed translating the German articles I selected from the mass of German papers (I do think that there is an much more interesting story of the

Montfort University and to Caroline Holmes of the Central Science Laboratory for their help with writing up the IENICA nettle project. Thanks to my wife Jill for putting up with being a nettle widow and for reading the manuscript and covering it with little kisses correcting my numerous mistakes.

I have enjoyed grasping the nettle and finally getting the fascinating information on this much misunderstood plant together for the first time in book form. It has given up some of its secrets to me but I hope this book will encourage my readers to do some further research on this fascinating but much maligned plant. The fact that a lot of poems and literature has been written about

The first frost on a nettle leaf. Notice that the ice crystals form on the hairs covering the leaf. The largest hairs are the stinging hairs and these appear as white lines on the upper surface of the leaf, the small white dots are the non-stinging hairs.

use of nettles in the first and Second World Wars but I could not do it because it has to be written by a German person interested in nettles who can research the German War Archives!). Thanks to Professor Ray Harwood and his wife Jane of De

the nettle shows that it makes a human impression, **but touch it and it stings!!!**

CHAPTER 1

INTRODUCTION TO NETTLES

HOW ARE NETTLES RECOGNISED?

This question was put to a class of students and they all answered 'by their stings'. Nicholas Culpeper, in his herbal, The English Physician (1652) says that nettles *are so well known that they need no description at all, they may be found by the feeling in the darkest night*. Culpeper's statement reflects his sense of humor whilst implying that nettles are recognized by their sting. However if the pain of getting stung is the only way the brain recognizes a nettle then it would not prevent a person getting stung again! Sight and smell association will also be stored in the brain. Few students remembered nettle details such as shape of leaves, leaf margin, flowers, fruits, etc, but recalled the clump growth and habitat. The brain records the visual gist of the nettle and future accidental stinging will add to and re-enforce this information (Fig 1.1).

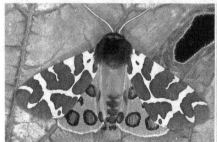

Fig 1.1 A photogram of the Roman nettle (Urtica pilulifera) with male and female inflorescences.

People are familiar with nettles through their stings but it is equally true that they know very little about these plants, either their morphology, or their ecological relationships with other plants and animals. The author has grasped the nettle and this book will enable readers to enter nettle patches and examine these fascinating plants and their often bizarre denizens, without getting stung!

BOYHOOD MEMORIES OF STINGING NETTLES

My boyhood was spent in North London during and after the 2nd World War. I had three friends and this was our gang. We were fond of a wild area bordering a stream called Pymmes Brook and this was where we built our camps. There were large clumps of nettles in the grassland away from the bank and nettles were also found along the pathways. We wore short trousers but we never complained about nettle stings and the nettle patch was regarded with respect, a place to show our bravado. If you didn't walk through the nettle patch you were a sissy. We used to apply a dock leaf after being stung but because we were 'townies' we didn't know about nettle chants. I must admit on occasions we took delight in using sticks to raze the nettles to the ground, only to find they grew back rapidly and rewarded us with even more virulent stings.

I was mad on natural history and one aspect of this was collecting butterflies and moths. At certain times of the year small moths used to fly out when we disturbed nettles. Using Hugh Newman's books from the library I identified these as the small magpie by its black, white and yellow colouration, and the mother of pearl, so named because of the rainbow effect when the wings were viewed at the correct angle (Fig 1.2). One day I laid flat on the edge of a nettle clump, parted the outer stems and looked in. The nettle stems looked like a miniature forest. It was then that I noticed the woolly-bear

Fig 1.2 The garden tiger moth

The woolly bear caterpillar

The small magpie moth

caterpillars. I raised these to produce the beautiful garden tiger moth with its great variation in wing pattern. I didn't know about the stinging nature of the shed hairs of these caterpillars until I rubbed some into my face which itched like mad. My face swelled up, was hot and inflamed, my eyes closed and watered (urticaria). This was ten times worse than the nettle stings. I was still made to go to school, but the garden tiger was worth it.

I found the webs of the gregarious small tortoiseshell caterpillars and raised them in roughly-made muslin cages in my bedroom. In replenishing the nettles I never wore gloves. The butterflies hatched out and flew around the bedroom ejecting large globules of blood (I later found out it was the excretory product called meconium) all over the curtains, etc. Mother was none too pleased! I searched the nettles but never did find the caterpillars of the peacock, red admiral or the comma.

I saved up my money to buy an antique brass microscope, my pride and joy, but never did look at nettles to find out about what caused the sting!

Later I went to university and read botany, which included plant anatomy; we never did look at the marvellous stinging hairs of the nettle! I remained ignorant of the beauty of the nettle and its microcosmic world until for some unknown reason in middle age, the crisis, I decided to write a monograph on the stinging nettle. My life gained purpose and I have not been disappointed!

CONTRASTING VIEWS ON THE STINGING NETTLE

Nettles you either love them or hate them. Try to ignore them and they sting you. Despised by most, these tormentors, command respect for their presence. The literature reflects these views.

A majority of authors, and many of the British public, hold the nettle in low regard mainly because of its stinging and weed properties, so terms such as ugly, vile, foul, obnoxious, and spiteful, a nuisance, etc., are common place. J. J. Rousseau (1794) in his 'Letters on the elements of Botany' addressed to a young lady, has expressed such a typical view and it is kept in the old English where $f = s$:-

His comments are understandable at a time when the wealthy gentry had established gardens, containing beautiful floral blooms from all over the world.

> "The ftinging nettles are to be found in the order Tetrandria of this clafs; but fuch vulgar ill-humoured plants may forgive your paffing them by, where you have fo many interefting and even great perfonages to attract your notice."
>
> ## J. T. ROUSSEAU 1794

The most prejudiced, virulent and condemning article I have come across was written by a highly regarded author and good naturalist **Grant Watson** in his book 'Walking with Fancy' (1943). The article is entitled 'Burdocks and Nettles' and the author gives a superb account of the burdock's leaves, unfurling like long tongues, but has little to say in favour of the nettle.

I cannot do justice to his article but just give my interpretation:-

Nettles are recognised particularly in the spring by their strong odour and this smell is one of the ways we recall them in the future. People can hardly like the appearance of this plant. Nettles seem to say, don't touch us, we suck up the richest nutrients from the soils where we grow, and we indicate the soil is very fertile, but you will have to share it with us. Unsuspecting humans have pulled back after their poisoned attacks; often young loving couples seeking a short cut have been surrounded and have had to go back as a result of these malignant plants. People find them irritating and frustrating and their dark-green to black leaves and tall growth give them a sinister appearance. Their smell, poisonous properties and clump like habit is threatening. They cover the soil like a suffocating blanket and their matted roots stifle out other harmless plants.

Nettles are ubiquitous and invasive, a threat to our horticulture. Their human equivalents are those that suppress and frustrate the ambitions of others.

I suspect that Grant Watson never bothered to take a close look at a nettle patch or its inhabitants and therefore missed the hidden beauty of this plant and the fact that many of our most beautiful butterflies are dependent on it.

All the people I have met who have studied nettles at close hand, speak enthusiastically about them, they get hooked or are nuts on nettles! This comes across in the articles they write, such as that of Lady Wilkinson (1858).

> *"The least ornamental objects are certainly not always the most useless nor the least interesting; an observation which especially applies to the nettle. Growing in waste and neglected places, boasting no beauty to attract the eye, no pleasant fragrance to delight the sense, shunned and neglected on account of its painful sting; it is yet when more closely considered not only a plant of the greatest utility but one which most amply repays microscopical examination by the unsurpassed beauty of its structure, while it acquires additional interest from the circumstance of its belonging to one of the noblest and most highly prized families of the vegetable kingdom."*
> **LADY WILKINSON 1858**

More recently, one of the best accounts of its uses, association with man and other animals is found in an article, 'The Fascinating World of the Stinging Nettle', in the small book 'Field and Moor' by **John Burton** (1976).

A Finnish wife of a friend of Burton's recounts that after the long cold and dark Finnish winter, without any fresh vegetables they developed a craving for greens. Once the snow had melted the tender young nettle shoots appeared and were gathered for a tonic because it was well known on the European Continent that nettles are rich in minerals and vitamins. The nettle tops were either made into a nettle soup or mixed with poached eggs.

Nowadays in Britain nettles tend to be a gimmick or considered good fun to consume at various annual dinners such as the Halloween feast of zoologist's at Oxford University in the early 1950's. Burton eat nettles on one such occasion but admits he was too incapacitated with dandelion wine and woodlouse sauce to care what he consumed.

He draws attention to the large number of insects that feed on nettles and concentrates on the various forms of camouflage, warning colours and patterns, warning scents as well as the role of stinging hairs of nettles in affording protection for their hosts. These insects are predated on and parasitised by other insects and birds in their turn feed on these thus the food passes up the food chain.

ᚦHE ᚦTINᚷING ᚦETTLE.

BOX 1.1 (If we cannot get through to the younger generation about how fascinating some of our common plants are, then we are failing. The Victorian books produced by the Religious Tract Society did inspire many children of this era. A good example is the 'Children's Flowers (S. L. Dyson, 1909). I include this piece, as a typical example of a plant description by a religious author from the creationist viewpoint, glorifying the nettle as a work of god. It shows the Victorian approach for young children). *My comments are in brackets and un-shaded.*

"UGLY and ill-nature weed! Is that what you call it? Why is it ugly? Is it because it has no beautiful blushing face, like Queen Rose; or because it has no sweet scent, like the violet; or is it because its dress is so coarse and rough looking?

Why is it ill-natured? Is it because it will not let you touch it without covering your hands with little white tingling spots. Or is it because it grows and spreads so fast, that you think it must be one of those 'ill weeds' that 'grow apace?"

(Although by present day standards the text is sentimental and attributes all to the hand of God it is the approach that I like! Throughout the author asks the child to question its prejudices, whilst at the same time wearing gloves to examine the nettle at close range. After all if you don't look you will never see!)

"Are you quite sure it is ugly? Perhaps you have never taken any trouble to find out its beauty."

(In relation to flowers) "But where are the flowers? There is no coloured face peeping out anywhere, all is dark green from top to bottom, But do you see hanging all round the top of the stem, and some distance from one another, rings of long slender green tails? Why, the tops of those stems are like the heads of those little girl's who wear long curls." (This might seem rather quaint, but is a good example of Victorian literature of the time, produced by the Religious Tract Society and designed to stimulate the curiosity of the child in looking at the wonders of God. After getting the child to look at the minute flowers of the male and female plants and pollination it continues). "Now that you have looked at the nettle all over, surely you will not call it 'ugly weed' any more." (Finally after having considered the uses of the nettle the author ends thus):-

"So that you may breakfast off Nettles; you may have them both to eat and drink at dinner; you may have your clothes dyed by them; you may feed your pigs and your hens with them; and you may have medicine from them when you are sick.

Surely a plant that does so much good cannot be called 'ill-natured.'

When you passed by those Nettles, and called them 'ugly and ill-natured,' you did not know what wonderful plants they were. No! little child, God makes everything with some kind of beauty, of some kind of use; so, whenever you see people whom you do not like very much, sit down and try to find out something good about them, as you have done about the Nettle."

Other balanced views include:-

In the 'Outline of Nature in the British Isles', edited by **Sir John Hammerton** in mid-1930's, there is an article 'A Handful of Nettles'. The frontispiece makes it clear that the only reason the stinging nettle was included in this series on our wild flowers is because it deals mainly with the more handsome 'dead nettles'. The article makes it clear that sooner or later most people become acquainted with it through its stings and therefore is known by everybody in the British Isles. Most people think of it as an unpleasant plant better done without. However it concludes that to the naturalist the plant is full of interest and should be looked at in more detail. The books contain articles on the stinging hair and butterflies which depend upon it.

Jean Palaiseul in his book 'Grandmother's Secrets' (1972) says the nettle does not deserve its bad reputation just because it stings, adding that the sting contains formic acid which causes the urticaria and that this should not prevent people from using it for its virtues as a medicinal plant. He compares

this to not eating sea urchins because they are covered in spines.

NETTLE RELATIONS – A LESSON IN POLLINATION

When I taught my students about insect pollination we looked at the structure of the buttercup flower (see the equivalent structure of the Quince) and then worked out the function of the various parts of the flower in relation to insects. This was followed by considering the rewards for the insects, nectar (for honey) and pollen (for a protein source) both for the adults and grubs. Insects were attracted to flower because of their certain colours, scents, patterns, shapes, available landing platforms,

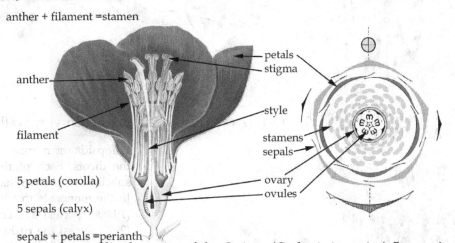

anther + filament =stamen
anther
filament
5 petals (corolla)
5 sepals (calyx)
sepals + petals =perianth
petals
stigma
style
stamens
sepals
ovary
ovules

Fig 1.4 Longitudinal section of the Quince (Cydonia japonica) flower & its floral diagram (Church 1909).

etc. all of which resulted in the insects inadvertently picking up the large sculptured pollen grains on their hairs and taking them to the next flower for cross pollination (Fig 1.4) and (Proctor, et. al. 1973, 1996).

However, when it came to wind-pollination not surprisingly the average student knew very little!

My usual lead into wind-pollination was the question, 'What do the flower of nettles, grasses and trees look like?' The majority of pupils replied that they had never seen flowers on these plants (see Fig 1.5). To make the lesson more dramatic I would produce from under the front bench, two jars containing nettles in flower. I pointed to the flowers but they still said 'They don't look like flowers'. We worked out that was because they were small, had no bright colours and didn't produce nectar, they would not attract insects, and that the only other agent that could carry the pollen was the wind. They noticed a difference in colour between the catkin-like flower masses of stinging nettle shoots in the two jars. They were astounded when told them that nettle clumps (clones) are either male or female so in this respect they are like humans -'vive la difference' (Figs 1.6 and 1.7).

THE NETTLE SUB-CLASS HAMAMELIDAE

There are two classes of plants, (1) class

Examples of wind-pollinated flowers

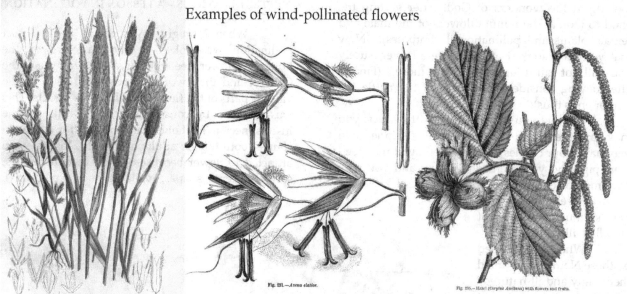

Fig 1.5. Grasses in flower
Anne Pratt (1905)

Oats (Avena elatier) and hazel (Corylus avellana) from Kerner (1895)

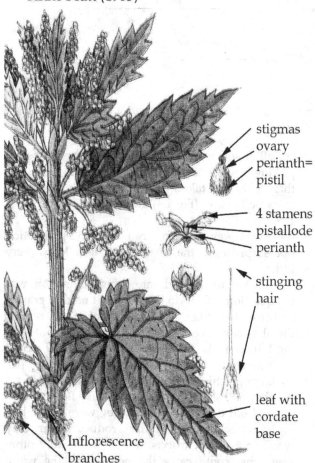

stigmas
ovary
perianth=
pistil

4 stamens
pistallode
perianth

stinging
hair

leaf with
cordate
base

Inflorescence
branches

Fig 1.6. The male nettle (U. dioica) and its flowers, a female flower is also shown (Horwood 1919)

Liliopsida the monocots, and (2) the Magnoliopsida, the dicots. Each of these classes contains a large subclass of predominantly wind-pollinated plants. In the monocots this is the subclass Commelinidae (19,000 species) that contains the families, Juncacae (297 species) the rushes, Cyperaceae (4,000 species) the sedges and the Poaceae (8,000 species) the grasses. In the dicots this is the subclass Hamamelidae. (In the past the nettles were placed in the group 'Amentiferae', meaning catkin –bearers. The 'Amentiferae' was an artificial group of diverse origin and Cronquist (1981, 1988), after having removed some unrelated order such as the Salicaceae, converted it into the subclass Hamamelidae). The flowers of this group are small, often unisexual and the perianth is reduced to mainly a single whorl of from 5-2 tepals, or absent altogether. The flowers, beautiful when magnified, are borne on catkins, or an amazing variety of often very beautiful inflorescences (Fig 1.6-7).

The Hamamelidae (Box: 1.2) contains about 3,400 species distributed between 11 orders and 24 families. Most orders are woody plants and the tree form predominates, with the exception of the nettle order the Urticales, members of which are rarely trees and more usually soft herbaceous plants. The Hamamelidae (excluding those of the Urticales that are dealt with next) contains many familiar trees of temperate areas, known for their beauty and the economic importance of their timber, for example, *Plantanaceae*, (sycamores), *Juglandaceae*, (walnuts,

6

Male inflorescence of Urtica dioica with flowers

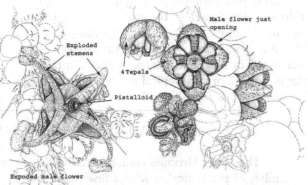

Male flowers of U. dioica in different stages of flowering

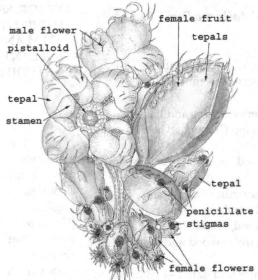

Fig 1.7. Urtica urens inflorescence with male and female flowers

Female inflorescence of U. dioica full flowering

hickories, pecans), *Fagaceae*, (oaks, chestnuts, beeches), *Betulaceae*, (alders, birches).

2 THE NETTLE ORDER URTICALES

The five main families of the Nettle order Urticales contain 2,200-2,300 species. Berg (1977, 1989) reviews the characteristics of the Urticales and

Box 1.2	THE CLASSIFICATION OF THE SUBCLASS HAMAMELIDAE	(based on Conquist, 1981, 1988)
Orders Families,	together with a few examples of familiar genera	
Trochodendrales	Tetracentraceae, Trochodendraceae	
Hamamelidales	Cercidiphyllaceae, Eupteleaceae, Plantanaceae (Sycamores), Hamamelidaceae, Myrothamnaceae	
Daphniphyllales	Daphniphyllaceae	
Didymelales	Didymelaceae	
Eucommiales	Eucommiaceae	
Urticales details)	*Barbeyaceae, Ulmaceae, Cannabaceae, Moraceae, Cecropiaceae, Urticaceae (see Box 1.3 for more*	
Leitneriales	Leitneriaceae	
Juglandales	Rhoipteleaceae, Juglandaceae (Walnut, Hickory, Pecan)	
Myricales	Myricaceae	
Fagales	Balanopaceae, Fagaceae (Oak, Chestnut, Beech), Betulaceae (Alders, Birches)	
Casuarinales	Casuarinaceae	

the natural relationships/phylogeny between and within the five families. The distribution, growth habit and the more commercially important genera, with the exception of the Urticaceae, are summarised in Box: 1.3. A large proportion of the order is tropical or sub-tropical and includes plants of great economic importance but there is no space

Parietaria judaica (pellitory-of-the-wall). Most flowers in the Urticales are unisexual (with or without vestigial pistils [pistillodes] or vestigial stamens [staminodes]). The perianth is reduced from five/four or two tepals. The pistil/carpel is formed from two carpels but one is suppressed so only one ovule is found in the ovary. There may one or two stigmas.

Box: 1.3 THE NETTLE ORDER URTICALES

The Order Urticales contains 2,200-2,300 different species (Berg 1977, 1989). The 5 families of the Urticales, with a few examples of the familiar and the commercially more important genera are shown.

(1) *Urticaceae. The nettles and nettleworts. (For more details see Box 1.4).*

(2) *Ulmaceae*. 15 genera. Widespread. Trees and shrubs.
The Elms (*Ulmus*), timber, Hackberries (*Celtis*), fruit, forage, fibre, and timber, *Zelkova*, timber, *Trema*, timber and fibre, *Holoptelea*, timber, and *Aphananthe* – timber.

(3) *Cannabaceae*. 2 genera. Temp. Eurasia to S. E. Asia, N. America. Herbs and lianes.
Hemp (*Cannabis*), Hemp fibre and pot/hashish/marijuana. Hop (*Humulus*), beer.

(4) *Moraceae*. 37 genera. Tropical and warm temperate and occasionally temperate climates. Trees, shrubs and lianes.
Antiaris, poison arrows, *Artocarpus*, Breadfruit and Jackfruit, *Brosimum*, Snake wood/Breadnut, *Broussonetia*, Paper Mulberry, *Ficus*, India rubber, Figs and Banyan tree, *Castilloa*, Panama rubber *Morus*, Fruit and silkworm food, *Pseudolmedia*, Barstard breadnut. Timbers from *Maclura*, osage orange, *Chlorophora*, iroko-wood and fustic.

(5) *Cecropiaceae*. 6 genera - Widespread in tropics - Trees, shrubs and lianes -
Cecropia - Wood and floats and association with ants.

---

to deal with them in this book.

FLORAL STRUCTURE IN THE URTICALES

Berg (1989) when considering the classification of the Urticales concentrated on the reproductive structures and aspects of pollination, floral protection and fruit dispersal. Many groups of the Urticales occur in tropical lowland vegetation such as rainforests and this has affected their structure, and distinguishes these from other wind-pollinated groups associated with temperate-subtropical conditions.

The primitive type of flower in this order is bisexual and this is found in the Ulmaceae, and rarely in the Urticaceae e.g.

MEMORIES OF THE BRITISH ELM AND PLANT STUDIES

I recount memories of one tree from the Urticales, the English elm (*Ulmus procera*), to show that the absence of attractive flowers, is made up for in other ways. The elm was a dominant feature in the British landscape until its demise in the 1970's due to the Dutch elm disease. These trees towered over 100 feet in height and were scattered as standards in hedgerows, enhancing the landscape. We took them for granted and it was amazing how, particularly in flat areas, the landscape became featureless after their demise. During boyhood my friend had an elm in his back garden, which we delighted in climbing to find the horned, lime-green caterpillars, of the lime hawk moth. Very early in the year the elms bore their clusters of pink flowers high up on their bare branches (Fig 1.8). Elms were abundant near farms and churches in small villages, where rooks built their communal nests and around which they squawked, cawed and circled. In the autumn the elm leaves turned a beautiful yellow and added their colour to the other autumn colours of the British countryside. I have carved many objects out of elm wood, freely available after their demise, and the beauty of these carvings arises from the intricate wavy pattern of the grain. I also broke both of my thigh bones whilst cutting down a large elm and this was in part due to the habit of the elm in suddenly dropping its great branches, which are often held almost at right angles to the main trunk.

Two studies (monographs) of the elm have been written (Wilkinson, 1978, Richens, 1983). These recount its history, the grandeur of the tree and its beauty as depicted in many paintings, its part in British life reflected in poems and folklore, herbal properties and the use of its timber, the elm as a plant, its wildlife and its place in the ecosystem.

With the advent of the study of ecology at the beginning of the 20th century, the study of plant communities (synecology) was the main plant study. Later in this century the study of plants had turned to the study of individual plants (autoecology). In England, the Natural Environmental Research Council's Unit of Comparative Plant Ecology (NERC) was set up in 1962. Two extensive vegetative studies have been brought together and published in a book 'Comparative Plant Ecology' (Grime, Hodgson and Hunt 1988) which is an 'Autecological Account of the common British species'. These accounts supplement or add to the autecological accounts, so far published as the 'Biological Flora of the British Isles' in the Journal of Ecology. Wilkinson's beautifully presented and illustrated book on the elm, backs up the approach of Grime and his workers, but more importantly makes some of these studies more attractive to the general public. This is shown again in the scientific monograph on the British Oak, the dominant tree of the ancient and original wildwood (Morris, Perrin, 1974). This book includes the physiology of the oak, the macro-fungi, fungal pathogens, insect life and galls, importance of the oak to birds and mammals,

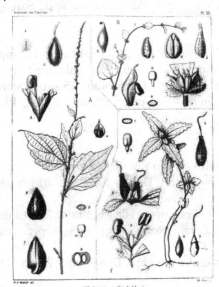

Fig 1.9.
Plate 20 of Weddell's 'Monographie des Urticees'

Fig 1.8 The elm (Ulmus campestris) from Kerner 1895.

thereby considering the ecology of the oak and its place in the ecosystem. It is these books and studies that have stimulated me to write my book on nettles, the backbone of which is the autecology of the common stinging nettle (*Urtica dioca* L).

3 NETTLE FAMILY URTICACEAE

Plant collections were amassed in the 18th and 19th centuries, as a result of the numerous voyages around the world and these were stored in museums. The French accumulated a large number of specimens of members of the nettle family. The first classification of the Urticaceae was that of the French botanist Gaudichaud (1830), this was followed up by his compatriot H. A. Weddell, who produced the classical monograph on the Urticaceae (1856-57). In a recent review of the Urticaceae the Danish botanist Friis (1989) concludes that Weddell's classification of the Urticaceae remains largely unchallenged (Fig 1.9). Friis's synopsis is outlined below and shows the five sub-families or tribes and the 48 genera, which contain approximately 900 species. The **five** tribes, genera and number of species are shown in (Box: 1.4). Descriptions and drawing of the Urticaceae can be found in journals, and floras from all parts of the world. Relevant to this work is 'The Biology of the Temperate Urticaceae', (Woodland, 1989), in which he points out there has been no complete contempory monograph of the Urticaceae. There has certainly been no monograph on the genus *Urtica*, which is surprising considering its abundance in Europe.

The majority of species of the Nettle Family (Urticaceae) are widely distributed in tropical and sub-tropical regions where they are associated with

9

the under-storey vegetation of forest habitats, or with forest margins. The largest number of genera and species are in tropical Asia. Fewer species occur

rarely small trees or vines

The members of the Urticaceae that occur in

Box 1.4   **THE URTICACEAE (NETTLE FAMILY)**

The five sub-families or tribes and the 48 genera contain approximately 900 species. (The shaded areas are the genera considered in this book).

1. Tribe Elatostemeae Pellonia - 50 spp., Meniscogyne - 2 spp.. Elatostema - 200 spp., Procris - 20 spp., Pilea - 250 spp., Achudemia - 1-3 spp., Aboriella - 1 spp., Sarcopilea - 1 spp., Lecanthus - 1 spp., Petelotiella - 1 spp.

2 Tribe Boehmerieae Boehmeria - 50 spp., Chamabainia - 1-2 spp., Pouzolzia - 50 spp., Hyrtanandra 5 spp., Neodistemon - 1 spp., Cypholophos - 15 spp., Sarcochlamys 1 spp., Touchardia - 1-2 spp., Neraudia - 5 spp., Pipturus - 20 spp., Nothocnide - 4 spp., Oreocnide - 15 spp., Debregeasia -4 spp., Archiboehmeria - 1 sp., Astrothalamus - 1 spp., Leucosyke - 35 spp., Gibbsia - 2 spp., Phenax - 12 spp., Maoutia - 15 spp., Myriocarpa - 18 spp.

3. Tribe Parietarieae.
Gesnouinia - 2 spp., Hemistylus - 4 spp Rousselia - 2 spp.
Parietaria - 20 spp.Subcosmopolitan. This includes the British pellitory-of-the-wall (*Parietaria judaica* L).

Soleirolia - 1 spp.,West Mediterranean Islands, Italy. In Britain this includes the garden escape, mind-your-own-business (*Soleirolia soleirolii [Req] Dandy*). (see Appendix 265-283.

4. Tribe Forsskaoleae Forsskaolea - 6 spp., Droguetia - 7 spp., Didymodoxa - 2 spp., Australina - 2 spp.

5. Tribe Urticeae (Urereae)
Urtica L.-45 spp. Subcosmopolitan, with most species in the northern temperate region. Annual or perennial herbs, sometimes shrubby at the base. This genus includes the 3 British nettles the small nettle (*Urtica urens* L), the common stinging nettle (*Urtica dioica* L) and the Roman nettle (*Urtica pilulifera* L) introduced and now probably extinct. .
Hesperocnide Torr. & Gray - 2 spp. California, Hawaii Islands. Annual herbs.
Nanocnide Blume - 2 spp. East Asia. Prostrate to creeping herbs.
Obetia Gaud. (Revision: Friis:1983). - 7 spp. Tropical and S. Africa, Madagascar, Mascarenes. Trees and shrubs.
Laportea Gaud. - 21 spp. Africa, Madagascar, E. Asia, E. North America. Most annual herbs, some perennial shrubs.
Discocnide Chew.(Revision Chew. 1969) - 1 spp. Mexico and Guatamala. Shrubs or small trees.
Girardinia Gaud (Revision Friis: 1981). - 2 spp Africa, tropical and E. Asia. Tall, short-living herbaceous plants.
Dendrocnide Miq. (Revision: Chew 1969) - 36 spp. Indomalayan region, W. Pacific Islands. Perennial, evergreen, soft-wooded trees.
Urera Gaud. - 35 spp. Tropical Africa, Madagascar, tropical America, Hawaii. Climbing shrubs, or small trees.
Gyrotaenia Griseb. - 4 spp. West Indies. Shrubs, or trees.

---

in temperate regions; however, this is compensated for by the fact that they are common and widespread. Nettles of the genus Urtica are found in the temperate areas of the Northern Hemisphere and in the more temperate climates in certain areas of the Southern Hemisphere. Most members of the family are herbs or small shrubs; more

Britain are: -
Tribe Urticeae. The nettles:-
Small nettle (*Urtica urens L.*), common stinging nettle (*Urtica dioica L.*) and the Roman nettle (*Urtica pilulifera L.*) which is probably extinct.
Tribe Parietarieae. The nettleworts:-

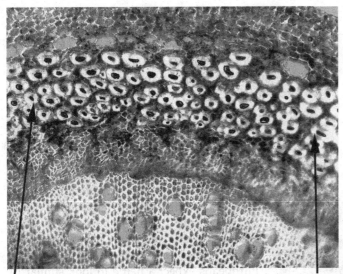

Fig 1.10. Bast fibres in the inner cortex of the stem of Urtica dioica.

Mind-your-own-business (*Soleirolia soleirolii [Req] Dandy*) and Pellitory-of-the-wall (*Parietaria judaica* L.)

For the natual history of these two plants see the Appendix at the end of the book, 270-287.

THE MEANING OF THE WORD NETTLE

The word Nettle is thought to have three closely related meanings, (i) According to Prior (1863) it is derived from the Anglo-Saxon and Dutch netel, Danish naelde, Swedish naetla and German nessel, the instrumental form of net which is the passive participle of ne, a verb common to most of the Indo-European languages in the sense of 'spin' and 'sew' (Latin nere, German na-hen, Sanskrit nah, bind). The word therefore refers to fibres in the nettle stem which in former times in Fries land, Germany and Scotland were extracted from Urtica dioica and spun, and the thread used to produce nettle cloth (Fig 1.10). The name could have come from the Anglo Saxon and Dutch Netel, a needle, (a) derived from Noedl, connected with the Greek neo to sew, since it provides the thread, (b) from the sharp sting or hurting, like the prick of a needle (Fischer, 1932). The name may have originated from the Anglo-Saxon netele; coquate with the Greek knadallo to scratch or 'scratcher' connected with the process of reaction to the sting?

WHEN IS A "NETTLE" A NETTLE?

The name nettle will be considered in relation to the following nettle characteristics, fibre, stinging and general appearance.

Fragments of nettle cloth have been found from the Bronze Age (1900 BC+) and in the 16th and 17th centuries in the Scandinavian and Germanic countries, as well as in Scotland. The imported 'Ramie' (in the form of 'China grass') from the Asian nettle (*Boehmeria nivea*) was also used at this time. Stinging fibre from the stinging nettle (*Urtica dioica*) was also used in the 1st World War and to a certain extent in the 2nd World War by the Germans. The feld gray uniforms contained up to 70% stinging nettle fibre and the rest of the 'ersatz' plant was also used for: food, fodder, oil, green and yellow dye, gas mantels, chemicals (sugar, minerals such as nitrate, potassium, etc.), junket for cheese, herbal use, etc. Various nettles of the Urticaceae throughout the world are used for their fibre; the fibre cells are generally taken from the outer layer (cortex) of the stem of the plant (Fig 1.10). The average person in this day and age is unlikely to associate nettles with fibre use and conversely the hundreds of plants used as fibre sources are not usually called nettles.

Many plants are called nettles because of their similarity to stinging nettles in their vegetative characters. These plants often grow in similar habitats to nettles and have heart-shaped leaves with serrated edges, such as many members of the family Labiatae: the white dead nettle (*Lamium album*), pink dead nettle (*Lamium purpureum*), yellow archangel (*Lamiastrum galeobdolon*), black horehound (*Ballota nigra*), common hemp-nettle (*Galeopsis tetrahit*) and other hemp nettles (Fig 1.11). They look like nettles in their vegetative state but mature plants, because of their attractive flowers which are insect-pollinated, should never be confused with nettles. Some are called dead nettles because they lack the sting of stinging nettles. A few people I have spoken to have been convinced that dead nettles do sting despite the fact they have attractive flowers.

Many plants belonging to the nettle family do not have the appearance of the common stinging nettle. Take for example the two British representatives of the Urticaceae, pellitory-of-the-wall (*Parietaria judaica*) and mind-your-own-business (*Soleirolia soleirolii*). They haven't the remotest resemblance to stinging nettles. People are always amazed when told these plants belong to the nettle family. They then reply, "But they don't sting", i.e., assuming that all members of nettle family do sting.

People associate nettles with the herbaceous growth habit. During the period of the round-the-world voyages of discovery, no man-eating plants were found, but when nettle trees were found in Australia they made headline news. Since then 36 species of nettle trees, belonging to the genus *Dendrocnide* (*Dendrocnide excelsa* being over 35m in height) have been found in the Indo-Malyan region and Pacific islands. The stings of these trees are much more virulent and long-lasting than those of our temperate nettles.

We associate nettles with their stings, but

White dead nettle (Lamium album) with U. dioica

Fig 1.11. Loasa a stinging plant called a nettle.

3 varieties of Soleirolia Mind-your-own -business

only one out of the five Nettle Tribes i. e. the Urticae, contains stinging plants (excluding genus *Gyrotaenia*). Many plants in the non-stinging tribes of the Urticaceae, however, look like nettles and are called nettles, e.g. herbaceous plants of the genus Boehmeria often have massive heart-shaped leaves.

Plants of the spurge family Euphorbiaceae (*Cnidoscolus, Tragia, Dalechampia*) and the Loasaceae (*Loasa,* etc.) do sting and are called nettles in the language of the people whose countries they inhabit. These are often different in appearance

from the European nettles with attractive insect-pollinated flowers, but have similar stinging hairs (trichomes) that produce on stinging the skin a very similar triple-response (pain/tingling, inflammation and swelling/wheal formation) as that of the European nettles.

In conclusion the word nettle is given to a plant that stings and elicits the characteristic skin reaction in humans, pain/tingling, rash/inflammation and swelling/wheal formation, (the triple response). Plants called nettles that grow outside Europe and do not belong to the Urticaceae, were probably called nettles because of their similar stinging reactions to the European plants that are called nettles. Most Europeans expect a nettle to look similar to the common stinging nettle (*Urtica dioica*). Botanists have found that nettles from the Urticaceae, Euphorbiaceae, Loasaceae and Hydrophyllaceae possess stinging hairs of a very similar structure (a case of parallel evolution). The way the stinging trichome/hair works can be compared with the action of the pipette/eye-dropper and hypodermic syringe and is an example of nature evolving a structure millions of years in advance of man. Designers now crib a lot of their designs from nature.

Whilst on the subject, in the course of my research on the common stinging nettle (Urtica dioica), a lot of work is published that uses the word nettle without any qualification. From what has been said above it is difficult to ascertain the species of plant in question. In many articles on fibre, the words 'nettle fibre' are used. The question remains "is the author referring to the fibre of Urtica dioica, or *Cannabis sativa,* or *Boehmeria nivea,* etc?" In the area of insects the problem is the same, since many larvae feed on members of the Labiatae, also called nettles. Thus there is a need to use the systemic/Latin in addition to the vernacular name.

THE UNIQUE EXPLODING STAMENS

All species of the Urticaceae share two characteristics: -

(1)   The ovary of the female flower contains one orthotropous ovule (see Fig 16.4) that is basally attached and there is only one stigma,

(2)   The male flowers have a unique type of pollen liberation (only found elsewhere in the Moraceae) in which the elastic filaments, inflexed in the bud suddenly reflex in an explosive manner to fling out the

powdery pollen.

When a student I worked in a plant nursery and one of the many things that delighted me was, when entering the greenhouse one morning, ready to de-bud the sweet peas, the soil in the flower pots emitted miniature puffs of smoke I had studied spore liberation in the fungi at college and on examining the surface of the soil found the small disc-like fruiting bodies of the cup fungi (Ascomycetes, see Chapter 11). The spore-bearing hymenium, on the upper surface of these cups,

clouds of pollen, very often thrown out in four puffs, each separated by a small time interval. The result is a display similar to the cup-fungi but far more dramatic, more like miniature rifle fire, thus its common name. Each nettle flower contains four, inflexed stamens and these can either explode together in a big puff or, in sequence, four small puffs one after the other!

The best way to see puffing in the common nettle is to place some male nettle shoots, gathered

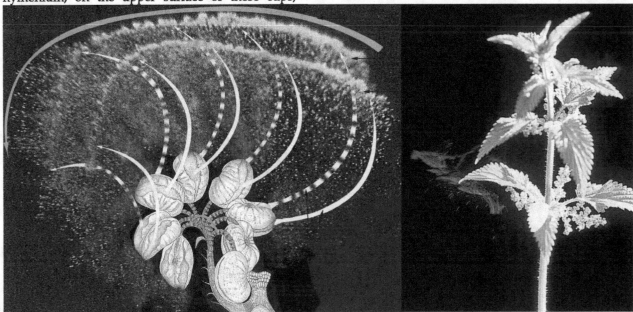

Fig 1.12. An exploding stamen of Urtica dioica throwing out two pollen masses-: Nettle shoot with exploding stamen

contains thousands of tubes (asci) each containing eight ascospores. The water pressure inside the ascus builds up overnight so that the vibrations I made around the greenhouse were sufficient to cause them to explode, throwing out their spores in a cloud, several centimetres into the air, a phenomenon called puffing. The object of this action is to get the spores into the turbulent air layer, which will then disperse them. A lot of these micro-fungi grow as saprophytes on dead nettle stems, together with other bizarre fungi (dealt with later in Chapter 11).

Male nettles also puff, especially early in the morning when the first rays of sunlight fall upon the minute male flowers (Fig 1.12). The Victorians were in an exciting age of discovery and many grew the artillery plant (*Pilea microphylla*) in their heated greenhouses, to amuse their friends. This plant belongs to the Urticaceae and its specific name denotes its small leaves which give it a fern-like appearance. When entering the greenhouse first thing in the morning Pollen explosion in nettle shoots greeted their owner with a succession of

when they are well in flower (mid-June), into a jar containing water and leave them overnight in a room with the curtains pulled. In the morning gently pull back the curtains so a small slit of light falls on the shoots. After a short time clouds of pollen are thrown out into the air several centimetres from the shoot and can then be seen swirling away in the convection currents of the turbulent air against the black background. The mechanism of pollen liberation was investigated by the German botanists in the 19th century but there is a need for further investigations using more modern techniques.

THE BEAUTIFUL INFLICTOR OF PAIN

The stinging hairs/trichomes of the common stinging nettle are found all over the shoot surface but are very small, 1-2mm in length. They are easily seen if, using gloves, the nettle stem is held up against the light. A hand lens (x10) will reveal enough to enable you to see the bulbous pedestal base and the hair shaft but a binocular microscope shows the plant in three dimensions revealing a forest of white hair shafts pointing in all directions. To see the detail of the hair compound microscope is needed and when I first viewed one through my antique brass microscope I was amazed by its beauty and the evolution of this structure to fulfill its function as an injector of poison into the human skin. It must rank as one of the most beautiful plant structures to be viewed by the microscope. The hair is even more beautiful when viewed through crossed polarizing filters, because the shaft, composed in a similar way to glass is transparent, and bends the path of polarized light splitting it up and making the hair colored. The color can be changed by rotating the microscope stage (Fig 1.13).

The principle hobby of the Victorians was microscopy and the art of making microscope slides of

However the best way to view the stinging trichome is to mount it alive in water. Looking through the transparent shaft the hair becomes alive with the random movement of cytoplasmic particles in a Brownian motion, and the streaming of strands of cytoplasm (cyclosis), which move up the hair to the tip on one side, and down to the base on the other. This is life at its basic level! When the pedestal base of a young hair is viewed, the central refractive nucleus is seen suspended by a matrix of delicate cytoplasmic strands which stream in different directions. These movements are most beautiful when seen using dark-ground illumination, when the objects appear white against a black background. This is

Plate 8 W. E. Kirby The butterflies & moths of Europe

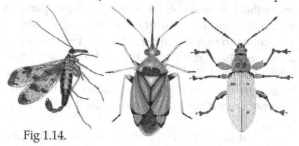

Fig 1.14.
Scorpion fly, Deraecoris ruber & Phyllobius pomaceus found on Urtica dioica.

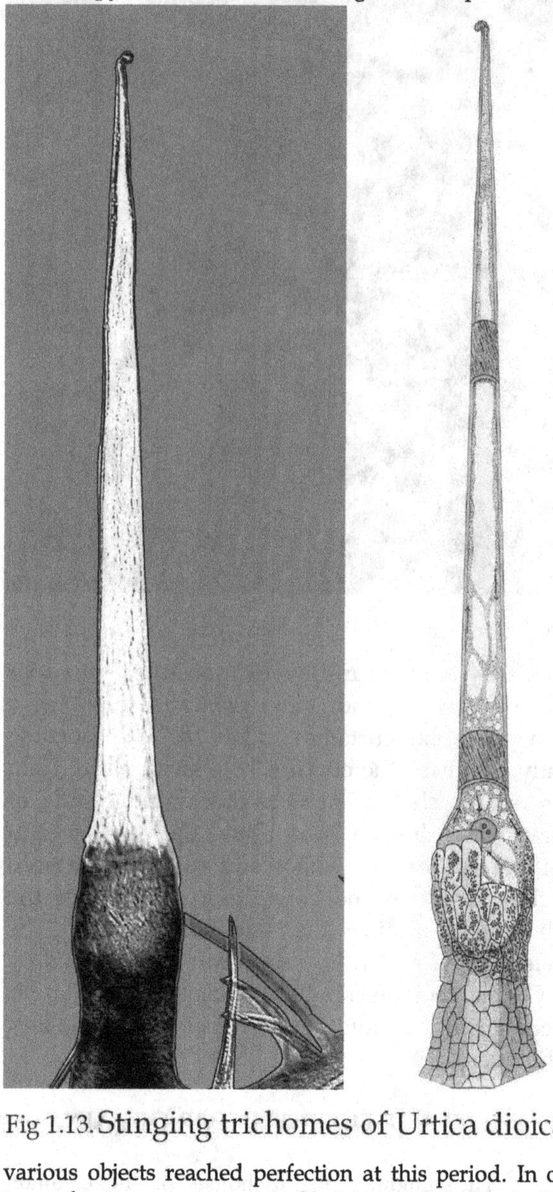

Fig 1.13. Stinging trichomes of Urtica dioica

various objects reached perfection at this period. In one type of preparation groups of hairs were killed in boiling water, decolourised and hardened in alcohol, then mounted in a cavity slide painted black. They were then viewed with reflected light, using the low power of a binocular microscope. In other preparations, from the alcohol stage they were mounted in resin and viewed under high power of a compound microscope, using transmitted light.

similar to a beam of sunlight passing through a gap in curtains into a darkened room; the white dust particles enlarged by the scattered light are seen against a black background. My students were spellbound when I showed them a live stinging trichome, magnified 500 times on a screen, using the micro-projector. If you can get young people interested in your subject that is half the battle; needless to say the stinging hair was not on the syllabus! Stinging power is undoubtedly the nettle's main weapon and therefore the focal centre of this book. A lot of recent research has been carried out on the relationship between stinging hairs and herbivorous insects, cattle, etc. and it makes a fascinating story.

INSECTS.WWW.CO.NETTLES

The relationship between insects and nettles started to be uncovered with the birth of entomology in the 18th century. Moses Harris in his famous book 'The Aurelians' (1766), produced beautiful watercolours to show the stages in the life cycles of many British butterflies and moths, and the plants the larvae fed upon. He established the importance of the nettle as the main food plant of some of our most beautiful butterflies: the small tortoiseshell, peacock, red admiral and comma (Fig 1.14). The relationship between the nettle and other insect groups was known by the mid-19th century. Kirby and Spence (1858) in their famous book 'Introduction to Entomology' say, in relation to the food of insects: -

"The common nettle is of little use either to mankind or the larger animals, but you will not doubt its importance to the class of insects when told that at least 30 different distinct species feed upon it'.

In his book 'Insects on nettles' Davis (1983) found that 31 species of insect are restricted to nettles, whilst 107 rely on nettles to a certain extent, either directly or indirectly for their food. These insects belong to the following orders (the number of insects associated with the nettle in each order is after the order), Coleoptera 15 (beetles), Dermaptera 1 (earwigs), Diptera 7 (flies), Heteroptera 26 (plant bugs), Homoptera 23 (hoppers, frog hoppers, aphids etc.), Lepidoptera 31 (butterflies and moths), Mecoptera 1 (scorpion flies), Neuroptera 1 (lacewings), Orthoptera 1 (crickets), Thysanoptera 1 (thrips), plus parasitic Hymenoptera (wasps). Other animal groups occur such as Mollusca (snails, slugs), Arachnida (spiders, havestmen), etc.

A good way to introduce a young person to the main groups of insects is to collect a sample from a nettle patch (see later Chapter 13). There is still a lot to be found out about these insects and their life-cycles and it is a worthwhile study, for any person, any age! These insects may be small; many only a few millimetres long, but magnified

under a binocular microscope many have an exquisite beauty. The success of insects comes as a direct result of their small size, which enables them to inhabit small habitats denied to larger animals and also enables them to avoid being stung by the nettle trichome! The fact remains that insects prefer nettles because they are rich in minerals, vitamins and proteins etc., that enable these insects to complete their life-cycles in a

Fig 1.15. The existence of nettles and cattle in a typical pasture

shorter time compared to other less nutritious plants.

A FOLLOWER OF MAN AND HIS ANIMALS

Nettles wouldn't be able to survive in a field full of cattle if they did not have some form of defence to stop them being eaten. Nettles trichomes sting cattle around the sensitive area of their nose, lips and mouth whilst they are browsing grass around a nettle clone, so it has long been assumed that it is the stinging trichomes that defend the nettle against being eaten by these vertebrate herbivores It is only recently that experimental evidence has shown that stinging trichomes of nettles, and not toxic chemicals or their smell, are an effective deterrent to these browsing vertebrate herbivores (Pollard & Briggs, 1984, Pullin & Gilbert, 1989). Even so, a few animals with horny lips and abrasive tongues, such as bison and gorillas relish them: even rabbits and cattle, after hard winters will eat the tender nettle shoots in the spring (Fig 1.15).

More would be known about the early evolution of flowering plants, if it was not for the soft nature of their flowers and leaves that soon rot; fortunately for the fossil record, the siliceous nature of their pollen grains and hardness of their fruits have resulted in their preservation. A table

showing the part of the geological time scale climate was a little warmer than the present but the

Era	Period	Epoch		Age started (millionsyears BP)	Urtica
Mesozoic	Triassic			c.235	
	Jurassic			c.194	
	Cretaceous			c.135	
Cenozoic	Tertiary	Palaeocene		65	
		Eocene		53.5	
		Oligocene		37.5	
		Miocene		22.5	
		Pliocene		5	
	Quaternary	Pleistocene		1.8	
		Holocene		0.02	

TABLE 1.1 After Anderson et al 1979

relevant (in bold) to this account (Table 1.1)

The Hamamelidae began to differentiate about 120 million years BP (before present) during the Lower Cretaceous period (70 million BP) in areas that had alternating wet and dry seasons. In adapting to the climate they evolved a deciduous habit which allowed them to revert to wind-pollination. This enabled them to migrate from the tropics to more temperate regions at a time when these areas were sparsely populated. Fossil evidence of members of the Urticeae from the Lower Cretaceous period consists of fruits (achenes) of Laportea, Girardinia and Urtica from the U S S R, Laportea from Germany and Czechslovakia, and Urtica from the Netherlands and West Germany (Collinson, 1989).

PREHISTORY OF THE NETTLE (URICA DIOICA)

(Table 1.1 after Anderton et al 1979, top of page): -

A brief look at the fossil evidence for Urtica in the Quaternary epoch is partially based on 'Historical Ecology of the British Flora' (Ingrouille, 1995). The Pleistocene began 2.2 million years ago and is an age of dramatic change with warm and cold periods, the latter including four glaciations in the later part of the epoch. The glaciations were separated by approximately 100,000 years.

In the Early Pleistocene, Urtica (nettle) is recorded from a site in Galway (Ireland), in a Karst limestone area, growing with sorrels (Rumex) and flowers of rock rose (Helianthemum), dropwort (Filipendula), umbellifers and roses.

Towards the end of the Pleistocene, the Anglian glaciation (450 thousand BP) left Britain with its present glacially sculpted landscape, and with deposits of glacial till, gravel and alluvium. The following Hoxnian Interglacial (400 – 367,000 BP) is rich in sites and well documented. The

flora was unremarkable. The Woodston deposit showed that there was a closed forest canopy and the vertebrate mammals included roe and fallow deer, beaver, Macaque monkeys and straight tusked elephants, the latter being destructive to tree saplings. In the 'elephant bed' at Clacton there were fruits of Urtica dioica (nettle) and Sonchus aspersa (prickly sow thistle) were found amongst the elephant bones - both of these plants are typical of disturbed and manured ground. The soil would have been rich in nitrogen and phosphate from the dung and bones. Phosphate is needed for the development of Urtica seedlings and this together with nitrate would have allowed rapid growth of this competitor plant. Urtica holds its own amongst other members of the tall herb vegetation and can grow to three metres or more in damp alluvial, slightly shaded situations.

Urtica would have grown on the flood plains, which were subject to disturbance and manuring by horse, giant ox, narrow-nosed rhinoceros that were preyed upon by the lion.

The end of the last glacial period of the Pleistocene gave way to the warm conditions of the late Devensian (14,000-10,000 BP). The summers of 13,000 BP were warm; the vegetation was open plains with masses of wild flowers, where herbivores were hunted by Palaeolithic hunters. Reindeer and horses were nearing domestication. Weedy and ruderal species such as the stinging nettle, which requires open, low competition habitats to establish, were particularly prominent.

The spread of the wildwood over much of the British Isles took place from 10,000 to 5,000 years ago. There was a decrease in herbivores with the extinction of the Irish elk, reindeer, arctic fox, and other herbivores such as red deer, roe deer, elk, auroch and wild boar lived on the woodland margins. The manuring and disturbance of these areas by herbivores would have favoured the establishment of the nettle. The nettle no doubt would have followed Mesolithic man and his animals as he encamped on the sides of rivers and lakes. The fruits of nettles growing alongside rivers would have dispersed their fruits in the water and these would have germinated and established themselves on open areas of gravel banks of meanders, in areas of alluvial silt and on the bare sides of banks. In the wet woodlands where there was only periodic flooding for a small part of the year, Urtica and alder dominated woodlands, developed on alder carr or reed fens.

Later the Neolithic culture entered the wildwood clearing parts of it and ending the dominance of trees. The disturbance here, together with the manuring from animals, would have favoured the establishment and growth of nettles in the more open areas or wooded areas up to 20% relative sunlight. The first 'landnam' forest clearance in the British Isles dates from 6,000 years ago at Ballynogilly with the construction of wooden houses and an arable phase, with cereal pollen being present, and lasting for periods up to 300 years. At this site the short clearance phase led to a steep decline in the elm and a rise in grass and Urtica dioica. Domesticated animals, cattle and pigs utilised the woods and prevented tree regeneration. These cattle feeding in open areas frequented by nettles could have moved into forest areas where they deposited their dung containing nettle fruits. Seedlings growing on the dung could have established themselves in less shaded areas.

NETTLES AS INDICATORS OF PAST HUMAN SETTLEMENTS

The chance of a nettle fruit developing into a nettle plant in a pasture is a rare event. Farmers can often tell you of past events that led to the establishment of nettles on their land and will admit that in the past it was due to bad farming practices such as burning hedge clippings or leaving these lying around, disturbance by pigs in pastures, ditching spoil alongside a ditch, rubble heaps, etc. (Bates, 1933). Nettles as followers of man grow near his dwellings and on his land and archaeologists know that where they persist on ancient woodland or pasture is likely to indicate a site of former human dwellings. In 'History of the Countryside' Rackman (1994) gives examples of some of these sites (Fig 1.16). Phosphate has many origins: dead bodies of vertebrates, human graves, spilt blood, burnt or decaying wood, human sewage, animal dung, fertilisers, etc. and it persists for long periods in the soil. A famous deserted village, Little Gidding (Huntingdonshire, England) still has an elm grove full of tall rank nettles. Rackman says, in relation to the plants growing in an English graveyard: -

"The nettles and cow parsley are a 'momento mori', for in them is recycled, while awaiting the Last Trump, part of the phosphate of 10,000 skeletons".

Dried up former castle moats are still marked by banks of nettles which grew on the phosphate and nitrate resulting from human sewage, refuse containing animal and fish bones, etc. thrown into the moat in former times. Moats not associated with castles but built in places across the countryside and inhabited by ordinary people are often marked by pollarded and ancient trees, and stinging nettles.

NETTLE MEDICINE, FOOD AND FODDER

These three topics are covered in detail later, so they are dealt with briefly here. Throughout man's history there have been wars, pestilence famine, poverty and starvation, and nettles in this connection have been ranked as famine plants. The association of nettles with

Fig 1.16. Nettles and Elder mark a derelict cow shed

human habitations and its ubiquitous nature are essential in times of adversity. Nettles are rich in vitamins, minerals and other food substances, essential in small amounts for survival during conditions of starvation. Numerous recipes including nettles were tried out during the 1st and 2nd World Wars and today they are included in menus more to promote conversation than for their culinary value.

Box 1.2. THE WORLD NETTLE EATING CONTEST takes place once a year on mid-summers' day. In 2003 it was held next to the Bottle Inn in Marshwood, West Dorset, England. This was televised and the naturalist, photographer and writer Chris Packham was commentator as well as a volunteer. The contestants had to sign a form stating that they did not have any heart, kidney, liver or any other condition needing medication. The nettles were reputed to have been collected at the cesspit of West-hay Manor! The nettles were in two foot lengths and if seed masses were present they were not eaten. Nettles that were old or covered with aphids were not accepted. The year 2003 was hot and dry and this made the nettles very drying to the mouth so most contestants washed them down with pints of Ale. Advice given by previous survivors was, if told they sting the lips it is nonsense, they only sting on the top surface of the leaf, so roll them into a ball with the lower surface upwards. The winner's strategy was to strip off a two foot length of leaves, roll them into a ball and eat them in one go! The champion ate twenty two foot of nettle stem in the one hour. Anybody throwing up was disqualified. Chris comments were: - "they instantly dried out and stung the inside of my mouth", "I'd rather lick the floor of a bus than do this again", "I felt sick after half and hour", "I pray for this hell to end". One person from the Continent said, "This British occupation doesn't take place on the Continent"! Another from a vegetarian was, "I shall stick to carrot cake in the future".

Farmers noticed that dried nettles will be eaten by livestock and often lead to an improvement in health as indicated by a sheen on their coats. The addition of small quantities of dried nettles to the diet was found to be beneficial. With the recent 'Green Initative' a Devon firm was advertising £1000 for a tonne of nettles. One cheese producer in Devon, 2003, has advertised for large perfect nettle leaves (i.e. those from shaded nettles) since they have traditionally been used to cover the outside of their cheeses (to improve the flavour) and

Fig 1.17. Frontispiece from Turner's Brittish Physician

they have experienced a shortage this year. In the past the nettle has been regarded as a cure-all, a panacea (Fig 1.17). With the advent of conventional medicine it has been largely disregarded except recently when there has been a resurgence of interest in the old herbal remedies. A vast amount of information on modern experiments to test the validity of previous nettle use can be found in scientific papers and on the internet. It is still used in most countries to a fuller or lesser degree and this is possibly due to its cosmopolitan distribution and ubiquitous nature. It acts by promoting the flow of urine (diuretic), as an anti-rheumatic, stops bleeding (anti-hemorrhagic), promotes milk flow, lactation (galactagogue), nutritive (it is full of vitamins and minerals, etc.), contains iron (anti-anemic), helps rectify a low glucose level in the blood (hypoglycemic), stimulates circulation, loosens phlegm (expectorant). Uses: skin problems (eczema), allergies e.g. allergic rhinitis (inflammation of the nose), loss of blood from the nose (epitaxis) and hemorrhages, e.g. in excessive menstruation, renal gravel (kidney stones), hair loss (alopecia), swelling of the prostate (begnin prostatic hyperplasia), infection of the bladder (cystitis), uric acid in the tissues (gout), soft bones (rickets), bronchitis, hay fever and anaphylactic shock. It is taken as a general tonic in the spring.

NETTLE ECOLOGY

Nettles can occur as scattered shoots in a hedge-bank, individual clones in pasture, or large patches made up of several clones which have joined during growth. A nettle patch or clone is similar to a wood but in miniature. In a similar way to a wood the nettle patch has a ground layer of herbs and small seedlings which vary during the season. Contrary to the opinions of many authors who describe the nettle patches as monocultures this is not true. Many plants of the ground layer are pre-vernal and show early in the year after which they die down, or remain hidden. The nettle is a perennial and the highly woody stems collapse each year and then break down to form a nettle litter. They are decomposed by saprophytic bacteria and micro-fungi and the humus and nutrients are returned to the soil to be recycled. The parasitic flowering plant the greater dodder (*Cuscuta europaea*) lives on the nettles alongside some rivers. Added to this are the soil animals and insects which live in the stems during the winter or feed on them and help to break them down. During its growth period insects live on it, together with their predators and parasites. Larger animal vertebrate quadrupeds and birds feed on other animals, shelter, avoid enemies or nest in nettles. I have studied a particular nettle patch over a number of years. These animals, plants and their inter-actions are dealt with in more detail later but I have included a flow diagram of nettle ecology to show possible inter-actions and food webs (Flow diagram 1.1).

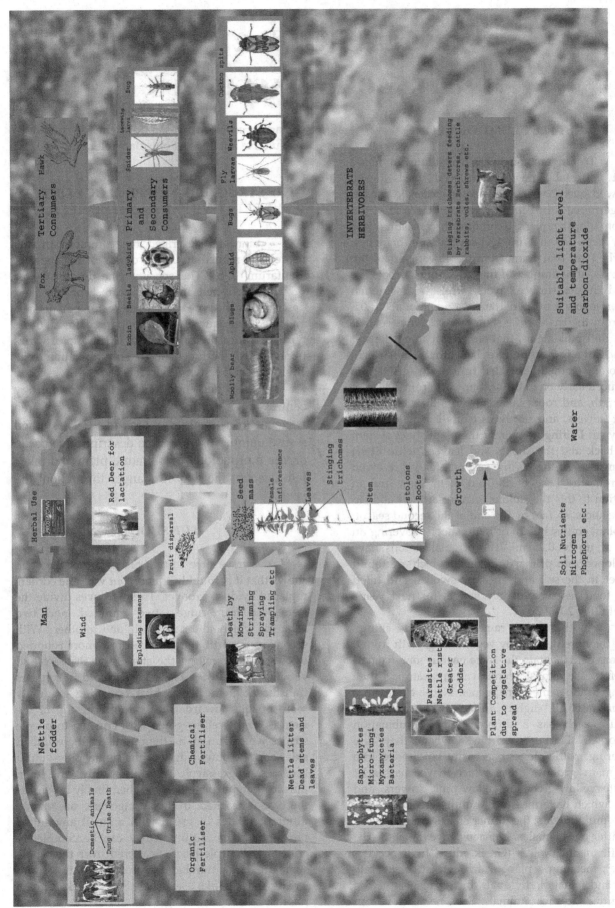

FLOW DIAGRAM 1.1 SHOWING THE ECOLOGICAL RELATIONSHIPS BETWEEN URTICA DIOICA AND ITS ENVIRONMENT

19

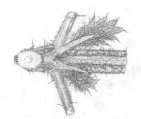

CHAPTER 2
IT NEEDS SOME DESCRIPTION

NETTLE CLUMP OR CLONE

To understand what constitutes a nettle plant its establishment from seed needs to be followed over 2 years. Seed sown in fertile garden soil germinates in February, and by the end of the season a bushy plant is produced, consisting of a main stem (up to 1 m) and several side branches, (nearly 1 m) that come from the lower part of the stem. A large number of fine adventitious roots are found in the surface layers, whilst a few much longer yellow roots penetrate to a depth of about 0.5 m. From the base of the stem there radiates several long, thin pink stems, that either run along the soil surface, or a few centimetres beneath it. These stems or stolons (sometimes called runners or offsets) are produced early on in the season, vary from 20-40 cm in length, and root mainly towards their ends. The plant flowers, and produces fruits if female, in the first year. During the winter the plant shoot system dies back and the shoots and leaves (nettle litter) decompose. In the spring, several shoots are given off from the base of the old stem base, and in addition to this the stolons turn up at their ends to form shoots, so that by the end of the second season the plant consists of 10 or more shoots, covering an area of up to 0.25 m². The original stolons have developed into primary rhizomes which are found deeper in the soil and are now swollen and filled with food reserves, mainly starch, for next year's growth (Fig 2.1, 2.2).

All the shoots/ramets of a nettle clump, since they are derived by vegetative growth from a single parent, contain the same genetic material and therefore are almost identical in appearance; they belong to the same clone/genet. Nettle clones in a pasture are all slightly different in appearance because each has a different gene combination (Genome). During mid-June, when they are flowering, nettle clones can easily be divided into two main groups, those which have masses of minute yellow-green or yellow-pink flowers, and those which have masses of minute green-white or green-pink flowers; the former clones are males and the latter ones females. Linnaeus gave the nettle the specific name dioica, (Greek, di = two, oecia = house), meaning a plant which consist of separate male and female individuals. In this respect nettles are similar to most animals. Each nettle clone can

spread to cover many square metres if conditions are suitable but it is just one plant/clone.

THE STRUCTURE/MORPHOLOGY OF THE VEGETATIVE PARTS OF THE NETTLE

Linnaeus described the common stinging nettle and named it Urtica dioica in his 'Species Plantarum' 1753. The specimen he described was probably collected from the nearest pasture and described as the type species (the lectotype), pressed and used subsequently as a comparison for all other types of Urtica dioica collected. Urtica dioica varies tremendously both genetically and in relation to its environment (i.e. it is very plastic).

This account of nettle morphology centres on a nettle clone growing in an area adjacent to a limekiln, which has been studied over a number of years The description is based on the morphology of a mature plant and takes into account the way it changes throughout the year.

THE SHOOT

A transverse section of the top of the stem shows that it is roughly square, but with the corners replaced by deep grooves. These grooves divide the stem into four ridges, two rounded, and two squares, which alternate with one another. With secondary growth, the stem becomes more rounded in shape. Illuminating the stem from the side and viewing it against a black background, it appears translucent at the top, whilst becoming gradually more opaque towards the bottom. The top of the stem is bright yellow-green with crimson to purple stripes which run along the middle of the rounded sides and the outer ridges of the square sides, but it becomes progressively more uniformly pink, then purple, then purple-black and then finally brown, as the base is reached. In the spring stems are mainly different shades of green with a small amount of pink, but in the autumn, they can be completely crimson to purple-black. Scattered over the whole stem are large numbers of thin long strips, and small stipple-like patches of dark green photosynthetic tissue (Fig 2.2).

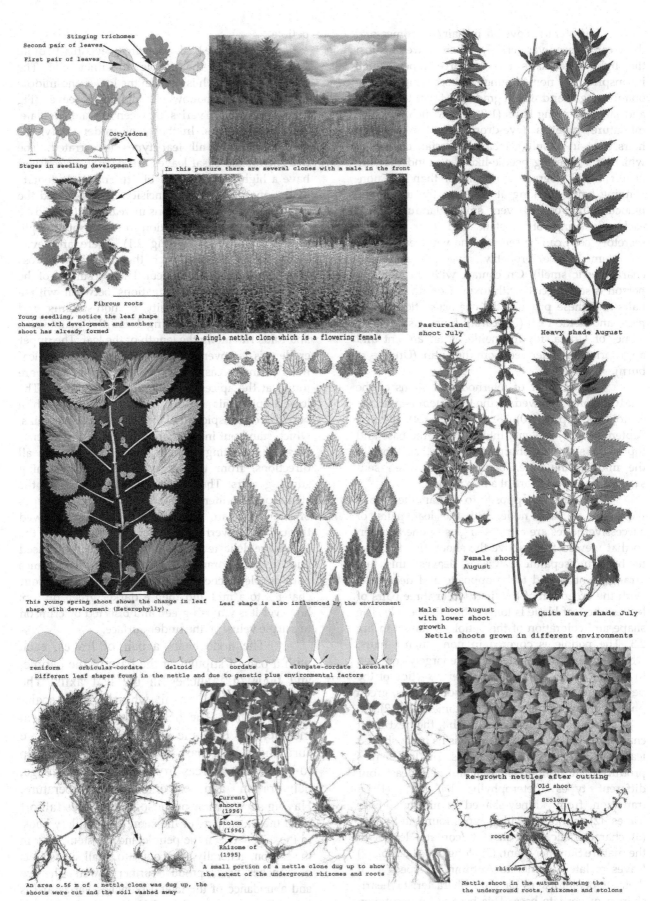

Stinging trichomes
Second pair of leaves
First pair of leaves
Cotyledons
Stages in seedling development

In this pasture there are several clones with a male in the front

Fibrous roots
Young seedling, notice the leaf shape changes with development and another shoot has already formed

A single nettle clone which is a flowering female

Pastureland shoot July

Heavy shade August

This young spring shoot shows the change in leaf shape with development (Heterophylly).

Leaf shape is also influenced by the environment

Female shoot August

Male shoot August with lower shoot growth

Quite heavy shade July

Nettle shoots grown in different environments

reniform   orbicular-cordate   deltoid   cordate   elongate-cordate   lanceolate
Different leaf shapes found in the nettle and due to genetic plus environmental factors

An area o.56 m of a nettle clone was dug up, the shoots were cut and the soil washed away

Current shoots (1996)
Stolon (1996)
Rhizome of (1995)
A small portion of a nettle clone dug up to show the extent of the underground rhizomes and roots

Re-growth nettles after cutting
Old shoot
Stolons
roots
rhizomes
Nettle shoot in the autumn showing the the underground roots, rhizomes and stolons

FIG 2.1 THE VEGETATIVE STRUCTURE AND GROWTH OF URTICA DIOICA

The stem is covered in hair/trichomes and these can be seen very clearly, when viewed against the light. The hairs are of three types, small inconspicuous non-stinging hairs, lying at an oblique angle, and which gradually taper to a point, and larger stinging hairs (1-2 mm), which look like miniature pipettes (eye-droppers). The stinging hairs start in a bulbous base/pedestal, on top of which is a tapering needle-like shaft; and they are nearer to 90 degrees to the stem than the non-stinging hairs. Looking at the stem through a x20 binocular microscope, very small glandular hairs, each consisting of a stalk and four rounded secretory cells can be seen on the younger parts of the stem (These probably give the nettle its characteristic smell). On contact with the nettle, a person is self-injected with toxins from the stinging hairs and these produce the characteristic burning pain, and nettle rash (Urticaria). Linnaeus's generic name, of Urtica, for the nettle, is an ancient and appropriate one, derived from the Latin, (Urere = to burn).

The number of internodes of stems of the Study 1 clone, followed by the total stem height, are as follows: April, (10) 38 cm, June, (24) 194 cm, September, (29) 208 cm.. Internodes at the base and top of the shoot are shorter in length than those in the middle, the latter being formed when self-shading and growth are at a maximum.

Two leaves, opposite to one another, leave the stem at each node, but the leaf pairs of successive nodes are at right-angles to one another, so that viewed from above the shoot, there appear to be four separate ranks of leaves; this leaf arrangement is said to be opposite and decussate. With the exception of the first two or three pairs of leaves, the leaf blade is longer than the petiole. The shape and coloration of the petiole is shown in Fig 2.3. The petiole is covered in non-stinging hairs, whilst numerous stinging hairs are largely confined to the top of the ridges. A transverse section of the petiole, shows the 7 vascular bundles/veins, green photosynthetic tissue and the trichomes (Fig 2.2).

Apart from its growth habit, the next most characteristic feature of the nettle is its heart-shaped leaves with their saw-like margins. The leaf shapes produced throughout the year are of at least four different types (heterophylly, Fig 2.1), (1) a transition from kidney-shaped (reniform) lower leaves, (2) round (orbicular) types found in Spring, (3) characteristic heart-shaped (cordate) leaves of the mature Summer plant, (4) elongated (lanceolate) leaves of late Summer to Autumn. Irrespective of their shape, all leaves have the characteristic heart-shaped or cordate base. This base is formed when the leaf margins extend well below the end of the petiole,

then curve back in an arc to eventually unite with the end of the petiole on either side. The cordate base, which is deep in the lower and middle leaves, is much shallower in the upper leaves (Fig 2.1). The margin varies between serrate, dentate, and crenate types. In the clone under study, the cordate base of all leaf types is serrated. The margins of the basal leaves are deeply incised and have a high proportion of bi, tri, and multidentate dentations. The depth of incision decreases and the number of simple dentations increases in the middle stem leaves, with a transition to the serrate margin of the topmost leaves (Fig 2.1). There are seven veins, which together with their subsidiary cross veins run throughout the leaf. The top surface of the leaf is thrown into corrugations between with a sparse but uniform density of non-stinging and stinging hairs. Non-stinging hairs the main veins and folds run along the length of the leaf. The upper epidermis is covered form a fringe along the leaf margin and occasionally small stinging hairs are found at the apices of some of the dentations. The lower epidermis of the leaf is covered with a network of conspicuous large veins and side veins, which stand out in relief and are covered in a dense mass of non-stinging hairs, whilst pointing in all directions, from the larger veins, are glistening stinging hairs. The young unfolded leaves of the stem apex are literally bristling with the two types of hair, and are beautiful objects when viewed through a powerful hand lens. In the spring the leaves are delicate shades of yellow-green, suffused with tinges of orange and crimson and sometimes with purple patches. Later in the year the leaf colour changes to a mid and then a darker green on top; however it is whitish-green and bisected by crimson to purple veins, on the under-surface.

The node bears a pair of leaves, each with a pair of stipules at the base of the petiole, and buds of branches in the leaf axils. The stipules are small, oval, whitish-green, scale-like structures. The delicate leaves and apical meristem of both the stem and the stolon are surrounded by a mass of these stipules that help to protect these areas from mechanical damage, dehydration and extremes of temperature. Having served their purpose, the stipules fall off from the older parts of the stem. The axillary buds, in the axil between the petiole and the stem, later in the season, generally grow out into small side shoots or branches, which produce further flowers. The size and abundance of the lateral branches varies and is dependant on the position of the shoot in the

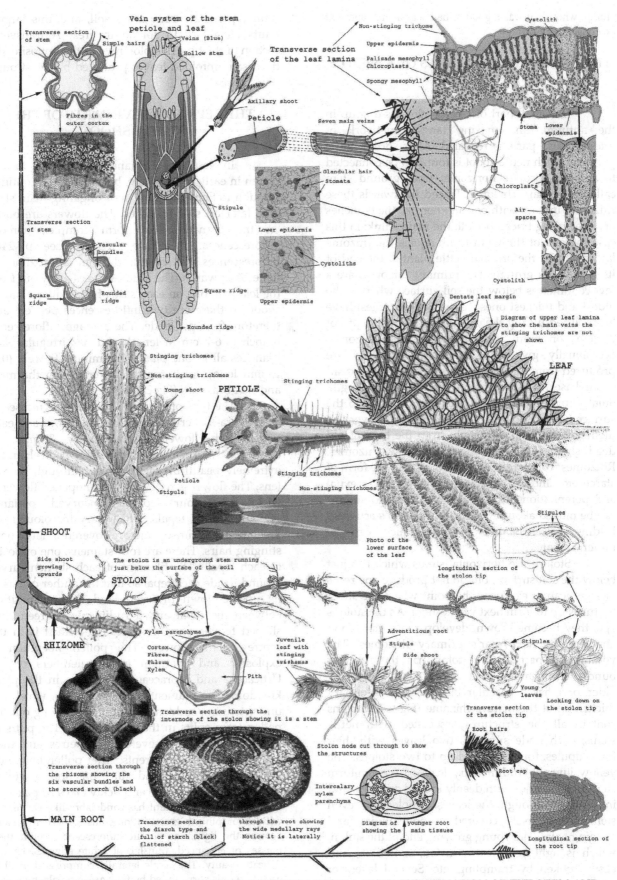

Transverse section of stem

Simple hairs

Fibres in the outer cortex

Transverse section of stem

Vascular bundles

Square ridge

Rounded ridge

Vein system of the stem petiole and leaf

Veins (Blue)

Hollow stem

Axillary shoot

Petiole

Stipule

Square ridge

Rounded ridge

Glandular hair

Stomata

Lower epidermis

Cystoliths

Upper epidermis

Seven main veins

Transverse section of the leaf lamina

Non-stinging trichome

Cystolith

Upper epidermis

Palisade mesophyll

Chloroplasts

Spongy mesophyll

Stoma

Lower epidermis

Chloroplasts

Air spaces

Cystolith

Dentate leaf margin

Diagram of upper leaf lamina to show the main veins the stinging trichomes are not shown

LEAF

Stinging trichomes

Non-stinging trichomes

Young shoot

PETIOLE

Petiole

Stipule

Stinging trichomes

Stinging trichomes

Non-stinging trichomes

Photo of the lower surface of the leaf

Stipules

longitudinal section of the stolon tip

SHOOT

Side shoot growing upwards

STOLON

The stolon is an underground stem running just below the surface of the soil

RHIZOME

Xylem parenchyma

Cortex

Fibres

Phloem

Xylem

Pith

Transverse section through the internode of the stolon showing it is a stem

Juvenile leaf with stinging trichomes

Adventitious root

Stipule

Side shoot

Stolon node cut through to show the structures

Stipules

Young leaves

Transverse section of the stolon tip

Looking down on the stolon tip

Root hairs

Root cap

Intercalary xylem parenchyma

MAIN ROOT

Transverse section through the rhizome showing the six vascular bundles and the stored starch (black)

Transverse section the diarch type and full of starch (black) flattened

through the root showing the wide medullary rays Notice it is laterally

Diagram of the younger root showing the main tissues

Longitudinal section of the root tip

FIG 2.2 THE MORPHOLOGY AND ANATOMY OF URTICA DIOICA, WITH THE VENATION OF THE STEM AND LEAF BASED ON GRAVIS 1886.

clump, whether it was a good or bad season etc., and will be considered later.

THE UNDERGROUND PARTS OF A NETTLE CLONE

If a small part of a nettle clone is dug up in the autumn, an amazing tangled network of underground parts is revealed. After sorting these parts out, each nettle shoot is found to be connected to a tough, brown, horizontal underground stem called a primary rhizome. Traced backwards these rhizomes unit up with one another like the branches of a tree being traced back to the main trunk; in this case the end of the main trunk equals the rhizome laid down by the original nettle plant at the end of its first year's growth. The primary rhizomes are a few centimetres below the soil surface whereas the oldest and thickest ones (secondary rhizomes) have been buried during the course of time to a depth of 20 cm. or more. The nodes of the rhizomes occasionally give off side shoots. Stolons are produced from the base of the previous year's dead shoot bases, and vary from 20-100 cm in length. Small brown adventitious roots are confined to the surface layers, and other thick yellow roots over one metre in length grow mainly from the base of old dead shoots and sometimes from the rhizomes. Rhizomes store large amounts of food in the form of starch etc., and are organs of clonal spread/asexual and perennation. Broken up rhizomes and stolons can be moved about by animals and man's activities leading to vegetative spread, which can be underestimated.

Stolons are horizontal stems which run just below the soil surface, but do not produce any roots of significance, except at the point where the shoot tip turns up to form next year's shoot. As the stolons age, they become brown, develop roots, store food and become next year's primary rhizomes. The young end part of the stolon has the vascular bundle arrangement of a young stem, whilst the older part has 6 vascular bundles and secondary thickening of the mature rhizome (Fig 2.2). Stolons contain all the structures associated with nettle stems; each node supports two leaves with their four stipules, four roots and up to two stolons. The yellow juvenile/rudimentary leaves have reniform shaped leaf blades with deeply incised margins, and interestingly enough, the leaves, petioles, and even stems are sparsely covered in non-stinging and stinging hairs. The young growing end of the stolon, which is light yellow to crimson, is delicate and easily broken by trampling, etc. Several layers of stipules, enabling the stolon to penetrate loose soil or surface debris, protect the delicate tip. The stolon cannot penetrate compacted soil, and this largely limits its ability to spread in area. A transverse section of the tip of a stolon reveals the opposite and decussate unfolded leaves protected by the stipules (Fig 2.2).

THE REPRODUCTIVE PARTS OF THE NETTLE SHOOT

In southern England, nettles are in full bloom in early to mid-June, but flowerings continue through to September on the elongating main stem and, later on side branches. The flowers are borne on the branches that form complex cymose inflorescences. In Study Area 1 (see p 240), inflorescences are produced from approximately node 14 upwards. The inflorescences grow out from the leaf axil, one on each side of the axillary bud or shoot, so there are two inflorescences per leaf and therefore four per node. The average inflorescence branch is 6-7 cm in length and has irregular side branches all in one plane. The minute flowers (0.5-1.0mm long) are borne in clusters along the main and side branches (Fig 2.3).

The tops of the male shoots have masses of candelabra-like crimson and yellow flowers at each node. Each flower, approximately 3 mm. in diameter, is borne on a short stalk or pedicel, and is extremely beautiful when viewed through an x10 lens. The flower is reduced. The unopened flower is enclosed in four separate, incurved, perianth segments called tepals, which vary in colour from green to dark crimson and are covered in large non-stinging hairs. There are four stamens, one opposite to each tepal. The filament of each stamen curves around inside each tepal so that the anther comes to lie upside down (inflexed) and held in position between the tepal and a rudimentary green cup-shaped female part, the pistillode which is in the centre of the flower. The pollen liberation is explosive and common to all members of the Urticaceae and Moraceae but unique in the plant kingdom. The filaments of the stamens, which are under tension, suddenly straighten, flinging out the pollen from splits in the pollen sacks. The puffs of pollen are shot out several centimetres and then wafted away on air currents. After pollen liberation the flower withers and falls off and a young expanding adjacent flower quickly takes its place.

The female plant has candelabra-like clusters of whitish or pinkish-green inflorescences. When viewed against the light, the rim-lit inflorescences, with their masses of enhanced, translucent white stigmas, have a delicate beauty. The single laterally compressed pistil of each flower is surrounded by four green tepals, two large ones covering the sides and two much smaller ones at the

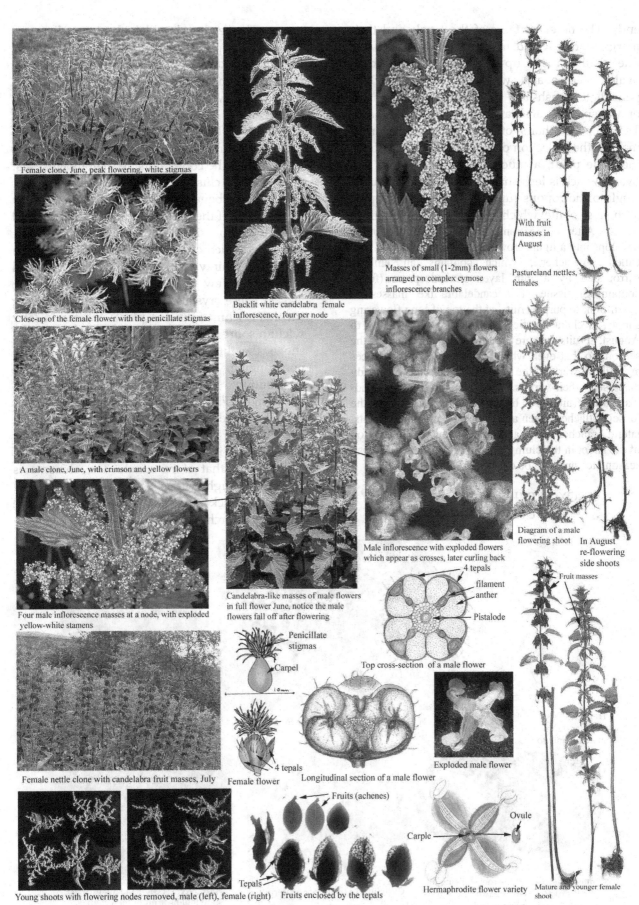

Female clone, June, peak flowering, white stigmas

Close-up of the female flower with the penicillate stigmas

Backlit white candelabra female inflorescence, four per node

Masses of small (1-2mm) flowers arranged on complex cymose inflorescence branches

With fruit masses in August

Pastureland nettles, females

A male clone, June, with crimson and yellow flowers

Four male inflorescence masses at a node, with exploded yellow-white stamens

Candelabra-like masses of male flowers in full flower June, notice the male flowers fall off after flowering

Male inflorescence with exploded flowers which appear as crosses, later curling back

Diagram of a male flowering shoot

In August re-flowering side shoots

4 tepals
filament
anther
Pistalode

Top cross-section of a male flower

Penicillate stigmas
Carpel

Female flower
4 tepals

Longitudinal section of a male flower

Exploded male flower

Fruit masses

Female nettle clone with candelabra fruit masses, July

Young shoots with flowering nodes removed, male (left), female (right)

Fruits (achenes)

Tepals

Fruits enclosed by the tepals

Carple
Ovule

Hermaphrodite flower variety

Mature and younger female shoot

FIG 2.3 THE REPRODUCTIVE SHOOTS OF MALE AND FEMALE URTICA DIOICA

ends. The outer surfaces of the tepals and their margins are covered in long non-stinging hairs. The pistil is made up of a minute (1mm long) oval-shaped ovary, which is capped with a penicillate (brush-like) stigma made up of masses of transparent, un-branched multicellular hairs. The stigmatic hairs offer a large surface area, making the collection of wind-blown pollen from the male plant, a much more likely event. The ovary, which is lens-shaped in section, contains a single orthotropous (upright with the micropyle at the top) ovule, which contains a single ovum.

After pollination and fertilisation the ovary develops into a light- brown, laterally compressed fruit called an achene, which contains an embryo surrounded by a thin layer of endosperm (food-containing) tissue. The candelabra-like masses of green-pink to purple fruits, at the top of long flowering shoots, is characteristic of nettle plants from July to August. Fruits mature continuously throughout the season, so that even when the topmost inflorescences are still flowering, the lowermost ones have already dispersed their fruits. The predominately wind-dispersed fruits are liberated enclosed within the loosely attached green and crimson perianth segments. lateral branches varies and is dependant on the position of the shoot in the clump, whether it was a good or bad season etc., and will be considered later.

BOX 1.1 BRIEF NOTE ON ANATOMY OF URTICA DIOICA

The reader should look at the diagrams and photographs (Fig 2.4). The basic number of vascular bundles is four (Gravis, 1886) but the mature stem has multiples of this number, and in the rhizome two bundles are split to give a basic number of 6. The most characteristic feature of the stem of Urtica is the incomplete rings of parenchyma in-between the xylem. Phloem fibres are found in the cortex outside the phloem. Most parts contain cluster crystals. Crystal aggregates of calcium carbonate called cystoliths are found in all members of the Urticaceae and have been used in classification since they vary in shape. These cystoliths which are irregular in shape in Urtica dioica are mainly found in the upper epidermal cells with a few in the lower epidermis of the leaves. These crystals may function in removing surplus calcium from the plant or act as a later calcium source. The transverse section of the leaf shows the three types of trichomes, glandular, non-stinging, and stinging and the chloroplast distribution in the palisade and spongy mesophyll (Fig 2.2). The breathing pores or stomata of the lower epidermis are shown in Fig 2.3. The root is laterally flattened; the vascular arrangement is diarch, with two large rays of parenchyma that store starch. The rhizome is extremely tough with six vascular bundles and secondary thickening, and it also stores a large amount of starch (Fig 2.4).

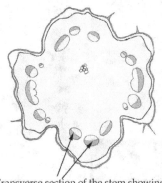

Transverse section of the stem showing vascular bundles. The very young stem has only four bundles.

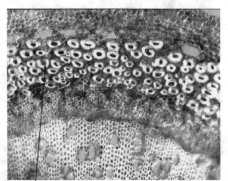

Transverse section of the stem to show the fibres in the inner cortex.

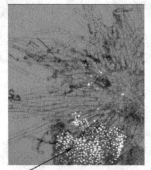

A squashed pistil showing the ovary with cluster crystals and the stigmas on top.

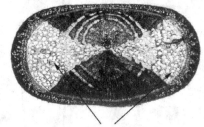

Transvers section of the root showing the diarch structure with the two xylcm arms separated by two wide medullary rays.

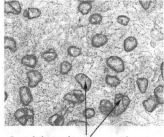

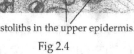

Cystoliths in the upper epidermis.

Fig 2.4

A transvers section of a mature stem showing the arms of the xylem parenchyma inside the xylem

AS A RUDERAL PLANT URTICA URENS IS GROWING AMONGST THE SAVOY CABBAGES.

CHAPTER 3
OTHER BRITISH NETTLES

DISTINGUISHING FEATURES OF THE BRITISH NETTLES

The following key enables the quick identification of the three British nettles and this is backed up by the illustrations (Fig 3.1a – 1b): -

1 ---Perennial plant with rhizomes and stolons: lower and middle stem leaves with a distinct cordate base: sexes generally on separate plants (dioecious). ……………………… ……*Urtica dioica*

1 ---Annual plant without rhizomes or stolons: leaves without a distinct cordate base: both sexes separate but on the same plant (monoecious)…….2

2 ---Height 20-100 cm: Inflorescences, separate male ones which are lax-flowered, and separate female ones with the flowers agglomerated into a spherical heads. ……………… *Urtica pilulifera*

2---Height 10-60 cm: Inflorescences catkins-like and each catkin has a mixture of male and female flowers………………………*Urtica urens*

THE ROMAN NETTLE (URTICA PILULIFERA L)

THE NAMES

The Roman Nettle is a former alien, unsuccessful in colonising the British Isles, and is now thought to be extinct; however, its chequered history is of great interest. Linnaeus named it Urtica pilulifera in 1753. Urtica is the Latin for nettle; it comes from Uro, to burn, which is one of the effects produced by its stinging hairs. The specific name pilulifera comes from the Latin, pila, ball, and fero, to bear, meaning globule bearing, which refers to the spherical heads of the female flowers.

When Julius Caesar invaded England, Camden says, he called the town where he landed Romania, which name was later corrupted to Romeney or Romny. From this, some authors e.g. Fernie, have concluded that Roman is a corruption of Romney (Kent), where U. pilulifera grows abundantly. Lyte in his Nievve Herball (1578), referring to U. pilulifera says,

"They do call al such strange herbes as be unknown of the common people Romish or Romayne herbes, although the same be brought direct from Sweden or Norweigh"

If this is true, why are there not more introduced plants having the word Roman, as a prefix to their common names? Neither of these

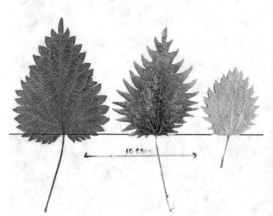

Fig 3.1a Leaves all to the same scale
U. dioica   U. pilulifera   U. urens

Fig 3.1b Inflorescences (not to the same scale, figures indicate the range in size of the inflorescence branches)
U. dioica (3-4cm) U. urens (0.5-1.5cm) U. pilulifera (4-7cm).

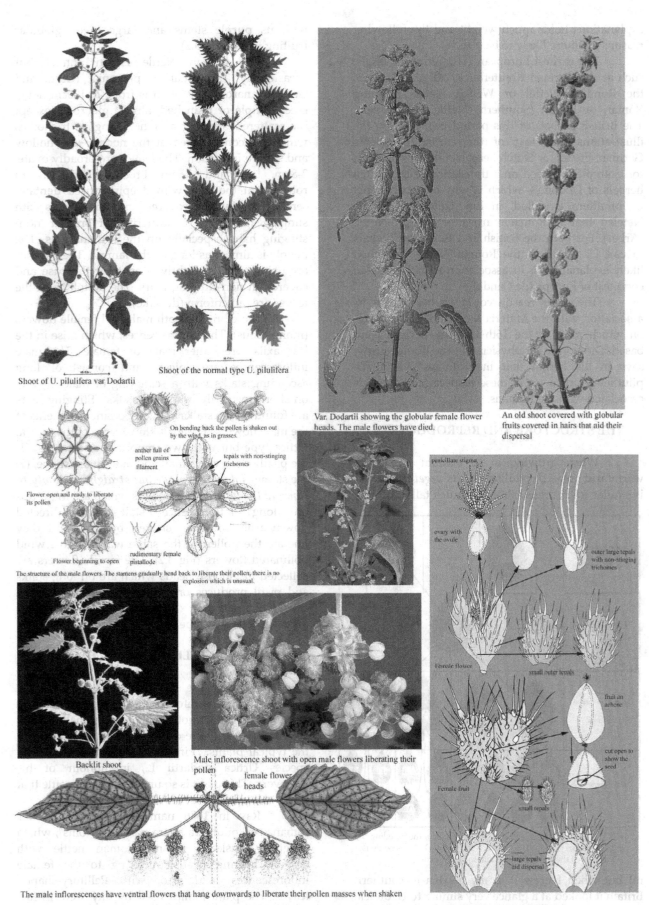

Shoot of U. pilulifera var Dodartii

Shoot of the normal type U. pilulifera

Var. Dodartii showing the globular female flower heads. The male flowers have died.

An old shoot covered with globular fruits covered in hairs that aid their dispersal

On bending back the pollen is shaken out by the wind, as in grasses.

anther full of pollen grains filament

tepals with non-stinging trichomes

Flower open and ready to liberate its pollen

Flower beginning to open

rudimentary female pistallode

The structure of the male flowers. The stamens gradually bend back to liberate their pollen, there is no explosion which is unusual.

penicillate stigma

ovary with the ovule

outer large tepals with non-stinging trichomes

Female flower

small outer tepals

fruit an achene

cut open to show the seed

Female fruit

small tepals

large tepals aid dispersal

Backlit shoot

Male inflorescence shoot with open male flowers liberating their pollen

female flower heads

The male inflorescences have ventral flowers that hang downwards to liberate their pollen masses when shaken

FIG 3.2 STRUCTURE AND REPRODUCTION OF THE ROMAN NETTLE (URTICA PILULIFERA)

29

explanations holds much weight and the following reasons are more likely to be true.

The earliest European 16th Century herbals, such as the German Kreuterbuck, call U. pilulifera, the Romifch Neffel or Welfch Nettle meaning Roman or Italian (Southern) Nettle, respectively. The British herbals of this period use, or copy the illustrations and text of the earlier European, German, French or Dutch herbals. Gerard's Herball, for example, is based on a translation of the Dutch herbals of Dodoen's, which is why he records that U. pilulifera is called, in low Dutch, Roomfche Netelen that is Romana urtica or Roman Nettle (Arber). For both the British and European herbals to call U. pilulifera the Roman Nettle, the most likely explanation, is its association with the Roman conquest of Europe (de Candolle).

The other reason could be because of its association with the Materia Medica of Dioscorides, on which most of the 16th Century herbals were based. Dioscorides, a physician of the Roman army, says in his herbal that the Romans call it (U. pilulifera) Urtica, so in these respects, this plant is associated with the Romans.

THE STRUCTURE AND REPRODUCTION

When growing in its natural habitat in warm arid areas U. pilulifera *in its vegetative state* is similar to U. urens (although much taller, up to 2

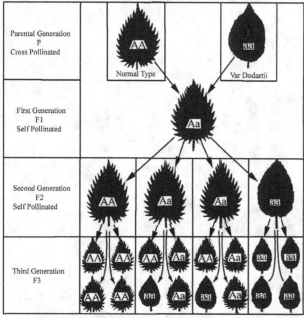

Fig 3.3. A graphic representation of the results of the breeding experiment of Correns (1909) which show that Dodart's nettle is a varriety of the Roman nettle and not a separate species (see text).

m) but when I grew it in my garden in southern Britain it looked at a glance very similar to U. dioica. Fully grown it is distinctive and quite attractive

with its purple stems and large green globular fruiting heads (Fig 3.2).

The Roman Nettle is an annual but occasionally a biennial or perennial (Gren. and Godr. Komarov). The stem is from 20-100cm. long, erect, simple or branched, almost glabrous (except for scattered stinging and non-stinging trichomes which are concentrated at the nodes); and hollow and square in section. The leaves are broadly ovate, 3-8cm. long and 2-5cm. broad, sub-cordate to rounded at the base with deeply incised dentate-serrate margins and covered on both surfaces with stinging hairs and a scattering of smaller non-stinging hairs especially on the leaf margins. The petiole is almost as long as the lamina. The stipules are oblong-ovate, slightly connate at the base and covered in non-stinging hairs. The cystoliths in the leaves are punctiform (dot-like).

The plant has both male and female flowers (monoecious). The inflorescences, which arise in the leaf axils, are either male or female. The male inflorescences are spicate and consist of long ascending stalks with a scattering of male flowers on short unequally branched stalks. Stinging hairs are found on the stalks and the perianth segments of the male flowers. The male flowers are of the typical Urtica type but with two important differences, (1) the pistillode is very small and of a square shape, (2) the stamens *do not explode but straighten slowly to liberate the pollen.* The flowers which are in groups on long inflorescence stalks are directed downwards, so when shaken by the wind they liberate the pollen in the same way as most wind pollinated flowers (Fig 3.2). The female flowers are collected in globose heads which are on long stalks and pistil produces one glistening brownish-black achene (2.5 mm long x 2.0 mm wide) with an outer mucilaginous envelope.

DODART'S NETTLE (URTICA DODARTII L.)

Early in the 17th Century, when large numbers of U. pilulifera plants were grown from seed, a Mr. Dodart noticed that occasionally plants appeared which were different in many ways from the typical plants. Linnaeus later named this new species Urtica dodartii L., in honour of his discovery. This plant is so unlike a typical nettle that it was called later the False Marjorum (Fig 3.2).

Ray in 1686 named this plant, "Urtica romana seu pilulifera altera parietaria foliis", which roughly translated means; Roman nettle with globule bearing heads (referring to the female inflorescences) and also, with Pellitory-shaped leaves. The plant names used by Ray were in fact mini descriptions of the distinguishing features of

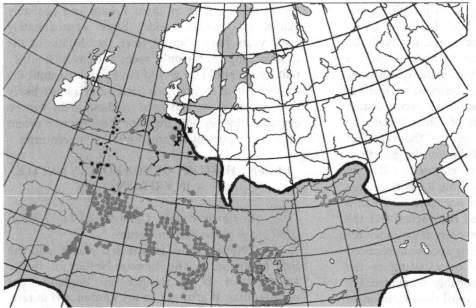

Fig 3.4 Map showing the present day distribution of U. pilulifera (green dots where it is extinct, orange where it is disappearing and red where it thrives). The purple shaded area shows th extent of the Roman Empire when at its maximum extent. ✖ = disappearing, ✳ =extinct in these areas.

the plant and really slowed the progress of botany until the introduction of the much simpler binominal system of nomenclature by Linnaeus.

In 1759 Linnaeus, in his 10th edition of the Systema Naturae, continues to treat this plant as a separate species under the name Urtica dodartii and this status is retained by Weddell in his Monographie des Urticees (1865). Weddell distinguishes this plant from Urtica pilulifera as follows: Leaves most commonly ovate, more or less entire but strongly waved and with very small teeth, female flower head not always solitary. The base of the leaf is also sub-cordate i.e. having two slight lobes at the base.

Sowerby's and Symes's English Botany, 3rd Ed. (1868) classifies the typical plant as genuina and this plant as var. Dodartii because it doesn't breed true. The seed from a single plant produces three different types of plants, those with (i) serrated-dentate leaf margins, (ii) partially serrated leaf margins, and (iii) completely entire margins, the latter being the Dodartii variety. On this evidence, H.C.Watson in his 'Cybele Brittanica' (1850?) concluded that it was impossible to regard them as two different species.

With the rediscovery of the Laws of Inheritance at the beginning of the 20th Century, the great German geneticist, Correns' became interested in the variety dodartii of the Roman Nettle and carried out some breeding experiments to look at the mechanism of inheritance. Taking the main difference, the leaf margin character, Correns

breeding experiments showed this to be controlled by a single pair of alleles. The dominant gene was responsible for the normal serrated/dentated margin, whilst the recessive allele, determined the almost entire margin of the dodartii variety (Fig 3.3). The inheritance follows that of a simple monohybrid cross, and the diagram shows why, very often, the plant doesn't breed true. The apparently normal plant of the 1st generation, because it carries the hidden recessive gene on self-pollination produces offspring in the characteristic 3:1 ratio. It is obvious that the dodartii variety carries two recessive genes and therefore on self-pollination will breed true. If cross-pollinated with pollen from normal-looking nettles, it could give rise to both types of nettle. However there are several differences between the normal and the dodartii variety, so it is likely that the genes for these are all linked together on the same chromosome.

HISTORICAL

EUROPEAN DISTRIBUTION

The extent of the Roman Empire, at the height if its expansion (A.D. 180), is shown on the Map 3.4. The conquering Romans will have carried with them live plants and seeds of many of the plants mentioned by Dioscorides in his Materia Medica (1st Century A.D.), and these will have been grown in the gardens they established. Dioscorides lists ten medicinal uses for Urtica pilulifera (and Urtica urens) and it is known that it was used, since early times, as an important nutritional plant or pot herb, so it is probable that it was employed by the Romans for either of these purposes. In any event it is likely to have been introduced into the northern European countries, either purposely or accidentally, as a contaminant to other medicinal or crop seeds grown, or by transport vehicles, etc., used at that time.

Sir Edward Salisbury's book on 'Weeds and Aliens' (1961) is the classical book in this area, and in relation to the spreading of weeds, he concludes that the cosmopolitan nature of many weeds is closely related to the ubiquity of man's disturbance of his environment and his efficiency as an agent of dispersal, either intentionally or accidentally. During the Roman invasion of Great Britain he emphasises the importance of the thousands of miles of Roman roads as a habitat for the growth of weeds. The roads were elevated with an embankment of soil on either side; the surface area of this initially bare soil, over not more than half a century, could have exceeded 6000 acres, and the southern slopes, must have been favourable for colonisation by the less exacting species introduced from southern Europe. The broadcasting of the grains of cereal by hand probably precluded the effective weeding by hoeing until the invention of the seed drill by Jethro Tull at the beginning of the 18th Century (Salisbury). In this connection it occurs as a weed amongst crops in Russia [Komarov]. Taking these things into account it is reasonable to conclude that Urtica pilulifera will have been given ample opportunity to be dispersed, and to establish itself, to the limits of the Roman Empire.

The present day distribution of Urtica pilulifera is:

Middle Europe

(SW France, Germany*, Holland*, Switzerland*, Austria*, Czechoslavakia*).

S. Europe/Mediterranean-

(Portugal, Spain, Balearic Islands, Corsica, Sardinia, Sicily, Italy, N. Africa, Saint Helena).

Balkans- (Hungary*, Rumania, Bulgaria, Greece).

Asia Minor- (Turkey).

Russia- (Crimea, Caucasus, Eastern Transcaspian). (The asterisks indicate that in these countries it is introduced/naturalised or casual).

The European distribution of Urtica pilulifera and the extent of the Roman Empire at its maximum are shown on Map 3.4. There is a similarity between the two but this might be co-incidental; however, taking the factors previously mentioned into account, it very likely to be due to the dispersal of Urtica pilulifera by the Roman Army. Weddell concludes that U. pilulifera seems to have originated in Italy, from where the famous Swiss botanist Alph. De Candolle supposes that it must have been transported to parts of Europe by the Roman occupation and that one way of looking at it is that the Italian and Roman Nettle are the same.

Urtica pilulifera at its northern limits has a scanty distribution and is regarded as a casual. It is regarded as extinct in Great Britain and probably extinct in Czechoslovakia. Since approximately 1,500 years have elapsed since the decline of the Roman Empire it would seem extremely unlikely that Urtica pilulifera would have survived until the present day at its northern limits, and a more likely explanation of its existence in these areas can be explained by periodic introductions in more recent times, i.e. especially during the 16th-18th centuries.

RECENT HISTORY OF THE ROMAN NETTLE IN BRITAIN

In Great Britain Gerarde, in his Herball (1597), says of the Roman Nettle:-

"Nettles grow in vntilled places, and the firft (referring to the Roman Nettle) in thicke woods, and is a ftanger in England, not withftanding it groweth in my garden.... It is rare, and groweth but in few places, and the feed is fent from other counteries, and fowne in gardens for his vertues." (f=s).

Parkinson (1640) in Theatrum Botanicum, after Camden, states it is found in the town of Lidde by Romney and the streets of Romney, Kent. Ray, Syn 29, (1690) says the plant was plentiful on the coast of Suffolk (near Aldeburgh), and in Norfolk (near Yarmouth). Thomas Green in his Universal Herbal (1820) says it is common amongst rubbish and stones, and has been found near the quay at Yarmouth, at Aldborough and Bungary in Suffolk, and at Romney in Kent. Mackay (1836) Flora Hibernica of Ireland, records it as growing amongst rubbish and under walls near the sea at Ballylickey near Bantry.

Sowerby/Syme edition (1868) records it, "By roadsides and in waste places near towns and villages in the east of England, but doubtfully native. The only places where I know it to be permanent in its stations, are by the side of the fish-houses, Lowestoft, Suffolk; Great Yarmouth, Norfolk; and perhaps at Copford, Essex, where both vars. occur. It has occurred in, or been reported from, the counties of Cornwall, Hants, Kent, Surrey, Middlesex, Cambridge, Stafford, Salop, Glamorgan, Anglesea, Lancaster, Durham, Northumberland; but I cannot discover that it has remained permanently established in any of these localities".

Babington (1881) records U. pilulifera, as about towns and villages on the eastern side of England and as being rare. Bentham and Hooker (1886) record it as a weed of roadsides and waste places in southern Europe, and farther north as an introduced weed in the neighbourhood of habitations. In England it is found ocassionally in the east. Clapham et al. (1960) state formerly it was found as a rare alien but at the present time in appears to be extinct.

This evidence shows that, in recent recorded history, it only took 400 years for U. Pilulifera to go from a position of being scantily widespread but plentiful in places, to one of extinction. The reasons for this are to be found in, (i) plentiful initially because of its use in the pleasure gardens of the 16th-18th Centuries and as a herbal medicine, (ii) reached extinction because of its unsuitability as an herbal medicine, and also, as a colonist of the British countryside.

AS AN UNSUCCESSFUL COLONIST OF BRITAIN

Many plants from southern Europe when introduced into Britain have successfully spread throughout the country e.g. Ivy-leaved Toadflax. The reasons why the Roman Nettle was not successful in spreading and establishing itself, in the British Isles, can only be guessed at, for even now little is known of its ecology. Principally an annual, it would need suitable conditions for growth and a long enough season to produce adequate seed. As an occasional biennial it may not have been able to survive the British winter, whilst the self-sown seeds produce seedlings appearing in May, and these may have been killed by late frosts (Salisbury, 1961)). The seeds are comparatively large, 2 mm in length, and are likely to have fallen near the parent and therefore were unlikely to have found suitable habitats, and so on. The fact that it was scarce, and has become extinct in parts of middle and northern Europe, may indicate unsuitable climatic conditions (still and rainy conditions would not favour the pollination method of this plant): in this connection its stronghold was in SE England, which has a climate approaching that of southern Europe.

FOR ROMAN USE AS A HERBAL PLANT

Camden's account of the Roman Army using U. pilulifera for flagellation of their bodies in cold weather. Most people agree that this is an amusing story, with little foundation, since Camden was principally a historian. It is obvious to any present day botanist that our perennial Common Nettle (U. dioica) of Britain, is admirably suited for flagellation, because of being found almost everywhere, readily re-grows after cutting, and is found growing almost all the year round. The Romans would have appreciated flagellation by this nettle with its mild sting, (but still effective ability to

" ...when Julius Caesar landed at Romney, the soldiers brought some of the nettle seed with them, and sowed it there for their use, to rub and chafe their limbs, when, through extreme cold, they should be stiff and benumbed, being told before they came from home that the climate of Britain was so cold that it was not to be endured without some friction to warm their blood."
WILLIAM CAMDEN 1607

bring blood to the skin surface or joints), to that of the more virulent and extremely painful sting of the Roman Nettle.

Equally there would seem little justification for using the Roman Nettle as an herbal medicinal plant, or pot herb, considering that our own perennial nettle is much more suited for forcing in the spring to produce tender shoots, and has similar medicinal properties to the Roman nettle.

BOX 3.1 THE ELIZABETHAN PLEASURE GARDENS, HERBALISTS AND THEIR CONNECTION WITH THE ROMAN NETTLE

Land and sea explorations led to the influx of a vast number of plants from all over the world, and the establishment of museums for herbariums, and botanic, physic and private gardens for ornamental and herbal plants, particularly in the 16th-18th Centuries. Coinciding with this was the rediscovery of the ancient herbals, followed by the printing and illustration of a number of modern versions, first in Europe and then in England. This led to an escalation of herb use and herbal gardens.

The Society of Apothecaries set up in London, provided for the correct recognition of "simples" or herbal drugs, and because of the importance of fresh herbs, the Society took upon itself the maintenance of a botanic garden, latterly, the famous Physics Garden at Chelsea, established in 1673 (Allen).

Gerarde had a renowned garden in Holborn, London, and in 1596, he published a catalogue of the plants, (which includes Vrtica Romana); the first ever published of the contents of a single garden. Other famous London gardens at this time were those of John Parkinson in the heart of London, John Tradescant's at Lambeth and

Mistress Tugg's at Westminster (Arber, 1938)). A fascinating account of the published lists of plants grown in famous gardens, based on manuscripts in the library of John Goodyer, is published in Early British Botanists by Gunther. Vrtica Romana is listed as growing in William Coys' garden in Essex (1621), and in John Tradescants' Garden at Lambeth (1634).

The variety of the Roman Nettle called Vrtica dodartii, was also grown at the Chelsea Physics Garden by Philip Miller. The latter was a brilliant custodian of the large collection of foreign plants. He says in his 'Gardener's Dictionary' (1741), Roman Nettles were "Preserved in many Gardens for Variety and he called Dodart's variety of the Roman Nettle, the Spanish Marjoram and says that it was *"most common in English gardens, where it was cultivated for making sport: many ignorant persons taking it for a Sort of Marjoram, are often severely stung by smelling into it; and others put it into the Middle of Nosegays amongst other Greens, which they present to Persons who are not acquainted with the Plant, and so by smelling to it they suffer in like manner as the former."* Miller says these Nettles *"should be transplanted out into Beds or the Borders of the Pleasure Garden, interspersing them amongst other plantd, so that they may not be so easily discovered by Persons whom there is design to deceive by gathering a Sprig from them to smell to."* No doubt its popularity as a fun plant resulted spreading it into wild adjacent areas where it was often mistaken for the typical Roman Nettle!

The Hortus Kewensis listing the plants grown at Kew in 1813 includes U. pilulifera, Native of England and U. dodartii, S. of Europe. Thomas Green in his Universal Herball (1816) gives instructions for growing the Roman Nettle, *"Sow the seeds in March upon a bed of rich light earth. When the plants are come up, transplant them into beds, or the borders of the pleasure garden. The seeds ripen in autumn and if the plants be permitted to scatter themselves, they will grow without further care."* He also lists Urtica dodartii.

From this, it can be seen that the Roman Nettle was a popular garden plant in the 17th Century, probably related to the practical joking which could take place using the variety dodartii. Seed continued to be available throughout the 18th Century from seed merchants and garden plants. Roman nettle plants found growing wild in the countryside or in the vicinity of human habitations could have resulted from seed dispersal or deliberate broadcasting of seed. Geoffrey Grigson relates how a Sir Thomas Brown in 1668 attempted to spread the plant, *"I have found it growing wild at Golston by Yarmouth, and transplanted it to other places."*

Bromfield in 1843 confesses to a similar practice after; a Mr. Gibson gives a list of plants found near Ventor, including Urtica pilulifera, in an issue of the Phytologist. Bromfield then confesses in a later issue of this journal, that he was responsible for scattering these seeds at this very spot. He added *"I would just beg to ask Mr. Gibson whether on examination he will not find his plant to be Urtica Dodartii"* he then goes on to condemn himself for thereby *"creating confusion in Vegetable Geography."*

Later, Bromfield, in his Flora Vectensis, which was quoted in the Phytologist (1860), says in relation to the Roman Nettle, *"Grows at Gosport somewhere on the way to Gomer Pond. The seeds are sold by London seedsmen under the name of Roman Nettle, I am told for some medical purposes though what that is I am unable to learn, as this plant does not form an official article in any of the London pharmacopoeia, nor is it worth cultivating for ornament. The knowledge of this fact favours a suspicion I have always entertained that U. pilulifera has in all its British Stations originated from the gardens of the growers of simples".*

In this connection Mc Clintock (1968) relates that after he wrote an article on extinct plants, including the Roman Nettle, in 'The Countryman (1957) that three years later a person wrote to him saying that a Roman Nettle had appeared in a chicken run in Wandsworth. Botanists were anxious to preserve it and it was recorded here for at least another eight years.

THE SMALL NETTLE (URTICA

URENS L

INTRODUCTION

NAMES

No doubt most people when stung by the small nettle whilst weeding in-between their vegetables recognise this nettle as different from the common nettle because of its small size. In places where both nettle species grow together the small nettle is generally completely overlooked. In the Kreuterbuch and in Gerard's Herball, it is called Vrtica minor which the latter author calls "in Engliſh, Small Nettle, and Small burning Nettle". Linnaeus, in 1753, calls this nettle Urtica urens, where urens means burning, acrid, and comes partially from the Latin uro, to burn.

DISTRIBUTION

Urtica urens is found throughout Europe except in the extreme north (Ball, 1964). It occurs in the Caucasus, W. and E. Siberia (adventive) and in the Far East (Komarov) and over almost the whole of Asia, Arabia, N. Africa, Abyssinia, Canary Isles, Madeira as well as South Africa(Greig-Smith).

It has been introduced and become naturalised in a number of countries, (i) North America where it is found in all Canadian provinces (Woodland 1974, 1982). It is widely scattered in the U.S.A. Sporadically naturalised in Florida and South Carolina (Miller, 1971), (ii) South America. It is widespread in most provinces of Chile (Navas), (iii) Australia, (iv) New Zealand where it was recorded by Hooker in 1864 in his introduced plants. It is stated to occur in waste places on both islands but is not common (Thompson, 1922).

In the Flora of the British Isles it occurs in 111 out of 112 of the vice counties and throughout Ireland as well as the Channel Islands. It is described as being not uncommon but of a local nature throughout the British Isles (Clapham W.and T., 1960).

In relation to altitude it is found in many areas in Britain between 300-500m but is regarded as a more markedly lowland species than U. dioica (Greig-Smith). In Europe it can be found up to about 2000m in the Alps (max. ht. recorded 2,700m), in Switzerland and Austria. At this altitude it often occurs in association with U. dioica in the vicinity of farms and chalets where the soil is rich in humus from dung heaps and cattle droppings (Newell-Arber, 1910).

STRUCTURE AND REPRODUCTION

The small nettle is an annual with a thick white fleshy taproot. There are no organs for asexual reproduction. Since plants are widely separated they develop large numbers of side-branches which give a bush-like appearance. Under very fertile conditions it grows to a height of 1 m, but in unproductive habitats, it only grows from 10-15 cm. The plant has glandular hairs but is largely devoid of small hairs (glabrous) and has scattered stinging hairs on the stem, petioles, inflorescences, and mainly on their top surfaces of the leaves. The leaves are ovate, with no cordate base and deeply incised to form serrated edges (Fig 3.1a).

The plant is monoecious (separate male and female flowers on the same plant) with mixed flowers occurring on the 4 short inflorescence branches at each node. The male and female flowers are similar to those of Urtica dioica and are produced very early on in development. In seedlings under controlled laboratory conditions they appeared 20-32 days after germination. The female flowers appeared approximately five days earlier than the males, enabling cross pollination by male pollen from other plants (Boot et al., 1986). The male and female flowers mature alongside one another (Fig 3.5) but the male flowers grow above the level of the females because they need space for the explosive pollen release. The inflexed stamens in the male flowers straighten explosively to catapult the pollen into the air several centimetres and well away from the female flowers.

All of these factors would tend to increase the chances of cross-pollination. Flowering takes place over a long period and under favourable conditions side branches form and the plant becomes bushy and can extend its area to 0.25 m. Even under stress conditions such as drought priority is given to flower production (Boot et al). The brown achenes are released from the perianth sometimes before or shortly after they are shed.

In relation to the habitats of U. urens, the older floras mention specific locations, whereas the more recent floras specify the broader habitat types. In analysing the habitats occupied by U. urens, 29 old and recent floras were consulted, and for each flora, a note was made of its habitats. The % occurrence in a particular habitat is as follows: - Waste Ground 17.7, Cultivated Ground 14.6, Dung Heaps 10.4, Human Habitations 9.4 , Roadsides 8.3, Sandy Places 7.3, Light Soils 6.3, Coast Formations 5.2, Gardens 5.2, Disturbed Ground 3.1, Refuse Tips 2.1, and Fields 2.1.

HABITATS

Of these habitats 65.2% are connected with human disturbance of soil or by domesticated cattle. In the Sheffield area U. urens is recorded in 0.4 of all habitats: arable (8), spoil (1) and bricks and mortar (6), (Grime et al). U. urens is absent from heavily shaded habitats, heavily grazed areas, wetland, woodland, skeletal habitats and pasture (Fig3.6). As a weed and a ruderal U. urens is in-between ruderal and competitive ruderal (Grime et al 1988).

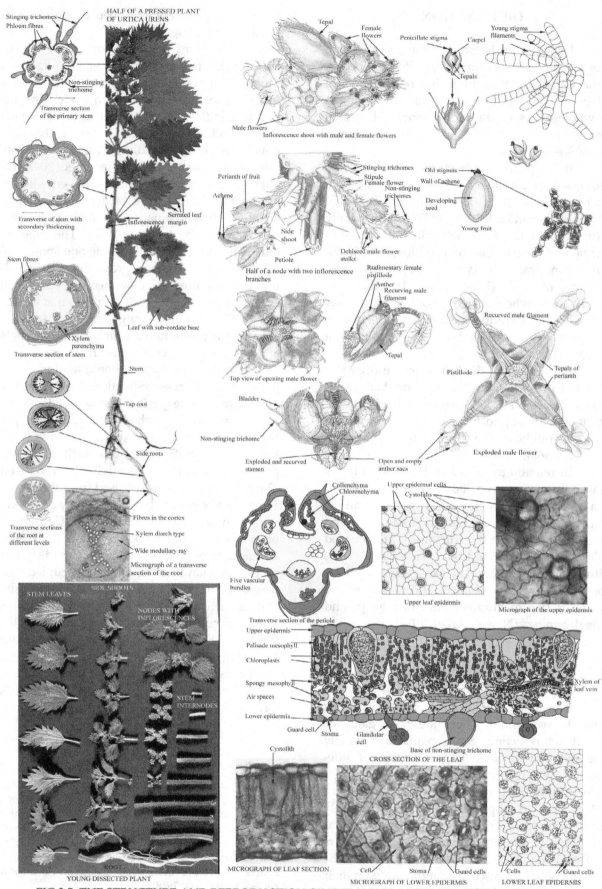

FIG 3.5. THE STRUCTURE AND REPRODUCTION OF THE SMALL NETTLE (URTICA URENS).

36

There is clear evidence that U urens is a nitrophyte, i.e. a plant with preference for nitrogen-rich habitats, and that this explains, to a large extent, its association with humans, human habitations and cattle. References to its nitrophily occur throughout literature but to quote a few, (i) especially found on soils containing a high organic content e.g. gardens and with horticultural crops (Salisbury), (ii) more generally confined to manure heaps and cultivated land and seldom in pasture, meadows or woods (Howard and Noel), (iii) abundant near alpine chalets where it is associated with soil rich in humus from manure and animal dung (Newell-Arber). In his classification of ruderal plants, Ellenberg places U. urens under strongly nitrophilous plants which are short-lived pioneers e.g. the Goosefoot-Mallow

cannot be used. In Cornwall it occurs frequently on the margins of potato fields where it grow dense mono-stands (Photo Fig 3.6). In field studies carried out in the Sheffield area (Grime et al., 1988) those plants most associated with U. urens are as follows: -Red Dead Nettle (*Lamium Purpureum*) 81%, Corn Spurrey (*Spergula arvensis*) 79%, Black Bindweed (*Fallopia convolvulus*) 77%, Field For-get-me-not (*Myosotis arvensis*) 76%, Scarlet Pimpernel (*Anagallis arvensis*) 74%.

GERMINATION

Grime and Jarvis (1976) carried out a series of experiments on the effect of light on the germination of species of contrasted ecology. Seeds

Fig 3.6. Two arable habitats of Urtica urens. Left on the outside area of a potato field Cornwall Devon. Right An organic field left to weed over where U. urens is quite dominant together with other weeds, pink dead nettle (*Lamium purpureum*), Sow thistle (*Sonchus arvensis*), field speedwell (*Veronica persica*), groundsel (*Senecio vulgaris*), shepherds purse (*Capsella bursa-pastoris*), etc.. I studied this field for years and the appearance of U. urens was sporadic and probably related to the seed bank and the disturbance of the soil.

community which also contains Nettle-leaved Goosefoot (*Chenopodium murale*), Stinking Goosefoot (*C. vulvaria*) and Dwarf-Mallow (*Malva neglecta*).

In a laboratory experiment the effect of high levels of nitrate on the growth of U. urens was to increase its yield almost four fold over the control. In the experiment plants of hoed gardens and the following crops responded strongly, e.g. Small Nettle (*U. urens*), Cockspur Grass (*Echinochloa crus-galli*), Bristle Grass (*Setaria pumila*) but the others did not, e.g. All-Seed (*Chenopodium polyspermum*), (Mayser & Walter in Ellenburg 1988).This experiment together with other field experiments (Jornsgard et al., in Ellenberg 1988) confirms the strong nitrophily of the small nettle and how it increases its chances of success (increased seed production) when growing with crops and other weeds on soil receiving high nitrogen fertiliser applications.

In the British Isles, as a weed of arable land the small nettle occurs particularly amongst broad-leaved crops such as potatoes, sugar beet, cabbages, etc., probably because in such situations herbicides

were exposed to three different light regimes referred to as 'light', 'shade' and 'dark', with a temperature of 20° C day and 15° C night The results for the germination of U. urens were as follows, 29% 'dark', 89% 'shade', and 3% 'light. The result for germination in the 'light' was unusual in that it showed a pronounced inhibition; in contrast to the, other weed species tested which showed high percentage germination. Lauer (in Ellenberg) investigated the germination of various weed species at various constant temperature levels. He grouped the weeds into two categories, those of summer crops and garden and those of winter cereals. Germination can be favoured by certain temperature regimes and plants can be divided broadly into, 'Warmth germinators' and 'Cold germinators', which germinate best at 20-30° C, and below 20° C respectively. Urtica urens falls into the category of a 'Warmth germinator' but it still shows appreciable germination in the range 10-20° C. Although U. urens can be found in cereal crops, it does not grow so well as when it grows amongst root crops. The reason for this is that spring crops have the advantage of higher natural nitrogen levels, and in addition, heavier fertiliser treatments that favour this plant. The percentage germination in particular areas varies each year and is linked to the disturbance of the soil (Roberts & Feast, 1972).

The structure of the achene and the stages in germination are shown in Fig 3.7. During germination the cotyledons absorb the food contained in the endosperm, the achene wall splits and eventually falls off, after which the cotyledons spread horizontally. The cotyledons differ from

(*Heterotoma Planicornis*) and (*Plagiognathus arbustorum*). Flies (*Agromyza reptans*)* and the larvae of the Nettle Midge (*Dasineura urticae*)*.

Of the eighteen species of insects recorded on U. urens, *Heterogaster urticae, Anthocoris nemorum, Lygus rugulipennis, Eupteryx urticae, E. aurata* and *Trioza urticae* were certainly breeding in addition to the aphids *Aphis fabae* and *Myzus persicae*, and the

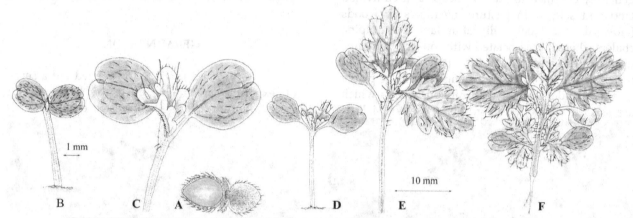

Fig 3.7 THE STAGES IN GERMINATION OF THE SMALL NETTLE (URTICA URENS)
(A) The achene with surrounding perianth. (B-F) Stages in growth of the young seedling which is similar to U. dioica but with the following differences (i) the cotyledons are longer and ovate-oblong, (ii) the leaves have fewer stinging hairs, (iii) the breadth of the leaf related to the length is much less, (iv) the cotyledons persist for much longer. The germination is epigeal and side branches appear very early in growth.

those of Urtica dioica in being longer and ovate-oblong in shape, and in common with many other rapidly developing annuals the cotyledons are retained in the young plant even up to the time of fruit liberation. In a similar way to foliage leaves the cotyledons contribute towards the production of food.

INSECTS ASSOCIATED WITH THE SMALL NETTLE

The main work on insects associated with Urtica urens is that carried out in Huntingdonshire (Davis & Lawrence, 1974). Larvae of the Silver Y moth (*Autographa gamma*) and the Red Admiral butterfly (*Vanessa atlanta*). Beetles, the flower beetle (*Brachypterus glaber*)* the weevils, (*Apion urticarium*)* and (*Cidnorhinus quadrimaculatus*)*. The Homopterans, included *Trioza urticae*,* leaf hoppers *Eupteryx urticae*,* E. aurata, and a few individuals of *E. collina, E.cyclops* and *Macrosteles variatus*. Aphids, *Aphis fabae, Myzus persicae* and *Aphis urticaria*.* Heteropterans included, Ground Bug (*Heterogaster urticae*), Common Flower Bug (*Anthocoris nemorum*), European Tarnished Plant Bug (*Lygus rugulipennis*), Common Nettle Capsid (*Liocorus tripistulatus*), Common Green Capsid (*Lygocoris pabulinus*),

lepidopterans *Plusia gamma* and *Vanessa atlanta*.

ECOLOGY OF THE SMALL NETTLE IN A NATURAL RUDERAL HABITAT

BOX 3.1 *THE SURVIVAL OF URTICA URENS ON SANDY SHINGLE ON A COASTAL HEADLAND*

In Devon, England, the Small Nettle (Urtica urens) is recorded in older floras, as occurring along estuaries and on coastal headlands. I have not been able to find them in some of these older locations, such as the coastal headland on the Exmouth side of the Exe estuary. The disappearance in this grassy sandy area is probably due to two changed factors, (1) it is not now grazed and (2) it is now mown.

In North Devon there is an area where the Small Nettle grows and I have studied this over the past year. Northam Burrows is at the head of the Taw/Torridge estuary and behind the burrows is a golf course where grazing by sheep, donkeys and horses is allowed. These grazing animals help to keep the turf short and fertilise it with their urine and droppings, but they also present trampling and grazing factors to the wild plants growing in the area (Fig 3.8).

There is a small inlet just before the estuary mouth, which forms a semi-circular area of mud flats at low tide. At one end of this area is a short sand and shingle headland (AREA 1). An artificial embankment runs alongside the other part of the bay and prevents the flooding of the low-lying golf course. At the base of this embankment, on the golf-course side, a number of sandy hollows are present which also support the small nettle (AREA 2).

Area 1 is my main study area and consists of a narrow strip of sandy shingle, sparsely covered in grass; the two dominant plants are Urtica dioica and U. urens but there are also large plants of the Slender Thistle (*Carduus tenuiflorus*). Other plants include, Silverweed (*Potentilla anserina*), Common Stork's-bill (*Erodium cicutarium*), Black Nightshade (*Solanum nigrum*), Prickly Saltwort (*Salsola kali*). Sea Knotgrass (*Polygonium maritimum*), Broad-Leaved Dock (*Rumex obtusifolius*) and Buck's Horn Plantain (*Plantago coronopus*). Behind this narrow strip lies

rain and sand, cold (although this area does not suffer from frost), and trampling. A second wave of germination in late March produced an enormous number of seedlings and a large number of these survived to produce young plants when I examined the area in mid-May. The majority of plants were 7-10cm in height but a few were 25-30cm high! All stages were flowering. On the large sandy areas where the trampling was most severe most plants had been destroyed but a lot were sufficiently large to be able to recover from this because of the substantial and deep tap root system. The grazing animals moved around the larger Common nettle clones and thistle patches so that the U. urens seedlings managed to survive in these peripheral areas.

As one moved along the strip the shingle became more abundant and the small nettle less

Fig 3.8.Growth of Urtica urens on a coastal headland the mouth of the Taw/Torridge estuary Northern Burrows, Devon. The turf is grazed heavily by cattle, horses and sheep which create disturbed open sand areas where they urinate and deposit dung. Left Urtica urens in the foreground and U. dioica in the background. Right close up to show U. urens amongst the trampling and dung.The soil is rich in nitrate which enables this nitrophyte to grow rapidly and produce a large amount of seed in order to survive in this hostile habitat.

the short grassland where scattered U. urens plants grow in very small sandy crevices between grass tussocks and around objects, such as large stones, posts, etc. They do not occur on the typical unbroken turf outside these areas. Since U. urens is a nitrophyte, without doubt, it could not survive in this sandy area without the nitrogen and other nutrients provided by the grazing animals and it is noticeable that they congregate in this area (a laird area) which is very rich in droppings and urine. The double-edged sword is that, on the one hand they help to create bare areas by their urine killing off the turf which is then slow to establish, whilst on the other hand, they destroy plants by their congregation and trampling of such areas.

My studies have shown that U. urens can only survive in this area due to its enormous production of seeds throughout most of the year and the germination and establishment of these seedlings over a long period from late autumn to early spring. Some autumnal seedlings did survive but the majority died over the winter due to driving

abundant and this may have been due to the inability of the taproot to penetrate this terrain. The common nettle and Creeping Thistle (*Cirsium arvense*) were found growing in the shingle together with Creeping Tormentil (*Potentilla reptans*) and this could be due to the ability of their stems to creep in-between the stones.

In Area 2 U. urens occurred in sandy hollows in the turf where it was the dominant plant and therefore the only one suited to survive; however even it could not survive in the badly disturbed areas. Other plants in such areas were U. dioica, Black Nightshade and in the peripheral parts Common Houndstongue and Black Horehound, the latter being badly grazed.

In conclusion U. urens survived in these areas because of its strategy of (1) its ability to flower at an early age and produce a large number of seeds over a long period of time, (2) germinating over the autumn-winter period which enabled its establishment and growth into large plants by the spring, (3) its comparatively rapid growth enabled

39

by the high levels of nutrients from faeces and urine, (4) the availability of open sandy areas, in which other plants could not survive due to disturbance and trampling, (6) its long tap root system allowed efficient water absorption in a habitat where the surface becomes dry and hot, (7) a most important factor was its stinging hairs which prevented it being grazed. Proof of this could be seen in short turf areas where large plants of U. urens succeeded in establishing and surviving. Some authorities question the significance of protective stinging hairs in this plant however, in this habitat and other habitats with vertebrate herbivores they are vital.

Plants in a similar way to the Common Nettle have good re-growth of side shoots in response to occasional grazing of top parts. This ruderal habitat exists due to disturbance by grazing animals, their urine and droppings that also contain seeds of U. urens and without these factors U. urens could not exist.

VARIATION AND GENETICS

There is very little information concerning varieties in U. urens. The varieties listed come from two sources which I will identify with symbols; (a) Druce (1928) * and (b) Ascherson and Graebner (1908-1913) #. (i) **parvifolia** */ **parvula** #. I presume these are the same because they stem from the word parvus meaning small, and refer to plants that are much smaller than the typical plant in all aspects. Typically they are found growing in dry infertile areas. (ii) **hispida** * appears to be similar to **Podolica** #. Both types are densely covered with stinging and non-stinging hairs. The latter variety also has round leaves 2-3.8 cm L x 1.7-3.2 cm B and inflorescence stalks 7 mm L. (iii) **montana** # Medium height with the stem largely unbranched. Leaves wedge-shaped, 5.2 cm L x 3.5 cm B. Scattered stinging hairs. Inflorescence stalks 0.4-1.0 cm L. (iv) **major** #. Much larger in all aspects than typical plants. Height 60 cm. Leaves 6.5 cm L x 5.0-cm B. (v) **iners** #. Plant almost without stinging hairs. Druce (1930) also mentions a variety, elegans, with variegated yellow-green leaves.

Somatic chromosome counts from material of U.urens in Canada and the United States found the diploid number to be 2n=26, and eight other chromosome counts in the literature were all 2n=24 (Bassett, Crompton and Woodland. 1977). Love and Love (1961) reported three chromosome counts, 2n=24, 26, and 52. This means that there are two basic chromosome genomes x=12, and 13, and that individuals with 52 chromosomes are tetraploid, (i.e. 4 x 13).

HERBAL MEDICINAL AND OTHER USES

It is generally claimed that Urtica urens has similar medicinal properties to Urtica dioica, and therefore only those medicinal properties specific to U. urens, are considered here.

U. urens is completely different from U.dioica in relation to its content of chemical substances called flavonids, (Saeed et al) the authors mention that U. urens is a troublesome weed everywhere and that it appears in gardens as soon as the winter is over. The plant was dried, powdered and then subjected to chemical analysis with the result that six flavonol glycosides were isolated, 3-O-galactoside, Patuletin 3-O-rutinoside, isorhamnetin 3-O galactoside, palulitrin, paluletin 3-O-glucoside and kaempferol-7-rutinoside, together with the rare flavonol, patuletin.

Severn flavonids isolated from U. urens were new to the Urticaceae. The aglycon patuletin, which represented the main compound, was tested for its antimicrobial, anti-inflammatory, analgesic and ulcerogenic effects. It showed significant inhibition of the growth of certain microbes (i) Staphylococcus and (ii) Streptococcus which cause infections associated with acute inflammation, pus, lesions and abscesses (iii) Escherichia coli, certain strains of which cause food poisoning and (iv) Candida albicans which is a fungus which can cause thrush. It reduced oedema, which is the retention of water in body tissue, and acted as an analgesic, i.e. a drug that relieves pain without inducing sleep- it had no side effect of causing ulceration. These properties help to explain the use of nettles in reducing inflammation and infection associated with burns sores and gangrenes.

In Turkey Urtica urens is called cincar, isirgan and dicirgen and is used in different regions as follows:- (i) for rheumatism (this refers to cases of rheumatoid arthritis which primarily affects the joints which become swollen, stiff and painful), used as the fresh herb directly applied, powdered, as a poultice or decoction which is drunk. The scientific basis for its use as a remedy against rheumatism in the western world as well as by Australian aborigines is linked to the discovery that U. urens contains immunoreactive leukotrienes (in tissues and the nettle stinging fluid). These are related to the prostaglandins, and like hormones, have profound physiological effects, (1) causing inflammatory responses involving joints, skin and eyes, (2) for hypoglycemia, which is a dangerous condition where the glucose level in the blood is too high, and can result in coma followed by death. The causes are various and I'm unaware of any research on the effectiveness of the nettle for this condition (Wetherilt, et al. 1992) The Common Nettle was used from the dawn of civilisation as a fibre plant.

U. DIOICA ON THE FLOOD PLAIN OF THE RIVER TAW, DEVON - MOVE ON

CHAPTER 4

FOLKLORE AND LITERATURE

COMMON NAMES

The most obvious characteristic of the nettle is its sting and this is embodied in its most widely used name Common Stinging Nettle although other similar adjectives such as Sting, Stingey or Stingy are occasionally used in different parts of Great Britain.

Grigson (1975) mentions the following common names for U. dioica together with the areas of origin or use:- Ettle (*Gloucestershire, Hampshire, Herefordshire, Northamptonshire, Warwickshire, Wiltshire, Worcestershire*); Cool Faugh (*Donegal*); Devil's Leaf, Devil's Plaything (*Somerset*); Heg Beg (*Scotland*); Hidgy-Pidgy, Hoky-Poky (*Devon*); Jenny Nettle (*Isle of Mann*); Naughty Man's Plaything (*Somerset, Sussex*); Tanging Nettle (*Yorkshire*). Fischer (1932) also mentions Devil's Apron, Gicksy, Hop Tops and Scaddie for U. dioica. In Devon it is also called Sting-Nittle (Lafont, 1984).

Hoky-Poky also means Hocus-pocus meaning to deceive, trick or impose upon – perhaps relating to the nettle's intrusion by way of its sting. Cool Faugh is an exclamation of disgust or contempt probably also associated with the nettle's stinging properties. Jenny Nettle means Common Nettle but is also associated with the Wren. Tanging comes from tang meaning a penetrating odour/stinking perhaps in relation to the odour giving off by fast growing nettles. Gicksey is applied to Wild Chervil, Wild Angelica and nettles, where Gick stands for a hollow stem of a plant. Hop-Tops liken female nettles, with their candelabra-like fruiting heads to the top of hops with their fruits (Fischer, 1932).

Friend (1883) gives a good account of the relationships between plants and the Devil, and I give a few examples here. He mentions in relation to the Giant Puffball (*Clavatia gigantea*) that it is called the Devil's or Old Man's Snuffbox where 'Old Man' is probably only a more polite and euphemistic form for 'Devil'. The inclusion of Devil in a plant name may refer to a characteristic associated with the Devil, e.g. Love in a Mist (*Nigella damascena*) is also called Devil-in-a-Bush because of its horned capsule. The Red Hot Poker (*Knophofia* sp.) is sometimes called the Devil's Poker because the flowering inflorescence has the appearance of a poker just taken out of the fire. Reference to the Devil is also found in plant names in connection to some unpleasant characteristic of the plant, e.g. Devil's Stinkpot referring to the Stinkhorn (*Phallus impudicus*) because of its nauseating smell. The Thorn Apple (*Datura stramonium*) is also called the Devil's Apple because it is poisonous and causes hallucinations, etc.

The names of Old Man's, Naughty Man's or Devil's Leaf or Plaything and Devil's Apron for Urtica dioica refer to its unpleasant, hurtful and protective stinging properties and likewise a nettle (*Urtica urentissima* now called *Dendrocnide moroides*) found in Timor. The sting of the latter is reputed to last a whole year or even cause death and is called the Daoun Setan or Devil's Leaf where Setan is the Semitic name for Devil. In a similar way the Yarrow (*Achillea millefolium*), which produces a tingling sensation when drawn across the face, is called the Devil's Nettle. It would seem appropriate at this point to consider the folklore regarding the association between nettles and the Devil, Puck and Fairies. In relation to Ogres, thistles and nettles are regarded as the Devil's vegetables. In Ireland the stinging hairs are thought to represent the tines of the Devil's pitchfork.

Although the nettle names that include the adjective Devil refer to its unpleasant stinging properties, most mythology centres on the beneficial and protective properties of this plant. It is believed to be a protection against evil spirits and in this connection; in Yorkshire (England) the leaves have been used in ceremonies to exorcise the Devil. The plant was sacred to Thor and the attachment of nettles to one's clothing, in times of danger, was thought to drive out fear and inspire courage. In relation to Gypsy life and lore it is thought that nettles grow in places where there are holes leading to subterranean passages in which dwell Earth-Fairies, the Pc,uvus. No doubt the nettle clump provides a place, protected by its stings, which is consecrated to the fairies and called Pc,uvus-wood. Gypsy children gathering nettles for pigs therefore sting:-

> *"Nettles, nettle do not burn*
> *In your house no one shall go*
> *No one to the Pc,uvus goes*
> *Drive, drive away the worms"*

Nettles are thought to protect against the evil spells of witches and house trolls and in this respect they are hung up in dairies to prevent the milk curdling. In the medicine practised in Anglo-Saxon times the nettle was considered effective against the green venom, one of the nine flying venoms which were thought to be responsible for the transmission of diseases.

The nettle is listed amongst the plants which guard against lightning and is used to this effect in the Tyrol and Italy, when during a thunderstorm, it is the practice to throw them onto a fire (Leach, M. 1950 and Wedeck 1973).

PLACE NAMES

Nettles grow most luxuriantly in places where there is a rich soil and indicate places suitable for crops and therefore human habitation. It is not surprising that habitations established in such areas where nettles are abundant (make their presence felt by their sting) should have been named after them. The word nettle might also have been included in a place name because of its former connection with producing nettle cloth, as a food in times of war or peace, and its use as a medicinal herb in more former times. The names also tell us of the abundance of nettles in past times. The place names indicate where nettles grew in past times and only the suffixes to the names need to be given:-

Nettlecombe, Somerset, Dorset. Combe = valley. (p viii).

Nettleton, Lincolnshire, Wiltshire, Humerside. Ton = farm.

Nettleham, Lincolnshire. Ham = estate or place.

Nettlestead, Kent. Stead = a place.

Nettleden, Hertfordshire. Den = haunt or dwelling.

The other place names are self-explanatory, and are as follows:-

Nettlebed, Berkshire. **Nettlestone**, Isle of Wight. **Nettlesworth**, Durham. **Nettlebridge**, Somerset. **Nettlehill**, Westmid.

Since nettles are sub-cosmopolitan, the word nettle in likely to occur in place names throughout the world. A few nettle names, accessed through Encarta are:-

In Germany, where the name for nettle is nessel: - **Nesselwang**, Bayern, Germany. **Nesseldorf**, Czech Republic.

In Spanish, Ortiga in the name for nettle: - **Ortiga**, Mexico. **Ortiga**, Bohria. **Ortiga**, Portugal.

In the U.S.A.: - **Nettle Creek**, Illinois. **Nettle Lake**, Ohio. **Nettleridge**, Virgina, **Nettleton,** Kansas, Mississippi, and Ohio.

This would be an interesting area for further research! In heraldry most people would expect that the objects used are chosen for good reasons, e.g. the crest of Sir Thomas Lipton Bart used both coffee and tea plants which helped him to build-up his immense fortune. However," a bunch of nettles vert" is present in the coat of Mallerby of Devonshire. The pun in the last case is apparent (Fox-Davies 1969). It might relate to the fact that people in the past have been connected with the nettle in various ways, e.g. its control, medicinal or fibre use for bows, etc.

Surnames also include the word nettle. Most people in this country are familiar with John Nettles as the handsome young detective in the T.V. series 'Bergerac' filmed in Jersey. Nettlefield may be derived from Roger de Netelfed 1221 Ass. Wo, as a dweller of the land overgrown by nettles (Reanbey, 1958).

LEGENDS AND FAIRY STORIES

In connection with nettle fibre we are reminded of Hans Christian Anderson (1805-1875). Born in Odense in Denmark and the son of a cobbler, he became the writer of the immortal Anderson's Fairy Tales. He would have been acquainted with the production of nettle cloth in Friesland (N. Netherlands), and the Scandinavian countries within fairly recent times and embodied this in his fairy story about 'The Wild Swans'. Most people have read this as children, and then later to their own children, and will remember it relates to a

beautiful Princess whose 7 brothers were changed by the wicked Queen into 7 swans. To release her brothers from the spell the Princess had to make 7 shirts from cloth produced from fibres of the nettles growing on graves in the churchyard, and then throw the shirts over the 7 swans. The story relates how she had to pull the nettles with her bare hands and then trample them with her bare feet to extract the green fibre to make the yarn, enduring the painful wheals and urticaria produced by myriads of nettle stings. Anderson was very optimistic about the simple method he gives for fibre extraction and conversion to cloth; however, they all lived happily ever after!

There is also the legend of the Rhine Castle of Eberstein, summarised here by Lady Wilkinson: -

"The hard-hearted castellan of Eberstein, who refused to let his little maiden marry until she had spun her own wedding-shirt and his winding-sheet from the nettles which grew on her father's grave, though he would never allow her time to weed or adorn it; of how her heart was almost broken - so their story goes - as she brooded over her apparently, interminable woes; until a good little old woman - he ancestress it is to be supposed of all the thrifty spinners and knitters of modern Germany - heard her tale and undertook the task of producing from the substance which had been hitherto believed to be so useless, two pieces of linen of extraordinary fineness. So the ill-natured castellan was called upon to redeem the promise which he had made on the conditions thus performed; while with that literal fulfilment of the requirements of justice which is peculiar to the realm of the imagination the same hour in which the bells rang out merrily, in the bright, clear air, for the maiden's bridal, was also that in which they sounded their solemn wail for the hard-hearted founder of the new ruinous Eberstein."

STINGS, SAYING AND CHANTS

Most antidotes involve the Dock (*Rumex species*) and this plant grows alongside nettles in most of its habitats and for this reason was probably the first plant at hand when antidotes were originally being tried out. In this connection it is interesting to read, in relation to U. dioica growing in the Himalayas, that the leaves of *Rumex napalensis* and *R. orientalis* which are found growing near the Common Nettle are rubbed over the affected parts to give relief after stinging (Chopra et al 1949). It would be interesting to know if this practice was introduced or was established before the British Colonial rule. In a similar way the Australian Aborigines have found an antidote to the sting of more vicious and dangerous nettle trees (*Dendrocnide* sp.) which grow from Queensland to N.S. Wales. This antidote is an occasional partner to the Stinging Tree, a small plant *Colocasia macrorrhiza* that the Aborigines call "cunjeroi", and to effect a relief, the affected area is rubbed with the large leaves of this plant for an hour or so. Also mentioned as an antidote is the inner bark of Dendrocnide (Petri 1906).

In certain parts of this country, e.g. Sussex, it is the custom to rub spittle over the affected part before applying the leaf. Interestingly enough in a similar way to the Nettle Tree, Lady Wilkinson says "it has a remedy in itself. Its own juice instantly allays the irritation"; however she doesn't mention how you obtain the nettle's juice without being stung in the process!

	CHANT	SOURCE	CHANT
Folklore of the northern countries Henderson 1879	*"Nettle in, Dock out, Dock in, Nettle out, Nettle in, Dock out, Dock rub, Nettle out"*	**Another version Friend 1883**	*"Nettle out, dock in, Dock remove the nettle-sting."*
Charm mentioned by Chaucer	*"Dock removes the Nettle sting! "*	**North Country the activity of the "auld wives"Friend 1883**	*"Docken in and nettle out, Like an auld wife's dishclout."*
Henderson 1879	*"In dock out nettles Don't let the blood settle*	**Black 1883**	*'Out Nettle, In dock, Dock shall have A new smock'*
Children of Wiltshire Wilkinson 1858	*Out 'ettle In dock. Dock shall ha'a a new smock, Ha'narran."* (None)	**Children of Wiltshire Thiselton-Dyer 1889**	*Out 'ettle In dock. Dock shall ha'a a new smock, 'Ettle zhant Ha' nanun.'*
Dorsetshire folklore Folk-lore 1859	*"Dock, dock, shall have a smock Nettle shall have nar a one."*		

A favourite childhood trick is often practised with success when a country child, familiar with country folklore, meets his opposite 'the towney'. Coming to a vigorous clump of nettles he casually mentions to the towney "Nettles do not sting this month." The gullable, green-behind-the-ears towney is amazed by this statement, and goaded into trying it out.

No doubt a practised country lad will carefully grasp and pull up a vigorous nettle shoot, thus showing that it doesn't sting, and then, when requested, lash the towney on a delicate part of his anatomy. The towney recoils, howls in pain and cries out, as his pride is badly dented. When the country lad has recovered from his laughter he says jeeringly "I said it wouldn't sting this month, I didn't say it wouldn't sting you." In a similar way, a person says, "Cuckoos do not sing this month." The listener expresses surprise or disbelief, and is then told, "They only sing Cuckoo."

At this point we can recall the trick practised in Elizabethan floral gardens, that of getting visitors to smell Dodard's variety of the Roman Nettle on the pretext it is a Spanish Marjoram. After being stung by this virulent nettle the visitor recoils in pain holding a red swollen nose, much to the amusement of their more knowledgeable host (Chapter 3 p 33-4). Interestingly enough, the Australian Aborigines practise a very similar trick, but in this case the much more dangerous and painful Nettle tree is used. This trick is recounted by K. Rowan, (1889) during her adventures searching for insects on that hostile continent (Chapter 8).

The phrase "grasping the nettle" crops up a lot in modern day news. It is a favourite term used by politicians in relation to various situations such as the "Irish problem" where firmness and a positive attitude are the necessary prerequisites needed when trying to find a solution satisfying both sides i.e. the nettle must be grasped firmly! It is based on the everyday experience that if you brush up-against a nettle, you are more likely to be stung than if you have the courage to grasp one firmly as in pulling up nettles from some odd corner of the garden. Only cissies wear gloves i.e. are guarded in their approach.

These observations are embodied in the profound phrase combining practical advice and shrewd philosophy in the poem 'Written on a Window in Scotland':-

> "Tender-handed stroke a nettle,
> And it stings you for your pains;
> Grasp it like a man of mettle,
> And it soft as silk remains.
> Tis the same with common natures,
> Use 'em kindly, they rebel;
> But be rough as nutmeg-graters,
> And the rouges obey you well." [1]
> Aaron Hill (1685-1750)

> "If they wad drink nettles in March,
> And eat muggings* in May.
> Sae many braw maidens
> Wadna gang to clay
> * = mugwort (Artemisia vulgaris)

In a similar vein the saying,

"Though you stroke a nettle ever so kindly, yet will it sting you"
And

"He that handles a nettle tenderly is sooner stung."

I am obviously biased in favour of the nettle, and having spent a vast amount of time in the field I thoroughly agree with the saying,

"Better to be stung by a nettle than pricked by a rose."

In place of pricked by a rose could be substituted pricked and scratched by thistles or holly or thorns or gorse, etc., or torn and tripped-up by a bramble! However, to be fair, at least most of these plants have more attractive fruits or berries.

When it comes to having fun it is not surprising that children's activities are more tied-up with nettles than those of adults (BOX 4.1).

On May 1st in Hitchin Hertfordshire, it was the practise to indicate your feelings in relation to your neighbours by decorating their doors before morning, either with branches of trees if they were popular, or with nettles or other obnoxious weeds it they were not liked!

St Babian's nettle is said to a favourite remedy for consumption, and the story of the mermaid of the Clyde who exclaimed when she

Nettle, Sowbread (*Cyclamen purpurascens*) and Hellebore (*Helleborus* sp.) were the ingredients of a popular love potion (since hellebores are poisonous I wouldn't recommend trying this one!).

BOX 4.1 OAK APPLE DAY

When his father, Charles 1, was beheaded his second son spent 19 years in France before Royalists in Scotland summoned him to be their king. He landed in Scotland in 1650 and 10,000 Scots marched into England where Cromwell at Worcester defeated them. At this time Charles escaped capture by hiding in an oak tree at Boscobel. After another 10 years in exile in France he was recalled in 1660 to become King, and on the 29th of May he triumphantly entered London. To commemorate the Restoration, the 29th of May, was called Oak Apple day and the custom was marked by wearing oak branches, twigs and leaves and also oak galls or apples. Most popularity for this event was lost by 1880 but still lingers on in modified form in certain areas today. The custom was celebrated in 29 counties and consisted of wearing the articles mentioned up to 12 o'clock. Failure to do this resulted in the person being punished in various ways, being kicked, being sodded, pelted with the eggs of wild birds, but understandingly, the most popular punishment was to be nettled.

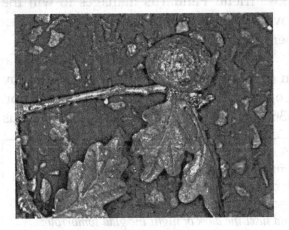

First of May is 'May-Doll' Day,
Second of May is Kissing Day,
Third of May is Sting-Nittle Day!
Lafont 1984

In Cleveland for example school children ran about with nettles tied to a stick, to nettle people not wearing oak leaves, etc The custom largely died out early in the 20th Century but some people remember the events: (i) one Cornish gentleman recounts that at, the turn of the century, Stinging Nettle Day (May 1st) was celebrated by eating a stinging nettle leaf wrapped up in a dock leaf, to keep you from harm until the next Stinging Nettle Day, (ii) in Brixham Devon, the 2nd of May was Stinging Nettle Day when the boys chased the girls with nettles (Vickery 1995) (iii) in the 1950's, a gentleman from Tiverton, Devon recounts that on the 3rd of May called Sting-Nittle Day it was the custom to ask people "Do you know what day it is?" and if they said "No" then you nettled them and cried "Sting-Nittle Day!." He also relates how his mother used to put a bunch of nettles on the breakfast table on May 3rd and how the children would chant (Lafonte 1984).

Probably with the demise of Oak-Apple Day the associated practice of nettling people, which was probably more fun, has persisted and largely replaced it, thus giving birth to Stinging Nettle Day/Sting-Nittle Day.

Opie .and Idal. in their 'Language of Children' mention that on Oak Apple Day, (i) in 1952, girls in Welshpool would run after another girl who was not wearing an oak apple and try to either nettle her or attempt to push her into a nettle bed (ii) nettling amongst children on Oak Apple Day (29th May) in Cheshire is mentioned as late as 1951. In relation to retribution amongst children country children mention the practices of 'Nettle walking', giving a 'Nettling', 'Slinging into nettles' and 'Hedging' which is similar. (African pun).

In medieval symbolism the nettle stands for courage and envy. In the 'Language of flowers' invented by the Victorians in relation to sentiments and symbolism, the nettle stands for (i) cruelty, slander and that you are spiteful - probably based on its defensive stinging properties (ii) you break my heart, and (iii) is thought to be a bad luck gift to a woman! (I cannot think of anybody, in his or her right state of mind who would contemplate the latter anyway!). Evidently to dream of being stung by nettles indicates vexation and disappointment but to dream of gathering nettles means that your family will be blessed with harmony or that somebody has a good opinion of you. The latter must by coincidence apply to me, however I add this paragraph for those interested, but personally, take it with a large pinch of salt!

LITERATURE THROUGHOUT HISTORY

Nettles have been used as food since very early times. The Roman lyric poet and satirist Horace 65-8 BC wrote his books of Satires 35-30 BC and Epistles 20BC.

In Epistles, 1, XII, 8 Horace writes to the steward of the Roman general and statesman Agrippa:

In Satire VI, 69, Persius a Roman poet asks:-

"If with rich dishes ready for your food,
You leave them and find grass and nettles good"

"Am I to have nettles cooked on holidays?"

These quotations provide evidence of the use of nettles as a potherb by the Romans; in this case undoubtedly they will have used young shoots of the Roman Nettle Urtica pilulifera which grows predominantly in the Mediterranean region.

The following is taken from 'A Book of Herbs' by **Dawn Macleod** (1968). She read a herbal in which the Saxon name for the nettle was *'Wergulu'* which she says sounds appropriate and suits its baleful appearance having not forgotten the painful experience of having fallen in a bed of nettle when young. However, the nettle improves with acquaintance and this irritating herb has more herbal properties than the saintly Angelica.

She quotes a monk **Walafred Stabo** - a thousand years ago;

*"**When last winter had passed and spring renewed the face of the earth when the days grew longer and milder, when flowers and herbs were stirred by the west wind, when green leaves clothed the trees, then my little plot was overgrown with nettles. What was I to do? Deep down the roots were matted and linked and riveted like basket-work or the wattled hurdles of a fold....."***

Sir John Harington in his 'Regimen Sanitatis Salernitanum (1607) sheds light on the herbal use of the nettle in the Middle Ages with the following poem:-

> *"The Nettles stinke, yet they make recompense,*
> *If your belly by the Collicke paine endures,*
> *Against the Collicke Nettle-seed and honey*
> *Is Physick: better none is had for money.*
> *It breedeth sleepe, staies vomit, fleams doth soften,*
> *It helpes him of the Gowte that eates it often."*

Chaucer's "Troilus and Criseyde" (Cressida), written inbetween 1382-1386, is regarded by many as the most beautiful poem in the English language. In this love story the Trojan prince Troilus, aided by his close friend Pandarus manages to win the love of Cressida but then tragically loses her to the Greek warrior Diomede.

There are two references to the nettle in this love poem using the translation by Coghill (1971), in the first Book 1 section 136, Troilus has just confided in Pandarus

> *"A soil that nurtures weeds and poisonous stuff*
> *Brings forth these herbs of healing just as oft.*
> *Next to the foulest nettle, thick and rough,*
> *Rises the rose in sweetness, smooth and soft;*
> *And next the dark of night the glad tomorrow;*
> *And joy is on the borderland of sorrow."*

about his love for Cressida. Pandarus is offering his advice, which is to stop brooding over his hidden love for Cressida and to do the opposite, change his frame of mind in order to win her love:-

And secondly in Book IV section 66, when Troilus is bidden to love another and let Cressida goes he replies to Pandarus:-

> *"It isn't in my power, my dear brother,*
> *And if it were I would not have it so.*
> *Can you play racquets with it, to and fro,*
> *Nettle in, dock out, and shift from here to there?*
> *Bad luck to her that takes you in her care!"*

As far as I know this is the oldest reference to the chant which is said when applying the dock leaf to the nettle sting for relief, but in this context it was a proverbial saying for inconstancy.

Shakespeare started writing his 38 plays round about 1590 and Eleanor Rhode

(1935) mentions in her book 'Shakespeare's Flowers' that he looks at flowers through the eyes of a countryman, in the fairest and grimmest aspects, and that the details of them that occur throughout his works is a testament to his acute powers of observation and his love and their beauty and fragrance, particularly of the Spring flowers. His wide knowledge of herbs and their uses and vegetables obviously stems from his love of his garden. He was thoroughly familiar with flowering plants and their habitats, such as the meadows, fields and hedgerows of Warwickshire, the banks of the Avon and the glades of the Forest of Arden.

Shakespeare refers to nettles several times using them in a proverbial sense:-

Relating to their hurtful stinging properties:

> **Leontes.**
> *"Goads, thorns, nettles, tails of wasps."*
> A Winter's Tale Act i, Scene 2.

> **Hotspur.**
> *"I tell you my lord fool, out of this nettle, danger, we pluck this flower, safety."*
> King Henry the Fourth. Part i, Act ii, Scene 3.

> **King Richard.**
> *"Yield stinging nettles to my enemies."*
> *King Richard the Second. Act iii, Scene 2.*

Referring to the rapid growth of nettles in May:

> **Cressida.**
> *"I'll spring up in his tears as 'twere a nettle against May."*
> Troilus and Cressida. Act i, Scene 2.

And stating the obvious characteristics associated with the nettle:

> **Menenius.**
> *"We call a nettle but a nettle and The faults of fools but folly."*
> Coriolanus. Act ii, Scene 1.

Lear, when mad, crowned himself with weeds, which were those found in corn fields. Hemlock is thought to be what we now call the Fool's Parsley (*Aethusa cynapium*), a very poisonous plant when fresh but harmless when dried. Cuckoo flowers refer to Creeping Buttercups (*Ranuculus repens*), whilst the nettles could refer to both the annual, Small Nettle (*Urtica urens*) and the perennial, Common Nettle (*Urtica dioica*):

> **Menenius.**
> *"Crowned with rank fumiter and furrow weeds, With Bur-docks, Hemlock, nettles, cuckoo flowers, Sarnel and all the idle weeds that grow In our sustaining corn.*
> King Lear. Act iv, Scene 4.

The nettle, which was one of the plants wreathed by the hapless Ophelia into her death garlands, in thought to be the White Dead Nettle (*Lamium album*):

> *"Cornflowers, nettles, daises, and long purples"*
> Hamlet. Act iv, Scene 7.

It was formerly believed that strawberries, which in Elizabethan day's refered to the wild strawberry, throve best near plants "of baser quality", thus in

Tusser's 'Five Hundred Pointes of Good Husbandry' (1577):

> *"Wife unto the garden and set me a plot*
> *With strawberry roots of the best to be got.*
> *Such growing abroade among thorns in the wood,*
> *Well chosen and picked prove excellent good."*

This observation is used by Shakespeare

This old observation has often been quoted but it is not until recently that attempts have been made to test its validity (p 212-13).

Robert Herrick was an English poet

> *"The strawberry grows underneath the nettle,*
> *And wholesome berries thrive and ripen best*
> *Neighbour'd by fruit of base quality."*
> King Henry the Fifth, Act I, Scene 1

and his chief work was 'Hesperides' (1648). One poem within this work, 'A Country life: To his Brother Mr Tho Herrick' congratulates him on his basic, rustic meals, and a willingness:-

> *"To taste boil'd nettles, colworts, beets, and eat*
> *These and sour herbs as dainty meat."*

Samuel Pepys is famous for his diary written in code, (1660-1669), and deciphered after his death. He makes one reference (Feb. 1661) to the nettle, which is often quoted; he obviously found them agreeable for he says:-

> *"We did eat some nettle porridge, which was made on purpose today for some of their coming and was very good."*

Thomas Campbell (1777-1844) the Scottish poet born in Glasgow, writes in his 'Letters from the South'. "Last of all my eyes luxuriated in looking on a large bed of nettles. *Oh, wretched taste!*, your English prejudice perhaps will exclaim; '*Is not the nettle a weed, if possible more vile than the Scottish thistle?*' But be not nettled my friend at my praise of this common weed. In Scotland I have eaten nettles, I have slept in nettle-sheets, and I have dined off a nettle-tablecloth. The young and tender nettle is an excellent potherb. Stalks of the old nettle are as good as flax for making cloth. I have heard my mother say, that she thought nettle-cloth more durable than any other species of linen."

Sir Walter Scott (1771-1844) wrote his famous novel 'Rob Roy' in which Andrew Fairservice says he was "bred in the parish of Deepdarly, near Glasgow, where they raise large Kail under glass, and force early Nettle for their Spring Kail." Rob Roy relates to the old Scotch song:-

> *"Cow the nettle, cow the nettle early,*
> *Gin ye be for lang Kai,l*
> *cow the nettle early.*
> *Cow it laigh, cow it sune,*
> *Just when it is in the blume,*
> *cow the nettle early.*
> *The auld wife with ae tuith*
> *Cow the nettle, cow the nettle,*
> *The auld wife with ae tuith,*
> *cow the nettle early."*
> (Cow = Pluck)

The toothless 'auld wife' would no doubt find the pottage much to her liking.

Since time immemorial man has used the nettle as an object for the release of pent-up feelings such as anger, frustration, etc., taking satisfaction from beating it down with a stick or trampling on it.

Jane Austin in her novel 'Persuasion' (1818, Chapter 10); Charles Hayter "was out of temper with his wife. Mary had shewn herself disobliging to him, and was now to reap the consequence, which consequence was his dropping her arm almost every moment, to cut off the heads of some nettles in the hedge with his switch;"

Thomas Hardy in his novel 'The Trumpet Major' (1880), Chapter 20, Robert Harding in following in the wake of the faithless and false Matilda, decided not to be steered by accidents any more, give up the pursuit of her and go home. "He picked up his bundle and switch, and retraced his steps towards Overcombe Mill, knocking down the brambles and nettles as he went with gloomy and indifferent blows."

In Feb. 1997, I was listening to Wogan on radio 2, talking to a **Ruth Scott.** Ruth was speaking about ways of controlling your anger or rage. She said you either slam somebody or learn to walk away and avoid confrontation. She admitted slamming doors was a better alternative, which is why most doors in her house do not shut properly-although this is regarded as childish by many people. The best solution she admitted was to grow a patch of nettles in a garden and to relieve rage simply go out and smash them to bits with a rake!

Lawson P. (1852), in his 'Synopsis of the Vegetable Products of Scotland', (Div, IV, Sect.1) quotes the following poem:-

> *"Where plots full of nettles be noisome to eie,*
> *Sow thereupon hemp-seed, and nettles will die."*
> Tusser

Hemp (*Cannabis sativa*) belongs to the family Cannabaceae, Order Urticales, and is therefore a cousin of the nettle. Previously widely grown in England, it grows rapidly and to a great height on a rich soil, and therefore shades the nettle out, so the advice is true - however since Cannabis is now illegal this control is academic!

Charles R Darwin (1809-1882) in his voyage around the world in the ten-gun brig The Beagle (1831-1836) visited the Chonos Archipelago (1834) off the coast of Chile. Darwin and his helpers collected plants, from two unnamed islands in this archipelago; one of the plants was a nettle. Darwin's original pressed specimen is listed by Eugenia Navas B., in his 'El genera Urtica En Chile (1961), and the information on the herbarium sheet is 'Archipelago de los Chonos, leg. C. Darwin, No 266 XII-1834 (CGE), (K) Tipo de Urtica Darwinii (Hook),' this shows that J.D. Hooker described this plant in his 'Flora Antarica', 343, 1847, and named it after Darwin (*Urtica Darwinii*). However according to the International Rules of Botanical Nomenclature, credit for a plant name can only be given to the first person who described the plant, and this was the Frenchman Poiret; he described the nettle brought back from the round-the-world-voyage of Commander F. Chesnard de La Giraudais (1767-1769) on the 480-ton storeship L'Etoile (in conjunction with Commander Louis Antoine de Bougainville). The botanist on the L'Etoile was Commerson and the herbarium sheet of his specimen reads, 'La Bay, Bougainville, Port Galant Leg. Commerson, 1767, Ex. Herbarium. Jussieu (P)'. The nettle is now called the Magellan Nettle (*Urtica Magellanica*) Poir. and is similar to our own common nettle but has male and female flowers on the same plant.

It was a pleasure to find a connection between nettles and the great Charles Darwin, whom every aspiring naturalist hopes to emulate. Darwin must have brushed up against nettles bordering his daily 'Sand Walk' and suffered many stings. He collected at least two things in Chile, a nettle and a curious barnacle. He left the nettle for me, I wonder why?

BOX 4.3 THE ENGLISH POET JOHN CLARE
John Clare (1793-1864) is famous as a Northhamptonshire peasant poet. His poems and diaries show that he was a first-class naturalist with a wide knowledge of plants and animals of the countryside. The countryside then was largely unspoilt and rich in number and species compared with our modern-day monoculture

prairies. Even so, Clare felt oppressed by the changes at that time against 'freedom to roam' - still a present day issue. Although he extols the beauty of our flowers, he did mention unattractive plants such as nettles, thorns, briars and thistles, but very often clumps them together as weeds or rank vegetation. The reasons for including unattractive plants in his poems are probably two-fold (i) his sympathy with the outcast and persecuted, associated with his own often wretched life, and his mental illness (ii) because of his accurate observations and descriptions of the English countryside and farming landscape.

Typical of the former is his sonnet 'Childhood'.- From 'Cowper Green' part of 'The Village Minstrel'

> "When nettles oft our infant fingers stung,
> And tears would weep the gentle wound away:-
> Ah gentle wounds indeed, I well may say,
> To those sad Manhood's tortur'd passage found."

> "Where uncheck'd the brambles spread;
> Where the thistle meets the sight,
> With its down-head, cotton-white;
> And the nettle, keen to view
> And hemlock with its gloomy hue;
>
> And full many a nameless weed,
> Neglected, left to run to seed,
> Seen but with disgust by those
> Who judge a blossom by the nose
> Wildness is my suiting scene,

Not for him the gardener's "cut-hedge and lawn adore" which have been levelled by his shears, he renews his love for Cowper Green with its "wildness and variety" and "Nature, when she blooms at will" The tall nettle growing up through the shaded hedge to get its flowers into the light, and with its clear view, is typical of the nettle.

This following poem was quoted by Clarence Druce in the 'Flora of Northhamptonshire' (1930). This is very similar to 'The Cross Roads'; a place where a young maid pregnant with child was buried. She was found earlier drowned in a pond and was thought to have been murdered. Her mother died of grief and the garden went to seed:

> "Yon nettles where they're left to spread
> There once a garden smiled."

> "And docks and thistles shake their seedy heads,
> And yearly keep with nettles smothering o'er: -
> The house the dame, the garden known no more:"

This is 'Sonnet' from his Epping Forest/Northampton Period:-This is 'Evening' from the same period as the last, and depicts a typical farmyard environment:-

> "Each wild weed, by the river side,
> In different motions dignified,
> Bows to the wind, quakes to the breeze,
> And charms sweet summers harmonies.
> The very nettle quakes away,
> To glad the summer's happy day."

> "The battered waggon wanting three
> Stands prop't with broken axle-tree
> A hen pen with two slats away
> And hen and chickens gone astray
> A barrow left without a wheel
> Since spring, which nettles now conceal"

Housman A.E. (1859-1936) was a classical scholar and famous for his poems and prose. Although born in Worcestershire he became famous largely through his book of poems, 'A Shropshire Lad' (1896) in which he expressed his pessimism through short usually melancholy poems of invariably tragic stories set in rural Shropshire which he grew to love as a boy. The poem from the Shropshire Lad which mentions the nettle is typical of his tragic stories. He probably chose the nettle for this poem not only for its tall swaying stems, which bend over in the breeze, but also because of its association with man and graveyards. The nettle is generally held in low esteem; one of the downtrodden, and therefore is more likely to be accepted as a symbol of sorrow in the eyes of many people.

> *"It nods and curtseys and recovers*
> *When the wind blows above,*
> *The nettle on the graves of lovers*
> *That hanged themselves for love.*
>
> *The nettle nods, the wind blows over,*
> *The man, he does not move,*
> *The lover of the grave, the lover*
> *That hanged himself for love."*

Prior to the invention of the modern mower and strimmer, graveyards used to be havens for wildlife. The nettle is frequent in this habitat because, as an opportunist, it quickly colonises such disturbed land, and once rooted between gravestones is very difficult to remove. Today nettles now rarely nod and curtsey over graves because modern graveyards are more like bowling greens; flowering heads, once raised, are swiftly beheaded, by swiftly rotating blades!

The second poem with nettles in it comes under the title of 'More Poems' (XXXII) published after his death. In this poem he is saying that whatever seeds are scattered by the sower into furrows, charlock will survive for two years, however, the nettle, the thonger of the land will remain whatever the weather and even grows in the grounds inhabited by Kings. In those days arable fields would have been colonised by both the common and the small nettle. However today, with deep ploughing, the common nettle cannot survive in the arable habitat.

John Betjeman (1906-1986) is one of England's modern poets and his poems centre around nostalgia for suburbia, the countryside and their preservation. He brings familiar plants into his poems such as the English Elm (formerly part of our landscape, but now almost gone due to Dutch elm disease) and of course nettles; these are mentioned mainly in passing and usually in his ecclesiastical poems, where they feature in graveyard. In 'Upper Lambourne' nettles in a graveyard cast a shadowed pattern over the gravestone of a horse trainer who died in 1923.

Edward Thomas (1878-1917) was born in London, and wrote about the natural history of the countryside he most loved – that of the south of England. Later in his short life he was a successful writer of poetry and prose. He joined the Artist's Rifles and was sadly killed in action at Arras in 1917. The poem on 'Tall Nettles' was characteristic of his style of unsentimental truth and an ability to appreciate both the beauty as well as the cruelty and grimness of nature.

> **Tall Nettles**
> *"Tall nettles cover up, as they have done*
> *These many springs, the rusty harrows, the plough*
> *Long worn out, and the roller made of stone:*
> *Only the elm butt tops the nettles now.*
>
> *This corner of the farmyard I like most:*
> *As well as any bloom upon a flower*
> *I like the dust on the nettles, never lost*
> *Except to prove the sweetness of a shower."*

In this respect it is typical that he chose the nettle, a follower of man, and keen to view, as part and parcel of the character of the corner of the farm he loved. As well as farmyard dust he could have been including the pollen which covers the male plants in yellow powder during the long flowering period (Louis Untermeyer, 'Modern British Poetry' 1920).

Henry Williamson (1895-1977). Almost everyone is familiar with Henry Williamson through his book 'Tarka the Otter' which shows his ability to 'look and see' and describe in minute detail (after his mentor Richard Jefferies), but also combine his passion for natural history with his vivid imagination to put to paper words/works of art. He captures natural scenes and moments in time in descriptions which will live forever. He was a true naturalist because he descried and treated all aspects of nature and life, pleasant and unpleasant. I have drawn on his main work, his autobiography; 'The Chronicle of Ancient Sunlight' where he is named Phillip Maddison and his parents are Hetty and Richard. There are thirty-four references to stinging nettles.

In relation to humour, Hetty on her honeymoon in a keeper's cottage in the evening wanted to relieve herself and was told by Richard who had forgotten his lantern that she would find the privy down the bottom of the garden but would have to be careful because it was surrounded by clumps of nettles. Fortunately the keeper found a light for her.

Young Philip Maddison spent most of his time bird nesting and refers to the whitethroat's nest built in the nettles and made of grass and a little horsehair, a nest you could almost see through;, and of the well camouflaged pheasant sun-flecked and sitting on her eggs in the middle of a nettle patch.

Philip had a thing about untidiness and mentions this on a large number of occasions. At Rookhurst the family home the gardens were overrun by thorns, hogweed and nettles. At Lucy's home a two-cylinder V-engine had nettles growing through the floor boards. Worst of all was the Norfolk farm where amongst the rubble lying around, pats of dung, fly-blown dead rats etc., were uncut nettles at the base of the walls. Rusting farm machinery was surrounded by burdocks and nettles.

He had a good understanding of the biology of the common nettle, his manager was worried about the nettle seed present in the soil being moved from the gupp,s (marshland) to unfertilised land but Philip said if nettles do come up we will plough them in as a green fertiliser. His most vivid description of a nettle is when he was removing a clump with a pitch-pole harrow on a tractor in his overgrown garden. The hanging nettle consisted of matted yellow ropes from which hung tentacles and the glistening spines on the leaves raised vicious white wheals on the forearm. The yard was half hidden by nettles and elder trees and even when rebuilt when he sat down and pondered he could feel the yard undergoing the same cycle of decay to eventually end up as it was before - the nettles would surely return!.

During the First World War he only mentions nettles a few times. He is diving into a trench amidst screeching noises similar to those of steam trains breaking and bombarded with earth thrown up by ear-piercing explosions to eventually come to rest when grass and nettles loomed up in his face and the earth vibrated through his body.

The Chronicles needs to be read when the reader will become immersed in his vivid elegant prose and living sense of the moment.

Small tortoiseshell	Comma
Map butterfly	Peacock
Red admiral	Painted lady

CHAPTER 5

A PURIFIER OF THE BLOOD AND A PANACEA

INTRODUCTION

Fig 5.2 A dried herbal preparation of U. dioica from Austria.

Before the advent of modern medicine, plants were used to provide herbal drugs available for alleviating the various diseases suffered by mankind. In the West herbal medicine was based on the gathering of herbal information by Dioscorides in his great book Materia Medica which drew on herbal use by the Ancient Egyptians and Greeks and the use of herbs by the Roman Empire at that time. Herbal use declined during the Dark-Ages. In the Middle-Ages monks kept the practice alive in their herbal gardens and copied manuscripts. A revival began in the 15th Century, first in Europe then in Britain, with the publication of numerous Herbals, and continued into the mid-18th Century.

Botanic and Herbal gardens were created such as the famous Chelsea Physick Garden run by the knowledgeable Philip Miller. The latter in his Garden Kalendar (1760) lists medicinal plants that should be gathered at different times of the year. **March** gather Brooklime, Elder Bush, *Nettle tops*, Coltsfoot flowers, Noble Liverwort, Primrofe, Rue-leaved Whitlow-grafs, Water-crefs and towards the end of the month Poplar buds. **August** gather *Nettle-feed*, Onion-feed, select Nightshade, Arum or Cuckow-pintle roots, Tobacco and Thorn Apple.

Disease is defined as the malfunction of the body and there are many causes, genetic, metabolic, injury, diet deficiencies, etc.; however, the majority are caused by pathogenic microbes.

Antibiotics that were discovered by Fleming (1928) are no longer effective against pathogens, due to the development of antibiotic resistance, as a result of mutations. Modern medicine has therefore failed. Since the beginning of the present century scientists continue to search the world's rainforests and target new families of plants in the never-relenting search for herbs as alternative medicines.

PAST AND PRESENT USES OF URTICA AS A MEDICINAL PLANT

1 *Vrtica Romana.*
Romane Nettle.

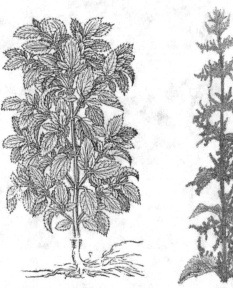

A   B   C   D

Fig 5.1. (A) Robert Turner's Brittish Physician 1664. (B) The Roman nettle (Urtica pilulifera) from De Materia Medica of Dioscorides 1st century A. D. (C) Urtica dioica from The Herbal of John Gerard 1597. (D) Male flowering shoot of U. dioica. showing accuracy.

Fig 4.3. Dried nettles (U. dioica) for nettle tea and as a tonic.

Although the nettle is no longer used widely in Western civilisations it is still an important herb in a large number of countries such as India, China, Russia and central Asia, Anatolia (formerly known as Asia Minor), Africa, North American, etc. Herbals very often list the nettle in the treatment of over 20 diseases and tend to give the impression that it is a panacea. I have looked here for any scientific evidence to back up these claims. With the development of new techniques a re-examination is taking place of plants such as nettles which grow on our doorsteps, so some recent scientific work needs to be made available to the general reader. In this historical account the word nettle refers to U. dioica and for other nettles their Latinised names are used. For modern nettle herbal equivalents see (Fig 5.3).

ANTIBACTERIAL AND ANTIFUNGAL PROPERTIES

Dioscorides (translation Gunther) says that the leaves of nettles smeared on with salt "does heal things bitten by dogs, and Gangranicall, and malignant, and cancrous, and ye foulness of ulcers and luxations tumours, ye Parotidas, ye Pani, Apostumations." Culpepeper says "The distinctive water of the herb affective for ...outward wounds and sores, to wash them, and to cleanse the skin from morphew, leprosey... The juice of the leaves or the decoction of them, or the roots, is very good to wash either old, rotten, or stinking sores; fistulas and gangrenes and such as are fretting eating and corroding, scabs, manginess and itch in any part of the body....."

Burns are said to be rapidly healed by using an alcohol tincture of the nettle, diluted with an equal part of water, allow this to soak into a linen cloth and then apply to the affected part; the cloth is constantly rewetted but not removed. In the previous U S S R a homeopathic preparation of the fresh plant was also used in the treatment of burns (Ossadcha-Janata, 1952). In Turkey a water-soluble Chlorophyllin from U. dioica leaves is the active principle in an anti-microbial ointment for wound healing. An alcoholic extract of U. dioica leaves is used (i) for Psoriasis, an inflammatory skin disease characterised by reddish patches and white scales, (ii) Eczema, an inflammatory skin desease attended by itching, lesions and water discharge and (iii) Seborrhoic Eczema, due to the increased secretion of fatty sebum from sebaceous glands at the base of hair follicles For regenerating skin, ointments and lotions containing an alcoholic and water extract of the roots of U. dioica are used (Wetherlilt 1992).

Dioscorides mentions, in relation to nettles, "but ye juice being gargarized doth keep down an inflamed Uvula". Which is what we would now regard as a symptom of a sore throat, (possibly caused by bacterial infections, such as streptococcus attacking the tonsils or pharynx), and most often associated with colds, etc. Leaf extracts from U. dioica can also be used as a mouthwash and in toothpaste. The toothpaste contains nettle extract used in conjunction with abrasives, binders, mild alkalis, flavouring oils and glycerine to give plasticity. The anti-microbial, anti-inflammatory, anti-plaque and anti-bleeding substances in the nettle act against the bacteria causing tooth decay and gum disease where inflamed and bleeding gums result from injury due to the build-up of plaque and bacteria (calculus) at the neck of the tooth.

For the scientific basis behind the use of nettles as an anti-microbial agents reference has already been made to the presence of flavonoids compounds in U.urens with their anti-microbial, anti-inflammatory, analgesic and ulcerogenic effects, and this is backed up by standard laboratory tests (p 40). The presence of anti-bacterial and anti-fungal agents in the rhizomes and roots of U. dioica, and their use as protection against insect herbivores and in genetic engineering are dealt with later.

BLOOD DISEASES

Hemostasis refers to the stoppage of bleeding, and the use of the nettle as a hemostatic is well documented. The majority of nosebleeds stop quickly; however some can be a problem, and in this respect Dioscorides recommends, "And ye leaves being beaten small and applied with the juice are good for ye fluxes of blood from ye nostrils." Culpeper advises the same use, but instead "The seeds or leaves bruised and put into the nostrils." Thomas Green in his Universal herbal (1816) says, "A leaf put on the tongue and pressed against the roof of the mouth will commonly stop bleeding at the nose." Quite frankly I don't think many people would fancy trying this last treatment! Dr. Leclerc reports that he used the nettle to alleviate bleeding in a case of haemophilia. To arrest bleeding he used 85 g of expressed juice as a dose.

These three different methods probably stop bleeding for different reasons because it is well known that the clotting of the blood is affected by at least 13 different factors. The cut blood vessels need to be plugged to stop blood loss. The first stage in this process is the formation of a loose platelet plug, and to help in this process, the blood flow can be slowed by the contraction of circular muscle in the wall of the blood vessel, thus decreasing its diameter (vasoconstriction). In this connection stinging hairs and leaf cells of the nettle have been shown to contain serotonin and prostaglandins (leucotrienes) which function as vasoconstrictors. The next process involves the formation of a 'cotton wool' mass of fibres made up of the protein fibrin, which infiltrates the blood clot. Calcium ions are needed for this process and if not present they would be available from the nettle juice. In the process of blood clotting the surfaces of the red blood cells become sticky and they clump together (agglutination) to form a mass or clot, enclosed in this case by the fibrin threads. As will be seen later, the roots, rhizomes and seeds of U. dioica contain a substance called a lectin, Urtica Dioica Agglutinin (UDA) which binds substances together. In this connection UDA causes red blood cells to clump together and therefore is likely to speed-up the clotting process (Chapter 11 p 158). So in these respects there appears to be some scientific evidence

of the nose the pulverised dry herb is used as a snuff (Lucas 1969).

Certain diseases of the blood are treated with nettles. In Turkey, U. pilulifera seeds, crushed and mixed with honey, are used in the treatment of leukaemia. U. dioica contains high levels of iron and traces of copper which are useful in the treatment of anaemia. This could only cure nutritional anaemia caused by lack of iron in the diet. It is difficult for the gut to take up iron but this ability is facilitated by the presence of copper. After iron uptake it travels to the bone marrow, where the iron is used to produce more haemoglobin to make more red blood cells which will carry more oxygen to the cells. In countries where nettles are not used as a potherb other green vegetables rich in iron could have the same effect.

ALIMENTARY DEAR WATSON

An extract of nettle acts as a mild purgative, i.e. results in bowel motion in cases of constipation. Dioscorides says "But ye leaves being sodden together with small shell fish, do mollify ye bellies, dissolve windiness" whilst Culpeper recommends a decoction of leaves or seeds in wine " killeth worms in children, easeth the spleen occasioned by wind and expelleth the wind from the body."

Also quoted by Fournier (1948) is the work of the German, Von Minko Dobreff (1924) on the discovery of a new 'Sekretin' in the Common Nettle

Table 5.1. The effect on gastric secretion, amount of free and total acid, of a 2.5g nettle extract injected sub-cutaneously into a female dog, 9.5 Kg in weight, (After Dobreff, 1924).

Time	Volume of gastric juice cc^2	Free hydrochloric acid	Total acid
9 ^{00} – 9 ^{30}	1.1		
9 ^{30} – 10 ^{00}	0.5	{70.0	{90.0
10 ^{00} Subcutaneous injection of nettle extract (2.5 g of substance) into the dog.			
10 ^{00} – 10 ^{30}	17.5	112.0	121.0
10 ^{30} – 11 ^{00}	29.1	128.0	138.0
11 ^{00} – 11 ^{30}	9.4	104.0	124.0
11 ^{30} – 12 ^{00}	1.0		
12 ^{00} – 12 ^{30}	0.2	{60.0	{86.0

to back-up the use of the nettle as a hemostat.

For women who have problems with their periods (menstruation) Dioscorides says "But ye decoction of ye leaves being drunk with a little myrrh, moveth menstrua. They move also ye menstrua being small beaten and applied with Myrrh, and ye new leaves laid to, do restore ye fallings down of ye matrix." In India and Pakistan it is used as a hemostatic for haemorrhages of the womb (uterus) such as excessive menstruation and the arresting of bleeding from internal organs such as the kidneys and the lungs. To check the bleeding

(Urtica dioica L.). 50 g of air-dried nettle was extracted using 5% sulphurous acid and placed in a demijohn, over a steam bath for 10 hours. 2.5 g of the extract was injected sub-cutaneously into a female dog which weighed 9.5 Kg and the effect on gastric secretion, amount of free and total acid, were measured at intervals (Table 5.1).

Table 5.1 shows that the 'sekretin' in the nettle increases the production of gastric juice, free and total acid, all of which are essential for full and adequate digestion of food in the stomach. Other workers measured the effect of intravenous injections of nettle extract on the pancreatic and intestinal secretions using dogs.

Fournier (1948) says that Dobreff discovered 'sekretine' and found it was abundant in the nettle and spinach. He maintains that the high level of 'sekretine' in the nettle makes it amongst the best stimulants known of stomach secretions, stomach and intestinal juices, as well as the muscular peristaltic movements of the intestines. (The 'sekretine' of Dobeff should not be confused with the hormone 'secretin' discovered by Bayliss and Starling). In this connection, spring nettles boiled in milk are recommended for the relief of constipation and also as a cure for diarrhoea.

Its use as a vermifuge (expeller of worms from the body) still takes place. Virendra Singh (1994) reporting on the ethnopharmacological resources in the Kashmir Himalayas found that worm infestation was a very serious illness due to poor sanitary conditions. Various folk medicinal herbs were used including Urtica dioica, as follows:
-

Commonly found in temperate region of Kashmir Himalayas from 1900-2400m. In September people of Karnah valley collect the roots in large quantities and thoroughly wash and dry in shady places. The fresh and dried roots are boiled in water about 2-3 h. Then extract is given to patient in the morning (one cup) about one week regularly against tapeworm. It is common belief that after taking this extract one can get relief from this illness." The conclusion is that traditional social herbal medicine provides essential healthcare and although it doesn't have the high prestige of modern medicine, is relatively inexpensive and widely available.

For haemorrhoids and enteritis nettle syrup is recommended (1 litre of half-boiling water poured over 250 g fresh leaves. Leave to infuse for 12 hrs; strain and add 500 g sugar; take 2-300 cc per day, between meals).

In Turkey (Iida Moriyuki et al 1993) herbal nettle preparations were being used for various conditions. For conditions concerning the alimentary canal U. dioica (locally called isigran, sitmaotu isigri, cincar, dirik, gijirtken, gezgezk) is used as follows: for **stomach-ache** the boiled herb is eaten as a meal: for **haemorrhoids** (1) decoction the herb drunk (U. pilulifera), (2) poultice of the herb is applied to the anus or to wash fistulas.

Some alimentary facts involving great naturalists and their recommendations for nettle medicine: -**Gesner**, advising the use of the root against jaundice, **Fabre**, using nettle seeds against dysentery, **Linnaeus**, when he was a doctor praised the nettle for its antidiarrhetic, binding properties.

PROBLEMS RELATED TO THE KIDNEYS

Dioscorides refers the use of the nettle as a diuretic, "But ye leaves sodden together with small shell fish...move ye urine." Culpeper (1805 Ed) says "The decoction (of leaves in wine) also or the seed, provoketh urine and has hardly even been known to fail in expelling the gravel and stones from the reins (ureters) and bladder" which is praise indeed! 20-30 g of seed is enough for this treatment. Most people know a friend who has suffered the agony of passing kidney stones, and although modern techniques such as ultra-sound or endoscopic surgery can help to break them up, little can be done, except to hasten their passing by the use of a diuretic. Nettles are also recommended as a diuretic for use in kidney diseases such as Nephritis, Cystitis, etc., where the flushing action of passing urine is likely to dislodge microbes and hasten recovery. The Chippewa Indians of the US use a medicine made from Stinging Nettle root and Lady Fern root for disorders of the urinary system. The Chippewa and Meskwak use the root to cure incontinence of urine, which leads us to the next topic (Leach 1950).

Jean Palaiseul (1972) says that, in France, the nettle is a country remedy for bed-wetting and recommends two methods, one of which I quote: Add 16gm of nettle seeds to 60gm of rye flour, mix to a paste with a little hot water and some honey; mould into six small portions, place in a baking tray and bake in an oven; give the child one of these cakes to eat every evening from 8-20 days.

The function of the kidney is not only to eliminate nitrogenous, toxic, metabolic waste such as uric acid, but also to regulate the amount of water in the blood and therefore the volume of tissue fluid surrounding the body cells. For the latter reasons it has also been used in the treatment of gout and oedema (edema).

Gout is a disease of metabolism characterised by the inflammation of the joint of the great toe which produces agonising recurrent pain and an excess of uric acid crystals in the joints (gouty arthritis), kidneys and soft tissues. I have only one piece of scientific evidence to back - up its use in this connection, Watt Breyer-Brandwijle (1962) who cites the work of Keeser on the therapeutic effect of nettles on gout. He found that extracts of nettle fed to duck and geese brought about the lowering of the uric acid content of the blood. This indicates that they act by stimulating an excretion of uric acid by the kidneys (however it should be kept in mind that birds normally excrete large amounts of solid uric acid in their droppings).

The accumulation of serous fluid in various tissues or organs of the body such as the lungs (pleural cavities) and eyes (retina) causes oedema. It is characterised by swelling, and results when the tissue fluid is 30% above normal. The causes are various. (*A sugar-type substance (polysaccharide) from a water extract of the root of U. dioica exhibited immunological activity in rat paw edema, lymphocyte transformation and complement tests, Sakai and Tani, 1988*).

CHESTY PROBLEMS

Dioscorides says "And ye seed...but being licked in with honey it helps ye Orthopneas and Pleurisies and Peripneumonies, and fetcheth up ye stuff out of ye Thorax. But being sodden with Ptisana doth bring up ye stuff from ye Thorax." Gerarde says "Being boyled with barley creame it bringeth up tough humours that sticke in the cheft, as it is thought, It is good for them that cannot breathe unlesse they hold their necks upright (*i.e. relating to asthma*), and for those that have the pleurisie, and for such as be sick of the inflammation of the lungs, if it be taken in a looch or licking medicine, and also against the troublesome cough that children have called the Chin-cough"

Nettles are used in various countries to alleviate the effects of colds and coughs. In Turkey a decoction of the herb is drunk to relieve shortness of breath and the effects of a cold. The Meskwaki tribe of N. American Indians makes a tea from the leaves of the rough nettle (*Laportea canadensis*) for severe colds. In Russia the treatments vary in different areas: (1) dried flowers mixed with lard are made into an ointment which is rubbed on the legs, after a foot steam bath, for colds, (2) the young flowers are brewed like tea and used as an expectorant, i.e. to enable loosening and bringing up of phlegm from the lungs. The young stems with leaves are brewed like tea and drunk for whooping cough in young children, i.e. the Chin-cough of Gerard (Ossadcha-Janata 1952).

The nettle is used as an anti-asthmatic where the expressed juices of the roots or leaves are mixed with sugar to alleviate bronchial and asthmatic problems; for the latter, dried leaves can be burnt and inhaled (Grieve, 1931).

In literature there are numerous references to doctors who have claimed success in the use of the nettle for curing Consumption, which is now called TB (Tuberculosis). TB is caused by a bacterium (*Mycobacterium tuberculosis*) which basically destroys the lung tissue and infects people with a low resistance, more likely when young or during old age, or who have infections such as AIDS, who are malnourished and living in dirty, dark unhealthy conditions. In the UK, children who have proved sensitive to TB are inoculated against it with a BCG injection at about the age of 12. TB is now on the increase and is very widespread in Russia. Rest and sunlight help, but a good diet is essential and the use of the nettle, which is a very nutritious plant and a tonic, no doubt helps in this respect. There is one famous account of a cure for TB by a Swiss doctor A. Vogel (1960) and here summarised from Lucas (1969). Dr Vogel recommended that a woman suffering from tuberculosis be given fresh chopped nettles every day with her soup. After a year she was considered a healthy woman. Her husband who had collected the nettles considered it well worthwhile getting stung all those time!

Modern medicines can cure TB in two phases, 'initial for 8 weeks' and 'continuation for 9 months', but since treatment involves many antibiotics, it is too costly for most under-developed countries.

Nettles have also been used with effect in cases of chronic catarrh, pleurisy and pneumonia.

RHEUMATISM

Rheumatism relates to a painful or aching state of structures such as bones, joints and ligaments, and muscles including their tendons. It also includes arthritis, which is a form of rheumatism, where the joints have become inflamed. Rheumatoid arthritis is produced by the body's own immune system attacking itself, to produce inflammation and damage to the joints which swell and become painful and stiff. Osteo-arthritis is stiffening of joints due to ageing, wear and abrasion.

This condition must have been prevalent in Dioscorides time so it is strange that he did not mention it under nettles, in his Materia Medica. In British herbals it is first mentioned by Culpeper (1653), "any part of the green herb... being applied to the limbs when wearied, refresheth them, and strengtheneth, drieth, comforteth such places as have been put out of joint after having been set again: as also such parts of the body as are subject to gout or other aches, greatly easing the pain thereof and the defluction of humors upon the joints or sinews."

Thomas Green in his Universal Herbal (1816), after describing the effects of the nettle sting, adds that it causes " considerable irritation and inflammation, having been employed as a rubifacient (producing redness or inflammation by irritation), a practice which was termed *urtication* and found of advantage in restoring excitement in paralytic limbs, or in torpid and lethargic affection. They are also admirable stimulants when applied externally to the patient in bed, in order to promote early rising. Paralytic limbs have been restored to their usual functions by stinging them with nettles."

It is commonly reported in the literature that when all else fails, for the alleviation of rheumatism the nettle should then be tried. The method that is used most frequently in Russia, Germany, Turkey, Britain and elsewhere is that of urtication or flagellation where the body is beaten or flogged with groups of nettle stems, or the shoots are rubbed on the painful joint areas. The result is the development of a nettle rash, characterised by red areas which are caused by the widening of blood vessels in the skin (vasodilation), and as a result more blood flows to the skin surface which causes it to become redder and hotter because of more heat loss. With more blood flowing to the joint there is an increase in its mobility. I remember having a similar treatment after I had broken both of my thighbones (femurs); one took 14 weeks to bind after which my knee joint was locked solid. The method, used by the physiologist for increasing the joint mobility, was to pack ice round it. After removal of the ice the blood vessels dilate, more blood flowed to the area increasing the mobility of the joint and lessening the chance of any damage to the ligaments. The nettle has a similar effect but with the added advantage of lessening the pain which is related to the numerous substances injected by the stinging hairs, (U. urens Chapter 3, Chapter 7). Many of these substances are also present in the leaves, which accounts for their use in other treatment methods for rheumatism. In Turkey for example either the boiled herb is directly applied as a hot poultice to the joints or the decoction of the herb is drunk. In Russia a similar treatment for rheumatism is to use the plant or root decoction in a bath. Whippings with a steam whisk broom of nettles, and nettle juice diluted with Vodka is drunk, to cure fever (see Internet on recent work on nettles and rheumatism).

Where I live in Devon England, urtication is still practised. I happened to declare my interest in nettles whilst chatting to a local farmer and he mentioned that his wife suffered terribly from arthritis. First she had tried bee stings without too much success, now he lashes her with nettles which have resulted in an improvement. It is ironic that a lesser pain can be used to alleviate a much worse one! Hatfield (1994) gives two other English treatments (1) to relieve lumbago first apply heat to loosen the muscles then a poultice consisting of nettle leaves and hot linseed oil (2) recommended

for sciatica and rheumatism is a tea made from stinging nettles. A decoction of nettle leaves can also be taken 2-3 times daily, over 6 weeks, for pain from cystitis.

THE MALE DISEASE
BENIGN PROSTATIC HYPERPLASIA (BPH)

This is a non-cancerous disease which affects 70-80% of men in their 70s and 80s. The prostate gland is chestnut-shaped and surrounds the base of the tube (urethra) leading through the penis. During ejaculation one to two drops of seminal fluid from the testes (containing 50-400 million sperms) mixes with two other secretions to make up the semen. 60% of the semen comes from the seminal vesicles, whilst almost the rest, comes from the prostate gland. These secretions basically activate the sperm and provide an alkaline medium to counteract the acid secretions in the female tract. The volume of seminal fluid ejaculated into the vagina of the female only amounts to 2-3 ml.

BPH is caused by the growth and enlargement of the prostate, which then presses on the urethral tube at the base of the bladder. The urethra becomes constricted thus slowing the flow of urine from the bladder; however, other complications are a feeling of urgency to urinate, frequent urination (also at night-nycturia) and retention of urine within the bladder. Most men have to put up with the condition but it does lower the quality of their lives. In severe cases the prostate is cut away using endoscope-type surgery.

At the present moment the precise cause of the condition is not fully known and the investigation continues into the search for the active principles contained in preparations which have been used to control the enlargement process. In Germany 90% of patients with BPH are treated with plant-based pharmaceutical drugs. One of these preparations, sold in Germany under a variety of trade names, contains an extract from the root of U. dioica and a lot of recent research into its effectiveness and mode of action has taken place (see the Internet).

The efficacy of Urtica has been established in placebo-controlled double blind studies i.e. unknown to the patients; half of them are treated with a preparation containing no drug (the placebo treatment) whilst the other half are given the drug. In an early Polish study, the patients of Tadeusz Krzeski et al (1993) were given two drugs known to be effective in BPH, Urtica dioica root extract and the bark extract from *Pygeum africanus*. 134 patients were given the extract twice daily for 8 weeks and three targets; residual urine, urine flow and frequency of nycturia measured efficacy. No adverse effects were found, but the three targets were all significantly reduced.

The triggering of the BPH condition is thought to be due to a shift in hormonal balance from the male hormone testosterone to the female hormone oestrogen. The two reactions are shown below:

(1) Testosterone $\longrightarrow$ Enzyme 5 alpha reductase $\longrightarrow$ Dihydrotestone (causes cell proliferation)

(2) Testosterone $\longrightarrow$ Enzyme aromatase $\longrightarrow$ Oestradiol (increases growth of prostate)

Studies showed that Urtica/Pygeum acts by inhibiting the enzymes in both of these reactions
A sex hormone binding globulin (SHBG), in addition to reactions one and two, is also needed for cell increase in the prostate.

(3) Sex hormone binding globulin $\longrightarrow$ receptor in prostate cell $\longrightarrow$ cell proliferation

It is thought that substances in the Urtica extract may bind with the SHBG preventing its action. Also it is thought that polysaccharides and lectins in the Urtica extract are involved, the former as an anti-inflammatory, and the later intervening in an immunologic and hormonal process.

Hryb et al (1994) in the USA confirmed that aqueous extracts of U. dioica roots inhibit the binding of SHBG to prostate cells and thereby reduce cell proliferation. Granßer and Spiteller (1994) in Germany isolated a number of chemical substances (pentacyclic triterpenes and secondary fatty alcohols), from the roots of U. dioica, which inhibited the enzyme aromatase, and therefore, oestrogen formation and prostate growth.

TUMOURS AND NEOPLASTIC DISEASES

So the search for chemical substances from U. dioica roots to produce more effective alleviation of BPH continues. Claims have been made in the past for the use of Urtica in treating tumours: Dioscorides says "But ye leaves …doe heal …malignant and cancrous …tumours. St. Hildagarde (12 th Cent.) mentions using the nettle root against ganglionated tumours and Culpeper using the seed or leaves in the nostrils says, "Takes away the flesh growing in them called polypus." Wetherilt (1992) mentions their use in Anatolian folk medicine for neoplastic disorders, cancers associated with hormones, and tumours of the mouth lung and alimentary canal.

It is interesting that a scientific basis for anti-tumour action of nettle extract has recently been discovered. Briefly, here, a substance called a lectin (UDA) was isolated from nettle rhizomes, roots and seeds in 1984. It was shown that UDA stimulates the immune response of the body and

causes it to produce an increase (due to its mutagenic activity) in T 2 lymphocytes. The latter in turn produce interferon which is an anti-viral and anti-cancer agent. Many of the old preparations, mentioned above in this connection and clamed to be effective, were prepared from the seeds, rhizomes or roots, thus backing up their supposed healing properties in this connection!

SEX

Dioscorides says "And ye seed being drank with Passumn (Wine) doth incite to conjunction" whilst Galen recommended it for impotency (one coffee spoon of powdered seeds in jam or honey). Palaiseul (1972) mentions a practice he considers heroic, that of flagellation of the erotic areas of the body with nettles which was practised at the time of Petronius who died AD 66 and was a writer and also planned much entertainment at Nero's court. Exhausted libertines to revive their flagging sexual appetites practised the rite of flagellation.

In England before the re-birth of the herbals, Andrewe Boorde the physician to Henry VIII gave some good advice on venery in 'A Dyetary of Helth' (1542) quoted below:

"*Priapismus* is the Greke worde. In Latin it is named *Erectio involuntaris virge*. In Englyshe it is named involuntary standyng of a mans yerd."

He goes on to outline the cause, and the first remedy, "Fyrst, anoynt the yerde and coddes with the oyle of luneper and the oyle Camphorie is good."

"β. Erection of the yerde to synne. A remedy for that is to leape into a greate vessel of colde water, or to put Nettles in the codpeece about the yerd and stones."

Gerarde follows Dioscorides in saying "others think it only powerful to provoke venery." In Germany nettle seed is considered an aphrodisiac (Leach 1950), and in southern Africa U. urens, called *im Babazane*, is one of a series of Zulu aphrodisiac drugs. Quoting material in the archives of the Folklore Society, Vickery (1995) records nettles being used as a contraceptive by a New Forest gypsy who proved it was effective in his case. The practise is to lay nettle leaves against the sole of the feet, put your socks on and wear them for 24 hours before engaging in intercourse. One could speculate a long time on its mode of action in this case!

G. Hatfield (1994) mentions a local farmer who lent him a book 'Farriery Improved' (1789) with the following:

"If you have any particular opportunity of a fine stallion when your mare is not naturally disposed to receive him, or will not stand to be covered: in this case, to provoke lust in her, give her drink of clarified honey and new milk mixed together, and then with a bunch of nettles pat her hinder-parts, and immediately after offer her the horse, which she will receive."

When later, Hatfield met an old man who used to look after Shire horse stallions and asked him about nettles, after a bout of uncontrolled laughter, he told him:

"They books, they get it all wrong! You beat the mare with the nettles after the stallion has been!"

MISCELLANEOUS

OTHER DISEASES

MILK AND DEER

Fournier (1948) says that the nettle has a certain value as a galactagogue, i.e. a stimulator of milk secretion in women. He relates to a case of a woman who was suffering from leukaemia (leucorrhee) and having taken a decotion made from 50 g of nettle leaves for this condition, developed a high pulse rate and temperature, accompanied by profuse sweating, with an apparent reduction in the production of urine over several days and a constant abundant secretion of milk over 8 days.

Jagdwiss (1988) observed the importance of the choice of U. dioica by grazing Red Deer. The does choose to eat a high proportion of flowers, and therefore seeds, of U. dioica during their high lactation period (June-August), and this is attributed to the galactogenic i.e. milk and health stimulating properties, of the nettle.

In relation to diet, the high calcium levels in the nettle would also be of benefit because they are an essential component of milk needed for bone formation of the developing embryo. In adults calcium is needed to replace that lost by the shedding of the antlers.

AS AN ANTI-VENOM

Gerarde says, "Nicander affirmeth that it is a remedie againft the venomous qualitie of Hemlocke, Mufhroms and Quick-filver. And Apollodoris faith that it is a counterpoyfon for Henbane, Serpents, and Scorpions." Culpeper says "The seed being drank, is a remedy against the stinging of venomous creatures, the biting of mad dogs, the poisonous qualities of Hemlock, Henbane, Nightshade, Mandrake and other herbs that stupify or dull the senses."

In South Africa the Sutos use U. dioica, and other Urtica species as ingredients in snakebite remedies (Watt and Breyer-Brandwijk, 1932). Iida (1994) reports that in Turkey there were cases where the fresh herb was directly applied, in one case to a swelling in the breast of a type of cattle and in the other a treatment of snakebite.

BEES AND FROGS

Fig 5.4 Frogs and bees

The earliest reference I can find on this subject is that of Barton and Castle (1877), in which Murray after Hagstrom (Argstrom?) states that, "the nettle in the neighbourhood of bee hives drives away frogs, which are said to be inimical to the swarming of these insects (bees)." Let us first consider the relationship between bees and frogs. The statement implies that if frogs are in the vicinity of hives they deter bees coming out. This is easy to explain because toads (and probably frogs) when it is near dark have been observed waiting at the entrance of bee hives that were placed too near the ground and consuming the last bees that returned home. 32 honeybees have been found in the stomach of one individual (Smith 1951). The studies of Cott (1936) showed that toads, after having been stung 6 times a day by bees, would take no more that day and after a week learnt to avoid them. He also examined the stomach contents of a large number of frogs and toads and found frogs stomachs to contain 4.4% bees, indicating that they do eat them in the wild.

Apart from the original observation of Murray there is only a small amount of circumstantial evidence to back up the hypothesis that nettles adversely affect frogs. Fernie (1914) says that an alkaloid has been isolated from the nettle which is fatal to frogs. It causes paralysis, beginning in the great nerve centres and then it finally stops the heart action (no reference is given).

The epidermis of the frog's skin is alive, full of blood vessels, and moist because it takes up oxygen and therefore is very sensitive. Nobody, as far as I know, has tested the effect of nettle stings on a frog, or their influence on its future behaviour. The ubiquitous nature of nettles and the fact they surround the edges of most ponds would not favour the frog's survival if they were affected adversely by nettle stings. Is anybody out there interested in nettles and frogs, who wants to do a PhD?

CHICKS AND CAPONS

Ray in his Flora of Cambridgeshire (1660) includes some interesting facts under the Common Nettle, which he names Urtica vulgaris urens.

"On more than one occasion we have seen not without pleasure and wonder (a fact that Aldrovandus records from *B. Porta Ornithologiae lib. 14. Cap. 1.*) a capon looking after a brood of chickens like a mother; summoning them with a clucking voice in the manner of hens, feeding tending and looking after them likewise. Nor does it cease from this work but it trains in turn some chickens excluded from the main group until he has done the duties to all of them whether fully grown or not. It is led to perform this task by rubbing its belly with leaves of nettle, the feathers having been first pulled off in the evening and then substituting the chicks one or two nights later until it begins to care for them. Do the chicks soothe the itching caused by the sting of the nettle with their heads? Or do they persuade by their complaining the one unfortunate to come to the aid of other unfortunates?"

Other diseases, given by the authors already quoted, which are capable of being cured or alleviated by nettles, are now given briefly. Some of these diseases which are related to diet will be dealt with in more detail, under food.

It is a favourite remedy amongst the Germans for neuralgia, where it is taken as a decoction, or crushed leaves as a poultice on the affected areas. Dr Vogel recommends it for chlorosis, rachitis (rickets), scrofula, and lymphatic troubles. It has a long traditional reputation for reducing high blood pressure, for which 28gm of fresh herb, added to one pint of boiling water, is taken twice a day. Hives, which is caused by disorders in the alimentary canal followed by a rash appearing on the skin and painful tingling and itching, has been cured by the nettle. Urtication gives relief to sciatica, incipient wasting, difficult breathing in some heart troubles, and lack of muscular activity and is invaluable as a measure which has been successfully used by the peasantry of Russia since time immemorial. In France a tincture is used for neglected herpes, leprosy, psoriasis, a remedy for hernia, and also for suffocation. It is efficacious in digestive toning and for inflammation of the eyes.

PURIFIER OF THE BLOOD

Having considered the medicinal properties of nettles it is no wonder that Culpeper regarded them as the plants most suited to purify the blood. In Russia a tea made from the leaves and roots of the fresh plant is prepared as a vegetable which is used to purify the blood, and a commercial product from Urtica dioica foliage is available, as water soluble tablets (Urtiphyllin), for the same purpose. According to John Gay (1685-1732) the English dramatist and poet, they were sold in the streets of London to cries of 'Nettles with tender shoots to cleanse the blood.' Mary Thorne Quelch (1945) says young nettles can be boiled in very little salted water, and what water remains in the saucepan, should be drunk in the morning as a health giving draught. In a similar way she says nettle tea is a pleasant alkaline spring tonic. To make, chop the young shoots of freshly gathered nettles

DOSAGE AND USE

In pharmacy the standard weight, which is equal to the weight of one barley grain, is the grain (gr.). The grain is equal to 0.0648 of a gram (g). I have quoted both weights in this account. In terms of the weight of seeds of Urtica dioica, each of which weighs 0.2 milligrams, one gram of these seeds would contain approximately 5000 seeds. A shoot of U. dioica, on the average, produces 40,000 seeds. The French and British herbalists seem to differ in the quantities of plant parts used and therefore I include both systems.

FRENCH DATA

This account is after Fournier (1948). High doses must be avoided because some people are sensitive to nettles. Fernie recounts a case where, a strong decoction, drunk too freely by mistake, produced strong burning all over the body, with inflammation and a feeling of being stung. Vesicles appeared on the skin and they eventually burst and discharged watery fluid. The attack subsided after 5-6 days.

The seeds The Italian herbalist Matthiole says the Ancients regarded nettle seeds as dangerous if not used as prescribed, because it only requires 20-30 gr (1.3-2.0 g) to produce purgation. Zanetti in the Italian Army (1797) employed the nettle against the fever and from his experience says 8-12 gr (0.5-0.8 g) per day must not be exceeded.

Infusion or decoction of leaves Use 30-60 gr (2-4 g) per litre to be taken between meals and only three cupfuls per day.

Free juice preparation. 60-125 gr (4-8 g) per day added to a little water before meals.

Syrup One pint of fresh juice boiled with one part sugar. 30-60 gr (2-4 g) per day.

Decoction of the root. As a diuretic and cleanser of the blood, 30-40gr (2.0-2.6 g) per litre of water, to be drunk over two days between meals.

BRITISH DATA

Homeopathic. Tincture. 2 onz. (56.8g) of the herb added to one pint (568 ml) of proof spirit. Powdered dried herb in doses of 5-10 gr (0.3-0.65 g)

Preparation. Fluid extract of the herb. 2-4 g

Infusion 1 onz. (28.4 g) to one pint (568 ml) of boiling water.   (Grieve 1931, Potter 1907).

Decoction. 1½-2 teaspoons. Simmer. Allow to stand for 10-15 mins. Take 2-3 times per. Day for 6 weeks. For cystitis and rheumatic pain.

Expressed juice. 1-2 tablespoons. Take 2-3 times per. day. For anaemia, physical exhaustion and as a spring tonic. (Launert 1981).

Decoction of nettle seeds. 1 onz. (28.4 g)* to 2 pints (1136 ml) of boiling water, reduced by simmering to 1 pint (568 ml), is an old remedy for TB. (Quelch 1948). * Although the amount of seed here is large, it is not being consumed as such.

In Homeopathy. A tincture prepared from the fresh plant is used externally or internally. Only Urtica urens is used. It is used for tumours, oedema, and diarrhoea, as a diuretic and for insufficient milk production after having given birth.

and place in a cup. Fill with boiling water to cover the leaves and infuse for 10 minutes. Strain into another cup and sweeten to taste. Why not give it a try yourselves!

More recent validation or disclaimers of some of the past claims by authors, for the cure of diseases of the body by nettles, can be found on the Internet where readers can form their own conclusions or give them a try!

CHAPTER 6
THE TALE IN THE STING 1
THE MARVELLOUS MICRO-PIPETTE
THE STRUCTURE AND MECHANISM OF THE STINGING TRICHOME

"Look through the microscope at the under side of a nettle leaf, and then you shall find it all full of needles, or rather long transparent pikes; and every needle hath a crystal pummel, so that it looks like a sword-cutler's shop, full of glittering drawn swords, tucks, ands daggers, so that here you may autoptically see the causes, as well as you have formerly felt the effects, of their netling. Something like them appear the prickles on Borrage leafs and stalks."

Dr. Henry Power 1664 (Experimental Philosophy

"We are mildly surprised when we recognize the principle of the hypodermic syringe in the poison fangs of snakes of the stings of insects. But we can surely call it fantastic when we see it perfectly developed in the stinging hairs of a plant, the nettle **Laudermilk (1952)**

INTRODUCTION

The first microscopes of the mid 17th century were hand - made and required some expertise in use, so to begin with, they were only in the hands of a few. They also suffered from optical defects such as chromatic and spherical aberrations, which resulted in fuzzy distorted images fringed with coloured halos. However the first microscopists were extremely privileged, because they were the first to see a whole new microcosmic world full of weird and beautiful objects, previously beyond the human eye. It is not surprising that when they gazed at the most transformed into miraculous structures full of design and beauty. Despite the poor quality of their lenses they were determined to reveal and record the structures and objects they were so privileged to see. When we look at the beautiful and extremely detailed drawings they produced we can imagine the hours they spent looking at their fuzzy objects and the eyestrain they had to endure. Any present day microscopist will know they were driven by man's innate curiosity to discover more and more about this miraculous new world, and make its wonders available to others. It is not surprising that one of the first things the microscopists looked at was the common stinging nettle, prompted no doubt by the age old questions "What causes the painful sting and how does it work?" Up to that time it is likely that few people had bothered to look at a nettle to find out how it stings, so the vivid descriptions of the first microscopists reveal the amazement at what they saw.

BOX 6.1. HOOKE, LEEUWENHOEK AND STINGING HAIRS OF THE COMMON NETTLE

Robert Hooke was a distinguished British scientist, member of the Royal Society and what we would now call a polymath. Amongst his numerous achievements he constructed a compound microscope (Fig 6.1). He became a microscopist of European fame and gave a powerful stimulus to microscopy in England. In 1665 he published his **"MICROGRAPHIA** *or Some Physiological Descriptions of* **Minute Bodies** *Made by Magnifying Glasses with Observations and Inquires thereupon."* I quote from his article "Obferv. Xxv. Of the ftinging points and juice of the Nettles, and fome other venonous Plants."

66

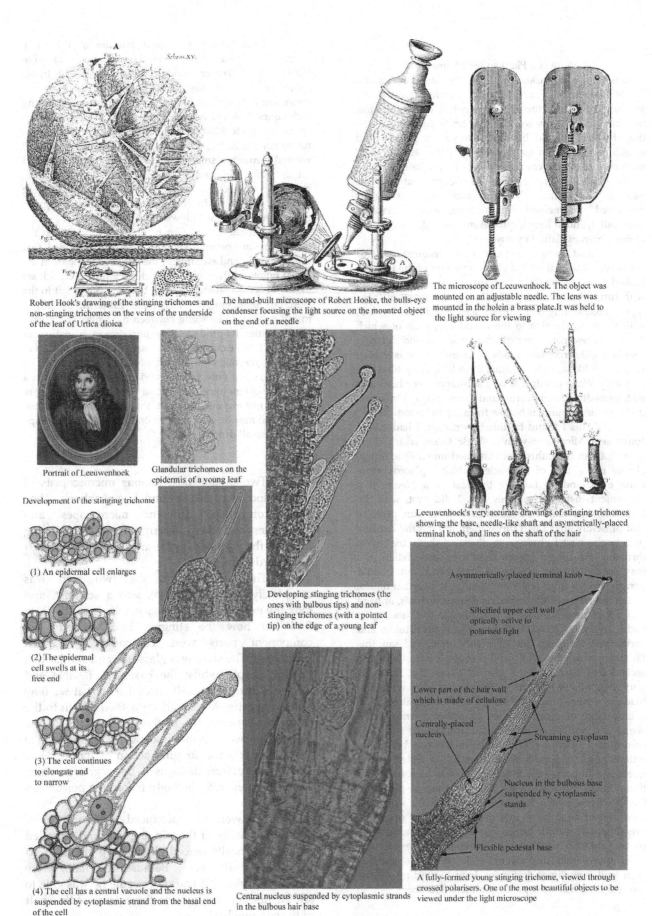

Robert Hook's drawing of the stinging trichomes and non-stinging trichomes on the veins of the underside of the leaf of Urtica dioica

The hand-built microscope of Robert Hooke, the bulls-eye condenser focusing the light source on the mounted object on the end of a needle

The microscope of Leeuwenhoek. The object was mounted on an adjustable needle. The lens was mounted in the holein a brass plate.It was held to the light source for viewing

Portrait of Leeuwenhoek

Glandular trichomes on the epidermis of a young leaf

Leeuwenhoek's very accurate drawings of stinging trichomes showing the base, needle-like shaft and asymetrically-placed terminal knob, and lines on the shaft of the hair

Development of the stinging trichome

(1) An epidermal cell enlarges

(2) The epidermal cell swells at its free end

(3) The cell continues to elongate and to narrow

(4) The cell has a central vacuole and the nucleus is suspended by cytoplasmic strand from the basal end of the cell

Developing stinging trichomes (the ones with bulbous tips) and non-stinging trichomes (with a pointed tip) on the edge of a young leaf

Central nucleus suspended by cytoplasmic strands in the bulbous hair base

Asymmetrically-placed terminal knob

Silicified upper cell wall optically active to polarised light

Lower part of the hair wall which is made of cellulose

Centrally-placed nucleus

Streaming cytoplasm

Nucleus in the bulbous base suspended by cytoplasmic stands

Flexible pedestal base

A fully-formed young stinging trichome, viewed through crossed polarisers. One of the most beautiful objects to be viewed under the light microscope

FIG 6.1 THE DEVELOPMENT OF THE STINGING TRICHOME OF URTICA DIOICA AND THE FIRST MICROSCOPIST'S VIEW

67

"A nettle is a Plant so well known to every one, as to what the appearance of it is to the naked eye, that it needs no description; and there are very few that a gentle and slight touch of the skin by a nettle, does oftentime, not onely create very sensible and acute pain, much like that of a burn or scald, but often also very angry and hard swellings and inflammations of the parts, such as will presently rise, and continue swoln divers hours. These observations, I say, are commom enough; but how the pain is so suddenly created, and by what means continued, augmented for a time, and afterwards diminish'd, and at length quite exstinguish'd, has not, that I know, been explain'd by any."

"And here we must have recourse to our *Microscope*, and that will, if almost any part of the Plant be looked on, shew us the whole surface of it very thick set with turn-Pikes, or sharp Needles, of the shape of those represented in (Fig 6.1). *Scheme* and first *Figure* by A B, which are visible also to the naked eye; each of which consists of two parts very distinct for shape, and differing also in quality from one another. For the part A, is shaped very much like a round Bodkin, from B tapering till it end in a very sharp point; it is of a substance very hard and stiff, exceedingly transparent and cleer, and, as I by many trials certainly found, is hollow from top to bottom."

"This I found by this Experiment, I had a very convenient *Microscope* with a single Glass which drew about half an Inch, this I had fastened into a little frame, almost like a pair of Spectacles, which I placed before mine eyes, and so holding the leaf of a Nettle at a convenient distance from my eye, I did first, with the thrusting of several of these bristles into my skin, perceive that presently after I had thrust them in I felt the burning pain begin; next I observ'd in divers of them, that upon thrusting my finger against their tops, the Bodkin (if I may so call it) did not in the least bend, but I could perceive moving up and down within it a certain liquor, which upon thrusting the Bodkin against its basis, or bagg B, I could perceive to rise towards the top, and upon taking away my hand, I could see it again subside, and shrink into the bagg; this I did very often, and saw this *Phenomenon* as plain as I could ever see a parcel of water ascend and descend in a pipe of Glass. But the basis underneath these Bodkins on which they were fast, were made of a more pliable substance, and looked almost like a little bagg of green Leather, or rather resembled the shape and surface of a wilde Cucumnber, or *cucumeris asinini*, and I could plainly perceive them to be certain little baggs, bladders, or receptacles full of water, or as I guess, the liquor of the Plant, which was poisonous and those small Bodkins were but the Syringe-pipes, or Glyster-pipes, which first made way into the skin, and then served to convey that poisonous juice, upon the pressing of those little baggs, into the interior and sensible parts of the skin, which being so discharg'd, does corrode, or, as it were, burn that part of the skin it touches; and this pain will sometimes last very long, according as the impression is made deeper or stronger" (Gunther).

Undoubtedly the most famous of the early microscopists was Antoni van Leeuwenhoek (lâý-vên-hôôk) a Dutch draper working in the city of Delft. In his spare time he ground small spherical lenses in a downstairs basement. Even with modern grinding techniques it would be difficult to equal his lenses which magnified up to 500 times. He mounted these in a simple microscope (Fig 6.1) that was held up to the light and viewed through a small hole. The objects were mounted on an adjustable needle (Payne 1966). It wasn't long before he trained his superior lenses onto the stinging hairs of the nettle. In 1687 he wrote on the "stings or prickles of nettles" as follows:

"At the time I first turned my thoughts to the nature of our common stinging nettles, I imagined that the great pain and swelling of the occasion arose from the sharp points of the stings or prickles, which are thick set on their leaves and stalks, being broken off and left in the skin: but happening one day, while gathering asparagus in my garden, to be stung between my fingers by a very small nettle, it produced so uncommon a pain and swelling, that I examined more narrowly the formation of nettles by the microscope, and I found that the stings or prickles are not only hollow, and contain within them a very transparent juice, but that, at the time when they are in their most vigorous growth, this juice issues from the stings, and may be seen to settle on the points in the shape of a very small drop or globule."

Two of the most famous microscopists of this period were Hooke and Leeuwenhoek. They used completely different microscopes and techniques and their description of the stinging hairs of the common nettle are best given in their own words (Box 6.1).

The approach of the two men was completely different: Hooke, was a scientist, and took the experimental approach, stinging himself to find out how the stinging hair worked. The component parts were compared to known substances. The shaft was glass-like and similar to a bodkin/hairpin whilst the base was flexible and reminded him of a small cucumber - what we now call a courgette. A comparison is then drawn to the similarity between the method of injection of the poison in a wasp or bee and that of the nettle. He even compares the stinging action of the nettle to that of the poison darts used by pygmies, which must first penetrate the body before the poison can act.

Leeuwenhoek produced a much more accurate drawing of the stinging hair and recorded its asymmetrically placed globular tip and showed the cells of the base. Because the hairs were mounted dry on the end of a needle he was able to see the lines or striations on the outside of the shaft of the stinging hair.

The botanical name for plant hairs is trichome, coming from the Greek, and meaning any hair-like growth of the epidermis, as a hair or bristle. Plant trichomes show great variety and beauty, and those shown in the frontispiece illustration have been taken from 'Anatomy of the Dicotyledons', (Metcalfe & Chalk, 1950&1979).

THE STRUCTURE OF STINGING TRICHOMES

INTRODUCTION

During the 19th century the optics of the light microscope were perfected and microscopy was the favourite occupation of the Victorians who made some superb dried microscopic preparations of the stinging hairs of the common nettle. Stinging hairs of various groups of plants (Urticaceae, Euphorbiaceae, Loasaceae, and Hydrophyllaceae) were also the favourites of some of the most famous German and French scientists. In the 19th century twenty-six major scientific works were devoted to the structure and stinging mechanisms of stinging trichomes. Perhaps the most famous one was that of G. Haberlandt (1886). In the 20th century, up to 1992, there were twenty-five papers; notable were those of Strasburger (1910) and Thurston (1974), (Table 6.1).

The resolution of the light microscope is limited by the wave-length of light to a maximum magnification of two thousand times. In 1933 E. Rusca invented the transmission electron microscope, five-hundred times more powerful than the light microscope, and later a scanning version was produced. The electron microscopes led to the study of the ultra-structure of cells and the discovery of their organelles, but strangely enough, it is only comparatively recently that the electron microscope has been used to look at stinging trichomes, Marty (1968).

THE DEVELOPMENT AND STRUCTURE OF THE STINGING TRICHOME/HAIR OF URTICA DIOICA

DEVELOPMENT

There are three types of hairs in Urtica dioica: glandular, non-stinging/bristle hairs/borsten haar and stinging hairs/brennhaar. The early development of these hairs can be studied by slicing off small portions of veins or viewing the edges of the topmost leaves at the 1-2mm stage. The hair destined to become a stinging hair very soon distinguishes itself from the non-stinging hair by developing a terminal globular swelling. In the further development of the hair cell the terminal knob remains approximately the same size whilst the hair increases enormously and develops a bulbous base (Fig 6.1).

Cell divisions take place at various angles in the epidermis and hypodermis and these continued divisions surround the basal hair bulb in a layer of cells and then raise it up on a cushion of cells called the pedestal. The cells of the pedestal tend to be rounded with large air spaces in-between (Rauter, 1872 Thurston, 1974).

Little seems to have been written on the function of the pedestal although its presence is thought to represent the highest development of stinging hairs. It certainly enables a certain amount of 'give' on impact by acting as an elastic cushion and in this respect the air spaces between the cells may be important. There is considerable variation in the angle of the hair cells and this is mainly brought about by different growth rates of cells on the two sides of the pedestal. In the stem for example the majority of hairs have an angle between 90°-70° but a few have angles of 30°-45° and point towards the tip or base of the stem. Stinging hairs with low angles occur on the veins on the underside of the leaves, and considering the leaf itself is at an angle, the hairs are probably at a good angle to sting the lips of browsing cattle. The single layer of cells around the basal bulb is important to give it support and elasticity which enable it to change shape and bring about the compression of the fluid in the bulb when animal contact subjects it to a force.

STRUCTURE

Having studied the development of the stinging hair it is clear that it consists of a single large cell embedded in a multi-cellular pedestal base. The stinging cell is an extremely large cell (1.8 mm long) whereas the size of an average plant cell is only 35μ (1μ=1/1000mm). The main part of the cell (1.6 mm long) is pulled out into a tapered needle (shaft) that is closed at the end by an asymmetrically placed hollow terminal knob/button/ball (14μ diameter). The shaft has a thick cellulose cell wall that is glass-like and brittle near its tip. The base is swollen into an

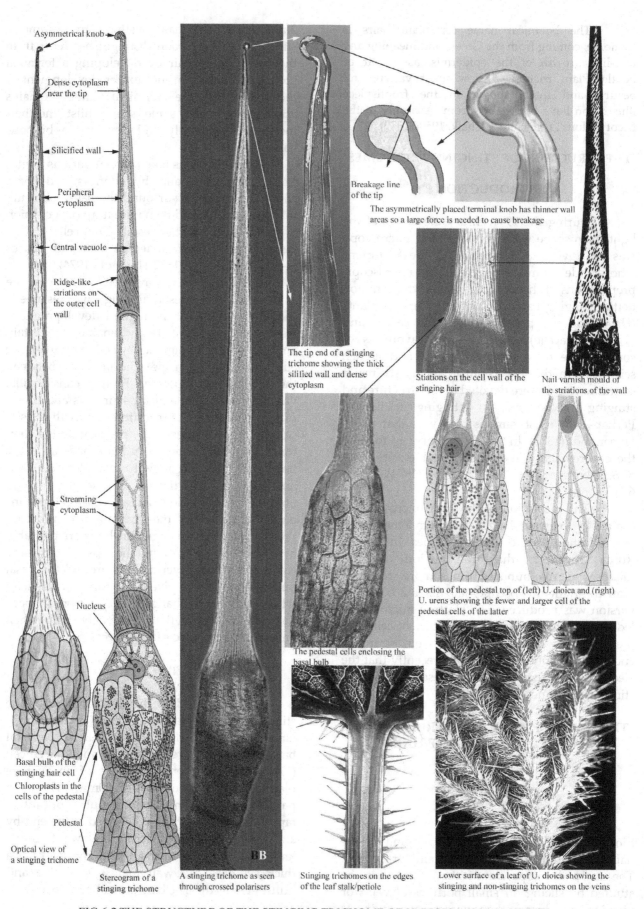

Asymmetrical knob

Dense cytoplasm
near the tip

Silicified wall

Peripheral
cytoplasm

Central vacuole

Ridge-like
striations on
the outer cell
wall

Streaming
cytoplasm

Nucleus

Basal bulb of the
stinging hair cell

Chloroplasts in the
cells of the pedestal

Pedestal

Optical view of
a stinging trichome

Stereogram of a
stinging trichome

A stinging trichome as seen
through crossed polarisers

BB

Breakage line
of the tip

The asymmetrically placed terminal knob has thinner wall
areas so a large force is needed to cause breakage

The tip end of a stinging
trichome showing the thick
silified wall and dense
cytoplasm

Stiations on the cell wall of the
stinging hair

Nail varnish mould of
the striations of the wall

The pedestal cells enclosing the
basal bulb

Portion of the pedestal top of (left) U. dioica and (right)
U. urens showing the fewer and larger cell of the
pedestal cells of the latter

Stinging trichomes on the edges
of the leaf stalk/petiole

Lower surface of a leaf of U. dioica showing the
stinging and non-stinging trichomes on the veins

FIG 6.2 THE STRUCTURE OF THE STINGING TRICHOME OF U. DIOICA AND U. URENS

70

TABLE 6.1. List of the authors of the main works on the stinging hairs/trichomes of the members of the Urticaceae and stinging members of other families. Placed in chronological order for historical reasons. (After Thurston and Lersten 1969, Updated to 1992 Wheeler).(*H*=Hydrophyllaceae, *U*=Urtica, *G*=Girardinia, *Ur*=Urera, *L*=Laportea, *C*=Cnidoscolus, *T*=Tragia, *D*=Dalechampia, *L*=Loasa, *B*=Blumenbachia, *C*=Caiophora, *W*=Wigandia).

Authors	Urticaceae				Euphorbiaceae			Loasaceae			H
	U	G	Ur	L	C	T	D	L	B	C	W
Hooke (1665)	*										
Leeuwenhoek (1687)	*										
Guettard (1745)	*				*						
Schrank (1749)	*										
Eble (1831)	*										
De Candolle (1832)					*						*
Meyen (1837	*				*			*			
Bahrdt (1849)	*										
De Jussieu (1849)	*				*			*			
Schleiden (1849)	*							*			*
Weddell (1854)	*	*	*	*							
Cruger (1855)					*						
Unger (1855)	*										
Wicke (1861)	*										
von Mohl (1861)	*										
Duval-Jouve (1867)	*							*			
Weiss (1867)	*				*			*			
Rauter (1872)	*										
Martinet (1872)	*				*			*			*
Sachs (1873)	*				*			*			
Delbrouck (1875)	*							*			*
Ducharte (1877)	*		*		*			*			*
Kallen (1882)	*										
Gravis (1886)	*										
Greinert (1886)								*	*	*	
Haberlandt (1886)	*			*	*			*			*
Stahl (1888)						*					
Kohl (1889)	*			*	*	*		*	*	*	
Ritterhausen (1892)						*					
Klemm (1895)	*										
Kuster (1903)	*										
Knoll (1905)								*	*		
Palla (19060	*										
Wiesner (1906)	*										
Solereder (1908)	*	*	*	*	*	*	*	*	*	*	*
Besecke (1909)			*								
Strasburger (1910)	*										
KusterWinkelmann,1914								*	*	*	
Rouppert (1914)	*	*		*				*	*	*	
Rouppert (1916)	*			*				*	*	*	
Jakovljevic (1929)								*			
Netolitzky (1932)	*	*	*	*	*	*	*	*	*	*	*
Korn (19440	*										
Metcalfe & Chalk (1951)	*				*	*	*	*			
Rao & Sundarara (1951)							*				
Tschermak-Woess &Hasitschka (1953)/(1954)	*										
Uphof (1961)	*	*	*	*	*	*	*	*	*	*	*
Barber & Shone (1966)	*										
Marty (1968)	*										
Thurston & Lersten 1969	*	*	*	*	*	*	*	*	*	*	*
Thurston 1974	*						*				
Thurston 1976	*										
Sowers & Thurston 1976	*										
Corsi & Gargari 1990	*										
Corsi 1992	*										

elongated sphere (0.2 mm in depth) with a flexible cellulose wall and forms the basal bulb.

The latter is sunk into a raised cylinder of cells called the pedestal/pedicule/zellenmass (0.5 mm long). The stinging cell contains a large central vacuole, and the nucleus with two large refractive nuclear vacuoles is generally in the centre of the basal bulb where it is held in

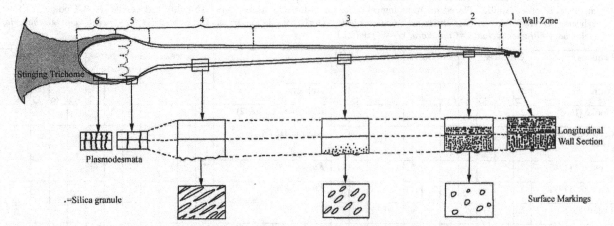

Fig 6.3. The diagram is based on the electron microscope studies, using Urtica dioica, on the formation of silica nodules by the endoplasmic reticulum and golgi bodies of the cytoplasm, and their deposition in different regions (1-6) of the stinging hair wall. The wall material, which is largely cellulose, remains free of silica at the base. The basal bulb doesn't contain pits but plasmodesmata are present and connect the cytoplasm of the hair cell with that of adjacent cells off the pedestal. The wart-like markings are elongated at the base but rounder towards the tip. (Thurston 1969).

place by strands cytoplasm which connect up with the peripheral cytoplasm layer. The cytoplasm streams in different directions but goes up the shaft on one side and down on the other and is one of the best objects for the study of cyclosis in cells. The granules in the cytoplasm are also in constant Brownian motion. The stinging cells have no chloroplasts but the pedestal cells are full of chloroplasts and starch grains. The stinging hair is one of the most beautiful objects of structure and design that can be viewed under the microscope, particularly when seen under polarised light and retarders or dark-ground illumination. It looks in essence like a miniature eye-dropper/pipette (Fig 6.2).

Leeuwenhoek drew the oblique streaks on the hair shaft and later they were investigated by Meyen (1837) and Bahrdt (1849), the latter says the stinging hair is covered by cuticle with wart-like spiral prominences, and adds these are also found in the non-stinging hairs. These spiral marks are best seen when a hair is viewed using oblique lighting. Alternatively they can be seen by gently pressing a leaf into nail varnish just before it sets and viewing the mould of the hair surface with oblique lighting (Fig 6.2).

A MUCH CLOSER LOOK

It was not until 1968 that Marty used the transmission electron microscope (TEM) to look at the structure of stinging hairs of Urtica urens and this study was added to by the work of Thurston (1969) on the ultra-structure of U. dioica (this will be looked at in the following section). Knowledge of the structure and composition of the stinging hair wall was also advanced by the work of Sowers &Thurston (1975, 1976). Earlier studies have spoken of the unique glass-like/siliceous nature of the top part of the stinging hairs which gives the wall it's rigid and brittle nature and enables the terminal

knob to fracture on impact and the needle-like tip to penetrate the skin. Using the TEM and taking into account the X-ray spectrum of the wall, the studies found that silica bodies are associated with the endoplasmic reticulum and golgi bodies, particularly in the dense cytoplasm towards the tip of the hair. The silica bodies, measuring 350-650 A°, comprise almost the entire cell wall at the tip and are arranged into two layers; the amount of silica decreases distally and is free from the basal part of the cell wall which is made mainly of cellulose (Fig 6.3),. Thurston also found that there was no calcium in the hair cell wall, as indicated by Haberlandt.

Sowers and Thurston (1976) studied the silica deposition in the stinging hair wall of Urtica pilulifera, in relation to silicic acid and its analogues, germanic acid and dimethyl siliciic acid. The latter workers showed that plant growth in practically silica - free solutions as would be expected show little ability to sting. The addition of silica to the solution, after a period of two weeks led to the development of stinging ability, assumed to be due to the hardening of the stinging hair wall by the added silica.

Silica is found particularly in the outer epidermal cell walls of grasses and accounts for the ability of a blade of grass to cut the hand when drawn across it. Silicon is a vital element as far as the nettle is concerned to give the wall of the stinging hair sufficient rigidity to penetrate skin.

BOX 6.2. THE ORIGIN OF THE TOXIN SECRETION IN THE STINGING TRICHOMES OF URTICA

The high power of the Transmission Electron Microscope has been used in an attempt to look for evidence that toxin secretion takes place in the stinging trichome cell. Thurston (1974) found that in Urtica dioica there are vacuoles in the nucleus; however, since the nuclear membrane is deeply lobed, this could be a mistake. The cytoplasm contains plastids with simple lamellar systems, osmophilic granules and small starch grains. No primary pits were found between the stinging cell and the basal cell, and the structure of the adjacent pedestal cells was morphologically similar to that of the stinging cell. Marty (1968) looked at the stinging trichomes of Urtica urens for evidence of secretory structures. The endoplasmic reticulum is first rough but later dilates to become smooth. Mitochondria and Golgi bodies are frequently found in the cytoplasm. The presence of a folded plasmalemma and granular vesicles both at the base of the stinging cell and in adjacent pedestal cells could be evidence of exchange of materials. Using cyto-chemical methods, acetycholine was found in the vacuoles and cavities of the endoplasmic reticulum. The secretory products produced in the ER and Golgi bodies are thought to be passed to the central vacuole where they are stored. These two works look at different species of Urtica and disagree on whether secretion of toxin takes place inside or outside the stinging trichome. More research, using the TEM, cyto-chemical techniques, etc, needS to be carried out on other species of Urtica, related members of the Urticeae, and other families of stinging plants.

STINGING HAIRS OF OTHER GENERA OF THE URTICEAE

There is a paucity of information on the structure of the stinging hairs of most species of the Urticeae. Most of the literature which is available was published towards the end of the 19th century and the beginning of the 20th century and little has been published since. Of the widely distributed species of the genus Urtica (45 species.) there are detailed accounts of only four species; Urtica dioica, U. urens and U. pilulifera and more recently Corsi

and Garbari (1990) have studied the morphology and ontogeny (development) of the stinging hair of Urtica membranacea Poiret (U. dubia Forskal). They found that the structure and development was similar to that of U. dioica but differed in two respects: - they report (1) pits between the stinging cell and those of the pedestal, as seen in surface view with the light microscope, (2) glandular hairs on the pedestal. These glandular hairs make their appearance early on (when the leaf is 1.5 mm) and increase in number with age and can reach a maximum of ten (Fig 6.4).

Very often there is a lack of detailed studies of the other hair types, which would help in elucidating possible evolutionary (phylogenetic) relationships. There are no anatomical studies of hair types for the following genera, *Hesperocnide, Nanocnide, Obetia, Discocnide, Laportea and Gyrotaenia* (73-spp. total).

Of the genus Urera (35 spp) there are only two works: Schleiden (1849) and Besecke (1909). The latter author describes the stinging hairs of Urera baccifera as having a basic structure and development similar to that of Urtica. The hair cell is sunk into a multicellular pedestal that contains latex tubes, and in a similar way to U. membranacea the surface is covered in small capitate hairs. Later in development a phellogen (cork initiating layer) is formed and due to its activity the greater part of the pedestal is shed – it should be mentioned here that this plant is a woody shrub. It has a terminal knob similar to that of Wigandria (see later)

Of the genus Girardinia (2 spp) of Africa

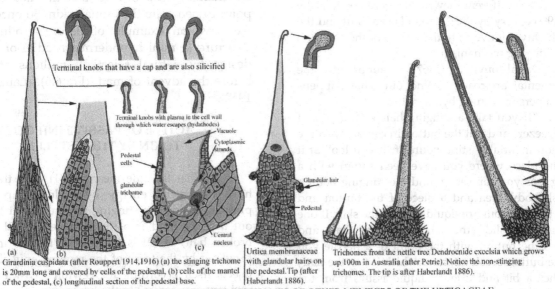

Girardinia cuspidata (after Rouppert 1914,1916) (a) the stinging trichome is 20mm long and covered by cells of the pedestal, (b) cells of the mantel of the pedestal, (c) longitudinal section of the pedestal base.

Urtica membranaceae with glandular hairs on the pedestal.Tip (after Haberlandt 1886).

Trichomes from the nettle tree Dendrocnide excelsia which grows up 100m in Australia (after Petrie). Notice the non-stinging trichomes. The tip is after Haberlandt 1886).

FIG 6.4. STRUCTURE OF THE STINGING TRICHOMES OF OTHER MEMBERS OF THE URTICACEAE

and tropical Asia, studies of the stinging hairs of *Girardinia cuspidata* were carried out by Rouppert (1914, 1916). Plants of Girardinia are indeed formidable and particularly when their *20mm* long stinging hairs are viewed against the light where they appear enlarged as glistening swords. Such an enormous hair cell needs support so it is not surprising that the basal pedestal covers $\frac{4}{5}$ to $\frac{8}{9}$ of the stinging cell (Fig 6.4). The outer cuticle layer of the pedestal cells is continuous with the cuticle overlying the wall of the stinging cell, and the marginal pedestal cells are reported to grow upwards (acropetally) in-between these layers. Finally they develop into an 'aril-like' mantle which forms a flexible connection with the basal part. Rouppert found very small droplets, thought to be small vesicles containing silica, appearing on the surface of the primary wall. He found silicification began in the apical regions and thereafter progressed downwards (basipetally). Using methyl violet stain in sulphuric acid he found that a 'plasma reaction' occurred in the upper regions of the stinging hair wall (Fig 6.4) and concluded that these areas function for the removal of surplus water (i.e. hydathodes) as witnessed by the exhudation of water globules in these parts. Rouppert's study is more valuable because he compared the structure of hairs on the vegetative and reproductive parts of Girardinia and concluded that they reached their greatest development on the latter parts. A more detailed study of the different types of hairs of this genus and also Dendrocnide, under the SEM and TEM would be worthwhile.

TOWARDS UNRAVELLING THE MECHANISM OF THE NETTLE STING
HISTORICAL

Two different viewpoints were taken in the mid-19th century by the German Haberlandt and the French Duval-Jouve as to the nature of the common nettle stinging mechanism.

Duval-Jouve (1867) adopted the experimental approach to find out what happens when a person is stung by the nettles.

"If you take a stinging hair with a pair of fine tweezers and put the button in contact with the skin you invariably sting yourself. If you look at it (i.e. the place where you have been stung) with a strong lens you can see around the stinging point a whitish body/area and a piece of the button and also a small amount of liquid spilt on the skin. If one places on a slide the whole stinging hair and touches the button with the point of a needle you see the button break off, after which it (i.e. the hair) stretches a bit and a jet of liquid issues from the rupture and shoots out a demi-millimetre or so."

Duval-Jouve makes the important discovery that the button at the tip breaks off *before* the entry of the hair into the skin. He also believed that the fluid in the hair squirts out because it is under pressure (see later); however he does say that "Bardht attributes the emission of the burning liquid to the pressure that the bulb undergoes on the moment of contact."

Gottlieb Haberlandt was a member of the German school of Physiological Anatomy founded by the famous Julius von Sachs. Haberlandt emphasises that the stinging hair has a rigid, but at the same time slightly elastic cell wall, with the top part of a glass-like nature due to rich deposition of silica (i.e. the main constituent of sand, quartz, glass, etc.). The silica in the wall decreases towards the base and is replaced with a deposition of lime/calcium carbonate (this is why this part dissolves in dilute acid and gives off bubbles of carbon dioxide). Although he doesn't include experimental data, he explains that the terminal knob (Köpfehen) is brittle and breaks off at the slightest touch, and he relates this to the structure of the terminal knob of Urtica dioica. He notes that the hair knob breaks along the plane of two areas of thinness in the knob wall (Fig 6.2, 6.6). The arrangement not only facilitates the detachment of the tip and leaves a point with a shape best suited to penetrate the skin. The fracture plane is oblique so the resulting point is lance-shaped and because it is glass-like is extremely sharp. It is clear when looking at the obliquely broken glassy tip that it is very similar to the tip of a hypodermic needle (Fig 6.6) which was carefully designed by the French physician Dr Charles Pravaz in 1853 to be the most efficient point to penetrate the human skin. So once again we have an example of nature producing a structure (a mini hypodermic needle) of perfect design by natural selection, millions of years before the advent of man! (Fig 6.6), (Laudermilk 1952).

ACTIVE OF PASSIVE INJECTION OF TOXIN BY THE NETTLE?

What the title means is (1) does the plant have to expend energy by building up turgor pressure inside the stinging hair sufficient to force out a jet of fluid into the skin penetrated by the broken hair, or (2) is the energy for the injection provided by the force of the moving animal which injects itself according to Newton's Law of equal and opposite forces? In the latter case, (a) a person's moving hand provides the downward force which breaks off the terminal hair knob, and this force is transmitted down the rigid hair to the flexible wall of the basal bulb, (b) this takes up the energy, changes shape and is compressed against the pedestal base, (c) this results in an equal and opposite upward force causing cell fluid to be injected from the broken tip into the open wound (Fig 6.6).

Duval Jouve's previous experiment supports an active process, and to verify this he did the following experiment (my words are in brackets):

"I mapped out very exactly, by means of the clear chamber, and very greatly enlarged (i.e. high power [X400 or more] of the microscope) a sketch of the lower half of an almost complete hair with the direction of its vacuoles (the spiral thickenings on the outside of the hair wall). Then I broke the point of the button and did a second sketch that I superimposed over that of the first. In every case, without exception I found that the diameter of the bulb remained the same whilst that of the stinging hair has diminished by 1/15th to 1/20th. I also found the angle of the spirals had risen by almost 2°. It therefore became for me very evident that there is, at the moment of rupture, a contraction which aids the expression/expulsion of part of the burning fluid and that the spiral disposition of the vacuoles coincides as well to the same effect."

Haberlandt (1886) reviews the experiment of Duval-Jouve and questions his procedure and interpretations. He says in relation to the decrease in the diameter of the hair and no change in the bulb diameter: - "In view of the fact that the walls of the hair are silicified or calcified down to the swelling whereas the membrane of the bulb comprises relatively pure cellulose the reverse would have been expected. In fact I never did find a constriction of the actual hair after breaking off the terminal knob, though indeed, a decrease in the transverse diameter of the bulb by 2-5%; frequently, however, the lowest part of the hair cell showed no change in diameter."

Haberlandt adds:-

"This clearly emerges amongst other factors from the fact that one can effectively prick (sting) oneself twice in succession with one and the same stinging hair. Obviously the turgor pressure does not apply in the second sting, although the latter, is no less effective than the former; the discharge of the poison occurs exclusively by the mode mentioned secondly", (i.e. due to pressure on the bulb). He concludes: -

"The usual case, however, of that in which the mechanism from both procedures combines.

When the stinging hair is touched only very gently - which often suffices to inflame the skin, the discharge of the cell fluid, however, is exclusively or mainly attributed to turgor pressure."

I devised another experiment to test to what extent an active and passive process injects stinging fluid into the skin (Fig 6.5), first carried out without a water droplet, here the pedestal base is suspended in air to eliminate any pressure on the bulb. In all cases with this set-up, the fluid collapsed backwards for some distance into the hair, after breakage of the tip. I concluded that, since the pedestal base was in the air, this caused water loss and the cell became flaccid due to a negative pressure, thus resulting in the cell collapse on hair breakage. To overcome this, I placed a small drop of water on the slide so that it made contact with the pedestal base and ensured maintenance of turgidity and in the majority of cases the breakage of the hair generally resulted in no change. In a few cases, however, after breakage a small drop of liquid extruded from the tip and then quickly solidified, showing the effect of turgidity before the wound was sealed.

My conclusion is that passive injection is the most important method of injection of stinging fluid, but the active method cannot be ruled out, but because the volume ejected is only minute, it could only work if the physiological reaction resulting from a sting could be brought about by a very small amount of fluid. Hairs lacking a high turgor pressure wouldn't work which would be a waste of resources.

Which model best represents the structure and action of the stinging hair? The typical plastic disposable hypodermic syringe is often referred to in relation to the stinging hair, hypodermic syringe is similar in structure and action since it had a basal bulb that is squeezed to inject the medicinal fluid. The nearest structure to the stinging hair is that of a pipette (eyedropper)-(Fig 6.6).

GENTLY GRASP OR BOLDLY GRASP?

The idea that you are more likely to be

> "Tender-handed stroke a nettle,
> And it stings you for your pains;
> Grasp it like a man of mettle,
> And it soft as silk remains.

stung by a nettle as a result of gently brushing up against it than if you grasp it firmly, is reviewed in the literature (Chapter 4) and most people are familiar with the poem of Aaron Hill (1685-1750). How many have bothered, or even dared to test the

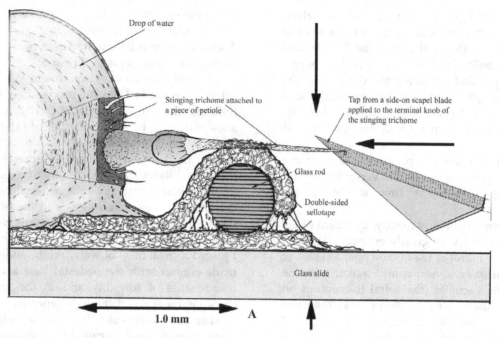

Drop of water

Stinging trichome attached to a piece of petiole

Tap from a side-on scapel blade applied to the terminal knob of the stinging trichome

Glass rod

Double-sided sellotape

Glass slide

1.0 mm   A

FIG 6.5 Experiment to test to what extent is the stinging mechanism of Urtica dioica due to an active process and/or a passive process (see text for the explanation).

validity of grasping the nettle, in a physical rather than in a metaphorical sense!

Schacht (1856) says "The hair shaft is made up of a lower flexible part and a terminal stiff part which is easily broken and from this it follows that you are more likely to be stung by a light touch than by seizing the plant.

In the first a light ouch causes the glass-like substance forming the wall of the tip to break off and the bitter liquid of the hair spills out into the wound. In the second case of seizing the nettle, this causes the flexible part of the hair to bend, so the rigid end piece with its little button cannot have a chance of penetrating the skin."

Duval-Jouve (1867) says "It is a common error to believe that nettles do not sting when grasped firmly. However quick and firm the contact of the hand is when the movement is from the top to the bottom (i.e. of the stem) the stings are just as numerous as when you grasp it weakly or slowly. I have stung myself enough times in this exercise to be an authority. What has caused this delusion is that when one grasps the nettle strongly and with the whole hand you usually do it from the bottom to the top, in which case you are hardly stung because of the direction of the but there is no equivalent to the movable piston in the stinging hair. On the other hand it is quite difficult to sting the palm of your hand because the skin is hardened by habitual use of a hard body, as for example carrying a cane or stick, but it is in the folds of the joints that stinging takes place. On the back of the hand and the arm the burning of the stings only lasts a few

hours at the most whilst on the palm of the hand, in the finger joint skin, because of the greater quantity of nerve cells and blood vessels, the stinging sensation is longer lasting and more than 24 hours afterwards you can still feel a tingling/stinging sensation.

In U dioica, stinging hairs are found all over the plant body, and vary greatly in their angle and density on different organs. The organs also are oriented in different planes, and when one considers the movement of the plant by the wind and the direction of movement of the animal, the 'potential nettle stinging volume' around the nettle is large and the chances of getting stung are high.

The hands are extremely sensitive to touch due to a high density of sensory receptors and free nerve endings which when stimulated are perceived as pain, so for people with thinner (less callused) skin on their palms, stinging can be extremely painful. I can add that in my experience the inside of the arms, the face, the legs and feet are very sensitive to nettle stings. If one considers the large mass of a human, its velocity and momentum even when slowly moving the magnitude of the forces are likely to be large and the needle point of the hair is designed to magnify this and facilitate entry into the tough skin. The direction of the force in relation to that of the hair is important: it would be expected that a force parallel to the direction of the hair is going to the most effective. As the force deviates more and more from this, the chances of breaking the hair tip and of penetration into the skin are

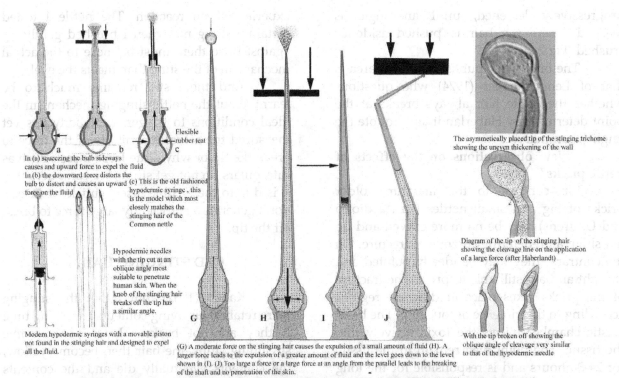

In (a) squeezing the bulb sideways causes and upward force to expel the fluid
In (b) the downward force distorts the bulb to distort and causes an upward force on the fluid

(c) This is the old fashioned hypodermic syringe, this is the model which most closely matches the stinging hair of the Common nettle

Flexible rubber teat

Hypodermic needles with the tip cut at an oblique angle most suitable to penetrate human skin. When the knob of the stinging hair breaks off the tip has a similar angle.

Modern hypodermic syringes with a movable piston not found in the stinging hair and designed to expel all the fluid.

The asymmetically placed tip of the stinging trichome showing the uneven thickening of the wall

Diagram of the tip of the stinging hair showing the cleavage line on the application of a large force (after Haberlandt)

With the tip broken off showing the oblique angle of cleavage very similar to that of the hypodermic needle

(G) A moderate force on the stinging hair causes the expulsion of a small amount of fluid (H). A larger force leads to the expulsion of a greater amount of fluid and the level goes down to the level shown in (I). (J) Too large a force or a large force at an angle from the parallel leads to the breaking of the shaft and no penetration of the skin.

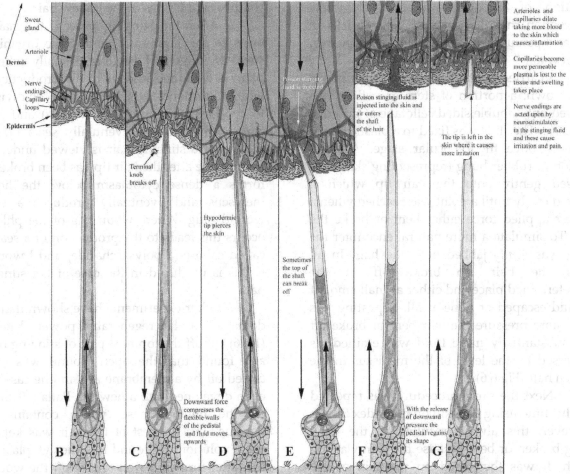

Sweat gland

Arteriole

Dermis

Nerve endings

Capillary loops

Epidermis

Terminal knob breaks off

Hypodermic tip pierces the skin

Poison stinging fluid is injected

Poison stinging fluid is injected into the skin and air enters the shaft of the hair

Sometimes the top of the shaft can break off

With the release of downward pressure the pedestal regains its shape

Downward force compresses the flexible walls of the pedestal and fluid moves upwards

The tip is left in the skin where it causes more irritation

Arterioles and capillaries dilate taking more blood to the skin which causes inflamation

Capillaries become more permeable plasma is lost to the tissue and swelling takes place

Nerve endings are acted upon by neurostimulators in the stinging fluid and these cause irritation and pain.

(B_G) Diagrammatic representation of the penetration of the skin by the stinging hair showing the breakage of the tip and the changes in shape of the pedestal and basal bulb as a result of the downward force of contact. This results in an equal upward force which expels the stinging fluid. After the release of the force the flexible bulb regains its shape and the fluid goes down drawing in air (E-F). There is debate as to whether the hair is broken off and remains in the skin, but it is likely that in most sases this does not happen..

FIG 6.6 DIAGRAMS SHOWING THE STINGING MECHANISM OF THE STINGING TRICHOME OF URTICA DIOICA

progressively lessened, until an angle is reached where the hair is pushed aside or crushed (Fig 7.9).

The only work published in this area is that of Lenggenhager (1974) who questions whether the nettle hair always breaks at the point determine by Haberlandt and I quote the English summary:-

"New observations on the effects of nettle pricks"

"In contrast to the literature, older pricks of big and small nettles (Urtica dioica and U. urens) may be no more curved and do not show a predetermined zone of fracture. On the contrary, they may be ideally pointed and straight and are still able to prick. The fracture of the pricks takes place at different regions according to the violence of touching. The basal elastic chamber injects the toxin actively into the tissue. The point may remain in the tissue for 24-36 hours and is responsible for the long duration of the pain and for the new observation that the pains of nettle pricks in human lips augment in cold and disappear in warm water."

I carried out a few limited experiments of my own: a portion of stem or petiole was pressed onto double sided cellotape of the edge of a slide. The slide was fixed to a plastic box to raise it above the binocular stage. A small portion of rubber bung (representing skin) was pressed gently onto the hair tip which it entered easily until a point was reached when a greater applied force either bent or broke the hair. To simulate a more natural encounter the bung was *gently* jabbed onto the hair. In all cases the hair tip broke off at the predetermined place and either a small amount of fluid escaped or none at all. Repeating this with more pressure the hair bent or broke off and substantially more fluid was emitted, as witnessed by the level of the meniscus in the broken hair (Fig 6.6).

Next the same procedure was repeated but this time using the skin on my index finger. However, this always resulted in the hairs being broken or bent because the skin was too tough. It was then tried on the skin of my finger joint, which then worked classically with the tip breaking off and an injection of fluid, but strangely enough I felt no pain and experienced no reaction. The nettle I tested certainly stung me when I brushed gently up against it, so there must be more to the actual mechanism of the sting than meets the eye!

And there still remains much to be learnt about the nettle stinging mechanism the ideal conditions to trigger it. Nobody has yet measured the actual magnitude of the force to break the tip or why quite large insects such as caterpillars do not get stung, we can guess that it is due to the flexible insect cuticle or insects don't generate a sufficiently large force to break off the tip.

OLD STINGING HAIRS

Kallen (1882) found that the stinging hairs retain their living contents for a long time if they are not broken. Later protoplasmic streaming stops, the hair then become yellow, the contents eventually die and the contents solidify on the sides of the hollow hair.

After the stinging process the hair is open to the ingress of pathogenic organisms such as fungi and bacteria. Usually when a plant is wounded it leads to the production of wound hormones, which stimulate cell division to produce a wound tissue (callus) and even cork formation that eventually seals off the wound. If a stinging hair is viewed under the microscope after the hair tip has been broken, it forms a dense cytoplasm below the liquid meniscus and eventually produces a solid wound plug. Where wounding of the phloem occurs this leads to the production of a sealant called callose (a polysaccharide) and I wonder if this is produced in the case of the stinging hair.

Other experiments have shown that the damaged hair has regenerative powers. Kuester (1916) cut off the topmost part of stinging hairs and found that the open wound was often closed off by a membrane and in one case this even developed into a new tip. Palla (1906) cut off the bulbous base, which contains the nucleus, and the rest of the hair was kept in sugar solution. He found that the cytoplasm of the latter formed a wall to seal off the wound, which is surprising in view of the absence of the nucleus.

FIG 7.1 LUCY'S FIRST ENCOUNTER WITH THE COMMON STINGING NETTLE

CHAPTER 7
THE TALE IN THE STING 2 STINGING SYMPTOMS AND POISONOUS PRINCIPLES

"I torment tormenters, but I torment none willingly;
Nor do I wish to harm anyone unless he first commits
A crime and tries to pluck my green stalk.
The limbs of the harmful man grow hot and swell;
Thus I repay his harm and take vengeance with stinging pains"
Aldhelm (Middle-Ages)

TROPICAL AND TEMPERATE TORMENTORS

Linnaeus's simple sexual and binomial system i.e. giving each plant just two names, led to an interest in botany and the spark once ignited caused a conflagration of botanical disciples to spread all over the world during the next half of the 18th century (Blunt 1971). This resulted in a sharp increase in herbarium specimens that needed to be described, classified and drawn. In 1874 Alphonse de Candolle's estimate of the number of species of flowering plants was inbetween 110,000-120,000 but J. Angely's estimate in 1956 was about 380,000 species.

NEW ZEALAND

Although botanists on early round-the-world voyages did not encounter any man-eating plants they soon learnt to respect the tropical nettles; unfortunately only a few of their experiences with these have been recorded. Captain Cook's first voyage included the famous botanists, Joseph Banks and Dr Daniel Solander, whilst the botanist on the second voyage was Anders Sparrman. The only reference to nettles in Captain Cook's diaries occurs in the second voyage, Nov. 1773. Before leaving Queen Charlotte's Sound (New Zealand) the sailors had trouble catching a male goat.

"at last the ram was taken with fits boardering on madness, we were at a loss to tell whether it was occasioned by any thing he had eat or by being Stung with Netles which were in plenty about the place, but supposed it to be the latter and therefore did not take the care of him we ought to have done; One night while he was lying by the

Centinal, he was seized with one of these fitts and ran headlong into the sea, but soon came out again and seemed quite easy, presently after he was seized with a nother fit and ran a long the beach and the she goat after him; some time after she returned but the other was never seen,…" (Beaglehole 1969).

It is now known that Urtica ferox a woody shrub commonly 3-4 feet and sometimes 10 feet high lives in this habitat and could have had this effect upon the goat. Aston (1923), more recently, states that the stinging hairs of Urtica ferox have been known to poison animals in New Zealand.

TIMOR AND JAVA

The French seem to have been particularly interested in the nettle family and made extensive collections of them on their round-the-world-voyages. Relevant to our story was the voyage to New Holland (Australia) and Van Diemen's Land (Tasmania) made by Commander Baudin, 1800-1804. The objects were two fold: firstly to establish a footing on the still unexplored coasts of New Holland and secondly it was one of the best scientific explorations organised, with 24 scientists-astronomers, geographers, mineralogists, botanists, zoologists, gardeners and draughtsmen on board.

The ship's gardener Anselme Riedlé remained on Timor and collected plants until his death in 1801 and was accompanied by the ship's botanist Leschenaulte de la Tour who was left sick on Timor in 1803. They became familiar with the nettle trees and the stories connected with them on Timor and the neighbouring island of Java. The effects of the nettle tree (Urtica stimulans) of Java are described well by Green in his Herbal (1820): "The leaves of this small shrub sting like our common nettles but much more violently so as to produce an inflammation in the skin. On every vein of the leaf are sharp pointed hollow prickles. The Japanese call it Kamadin and Dutch colonists Buffelblad or Buffalo-leaf because it is customary with the Javanese princes on holidays, by way of diversion, to turn out a tiger and a buffalo to fight in an area fenced with planks. When the buffalo is tardy in attacking his adversary he is flogged with this plant, which causes such a heat and inflammation in his skin that he soon becomes quite outrageous. When anyone is stung with this Nettle tree they anoint the part with oil or with rice boiled to a soft consistency, as water would only render the pain more intolerable."

A Smålander, Carl Peter Thunberg, one of Linnaeus's apostles, managed to collect plants by attaching himself to the Dutch East India Company. In 1775 he travelled to Japan via Java and in the latter island collected branches of a nettle tree which Linnaeus described and named *Urtica stimulans* (burning stinger) in his supplement of 1781. Chew (1969-1971) renamed this plant *Dendrocnide* (tree nettle) *stimulans*. It is a dioecius tree which grows to a height of 7 metres (23 feet) with widespread branches and stinging hairs on the veins of the leaves, petioles and male and female inflorescences.

Whilst in Timor, Leschenault learnt from the natives of a nettle tree of unsurpassed virulence which they called Daoun Setan, Devil's Leaf or Feuille du diable (*Urtica urentissima*, this could now be called *Dendrocnide moroides*), the effects of which are said to last one year or even cause death (Lindley 1853).

INDIA

During his travels in India Leschenault (Mem. Mus. 6 362) describes the effects of gathering the nettle *Urtica crenulata* in the Botanic Gardens of Calcutta, "One of the leaves slightly touched the first three fingers of my left hand: at the time I only perceived a slight pricking, to which I paid no attention. This was at seven in the morning. The pain continued to increase; in an hour it had become intolerable: it seemed as if someone was rubbing my fingers with a hot iron. Nevertheless there was no remarkable appearance; neither swelling, nor pustule, nor inflammation. The pain rapidly spread along the arm as far as the arm-pit. I was then seized with frequent sneezing and with a copious running of the nose, as if I had caught a violent cold in the head. About noon I experienced a painful contraction of the back of the jaws which made me fear an attack of tetanus, I then went to bed hoping that repose would alleviate my suffering, but it did not abate; on the contrary it continued during nearly the whole of the following night; but I lost the contraction of the jaws about seven in the evening.

The next morning the pain began to leave me and I fell asleep. I continued to suffer for two days; and the pain returned in full force when I put my hand in cold water, I did not finally lose it for nine days."

This plant was classified later by Gaudichard as *Laportea crenulata* and this was retained in The Flora of British India where it is called the Devil Nettle, Elephant Nettle and by the English coffee planters as the Fever Nettle. Chopra et al (1940) says that this nettle plant is perhaps the worst of all stinging nettles found in India. Brushing against this plant produces severe burning pain which can last several days and is greatly aggravated by bringing the stung area in contact with water. The sting is reputed to be worse during the flowering season when it causes violent sneezing, sleeplessness and fever. Although Chopra always found it to sting it is said by some to drop its hairs at certain seasons and is then innocuous. Sneezing, violent catarrh and ultimately vertigo often attack coolies working in Sikkim terai where it is prevalent, apparently from inhaling the numerous minute hairs.

The fresh juice is used together with that of the Upas tree (*Antiaris toxicaria* [Pers.], Lesch. also a member of the Urticales) by Negritos of Malaya to poison their darts. The leaves and flowers are mixed with cakes, in Kelantan, to bring about criminal homicide. Chew (1969-1971) classifies *Laportea crenulata* as (*Dendrocnide sinuata* [Bl], Chew.). Its name comes from the crenulate/sinuate leaf margins. Trees are 10 metres (33 feet) high. Irritant hairs are found on the leaves, petioles and on the male and female inflorescences. Distribution: India, Ceylon, China through to SE Asia to Malay Peninsula, Sumatra, Java and Bali.

Joseph Dalton Hooker (1817-1911) explored the Sikkim province of the Himalayas in 1847-1851. At one point whilst crossing the posts in the forest which divide Sikkim from Nepal he descended into the remarkably fine Myong valley and describes the scenery as the most beautiful he has known in the lower Himalayas. "The villages, which are merely scattered collections of huts, are surrounded with fields of rice, buckwheat, and Indian corn, which latter the natives were now storing in little granaries, mounted on four posts, men, women, and children being all equally busy. The quantity of gigantic nettles (*Urtica heterophylla*) on the skirts of these maize fields is quite wonderful, their long white stings look most formidable, but though they sting virulently, the pain only lasts half an hour or so. These, however, with leeches, mosquitoes, peepsas, and ticks, sometimes keep the traveller in a constant state of irritation."

(The remarkable stinging hairs of the nettle Hooker mentions (*Urtica heterophylla*, later called *Girardinia heterophylla*) have been described in Chapter 6. It is now called *Girardinia diversifolia* (Link) Friis The genus Girardinia has recently been reviewed by Friss (1980). Plants collected by Leschenault and later called Girardinia Leschenaultiana were also included which is the fate of so many plants named after earlier collectors It is a tall herb 1-2 m (4-6 feet) high, short lived and covered in long sharp stinging hairs. The leaves are heart-shaped (cordate) and deeply lobed 10-30 cm (4-12 inches) long. Male and female flowers are on the same plant (Fig 7.2). It yields a very strong fibre but its extraction is hindered by the difficulty in its collection! Its abundant stinging hairs make it a great annoyance to travellers because the slightest touch produces smarting and itching which fortunately are of short duration but worse than that produced by the common nettle. It is used as a pot herb by boiling twice and then throwing away the water.

Hooker describes the remarkable flora of mixed temperate and tropical plants growing in the bottom of the valley at Chakoong (4,400 feet), "The birch, willow, alder, and walnut grow side by side with wild plantain, *Erythrina*, *Wallichia* palm, and gigantic bamboos: the *Cedrela Toona*, figs, *Melastoma*, *Scitamineae*, balsams, *Pothos*, peppers, and gigantic climbing vines, grow mixed with brambles, speedwell, *Paris*, forget-me-not, and nettles that sting like poisoned arrows."

On the way down the Lachen-Lachoong he found that the temperate flora of northern Sikkim was being replaced by tropical forms and of these the nettles were most numerous in the woods. After crossing the Teesta valley and continuing along the east bank to Tucheam (2000 feet above the river) he says, "The great shrubby nettle (*Urtica crenulata* now *Dendrocnide sinuata* (Bl) Chew) is common here: this plant, called 'Mealum-ma' attains fifteen feet in height; it has broad glossy leaves, and though apparently without stings, is held in so great dread, that I had difficulty in getting help to cut it down. I gathered many specimens without allowing any part to touch my skin; still the scentless effluvium was so powerful, that mucous matter poured from my eyes and nose all the rest of the afternoon, in such abundance, that I had to hold my head over a basin for an hour. The sting is very virulent, producing inflammation; and to punish a child with 'Mealum-ma' is the severest Lepcha threat. Violent fevers and death have been said to ensue from its sting; but this I very much doubt."

As a footnote he adds "The stinging hairs are microscopic, and confined to the young shoots, leaf and flower-stalks. ....I frequently gathered it with impunity on subsequent occasions, and suspected some inaccuracy in my observations; but in Sihet both Dr. Thomson and I experienced the same effects in autumn"

Roy Lancaster (1981) in his book "Plant Hunting in Nepal' mentions a small incident involving a nettle which took place one morning whilst they were camping near a virgin forest above Hatia. The incident happened accompanied with a loud shriek which came from a porter in the act of relieving himself. He thought he had been bitten by a demon and showed a large red mark on his backside. Roy returned to the area to be confronted by a number of giant stinging nettles bristling with stinging hairs; the feared Girardinia diversifolia 10-15 feet high a worthy demon. Evidence of the lasting effect of the stings was the fact that the porter for several days preferred to eat his meals standing up.

AUSTRALIA

With the opening up of the interior of Australia it was not long before the nettle trees were encountered, especially by workers laying railway lines, telegraph and telephone routes. Hard work and hot conditions meant that little clothing was worn, and therefore severe stinging took place on the more tender parts of the body! The men had to suffer inexorable and enduring pain and "after being nettled, one is reminded of the fact for several days and in exceptional cases for weeks whenever the nettle part is wet" (Bancroft 1889). When horses and cattle were badly stung they often became enraged, violent and uncontrollable. Horses proved to be more susceptible than cattle, and in some cases, the limbs and bodies of horses travelling through the bush, when severely stung, became so swollen that they had to be rested for several days and in some cases they died.

Victorian England was an exciting place and time awash with travellers' tales from all over the world and these were reported in a vast number of magazines and journals. It was not long before news of the dreaded Nettle Trees of Australia hit the news, with the following article in 'The Gardeners Chronicle' under **Variorum** (1875) but taken from 'Cassell's Illustrated Travels' for December –the author was not given.

"THE STINGING TREE. - One of the torments to which the traveller is subjected in the North Australian scrubs is the Stinging tree (*Urtica gigas*)*, which is very abundant, and ranges in size from a large shrub of 30 feet in height to a small plant measuring only a few inches. Its leaf is large and peculiar, from being covered with a short,

82

silvery hair, which, when shaken, emits a fine pungent dust, most irritating to the skin and nostrils. If touched it causes most acute pain, which is felt for months afterwards -a dull, gnawing pain, accompanied by a burning sensation, particularly in the shoulder and under the arm, where small lumps often arise. Even when the sting has quite died away, the unwary bushman is forcibly reminded of his indiscretion each time that the affected part is brought into contact with water. The fruit is of a pink, fleshy colour, hanging in clusters, and looks so inviting that a stranger is irresistibly tempted to pluck it; but seldom more than once, for, though the Raspberry-like berries are harmless in themselves, some contact with the leaves is almost unavoidable. The blacks are said to eat the fruit, but for this I cannot vouch, though I have tasted one or two at odd times, and found them very pleasant. The worst of this Nettle is the tendency it exhibits to shoot up wherever a clearing has been affected. In padding through the dray tracks cut through the scrub, great caution was necessary to avoid the young plants that cropped up even in a few weeks. I have never known a case of its being fatal to human beings but I have seen people subjected by it to great suffering, notably a scientific gentleman, who plucked off a branch and carried it some distance as a curiosity, wondering the while what was causing the pain and numbness in his arm. Horses I have seen die in agony from the sting, the wounded parts becoming paralysed; but, strange to say, it does not seem to injure cattle, which dash through scrubs full of it without receiving any damage. This curious anomaly is well known to all Bushmen." *(Urtica gigas is now Dendrocnide moroides).

It is interesting how similar customs crop up quite independently in different parts of the world, but most people would agree that the practice, of Elizabethans of using a stem of Dodart's Nettle in a bunch of flowers to sting the noses of unsuspecting persons smelling them would not be so funny if it was a twig from a nettle tree which was used instead! The Aborigines and some Australians have a slightly different sense of humour, as was reported by K. Rowan (1889?), "I had the pleasurable excitement here of being introduced to the Nettle Tree some branches of which I picked not knowing what it was, my hand and arm ached for many days afterwards." and "Another thing to be warned against is the Nettle Tree. A gentleman thinking he would play an amusing trick on me gave me some of its branches in the dark with some other flowers and I took it in my arms not knowing what it was; it brushed against my face and next morning my whole head was swollen and I could not see out of one of my eyes for some days. The pain was intense and I suffered for more than I care to acknowledge. Horses have been known to have died from the stings of this tree and they are also sent mad sometimes with the pain."

AUSTRALIAN STINGING TREE SYMPTOMS

Petri (1906) who investigated the stinging properties of the Giant Nettle Tree (Dendrocnide excelsa) says that being stung by this tree results in pain which gradually increases in severity and occasionally lasts several days. Children have been known to be ill for weeks with the pains of the sting, and it seems to be more severe at certain seasons when it earns its popular name of 'Mad Tree.'

Although the Shining-Leaved Nettle Tree (Dendrocnide photinophylla) has only a scattering of stinging hairs, it is described as a dangerous plant to man and beast and a cause of great pain when touched.(See Everist)

BOX 7.1 AUSTRALIAN NETTLE TREES
(1) GIANT STINGING TREE, STINGING TREE, NETTLE TREE, FIBREWOOD
Dendrocnide excelsa (Wedd.) Chew, previously (Laportea gigas Wedd.).

Distribution: It is endemic to Australia. Found along the east coast of Australia, in the brush forests of southern New South Wales up to the rainforests of northern Queensland.

Description. A soft wooded tree up to 35 (114 ft) metres high and with a stem diameter of over 180 cm. Stem fluted or channelled, particularly at the base (buttressed). Young shoots, branchlets and leaves covered with stinging hairs which tend to disappear from the leaves of large trees. Leaves heart-shaped (cordate) and the blade can reach up to (10-) 13-20 (-25) cm long by (5-) 10-12 (-18) cm broad with toothed margins. Sexes on separate trees (dioecious). The fruit is an achene but the stalk of the fruit is fleshy so that groups form into succulent pink or white masses (Fig 7.2).

Uses. The timber is very light and used for bitumen sealed floats or cases. (Note: It seems incredible that Francis found an absence of material in the Queensland herbarium and had to resort to Bentham's Flora Australiensis for his description!).

(2) SHINING-LEAVED STINGING TREE, SMALL-LEAVED NETTLE TREE, STINGING TREE, FIBREWOOD.
Dendrocnide photinophylla (Kunth.) Chew, previously (Laportea photinophylla [Knuth.] Wedd.). Specific name, Greek, photeinos, shining,and phyll, leaf.

Distribution. Endemic to Australia. Coastal scrubs from Bateman's Bay, New South Wales to far northern Queensland. One of the commonest trees in the rain forest of the foothills and ranges, Sarina district and common in the Rockhampton and Moreton districts of Queeensland.

Description. Soft-wooded tree reaching a height of 20 m (65 ft) and a stem diameter of 75 cm. Stem often fluted but not buttressed. Nearly all parts of the tree are free of hairs (glabrous). Leaves (6-) 8-12 cm (-18) long and

(3-) 4-6 cm (-10) broad, ovate and devoid of stinging hairs. Irritant stinging hairs are only on the flowers or their stalks. Male and female flowers generally in separate inflorescences on the same or separate plants. Fruit an achene with a persistent perianth.

Use. Same as for D. excelsa.

(3) GYMPIE BUSH, GYMPIE GYMPIE, GYMPIE NETTLE, MULBERRY NETTLE TREE.

Dendrocnide moroides (Wedd.) Chew, previously (Laportea moroides Wedd.) Specific name from Latin, Morus, Mulberry, referring to the leaf shape which is like that of a Mulberry Tree.

Distribution. Southern Moluccas and north Eastern Australia i.e. from northern New South Wales to northern Queensland in the coastal brush forests.

Description. Shrubs or trees capable of reaching a height of 10 m. (32 ft) the whole plant is covered in dense irritant stinging hairs. The leaves are (10-) 14-20 (-38) long and (9-) 12-18 (-30) broad, broadly ovate with a cordate base. The leaf stalk joins the blade within the leaf margin at the base (peltate). The margin is dentate. The inflorescences are bisexual with 10-20 female flowers around each male. The fruit is an , bloated with a warty covering (pericarp) and borne on greatly swollen stalks, purplish-red in dense clusters.

(4) GYMPIE *Dendrocnide cordata (Warb. Ex Winkl.) Chew.*

Chew (1969-1971) also includes another nettle tree in the Australian Flora; this is *Dendrocnide cordata*. Vernacular names: Gabu, Salat and Sisik (Papuan), Gympie (Australia) and Leswatan Alas (Timor). He says this is closely related to D. moroides but differs in (1) the plant being less irritant (b) the leaf blade is not peltate (c) the inflorescences are mainly either male or female. This plant occurs in Timor, Tanimbar Islands, New Guinea, New Britain (Bismark Archipelago) and Queensland (Australia). It was collected by the French on the Voyage of the l'Uranie (1817-1820) and was named after Gaudichard as *Laportea Gaudichaudiana*. Winkler (1922) in his study of the New Guinea Urticaceae mentions a human fatality from the sting of *L. cordata* Warb.

SYMPTOMS OF THE GYMPIE NETTLE OR BUSH

The Gympie Bush (*Dendrocnide moroides*) is reputed to have the most virulent sting of the Australian Nettle Trees and the sting from it lasts for weeks after contact, compared with about 24 hours for the other two species. During the gold rush of the 1860's the miners in the vicinity of the gold town Gympie were often badly stung by this bush and hence its name Gympie Bush. It should be added, however, that the Aboriginal name Gimpi Gimpi was their name for the Shining-Leaved Stinging Tree.

Francis (1955) was the first to describe the stinging symptoms from the Gympie Bush in some detail. For the first 2-3 days there is an intense irritation, and a recurrence of the stinging effects can be felt up to 3 months after, on washing in cold water or during cold weather. Severe stinging on the arm or leg can also lead to pain in the armpit and groin respectively, due to swollen lymphatic nodes. Violent sneezing also occurs during brush clearing when large numbers of Gympie bushes are being cut back.

Robertson and Macfarlane (1957), Macfarlane (1963a, 1963b), in their structure of the 'Pain-Producing Substances from the Stinging Bush *Laportea moroides*', give the first scientific description of the stinging symptoms of this feared tormentor. The forearm skin of 6 human subjects was tested with either individual stinging hairs using forceps, or with an injection of 0.02-0.04 ml of a saline extract of stinging hairs; normal saline was used as a control.

SUBJECTIVE EFFECTS

As with Urtica species, the hairs will not penetrate callosed skin of the palms of the hands or soles of the feet, but all thinner skin is penetrated on gentle contact. Under natural conditions, the movements of the plant and hand on contact are sufficient to break off the terminal knob, but in artificial stinging with a single hair, lateral movement was needed to break the tip. After stinging there is a latent period of 20-40 sec, which is followed by a slight itch, and then a severe prickling sensation.

The first burst of sharp pain develops into intense radiating stabs that pass outwards from the stinging point. If the stinging takes place on the arm, pain is felt in the arm pit, and referred pain appears to come from the face and opposite limb. A sharp diffused pain continues, and in addition to this are periodic acute radiating bursts. The stabbing pain varies in duration from 20 min-3 hrs and the diffuse pain persists for 2-3 days. The duller pain turns into a prickling pain when the stung area is gently rubbed or exposed to cold or cold water, and this reaction is felt for periods up to 8 weeks after stinging. The lymphatic nodes in the groin and arm pit become tender and swollen and a diffuse pain is felt along lymph channels to these regions.

OBJECTIVE REACTIONS

The area stung develops small red dots within a minute. These increase in area and unite to form a pink(erythematous) area. Within 10 minutes, widening of blood vessels (vasodilation) over a zone 2-3 cm greater than that of the erythema, is brought about as a result of reflex nerve impulses passing along nerve cell axons. The erythema lasts 12-36 hours. In the inflamed area, increased blood causes profuse sweating which develops after 5 min and in

FIG 7.2 THE AUSTRALIAN NETTLE TREES (A) the giant nettle tree (Dendrocnide excelsa Wedd. Chew) is up to 35m in height and buttressed at the base. The wood is very soft. The tree is dioecious. (A1) The fruit is an achene with a warted pericarp. (A2) The fruit consists of a swollen flower stalk with the fruit and the remains of the stigma. (A3) The young fruit with ovary tipped by a stigma. (A4) twig with female inflorescence.(B) the shining-leaved nettle tree (Dendrocnide photinophylla Kunth Chew) (B) the tree is up to 20m tall and has a soft wood. It is dioecious. (B1) the twig with female ovary and stigma. (B2) the young fruit with ovary and stigma. (B3) the mature with swollen fleshy flower stalk and the fruit with the remains of the stigma. (C) Gympie Bush (Dendrocnide moroides Wedd Chew) (C1) twig with male and female flowers (C2) young fruit with ovary and stigma (C3) mature fruit with achene and warted pericarp. (after Chew & Francis)

GIANT STINGING TREE

SHINING -LEAVED
STINGING TREE

GYMPIE BUSH OR
MULBERRY NETTLE TREE

A

B

85

most active after 6 hrs; it persists for 26-30 hours. Hairs 'stand on end' (piloerection) in the red swollen area during the first 10 hours.

Injection of 0.01ml of saline extract of the stinging hairs produces the same pain and sequence of events as are produced by stinging with individual living hairs; however, the effects persist for a shorter time. After injection, pain develops after a latency of 20 sec, and piloerection occurs within one minute. Most signs and symptoms are lost after a period of 3 weeks.

Inhalation of dust from the dried leaves of broken hairs causes violent sneezing. A watery mucous discharge takes place, within 3 hours there was nasopharyngeal pain and after 26 hours an acute sore throat, like tonsillitis. Aching sensations in the sinuses occurred and sneezing continued. The nasal mucous membranes began to slough together with blood and pus, and this continued for 10 days. After this the work was carried out with a gas mask, thick rubber gloves and a thick gown. Despite the fact that a negative pressure hood was used for the preparation, occasional invasion of the operator took place; I wonder what incentives were offered to the poor human guinea pigs?

ANTIDOTES

Four subjects were used to test the effectiveness of antidotes used by Aborigines and others. Similar stings were induced on each arm either by an actual stinging hair or by injection with a saline nettle extracts. One area was treated with the test substance and the other with a placebo, the treatments being unknown by the subjects. The following antidotes were tried: rubbing the juice exhuded from the leaves, stem and root of *Alocasia macrorrhiza* (cunjevoi) into the nettled part; treating with the bark of *Dendrocnide excelsa* (*Laportea gigas*) and the root of *Bowenia spectabilis*; a saturated aqueous solution of picric acid or sodium carbonate; application of the alkaline ammonium hydroxide and using adrenaline and mepyramine cream. Two minutes after application, individually, of all antidotes the pain returned, with the exception of ammonium hydroxide which gave partial relief in two out of the four times it was used.

ALLEVIATION

Some relief comes from the local use of anaesthetics or antihistamines but their effects are short and incomplete. Aspirin and similar analgesics are ineffective in ordinary doses. No doubt the most popular and readily available remedy used by Bushmen and timbermen is alcohol, used to 'drown

your sorrows.' Morphinomones are useful for the alleviation of the chronic aspect of pain.

Francis (1955) reported every Australian's nightmare, that of a man who fell into a stinging shrub and remained unconscious for some time afterwards!

TEMPERATE TORMENTORS

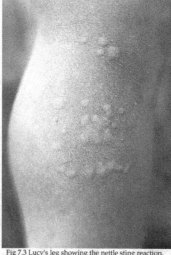

Fig 7.3 Lucy's leg showing the nettle sting reaction, wheal formation and rash.

Temperate nettles belong mainly to the genus Urtica and have been spread, deliberately or accidentally, by man to most other countries. Their cosmopolitan distribution makes them familiar members of most floras throughout the world, and there are few people who are not familiar with the stinging symptoms of the common nettle. The sting of the latter is mild compared to that of its tropical relatives, it is simply an irritation or annoyance, and its effects are quickly dissipated.

First impressions or experiences are always the most vivid and I well remember the first encounter of my three year-old daughter Lucy with the common nettle (Fig 7.3). I was, as usual, caught up examining some nettle clones in a pasture when there was a sharp cry, and there was Lucy, in her short blue and white skirt, rubbing her leg. Her face was screwed up and tears rolled down her cheeks as she cried bitterly. "Look what that nasty plant did daddy" and pointed first to the nettle tormentor and then to the red areas, with their scattered raised pink wheals, spreading on her leg. Never one for missing a photographic opportunity I recorded this event first, then quickly consoled her by saying it was only a nettle sting and that we would have to look for a dock leaf to make it better. Sure enough there was the dock, I crushed a leaf and got her to rub it over the nettled area, after which a second shot was taken (see p 79 and Fig 7.3). After being the focus of attention and having her photograph taken twice, she soon recovered, but the nasty nettle was not forgotten, the experience and the nettles appearance had been imprinted on her mind to enable her to avoid future close encounters.

Familiarity breeds contempt and this was backed up by the fact I could not find in the literature any *scientific*, subjective and objective account of the skin reactions to the sting of the common nettle. I have read all the recent scientific accounts, relating to the search for the substances responsible for the stinging effects of different members of the Urtica genus, but none of the authors considered it worthwhile recording the symptoms of each species; perhaps they thought that we are all too familiar with the symptoms of common nettle sting.

Long (1924) states that Urtica dioica is said to have poisoned dogs in Germany. Fyles (1920) in (Poisonous Plants of Canada) quotes Chesnut who reported that the perennial nettle, *Urtica gracilis*, covered 100's of acres of land in Michigan and Wisconsin and that their dense growth made the land worthless. Horses refused to pass through it to cultivate the soil. He has reported (1900) that in California, the stings of the perennial nettle, *Urtica holosericea,* were responsible for the death of several horses. Urtica chamaedryoides Pursh., an annual nettle growing in the south eastern states of the U.S.A., is reputed to have produced a syndrome in hunting dogs which is characterised by excessive salivation pawing at the mouth, vomiting, respiratory distress, slow and regular heart beat and muscular weakness (Davis 1958).

The Wood Nettle *Laportea canadensis*, ranges in Canada from Saskatchewan to Newfoundland, and in the U.S.A., south to Louisiana, northern Florida and the eastern Mexican highlands. As its common name suggests it is found in mixed hardwood forests. It is a perennial and varies in height 30-120 cm (1-4 feet). Masias and Positano (1990) report a case of reaction to the Wood Nettle stings contacted on a man's feet, from brushing up against these, whilst walking barefoot in a park. He stated that there were tiny needles on the plant and the symptoms recorded: immediate redness, burning and itching (pruritis) within 2-3 min. and small hives. Examination of the foot revealed erthyema, slight edoema and multiple wheals 2-3 mm. A cool compress caused relief, and because of the short duration of the reaction anti-histamines or steroids were unnecessary. Approximately one hour later all symptoms had disappeared. The reactions developing within 30 sec were a severe burning sensation, skin becomes red (erythymatous), 1-5 mm wheals; the dermatological reaction such as tingling pallesthesia may last up to 12 hrs or more and sensitivity and redness up to 1-2 days.

This review of the literature shows that there is a paucity of accurate information concerning the stinging symptoms produced by different genera and species of the Urticeae, and that there is a need for a *comparative*, subjective and objective study of the stinging symptoms from a cutaneous and physiological viewpoint. Chemists have chosen some interesting members of the Urticeae to look at in an effort to find the toxins involved in the stinging process, but the majority have not, at the same time, grasped the nettle and recorded the relevant stinging symptoms; a much broader approach is needed!

THE SEARCH FOR THE IDENTITY OF THE TOXIC SUBSTANCES PRESENT IN PLANT STINGING HAIRS

Much has been written about poisonous plants and animals because this is an area of interest to the general public. This is not so in the case of the poisonous substances in stinging plants, and the first comprehensive review of the 'Toxicology of Stinging Hairs' is that of Thurston and Lersten (1969); see Table 7.1

Progress in biology has always depended upon advances in techniques made mainly in the fields of chemistry and physics. In the 19th century biochemistry was in its infancy and techniques were not available for the analysis of the chemical constituents of very small quantities of plant material

ACID OR ALKALI?

The burning properties of acids and alkalis have been known since very early times, and the discovery that certain natural dyes change colour, according to whether the solution is acidic or alkaline, led to the development of litmus paper. Bahrdt (1849) says that on pricking himself with liquid from the bulb of the stinging hair he felt an ordinary burning of short duration, whilst, when this was repeated with liquid from the tip of the stinging hair, the burning was more frequent. Liquid from both areas gave an acid reaction with litmus paper but was stronger from the button area.

PHARMACOLOGICAL BIO-ASSAY TECHNIQUES INTRODUCTION

In the first half of the 20th century, standard chemical tests required relatively large amounts of the purified substance for positive identification. Fury's work gives some idea of the labour involved in extracting even a small amount of fluid from stinging hairs whose individual volume is just 0.009 ml (9γ ml).

Authors Chronological order	Formic acid	Acetycholine	Histamine	Serotonine	Alkaloid	Acetic acid	Enzyme	Glucoside	Protein	Tartaric acid	Resinic acid	Calcium	Salt
Hooke (1665)													U
Gorup-Besanez (1849)	U												
Rauter (1872)								U					
Bergmann (1882)	U												
Haberlandt (1886)							U						
Tassi (1886)							L						
Gibson & Warham (1890)										U			
Ritterhausen (1892)	T												
Giustiniani (1896)					U								
Dragendorf (1905)	U						U	U					
Knoll (1905)									T				
Petrie (1906)	UD					D							
Winteritz (1907)	U												
Flury (1919)	U												
Nestler (1925)	U						U						
Flury (1927)												U	D
Kroeber (1928)								U					
Starkenstein & Wasserstrom (1933)					U			U					

Table 7.1. THE CHEMICAL CONSTITUENTS REPORTED IN PLANT STINGING HAIRS URTICACEAE – URTICAE. U=*Urtica*, G=*Girardinia*, D=*Dendrocnide*, O=*Obetia*, LOASACEAE, L=*Loasa*, EUPHORBIACEAE, T=*Tragia*. (After Thurston & Lerston, 1969).

Chromatography was in its infancy, so the problem of the identification of minute amounts of chemical substances was a major one. The fact that a single stinging hair can produce the symptoms associated with the nettle sting shows that animal tissue is extremely sensitive to small amounts of toxins. At the time it was known that the bodies of larger animals produce extremely small amounts of substances e.g. hormones, enzymes, neurotransmitters, etc. which have large physiological effects. This led scientists to develop a technique that could be used to identify extremely small amounts of a chemical substance; all that was required was a known concentration of a known chemical, say X, and living animal tissue.

BOX 7.2
NO, TO FORMIC ACID, AS THE STINGING NETTLE TOXIN

When tests for the identification of the organic acids became available, it is not surprising that chemists decided to apply these to the acidic sap of nettle stinging hairs. Gorup-Besanez (1849) and Bergman (1882) used the standard tests then available and applied them to the volatile organic acid component produced by distilling large amounts of the leaves of Urtica urens and U. dioica. Formic acid was isolated and it was concluded that this could be the cause of the burning sensation produced by nettle stings. At that time it was known that ants produce formic acid and introduce this into the skin when they bite, and attributed this substance to the painful burning reaction which is produced.

Haberlandt (1886) came to the conclusion that a stinging hair of Urtica dioica holds 0.007-0.008 ml, but the amount injected is only 0.0003 ml, and therefore, the amount of formic acid which could possibly be injected into the skin is much too little to produce the symptoms noted. He worked out that when a nettle stings, 0.0006 mg of formic acid could be injected into the wound from one hair. Formic acid would therefore have to be an extremely poisonous substance if it could produce the usual skin inflammation working so quickly and in such tiny amounts. With a fine needle point he tested an 11% formic acid for its irritant effect on the skin, "The stinging feeling was very slight, small marks appeared on the skin." Against the formic acid theory must be mentioned the fact that in some tropical Urtica types (*U. stimulans* on Java, *U. urentissima* on Timor, etc) the sting of the nettles is accompanied by extremely violent poisonous action which cannot possibly be attributed to formic acid. According to Haberlandt, the poison in the hairs of U. dioica consists of an albuminoid (egg-white like) substance dissolved in the cell fluid, and this substance, because of its many properties (i.e. solubility), is able to attach itself to the unformed ferments and enzymes; it is destroyed by boiling for a short time; it is soluble in water and glycerine, and alcohol causes it to precipitate.

Dragendorf (1905) using Urtica dioica and U. urens found abundant formic acid along with an enzyme and a glucoside. The search was continued in Australia by Petri (1906), who applied organic acid tests to the Giant Nettle Tree (*Laportea gigas*, now called *Dendrocnide excelsa*) and the small Nettle (Urtica urens). The results showed that the fresh leaves of the Giant Nettle Tree contained 0.002% formic acid and 0.177% acetic acid in free form, and the rest was tied up as salts, e.g. 0.082% potassium formate, 0.067% potassium acetate and 0.406% calcium acetate. The fresh leaves of the Small Nettle contained 0.002% of the free formic acid.

The leaves of Urtica dioica contain high levels of potassium (Chapter 6) and Winterritz (1907) suggested that this was the active agent in the stinging hair.

Nestler (1925) attempted to continue Haberlandt's work, to ascertain whether formic acid and/or a ferment/enzyme are involved in producing the symptoms of the nettle sting. Using Pravaz's hypodermic needle and syringe, after introducing 9% formic acid into the skin he immediately felt a violent pain and in a few seconds blisters appeared. The wound made by the needle was large so he tried scratching the skin and then dabbed the skin with 9% formic acid – there was a momentary violent pain; then blisters appeared along the line of the scratch. He determine to continue the experiment using actual stinging hairs to ascertain the differences between the effect of the (1) fresh intact hairs, (2) a hair without any effective irritant substance.

The procedure for (2) was as follows:. A fresh shoot was left in alcohol for 6 days, taken out and left at room temperature for 24 hrs., then the stinging hairs were tested on the inner upper skin of the arm. This led to an immediate burning sensation and then blister formation, but not as pronounced as with fresh hairs. It was assumed that the alcohol must have removed the formic acid and therefore the reaction was due to an enzyme. Using the fact enzymes are destroyed by high temperatures, he heated U. urens shoots in a sterilising apparatus to 150°C. The upper surfaces of the leaves were rubbed along the skin. A sharp pain was felt as the hairs entered the skin and a few seconds later a burning feeling, blister formation and then red dots on the skin. He showed that on boiling shoots, or letting them wilt, they could not sting because the collapse of the basal bulb caused them to lie flat on the plant epidermis.

The action of an enzyme is discounted, and he states earlier that formic acid would have been evaporated at 150°C – however its action is not stinging hairs. Flury (1927), in a labour of love, isolated the stinging hairs from 100 Kg of fresh nettles (Urtica dioica) to obtain 40 gm of material, i.e. 100 hairs weigh approximately 1 mg. The protoplasm of the stinging cell was alkaline whilst the sap of the central vacuole was acidic and contained a small amount of formic acid accompanied by acetic, butyric and other volatile fatty acids. The real poison was thought to be a non-volatile unsaturated acid substance containing no nitrogen and allied to the resin acids. It was thought to be allied to the irritant substances of the Primulaceae and Rhus toxicodendron, and it was found that less than 0.0001 mg of nettle extract produces a reaction with human skin. Intravenous injection of the nettle extract into rabbits proved to be very toxic and the main symptoms were respiratory paralysis. Drying or heating the extract destroyed the substance responsible for wheal formation. Fury ruled out formic acid, an enzyme and a toxalbumin as being the toxic substances in stinging hairs.

Using a technique evolved, called bio-assay, it was possible to find out (1) if the unknown substance was likely to be substance X, and (2) to work out its concentration.

No doubt many people are familiar with the use of the frog to demonstrate the contraction of muscle, such as those of the calf (gastrocnemeus) and heart (cardiac), and recording this on the smoked paper of a rotating drum (kymograph) see Fig 7.5. I have in front of me a student's laboratory textbook 'Experimental Physiology' by George H. Bell, the 4th edition of which appeared in 1947. In the section dealing with the cardiac cycle of the frog the student records the normal heart beat, the inhibitory effect on the heart beat of stimulating the vagus nerve and the effect of drugs on the heart muscle. Dripping a 1 in 500 concentration of acetylcholine in Ringer's solution (a solution of similar composition to that of the body), onto the heart suppresses its action, but, the addition of atrophine (the toxin from Deadly Nightshade [Atropa belladona]), inhibits that of acetylcholine, and reverses this effect – all of which can be deduced by the kymograph traces.

This is an example of how extremely small quantities of known substances can effect the body, in this case the heart action, and this led to the technique of bio-assay. Using the same set-up, if an unknown substance had the same effect on the frog heart muscle as acethylcholine, then it could be concluded that it contained a chemical that was acetylcholine-like, and further chemical tests could make its identity more certain.

The triple response of a nettle sting (wheal, inflammation and flare) is produced by pricking histamine into the skin. Pharmacological studies (Feldburg and Kellaway, 1937), involving the perfused lung of guinea-pig, had shown that an enzyme in bee venom leads to the liberation of histamine in the lung tissue. Considering these two facts Emmelin and Feldberg wondered whether, in a similar way, a substance in the nettle sting could liberate histamine in the skin. This led to a study, which resulted in a paper, 'The Sting of the Common Nettle (Urtica urens); 1947.

THE CLASSICAL STUDY OF EMMELIN AND FELDBURG

The reasoning and development of their ideas is best given in the words of Feldburg (1950) and I quote a small piece from this article.
"A Suggested Approach to the Problem"
"The author well remembers a discussion which he had one evening, about this problem, with Dr. Niels Emmelin, who had come from Sweden to work with him in Cambridge. Why should it not be possible, it was argued, to 'sting' a smooth muscle preparation, for instance, a piece of a guinea-pig's intestine suspended in a bath of physiological saline solution and why had this simple experiment never

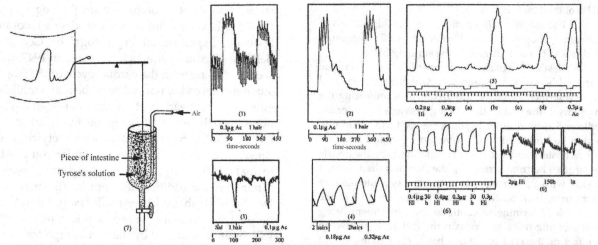

FIG 7.4 Comparison of the effects of stinging hairs of Urtica urens with that of acetylcholine (Ac.) on: - (1) rabbit's intestine, (2) guinea-pig's intestine, (3) arterial blood-pressure of a cat in chloralose anaesthesia. (4) eserinized frog rectus muscle. (Sal.= saline solution). (5) Contractions of the isolated guinea-pig's intestine in 10 ml bath. Immersion for 1 min of a piece of nettle leaf with three hairs. (a) hairs left intact; (b) hairs broken in bath; (c) hairless leaf; (d) extract from same piece of hairless leaf. (Hi and Ac = Histamine and Acetylcholine time in 30 sec). (6) Assay of nettle hair extract (H) against histamine on atropinized guinea-pig's intestine (upper tracing) and on arterial blood pressure of atropinized cat in chloralose anaesthesia (lower tracing). Time in upper tracing 30 sec. (After Emmelin and Feldburg 1947). (7) Diagram of the apparatus for testing substances that bring about the contraction of smooth and striated muscle. The contraction of the muscle brings about the movement of the lever and this is recorded on the paper of the rotating kymograph drum (After Feldburg 1950).

been performed? Naturally one has to realise that the intestinal muscle will respond differently from the human skin. For instance, histamine, which causes the characteristic weal on the skin, causes contraction of the guinea-pig's intestinal muscle."

Next day the guinea pig intestine was set up as in (see Fig 7.4) and a broken stinging hair added to the bath caused quick contraction. Renewing the bath and repeating the experiment several times lead to the same effect.

ACETYLCHOLINE

When the experiment was repeated with rabbit intestine the same contraction was recorded, however, it was back to square one because the **rabbit intestine is insensitive to histamine.**

At the time it was also known that acetycholine, which is found throughout the body, will bring about the contraction of the intestines of both guinea-pigs and rabbits, so could this substance be present in the nettle sting? When a single nettle hair was placed in the bath, containing the suspended intestine of either animal, a strong contraction occurred. Further confirmation that the substance was likely to be acetylcholine came from 5 other tests.

The acetylcholine contents of hairs from stalks and upper and lower surfaces of leaves were calculated by bio-assay', for the same and different plants, and although there were great variations, the average content per hair for the stalk was 0.1 microgramme/µg and for the leaves, a $\frac{1}{3}$ - $\frac{1}{2}$, of this. The fluid content per hair was estimated to be 9

microgrammes/µ³. This means that the concentration of acetylcholine in each stinging hair is 1 in a 100 which is an extremely strong solution since it exerts its pharmacological effects in concentrations of 1 in a 1,000,000 or less! However, when a drop of acetylcholine, 1 in 100, was placed on the forearm, and pricked in with a needle, no reaction was seen or felt. It was necessary for them to do a re-think, since a high concentration of acetylcholine in the hair had not explained the nettle sting.

HISTAMINE

The similarity in the triple response produced by histamine and the nettle sting suggested to the researchers that histamine might actually be present in the stinging cell. All that needed to be done was to render the guinea pig's intestine insensitive to acetylcholine without affecting its sensitivity to histamine, and as we have seen this was easily achieved using atropine. It was found that 0.1-0.2 ml, taken from an extract made from 300 stinging hairs in 2 ml, added to the bath containing atropinised guinea pig intestine; caused the intestine to contract, showing that it was very likely that histamine was present. Further experimentation showed it was in a concentration of 1 in 500 to 1 in 2000.

Further evidence that the substance was histamine came from 4 other tests. What was also interesting, was when leaf tissue was assayed it was found to contain 0.018-0.027µg of acetylcholine and 0.019µg of histamine per. mg of *leaf tissue*. So the possibility remains that these substances could be made in the leaf tissue and transported to the stinging hairs, where they are concentrated.

Another substance causing the contraction of smooth muscle was also present in the stinging hair fluid, but only produced its effects when large amounts of extract was used; it was not possible to identify this substance.

All that remained now was to test the effect of a mixture of histamine and acetylcholine on the skin. The effect of histamine, a 100 times weaker than that in the stinging hair, had already been tried on the skin. It produced the typical weal, inflammation and flare (triple response) but in one respect it differed from the actual nettle sting; although histamine produces a strong itching which begins 30 sec after the prick, it does not produce the burning pain. The latter is so characteristic of the nettle sting that the German name for the nettle is Brennessel, (brenn = burning and nessel = nettle), meaning the Burning Nettle.

It was known that acetylcholine by itself produces no symptoms when pricked into the skin, but what would be the result of using a mixture of histamine and acetylcholine in the same proportions as they are found in stinging hairs? When a drop of the latter solution was placed on the skin and pricked through, the reactions produced in the skin of the forearm were: after 20 sec burning after 40 sec burning more pronounced like a nettle sting, after 60 sec violent itching starts and after 120 sec itching without more burning. The effect was similar to the actual sting but weaker; however, it must be remembered that they had failed to find the smooth muscle contracting factor.

In the absence of the identity of the 3rd factor they tried adding 1 % formic acid to the histamine solution, with and without acetylcholine, but no effect was produced (even a 1% soln. of formic acid made it more acid than the stinging hairs natural acidity).

At the time it was known that acetylcholine in small amounts can initiate impulses from the sensory nerve endings in the skin, and also, the injection of a 2% solution of this substance into an artery causes excruciating burning pain. Histamine causes the capillaries to dilate and become more permeable, causing the weal, but at the same time it may enable the acetylcholine to reach the nerve endings in sufficiently high concentrations to cause the stimulation leading to burning pain. It might also be that nerve endings become sensitised to acetylcholine, when under the influence of histamine. Emmelin and Feldburg raised a number of questions, (1) what is the nature of the 3rd substance? (2) Are there metabolic pathways and enzymes, in nettles and other plants, for the production of histamine and acetylcholine? (3) Are there evolutionary stages such as non-stinging hairs in plants containing these substances?

FLOW DIAGRAM 7.1 THE PHYSIOLOGICAL EFFECTS OF THE STINGING TOXINS PRESENT IN THE STINGING HAIRS OF URTICA DIOICA ON THE BODY OF VERTEBRATE ANIMALS

SEROTONIN (5-HYDROXY-TRYPTAMINE/5-HT)

The chemical properties of a pain-producing substance, 5-HT, had been subsequently described, and Collier and Chesher (1956), recognised that these fitted the six properties of the 3rd unidentified substance found by Emmelin and Feldburg: namely constriction of blood vessels of the rabbit's ear; stimulation of *in vitro* preparations of rabbit's and guinea pig's small intestine; lowering of rabbit's blood pressure; solubility in ether; and instability of boiling in alkaline solution.

TABLE 7.2 Chemical Toxins in the nettle sting in different members of the Urticeae. Data since 1947.

Plant name	Researchers	Date	Identification Technique	Extraction from	Skin test	Acetylcholine	Histamine	Hydroxy tryptamine	Leucotrienes	Others
2 D. excelsa	Lindikeit&Jung	1953	8,4	H		.2*	1-0.13*			
4 D. moroides	Robertson&Macfarlane	1957	8	H		0.01-0.025*	0.025-0.05*	0.001*		Pain producing substance
11 D. moroides	Oelrichs & Leung, Williams, Barna, Foti.	1986	,13							Peptide MOROIDES
6 G diversifolia	Pramod,Saxena, Tangri,Bhargava	1965	1,8			40.0†	3.75†	0.15†		Negative for histamine liberator.
10 O. pinnatifida	Maitai, Talalaj S.&D. &Njoroge	1981	2,8			75† hair	1000† hair	Trace		3 unidentified substances
9 U. cubensis	Regula & Devide	1980	1,2,9,10,6					0.42†		Tryptaphan
2 U. dioica	Lindikeit&Jung	1953	8,4	H		0.2*	0.03*			
3 U. dioica	Collier & Chesher	1956	1,8	,H				0.003-0.005*		Calcium sensitive factor
5 U. ferox	Pilgrim	1959	8			0.3-0.9*	?	?		Tryptaphan
9 U. ferox	Regula & Devide	1980	1,2,9,10,6					0.33†		Inconclusive
9 U.massaica	Maitai, Talalaj, Njoroge & Wamugunda	1980	8			Low	Low	?		
10 U. membranacea	Regula & Devide	1980	1,2,9,10,6					0.26†		Tryptaphan
13 U. membranacea	Corsi	1992	6			+	-	+		K++,lipids, proteins, pectin & alkaloid-like substances
6 U. parviflora	Saxena, Pant, Kishor & Bhargava	1965	1,8			318.4†	38.8†	0.25†		Suggested histamine liberator
7 U. pilulifera	Regula	1970						+		Tryptaphan
8 U. pilulifera .	Regula	1972								Bufotenine 5-HT methylated der.
9 U. pilulifera var dodartii	Regula	1980						+		
9 U. thunbergiana	Regula & Devide	1980	1,2,9,10,6					0.31†		
1 U. urens	Emmelin & Feldburg	1947	7,8	,H		18-27† 0.13-0.03*	19-50† 0.005-0.022*			3rd unidentified substance
9 U. urens	Regula & Devide	1980	1,2,9,10,6					0.00†		
12 U. urens	Beale, Czarnetzki. Thiele.& Rosenbach	1990	5,11,12				1.43† hairs 1.57† leaf		+	LTB4 2.4-1.8°* LTC4/D4 3-8°*

Identification Techniques, [Chromatography 1 = Paper, 2 = Thin layer, 3 = Column, 4 = Paper Electrophoresis, 5 = Reverse Phase High pressure Liquid (RP-HPLC)]. 6 = Histochemical Tests. 7 = Standard Chemical Tests. 8 = Pharmacological Tests. 9 = Spectrophotometry. 10 = Spectrophotofluorimetry. 11 = Radioimmunoassay (RIA) 12 = Vitro Neutrophil Chemotactic Activity. 13 = H & CNMR & Mass Spectroscopic Studies.Generic Plant Names, D = Dendrocnide, U = Urtica, O = Obetia, G = Girardinia, W = Whole plant, L = Leaf, H = Stinging hairs. Skin test with artificial stinging fluid, + = yes, - = none. Quantities of acetylcholine, histamine, 5-hydroxy-tryptamine, µg per. hair = *µg per.g = †, ng/ml = °*,Shaded = Tropical

Using paper chromatography and pharmacological techniques they identified the substance as 5-HT in this case using Urtica dioica. An enzyme was found in the nettle leaf extract, which quickly destroyed serotonin. There was little evidence for a 4th smooth-muscle stimulating substance. It was worked out, on the basis that the nettle sting contains 7-9µg fluid, that, 3.4-4.9µg of 5-HT per sting, provides a concentration more than sufficient to evoke pain in human skin; Jaques and Schachter (1954) found a similar concentration in wasp venom. It's a pity they didn't test the effects of 5-HT, in conjunction with acetylcholine and histamine, on the skin.

INTERPRETATION OF OVERALL RESULTS

Up to 1990, thirteen different species (out of approx. 90) from three different genera of the Urticeae have been tested for stinging hair toxins. For the majority of these there is only one set of results (Table 7.2).

There is now sufficient evidence to show that the toxins acetylcholine, histamine and serotonin occur fairly universally in the stinging hairs of the Urticeae. Further studies, using modern analytical techniques and of a comparative nature such as those of Regula & Devide (1980) are needed. No data is yet available for the genera Laportea, Hespercnide, Nanocnide, Disconide and Urera (approx. 76 species).

THE TRIPLE RESPONSE

Lewis (1927) during his investigations of skin reactions discovered the triple response which develops in the skin when it is stroked very heavily or scratched;

(1) After a short latent period a red line appears in the track of the stroke and is due to the dilation of the blood capillaries,

(2) About half a minute later there is a flush or flare over a large area on each side of the line, again resulting from dilation of the arterioles, causing the area to become hot and inflamed,

(3) A little later a weal i.e. a raised fluid filled area (oedema), develops along the red line. As the weal becomes larger the blood vessels are compressed and the area becomes pale. The weal is caused by an increase in permeability of the blood vessels, which leak out blood plasma. Lewis showed that the triple response could be produced by the injection of a minute amount of histamine into the skin and is antagonised by anti-histamine drugs.

This triple response, characteristic of urticaria, has already been studied in relation to the nettle stinging symptoms and is also a result of allergic reactions mentioned here and brought about by the introduction of histamine, or a histamine liberator (H-Substance), into the skin.

PHYSIOLOGICAL EFFECTS OF STINGING SUBSTANCES ON ANIMALS

The physiological effects of the stinging hair toxins on the body of animals are fairly well known, but apart from the few experiments mentioned, not enough is known of their cutaneous effects and more work in this area is needed. To recap briefly, Emmelin & Feldberg found that acetylcholine, in the amounts found in the stinging hairs of Urtica urens, when pricked into the skin produced a weak sensation of pain and generally no weal formation. Histamine when pricked into the skin in the correct concentrations produced the triple response and itching, indistinguishable from that of the nettle but with no burning sensation. However when acetylcholine and histamine were mixed together and pricked into the skin a burning sensation was produced after 15-25 sec. These simple experiments show that when acetycholine and histamine are mixed, their effect is different from when tested separately. Most people nowadays are familiar with the function of acetycholine as a neurotransmitter in nerves, and with the fact that when its job is finished, it is broken down and inactivated by the enzyme cholinesterase. The latter enzyme was not present in plant tissue, but if present in the skin it could inactivate the aceylcholine injected by the nettle sting. It is possible that the effect of histamine is to act as a potent vasodilator, increasing the permeability of the capillaries and causing blood plasma to pass into the skin to, (1) protect the breakdown of acetylcholine and, (2) by bringing it into contact with nerves, to initiate the burning sensation. The injection of a 2% solution of acetylcholine into the arteries of man causes an excruciating burning pain for a few seconds along the course of the artery (Ellis & Weiss 1932). Serotonin is also a neurotransmitter and like acetycholine produces pain and dilation of small blood vessels.

LEUCOTRIENES

Regula & Devide (1980) in their comparative study of the presence of serotonin in the Urticeae failed to find this substance in the stinging hairs of Urtica urens. Czarnetzli M.Beate et al (1990) recognised the third substance in Urtica urens, mentioned by Emmelin & Feldberg (1947), to have similar characteristics to that of the slow reacting substance leucotriene LTC4/D4. They found leucotrienes LTC4 and LTB4 in this plant, in concentrations where they are known to exert potent biological activities, such as inflammatory responses, pain and fever.

THE INGENUITY OF NATURE'S NETTLE STINGING HAIRS AND THEIR EVOLUTIONARY IMPLICATIONS

Evolution in animals is thought to go hand in hand with their ability to detect and kill pathogens. The defence mechanisms and immune systems of the body are essential for the continued survival of the species.

Injuries such as cuts or abrasions must be quickly repaired, to prevent loss of blood and to seal the body against the ingress of pathogenic organisms. Platelets play the main part in plugging a damaged blood vessel. They contain (1) alpha granules containing clotting and growth factors which stimulate cells in the blood vessels to proliferate and repair damage, (2) dense granules which contain *serotonin*, enzymes that produce prostaglandins and factors for the clotting process to stabilise the fibrous strands which bind together the clot. Platelets have the ability to adhere to the wall of the blood vessels and to one another and to secrete prostaglandins, *serotonin* and *thrombaxane A2*

which function as vasoconstrictors and decrease blood flow to the injured area.

In injuries and allergic reactions, the all important thing is to inactivate and destroy germs and foreign proteins (antigens) with the antibodies made by lymphocytes, and also for other white blood cells, phagocytes, to flow around foreign objects and enclose them within their cytoplasm. It is imperative that white blood cells in the blood vessels can reach the infected areas as soon as possible, and for this to take place, the blood produces substances to bring about vasodilation and increased blood-vessel permeability. One such substance is *histamine*, (found in most body cells but more so in mast cells, basophils, phagocytes and platelets), released in response to injury. Histamine and kinins causes vasodilation and increased permeability and prostaglandins intensify these effects and may help the migration of white cells through the wall of blood vessels. *Leucotrienes* produced by basophils and mast cells bring about vasodilation and function in adherence and chemotactic (movement towards a chemical) agents for phagocytes (Tortora &Anagnostakos 1990).

It is interesting therefore that the nettle sting contains the very substances, histamines, serotonin and leucotrienes, produced by animals in the

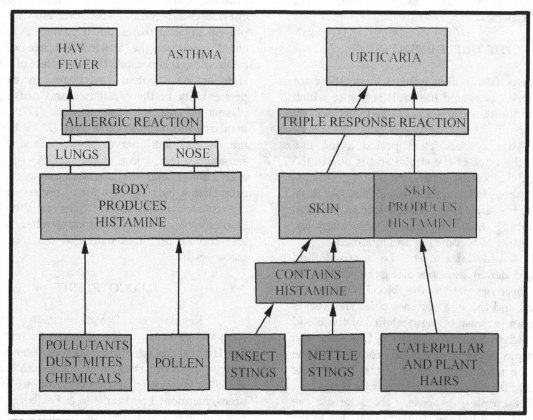

FLOW DIAGRAM 7.2. Reaction of the skin and body to allergens, insect and nettle stings

defence of their bodies and including immune responses. To be effective the nettle sting must act on the body quickly therefore the nettle toxins are in concentrations that are physiologically active. The substances acetylcholine and serotonin are also known in connection with the transmission of the nervous impulses, and enable the electrical impulse to pass from one nerve cell to the next, i. e. they are neurotransmitters. It is likely that they are involved in the burning pain produced by the nettle sting, and also for the later itching and tingling sensations, which need more study. The most remarkable part of the story is that the nettle sting should contain the exact chemicals that produce such powerful effects in the bodies of animals; however, this is all tied up with the evolutionary process (Fig 7.2).

Plants and animals share a common ancestry and it is well known that the cells contain very similar organelles, e.g. nuclei, mitochondria, etc., and that they have very similar chemical (metabolic) pathways. It is therefore of no surprise that plants produce, as by-products of their metabolism, substances which although of little use to them do have profound physiological effects in animal bodies. During evolution this has resulted in these substances being selected by certain plants and animals to ensure their survival.

Firstly, in relation to animals some of the most virulent toxins produced by venomous animals rely on the very potent physiological effects they have on the body chemistry of other animals. Many toxins affect the nervous system, or the transmission of nervous impulses from one nerve cell to the next, which depends upon the neurotransmitter acetylcholine and interference with the latter often stops breathing and causes death. The black widow spider produces the neurotoxic venom α-latrotoxin, which causes a mass release of acetylcholine at the neuro-muscular junction, whilst the most feared food poisoning is caused by the bacterium *Clostridium botulinum* which inhibits the release of acetylcholine.

In a similar way insect venoms contain *histamines, serotonin, acetylcholine*, etc., which affect the cardio-vascular system, central nervous system and endocrine systems of other animals. 2% histamine is present in the venom of the wasp-like insect Paravespula. Serotonin is found in high levels in the venom of social wasps and in hornets; Vespa orientalis contains 3.5% 5-HT. Venoms of many insects however contain an array of enzymes which are macromolecules and smaller units called peptides (Schmidt 1982).

NETTLE TREE TOXINS

Robertson & MacFarlane (1957) have shown that when an extract of stinging hairs of the nettle tree Dendrocnide moroides was dialysed to remove histamine, acetylcholine and serotonin, its stinging effects were hardly diminished. They identified the chemical characteristics of the pain-producing substance, which was a stable, non-dialysable substance, resistant to heat, neutral in reaction, unattacked by proteolytic enzymes (they breakdown proteins). It induced sweating, erection of hairs and arterial dilation.

Leung, Williams, Barna, Foti and Oelrichs (1986) continued this work, using a series of chemical, H &C NMR and mass spectrometric studies; they elucidated the structure of one pain-producing substance in the nettle tree *Dendrocnide moroides*,

FIG 7.5 On a walkway in a Queensland forest area

which they named *Moroidin*. Moroidin turned out to be a tricyclic octapeptide with C-N linkages between tryptophan and histadine residues. Cutaneous reactions, to the injection of moroidin, were tested by injection into human forearms, and the reaction (pain, redness and duration) was rated on the same 5-point scale that was used by Robertson & MacFarlane. Injection of 5μg gave a moderate reaction, rated 2, whereas, 10μg gave a severe reaction, rated 4 and they admitted the roughness of the guide. Moroidin was not as virulent as the crude extract and they identified a fraction from column chromatography not containing moroidin that produced a severe reaction on the human forearm.

The study of the chemical constituents of plants has shown that many plants contain, physiologically active substances normally found in animals, e.g. soya beans, potato tubers and wheat germ oil are known to contain respectively lipoxygenase, arachidonic acid and prostaglandins. The investigations on nettle toxins have shown that they, and their precursors, are found in the leaf and stem tissues adjacent to the stinging hairs (see Chapter 6). It seems likely that during evolution these substances moved from the leaf tissues into the bristle hairs, many of which had sufficient strong walls to penetrate animal skin, and therefore cause allergic responses. Those plants endowed with these hairs would have a selective advantage because they would be less likely to be eaten by herbivores, and therefore, more likely to pass over their genes to the next generation than plants with ordinary hairs. Further mutations, over long periods of time, producing hairs with more virulent toxins, stiffer hairs, hairs with sharper breakable tips, with compressible bases, etc., and the selection of those most suited to deter herbivores, could have produced the perfected nettle stinging hair. The presence of serotonin, acetylcholine and histamine in four different genera of the Urticaceae is evidence that they shared a common ancestor. The more virulent pain-producing toxins found in the Dendrocnide and the discovery of leucotrienes in Urtica urens, should stimulate more research into the toxins present in stinging hairs within the Urticaceae and lead to the elucidation of more substances which have profound physiological effects on the bodies of animals. The Map butterfly (*Arashnia levana*) once introduced into Britain but then purposely destroyed.

FIG 8.1. Nettles, vertebrate and invertebrate herbivores, and tropical tormentors showing the stinging effects on the human fore-arm of stings from Blumenbachia hieronymii (Euphorbiaceae).

97

CHAPTER 8

THE TALE IN THE STING 3
HERBIVORE INTERACTIONS
AND OTHER FAMILIES OF STINGING PLANTS

"Less than three dozen papers have appeared on all aspects of stinging hairs in this century; only a scant dozen of these has been published in the last 25 years. Nineteen of the 29 genera reported to have stinging hairs have never received even superficial study. This slow increase in knowledge is unfortunate, because stinging hairs offer convenient material for the study of a number of processes of current interest: silica deposition (Urtica), secondary wall formation (Cnidoscolus), crystal formation (Tragia), endopolyploidy (Urtica). They are also a spectacular example of convergent evolution, and worthy of study for that aspect alone.

Stinging hairs, far from being merely classical textbook objects, are instead complex structures with unusual characteristics and unsolved problems at all levels of organization."

Thurston and Lerston (1969)

INTRODUCTION

Traditionally plants and animals have been studied separately. With the publication of the 'Biological Flora of the British Isles' (1913) interactions with animals were included. More recently there has been escalation in the number of papers and books on plant/animal interactions, especially in the area of 'Plant Herbivore Relationships.' Some of the most fascinating biological stories concern plant and animal interactions and this is evident in relation to herbivores and stinging hairs.

FUNCTIONS OF TRICHOMES

The natural chemicals useful to plants and man are mainly produced by glandular trichomes which synthesise or accumulate and secrete terpernoids, phenolics, mucoproteins and resins, some of which deter plant feeding (phytophagous) insects. Trichomes also afford protection from excess temperature drop or water loss by covering the plant surface with trapped air space. Stinging trichomes of nettles and other plants, act defensively by deterring certain herbivores.

VERTEBRATE / MAMMALIAN HERBIVORES

1 THE STINGING PLANTS OF THE URTICACEAE
DO STINGING HAIRS OF URTICA DIOICA DETER LARGER HERBIVORES?

In their book 'Introduction to Entomology' (1858) Kirby & Spence say, **"The common *nettle* is of little use to either mankind or larger animals; but you will not doubt its importance to the class of insects, when told that at least 30 distinct species feed upon it."** The authors make the point, that although the nettle is a food for insects, it is useless to larger herbivore animals.

It is known that nettles grow and survive, largely unharmed in pastures which harbour cattle so why do herbivores insects eat the nettle whereas vertebrate herbivores do not? Evidence indicates, that, (1) the large populations of insects (including 31 specific species) feeding on the nettle, either cannot be stung or either are suited by their size or behaviour to avoid being stung by stinging trichomes, (2) nettles thrive in pastures grazed by cattle (only occasionally do they appear to be lightly browsed) so could be due either to the plant being distasteful to them or to the deterrent action of its stinging trichomes. Man avoids the nettle because of the pain and skin reaction it inflicts, and it is logical to conclude that other vertebrate herbivores with highly developed brains will react in a similar way. Plants have a limited energy budget, the survival of the nettle plant would be jeopardised by using food to produce stinging hairs if this was of no use, when it could be used in increasing seed production or stored in the rhizomes for next year's growth. Some animals are adapted to eat nettles such as goats, bison, and mountain gorillas (Schaller 1963) and this could be due to the leathery nature of their lips and copious saliva production.

EXPERIMENTAL STUDIES

Pollard (1981) was able to use the Stingless Nettle (*Urtica dioica* var. *galeopsifolia*), to extend his range of clones with different densities of stinging trichomes, to test the hypothesis that stinging trichomes provide a deterrent to grazing by mammalian herbivores e.g. rabbits, and sheep. Experiments were carried out under artificial conditions using domesticated animals in captivity, and by means of experimental field trials under natural conditions.

USING DOMESTICATED HERBIVORES

Prior to the experiment 11 nettle clones each with different hair densities were propagated vegetatively in pots in sufficient quantity for the replicates in the experiment. For each clone the hair density was calculated from the mean number of stinging hairs per cm² on upper and lower surfaces, in the sun and the shade. The rabbits and sheep that normally fed on pellets and hay had this withdrawn 24 hr before each experiment.

RABBITS

Six rabbits each kept in individual wire cages were presented with cut nettle shoots, which passed through the wire floor, into containers of water underneath. Two shoots of contrasting stinging hair density were given at any one time, and left for a period of 24 hr, after which the total number of leaves or portions of leaves consumed from each shoot was noted.

SHEEP

The sheep were kept in groups in a concrete paddock, and nettle plants in pots, were presented to them in rows. Grazing was scored, as for the rabbits, and the plants were removed at the end of a week. The experiment was repeated several times (replicated) and the pots were randomised.

Observation of both sheep and rabbits showed that they occasionally exhibited immediate pain response on contact with the heavily-armed nettle clones, including jumping back, shaking the head, licking the lips, and in the case of rabbits, rubbing the nose, mouth and ears with the fore paws. Even so, on some occasions, there was considerable grazing of such plants; on the other hand pain responses, produced by the biting off of small portions of one or two leaves, was followed by cessation of grazing.

For both rabbits and sheep the results showed that, as stinging hair density became less then more grazing took place, and the relation was significant. Since these domesticated animals hadn't come into contact with nettle plants prior to the experiment and therefore developed avoidance behaviour, the results clearly showed that stinging trichomes acted as a deterrent to grazing of the nettle plants. Because of the artificiality of these trials it was decided to follow them up with more realistic field trials.

FIELD EXPERIMENTS UNDER NATURAL CONDITIONS

Field experiments took place on Cavenham Heath National Nature Reserve, Suffolk. Six clones of varying hair density were chosen and propagated vegetatively to produce sufficient pot-grown replicate plants for the experiment. The potted plants were sunk into the soil in three different areas, 10 localities on the heath (some in the vicinity of rabbit burrows and dung areas), 4 sites in pre-existing grazing enclosures and enclosed sites surrounded by rabbit-proof wire fencing. The experiment started in September 1978; results were recorded in May to July 1980 when there were signs of grazing, and recorded as numbers of leaves, portions of leaves, shoot apices or whole shoots removed from each clonal plant.

The results enable comparisons of grazing (principally by rabbits) between the open and enclosed sites, and they reveal that grazing was more severe in the Wicken Fen 'stingless' varieties than on more heavily-armed plants.

The results raised a number of areas, requiring further investigation. It might be expected that the nettle clones established in pastures inhabited by cattle and therefore under grazing pressure, would have survived or been selected because they have sufficient density of stinging hairs to deter severe injury by the cattle. On the other hand avoidance of nettles by herbivores might enable pastureland clones with low hair densities to exist on a type of mimic basis. The stinging strategy is elegant because the toxins reach the mammalian nervous system quickly, produce pain and burning sensations, and results largely in future avoidance of this plant. The existence of relatively 'Stingless' nettle clones at Wicken Fen, could be explained by the fact that in the fen carr habitat, these nettles have virtually no large mammalian herbivores to feed on them. Under the latter circumstances the expenditure of energy in producing high densities of stinging hairs is not of survival value.

MORE GRAZING STUDIES

This was followed by a paper on a study of the relationship between trichome density in Urtica dioica, and herbivore and mechanical damage (Andrew Pullin 1989). The first part of the research parallels the work of Pollard on *Cnidoscolus* (see later). The hypothesis chosen was that vertebrate grazing has led to the selection of heavily armoured nettle clones in grazed areas whilst natural largely grazed areas favour less well defended plants.

EFFECT OF LONG TERM GRAZING PRESSURE

Trichome density was measured from the same part of the leaf and over an area of 2 cm² and also from 1 cm lengths of internodes. Clones were chosen from 8 natural areas, mainly from waste ground in the vicinity of Oxford, England, and an equal number of clones in three nearby fields where grazing was long established and well-documented grazing regimes. The main livestock in the fields were cattle and horses with a high stocking density and therefore heavy grazing pressure on the nettle clones. All clones were in the open sun, and samples were taken in the in the summer.

The results clearly showed that clones of Urtica dioica in pastures under heavy grazing have a greater density of stinging trichomes than those in waste areas outside pastures where the herbivore pressure is lower. In this respect the results back up the findings of Pollard & Briggs (1984 b) and Pollard (1986).

Pullin's observations are also agree with my own field studies, in that, there are other environmental factors operating in a pasture which can bring about an increase in trichome density. These factors damage due to trampling by cattle, and also spraying or mowing of nettle clones at different times during the year. The second hypothesis that Pullin tested is, whether U. dioica can increase trichome density, after experiencing some grazing damage.

EFFECT OF SIMULATED HERBIVORE DAMAGE ON STINGING TRICHOME DENSITY

To simulate herbivore damage, or damage by man some nettles were cut down and the trichome density of nettle clones were measured before and after cutting. Clones in open situations were cut back to a height of 20 cm in mid-July and then left for 10 weeks to re-grow.

The results show that, 2 out of the 3 clones sampled, had significantly higher stinging trichome densities on the re-growth shoots compared with densities on the initial shoots. This agrees with the prediction that, simulated herbivore-damage, would be expected to result in shoots with higher trichome densities.

VARIATION IN STINGING TRICHOME DENSITY IN CENTRAL AND PERIPHERAL

AREAS OF NETTLE CLONES

When herbivores brush up against nettle clones or gaze around their edges, they do a certain amount of damage to the peripheral nettle shoots, whereas those shoots centrally placed are largely unaffected. It might be expected that this peripheral damage, as opposed to little central damage, would be reflected in high stinging trichome densities on the outside shoots compared with those of the centre. To test this prediction, the shoots of six clones, of a heavily grazed pasture, were sampled at the centre and on the periphery for trichome density).

The results show that the prediction was true for most of the clones, however, Pullin did not rule out the possibility that these results could be explained, (1) by the greater shading of the central shoots or, (2) the up-growth of shoots with higher stinging trichome densities later in the year in the peripheral areas of the clone. This is an area where further research could be rewarding.

Whether the chemicals causing the smell come from the epidermal cells or from the glandular

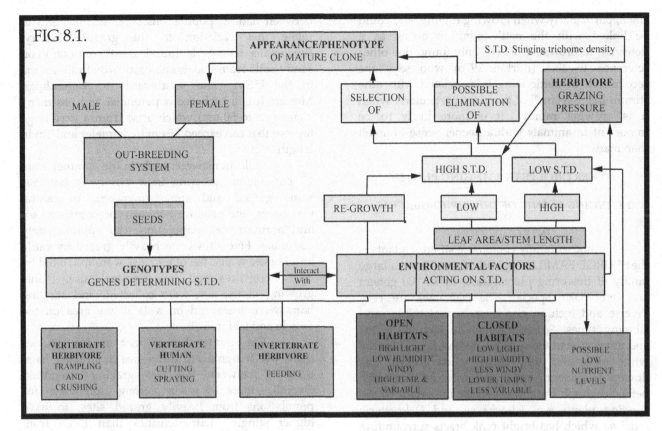

FIG 8.1.

S.T.D. Stinging trichome density

FIGURE 8.1 Flow diagram of the effect of biotic factors (vertebrate and invertebrate herbivores) and environmental climatic and soil factors, and genetic factors on the stinging hair density of Urtica dioica (i.e. phenotype =genotype + environment).

hairs, it would be interesting to know. The nettle scent might also stimulate urination and defecation in the region of nettles and therefore be to their benefit. These interactions are shown in the flow diagram 8.1.

EFFECT OF CUTTING AND NUTRIENT LEVEL ON STINGING TRICHOME DENSITY

A single nettle clone was separated into 20 blocks, transferred to seed trays, and placed in a greenhouse. When the plants were of sufficient height they were cut down to 5 cm, four treatments were applied and the plants moved at intervals. Treatments as follows:

Unfertilised and allowed to re-grow for 140 d.

Fertilised and allowed to re-grow for 140 d.

Unfertilised, allowed to re-grow for 70 d. then cut again and allowed to re-grow for a further 100 d.

Fertilised, allowed to re-grow for 70 d then cut again and allowed to re-grow for a further 100 d.

The results of the experiment can be interpreted in different ways but the fact that debate is stimulated is good. Pullin concludes that in relation to the unfertilised plants, the decrease in stinging hair density of group 3 compared to that of group 1, could be due to the fall in nutrient levels and that this 'potentially makes the plant vulnerable to herbivore attack.'

I have noticed that when nettles are damaged or cut down by farmers the cattle are attracted to these open areas which they use as urination and dung areas. The stems of the re-growth nettles in these high nutrient areas are invariably covered with extremely high stinging trichome levels. Based on the nutrient allocation theory, the allocation of nutrients to produce such high stinging trichome densities would appear to be a waste of nutrients, but it is likely that it is due to rapid growth, high nutrient levels, hormones, and light which stimulate trichome expression and growth.

Another area neglected in relation to grazing is how do these animals recognise the nettle apart from its sting? Their panoramic black and white vision is geared to registering the positions of moving animals, and therefore less suited to details of nettle morphology; however they are likely to be able to recognise it as a clump plant. More likely, during grazing, is the stimulus of the smell of the nettle at close quarters. It has a distinctive, cat-urine smell, particularly when growing rapidly, and could be linked with the nettle sting in acting as a deterrent to browsing. I have only found one other reference to this (Burton 1976) who says the recollection of nettle sting is associated with othe stimuli like the smell of the plant particularly when it is growing rapidly. It is more likely to be important in animals with a keener sense of smell than man.

OTHER GROUPS OF STINGING PLANTS

2 *STINGING PLANTS OF THE EUPHORBIACEAE*

INTRODUCTION

Another family containing stinging plants is the SPURGE FAMILY Euphorbiaceae. This is a large family of flowering plants made up of 300 genera and over 5,000 species. The trichomes are very diverse and include glandular, non-glandular and stinging types. Secretions include tannins, resins and mucilage but the spurges are best known for the white milk/latex they exude when broken. The flowers are generally small and unisexual; most lack petals although these are present in certain of the stinging plants e.g. *Jatropha sp.* and *Dalechampia roezliana* which has bright pink bracts surrounding the small flowers. Stinging hairs are found in the following genera of the **Euphorbiaceae**: *Cnidoscolus (Jatropha), Tragia, Dalechampia, Platygyna, Acidoton, Cenesmon, Pachystylidium, Tragiella and Sphaerostylis.*

THE BULL NETTLE AND HERBIVORES

Pollard (1986) followed up his study on Urtica dioica that stinging hairs have evolved as defence against mammalian herbivores, with a similar study carried out in the U.S.A., this time looking at a stinging plant The Bull Nettle, Spurge Nettle or Mala Mujer, from a completely different plant Family. The Spurge nettle (*Cnidoscolus texanus* (Muell. Arg.), as its name suggest, is a member of the Euphorbiaceae and is covered in stinging trichomes which are very large, 5-8 mm long, and are found in greatest densities on the stems, petioles, leaf mid ribs, pedicels and fruits.

Examination of herbarium material of C. texanus revealed variation in stinging hair density between plants, but the plant is different from Urtica dioica, in that it produces a latex which may contain, linamarin (a cyanogenic glycoside), β-amyrin (a triterpenoid) and a diverse flavonol glycoside, and therefore appears to have a very effective herbivore defence system. For these reasons, Pollard decided to carry out a study of variation in stinging hair density within and between natural populations of *C. texanus*, and to relate this variation to the grazing history. *Cnidoscolus texanus* is found most commonly on sandy soils from Oklahoma eastwards to Louisiana in the U.S.A., and southwards to Tamaulipas, Mexico. It is a herbaceous perennial and has many stems (up to 50 cm) which arise from a very large taproot that can exceed 15 cm in diameter and 1m in length.

Collections were made in the summer from 12 populations growing in a variety of habitats, some grazed and some ungrazed, in central Oklahoma; the distance between the southernmost and northernmost population was approximately 150 miles. Five sites were heavily grazed by cattle and horses, whilst the other sites, were inhabited by wild herbivores and low livestock use. Plants growing in the sun were collected, and stinging hairs were measured on a 1x20 cm, area on the petiole and leaf midrib.

The results showed that on the petioles there was a significant difference in stinging hairs densities between the two grazing categories. Overall, there was a strong tendency for populations from heavily grazed sites, to have higher stinging hair densities than those from ungrazed sites. This implies that local adaptation has occurred as a result of the selection of features that discourage grazing. Pollard did not actually observe cattle eating C. texanus.

A CLOSER LOOK AT THE STINGING TRICHOMES OF CNIDOSCOLUS DEVELOPMENT AND STRUCTURE

Thurston (1969) investigated the anatomy and development of the stinging trichomes of *Cnidoscolus stimulosus* at the light and electron microscope level (Table 8.1). During development Cnidoscolus differs from Urtica in that the bulbous tip develops at a later stage after cell elongation has started. Thurston distinguished between two different stinging trichomes, type A on the stem and type B on the leaf margins. The mature hair is remarkably similar to that of Urtica but the terminal knob is symmetrically placed (Meyen 1837). Haberlandt (1886) accurately described and illustrated the structure of the tip. The cellulose wall of the stinging trichome is impregnated with lignin, the substance that gives the strength to wood. The hair invariably breaks along the line

Shown i.e. below the constriction found at he base of the swollen apical part where the cell wall is lignified and therefore more brittle than elsewhere.

TABLE 8.1. Comparison of selected characters of some stinging cells, of members of the Urticaceae, Euphorbiaceae, Loasaceae, from original (Thurston 1969) and published observations (After Thurston & Lersten 1969). [+ = present, - = absent] = unknown, E = epidermal; SE = sub-epidermal].

| CHARACTERS | URTICACEAE | EUPHORBIACEAE | | LOASACEAE |
	URTICA	CNIDOSCOLUS	TRAGIA	LOASA
AVERAGE LENGTH μ	**1000**	**4150**	**400**	**1600**
MEAN DIAMETER μ	**90**	**200**	**15**	**75**
WALL STRUCTURE & COMPOSITION				
CALCIUM	+	-	-	+
LIGNIN	-	+	-	-
SILICA	+	-	-	+
CUTICLE-LIKE LAYER	+	+	+	+
EXTERNAL WALL MARKINGS	+	+	-	-
CELLULOSE CELL WALL	+	+	+	+
PITS	-	+	-	-
PIT FIELDS	+	-	-	+
ONTOGENY				
ORIGIN	E	E	SE	E
TIP DIFFERENTIATION PRIOR TO ELONGATION	+	-	?	?
MISCELLANEOUS				
CALCIUM OXALATE CRYSTAL	-	-	+	-
SYMMETRICAL BULBOUS BASE	+	+	-	+

In a similar way to Urtica the shaft of the trichome is covered externally in elongated, spiral, wart-like markings and has a thin, compressible wall forming its bulbous base. The pedestal is comparatively larger and more irregular than that of Urtica and lacks the central columella (Fig 8.3A).

BOX 8.1   STINGING SYMPTOMS OF CNIDOSCOLUS URENS

I can only find one reference to the stinging symptoms of Cnidoscolus and this applies to *C. urens*, commonly called Ortiga, Ortiga Brava, or Chichicaste (Lutz 1914). This is the most abundant Euphorbiaceous plant growing in and around the savannahs of the Pacific coast of South America. Its abundance is thought to be due to its avoidance by cattle and the indolence of the local farmers. It has the reputation of being extremely dangerous on account of its poisonous effects.

This plant is 0.5-1.5m high, regularly branched, with simple palmate leaves, white flowers and 3-celled fruit capsules. All parts are covered in long hard glowing stinging hairs. Lutz gives this account of his encounter with this plant!

"Which protect the plant as barbed wire protects the fortifications of today. It would seem as if the remarkable glossiness of the stinging hairs might warn the curious against approaching or touching. As a matter of fact, the animals either by instinct, or on account of the wisdom acquired through some previous experience, avoid contact with it. "

"On an excursion along the San Felix River, in eastern Chiriqui, with Dr. MacDonald, geologist of the Canal Commission, the writer became acquainted with a single specimen of the plant. All at once he felt an intense burning on the left hand, where about 10 of the stinging hairs had entered pretty deep into the skin. The inflammation produced by this touch was very similar to that produced by nettles, but the pain soon increased, the whole hand began to swell and inside of half an hour had assumed a monstrous shape. Then the arm commenced to swell also, the right hand and arm, without having been inoculated, yet showed the same abnormal symptoms, and a very strong itching sensation was felt all over the upper part of the body. At about the same time parts of the face, around the eyes and nose, swelled considerably. The itching sensation rapidly spread over the abdomen and the lower extremities and red pimples appeared everywhere. In less than an hour the poison had extended over the whole surface of the body, and its entrance into the blood current was indicated by the corresponding physiological reaction of the interior organs. The palpitation of the heart became extremely accelerated and the mind was soon overcome by an agonising depression. The respiration seemed to be delayed as if under a great pressure, cold sweat broke out, and the patient gave way altogether, remaining unconscious for more than and hour, except for feverish dreams. After coming back to his senses, he had several fits of copious vomiting, from which it may be surmised that the poison was slowly eliminated from the organism. The weakness, however, remained for several days. A case of such extreme effects, which might have killed a man of less strength than the writer, has never been recorded..."

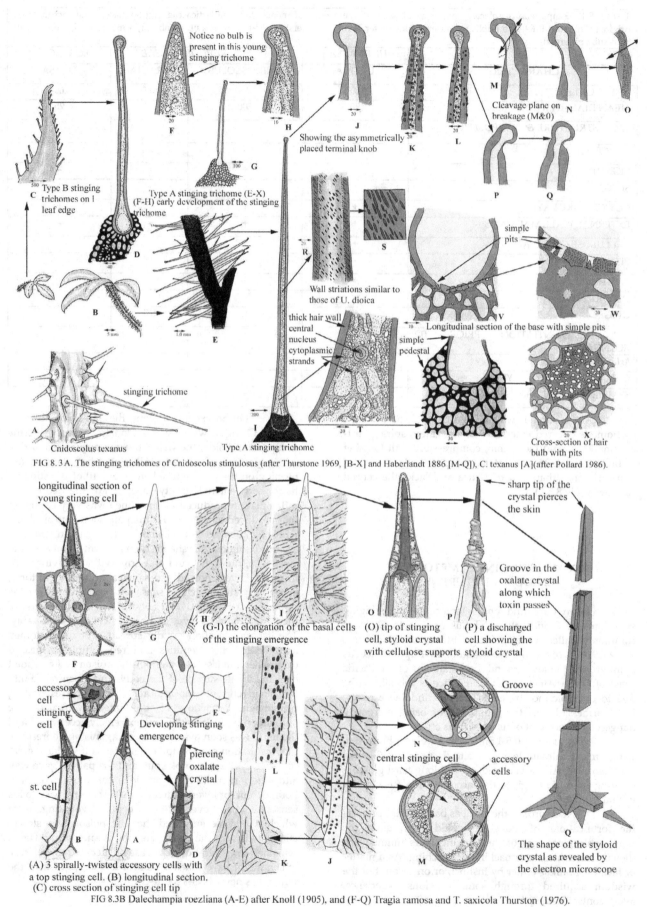

Notice no bulb is present in this young stinging trichome

Showing the asymmetrically placed terminal knob

Cleavage plane on breakage (M&0)

Type B stinging trichomes on l leaf edge

Type A stinging trichome (E-X) (F-H) early development of the stinging trichome

Wall striations similar to those of U. dioica

simple pits

thick hair wall
central nucleus
cytoplasmic strands

simple pedestal

Longitudinal section of the base with simple pits

stinging trichome

Type A stinging trichome

Cnidoscolus texanus

Cross-section of hair bulb with pits

FIG 8.3A. The stinging trichomes of Cnidoscolus stimulosus (after Thurstone 1969, [B-X] and Haberlandt 1886 [M-Q]), C. texanus [A](after Pollard 1986).

longitudinal section of young stinging cell

sharp tip of the crystal pierces the skin

Groove in the oxalate crystal along which toxin passes

(G-I) the elongation of the basal cells of the stinging emergence

(O) tip of stinging cell, styloid crystal with cellulose supports

(P) a discharged cell showing the styloid crystal

accessory cell
stinging cell

Developing stinging emergence

Groove

piercing oxalate crystal

central stinging cell

accessory cells

st. cell

(A) 3 spirally-twisted accessory cells with a top stinging cell. (B) longitudinal section.
(C) cross section of stinging cell tip

The shape of the styloid crystal as revealed by the electron microscope

FIG 8.3B Dalechampia roezliana (A-E) after Knoll (1905), and (F-Q) Tragia ramosa and T. saxicola Thurston (1976).

104

CHEMICAL CONSTITUENTS

It is a great pity, considering this remarkable case of convergent evolution that the, search for similar toxic constituents in the stinging trichomes carried out on the Urticacae, have not been applied to the stinging plants of the Euphorbiaceae. An initial study of Willis (1969 unpublished M.Sc.), using chromatographic techniques, was unable to confirm the presence of acetylcholine, histamine and serotonin, in Urtica and Cnidoscolus; he did however, isolate an unidentified substance common to both. This is another area awaiting further study.

THE UNIQUE STINGING PLANTS OF THE EUPHORBIACEAE THAT GIVE VERTEBRATE HERBIVORES THE NEEDLE

INTRODUCTION

These unique stinging plants belong to several genera of the Euphorbiaceae, but only the genera Tragia and Dalechampia have received any study (Table 8.2). The stinging structure and mechanism is completely different from that of other stinging plants where convergent evolution

THE STRUCTURE OF THE STINGING EMERGENCE

Knoll (1905) carried out an extensive morphological study of *Tragia volubilis* and found that it consists of three elongated accessory cells surrounding a central stinging cell. The latter cell is extended beyond the accessory cells, for almost a ⅓rd of their length, and forms an apical cone which contains a needle-shaped calcium oxalate crystal suspended by strands of cellulose. He believed the accessory cells were multinucleated whilst the central cell was uninucleate. The stinging cell was found to be of sub-epidermal origin.

Knoll found that *Dalechampia roezliana* had a similar structure and development to that of T. volubilis (Fig. 8.3B). Thurston (1976) studied the structure of *Tragia ramosa* and *T. Saxicola* at the light and electron microscope level. Histochemical tests were used to determine calcium oxalate (silver nitrate-rubeanic acid) and protein distribution (acrolein/Schiff). The crystal is an elongated tapered tetrahedron, pointed at the apex and with radiating needle-like

Table 8.2. stinging plants of the genera Tragia and Dalechampia (Euphorbiaceae) whose stinging trichomes have been studied.

Species	Country	Author	Year
Dalechampia roezliana	?	Knoll	1905
Tragia volubilis	?	Knoll	1905
Tragia cannabina	India	Rao & Sundararaj	1951
Tragia saxiicola	U.S.A. Florida	Thurston	1969
Tragia ramosa	U.S.A. Texas	Thurston	1974

has resulted in an 'Urtica type' stinging trichome. The stinging structure/emergence in this case, since it is sub-epidermal in origin, cannot be classified as a stinging trichome, but for traditional reasons is included within this group (Thurston & Lersten 1969, Thurston 1976.

Tragia cannabina is a trailing plant of frequent occurrence in black cotton soils in India. The plant has unicellular and multicellular hairs, and the stinging emergences, which vary from 0.5-1.0 mm in length, are found over the whole plant but in greatest density on the calyx and ovary of the flowers. With increasing age of the shoot or fruit they tend to fall off or lose their contents and stinging properties. *Tragia ramosa* and *T. saxicola* are morphologically similar and the stinging emergences are found all over the plant.

projections at its base; these projections are enclosed by an inner cell wall that holds the crystal in place when contact with an object is made. A rectangular groove 1.6μ depth and 0.8μ width is found along the mid-line on one side of the crystal and this groove ends about half-way down from the top (Fig 8.3B q).

The stinging cell originates from a sub-epidermal cell and the accessory cells are formed from adjacent epidermal cells that elongate with the stinging cell (Figs 8.3B e).

THE MECHANISM OF THE STING

Very little is known of the mechanism of the sting and this account is based on that of Sakharam and Sundaaraj (1950). When a vertebrate makes contact with the hair, the force of the impact causes the apical part of the stinging cell to peel back and the needle-sharp point of the crystal penetrates the skin. It appears that the crystal, very often, breaks a little below the middle and the broken tip remains in the skin. This is verified with a binocular microscope which shows the broken crystal in the skin together with small globules, perhaps resulting from the peeled back part of the cell. Old dead stinging emergences or dry parts of the plant, on contact with the skin, do not produce irritations, and this indicates that it is not the calcium oxalate crystal that produces the stinging symptoms. Thurston found that proteins were concentrated around the crystal and in the crystal groove and proposed that this groove might actually channel the 'poison fluid' into the wound in the skin.

Thurston states that the physiological reactions produced by the sting of Tragia are similar to those produced by other stinging plants.

EVOLUTIONARY RELATIONSHIPS

Calcium oxalate crystal formations e.g. raphides, druses, crystalline sand and styloids, are found imany plants and could deter or slow sown grazing by herbivores e.g. slugs and snails. Packets of needle-shaped calcium oxalate crystals, called raphides can be shot into an animal aggressor such as a slug or snail. I am unaware of further work on raphides as herbivore deterrents, but it does point to a possible route for the evolution of the crystal stinging emergences of Tragia and Dalechampia. Perhaps they could have first evolved as surface structures capable of deterring browsing gastropods, but later mutations produced elevated structures with poisonous principles, more suited to deter the potentially more harmful vertebrate herbivores.

3 STINGING TRICHOMES OF THE LOASACEAE
INTRODUCTION

The Loasaceae is a small plant family with only 15 genera and 250 species. The family is almost entirely confined to America with numerous species in the south-west U.S.A. and Mexico. The main genus Loasa (100 species) extends from southern Mexico and the West Indies southwards to Patagonia; they are characteristic of the flora of the Andes. One genus, Kissenia (2 species) occurs outside America and is found in Africa and Arabia.

The family is mainly composed of herbs, many are woody twiners and a few are tree-like. Many are rough to the touch because they are covered with barbed hairs e.g. *Petalonyx* the sandpaper plant and others have to be handled very carefully because they are bristling with virulent stinging trichomes that can deliver a severe sting. Just under half of the genera are stinging plants, as follows: *Loasa, Blumenbachia, Caiophora, Eucnide, Gronovia, Cevallia* and *Fuertesia*.

They have beautiful insect/animal pollinated flowers and because of their hardy nature and strange attraction deserve to be grown more in temperate gardens. The flowers are hermaphrodite, often yellow, occur singly or in cymes and are symmetrical with 5 (4-7) boat-shaped petals which may be fused or free. In Loasa the stamens are numerous and in bundles, and the ovary is surrounded by conspicuous, often brightly coloured staminodes that secrete nectar. The ovaries ripen into spectacular special twisted capsules often covered in long non-stinging hairs.

HISTORICAL

Loasa vulcanica was first discovered by Berthold Carl Seemann (1825-1871) near Gonzanama in Ecuador; however Loasa tricolor was described by Meyen in 1836. Meyen described the trichome as being very similar to that of Urtica, with an asymmetrical terminal knob and supported at the base by a multicellular pedestal. His accurately drawn diagrams also show, bristle, anchor and glandular trichomes (Fig 8.4). Haberlandt (1886) using material preserved in alcohol drew the trichome tips of *Loasa hispisa, L. papaverifolia, L. tricolor. Blumenbachia*

106

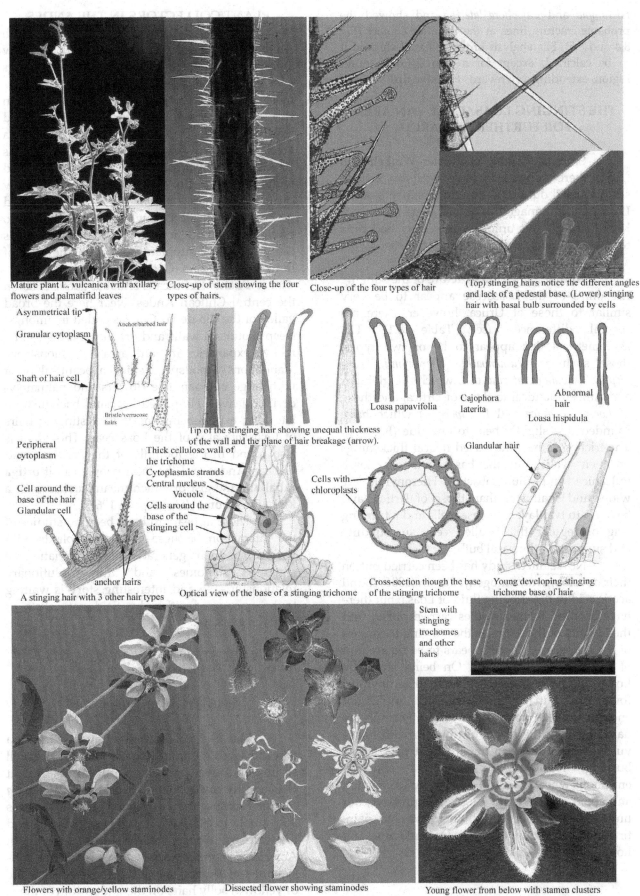

Mature plant L. vulcanica with axillary flowers and palmatifid leaves

Close-up of stem showing the four types of hairs.

Close-up of the four types of hair

(Top) stinging hairs notice the different angles and lack of a pedestal base. (Lower) stinging hair with basal bulb surrounded by cells

Asymmetrical tip

Granular cytoplasm

Shaft of hair cell

Anchor/barbed hair

Bristle/verrucose hairs

Tip of the stinging hair showing unequal thickness of the wall and the plane of hair breakage (arrow).

Loasa papavifolia

Cajophora laterita

Abnormal hair

Loasa hispidula

Peripheral cytoplasm

Cell around the base of the hair Glandular cell

anchor hairs

A stinging hair with 3 other hair types

Thick cellulose wall of the trichome
Cytoplasmic strands
Central nucleus
Vacuole
Cells around the base of the stinging cell

Optical view of the base of a stinging trichome

Cells with chloroplasts

Cross-section though the base of the stinging trichome

Glandular hair

Young developing stinging trichome base of hair

Stem with stinging trochomes and other hairs

Flowers with orange/yellow staminodes

Dissected flower showing staminodes

Young flower from below with stamen clusters

FIG 8.4 THE STRUCTURE OF THE FLOWERS AND STINGING TRICHOMES OF LOASA VULCANICA

107

Hieronymi and *Cajophora lateritia* and showed the probable fracture lines at the tip after contact (Fig 8.4 and 8.5). His analysis of the cell wall showed it to be calcified, except for a thin siliceous outer region, extending downwards from the tip.

THE STINGING LOASACEAE – AN AREA FOR FURTHER RESEARCH

Since the work of Kuster–Winkelmann (1941) there appears to have been no serious study carried out on the stinging members of the Loasaceae. I managed to obtain some seed from Kew Gardens, but unfortunately, only had time to make a brief study of the structure of the stinging trichomes (Figs 8.4 - 8.5).

At first glance the structure of the stinging trichomes of the Loasaceae appear to be very similar to those of Urtica, however, there are several differences (see Table 8.1). The asymmetrical tips appear to be of two types, those such as *Blumenbachia Hieronymii*, *Loasa hispida*, *Cajophora laterita*, etc., which are globular and almost identical to those of Urtica, and those of *Loasa vulcanica* and *L. paperifolia* which have rounded tips slightly bent to one side (Fig. 8.4). The trichomes have no raised helical thickenings on their walls and the basal bulbs of Loasa vulcanica and Blumenbachia Hieronymii are wider and shallower than those of Urtica; and have up to two layers of basal cells and a fringing ring of regular thick-walled cells surrounding and supporting the basal bulb.

No detailed study has been carried out on their development/ontogeny. Tassin (1886) found acetic acid in the stinging fluid of Loasa, but there have been no further studies carried out to find the identity of the toxins in the stinging trichomes of the Loasaceae. There appears to be no account of the stinging symptoms. On being stung by Loasa vulcanica and Blumenbachia Hieronymii I found the initial pain sharp and unpleasant enough, to lead to a quick withdrawal of my hand. Lashing the inside of my arm with Loasa vulcanica produced an initial, slight pain and a burning, followed by erythrema and an enormous wheal, about 15 cm long by 10 cm wide and about one cm high, it looked impressive, but unlike the sting of Urtica, there was no pain, tingling or irritation, and it disappeared after and hour or so.

PLANT COLLECTORS IN THE ANDES

The deserts on the west-coast of South America are some of the driest on earth. In a few areas of these deserts of Peru a dense fog hangs over the coastal hills and plains. The soil becomes moist and in wet spots short-lived vegetation springs up to form 'meadows of the desert' called locally '**lomas**'. Between Chimbote and Lima green lomas are found. In the Lachay lomas Goodspeed found areas covered in yellow and white-flowered Loasa species. Great yellow carpets of Loasa similar to yellow mustard covered the hillside through the fog at Pasomayo extended down to the ocean beach. In some areas the yellow was supplemented with the blue of flowers of Solanum (Goodspeed 1961).

Puente Del Inca is situated above 8000' in the central Chilean Andes. Near here the broad valley of the Rio de las Cuevas ended in amongst steep mountain walls and growing on the sandy, rocky expanses. In an area of monstrous 'dandelions' Goodspeed spied a beautiful plant with large campanulate flowers and palmately-divided leaves. He pulled his hand back just too late after experiencing the violent stinging hairs of *Cajophora* also of the Loasaceae. This plant is also found in the foothills of the Peruvian and Chilean Andes and the local people call it **ortiga caballana** the gist of which means '**nettle with a kick like a horse**' (Goodspeed 1961).

There appears to have been no studies of the interaction of these fascinating plants with herbivores, their general ecology, variation of stinging trichomes and the evolutionary relationships, so and interesting story is waiting to be uncovered either by field naturalists or research workers.

4 THE STINGING PLANTS OF THE HYDROPYLLACEAE.

THE HYDROPHYLLACEAE

This is a small family of about 18 genera and 250 species, annual or perennial herbs, small shrubs and trees, mainly North American but with a fairly cosmopolitan distribution. *Wigandia* contains six species of evergreen perennial shrubs and small trees that occur in woodlands and roadsides in tropical USA, Central and South America. *Wigandia caracasana / urens* are soft-stemmed evergreen sub-shrubs covered in white or yellow woolly hairs on the underneath of the

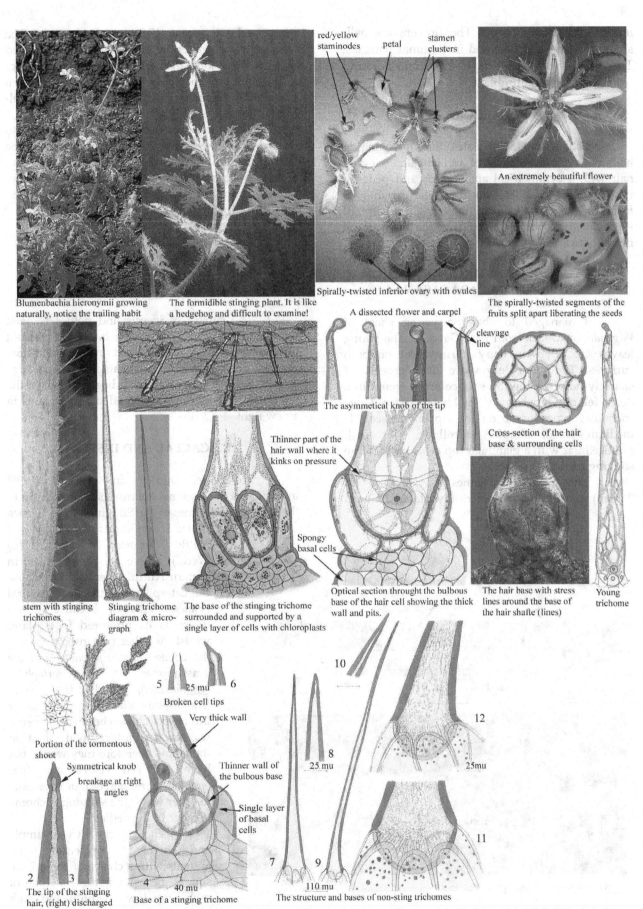

red/yellow staminodes

petal

stamen clusters

Blumenbachia hieronymii growing naturally, notice the trailing habit

The formidible stinging plant. It is like a hedgehog and difficult to examine!

A dissected flower and carpel

Spirally-twisted inferior ovary with ovules

An extremely beautiful flower

The spirally-twisted segments of the fruits split apart liberating the seeds

The asymmetical knob of the tip

cleavage line

Cross-section of the hair base & surrounding cells

Thinner part of the hair wall where it kinks on pressure

Spongy basal cells

stem with stinging trichomes

Stinging trichome diagram & micrograph

The base of the stinging trichome surrounded and supported by a single layer of cells with chloroplasts

Optical section throught the bulbous base of the hair cell showing the thick wall and pits.

The hair base with stress lines around the base of the hair shafle (lines)

Young trichome

Portion of the tormentous shoot

1

Symmetrical knob
breakage at right angles

Very thick wall

Thinner wall of the bulbous base

Single layer of basal cells

5   25 mu   6
Broken cell tips

2 3
The tip of the stinging hair, (right) discharged

4   40 mu
Base of a stinging trichome

10

7   9   8   25 mu   110 mu

12   25mu

11

The structure and bases of non-sting trichomes

FIG 8.5 THE STINGING TRICHOMES OF BLUMENBACHIA HIERONYMII AND WIGANDIA CARACASANA (1-12)

leaves and on the stems. The flowers are bell-shaped, white and lilac and in terminal panicles. The plant grows to 3-4 m (10-12 ft) and is found from Mexico to Columbia.

HISTORICAL

Schleiden (1849), states that the stinging hairs of Wigandria consist of an elongated stinging hair with a symmetrical apical knob and pedestal base. Haberlandt (1886) illustrated the variation in form of the apical tip of the stinging hairs of *Wigandia urens* but the fracture of the tip was not investigated.

STRUCTURE OF THE STINGING TRICHOME OF WIGANDIA CARACASANA

I managed to obtain a young shoot of *Wigandia caracasana* from Kew Gardens. The young leaves are intensely hairy (tormentose) on both surfaces. The older leaves are dark green and sparsely hairy on the top surface and covered in a dense felt of white hairs on the lower surface. Three trichomes types occur on the upper surface, (1) medium sized, simple, unicellular, (2) small multicellular with a glandular top cell, and (3) large stinging trichomes (Fig 8.5).

The stinging trichomes vary in size (1-2.5mm) and have a symmetrically placed bulbous

Fig 8.6 Aphids and the stinging hairs and other hairs on the surface of Loasa vulcanica

tip capped with a cone (17.5μ long X 15μ wide). The terminal knob generally breaks at the constricted point where it joins the hair shaft (Fig 8.5), however I did find broken tips where fracture had taken place along the sides of the bulb to leave a chisel-like cutting edge (Fig 8.4).

The portion of the plant was too young to test whether these hairs sting. There appears to be no information on the following: wall composition, stinging mechanism, stinging symptoms, herbivore relations and general ecology of these plants, again an area for further research.

DO STINGING TRICHOMES DETER INVERTEBRATE HERBIVORES?

(1)   INSECTS

The subject of insects and nettles is dealt with, in detail in the chapter on insects. It was not until comparatively recently that an interest in how plants defend themselves against herbivores developed, and then researchers began to look at the relationships between insects and stinging plants in a new light.

URTICACEAE AND INSECTS

Tuberville, Dudley and Pollard (1996) investigated the responses of insects and molluscs to the stinging trichomes of the Stinging Nettle (Urtica dioica L. ssp. dioica) and the Wood Nettle (*Laportea canadensis* (L) Wedd) native to moist areas in eastern North America. They chose the caterpillars of the Red Admiral (*Vanessa Atlanta*) because Urtica dioica is its preferred food plant, whilst the other two insects chosen, the beetle (*Popillia japonica*) and the grasshopper (*Chortophaga viridifasciata*), and the snail (*Anguispira alternata*). The latter three were chosen because the nettle was an unfamiliar food plant to them, and therefore they would not have evolved behaviour that enabled them to avoid, or overcome in other ways, the stinging trichome defence of the nettles.

The experiment was simple and involved presenting the animals with a choice of three 2 cm square pieces of nettle leaf (one of each with low, medium and high trichome densities) on moist filter paper in a petri dishes and then measuring the leaf areas before and after feeding.

The experimental results showed there was no significant difference in insect herbivore preference or deterrence in relation to nettle leaves with different stinging trichome densities (for the snail, see later). There was therefore no evidence for a deterrent role of stinging trichomes against insect herbivores. They concluded that small size, low body mass and rigid body exoskeleton act to prevent the body being pierced by stinging trichomes. Small insects can walk and or clamber over stinging trichomes whilst large insects such as caterpillars chew off the stinging trichomes at their base, although some whole trichomes are found in their droppings and therefore must have been ingested. Differences in trichome density are therefore unimportant to insects which feed specifically on nettles (Fig 8.6).

THE 'EVIL WOMAN': THE ULTIMATE DEFENSIVE PLANT

Dillon, Lowrie & McKey (1982) produced a fascinating paper on the ways in which the caterpillar of the hawk-moth Erinnyis ello L. (Sphingidae) has evolved a mechanism to overcome the defences of its host plant *Cnidoscolus urens* (Euphorbiaceae). Cnidoscolus urens (L. Arthur ssp. urens), roughly translated the systemic name means 'burning nettle,' however, in Costa Rica the people call it 'mala mujer' meaning the 'evil woman' probably because of its virulent stinging properties. It is an herbaceous perennial (0.5-1.25m ht.), occurs in dry open pasture with scrub vegetation where it grows in clumps that cover an area of approximately 0.75m². Large stinging trichomes (mean 6 mm) cover the leaves, stem and fruits, but in addition to these it has a sticky latex sap which flows out through any break in the epidermis and soon coagulates, and this effectively deters both piercing and chewing insects. During insect studies in the field it was noticed that the leaves of Cnidoscolus plants were being consumed by the larvae of the hawk-moth *Erinnyis ello*, and that, almost fully grown (4th instar) individuals could consume a whole plant in one day.

It is unlikely that this large caterpillar is in any danger of being stung by the stinging trichomes but they do present a mechanical barrier to its

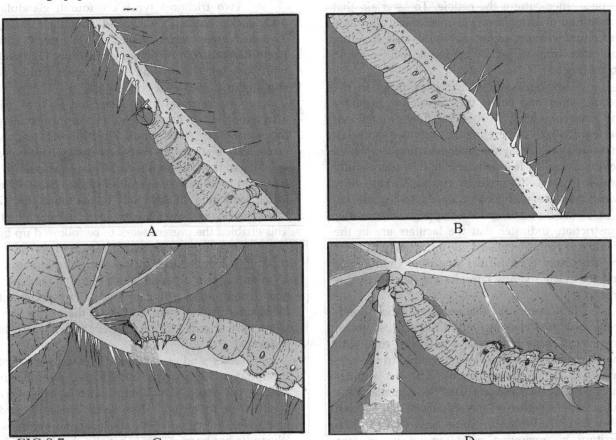

FIG 8.7
Interaction betweeen the spurge hawk-moth caterpillar and the stinging plant Cnidoscolus urens. (A) first the stinging hairs are chewed off at their bases, (B) the caterpillar moves up the petiole to near the lamina, (C) it chews off the bark (i.e. including the phloem) which stops the flow of poisonous latex, (D) it can then feed on the leaf minus its poison.

movement and in this respect, it is seen to chew these off during its progress along the petiole. A small amount of latex results from the plant injury resulting from the chewing off of stinging trichomes, so the larva stops periodically to remove this from its pro-legs and mandibles. When it reaches the base of the leaf it remains inactive for sometime and then begins chewing of scraping the petiole epidermis 1-2 cm below the blade base. It crushes the petiole around the external surface without severing the leaf from the plant and then moves onto the leaf blade where it chews off the stinging trichomes before feeding on the edge. Sometimes a small stem is constricted, in which case, it feeds off the leaves above this point. The larva must still contend with the small amount of latex in the leafbut this does not appear to influence its feeding.

To test whether constriction influences the supply of latex to the leaf, latex flow was measured by cutting the petiole 1 cm. above (distal) the constriction, and then from a second cross-section 1 cm below (proximal) the constriction. Latex flow was standardised as the number of millimetres of latex caught in a capillary tube during the first 15 seconds after cutting the petiole. To ascertain that prevention of latex flow was mechanical the same procedure was carried out, but in this case abrading the outer 1mm of petiole epidermis with a nylon string (Fig 8.7).

The results show that latex flows in the petiole above and below the constriction made by the larva completely shut off the flow of latex into the leaf (P<0.001). Therefore the authors hypothesis, that the larva's behaviour in constricting the petiole before eating the leaf, is to enable it to successfully exploit Cnidoscolus urens by cutting off latex flow which interferes with feeding, appear to be correct.

The flow rate and the stoppage of latex after constriction, indicates that the lactifers are in the vicinity of the phloem and are more likely to be of the articulated type; further studies of Cnidoscolus and the related genus Jatropha are needed in this area.

It is mentioned that very few other insects were observed feeding on Cnidoscolus urens, however, a study of these and how they cope with the latex problem would be interesting. In the area described the authors mention that the stipular thorns of acacia trees are used as domatia (little houses) by a genus of ants Pdeudomyrmex (Janzen 1966 & 1967, Willmer). These ants defend their territory by removing plant species in an area surrounding the tree base, however, they could not remove the 'evil women' and the reason for this was revealed when on closer observation, a large number of dead Pseudomyrmex larvae were found with their mandibles embedded in the latex on the stems.

A large number of dead insects including butterflies, moths and katydids (related to the grasshoppers) were recorded as caught on leaves and stems and noted as a testification to the effectiveness of the stinging trichomes in impeding potential herbivores and ovipositing female insects.

INSECTS HERBIVORES CHOOSE THE STINGING PLANT WIGANDIA URENS

Wigandia urens if a perennial shrub that usually colonises disturbed and open sites. In a study of variation in leaf trichomes and nutrients of Wigandia urens and its implications for herbivory Cano-Santana & Oyama (1992) chose an area near Mexico City. The vegetation was classified as xerophytic scrub with more than 300 plant species. Wigandia urens, as reviewed previously, is an extremely hairy plant and populations as well as individual plants show great variation in trichome density in relation to their ontogeny and other factors.

Two trichome types are found, glandular with sticky heads (0.7-1.0) and stinging (3.0-6.0). Two leaf types were categorised (1) *Smooth* with glandular hairs but no stinging trichomes (2) *Bristly* with both types of trichomes (only ones with > 40 stinging trichomes were chosen).

Grazing rates were calculated as % of leaf area removed per. day from leaves of approximately the same age. A previous Ph D thesis, on the ecological relationships between insect herbivores and Wigandia, (unpublished of Cano-Santana 1987) had been produced as a result of studies carried out in the same area. In this study it was found that 17 insect herbivores use different parts of this plant. This enabled the present work to be followed up by using plants in the same plot, as well as insect collections from chosen leaves along 6 transects of 25 m during two different seasons, and in the centre and fringe areas. In the study 14 species of herbivores insects were found, of these only two were host specific (*Sphinx lugens* and *Aconophora pallescens*).

Other studies included (1) measurement of precipitation (2) analysis of nitrogen, phosphorus and % of water, (3) chemical tests which were positive for esteroids, flavonoids, phenols and glucosides, but negative for alkaloids and saponins. Wigandia has been shown to contain the **flavonoids** 5, 4/ -dihydroxi-7, metoxiflavona and 5, 4/ - dihydroxi-6, 7-dimetoxiflavona, and **terpenoids**, farsenol quinona and wigandol (Gomez et al 1980).

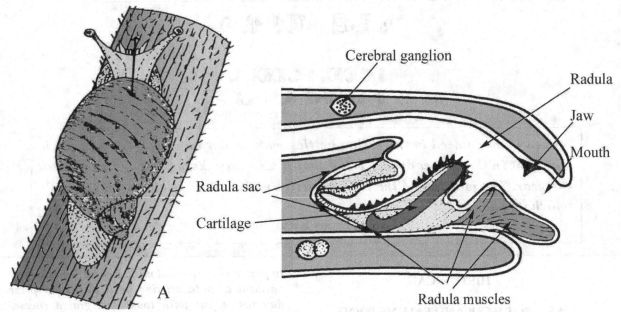

FIG 8.8 MOLLUSCS AND THE STINGING NETTLE (Urtica dioica). see text.

These chemicals are reputed to be effective against pathogens and herbivores.

Grazing rates were lower on smooth than in bristly young leaves (these contained high nitrogen, phosphorus and water levels), but the rates were similar in mature leaves. These results (1) do not fit the suggestion, that leaf pubescence may play a role in reducing insect herbivory by serving as a physical barrier or emitting toxic or repellent compounds (Levin 1973) and (2) indicate that stinging trichomes do not deter insect herbivores.

I would like to conclude this section by quoting Richard Southwood's article on "Insect Communities on Urticaceous Plants" (1986). He starts the article by arguing that in the absence of vertebrates there will be more resources available for insect communities. This could result in time (1) in the production in insect communities that are richer than on plants shared with mammals (2) that insect herbivore population levels would become higher than on those plants grazed by vertebrate herbivores.

(2) MOLLUSCS – GASTROPODS

SLUGS, SNAILS AND STINGING TRICHOMES

In a comparative study, of the palatability of the snail *Cepaea nemoralis*, to a wide range of plants (Grime, Macpherson-Stuart & Dearman 1975) it was found that there were no significant differences in relation to hairy and non-hairy plants. There was little evidence to suggest that trichomes inhibit the passage of food through the gut. It was suggested that further experiments are needed to determine why gastropods are undeterred by plant stinging trichomes. Urtica dioica was also found to be highly palatable to the slugs *Arion fasciatus* and *A. subfuscus* (Jennings & Barkham 1975). The mucous trail enables the gastropods to glide over the top of stinging hairs and the file-like radula rasps away the surface including stinging hairs.

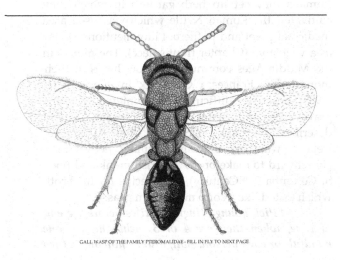

GALL WASP OF THE FAMILY PTEROMALIDAE · FILL IN FLY TO NEXT PAGE

113

"When young indeed in the spring nettles make a not unpleasant food, which many eat in the further devout belief that it will keep disease away throughout the year. The root too of the wild varieties makes more tender all meat with which it is boiled."

Gaius Plinius Secundus (AD?)

HISTORICAL

AS A POT HERB AND FAMINE FOOD

HISTORICAL

AS A POT HERB AND FAMINE FOOL

The common nettle (Urtica dioica) needs disturbed and heavily manured soil for their establishment; therefore since civilisation began they have been associated with animals and human habitations. Together with other members of the herb flora, they would have been used by man for medicinal purposes or eaten as a vegetable. In times of hardship such as occurred during glacial and interglacial periods, moraine soils were colonised by weeds, and it is likely our early ancestors would have eaten some of these as famine foods.

Nettles were undoubtedly used by the Ancients as a vegetable because they are mentioned by Dioscoroides in his Materia Medica (Gunther, 1933). After the invasion of the British Isles by the Romans they set up herb gardens in which they cultivated the Roman Nettle which was used as a medicinal plant and potherb. Pliny mentions its use as a vegetable (Chapter frontispiece). The monks in the Middle-Ages continued to grow herbs in their monasteries. Francesca Greenoak in 'Gods Acre' (1985) describes difficulties encountered in some graveyards and states that an ancient legend describes St Patrick (389-461?), the Apostle of Ireland, watching a woman pulling nettles in a churchyard to make broth. An Irish monk and poet, St Columba (6th Century) left a recipe for his broth which tasted like a soup made from peas:-

"Pick young stinging nettles before the end of June, when they are 4 or 5 inches high – one handful for each person. Boil, drain, chop and return to pan with water and milk. Reheat; sprinkle in fine oatmeal or oats, stirring until thick. For present-day tastes, eat with toast and grated cheese, or peeled soft-boiled egg" (Mabey, after Don, 1996).

They continued to be used as a potherb up to the 16th Century in Britain, after which they gradually fell out of use except with the poor and hungry and people living in country areas. Culpeper in his Herbal (1652) says "then you may know as well the reason why Nettle-tops eaten in the spring consume the phlegmatic superfluities in the body of man, that the coldness and moistures of winter hath left behind." In the 18th Century herbal gardens, such as the Chelsea Physic garden managed by Philip Miller, often included in their kalendars the gathering of nettle-tops in March for use as a potherb.

Although nettles were hawked on the streets of London in the early 18th Century their use declined in the 19th Century, except in Ireland, where no doubt, they saved many Irish lives. In the early 1840's *"The cottiers lived on potatoes, on food inadequate for cattle but good enough for man. From the substance of the potato alone was built up the stuff of human bone, muscle, sperm and milk for the young"* (Large, 1940). The Irish population had almost doubled inbetween 1800-1845 and the high rents from landlords meant a labourer had an income of about £2.18.0 *per annum*. When the Irish put all their eggs in one potato basket they did not take into account the Irish weather and Potato Murrain (now called the Potato Blight). With the failure of the potato crop in 1845-1847, after death from starvation and some emigration to America the population decreased by 2 million. Large was not quite correct in his statement above because he forgot to include the saving grace of many Irish people – the Irish weed flora. Susan Drury (in Vickery, 1984) gives a good account of the use of

'Wild Plants as Farm Food in 18th Century Scotland and Ireland'. She quotes from a pamphlet 'The Necessity of Tillage and Granaries' (1741), *"The food of the poor in the island of pasture, is buttermilk, curds, sorrel, nettles and watergrass (i.e. watercress)."* Skelton, Co., Tyrone (1778) states that hardly a family in the parish was free from disease, "in many houses, there was not one able to attend the rest, or search the fields, or ditches, for sorrel and nettles to relieve a perishing parent of child." Drury says although no written account is available for the use of nettles there can be no doubt that in times of famine, trends point to their former use as regular articles of diet. Fortunately also for the Irish was the fact that the British Rev. N.J. Berkeley and the French Dr. Montague were responsible for proving that a fungus (then called *Botrytis infestans*) was responsible for the Late Blight.

In a similar way they were eaten regularly in Scotland where in the late 18th Century the poor lived mainly on barley bread or oatmeal made into porridge with peas and potatoes. There is no doubt however that this diet was supplemented with weeds, and it is reported that in the Orkneys (1884) wild plant seeds were included in the black oats to make porridge. When the year's crop was below average special care was taken to gather the seeds of wild plants. Other wild plants used to supplement the grass. These included nettles gathered in the summer to make a broth. To make this nettle leaves were boiled with a little oatmeal and other plants, such as periwinkle and the tops of wild spinach, might also be added (Drury, in Vickery, 1984). To this can be added the usual famous quotes of Herrick (1648), Pepys (1661), Campbell and Scott early 19th Century (Chapter 5).

Nettles also came to the forefront during the 1st and 2nd World Wars when they were put to great use in Germany and to a lesser extent in Great

Fig 9.1. The Irish Potato Famine. The Irish small holder's digging for potatoes. London Illustrated News 1849

> **IRISH POTATO FAMINE**
>
> **FAMINE AND EXPORTATION**
> By John O'Hagan
>
> Take it from us, every grain,
> We were made for you to drain;
> Black starvation let us feel,
> England must not want a meal!
>
> When our rotting roots shall fail,
> When the hunger pains assail,
> Ye'll have of Irish corn your fill –
> We'll have grass and nettles still!
>
> We are poor, and ye are rich'
> Mind it not, were every ditch
> Strewn in spring with famished corpses,
> Take our oats to feed your horses!
> (3 of 14)

Britain (Chapter 10). At this time in Britain there was a resurgence of books on herbs, which encouraged their inclusion, as supplements to the diet, and some of these are considered later. During the early and mid-19th Century, Campbell accurately summed up the prejudiced attitude of the English towards nettles. This attitude worsened during the 20th century with the increasing affluence of British society; however it is also due to the conservative nature of the British, e.g. they wouldn't eat wild toadstools for fear of being poisoned by them!

Things have changed radically within recent years as most affluent societies have become obsessed with their health. There has been an explosion of literature, films, videos, TV, educational programmes, etc., on health – health foods, herbs, dieting, low-fat cookery, exercise, and alternative medicines. The nettle on occasions has received some limelight but largely because it is considered as a gimmick, something that is likely to make the headlines in newspapers, to raise eyebrows and to stimulate conversation when included in the menu at society dinners, etc. It is one of the main objectives of this book to put across a balanced view of this plant.

ON THE CONTINENT

On the Continent a similar trend to that of the British Isles seems to have taken place. Fournier says that nettles were eaten almost everywhere up to the 16th Century. Burton (1976) writes that his wife says that in Germany, at the end of the 2nd World War, when everybody was desperate for food, nettles became an important part of the family diet and that she helped her mother to gather them from the surrounding countryside. As a vegetable and medicinal plant the nettle is still consumed widely today by the people of the Northern and Eastern Anatolian Regions of Turkey (Wetherilt, 1992). In the old USSR they were regarded as edible plants and the young shoots were used to make soups, mash, and gravy and mixed with dough (Ossadcha-Janata 1952) and they are still eaten by the poorer people of the new Russia today. They are still welcomed as a spring vegetable and a tonic in Scandinavian countries at the end of their long winters. (Burton, 1976).

Andre Piedalles (1921) who wrote the book 'Wild Vegetables' declared that the young nettle shoots cooked in water made a good vegetable like spinach. He recounts that he was able to see, in a spring visit to St Petersburg in Russia, very large quantities of nettles being brought into the market place for sale as a vegetable. Even in 1948 considerable quantities arrived at the markets of numerous towns of Eastern Europe e.g. Lemberb (Fournier, 1948). In France during the summer the leaves of U. Urens generally replace those of the Common Nettle as a vegetable. Fernie (1931) says that in Italy nettles are esteemed as nourishing and medicinal and they are made into either herb soups (herb knodel) or round balls similar to our dumplings in size and consistency and high in flavour.

In Russia after perestroika and glasnost came the downfall of communism. The USSR was dissolved in 1991 and replaced by the Commonwealth of Independent States (CIS). President Yeltsin brought in his economic reforms and the following was recorded from a BBC I TV programme on Nov. 1996 – yet another example of the relationship between mankind and nettles (Box 9.1).

AS A FOOD

Generally speaking mankind, throughout history, has looked to the nettle as a food for the following reasons: (1) medicinal purposes to alleviate disease (Chapter 5), (2) as a springtime tonic and supplement to the diet through its micronutrients –vitamins and mineral salts, (3) as a survival food in times of starvation caused by war (Chapter 10), crop failure (due to adverse climate, pests, diseases, etc.), or economic crises which result in extreme poverty, (4) indirectly, as a food from domesticated animals, which have had nettles included in their diet as a fodder. For these reasons the nettle, which is generally despised, can gain respect and become a friend of mankind. Under these circumstances its ubiquitous nature is an advantage. Its long roots and extensive storage rhizome system also enable it to continue to grow and remain healthy when many crop plants, such as grasses with shallow rooting systems, have died.

Eogory Doniov said Russia faced a catastrophic decline in their armed forces' combat readiness. The Russian navy used to be one of the world's most feared fighting forces but now many sailors aren't even paid readily and have a problem feeding and housing their families. Russia's Baltic fleet faces a response to a simulated enemy attack but according to defence ministers Moscow's military machine just isn't up to the job. Mothballed Moscow's front line is now used mainly for hanging out the washing. In the port of Baltese 80 warships have been laid up for more than a year. With no fuel to go to sea they are increasingly used for homeless families of officers and ratings which the navy can no longer afford to house.

As far as the children are concerned they complain that their footballs keep going over the side and there is no other place for playing. After months of living together below deck in cramped conditions the officers and their families have been promised proper accommodation by next year but no one believes it. Disillusionment has spread from the lower ratings to the highest commanders.

Interviewed one said "I used to love the navy and doing the work, I want to serve but when I see my ship in such a dire position well what can I say. No one here has been paid since August, we feel abandoned and hardly in a mood to fight for our country and there hasn't been enough food to eat."

"We are in a three meal system, Mondays, Wednesdays and Fridays. There's always the nettle, there's plenty of them to eat." (The film shows officers/ratings cutting down nettles, placing them in a dish and washing, prior to cooking.)

"In fact eating nettles is what the pride of the Russian Navy has been reduced to. It has soured the moral of the unhappy fleet and high-lighted the military disintegration that's fast becoming Boris Yeltsin's biggest headache."

This of course immediately roused the sympathy of the British public thinking of the poor Russians being forced to eat nettles; however the fact is, the Russians are well used to eating nettles and appreciate their good nutritional and health qualities!

LITTLE, OFTEN AND ESSENTIAL

A balanced diet must contain all the essential nutrients, carbohydrates, proteins, fats, water, mineral salts, vitamins and roughage in the correct amounts for our daily requirements. The micro-nutrients cannot be stored in the body and so are needed, each day, in the order of milligrams, to replace their loss in sweat and urine. They are essential as components of important body compounds, or as parts of enzymes which speed up the reactions of the body and their absence leads to deficiency diseases. Vitamins cannot be made by animals, (except B12), and therefore they have to be obtained by eating plants.

The micro-nutrients in the fresh and dried leaves of Urtica dioica and the seeds of U. pilulifera are shown in Table 9.1 based on Wetherilt (1992). There was a substantial loss of Vitamin C and Pro-Vitamin A on drying, but the fresh material, in agreement with other published analyses, showed the fresh leaves to be one of the best natural sources of Vitamin C, K, and Pro-Vitamin A. The mineral content of the leaves was remarkably high, especially in important ones such as potassium, calcium and iron. The results clearly show the nutritional value of fresh nettle leaves as sources of important micro-nutrients.

Table 9.1 Analysis of the seeds of Urtica pilulifera, and the dried flowers and freshleaves of Urtica dioica (mg per 100g), showing their vitamin and mineral salt content (after Wetherilt 1992).

NUTRIENTS	CHEMICAL NAME	URTICA Pilulifera SEEDS	URTICA DIOICA	
			DRIED FLOWERS	FRESH LEAVES
Vitamin C	Ascorbic Acid	6.00	0.00	238.000
Pro-Vitamin A	b-Carotene	0.70	1.90	5.000
Vitamin E	a-Tocopherol	20.20	16.90	14.400
Vitamin B1	Thiamin	0.13	0.03	0.020
Vitamin B2	Riboflavin	0.22	0.76	0.230
Vitamin B3	Niacin	1.79	1.86	0.620
Vitamin B6	pyridoxine	0.15	0.10	0.070
Iron		33.00	43.00	34.500
Zinc		4.30	2.60	2.500
Copper		0.90	1.20	0.3600
Calcium		2170.00	2980.00	609.000
Phosphorus		642.00	400.00	200.000
Magnesium		352.00	325.00	256.000
Manganese		6.00	19.00	8.00
Sodium		24.00	24.00	42.500
Potassium		666.00	1490.00	1415.000
Selenium		0.08	0.002	0.007

VITAMIN E

A few results from a fairly recent analysis of the tocopherol (Vitamin E) content of 53 vegetables and fruits (Booth and Bradford 1963): the authors state that the leaves of the stinging nettle are included because they are sometimes eaten as a potherb in a similar way to spinach. The Vitamin E values varied from 240(50) in March, to 1070 (215) in June-July, to 550(105) in November. The nettle contained the highest Vitamin E content of the 53 plants tested.

BOX 9.1 VITAMIN C - SCURVY, THE SEAMANS SCURGE

In retrospect it is ironic that the main danger facing seamen on the early round-the-world-voyages resulted from the simple lack of one micronutrient in their diet and produced the disease scurvy which led to a slow painful death. Early experiments to find the cure for scurvy were carried out by James Lind in 1753, and for this, the reader is referred to an article by Hughes (1975). Lind experimented on seamen suffering from scurvy – in his own words:

"On the 20th of May, 1747, I took twelve patients in the scurvy, on board the *Salisbury* at sea. Their cases were as similar as I could have them. They all in general had putrid gums, the spots and lassitude, with weakness of the knees. They lay together in one place, being a proper apartment for the sick in the fore-hold; and had one diet common to all....."

He gave them six diets based on those currently favoured by ship surgeons and found that the diet of oranges and lemons was the best. He could have chosen the six remedies from John Wesley's Primitive physic (1754), six of which are given below:

Three spoonfuls of nettle juice daily
A cupful of goose grass juice daily
Sweetened pulped whole orange
Juice of half an orange in milk daily
Two spoonfuls of lemon juice and sugar daily
Water and garden cresses, mustard and scurvy grass.

Wesley's notes make it clear that he had already compared the virtues of some of his different remedies; he wrote in relation to the nettle-juice preparation, "tried last year, I knew many persons cured by it."

Hughes writes "The vitamin C content of Wesley's remedies is; (mg vitamin C/100g fresh material); nettles 160, goosegrass 78, water cress 60, mustard 70, lemons 45k, oranges 55." The daily quantities of nettle are advocated by Wesley would therefore have afforded adequate protection against scurvy.

Although not directly connected with the nettle, but to complete the scurvy story, I quote from the diary of Captain Cook's Journal, in his 2nd around-the-world-voyage in the *Resolution* (Beaglehole 1969). On this voyage he met up with Captain Furneaux on the *Adventure*. Cook prepared well to prevent scurvy by including in the victualling, July 1772. "But few of the anti-scorbutick articles before mentioned have been interduced into the Navy...Sour Krout, is cabbage cut small, and cured by going through a state of fermentation...it is a very wholesome food and a very great antiscorbutick, a pound is served to each man each Beef day, it is much use (d) in several parts of Germony...Saloupe and Rob Lemons and Oranges are intended for the sick and scorbutick only."May, Wed 19th, 1773, Queen Charlottes Sound, New Zealand. "Knowing that sellery and Scurvey grass and other vegetables were to be found in the Sound ...is extremely beneficial in cureing and preventing the Scurvey I went my self at daylight in the Morn.... And returned ... with a boat load." The same was collected on May 22nd. July 1773 Thurs. 29th, "20 Men Sick with the Scurvey" on the *Adventure*.

There was only one man sick from scurvy on the *Resolution* due to Cook's attention to a vegetable diet. Cook advised Furneaux "to in large their allowance of Sour Krout" ... he adds the crew of the Resolution "being more Scorbutic when they arrived in New Zealand than we were and their eating few or no Vegetables whilst they lay in Queen Charlottes Sound, partly for want of knowing the right sorts and partly because it was a New diet which alone was sufficient for Seamen to reject it."

Tahiti Aug, 1773, " The fruits we got here contributed greatly towards the recovery of the *Adventure's* Sick many of whom were so weak when we put in as not to be able to get on deck without assistance were now so far recovered as to be able to Walk..." Then Cook writes to the Admiralty Secretary he praises the Sour Krout to be used as an antiscorbutic to be included in the naval diet.

Vitamin C is associated with the formation of the body's most abundant protein collagen, which is organised into fibres of great strength. These fibres form components of bone, teeth, cartilage, tendon, ligaments and matrices of blood vessels and skin. The 3-D structure of collagen depends on the enzyme Prolyl hydroxylase and this enzyme requires Ascorbic Acid (Vitamin C) to maintain its activity. Without it collagen synthesis cannot form fibres properly and scurvy results. The consequence is skin lesions poor wound healing and fragile blood vessels.

VITAMIN A

Vitamin E is fat-soluble. It is involved in the formation of cell structures, membranes and in the construction of DNA, RNA and red blood cells. Deficiency of the vitamin causes cell abnormality and functions and the breakdown of red blood cells, leading to development of one type of anaemia. Lack of it causes muscular dystrophy in monkeys and sterility in rats.Carotene the precursor of Vitamin A is fat-soluble and also present in U. dioica in large amounts. Everybody knows that carrots are good for your eyes and they aided the night vision of fighter pilots in World War 2. This is because the orange pigment carotene they are rich in is changed into Vitamin A. by the body. Deficiency of this vitamin leads to dry scaly skin and increases the chances of infections of the body organs and nervous disorders.

Other vitamins found in U. dioica by other research workers are Vit. B5 (Pantothenic Acid), and Vit. K1. For the people of poorer countries where vitamin tablets or supplements are not available the fresh juice of nettles is an excellent vitamin source.

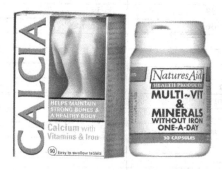

MINERALS MATTERS

BONES AND TEETH
CALCIUM, PHOSPHORUS AND MAGNESIUM

Nettles contain large amounts of the minerals calcium, phosphorus manganese and magnesium, which provide materials for the formation of bone and tooth. However, these minerals can only be absorbed from the gut, if Dietary Vitamin D, or Vitamin D formed by the skin is present. Vitamin D is the only vitamin, which can be made in the human

Dehydrocholesterol ⟶ Cholecalciferol (Vitamin D3)

This is converted into Vitamin D as follows:

Cholecalciferol ⟶ 25-hydroxycholecalciferol ⟶ 1,25-hydroxycalcierol
(Active form of Vitamin D)

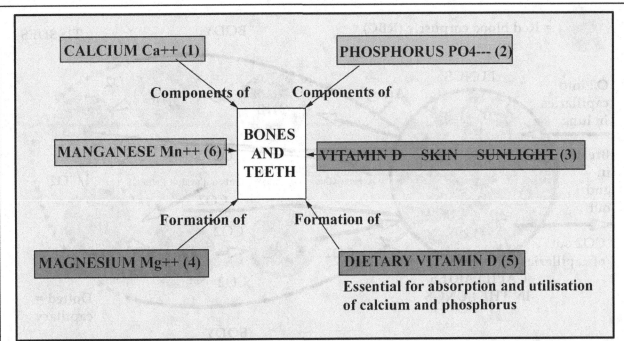

Flow diagram 9.1 to show the interaction of minerals and vitamins to enable bone and teeth formation

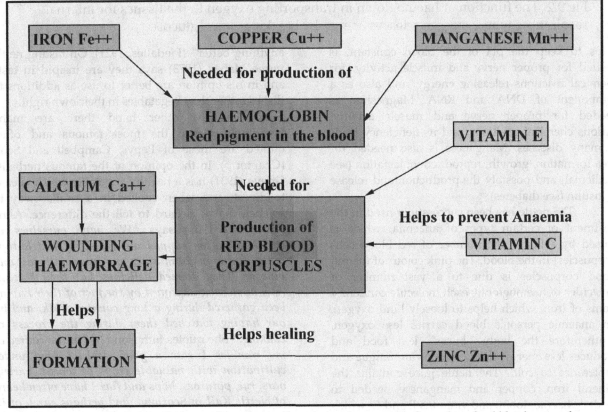

Flow diagram 9.2 to show the interaction of minerals and vitamins to enable formation of red blood corpuscles

body. When sunlight shines on the body a substance in the skin called dehydrocholsterol is eventually converted into Vitamin D, in a chain of reactions shown in the equations to the left: -

The flow diagram 9.1 pp 119 top, shows the various interactions involved in bone and tooth formation Blockage of any of the reactions (1 – 6) could lead to **rickets** which, particularly in children, results in soft distorted bone formation, tooth decay and lax muscles.Calcium is also needed for normal nerve and muscle activity and other chemical reactions taking place in cells. Phosphorus also

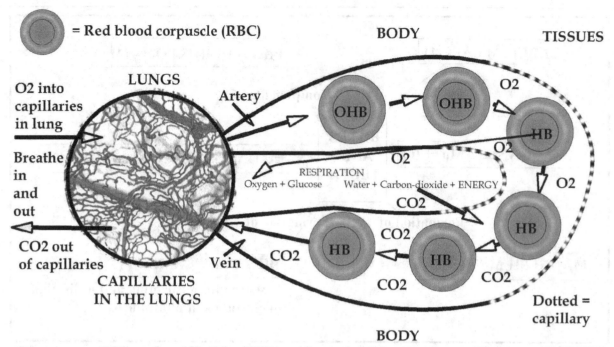

= Red blood corpuscle (RBC)

BODY   TISSUES

O2 into capillaries in lung

LUNGS

Artery

Breathe in and out

CO2 out of capillaries

CAPILLARIES IN THE LUNGS

Vein

RESPIRATION
Oxygen + Glucose   Water + Carbon-dioxide + ENERGY

Dotted = capillary

BODY

O2=oxygen, CO2=carbon-dioxide, OHB=oxyhaemoglobin, HB=haemoglobin   TISSUES

Fig 9.2 The function of haemoglobin in transporting oxygen to the tissues for internal respiration where oxygen releases energy by breaking down glucose.

helps to keep the pH of the blood constant, is needed for proper nerve and muscle activity, for chemical reactions releasing energy, and also as a component of DNA and RNA. Magnesium is needed for proper nerve and muscle activity, various chemical reactions, and its deficiency leads to many diseases. Manganese is also needed for urea formation, growth, reproduction; lactation (see medicinal) and possibly the production and release of insulin (see diabetes).

The nettle has been successfully used in the treatment of certain types of anaemia, which is caused by a fall in the number of red blood cells (corpuscles) in the blood. The pink colour of the red blood corpuscles is due to a vast number of molecules of haemoglobin; each molecule contains 4 atoms of iron, which helps to loosely bind oxygen. An anaemic person's blood carries less oxygen, andtherefore the body "burns" less food and produces less energy; the symptoms are fatigue and intolerance to cold. The nettle juice contains the mineral iron, copper and manganese needed to produce haemoglobin, and vitamins E and C, which help to prevent the breakdown of red blood corpuscle's and therefore the likelihood of developing anaemia (Flow chart 9.2 pp 119).

NUTS OVER NETTLES

"I have eaten them several times and I must state that it is an acceptable food in the absence of anything better" (Piedalles, 1921). On tasting nettle puree Mabey (1973) says they are insipid in taste and in his opinion are better to use as additions to dishes rather than vegetables in their own right.

On the other hand there are many favourable views: the most famous and often quoted are those of Pepys, Campbell and Scott (Chapter 5). In the opinion of the famous herbalist Grieve (1931) it is a healthy vegetable which is easy to digest, and when cooked in a similar way to spinach that it is hard to tell the difference. Anne Pratt (1899-1905) **says** *"We have ourselves in childhood often supped on a dish of Nettle-tops boiled for about 20 minutes and eaten with salt and vinegar. They seemed delicious but their flavour may have been improved by the fact of their having been gathered during a long country walk, and by our having watched them during the process of cooking."* She quotes Simpson (?), *"In the course of my rambles I saw a good deal of land under cultivation with valuable crops of wheat, barley, oars, rye, potatoes, hops and flax I have often heard of Nettle Kail in Scotland, and perhaps eaten of it, but never till I visited the banks of the Lena had I found nettles artificially grown as greens. At Sitka I had partaken of them dried and preserved and to my taste they were excellent vegetables."* MaryThorne Quelch (1946) describes it as a delicious vegetable and Fournier (1948) says that it must be regretted that the plant no longer appears on our tables except in exceptional circumstances. It should come in the

120

same class as spinach; for preparations of this sort however, the Small Nettle, which is less fibrous, should be chosen.

RECIPES FOR FOOD DISHES

If you have sufficient garden space, why not grow some common stinging nettle clumps which can be cut back at intervals, so that you have re-growth for yourselves as well as other wildlife. The Small Nettle can be used also.

NETTLE SOUP 1lb (448 g) nettle-tops: 6 small spring onions: 1 clove of garlic: Butter. Flour: Milk. *(After Quelch 1946)*

NETTLE QUICHE 8 oz (225 g) nettle tops:1 oz (30 g) butter:1 oz (30 g) grated Parmesan cheese:3 eggs: 8" ("20 cm) pastry case: ½ (550cc) pint milk or cream: Salt, pepper and nutmeg. *(After Streeter 1982)*.

NETTLE PORRIDGE/PUDDING Method 1 :1 gallon nettle-tops: ¼lb (110g) rice :2 large leeks/or onions :Gravy/or butter :Small cabbage/or Brussels sprouts/or 2 head broccoli.*(After Grieve 1931)*.

NETTLE PORRIDGE/PUDDING Method 2 Barley 1 handful of dandelion leaves 6 handfuls of nettle leaves Small bunch of watercress Small bunch of sorrel leaves 8 black current leaves 1 onion Butter Salt and pepper Sprig of mint and spray of thyme. *(After Hatfield 1975)*

(Urtica urens) is recommended by continental cooks and can be grown on arable ground, but since it is an annual, it will naturally re-seed itself in future years. Procure seed either from a dealer or collect from plants in the wild. Some authors say that older nettles just prior to flowering can be used but if these are used only select the topmost parts. Never use older growth because it is fibrous, full of crystalline cystoliths made of calcium carbonate/oxalate, tannins and phenolic compounds, which are designed to lessen the chances of being devoured by insects, and have the same effect no doubt, on humans. To avoid being stung wear gloves, and once cut wash thoroughly, because you will be amazed at the variety and number of small insects which feed upon it. As advised by Walter Scott you can earth-up the young shoots or on a large clump drive in a bamboo cane at each corner, cover with a black polythene sheet, and make a few holes in the top to allow some light in.

NETTLE BEER
1 peck (9 L) young nettle tops
1 oz brewers yeast
1 handful of dandelion
1 handful of coltsfoot (leaves?)
1 oz (30 g) fresh ginger
2lb (900 g) brown sugar
1 oz cream tartar (no author or date)
Method 1
With the ingredients ready plus "three gallons of boiling water, Infuse the herbs in the boiling water. And when cold, strain the liquor. In it dissolve the cream of tartar and the sugar, adding the yeast and bruised ginger. Let the whole work about twelve hours, skim the liquor carefully, and bottle in champagne bottles. Close tightly with good corks softened in boiling water, and tie the corks down. After a few days the beer is ready for use."

Method: 2 lb (900g) young cut nettles: 1 gallon (4.4 l) water: 2 lemons: 1 lb (450g) demerara sugar: 1 oz (30g) cream of tartar: 1 oz (30g) brewers yeast 2 *(After Hatfield 1975)*

NETTLE WINE: 2 (2.2 l) quart of young nettle tops: 1 gallon (4.4 l) water: 4 lb (1.8 Kg) best white sugar: 2 lemons: ½ oz (15 g) root ginger: 1 oz (30 g) brewers yeast. *(After Hatfield 1975)*

Nettle beer is reputed to be good for gouty and rheumatic pain. (See also additional food recipes used during the 1st and 2nd World Wars [Chapter 10]).

JUNKETS

Rennet can be bought from health shops and is used to make junket. It contains the enzyme rennin which is derived from the stomach of young animals such as calves, lambs and kids. The soluble protein caesinogen in the milk is changed into insoluble caesin by rennin, and this causes it to stay in the stomach longer, where the enzyme pepsin helps to break it down. The addition of rennet to milk has the same effect, causing the milk to clot or coagulate to form a solid mass (curd) to make junket, which can be flavoured with lemon, orange or coffee; once popular, it is now largely replaced by yoghurt.

Milk contains harmless bacteria which multiply under warm conditions; two of these Streptococcus lactis and Lactobacillus, produce lactic acid which causes milk to sour (In the production of yoghurt two bacteria *Lactobacillus acidophilus* and *Streptococcus thermophilus* have a similar effect). In the souring process the soluble caesinogen is converted into solid caesin which clots the milk forming a solid curd, this then absorbs the fats and sugar leaving behind liquid whey. The separated curds are compressed and left to cure, produce cheese.

Pratt (1899-1905) says, "Rennet made of a strong decoction of Nettles, of which three pints are added to a quart of salt, is often kept in bottles for use. Of this liquid about a tablespoonful is put into a large bowl of milk that readily coagulates, forming a very pleasant beverage, quite free from any flavour of the Nettle." Brenchley (1919), considering the uses of wild plants during war time, mentions the use in Picardy of fumitory (*Fumaria officinalis*), nettles and goosegrass (*Galium aparine*) to curdle milk. Grieve (1931) says a decoction formed by boiling the nettles in a strong solution of salt or the fresh juice will curdle milk, and provide the cheese maker with a good substitute for rennet. Many modern cheeses are also flavoured by adding herbs such as sage, parsley, nettles and other herbs (Caesin can now be used commercially to produce paints, glue, textile sizes and even plastics). Here again the nettle finds a use in times of economic crises, during periods of starvation and war.

FODDER AND THE NEW CROP

Man has noticed that when nettles are cut they lose their stinging properties and can then be eaten by domesticated animals. Since nettles frequently colonise grassland they can therefore be included in hay and silage as a fodder. Turner R., in his Brittish Physician (1664) says " give Hens dry Nettles cut small amongst their feed in Winter, and it will make them lay Eggs the more plentifully." Lady Wilkinson (1858) says: -

"Many animals will not eat the nettle when in a growing state; but when partially or wholly dried it forms a most valuable food in the scarce time of early spring. It is more especially adapted for cows, as it increases the quantity and improves the quality of the milk; and a pint of milk is in rural districts, an equivalent for the permission to cut the nettles in their hedgerows, rickyards, etc. In, Russia, Sweden, and Holland, it is largely cultivated for this purpose, and is mown 5 or 6 times a year. In the north of England it is boiled as a food for pigs; and every thrifty farmer's wife knows how eagerly, and with how good a result the chopped leaves are devoured by poultry. Indeed, they are almost an essential article of diet to your turkeys, although their sting is usually fatal to the tender little creatures who if not regularly supplied with them in their food seem as if by an intuitive want to wander off to the nettles beds where they perish miserably."

In France De Gubernatis (1882) says that they are also eaten by cattle, and relished by young turkey cocks when mixed with flour. Nettle seeds excite the appetite of poultry fowls, and horse dealers will sometimes add nettles to a certain quantity of oats to give horses a lively look and a shiny coat. Fournier (1948) says a happy effect of nettles is as a food in the raising of poultry, which has been known for a long time and has been explained by the discovery of sécretine by Dobreff (1924). He showed that the sécretine of nettles is counted amongst the best stimulants known of stomach, pancreatic, bile,

intestinal secretions, as well as peristaltic movements of the intestine, and therefore is important from a nutritional point of view. Grieve (1931) says that nettles dried and powdered, as well as some seed, when added to the food, help to keep poultry healthy and increase their weight and egg production. This is attributed to the sodium and calcium in the nettles, which being in the correct proportion, increases their egg laying power.

The use of the nettle as a fodder plant came into its own during the 1st and 2nd World Wars, the period 1914-1945, see (Chapter 10).

The development of intensive farming methods during the post war years has led to food-mountains and general over-production at the expense of our countryside. As a result the use of the nettle as a fodder plant is generally not needed in an age of animal feed stuffs with added minerals, vitamins, hormones, etc. However it is still used in relatively underdeveloped countries which retain the old style of farming and some recent research still continues into the nutritional value of the nettle.

Experiments involving using nettles as a fodder supplement have been carried out on rabbits. In Germany, Bruggemann (1937) found, using rabbits that results for digestibility were somewhat better with nettles than lucerne hay and much better than meadow hay; digestibility coefficients were respectively 63, 61 and 47.

In England, Wilson W. K., (1941) using rabbits found that they will not eat fresh growing nettles but mown ones dried for 3-4 weeks were eaten. 20 rabbits, 2 months old, were divided into two groups; one group was fed green food, roots, mash and hay (control), the other group the same but with nettles substituted for the hay. The experiment lasted 8 weeks, and after this time the rabbits fed nettles, were 8.7% (= 17% expressed as % growth over the controls) heavier than the control group. In those fed on nettles, the body condition was excellent (control quite good) and the coat moulty but glossy and silky textured (control, moulty and rough).

The feeding value of nettle was compared with that of crimson clover in an experiment with 2

Table 9.2a protein content of *leaf nettle whole meal* (NLWM) from nettles harvested at different times of the year, Table 9.2b nutrient content of NLWM and nettle leaf proteint concentrate (NLPC), (After Hughes, [1980]).

TABLE 9.2a

Annual pattern of protein content of whole leaf nettle meal

	Protein (%)
Jan	27.6
Feb	28.0
March	33.5
April	36.0
May	31.0
June	22.6
July	22.8
Aug	24.9
Sept	26.8
Oct	23.0
Nov	23.2
Dec	20.9

TABLE 9.2b

Composition of nettle leaf whole meal (NLWM) and nettle leaf protein concentrate (NLPC)

	NLWM	NLPC
Prox. comp. (g 100 g-1)		
Crude protein (N x 6)	29.7 2.7	53.4 1.4
Ether extract	5.6 0.6	1.8 0.35
Dietary fibre	49.4 1.3	ND
Sugars	0.5 0.01	ND
Total ash	14.8 0.2	8.0 0.4
Amino acid comp.(g 16 g-1 N)		
Aspartic acid	4.35	10.96
Threonine	2.18	4.92
Serine	1.86	4.24
Glutamic acid	5.28	11.82
Proline	1.95	6.00
Glycine	2.66	5.98
Alanine	2.69	6.95
Valine	2.91	6.75
Methionine	0.35	0
Isoleucine	1.98	5.72
Leucine	2.98	9.67
Tyrosine	1.63	3.32
Phenylalanine	2.75	6.88
Lysine	5.60	5.93
Histidine	1.18	2.62

lots of 6 cockerels each, which lasted 63 days. One lot of cockerels consumed 10.3 kg of bran, 5.4 of nettles and 9.8 kg. of corn, the total ration having a starch value of 15.72 kg, whereas the other lot consumed 10.3 kg of bran, 5.4 of crimson clover, and 9.8 kg of corn having a starch value of 14.92 kg.

The first lot made average gains in the test of 0.537 kg per head, as compared with gains of 0.499 kg for the second lot. At the start of the test the average weight of the birds in the respective lots were 0.232 and 0.25 kg. The author concludes that nettle has shown itself to be superior to crimson clover for growth and development of cockerels (Mollo, 1923).

Cappa (1965) carried out a study to find out the nutritive value of U. dioica, by feeding some broilers, (F1 hybrids, New Hampshire x Leghorn White) their usual feed of dehydrated lucerne meal, and others dehydrated nettle meal. He found that chickens fed on nettle-meal pellets became sexually mature quicker than birds fed alfalfa meal pellets.

Hughes et al (1980) says, in relation to using U. dioica as a dietary supplement in animal feed, that it has the advantages of being widespread with a prolonged growing period, easy harvesting and has a comparatively high protein content. In relation to poultry he says it is one of the few plants that grow on poultry droppings and its abundance in these areas could be coupled to it being added to poultry food.

In a series of experiments he prepared a nettle leaf protein concentrate (NLPC), which was a protein coagulate prepared by the extraction of juice from nettle leaves, and a nettle whole leaf meal (NLWM) which was basically powdered dried nettle leaves. Table 9.3a, 9.3b, show the composition of these two concentrates.

The results found that U. dioica was a good protein source, with a value of 25 % protein content for NLWM, at the height of the season. The NLPC was difficult to extract, it was high in aspartic acid and leucine, low in histidine and lacked methionine which had to be added to the diet for the growth of young rats to continue. With methionine supplementation the protein efficiency ratio (PER) exceeded that of casein.

The nettle leaf meal, which accounted for 66% of the total protein, supported the growth of

Table 9.3. Macronutrient composition of seeds (*Urtica pilulifera*), dried flowers (*Urtica dioica*) and fresh leaves *(Urtica dioica)* (%), (After Wetherilt 1992)

Nutrients	Seeds of Urtica pilulifera	Dried flower of Urtica dioica.	Fresh leaves of Urtica dioica.	Literature for leaves,(fresh weight) of Urticadioica.	
Water	8.5	11.0	76.9	76.0	(Franke et al)
Fat	25.0	12.1	6.7	5.6	(Hughes et al)
Protein	21.9	19.3	28.1	20.9-36.0	(Hughes et al)
Nitrogen-free extract	26.4	35.2	17.9	10.3	(Duke)
Fiber	11.4	16.6	23.2	39.6	(Duke)
Ash	6.8	16.8	24.1	14.8	(Hughes et al)
Ash				11.7-17.7	(Erstic-Pavlovic et)

young rats, mice and guinea pigs. When presented to young cockerels as a *sole* source of dietary protein, the nettle meal produced only half the growth rate of commercial pellets containing 13% protein (In this experiment the nettle diet was 44% starch, 5% sucrose, 5% maize oil, 33% NLWM, plus adequate minerals, vitamins and sawdust. The basic commercial meal was based on bran, grass, oats and white fish-meal). For animals fed on the nettle leaf meal diets there were significant increases in the weight of the kidneys. However the general conclusions were that nettle meal is a good source of protein and that it could be incorporated as a supplement in established animal feeds. It could also be used to advantage as a supplement vegetable to human diet in terms of vitamins, fibre and protein content. Its digestibility has yet to be characterised and further experiments are needed to ascertain any toxicity. It should be mentioned that insects grow very rapidly on different parts of the nettle!

Perhaps, Wetherilt (1992) wrote the most important article compiled on the evaluation of Urtica species as potential sources of important nutrients. He gives an excellent summary of the European literature concerning the herbal, nutritional and food uses, where most of the information concerns U. dioica. This is backed up by his experimental contribution that is an analysis, of the leaves and dried flowers of U. dioica and the seeds of U. pilulifera, as important sources of nutrients. I have already considered his results for vitamins but will present the other data here.

The macronutrient results (Table 9.3) showed, as would be expected, that the seeds of U. pilulifera were rich in fat and protein. The 'flowers' of U. dioica had more fat than the leaves because they probably contained either developing or fully formed seeds. The mineral levels were very high but this was attributed to the high silicon levels found in plants in Turkey and Yugoslavia (Erstic - Pavlovic 1985).

The amino acid composition of the proteins extracted from the seeds and dried flowers of U. pilulifera and the leaves of U. dioica was investigated (Witherilt, 1992). Although the protein content of U. pilulifera is high because of its use as an anti tumoural agent, it is sold at a high price and therefore is not a viable proposition as a protein source. U. dioica on the other hand is abundant, and with its high protein content (6.5%) should be investigated more thoroughly in relation to its use as a potential protein source. Wetherilt considers their protein quality better than all greens used as vegetables. He says the high lysine content of U. dioica protein could make it an important supplement to the Turkish diet, which is based on cereal and bread that is low in lysine.

The fatty acid composition of U. pilulifera seed compared to those of U. dioica (Lotti, et al, 1982). The main oils in both were Linoleic followed by Oleic acid. Both plants have a reasonable amount of the saturated long chain behemic acid which does not occur in quantity in common fats and oils. Oil expressed form nettle seeds yields a burning oil which has been extracted and used in Egypt in the remote past (Grieve, 1931). The seeds also contained reasonably high levels of vitamins and minerals. The inclusion of seed in nettle feed cetainly provides oil of high energy level. The problem with Urtica is that the seeds are very small and mature and fall off the plant throughout the prolonged flowering period so would be difficult to gather; however it was used by the Germans during the war periods (Chapter 10).

Hanczakowski and Szymczyk (1992) show that U. dioica has higher overall total nitrogen and amino acid concentrations than most plants but that its nutritive value and digestibility were low. Wetherilt suggests that this could be due to oxalates in the leaves which tend to bind minerals and thereby reduce their absorption by the gut wall. If nutrients could be extracted free from oxalates their processing into supplementary drugs could yield nutritional and economic benefits –such as the urtiphyllin tablets from U. dioica preparations from U. dioica in Russia.

Hanczakowski and Szymczyk (1992) investigated the nutritive value of a number of plants, including the nettle (U. dioica), in relation to their use as fodder supplements. The extracted juice was broken down (hydrolysed) with acid after which its total nitrogen and amino acid composition was analysed. To measure the nutritive value the juice was added to a diet, based on barley, and fed to rats, and their increase in weight over a period of time was measured in relation to that of controls.

The results show that although the nettle had the highest values for nitrogen and amino acid content ihad the lowest digestibility (TD). This means that there must be factors operating in the gut which are preventing the uptake of the amino acids liberated from the nettle juice. As a result its (BV) is lowered to 45 which is only slightly lower than that of Lucerne 48 which has an acceptable nutritional value. This means that the nettle could be used as a diet supplement but if its (TD) could be improved its (NV) would also benefit.

ROUGHAGE

From school biology it is known that roughage is an important component of the diet for several reasons, (1) To provide bulk which allows the gut muscles to act on the contents during peristalsis and thereby expel the faeces thus preventing constipation, (2) To lessen the chances of diverticulitis (infective pockets in the gut), cancer of the large gut (colon) and colitis (inflammation of the colon), (3) Control in the blood of sugar and fats (lipids), reduction of acids from the bile and absorption of minerals.

Juice containing proteins can be extracted from a nettle leaf. The biomass left after the nettle leaf deproteination is called the NDB and Leo et al (1993) realised that this could also be converted into an animal feed supplement. It would serve two purposes: (1) To provide a source of roughage, and, (2) if it could be partially broken down into sugars, then these would be a good energy source. They extracted from the NDB a

non-starch polysaccharide fraction (NSP) which was made up of polysaccharides, pectins, celulloses and hemicelluloses and an ethanol/alcohol insoluble residue which they called (EIR) –see Diagram X.

The results show that for the best enzyme treatment (F) there was an increase compared to the control of solubilised total sugars equal to 662.8 g kg -1 of NDB; of these, 205.1 g kg -1 were glucose. Therefore these treatments show a good improvement in NDB for ruminants' feed but also for other animal species. The results also show that NDB could be utilised as a source of simple fermentable sugars and bioenergetic production. Thus the process of utilising Urtica species for food or fodder continues. If the battle is won the increasing abundance of U. dioica could be put to good use. Perhaps the answer to the digestibility problem might lie in the study of those insects that normally feed on this species to see how they solve the digestibility problems that higher quadrupeds have to face!

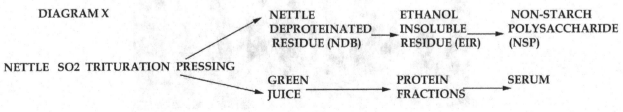

DIAGRAM X

NETTLE SO2 TRITURATION PRESSING

NETTLE DEPROTEINATED RESIDUE (NDB) → ETHANOL INSOLUBLE RESIDUE (EIR) → NON-STARCH POLYSACCHARIDE (NSP)

GREEN JUICE → PROTEIN FRACTIONS → SERUM

CHEMISTRY OF URTICA SPECIES
(1) *URTICA DIOICA*
(A) FOLIAGE

CHLOROPHYLL a   ASCORBIC ACID   ACETYLCHOLINE FORMIC ACID
CHLOROPHYLL b   PANTOTHENIC ACID   CHOLINE   ACETIC ACID
PROTOPOTPHYRIN   VITAMIN K1   HISTAMINE   BUTYRIC ACID
b-CAROTENE   METHYLHEPTANONE   5-HYDROXYTRYTAMINE   CITRIC ACID
VIOLAXANTHIN   ACETOPHENONE SEROTONIN   FUMARIC ACID
XANTOPHYLL   NICOTINE   GLYCERIC ACID
ZEAXANTHIN   THREONO-1,4-LACTONE   MALIC ACID
LUTEOXANTHIN   OXALIC ACID
CAFFEIC, p-COUMARIC
SUCCINIC ACID, THREONIN
.   *CHAURASIA (1957), KUDRITSKAYA et al (1986)*
TANNIN   *ERSTIC-PAVLOVIC et al (1985)*
NEUTRAL AND ACIDIC CARBOHYDRATE-PROTEIN POLYMER   *ANDERSON (1978)*
TRIGALACTOSYL Di-GLYCERIDE with antigenic activity   *RADUNZ et al (1976).*
KAOMPFEROL, ISORHAMNETIN, QUERCETIN and their GLYCOSIDES   *ELLNAIN-WOJTASZEK et al (1978)*
LIPASE in leaves and inflorescences   *KORCHAGINA et al (1973)*

(B) ROOTS

OLEANOL ACID   3b-SITOSTERIN and derivatives   GLUCOSIDES
SCOPOTETIN   HOMOVANILLYL ALCOHOL
SECOISOLARICIRESINOL GLUCOSIDE
NEO-OLIVIL and its derivatives and GLUCOSIDES   *CHAURASIA (1957)*
LECTIN (URTICA DIOICA AGGLUTININ)   *PEUMANS et al (1984), MOAL et al (1988)*
                                      ,BROEKART et al (1989) (Chapters).
POLYSACCHARIDE split into 35% sugars (below). 1% PROTEIN and 35% URONIC ACID.
GLUCOSE. GALACTOSE, RHAMNOSE, MANNOSE and XYLOSE   *WAGNER et al (1989)*

(C) XYLEM SAP

CYTOKININ COMPOUNDS ZEATIN
ZEATIN NUCLEOTIDE   DIHYDROZEATIN
ISOPENTANYLADENINE   ISOPENTENYLADENOSINE
ISOPENTYLANENINE NUCLEOTIDE   *FUSSEDER (1988)*

(2) *URTICA URENS*
Hairs   LEUCOTRIENES LTB4 and LTC4   *CZARNETSKI (1990)*

(3) *URTICA CANNABINA*
STACHYDRINE   *VISHNEVSKII et al (1989)*

(4) *URTICA PILULIFERA*
ALKALOID BUFOTENIN   *REGULA (1972)*

126

DENIZENS OF THE NIGHT

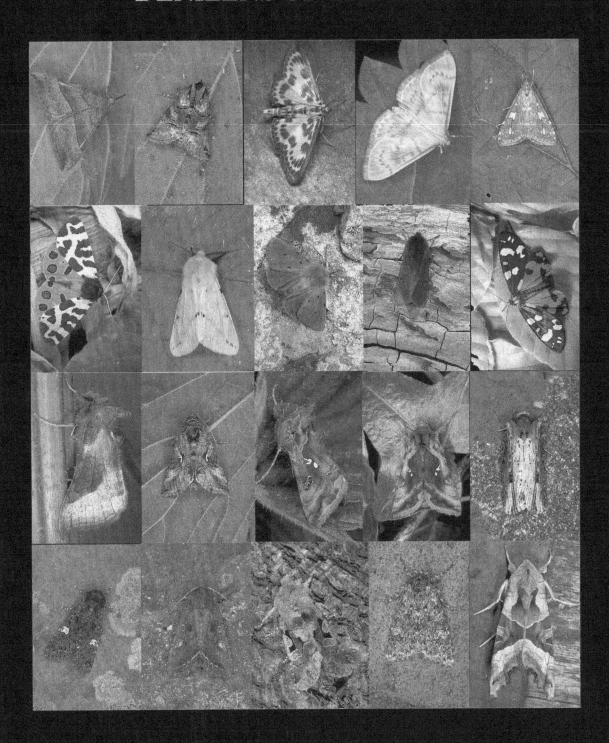

ASSOCIATED WITH URTICA DIOICA

CHAPTER 10

AS A FIBRE PLANT IN PEACE AND WAR

In her book 'Herbs and how to enjoy them' Mary Thorne Quelch says that the nettle is a valuable medicinal herb but people may be reticent to use it because of its 'unpleasant sting!' She recounts that at the beginning of War II journalists wrote an article saying that 'Hitler had advised the Germans to eat nettles' and that this advice was 'the last word in absurdity'. Miss Quelch refutes this statement and says 'it is not often praise can be awarded to the most hated person in the world' but in this case it was sound advice. She claims that many English people eat nettles and are 'all the better for it'.

Mary Thorne Quelch 1946

INTRODUCTION

Nettle fibre is often mentioned in the literature but it could be referring to fibre from a variety of genera and species within the Urticales and Urticaceae. Hemp is produced from *Cannabis sativa* (Family Cannabaceae). The nettle family (Urticaceae) contains the tribe Boehmerieae which includes Boehmeria nivea from which Ramie (China grass) is produced. Tribe Urticeae contains many genera of fibre-producing plants (Table 10.1). Fibre from Urtica dioica should be called stinging nettle fibre to distinguish it from the other types of nettle fibre each one of which should be followed by the systemic name of the plant.

Cannabis sativa, a native to India and Persia, has been grown in China for the production of hemp for 4,500 years and is one of the oldest fibre plants. In Western Europe it was cultivated principally for its seed which was used as a food. In Britain, Hemp was probably introduced at the time of the Norman Conquest but came into its own with the advent of sailing ships and the need for rope, cordage and sails. Flax was grown for the production of linen for sails, and Cannabis for the production of hemp for ropes, and Henry VIII required everyone with 20 acres (8 hectares) of land suitable for cultivation to grow one or other of them. Ray (1660) mentions Cannabis sativa in his 'flora of Cambridgeshire'. It grew particularly well on the fen soils but had to be weeded. After harvesting manually it was allowed to dry, then wetted and re-dried before it was taken in. Hemp was used for cordage, sacking and canvas. In Europe hemp is being grown again but it needs to be policed! Ray also mentions that flax (*Linum usitatissimum*) was also grown but only on loam and clay soils.

INTRODUCTION TO FIBRE EXTRACTION IN NETTLES

With the general availability of flax, hemp, ramie, cotton and wool the use of any other naturally occurring fibre would only be on a small scale and of local/domestic importance. There are records of stinging nettle fibre being made locally in Europe from the 16th to the 19th century.

HISTORICAL

The fibres found in nettles are bast fibres and they are found just outside the phloem, in the soft outer tissue of the stem called the cortex (see Fig 10.1). The cortex (bark/bast) covers the central cylinder of wood/xylem. If a stinging nettle stem is gently scraped with the edge of a blunt knife the soft tissue of the cortex is peeled away revealing the fibre layer. More scraping would remove the fibres and the cylinder of wood would remain. To remove the fibres therefore the soft tissues and the wood must be removed, whilst keeping the fibres arranged in their longitudinal bundles. There are about sixteen bundle groups in the stem of U. dioica. The individual fibre cells are from 50-75mm

Sytemic Name	Common Name	Distribution	A or P	H/S /T	Fibre Information	REF
TABLE 10.1 Fibre plants of the True Nettles, Nettle Tribe URTICEAE. (Excluding Urtica dioica and U. urens).						
Urtica holsericea		West N. America	P	H	For the manufacture of cloth.	1
Urtica Lyallii		West N. America	P	H	Indian tribes in western Washington use the fibre.	1
Urtica Thunbergiana		Japan		H	Fibre used for cordage and cloth.	1
Urtica parviflora		N. America	?	S/H	Used for thread and cloth.	,7
Urtica Cannabina		India	P	H	Various purposes. Thread and cord for fishermen.	1
Urtica platyphylla		Iran, Siberia	A	H	Ainu and Sakhalin, long used it as a source of fibre.	8
Laportea canadensis	Wood Nettle	N. America	P	H	Meskwaki Indians used it as strong twine.	,7
Girardinia bullosa	Kibanzoou	Congo, Ethiopia	P	H	For sewing.	1
Girardinia palmata *	Nilgiri Nettle	Nepal, Malaysia	P	H	For bags, sacks, fishing-nets, jackets, etc.	,4,5
Girardinia heterophylla *	Nilgiri Nettle	India	P	H	Fine thread , resembles ramie, makes a white clothe when mixed with cotton	,5
Girardinia condensata *	Nilgiri Nettle	Africa, Madagascar	P	H	Cultivated for its fibre, 'Lukaha' for twine and ropes.	,7
Dendrocnide † excelsa	Giant Nettle Tree	Australia	P	T	Bark yields fibre.	1
Dendrocnide † photiniphylla	Shining Nettle Tree	Australia	P	T	Aborigines use it for cordage, dill bags, fishing nets.	1
Dendrocnide † sinuata	Chor Putta, Surat	India, China, Mal. Arch.	P	T	Hill tribes use the fibre for fabricating coarse cloths.	5
Urera baccifera	Ortega de caballo	C & S America	P	S	Rope and twine	1
Urera oligoloba		Madagascar	P	S	Resembles ramie, used for bags and cloth.	1
These former species are now grouped as Girardinia diversifolia. † Genus was originally Laportea. A = annual, P = perennial. H = herbaceous, S = shrub, T = tree. 1 = Uphof 1968, 2 = Hutton 1923, 3 = Leach 1950, 4 = Canning & Green 1986, 5 = Royle 1855, 6 = Felix & Rabéchault 1948, 7 = Kirby 1963, 8 = Komarov 19						

in length but these cells are cemented together horizontally and vertically to make up the sixteen strands which run the length of the stem.

The soft tissue is generally removed by the process called retting. The cut stems are either left in humid conditions or submersed in water, during which time bacteria and fungi produce enzymes that dissolve the calcium pectate which cements the cells together. Retting should not be too long otherwise the fibre cells will also become separated. The long fibre bundles and the xylem will remain. To remove the wood from the fibre (scutching) the stems are dried and the wood is either removed by passing the stems through a machine which crushes them between fluted rollers, or in a machine called a decortifier (decortication) where blades rotating at high speeds do the same job but much faster and more effectively on dried nettle stems.

STRUCTURE OF THE STEM AND FIBRE EXTRACTION IN NETTLE

Fibre separation is simple with flax and hemp but more difficult with nettles such a *Boehmeria nivea* and *Urtica dioica*, because in these the fibres are contaminated with various substances such as gums and pectins and these need to removed. Several methods for de-gumming were devised and will be dealt with later.

16TH AND 17TH CENTURY SCOTLAND

In the 16th and 17th centuries nettle fibres were still used in Scotland and the historian Westmacott (---) says, "*Scotch cloth is the only housewifery of the nettle*". The famous words of the poet Campbell (1840): "*Last of all my eyes luxuriated in looking on a large bed of nettles. Oh, wretched taste,* your English prejudice perhaps will exclaim; *'Is not the nettle a weed, if possible more vile than the Scottish thistle?'* *But be not nettled my friend at my praise of this common weed. In Scotland I have eaten nettles, I have slept in nettle-sheets, and I have dined off a nettle-tablecloth. The young and tender nettle is an excellent potherb. Stalks of the old nettle are as good as flax for making cloth. I have heard my mother say, that she thought nettle-cloth more durable than any other species of linen."*

16TH AND 17TH CENTURY IN EUROPE AND RUSSIA

In former times it was used by the Germanic and Scandanavian nations before the introduction of Flax and Hemp, and in Friesland until a late period. The definitive work on the nettle as a culture plant in Denmark was written by Margrethe Hald (1942). This account is based on her work. She quotes several works written towards the end of the 18th century, including that of a clergyman of Sealand, Wedel, (1796). The latter author recommends the use of the nettle by country people and parsons and gives full details of the preparation of nettle stalks, "experience will show that the fibres of nettles are finer than those of common flax." The method given is as follows: -

"The nettles are collected at the end of August, as well as in September, according as the

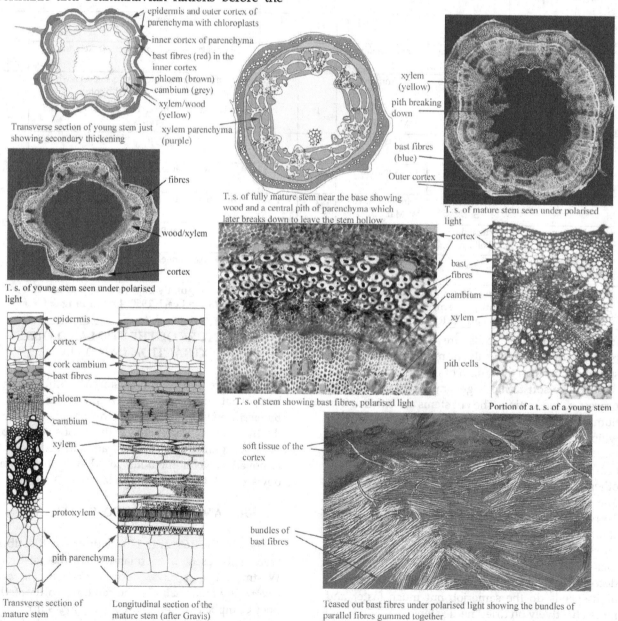

epidermis and outer cortex of parenchyma with chloroplasts

inner cortex of parenchyma

bast fibres (red) in the inner cortex

phloem (brown)

cambium (grey)

xylem/wood (yellow)

xylem parenchyma (purple)

Transverse section of young stem just showing secondary thickening

fibres

wood/xylem

cortex

T. s. of young stem seen under polarised light

epidermis

cortex

cork cambium

bast fibres

phloem

cambium

xylem

protoxylem

pith parenchyma

Transverse section of mature stem

Longitudinal section of the mature stem (after Gravis)

xylem (yellow)

pith breaking down

bast fibres (blue)

Outer cortex

T. s. of fully mature stem near the base showing wood and a central pith of parenchyma which later breaks down to leave the stem hollow

T. s. of mature stem seen under polarised light

cortex

bast fibres

cambium

xylem

pith cells

Portion of a t. s. of a young stem

T. s. of stem showing bast fibres, polarised light

soft tissue of the cortex

bundles of bast fibres

Teased out bast fibres under polarised light showing the bundles of parallel fibres gummed together

FIG 10.1 THE ANATOMY OF THE STEM OF URTICA DIOICA SHOWING THE STRUCTURE AND ARRANGEMENT OF THE BAST FIBRES

weather has been damp or dry. When you see the leaves beginning to droop and wither, the stalks turning yellow, and the seed falling out of the pods, the stalks are cut off with a sickle close to the root without damaging the root, which later on every year gives out more fresh stalks. The nettles thus gathered are now spread out in the open air, being left to dry for two days, that the leaves may easily be detached from the stalks. Then you shake them like hemp, tie them into bundles and let them lie for 6 or 7 days, more or less according to the nature of the weather, in running water."

"After this shaking they must be allowed to become fairly dry.... consists in the preparation of the long fibres, using the same implements as for hemp..... The linen made of it will bleach not only whiter but also quicker than hemp linen. A kind of very fine calico may also be made of nettle thread, the chief thing being that the fibres are properly broken so that what is most woolly can be kept by itself."

This accounts for the nettle's inclusion in the 'Fairy Tales' of Hans Christian Anderson (1835), where reference is made to its use in producing cloth, in the story of the 'Wild Swans' (see Chapter 4). Anderson may have heard of the use of nettle fibre from the pauper women's spinning rooms at Odense, or through family channels, that nettle linen was once made in the northern plains of Fyen.

THE FISHERMAN

> "Excuse me, my child, I am somewhat late.
> In the daytime I have to earn my bread.
> You know it is but thinly cut for me.
> I pluck the nettles in the ditch.
> What my wan withered fingers gather
> Will later cover snow-white bosoms.
> Alas – such are the ups and downs of life."
>
> **Oehlenschlaeger**

Wille (1786 see Hald), a Norwegian Pastor, gives the following account of the nettle:

"Urtica urens, poison-nettle, and Urtica dioica, nettle, are used by all poor people for cabbage...Wiser are they who make very tolerable linen of it, called strie; they sow a piece of useless meadow with it, enclose it, and when this field is ripe, they treat it as other flax. Since this linen is very good and strong it would be desirable that the nettle, otherwise so despised, should be used for this purpose everywhere."

That the nettle (Nosle) was cultivated in Norway is evidenced in place names Nosleland and Naadland. There is also evidence of the Common Nettle being used by the Swedes, in the late 18th century, to produce fibre, together with other plants, for spinning.

Hehn (1874 see Hald) states that Urtica dioica was used by the Russian, Bashkirs, Koibales and Sagai Tartars to weave nets and sewing threads and also for larger pieces of linen. For this purpose nettles growing in rich soil round houses were treated in the autumn like hemp, pulled, dried, and soaked. The bark (bast) can usually be treated by hand, by a kind of maceration: it is then freed from the wood, and is finally pounded in a wooden mortar. The Vogulians and Kamchatkans (end of 18th century) used linen from the nettle for their underwear.

Wedel (1796) records that a Swiss parson's wife used the Common Nettle to make linen. After drying and hackling she has treated them like cotton by carding and spinning them, to produce knitted stocking both fine and strong. She also found that nettle yarn dyes well. Haberlandt M. and A., (1928) also record that peasants of the Tyrol produced nettle linen for use as late as 1917.

18th CENTURY ENGLAND

Thomas Green in his Herbal (1820) gives an excellent account of the growth of nettles and their habitat at that time, and the extraction of the fibre, and also making paper from the lint. The detail reveals that this is a method passed down for extraction from stinging nettles and not simply based on the same techniques used for flax and hemp (see Box 10.1).

131

NETTLES AND THE FIRST WORLD WAR
1914-1918

GERMAN PRELUDE

Schiller (1915?) in an article about fibre production from the stinging nettle (Urtica dioica) refers to its use in the past and work which took place towards the end of the 19th century to try to solve the problem of the extraction of this fibre on a commercial scale.

Schiller mentions that in the 18th and 19th century in Leipsic and Picardy in France families produced handkerchiefs, and table cloths of great beauty. The main problem was to discover a method to obtain fibre by the rotting method.

In 1877 a special body, the German Committee for Commencing the Growing of Nettle and the Technical Use and Employment of Nettle Fibre, was appointed. But the reliable working and cheap means by which the fibre could be produced and compete with the other kinds, was not found even when the German Empire Government offered prizes. Bouché (Inspector of the Botanic Gardens in Berlin) proved that the nettle was capable of culture and he found that un-manured soil could support nettles for up to 10 years, without any shortage of crop. This is perhaps accounted for by the fact, discovered by Prof. Molisch of Vienna, that, the nettle plant singularly can exist on soil containing the least traces of nitrate. It loves some shade and with it yields especially where there exists a good deal of dampness, enormous crops. Wherever man congregates there the nettle flourishes as it is very fond of the urine.

BOX 10.1
EXTRACTION OF FIBRE FROM THE NETTLE
(URTICA DIOICA) BY T. GREEN (1820)

"The growth of nettles is general throughout this country particularly in strong fertile soils where on every bank ditch and place which cannot be reduced to tillage they are produced in such abundance that the quantity collected could be of great magnitude. The cultivation of them might be encouraged in such waste places or a vast quantity of land of that description might, at a moderate expense be made to produce a valuable crop of a useful article (from a plant) heretofore regarded as a nuisance. **The harl or fibre** of the plant is very similar to that of hemp or flax, inclining to either according to the soil and different situations in which it grows; and it has been shown by experiment that they may be used for the same purpose as hemp or flax, from cloth of the finest texture down to the coarsest quality, such as sail-cloth, sacking, cordage, etc.

Another use of great magnitude is the application of the fibres of nettles to the **manufacture of paper** of various qualities. The impediments to foreign commerce having depended on a supply of linen rags, and the paper manufacturing, the quality of writing and printing papers has been materially deteriorating. It is therefore on this account desirable to find some abundant substitute for hemp. For the purpose of writing and printing papers, the nettles might be gathered twice in one season; as for these purposes an extraordinary length of staple is not required and the fibre would be increased in its fineness, and in point of colour the prudent use of bleaching would render them a delicate white without injuring them.

The kind of nettle capable of being manufactured into cloth etc., it is scarcely necessary to say is that which in general is called the Stinging Nettle. The most valuable sort in regard to length, suppleness, fineness of the **lint** (fibre bundles), brittleness of the **reed** (wood), which dresses most freely, with least waste of fibre and yields the greatest produce of fine strong harl is most common in the bottom of ditches amongst briars and in shaded valleys where the soil has been a blue clay or strong loam. In such situations the plant will sometimes attain the height if 12 feet and upwards to 2 inches in circumference, in general they are 5-9 feet in height and those growing in patches on a good soil standing thick and in a favourable aspect will average about $5\frac{1}{2}$ feet will work kindly; they produce lint more coarse, harsh and thin. In every situation and different soil the most productive nettles are those which have the smoothest and most concave tubes, the largest joints, the fewest leaves and procure the least quantity of seed.

In gathering them, as they are perennial plants, they should not be pulled up by the roots, but cut down with a view to obtain a 2nd crop where the situation will allow it and to secure the propagation of them the subsequent year. The most favourable time for collecting them is from the beginning of July – the end of August, but it may be continued even to the end of October, only the last of those that remain growing till that time will be less supple and will not work so freely; and if the season happens to be unfavourable it is probable there will not be sufficient time to steep and grass them in which case they should be dried by the heat of the atmosphere or if the state of the weather would not permit that then by means of artificial heat; and when dried they should be housed or staked till the spring when they might successfully undergo the same operation of steeping as those of the first collection.

Such stems in grass fields where the grass is intended for hay should be cut when the hay is cut in order to prevent them being spoiled by the cattle when feeding; the harls of which would be fine in quality and well suited to be wrought up with the 2nd crop may be obtained after those of the first cutting where the situation will admit of their being preserved.

After the nettles are gathered they should be exposed to the atmosphere till they gain some firmness in order to prevent the skin being damaged in the operations of dressing off the leaves, the lateral branches and seeds which should be done a handfull at a time, and afterwards sorted, viz those which are long and fine by themselves, those which are both short and coarse by themselves, then made up into bundles as large as can be grasped with both hands a convenient size for putting them in water and taking them out, for this purpose a place should be previously prepared and may be either a pond or a pit free from mud or a brook or river. The bundles should then be immersed and placed aslant with the root end uppermost and to prevent their floating on the surface some weight should be laid upon them.

The time required for steeping them is 5-8 days but it is better they should remain rather too long in the water than too short a time; yet great care should be taken that they are not underdone, when the fibre approaches to a pulp and will easily separate from the reed, and the reed becomes brittle and assumes a white appearance the operation is finished. The bundles should then be taken out singly, very carefully, to avoid damage to the fibres and rinsed as they are taken out of the water to cleanse them if the filth they may have contracted; they must next be strewed very thinly upon the grass and be gently handled. When the surface has become sufficiently dry and the harl has obtained a degree of firmness they should be turned repeatedly till they are sufficiently grassed; the time required is only known by experience, so much depends upon the state of the weather during the process; when they are sufficiently done, the hard blisters and the stems become brittle they must then be taken up and made into bundles and secured from the weather. The harl is now to be separated from the reed after the manner practised on flax and hemp either manual labour or machinery now in use in those manufacturers.

The harl being separated from the reed it requires next to be beaten that it may become more ductile for the operation of dressing and which may be performed with such implements as are used in dressing flax or hemp. This operation being accomplished, the produce of the nettles is arrived at a state ready for spinning and may be spun into yarn either by hand or machinery constructed for the purpose of spinning flax of hemp, and which yarn may be successfully substituted for manufacturing every sort of cloth, cordage, etc., which is usually made from hemp or flax, and this new material is particularly calculated for making twine for fishing nets equal to the best Dutch twine imported for that purpose, the fibres of the nettles being stronger than that of flax and not so harsh as the fibres of hemp.

The most favourable condition of the lint? With a view to the **paper manufacturing** is to begin with, i.e. after it is hackled; in order that the fibres may be divested of the skins which enclose them; as when it is intended to make white paper, having gone through that process would greatly facilitate the bleaching and render it more easily disencumbered from gross particles. After the lint? is bleached it should be reduced to a proper length for the paper and then macerated in water after the manner of rags and undergo similar processes until the substitute is converted into paper which may be easily accomplished by the manufacturers and the substance of nettles made to produce substitute paper of the 1st quality."

THE FIRST WORLD WAR (1914-1918)

Many British had the impression that the use of nettle fibre by the Germans during the world wars was a panic measure organised at the last moment. The evidence from the previous section shows that this impression was just not true. The Germans were serious about producing their own 'cotton-type' fibre product of German origin, from a suitable native plant. The plant most suited for this purpose was the stinging nettle (Urtica dioica). The German Nettle Committee of 1876/1877 was worried about *the increasing levels of cotton that were being imported into Germany*. A lot of valuable work was done by this Committee and it was extended into the 20th Century to include studies on cultivation, growth and finding processes for extraction of the fibre to produce 'nettle cotton'. This long-term work programme was simply accelerated by the Great War.

EXTRACTION OF NETTLE FIBRE

Dr. Oswald Richter was Professor of Botany at the University of Agriculture in Vienna had begun his studies in 1910 to find an economic method of separating fibre from Urtica dioica. By 1915, he had succeeded into putting into action on a commercial scale a plan that was claimed would make Germany self-sufficient, in terms of fibre production, using nettle fibre almost entirely. This story must rank equal to other efforts on the German Home Front and is best told by Dr. Schiller of Vienna who gives the flavour of the German nationalism existing at that moment in time.

'The Solving of the Problem of the Sting-Nettle' (Dr. Richter)

"At the beginning of the Great War it seemed as if economic and scientific life would be completely laid idle. All forces seem to have to combine to beat the enemy and to throw him back so as to finish the war as quickly as possible. When the enemy soon realised the spiritual superiority of the Central Powers, they employed the well known means to overpower us by starving us, and cut off the necessary overseas raw products for the manufacture of war-material. Then German Science, technique and organisation stepped into battle with the same glorious success as our armies, they obtained the finest results and nullified so far all endeavours of our enemies. Just now (March) a fresh and glorious victory has been gained in the battle against the English policy of throttling which has to go to the credit of Austria, viz. the requirement of textile raw material has been assured. After years of preparatory and difficult labour an Austrian experimentalist has succeeded in the solving of the problem of the sting-nettle.

Prof. Dr. Oswald Richter has found means by which, in a simple and cheap manner the fibre of the sting-nettle can be obtained suitable for spinning, and has obtained together with F. Pick of Vienna the Austrian Patent No 687822 and the German Empire Patent No. 284704. The Hungarian and the United States Amer. Patents are expected shortly.

By the year 1900 Prof. Richter has discovered that concentrated ammonia could be used to treat plant fibres, and after a few hours or more the ammonia caused the disintegration of the weaving elements and fibre cells were obtained. The cells and their contents are unharmed by this process; the bass fibres suffer no damage or faulty change in their chemical structure and physical properties.

With ammonia therefore Prof. Richter could already years ago isolate the fibre of the sting-nettle. But this method had no practical importance. It was too dear. A cheapening of the process for winning fibre has to be thought of, for which purpose trials were made with diluted ammonia, which showed equal favourable results, even still then, when only traces of ammonia were in operation.

So it was found that water alone also fulfilled the aim, and with this the old problem of sting-nettle, on which Germany has worked so long, was solved in the imaginable simplest and cheapest way.

It is immaterial whether fresh gathered green nettle is employed to secure success, or dried nettle (nettle straw). The stems, cleaned of their leaves, need lie only for half an hour to two hours in water of usual temperature. Thereby the layer of rind swells quicker than the wood loosens and separates from the same, so that one can commence at once with the machine work. In rotation the water-treated material of the stalks goes through the skinning, breaking and combing machines, which within a few hours furnish the beautiful, long and

unusual firm fibre ready for spinning. It is of special importance, that no new machinery is necessary, but the nettle-fibre can, as is already done in Austria, without ado undergo the treatment by machines in the hemp factories used for similar processes.

In Germany numerous establishments have already spent much money, time and trouble over the separating of the nettle-fibre and always employed the same treatment as that for flax, the retting. It sometimes produces fibre, but the success was never sure, and the reasons for this singular behaviour could never be ascertained.

But the Austrian Scientist has now beside the ammoniac and the water treatment discovered a rotting process for the sting-nettle fibre production, which latter proves just as cheap as the water treatment and besides offers other advantages, which will be mentioned later.

With the flax-rotting it is well known that the separating of the fibre is obtained by the activity of bacteria (rotting bacteria). These exist also on the nettle stalks, but beside them also cellulose destroying bacteria, which destroy the substance of the fibre, the cellulose. If therefore one puts the nettle stalks into water like the flax stalks to rot, the fibre nearly always is destroyed after shorter or longer time and floats away on the water. What is the reason of this?

Prof. Richter detected high sugar-contents in the rind and it was proved that the rind of the sting nettle has on the average, contained up to 8% 'laevulose', valuable fruit sugar, this nettle therefore represents our richest sugar-yielding plant. If therefore the sting nettle is laid into water, it extracts the fruit sugar that favours the cellulose destroying bacteria so strongly, that the rotting bacteria cannot flourish, and the cellulose of the fibre is spoiled. If one leaves the rind or stalks in cold water for 12 hours and then puts them in fresh water, then the rotting bacteria reach a strong development and the separation of the fibre takes place in the desired way. With the rotting treatment O. Richter obtains the sugar as a bye product (Patent of 5 Feb. 1915).

FIBRE PROPERTIES AND SPINNING

On this fibre, obtained as just described, one now and then finds, as ascertained by microscopic observations, single cells of the structure from next to the fibre. If one desires also to eliminate this impurity, a simple means is to oil the fibre in a soap solution (0.5-2.0%) and so obtains the desired quickly.

The quality of the nettle fibre is almost the mean between linen and ramie fibre. Its thickness is 0.02-0.03 mm. The length depends upon the gathering and can be from 6-30 cm. The fibre, especially after the soap-boil, feels very soft and like silk, takes a high polish and permits all those procedures, which with linen and ramie fibre command such multitudes of effects. Its strength surpasses considerably that of linen fibre. One fibre, according to Prof. Richter's statement, carries 70 g, a threefold twisted thread did not break even with a weight of one kg. The fibre has a very small interior, the wall is thick and doubly criss-cross striped. The bleaching of the yarn or web has naturally offered no difficulty. It is of textile technical importance, that the microscopic difference between the nettle fibre and the linen fibre is an easy one.

With regard to the present conditions it is of the highest importance, that the spinning and weaving of the nettle fibre can be commenced directly with the machines already running in our textile works of by making quite insignificant and quickly executed alteration. Especially is this so, if the nettle fibre, mixed with cotton, is to be worked in the cotton mills or weaving works, or with linen fibre in addition is used in the flax mills.

The spinnings in the Austrian and Hungarian textile works produced yarns of the roughest to the finest numbers and besides rough 'plachen' - sack trousers of finest webs like linen were made. As already mentioned above, the tensile strength of the nettle fibre is much greater than that of the linen fibre and trousers made of it will even puzzle the boy most experienced in trouser tearing. In the whole of Austria-Hungary since summer 1915, the collecting of sting nettle has been going on by desire of the Minister of War, and soldiers, prisoners of war, and fugitives, and also school-children were employed in it, and the quantity brought in so far is estimated at 10, 000 metre zentners (50 Kg), of which part has been handed over to the manufacturers. At a lecture recently held at Vienna Prof. Richter drew the attention to the fact that several by-products could be obtained from the sting nettle exploitation. The treatment for fruit-sugar is already protected by patent.

NO SUCH THING AS WASTE

The waste of the stalks coming from the breaking and combing machines has been tried as fodder for cattle, which took it with an appetite creating the greatest astonishment and even preferred it to other usual feeding stuffs. From the seeds of Urtica dioica the 'nettle water' is prepared as is well known used for the damping of silk, and the 'China green' for colouring liquers. The extract of nettle seed is said to increase the laying of eggs by poultry. We therefore possess in the nettle fibre a splendid means to stretch and to increase our textile raw material, and for the nearest future need have no care about the development of the Cotton Question. Should the war last longer still, steps for the cultivation during the coming time will be taken, by which we can cover our inland requirements for textile fibre, in case of need all the more as we can obtain from Hop and in large number in quantity growing wild plants existing in Middle Europe other textile fibre of equal quality, to be treated on the Richter methods about which further reports are to be made."

FIBRE USES

An interesting article appeared in the 'U. S. Commerce Reports,' 24/4/1916, written by Consul General, A. Halstead, Vienna, and reports on a lecture given by Prof. Richter: -

"During the lecture Prof. Richter exhibited articles made from the nettle fiber. He showed the simple fiber, which had the appearance of hemp and then the thread on large spools that seemed to differ in no respect from cotton thread (=nettle thread). A ball of cotton yarn next attracted attention, and finally a pair of socks knitted from this cotton, which the Wiener Tagblatt, in its issue of March 30, says were dazzling white and fine texture. Cord looking like the ordinary coarse cord was also shown, as was 'cotton batting,' which would be useful for dressing wounds. Continuing the Tagblatt stated: -

Prof. Richter explained other attributes of the nettle textiles, mostly of a chemical nature but of great practical importance. Thus, because of its great receptivity for certain elements it is adapted for the mantles of the Welsbach lights. Furthermore, it absorbs many colors and can therefore be dyed well. Finally, it can easily be made waterproof. It need not be mentioned how significant this is just at the present time. Experiments have shown that its impermeability may become essentially greater than that of other textiles."

Grieve (1931), in her Herbal, written between the wars gives an interesting account of nettle fibre production and use during the Great War.

Cloth made from Nettle fibre was employed in many articles of army clothing, 40 Kg of fresh nettle were calculated to provide enough fibre for one shirt. In 1917 two captured German overalls marked with the dates 1915 and 1916, were woven of a mixed fibre consisting of 85% of the Stinging Nettle and 15% of Ramie fibre. The latter was used in the manufacture of gas mantles, artificial silk, and gas masks in wartime.

In German army orders dated in March, April and May of 1918 Nettle is described as the only efficient cotton substitute, and as essential to the supply of underclothing and other garments for the army. Landstrurmers, convalescent soldiers and troops in rest billets were to be employed in the work of collecting nettles in all occupied territories, together with the local population, if necessary by compulsion (Grieve 1931).

Brenchley (1919-1920) reports that, in 1916 the Central Powers had developed the industry to such an extent that nettle fibres were reported to cost 60% less than imported cotton. The War ministries were using it for the production of wagon-covers, sackings, tents, clothing material and even cloth for military underwear.

SUITABLE AREAS FOR NETTLE CULTIVATION

Three Nettle Companies were set up, (1) Nesselfaser Verwertungs Gesellschaft, The Society of Nettle Utilisation, (2) Nesselaubau Gesellschaft, The Society of Nettle Cultivation, (3) Bayerische Nesselfaser Gesellschaft, The Bavarian Nettle Fibre Society.

Nesselaubau Gesellschaft, the Society of Nettle Cultivation

The U.S. Commerce Report, 9/1/1917, G. N. Lfft Stuttgart, reports, firstly from Dr. Richter's lecture that:

"During 1915 and in the spring of 1916 experiments were made in the cultivation of the nettle in numerous districts along the Danube in Austria and Hungary, and all with splendid results. As a result of these experiments the question was taken up whether there was in Austria and Hungary a sufficient area of suitable soil which does not come into question for the cultivation of other crops. Prof. Marchet has through thorough investigation established the fact that in the Niederwald in Austria there are 10,000,000 acres, splendidly adapted to the cultivation of the nettle, and which up to the present have not been utilized for any purpose."

"According to Dr. Richter's estimates this is twice the area needed to produce sufficient nettle fiber to replace the cotton imports of both Germany and Austria-Hungary. Samples of cloth which were shown are considered by him as proof that fabrics can be produced from nettle fiber without any admixture of cotton, and that they can be used for any purpose for which pure cotton fabrics have heretofore been used."

"In 1915 1.3 million Kg of this material were collected in Germany, a quantity which increased to 2.7 million Kg in 1916 and this without any attempt at systematic cultivation. The quantity of nettles grown wild in Germany was estimated at 60,000 tons, but as time went on, it was found that self-sown nettles were insufficient in quantity for the need and that their quality could be improved by cultivation and great efforts were made to increase production. The Government therefore determined to begin the cultivation of nettles on a large scale, beginning with the autumn of 1916. A special Nettle Growers' Company was founded with a capital of nearly £1,000,000 which paid a premium of £8.2s.0d per acre for properly cultivated nettles, guaranteeing to purchase the crop and cultivating 69, 000 acres of its own and using a large number of the most modern machines for preparing the soil. An official report stated that about 2 tons of dry Nettle stalks could be grown per acre, yielding 4 cwt. of finished fibre, the total amount of yarn varying from 90-140 lbs. (Grieve 1931).

Nesselfaser Verwertungs Gesellschaft, the Society of Nettle Utilisation

The U.S. Commerce Report, 10/1/1917, H. G. Seltzer, Breslau, reports: -

"The Breslauer Zeitung, reports upon, the results of the collection of nettles, for textile purposes. "There are 1,650 tons of dried nettle stalks," it states, "in the storerooms of The Society for the Use of Nettle Fibers (Nesselfaser Verwertungs Gesellschaft) and considerable quantities are still lying in the various branch stores". Inasmuch as the society is of very recent origin and as nettles were formerly considered useless weeds, the results of the crops may be called very satisfactory."

"There are 12,000 trustees in Germany who are promoting the collection of nettles, and officials as well as the industries concerned and the daily press are interested in it. Throughout the Kingdom of Prussia the landrats in the various rural districts and the burgermeisters in the towns have established central collecting stations. Similar organizations exist in the other States of Germany, and all are doing their utmost in collecting nettles as a substitute for cotton."

The British, Board of Trade Journal and Commercial Gazette, 3/1/1918 takes a more critical look at the German claims about a textile substitute using fibre from the common nettle. The point is made that the shortage of cotton, caused by the war, has led Germany, Austria, Denmark and Switzerland to use nettle fibre as a raw material for their textile industries.

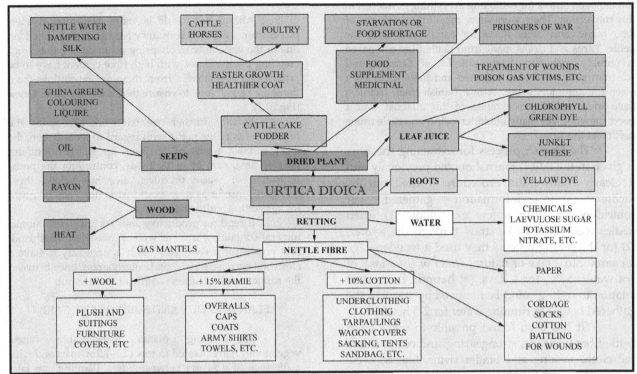

FLOW DIAGRAM 10 1 THE USE OF URTICA DIOICA FOR FIBRE AND ERSATZ MATERIAL IN WORLD WARS 1 AND 2.

"The danger of ignoring a substitute is the possibility that by scientific experiments and research it may become a serious competitor with staple industries, before the full extent of the risk has been appreciated." The new German Society of Nettle Utilisation, (Nesselfaserverwertungsgesellschaft) by order of the Bundesrat, 27/7/1916, fixed the price of stinging nettles for fibre at 14 marks per 100 kilogs and dried nettle leaves for medicine and fodder at 25 marks per 100 kilog. The yield of fibre varied from 30 % in cultivated down to 10 % in wild nettles. The War Nettle Fibre Company claims that nettle fibre when - "mixed with wool, a cloth of soft texture, hardly distinguishable from expensive woollen material, much cheaper and easily dyed, is said to be produceable, the cloth being suitable for use in the manufacture of furniture covers, plush and suitings. There is, however, no confirmation of this claim; although there is no doubt that the fibre has been used to make linings for caps, coats, etc., for sandbags and probably for Army shirts and towels."

The Society of Nettle Utilisation offered for every Kg of dried nettle stalks a bonus of one roll of half-nettle sewing thread over and above payment of the current price (Grieve 1931).

The British Board of Trade Journal quotes two adverse reports from German sources although these are not mentioned by name. A German agricultural expert states that the cost of production rules it out because of the immense amount of labour involved in ploughing and planting nettle slips when farmers should be engaged in preparing more valuable crops. It was considered however prisoners of war could help in the cultivation of waste land. The results of this authority's experiments in the use of the fibre in place of cotton were said to be poor in the extreme.

At the end of the war it was estimated that the total yield of dried fibre was between 1,000-2,000 tons, with a value of between 2-3 million marks. This was used principally in the manufacture of textiles, with 3,000 tons of leaves for food, and 3,000 tons of by-product split between paper, chemicals, lignin, chlorophyll, potassium and even gas mantels (Metcalfe 1942). See Flow Chart 10.1 for the use of nettle fibre as an 'ersatz' plant.

DANISH EXPERIMENTS ON NETTLE FIBRE AS A TEXTILE MATERIAL

The Danes, like the Germanic nations, have a fairly recent experience of producing nettle fibre, so it is not surprising that, in 1916, they decided to follow the example of Germany. I quote a piece from an article in the U.S. Commerce Reports, 9/10/1917, from E.W. Thompson, Copenhagen: -

"The Berlingske Tidende, one of the largest newspapers in Denmark, has devoted considerable space to the promotion of the gathering of nettles by country people and their delivery to the Government Committee. The newspaper gave the use of a large room in its

Copenhagen offices for exhibiting everything of interest in this connection. There were show cases full of exhibits of flax, ramie, and other fibres for comparison with the nettle. Yarns and cloths made from nettle fibre compared favourably with flax. Some samples of German and Austrian goods had been collected and these included a piece for automobile tire. A few Danish linen factories have spun and woven samples of this material, and a good showing was made of binder twine, an article much needed at this time."

The Danish process for extracting the fibre is given in the B.O.T. journal quoted previously and it clearly follows the procedure worked out by Richter, from information gathered, or coincidentally. With a few exceptions, (1) dried nettles were staked like straw through the winter, (2) for the retting process they used a wooden cage (a) sunk into a lake or natural water or (b) a tank of hot water, 30°C, for 4 days, (3) harmful bacteria in relation to retting could be removed by steeping the gathered nettles in running water for 2-5 hours.

"It has been found possible to make from nettle fibre fine rope, strong string, and coarse linen, sail cloth, sacking and binder twine. Sheets, cycle tyre covers, and fine material suitable for clothing can also be made, but have not as yet been produced in Denmark owing to lack of expensive delicate machinery."

NETTLE FIBRE STUDIES IN GERMANY LEADING UP TO THE WORLD WAR 11

At the end of the Great War the Nettle-Cultivation Company Ltd had 300 ha (740 acres) of nettles growing in fields on three estates. The programme continued until 1921 when the import of cotton was re-started. This did not mark the end of Germany's effort to produce 'nettle cotton' on a peacetime basis that work was to fall on the shoulders of a scientist, G. Bredemann, in 1919.

Bredemann explains why the effort to make Germany's own 'nettle cotton' did not continue after the WW1. During WW1 there was no time to cultivate the nettle (apart from a small piece of land owned by the Nettle Cultivation Company) so it had to be collected by volunteer groups from riversides, woods, etc., therefore the fibre was of mediocre quality. Little was known about the nutritional requirements of the nettle and the gathering in procedures. There was no time for scientific investigations. The nettle has a low fibre content; 4-5% for cultivated nettles and 3% for wild; not the quoted figures of 15-20% which are found in flax and hemp.

BOX 10.2. CULTIVATION OF THE NETTLE AS A FIBRE PLANT, BREDEMANN (1937)

Although it would be more convenient to raise plants from seed, seed constancy has not been reached yet due to the variability in offspring produced by these out-breeding plants. Plants with high fibre content have to be propagated vegetatively from rhizomes or cuttings from the same plant/clone to ensure they have the same genes. (Fig 10.2).

Equally, further research work concerning the requirements of the nettle with regard to its nutrition, the most suitable forms of fertiliser for it, the optimum harvest time, care of nettle fields, controlling the pests, utilisation of waste products, etc., has solved these questions, insofar as now exact instructions can be given for agricultural cultivation.

It requires productive soils such as loose humic, mineral-containing areas as well as low-lying marshland. It is grown for several years so it is necessary to have a clean soil because weeds, particularly grass, once between the runners and rhizomes is difficult to clean out.

PLANTING OUT AND SUBSEQUENT CARE

The young plants (presumably raised vegetatively?) are planted in rows 1.5-1.2m apart and with a distance of 0.5-0.6m between rows. Planting can take place from May-Aug. but dull, rainy humid conditions are best for rapid growth at this stage. Spring plants can result in plants large enough for appropriate yields. If stalks are not utilised they can be flattened to give the shoots winter protection. After cutting the weeds must be removed and soil loosened but care must be taken not to disturb the runners which begin to grow out about the beginning of August.

In the 2nd year the plants merge into continuous rows, and the space between them decreases, due to lateral runners which upturn to form shoots. To prevent complete merger strips between rows must be torn up with a porcupine roller. Further care is weeding, loosening the soil and the addition of fertiliser.

HARVESTING

The harvesting of stalks begins about the middle of August. All the clones grown were female or hermaphrodite so ripeness for cutting is indicated by the falling off of leaves up to the level of the inflorescences. If left for too long the upper stem produces branches.

Small crops can be cut, as deep as possible with scythes. It is important the stalks fall parallel, which can be achieved by a 2nd person bending the stalks down towards the next row. Machine lawn-mowers can be used, provided with a manual stacker and side catching device (reaper bundlers are of no use).The stalks are left for a few days, gathered into small bundles and stood in stooks for drying. They are then brought in as soon as possible to prevent spoilage of the fibre.

After cutting the nettles rapidly produce new shoots which grow sufficiently fast to provide a good fodder crop if cut in mid-Oct. They can be used fresh or as ensilage, dried and as chaff.

PESTS

These will be considered later under insects and parasites (Chapters...). They include the nettle Rust (Puccinia caricis) which does not cause a drop in yield. The weevils (Cidnorrhynchus and Ceutorrhynchus sp.) which eat the young leaves and give the plants a sieve-like appearance and are only a nuisance, if in large numbers, on young plants. They can be sprayed with lead arsenate. The male blossoms can be eaten and completely destroyed by the flower beetles (Brachypterus sp.) but this does not matter because seed is not required. The caterpillars of the Small Tortoiseshell (Aglais urticae) and Peacock (Nymphalis io) butterflies form communal nests and if allowed to spread defoliate large areas. To deal with this the shoots with webs are bent to ground level and then trampled.

Simultaneously with the agricultural and botanical research work the industrial production of fibres and their treatment has made further progress. The fibres of the nettle are in the rind, not combined to fibre strands as in flax and hemp, but lying as individual fibres in the rind, at most combined to a few, similar to ramie fibres. Their isolation, therefore, does not produce long fibre bundles comprising individual fibres as in the case of flax and hemp. But the fibre material obtained from the nettle stalks consists of individual fibres, each about 3-5 cm long, occasionally laterally joined to a few others.

The material strongly resembles cotton. Obtaining the fibres from the nettle stalks is achieved by a mechano-chemical method. The necessary machines have been constructed by the industry and function perfectly.

Spinning the pretty, firm and cotton-like fibres is carried out on the usual cotton spinning-machines, in a pure state, or as arbitrary mixture with cotton, spun rayon or other relevant fibres. So far, corresponding to the present limited amounts of nettle fibres, only small amounts of the most diverse fabrics have been produced from pure nettle – fibres and mixtures. They have met with general approval and have proved themselves very well in use.

After the work of cultivation had progressed so far, the best fibre-rich varieties of cultivated fibre-nettles were increased, in order to be able to lay out larger areas. Today we have planted 40 ha in Germany with these cultivated fibre-nettles, scattered over more than 50 places all over Germany under the most diverse conditions of soil and climate, in areas of several hectares up to about 100 square metres. This year, special trial plantings in lowland marshes have also been undertaken with the cultivated fibre-nettles that had meanwhile been recorded in the register of species at the instigation of the *Reichs*-Food Estate. There its yield in fibres compared with hemp cotonine (cottonised hemp fibre) will be tested and, at the same time, the quality of the fibres of the nettle-fibres grown in the lowland marshes compared to those grown in mineral containing soil.

All this work has been undertaken in order to create a new fibre-culture plant that will produce a natural fibre on German soil at least equal to cotton and immediately ready for spinning on cotton spinning-machines and that should make us more independent from other countries in our textile industry, not only at times in which we were placed into a position of great fibre shortage, such as during the World War, but altogether in the interest of the national economy. According to past experiences the nettle-fibre as a high-quality natural fibre besides other 'fibre additives' (in order to avoid the term "*Ersatz*"-fibre), will be able to contribute considerably to the provision of raw materials for our cotton spinning-plants. Every fibre for its special purpose! The position is that spun rayon and cottonised flax and hemp fibres, if they cannot be spun in a pure state for special purposes, require a more or less large addition of cotton for any other purposes. The nettle fibre could just possibly help to save these required quantities of cotton.

SCIENTIFIC STUDIES ON THE GROWTH AND HARVESTING OF THE NETTLE

The following account is based on Bredemann's account of 'The Nettle as a Fibre Plant' (1938) which is a summary of his work up to that time, (Box 1.2). The first task was to find out ways of changing the wild-growing plant into a cultivated plant, and it was clear that this would take time, because after a breeding experiment the plant has to grow for 4 years before the fibre content can be assessed.

The wild growing plants have an average fibre content of between 4-5%, however, male and female clones can be found with higher fibre contents and when these are crossed it was possible to get plants with 13% fibre. This fibre content is similar to that of hemp but with further crosses it should be possible to improve on this.

As a result of nettle cultivation techniques discovered by Bredemann after WW1 the yield of cultivated nettle has increased to 6,000-8,000kg of air dried stalks per hectare (247acres) which with high 13% fibre content produces 750-1,00kg/ha of fibres which is similar to that of flax and larger that that of cotton. Just after WW1 plants of fibre content 4-5% and up to 3,200kg/ha of dried stalks only gave 125-160kg/ha of fibres.

After processing the stalks 65-70% of wood is left i.e. 4,000-5,000kg/ha of wood per year. This is greater than a wood which is 2,300-3,100kg/ha wood per year. The wood is mainly used for fuel but is usable for paper, cellulose and more uses will be found no doubt.

139

Fibres

Fibres

Cutting taken from
a small stem portion

A

High fibre nettle
stem 13% fibre

Normal wild nettle
stem 4-5% fibre

B

C **D**

(A) Wild nettles generally have a small fibre content but there is much variation in this out-breeding plant. The % fibre can be estimated by looking at a section of the stem. Wild nettles with a high fibre content are selected and grown in field trials (B). The best clones are then allowed to grow into large clones the individual stems of which have the same genes (C). Stem cuttings of two internodes are taken (D).

E **F** **G** **H** **I**

(E) The cuttings are potted up and after a few weeks the stem has produced adventitious root and side shoots with leaves and is now ready to be planted out (F&G). A tractor with transplanter for a cabbage crop is used to plant the young nettles all of the same clone and genotype The field has been prepared by ploughing in farmyard dung and adding chemical fertiliser containing nitrate and phosphate (H). (I) A young nettle crop in its first year, they take two to three years for the nettle canopy to be 100%.

Stolons grow outwards
from the base of the shoot.

J **K** **L** **M** **N**

(J) The young plants (I) tend to branch out as shown here which is not wanted because fibres extraction is more difficult, however when the plants spread vegetatively by shoots coming up from stolons (K) the crop begins to close up. The stolons have to be hoed back to leave some space between the rows. (L) Pest such as the gregarious caterpillars of the Vanessid butterflies are got rid of by bending down the shoots and stamping on them. (M) The nettles spread and flower in the first year. (N) In the second year the nettles grow to form a closed canopy and shading prevents the formation of side branches, the stem grow to 2-3m in height.

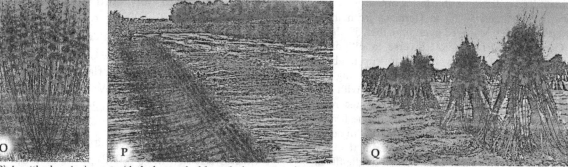

O **P** **Q**

(O) A nettle clone in August with the leaves shed from the lower stem due to mutual shading and the tops of the female shoots with fruits, at this stage the nettle is ready to harvest for the fibre. (P) First the stems are cut off at ground level and left to dry for a few days they could also be turned at this stage. (Q) Finally they are tied in bundles and stacked into stooks to dry further before being loaded for dispatch to the fibre separation plant. (N-Q) are based on Bredemann (1937).

FIG 10.2 STAGES IN THE CULTIVATION OF URTICA DIOICA AS A FIBRE PLANT IN GERMANY 1937

THE SECOND WORLD WAR (1939-1945)

ON THE GERMAN FRONT

At the beginning of the Second World War, as outlined by Bredeman (1938), the Germans had just about perfected their long term aim of converting the wild nettle into a cultivated nettle with fibre content similar to hemp, flax, etc. They had also perfected their technique of extraction of 'nettle-cotton' and had machinery adapted to spinning up the fibres. The publicity given to the use of the nettle as a fibre plant during the 1st World War was now old hat, and because of the different nature of the 2nd World War, it was probably considered as of minor importance in relation to the rapid progress of this war. Consequently I can find very little reference, in British reports, of this industry, and the only references tend to provide circumstantial evidence. No doubt the story is locked away in the German War Department Archives.

At the start of the war The German Government appealed to the general public to start collecting wild nettles (anon Jute Extracts, 1939). Despite Bredemann's work it would have taken time to plant out the cultivated strains and the question remains as to whether farmers were prepared to free good agricultural land for this process. The Daily Express, 8/6/42, reported that the nettles must still be in use with success because it was relayed from Stockholm that 5,000 railway carriage loads of stinging nettles will be collected in Hungary this summer for use as raw material for textiles. There is also the front-piece quote, in which Hitler asks the German people to eat nettles in 1946. My next-door neighbour, who spent sometime in a German concentration camp also tells me that they were frequently given food containing nettles and that one of the commonest dishes was nettle soup.

I can find very little information on the use of nettles in the 2nd World War and it seems that they did not play such a prominent role as in the Great War. This was no doubt largely due to the use of rayon, in place of nettle fibre used in the Great War, as a synthetic fibre in the German Military Uniform.

The German Army "Einheitstuch," Standard Field Cloth Gray (19/6/45), reveals that at the beginning of the war the uniform consisted of 95% wool and 5% rayon staple fibre (Zellwolle), but due to the scarcity of wool towards the end of the war the Zellwolle component rose to 65%. The process for the production of rayon in Germany was in place at the beginning of the 2nd World War. The source of the cellulose needed for rayon production could have been obtained from the straw left over from crop harvesting, but it is likely that a number of plants sources were used, including nettle stem pulp. With the blockage of cotton, no doubt the nettle was used again as an 'Ersatz' material; obvious uses would have been to produce green dye for camouflage, human food and fodder, medicines, paper manufacture, chemicals, and to a lesser degree as a fibre in conjunction with other fibres.

Bredemann/Derselbe continued his scientific research throughout the war and published papers on 'Fibre Content and Fibre Output of the Nettle Fibre Plants of Different Crops and Different Stalk Heights' (1940), 'The Growth of Nettle Fibre in Relation to the Absorption and Utilisation of Nutrient Substances' (1942). His work continued after the war and he produced a paper on 'Investigations on the Influence on the Fibre Content of the Scion of Grafting Nettles (U. dioica L) of Respectively High and Low Fibre Content" (1953). However it is a pity that he does not appear to have kept his promise of publishing a detailed summary of all of his work of the nettle as a fibre plant.

ON THE BRITISH HOME FRONT

In Britain in the interlude between the two Great Wars 90% of herbs needed for medicines were obtained from Europe and America. At the outbreak in 1939, of the Second World War, the British Isles was cut off from European and Far-Eastern Suppliers, and the Government soon realised there would be a severe shortage of vital drugs. The Ministry of Health appointed a National Herb Organiser, Dr Butcher who organised voluntary collections through Country Herb Committees as well as through the National Federation of Women's Institutes (6000 Branches), the Women's Volunteer Services, Boy Scouts and Girl Guides, and schoolchildren.

Germany during the wars had worked up her herbal and synthetic drug industries under the Bureau of Health and this also applied to France and other European countries. It is not surprising therefore, because of these facts, and the difference in living standards, that it was cheaper to import dried stinging nettles into this country from Europe just before the war, than to collect them from the British countryside! The stinging nettle is particularly rich in chlorophyll and this was used to give green colour to soap and other toilet preparations but was used to a lesser extent in medicine (Metcalfe 1942).

Over 10 tons of herbs were collected in Britain in 1941, and with the setting up of the Vegetable Drugs Committee of the Ministry of Supply in 1942, it was a record year for the Herb Industry. A national appeal was sent out for 100 tons of dried nettles for the extraction of chlorophyll for dyeing army uniforms and textiles for camouflage purposes, and as a result 90 tons were sent to manufactures. Nettles were also used as a tonic and other medicinal purposes. Considering that about 80% of the plant is water and because of its stinging properties, this nettle gathering involved a tremendous national effort (Ranson, 1949).

Roy Vickery's book on Plant Lore (1995) compiled to a large extent from the present-day British people includes many records on nettle collectors at that time, of which I quote two: -

"I well remember one hot summer being organised in parties from our school in Sussex to go out foraging for stinging nettles during World War II. We returned with massive bundles and innumerable stings, and covered the playing fields with them – cricket was abandoned for that week." After drying they were dispatched possibly to help to make green 'blanco' for the use of our forces (Hexham, Northumberland, August 1989).

"Then I was at school during the war we used to collect things - LIME flowers, stinging nettles and (DOG) ROSE hips. They used to dry the stinging nettles, laying them out on sort of big canvas sheets. I didn't like collecting stinging nettles. On the list of clothing we had to take to school were stinging nettle proof gloves – they were terribly difficult to get. (Chiswick, London, February 1991)."

BOX 10.3. ON THE BRITISH HOME FRONT (1939-1945)

FOR FOOD

The use of the nettle as a food has been considered in Chapter 6, but it should be mentioned here that in Britain and Germany many food recipes involving nettles were thought up during the war periods to improve the palatability of this nutritious and health giving plant. As a result of war-time use of herbs such as the nettle, a host of books on herbs as medicinal plants and for food recipes appeared. One such book, 'They Can't Ration These' (1940) was written by Vicomte de Maudit, the son of a valiant French General of the Great War. In the foreword, the Rt. Hon. D. Lloyd George says, "It is a valuable contribution towards our national defence. Days may lie ahead when it will be a matter of life and death to secure the maximum food supply from those things which grow in our country-side."

Maudit gives recipes for Nettle Soup, Nettle Beer, and the use of nettles in making home-made Tobacco and of Nettle Tea for rheumatism. I include the following recipes of his here: -

NETTLE CAKE

Wash the nettles and then wash in water containing a little salt, keep on the boil for 10min. Put a layer of browned bread crumbs on a greased pie dish and fill with layers of chopped meat and nettles. After cover with a layer of bacon rashers, bake in the oven for 20min. A little water in which the nettles were boiled could be added every 5min to keep the cake moistened.

PURÉE OF NETTLES

Wash nettles and 'steam them in a little cold water'. Drain and then 'rub them through a sieve'. Place them back in the saucepan, add a little butter, salt, and pepper and stir to form the puree.

NETTLE TOAST

Collect two pounds of young nettle leaves and tops. Chop up and fry in a pan of butter (1onz) with lemon juice, salt and pepper to taste. Put on top of buttered toast.

A highly amusing book on the 2nd World War is 'The Phoney War on the Home Front' (Turner, 1961) and shows the British sense of humour in times of adversity. I quote a little from the Chapter 'Who's For Nettle Toast': -

Grieve (1931) says at the beginning of the war the general public were coaxed by journalist to supplement their meals with 'unrationed, titbits as nettles, nasturtium petals, lime blossoms, dandelion leaves, seaweed and bracken' and the Sunday Times recommended 'hot pea-pod soup, potato-and–chocolate pudding, soya bean loaf, vegetable mould and nettle toast.' The last recipe was similar to that of Maudit but more luxurious with the addition of an egg and a rasher of bacon!

DYES

Grieve in 1931 recommended the use of nettles as a dye, the leaves produce a beautiful green dye much used in Russia for woolen stuffs: 'the root boiled in alum produce a yellow dye' used to dye yarn and by the 'Russian peasants to stain eggs yellow on Maundy Thursday.'

The chlorophyll extracted from the leaves can give different shades of green according to the type of mordant used; alum gives a yellow-green and iron will produce a grey-green. The nettle tops are placed in a net bag and placed in a bath together with the clean wetted wool. This is left to simmer for $\frac{1}{2}-\frac{3}{4}$ hr during which time the bag is lifted out of the bath frequently and the wool worked to keep the dyeing even. The wool in rinsed twice then dried (Robertson, 1973).

Nettle fibre on a small scale was extracted at the Royal Botanic Gardens, Kew around about 1940 and tests fully confirmed that this fibre is remarkably strong and consists of a very pure form of cellulose. The comment is made however that the availability of more familiar fibres have closed our eyes to the possibility of using this common and troublesome weed (Metcalfe, 1942).

PAPER MAKING

The nettle fibre can be used in making paper and in this connection has been used for a long time in Siberia, and a very superior nettle paper has been manufactured in Germany. In Britain it is considered to be inferior to that produced from linen, hempen or woollen rags (Pratt, 1900). In 1941 large samples of nettle fibre were prepared and examined by paper making firms in Scotland and one of these undertook to purchase 1,000 tons of nettles at £10 per ton, whilst another firm wanted to buy 200 tons for experimental purposes. Steps were also taken to cultivate several acres of nettles on land unsuitable for crops (World's Paper Review, 15/5/42). It is reported that many of these trials failed as a result of the nettle crops being eaten away by caterpillars, such as those of the Small Tortoiseshell and Peacock butterflies. The low yield of nettle fibre, 8-10% of the dry weight of the stem, meant that the wild nettles available could only satisfy a fraction of the British requirements for paper. It was thought that it would be worthwhile to produce it on a small scale, from wild nettles, for use as a good quality paper such as those used in electrical insulation. There was also the possibility of using the other parts, as in Germany, as *Ersatz* material by using the leaves as a fodder and for chlorophyll extract. The anatomical properties of nettle fibre were investigated at Kew and it has been established that rayon can be made on a laboratory scale from the wood of the stem, which is generally burnt as a waste product (Metcalfe, 1942, and Metcalfe & Chalk, 1950).

A number of top secret uses of the nettle were considered and I quote part of this interesting story as researched by Milne and Hastings, (1998).

They looked at papers between Kew Gardens and the Ministry of Supply during WWII and found that stinging nettle fibre was used to make paper and this paper was used to re-inforce plastics with a view to making it available for use as panels for planes as well as for "gear wheels and other machine parts – samples of such gear wheels were almost as strong as steel." Nettle fibre is one of the strongest natural fibres which is why it was considered together with the fact it was readily available! (see later the European Fibre Crop Project).

What comes across, when studying the use of the nettle on the British Front, is that we just did not have the know-how on growing or using the nettle as an 'Ersatz' material, such as was built up by the Germans in the Great War - it was often simpler to consider other alternatives.

Ramie fibre was available in Britain in the 2nd World War because $\frac{1}{2}$ million lb. (227,272 Kg) was used in covering hose-pipes, and later on, $1\frac{1}{2}$ million lb. (681,818 Kg) for parachute cords, and gas mantels (Kirby 1963).

THE STINGING NETTLE (*URTICA DIOICA*) AS AN INDUSTRIAL CROP PLANT

INTRODUCTIONTHE INTERACTIVE EUROPEAN NETWORK FOR INDUSTRIAL CROPS AND THEIR APPLICATIONS (IENICA)

Completed at the beginning of 2005, the IENICA project was set up in 1997 under European Commission funding. It involved the development of renewable raw materials for industrial uses (to replace non-renewable products) from crops throughout Europe. Other objectives were to enable interchange of information, to disseminate unpublished data and to assess the European Member states in relation to industrial crops. The UK coordinated IENICA and the Central Science Laboratory CSL is an Executive Agency of the UK Government Department **DEFRA** (Department for the Environment Food and Rural Affairs). 26 partners formed the IENICA network, involving the European Union Member States (Within IENICA there are about 63 partners (www.ienica.net/links) A number of IENICA partner countries (i.e. Austria, Finland, Germany, Italy and the UK) have reported fibre nettle activities; many of these are discussed here.

THE DEVELOPMENT OF THE STINGING NETTLE PROJECT GERMANY AND AUSTRIA

After the formation of The German Nettle Committee of 1876-77 a policy of using native plants to produce materials, rather than importing expensive alternatives from abroad, was introduced. This has resulted in a continuing programme to produce 'nettle cotton' from *Urtica dioica* to act as a substitute of expensive imported cotton.

NETTLE (*URTICA DIOICA*) CULTIVATION AS AN INDUSTRIAL CROP PLANT

PRINCIPLE AIMS AND FIBRE NETTLE CLONES

After the Great War the nettle programme was handed over to Mr. G. Bredemann (Institut für Angewandte Botanik der Universität Hamburg) to conduct experiments to find out the best conditions for nettle crop growth and this led to the selection and breeding of high fibre nettle clones; these studies ran from 1927-1950. Interest in the nettle as a fibre crop was rekindled at the University of Hamburg in 1992 with the study of 27 nettle fibre clones and further nettle projects

Fig 10.3 Harvest time for the nettle crop after two years growth in Austria 2002.

from 1997-2004 with a view to producing nettle cotton for the textile industry (Fig 10.5).

The main research at Hamburg University is that of J. Dreyer, G. Dreyer and F. Feldmann (1998) and the result of this work is now briefly reviewed. The economical reasons for the cultivation are (1) its low resource input in terms of fertiliser and pesticides, (2) a raw fibre as a component of compound materials, (3) use for pulp, (4) potential for cultivation on greenland areas, (5) to improve over fertilised soils, (6) to decrease soil erosion and (7) promote the diversity of local flora and fauna.

The methods are considered later but involved the cultivation of 27 of Bredemann's nettle fibre clones. After harvest the stems were separated from leaves and

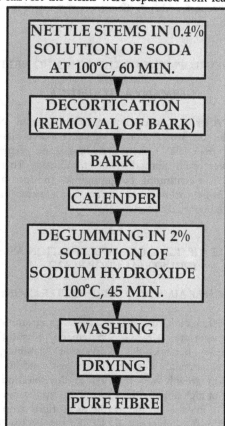

Flow diagram Fig 10.4 Chemical method for nettle fibre separation

shoots, dried at 105°C and weighed. The fibre content was calculated after fibre extraction by a chemical method (Flow diagram 10.4). Thirteen of the clones had high fibre content and of these clones 1 (fibre content 11.8% and woody core 71.5% with pure fibre 8.1-9dt/ha) and 13 (fibre content 14.1% and woody core 62.4% with pure fibre 14.3dt/ha) had the highest. The fibre is remarkable for its high tensile strength and has the potential to replace glass fibre in polymer matrix composites.

In Austria, A Hartl and C. R. Vogl working at the University of Agricultural Sciences, Vienna, carried out a study on five Bredemann nettle fibre clones (2002). However the same authors later produced the definitive summary of the nettle fibre project to date (2003) and I will therefore use this work. The authors' research had the following aims: (1) awareness of toxic residues in textiles, (2) unacceptable Third World textile production using pesticides and defoliants, (3) the increasing demand for textiles, (4) the use of plants in the home area to produce textiles, (5) 'new' fibre material to enable regional production, (6) using the nettle for a multitude of other uses, i.e. an ersatz material.

Recently finished research projects on nettle fibre carried out by partners include:

(a) cultivation methods, fibre processing, production of yarns, knitted clothes and marketing nettle clothes – **Agricultural Research Center of Finland; FinFlax; Kalajokilaakso Vocational College,**

(b) cultivation methods in organic farming testing spinning, weaving, and manufacturing clothes, **Paptex GmbH & Institute of Agrobiotechnology, Austria, Ertex GmbH, Germany, Zucchi S. p. A. Italy, Heinrich Rimml & Textilpflege Switzerland,**

(c) producing clothes from cultivation to manufacturing, **Institute of Plant Production University of Göttingen; Thurigisches Istitut fur Textil, University of Hamburg, Spremberger Tuche GmbH; Langhein-Textil GbR Germany.**

Research on the fibre content of the fibre nettle is as follows:-

(1) **Chemical processing;** (a) 1.8-12.7% fibre, 27 Bredemann fibre clones, Dreyer et al. 1996, Drey and Dreyling 1997; (b) 1.2-12.7% fibre, 6 Bredemann fibre clones, Bredemann 1959, Dreyer et al. 1996; (c) 5.5-9.0% fibre, One Bredemann clone, Bredemann 1959, Köhler et al. 1999; 7.4-14.5% fibre, 3 Bredemann clones, Bredemann 1959, Schmidtke et al. 1998.

(2) **Adapted Heyland et al. method;** 12.6-15.4% fibre, 2 clones Dornburg 1 and 5 clones, Francken-Welz et al. 1999.

(3) **Mechanical decortication opening & chemical processing** – alkali boil-off; 8.1-16.0% fibre, Hartl and Vogl 2002.

STINGING NETTLE CULTIVATION METHODS (C. R. Vogl & A. Hartl, 2003)

Soil requirements are fertile soils with a high organic content and poorly drained and acid soils should be avoided. Best in areas of high rainfall and in the first year watering may be necessary. If seeds of fibre clones are used then plant growth differed by up to four weeks and a 2% reduction of fibre content resulted. For clonal purity top shoot cuttings are grown in greenhouses and then planted out with spacing between individual plants of 75cm x 50cm and with 100-150cm between rows. They are planted out in April and May. In relation to crop rotation the best preceding crop is legumes because of their nitrogen fixation, although other crops could be root crops such as potatoes (*Solanum tuberosum*) or sugar beet (*Beta vulgaris*).

Because of the nettle's high biomass and its removal, further growth of this nitrophilous plant on organic farms is best by including under-sown legume crops such as common vetch (*Vicia sativa*) and crimson clover (*Trifolium incarnatum*) or cattle slurry or silage. Low mineral N may be added at intervals. Weed management in the first year of the fibre crop is by frequent harrowing and grass can be a problem. Narrow plant spacing promotes suppression of weeds whereas wide spacing allows inter-row cultivation.

The relationship between the dry weight and fibre nettle yields for various managements are as follows: (1) stem 4.4 – 7.3 Mg ha^{-1}, fertiliser calcium ammonium nitrate 200kg N ha^{-1} in spring and 100kg N ha^{-1} after first cutting in autumn, spacing 50cm x 50cm, **Vetter et al 1996**; (2) stem 4.88 – 11.52 Mg ha^{-1}, fibre 0.14-1.28 Mg ha^{-1}, 20 Mg ha^{-1} stable manure row spacing 100cm, **Dreyer et al 1996**; (3) stem 2.19-4.93 Mg ha^{-1}, fibre 0.30-0.60 Mg ha^{-1}, 2.86 plants per m² rows 70cm apart mechanical weed control and no mineral fertilizers, **Schmidtke et al. 1998**; (4) stem 2.66-5.52 Mg ha^{-1}, fibre 0.21-0.49 Mg ha^{-1}, 2.86 plants m² , no mineral N, **Schmidtke et al. 1998, Kohler et al. 1999**. (5) stem 1.7-4.4 Mg ha^{-1}, fibre 0.53 Mg ha^{-1} max, organic farming, rows 150cm apart, 2.86 plants m² three manuring systems (a) under-seed *Trifolium incarnatum* plus stonemeal, (b) compost, (c) cattle slurry and manure, **Lehne et al. 2001**; (6) stem 2.3-9.7 Mg ha^{-1}, fibre 0.3-1.02 Mg ha^{-1}, organic farming under-sown with *Trifolium incarnatum*, cattle slurry (150 kg N ha^{-1}), **Hartl and Vogl 2002**; (7) stem 1-10 Mg ha^{-1}, organic farming, spacing 75 x 50 cm organic fertilizers, **Ruckenbauer et al. 2002**.

There are few pest problems except the gregarious webs of butterfly larvae e. g. *Aglais urticae, Inachis io, Vanessa atlanta, Cynthia cardui*; and *Doralis urticaria*. The mildews are *Peranospora debaryi* and *Pseudoperanospora urticae*. (I have found whilst growing nettle in fields that the weevils *Cidnorhinus quadrimaculatus* and *Ceutorhynchus pollinarius* can make holes in leaves and the larvae live in the petioles and then the stem but they do not seem to affect growth. The aphid *Microlophium carnosum* specific to the nettle can decimate nettles in certain years but they do recover quite quickly).

In the second year nettles are harvested between mid-July and early August or early until late August (Fig 10.3). Alternatively they can be harvested when the seed matures on the lower nodes of the stem in female plants, or when the stem has made the equivalent of 80% of its average biomass. Machines with cutter bars which are used to harvest hemp can be adapted to do the same with nettles.

Yields depend upon the fertilizer regimes and the year of growth. Hartl and Vogl (2002) found that under extensive cultivation but without N fertilizer addition, in the second year yield was 2.3-4.7 Mg ha^{-1} and in the third year 5.6-9.7 Mg ha^{-1}. The latter increase was due to increased height and greater density due to runners/stolons. Legume crops also have a positive effect on nettle growth. The duration of a nettle crop is not really known and in the undisturbed state wild clones can live for 50 years or longer; however in cultivation four years is estimated.

STINGING NETTLE FIBRE PROCESSING

Retting by leaving cut nettles in fields where in moist dew conditions enzymes will breakdown the substances which hold the fibres together does not work for

Fig 10.5 To the right of the nettle leaf is some nettle 'cotton' fibre.

nettles because the fibres are held together with gummy substances and they are also prone to over retting. The methods in place (2002) are:

(1) **Mechanical processing methods** - however, the fibres processed by this method cannot be used for textiles but only for alternative lower value purposes;

(2) **Physico-chemical processing methods** which include (a) the cottonising method where fibre length is equalized, (b) the steam explosion method. Decorticated nettle fibres must be used in these methods but the fibres produced can be used for textiles; (3) Microbiological-enzymatic processing methods - these depend on the breakdown of the gummy substances holding the nettle fibres together but without breaking down or weakening the fibres.

The fibre content and fibre yield depend upon (1) the fibre nettle clone and this is due mainly to its genotype or to a lesser degree the environment; (2) fibre yield increases with an increase in stalk density; (3) harvesting can only be carried out once a year and is best before the side shoots appear; (4) the upper part of the stalk has the higher percentage of fibres so this part could be used for textile production whilst the lower half is used for other applications; (5) the effect of N fertilization is unknown; (6) processing methods will affect the quantity as well as the quality suitable for spinning.

STINGING NETTLE FIBRE FOR NATURAL TEXTILES (2003-4)

The Austrians (C. R. Vogl & A. Hartl, 2003) (Bredemann fibre clones) concluded that the main obstacles to the stinging nettle becoming a fibre plant are lack of suitable harvesting technology, large scale fibre processing and textile processing.

The Austrian IENICA Report (2004), discusses how after all the hard work of Professor Peter Ruckenbauer (University of Life Science and Natural Resources, Austria), (Austrian clones), in relation to making the stinging nettle a fibre plant, they have had to pull out of the fibre programme due to lack of financial support, despite the fact that there is a great demand from the Italian textile industry for nettle fibre but no raw material for the spinning industry is available at present. In the German IENICA Report (2003), they report that three hectares were under stinging nettle fibre crop, which produced 3.3 fibre tonnes, with a fibre yield of 1.12 tonnes per hectare; straw yield was 6.53 tonnes per

geotextiles, fibre-reinforced concrete, fibre-reinforced polymers, paper production and energy use.

Professor Ray Harwood and his wife Jane, based at the De Montfort University, Leicestershire coordinate the UK research programme STING. 'Sustainable Technology In Nettle Growing', STING is a LINK project sponsored by Defra through the Sustainable Technologies Initiative and carried out by De Montfort Univeristy, along with CSL and a number of other partners. It is investigating the usefulness of nettle fibre and its potential in the textile market and as a UK crop. STING has its first public presentation at the 2004 Royal Agricultural Showground at Stonleigh, Warwickshire. As part of a 'natura fibre' fashion show organized by CSL, De Montfort textile design student Alex Dear modeled a bikini she designed, made from stinging nettle fabric she produced for her final year project. Alex modeled har pink camisole top and nettle knickers and appeared in most newpapers in the UK (Fig 10.7).

In 2004 the Italian fashion house and textile company, Corpo Novo, Grade Zero Espace, completed a fashion line from stinging nettle fibre obtained from nettle crops grown in the Rhine Valley, Germany. The garments were exhibited in various venues including the Eden Project (www.edenproject.com) and the Science Museum London and were included on the National 'Be Nice to Nettles Week', UK, May 2004 (www.nettles.org.uk). The

Fig 10.6 Dan with stinging nettle top and right a young lady with stinging nettle jeans displayed at the Eden project, UK. From the Italian fashion house and textile company, Corpo Novo, Grade Zero Espace, 2004.

hectare. In the Italian IENICA Report (2003), it is mentioned that there have been some experiments on development of the stinging nettle. The Finnish IENICA Report (2003), reports that the stinging nettle is a potential long fibre crop in Finland and is estimated to increase in the next few years. At present the crop was 0.01 hectare with a yield of 2-4 tonnes/ha with 20-40 tonnes for domestic production. In the UK IENICA Executive Summary Report for the European Union 2004, the stinging nettle is mentioned as being grown on ADAS sites in southern England (1995-97) with a programme in place to determine its technical and economic viability as feedstocks for forest products and textile industries (see Plants For a Future www.scs.leeds.ac.uk/pfaf/) The programme includes establishment costs, prevention of high weed content of the crop, harvesting systems, retting and decortication, storage and drying systems and costs; to establish whether this long fibre stinging nettle crop could become competitive with wool and cotton. The programme is guaranteed support over the next 20-25 years. Statfold Seed Oil Developments include the stinging nettle in their list of 59 cold-pressed products. Industrial uses for fibre include insulation material ropes,

stinging nettle garments were shown on the website www.nf-2000.org/) (Fig 10.6). Lochcarron kilt makers from Galashiels, the World's largest manufacturers of authentic tartans, produced a stinging nettle kilt for the nation's 'Be Nice to Nettles Week'.

MULTIPLE PURPOSE USES OF THE STINGING NETTLE

AS A NETTLE FIBRE CROP OR A NON-FIBRE STINGING NETTLE CROP

The experimental work of Friederike Weiß on the "Effects of varied nitrogen fertilizer applications and cutting treatments on the development and yield components of cultivated stinging nettles" (1993), was aimed at the use of *Urtica dioica* as a herbal medicinal plant and animal fodder supplement. To gather wild nettle is time consuming and they are likely to contain pesticides and high nitrate levels due to fertilizer run off (Franz 1982, Rosnitschek-Schimmel 1985, Teckelmann 1987 and Pank 1991). In this study to grow a stinging nettle crop wild-grown nettle rhizomes were used and these took a year to establish. Different quantities of nitrate application up to 440 kg N/ha resulted in an increase in growth (dry wt.) but even so the optimal growth was not reached in this nitrophilous plant. The nitrate stored in the plant tissue was related to the nitrate applications, with the stem containing higher amounts than the leaves. Over a two-year period four harvests were achieved but growth fell off sharply for the last two harvests and this was more marked in the second year (mean growth per harvest, 1990 [185. g/m²] and 1991 [181 g/m²]). The experiment showed the remarkable re-growth capability of the nettle. Disadvantages are the high cost of nitrate application, high nitrate content of nettle tissue and it is questionable whether four harvests could be maintained without severely depleting the underground rhizome system, since periodic cutting of nettles is generally a method of eradicating nettles! Two harvests with lower nitrate or organic slurry application would probably be better. The fibre nettle crop could also be used for other purposes by using the first year crop; however, fewer nutrients would be stored in the rhizome

Fig 10.7 Alex Dear shown above modelling her camisole top and nettle knickers made from German stinging nettle fibre.

system for next year's growth.

The potential uses of nettles are found in this book (Chapters 5, 9 & 10). However for more modern herbal uses (see up-to-date papers on www.rain-tree.com, www.healthy.net, and www.ahealthyme.com and the

medicinal herbal use of the nettle (*Urtica*) in a monograph, Patten G., 1993) and industrial uses are included here. It is likely these markets will expand once the nettle is grown as crop and non-crop plant. Some uses are: -

Roots: used to make yellow dyes (pp. 142), and in conjunction with other plants in the treatment of benign prostatic hyperplasia. Recent studies show it inhibits the growth of prostate cells by 30% and is even more effective when combined with *Pygeum* (pp. 62-63).

Leaves; (1) **Human food supplements** - because it is rich in vitamins (vitamins, E, C and A, pp. 116-18) and minerals (Calcium, Phosphorus, Magnesium and Iron pp. 118-20) for blood to prevent anemia and to promote bone growth, etc, it is used as a tonic in tablet form or nettle tea (pp.116-120). It can be used in soups, quiches, porridge, puddings and to make junkets, (pp. 120-121), also nettle cake, nettle purée, nettle toast (pp. 142) and there are many modern recipes with the inclusion of nettles in cheeses, breads, sausages tarts, ice creams, biscuits etc (see France's Friends of the Nettle Association and annual festival the Orties Folies www.franceguide.com for example). (2) **Herbal medicine, leaves roots and seeds** - consumers and practitioners are using nettle products for their herbal/medicinal properties, for rheumatism and arthritis where it can be taken internally where it interrupts the production and action of inflammatory-producing immune cells in the body or applied to joints directly (Schulze-Tanzil G. et al, 2002, Broer J., Behnke B. 2002). As a hemostatic to stop nose bleeding and internal haemorrhaging from internal organs including excessive menstruation, and in this connection helping women in their peri-menopausal and menopausal age as a herbal use rather than standard hormone replacement therapy (Stella M, Dantas MD, 1999); (pp 57-8). As a diuretic and hypertensive, e.g. in rats it caused an increase of diuresis, lowered the blood pressure and reduced the heart rate, (pp.59-60), (Abdelhafid Tahri, et al., 2000, H. Jouad, et al., 2001), anti-septic, anti-oxidant anti-ulcer and anti-inflammatory properties (İlhami Gülçin[a], et al., 2003), (pp, 57,62), anti-diabetic (R. Petlevski, et al., 2001), for treatment of allergic rhinitis, hay fever, hair loss, gout, dropsy, and weight loss, etc., (see also the EU Traditional Herbal Medicine Guideline (Gaizia, 2003). (3) **As a supplement in animal fodder** for feeding to poultry, cattle, horses and pigs, dried, milled or as silage (pp. 122-26). It is rich in chlorophyll used to make a green dye (pp. 141-42). (4) **Other uses - paper** production from the wood and oil from the seeds for repellent and water-proofing (25-33% oil), see also (pp. 137, 143), **horticultural** uses as a fertilizer and insecticide and fungicide (pp. 158-60, 212-13), **culinary** e.g. hair shampoo.

"It was suggested in 2000 that the stinging nettle is one of the most undervalued of economic plants with potential applications in a wide range of uses. If technical problems are solved the nettle has greatest potential for long fibre pulping and textile markets".

Top left Puccinia carcina (nettle/sedge rust) on petiole of nettle, Top right Micro-fungus Dasycyphus sulphureus on nettle
Bot. left Cuscuta Europaea , flowers/fruits on a nettle stem   Bot. right haustoria of Cuscuta Europaea into the nettle stem

148

The river Avon, Wiltshire showing a patch of nettle dodder parasitising the nettles on the river bank.

Nettle dodder on nettles in the shade of a willow growing on the edge of the river bank.

The twining stems of the nettle dodder spreading out over a nettle clone from the dead stems of last years infection.

Nettle dodder showing the abundant cluster of flowers and fruits attached to the spiraling stems around the nettle.

A nettle patch attacked by the nettle dodder is putting up re-growth shoots around the edge of the infected area.

Close-up of the masses of dodder stems that twine around one another and must lead to much wastage of resources; they even send haustoria into one another.

Nettle dodder at different stages of development with masses of flowers and fruit masses but notice the bright green nettle foliage which indicates that they don't appear to be too adversely affected by this parasite.

Young nettle shoots growing up amongst last year's dead nettle shoots still covered in fruits masses. The large size of nettle clones and underground storage still enables them to send up new healthy shoots the following year.

The masses of fruits and flowers on the small area of nettle dodder stems shows the characteristic high reproductive capacity of parasites in general and essential for their survival. The seeds are also relatively large for seedling establishment.

The twisting nutating nettle dodder shoots emerging above the healthy nettle shoots of a nettle clone growing along the top of the bank bordering the river Avon, Somerset, Wiltshire. With its cousin the twining greater bindweed.

FIG 11.1 THE HABITAT AND GROWTH OF THE GREAT DODDER (CUSCUTA EUROPAEA) ON URTICA DIOICA

149

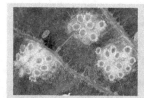

CHAPTER 11

PARASITES AND SAPROPHYTES
NETTLE DODDER, RUST
AND MICRO-FUNGI

"Round sire and sons the scaly monster roll'd,
Ring above ring, in many tangled fold,
Close and more close their writhing limbs surround,
And fix with foaming teeth the envenom'd wound."
Erasmius Darwin 1825

PARASITIC FLOWERING PLANTS

All parasitic flowering plants share one feature in common and that is the *haustorium*. This is a specialised structure that grows out from the body (root or stem) of the parasite and penetrates the tissues to make contact with the host's vascular bundles: the xylem supplies the parasite with water and minerals and the phloem with food substances. The haustorium is therefore a bridge along which flow nutrients from the host to the parasite, and it is possible that it could have originated from a root structure. In this case the plant is feeding in a similar way to most animals, taking in ready - made food, and is therefore a heterotroph. Some parasitic plants lose all of their chlorophyll to become holoparasites whilst others retain some chlorophyll and are called hemiparasites. In the British Isles everybody is familiar, at Christmas time, with the pale green sprigs of Mistletoe (a hemi-parasite), and those visiting the coast may have seen the masses of yellow or pink threads of the Lesser Dodder (a holo-parasite) spreading over the evergreen gorse bushes, where their masses of small pink flowers are scattered amongst the yellow gorse flowers.

Parasitic plants belong to 17 families. During evolution over 3000 species of flowering plants have become parasites. Little is known about most of these parasitic flowering plants, so they provide a good area for field research (Kuijt, 1969).

DODDERS: CUSCUTACEAE

They have a worldwide distribution and the family Cuscutaceae (Solanales), sometimes included in the Convolvulaceae, comprises 140-150 species. Most temperate Cuscuta species (dodders) are annuals but some tropical ones are perennials. They are herbaceous and attack stems with their characteristic haustoria (Table 11.2). Very little seems to be known about the ecology of dodders (Verdecourt, 1948, 1950, M. C. & J. D. Graves, 1995).

THE GREATER DODDER
(CUSCUTA EUROPEA L.)

In relation to *Cuscuta europaea* only one ecological study exists, (Verdcourt, 1948, 1950), and it is fortunate that this study is extremely good.

DISTRIBUTION

It occurs throughout Europe to 60° 20' N in Norway, 63° in Finland and 64° N in Sweden. Also found in Siberia, N. Africa and the temperate Himalayas. In Europe it occurs up to 5,500 feet (1,680 m), whilst in Tibet and the Himalayas it is found up to 10,000 feet (3,048 m). It is confined to southern Britain up to approx. 52-54°N. Its distribution follows that of the main rivers, the Bristol Avon valley, the Thames valley and the Mole valley in Surrey. In other counties up to the Wash it occurs sparingly by rivers and streams. It is classified as a lowland species in Britain with 95% of the records, 0-150 feet (0.46 m) and only 5% at, 150-400 feet (46-122 m). It is recorded as being distributed throughout Europe, except the extreme north and some of the islands, and of occurring

Dodder on nettles growing on the bank of the River Avon, Staverton, Wilts.The orange filamentous stems can be seen spreading out over the nettle tops

Nettle stems covered in the twining thread-like orange stems of Cuscuta europaea. The lower nettle stems are covered in the globular masses of dodder fruits whilst on the upper stems are the globular masses of white or pink flowers. On the extreme edge of the bank with the water beyond.

The twining stems with scale leaves, buds and globular masses of pink flowers on the host nettle stem which is covered with the parasites haustoria.

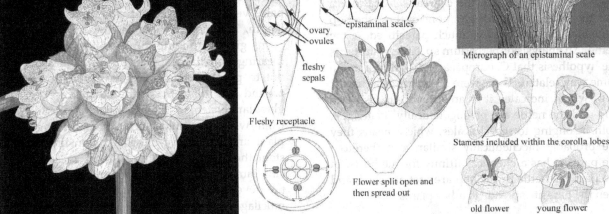

Micrograph of an epistaminal scale

Stamens included within the corolla lobes

old flower   young flower

A globular mass of dodder flowers many of which are open showing the two crimson stigmas in the centre, the four stamens inbetween the four petals and the epistaminal scales

Dissections of the flower to showing the structure. The tops of the pedicel is fleshy and short the ovary is two celled, each with two ovules, the 4-5 sepals are obtuse, the 4-5 petal are free the 4-5 stamens are included and epipetalous with epistaminal scales at their bases and closing the flower tube. The two stigmas are free, included and shorter than the ovary

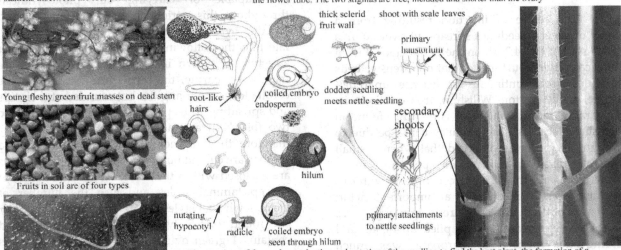

Young fleshy green fruit masses on dead stem

Fruits in soil are of four types

A young seedling with a hypocotyl of 11mm with a tip that nutates in search of the host

The structure of the seed, germination and nutation of the seedling to find the host plant, the formation of a primary haustorium and then shoot formation to find other stems of the host plant or other plant species to scramble across to find more host plants

FIG 11.2 CUSCUTA EUROPAEA THE FLOWER, FRUIT, SEED GERMINATION AND FINDING THE HOST

HABITAT

Verdcourt found that it has a strong preference for the vicinity of running water, and for luxuriant herbage or scrub on alluvial soils, by rivers and streams. In a study of 6 widely separated areas he found it was growing within a yard of the water (Table 11.1 and 11.2 p 161). In a study of herbarium specimens of 115 records, 95 were from places where there were large rivers, 14 near large streams, 3 inconclusive and only 3 from areas with no running water. He says shade might be necessary, and qualifies this to mean the shade of bridges, hedges or dense herbage.

THE HOST PLANT

From study of habitats and herbarium specimens, Verdcourt came to the conclusion that in Britain, and probably in Europe, Urtica dioica is the most important host. In the 6 areas, Urtica dioica was the main host, although in one of these the hop (*Humulus Lupulus*) was as much parasitised as the nettle. An analysis of herbarium specimens supports the hypothesis that C. europaea and U. dioica are in some way related. There were 23 occurrences on the hop, which indicates it is an important host. The hop and the nettle are phylogenetically related, i.e. both belonging to the Urticales, which means they are probably biochemically similar, and therefore the parasite has a chemical affinity for the hosts. In the field the nettle or the hop are first attacked, and then the parasite spreads to other plants.

GENERAL ECOLOGY

The centre of infection resulting from a single or several seedlings spread out over an area of 2-5 sq. yd. (1.7-4.3m^2) on the nettle clone, but in some cases Verdcourt found, that on extensive beds of nettles, it was continuous for distances up to half a mile, e.g. Staverton, Wiltshire. It is erratic in its appearance and in some years is not to be found in its usual place. Its disappearance could be due to drought, e. g. it was observed that when a small streamlet dried up it made no appearance in its usual place, and that it is scarcer in years with dry summers. Disturbance is also an important factor: (1) it was noticed that after dredging along the R. Ouse nettles increased in the piled up debris and during this period C. europaea was much commoner in its Surrey and Berkshire localities, (2) J. W. Hames made observations on a hedge

containing hop which was parasitised by C. europaea. It was present from 1915-1919, but in 1920 when the hedge was severely cut - back, the hop and its parasite were not seen until the hop grew again in 1923; this sequence was repeated on cutting in 1933 and 1943. J.C. Grose (1957) noted that it was definitely absent from part of the Avon at Staverton in 1937 but occurred in abundance in 1941.

LIFE CYCLE

FLOWERS AND POLLINATION

The mature plant body is very simple and the stem consists of thin crimson threads (0.5-0.9 mm diam) which coil around the stem, generally in an anti-clockwise direction. Tight coils of the stem indicate haustorial penetration, and above these are looser coils and branches that twine over one another and the surrounding nettle stems to form a crimson massed network. The tips of the stems are pale yellowish-green. At intervals along their length, but more noticeable towards the tips, the stems give off minute transparent scale-like leaves (bearing stomata) and later buds in their axils grow out to produce side branches. The Cuscuta stems around the tops of a nettle stem are covered in globular clusters of flowers (1 cm diam) which vary from white to pinkish-crimson according to the plant and its habitat. Further down on the nettle stem the globular fertilised flower masses (1.2-1.5 cm diam) are capped with brown dead corollas and the developing fruits have distinctly green swollen mucilaginous bases. These fruit masses remain green for long periods, even after their stems and the nettle stems are dead and brown; I suspect they are capable of carrying out photosynthesis throughout this period. The nettle stems, bound together by Cuscuta stems, can remain as such until late into the following year (Fig 11.2). The flower structure is shown in Figs 11.2. The flowers are mainly 4-5 partite, the sepals are obtuse, and the corolla lobes are triangular but rounded at their tips and spreading. The epi-staminal scales are split into two (bi-lobed) and adpressed to the corolla tube; therefore they do not close its mouth. The two stigmas are curved but not twisted, and the stamens are enclosed within the corolla. Variation occurs in the epistaminal scales and also the number of stigmas where 3 styles are frequent, and one flower was found with 5 styles. The ovary is globose and contains 4 green ovules. The base of the ovary is large, succulent and green. Yuncker (1921) and Verdcourt failed to observe any insect visitors, and self-pollination appears to be the rule (Fig 11.2). In

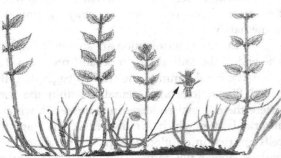

This diagram is based on a sketch in situ of part of a nettle patch, growing on a steep bank of the River Avon, Wiltshire, and recently parasitised by Cuscuta europaea. The primary haustorium was 1cm above soil level and shown in more detail above. From the primary haustorium shoots were given out in all directions and these formed haustoria on grass shoots in the vicinity before finding the preferred host the nettle where at this stage they are in the process of twining their way up the stems.

Dodder stems entwining nettle leaves have produced haustoria some of which have penetrated the leaf whilst others are still on the surface. There are abundant buds present.

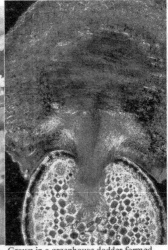

Grown in a greenhouse dodder formed haustoria on many plants including here Polygonum persicaria, the haustorium has penetrated through the vascular bundle into the central pith.

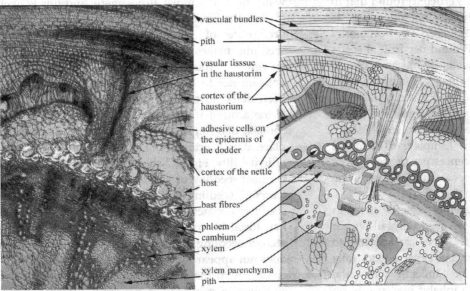

vascular bundles
pith
vasular tisssue in the haustorim
cortex of the haustorium
adhesive cells on the epidermis of the dodder
cortex of the nettle host
bast fibres
phloem
cambium
xylem
xylem parenchyma
pith

(Left) a micrograph of an haustorium penetrating the stem and vascular tissue of Urtica urens (under experimental greenhouse conditions) and (right) is a diagram based on the micrograph to give clarity to the tissues involved.

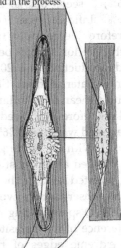

Longitudinal section through a grass and haustourium showing how it splits the cells apart and the cell on the surface which must aid in the process

surface cells of the haustorium

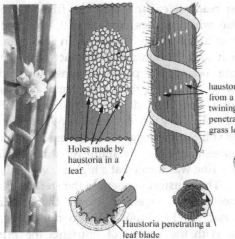

Holes made by haustoria in a leaf

haustoria from a twining stem penetrating a grass leaf

Haustoria penetrating a leaf blade

Stereogram showing the three dimensional nature of the haustria on a trailing stem of Cuscuta europaea. Notice the bubbble-like cells on the surface which may aid adhesion, produce a growth force on expansion or secrete enzymes.

The photo and diagrams here show the structure of the haustorium more readily seen as it penetrates a blade of grass. It shows that the haustorium has the shape of the tip of a knife blade which concentrates the growth force over a small area thereby increasing it and enabling it sufficient to penetrate the host stem and tissue. This process splits the tisssue which is prised away and this is also facilitated by enzymes action at the same time.

FIG 11.3 STRUCTURE OF THE HAUSTORIUM OF CUSCUTA EUROPAEA AND ITS PENETRATION OF THE HOST

older flowers the filaments bend the stamens towards the centre of the flower where pollen falls on the stigmas. Cleistogamy is frequent and Kerner, (1894) found pseudo-cleistogamy where pollination takes place in flowers kept closed during rainy weather. Cuscuta europaea has a very strong nectar-like smell and it maybe that some cross-pollination is brought about at night since I have observed snails and woodlice moving across the flower masses. This is possible because quite often an infected nettle patch is formed from many Cuscuta seedlings.

SEEDS AND SEED DISPSERSAL

Flower buds appear, and the first flowers open, about the middle of July. Flowering continues until the middle of October. Verdcourt found that in material from Bedfordshire fruits contained 4 seeds 25%, 3 seeds 41.7%, and 2 seeds 33.3%. In material from Staverton, Wiltshire, I found per fruit, 4 seeds 37.6%, 3 seeds 32.3%, 2 seeds 19.7% and 1 seed 10.5%. Inflorescences contained 26 flowers and therefore theoretically produce 76 seeds in total. With 20 inflorescences per metre of stem, this means seed production is 1520 seeds per metre of stem. Using material from Stoke Limpley, Wiltshire I found a mean of 55 inflorescences per metre of stem and therefore 4252 seeds per. metre of stem. The mean seed weight is 0.365 mg.

With the binding together of nettle stems in the infected areas, most of the seed will fall within the infected area, although some spread due to wind/censer action would be expected to take place. Dispersal might be linked, with the preference of the parasite to inhabit host plants on the extreme edges of river banks, and therefore making the dispersal of seeds by water possible.

GERMINATION AND ESTABLISHMENT

Little information is available. Authors have stated that seed can lie dormant for 5-6 years. Verdcourt obtained 30-50% germination from one year - old seeds and up to 3% germination from 7 - year old herbarium specimens. Germination takes place in the surface layers and seldom occurs in seeds below 1.3 cm of the surface. This makes sense because if seed did germinate at any distance below the surface the maximum extension of the seedlings above the soil would be restricted, and the chances of finding a host even less. I suspect the hard outer seed coat restricts/delays germination until it becomes broken down, because when I separated

seeds through a sieve, I noticed that the seeds where the testa had been worn away germinated immediately.

Stages in germination are shown in Fig 11.2. The end of the radical has 'root hair' processes that attach the basal 2 mm to the soil. To begin with the coiled filamentous stalk remains within the testa where the external endosperm is broken down and absorbed, after which it falls off. At this stage the cells are rich in oil globules and starch grains. The portion above the radical (i.e. the basal swollen piece Fig 11.2), the lower 'hypocotyl', elongates rapidly, but this elongation is retarded by direct sunlight. The seedling is greenish-yellow and contains chlorophyll; therefore diffuse light is beneficial probably because it enables limited photosynthesis to take place. The most important factor for the survival of the seedlings is free surface water or a very moist atmosphere, and this is likely to be the main factor determining its habitat preference of being near running water. The seedling makes extensive but irregular nutating movements from side to side but rarely in a circle. It appears not to twine around dead objects but has been noted to touch a host plant and then not to twine around it, or even to un-twine after a loose contact; this might indicate that twining only takes place after a certain point in growth or at high levels of irritability. Fig 11.2 shows stages in attachment to the host seedling of Urtica dioica but notice that the Cuscuta seedling did not twine around the first seedling contacted, although a complete coil and haustorial formation occurred on contact with the second seedling. Contact with the side of the stem does not appear to as effective in eliciting coiling as contact with the stem tip. In this example the first coil was in a clockwise direction whereas coiling above this was anti-clockwise. This first 'abnormal' coiling reaction ensures that the first side of the parasite which makes contact with the host will result in a coil around the host. In this example I found it took 24 hours after contact with the first seedling before the parasite twined around the second seedling and then a further 5 days before haustoria were formed. The first haustorial ring is formed only a few cm above soil level, but since the stem is still elongating at this stage examination at a later stage, might give the impression that the initial primary ring was formed at a higher level.

The haustoria penetrate the stem as a result of mechanical pressure from the blade-like haustorial tip (Fig 11.4) and also due to enzyme action. With the uptake of nutrients the primary ring coil swells up and after about 2 weeks shoots arise from this and these elongate and nutate. Fig 11.3 shows that low growing plants such as grass can act as secondary hosts or bridging posts before the primary host Urtica dioica is located. The parasite coils around the stems of U. dioica and forms haustoria at intervals in its ascent. Although nutation is the most effective way of finding a host, the net result when an adult Cuscuta plant is observed is that a lot of energy is wasted in producing Cuscuta stems which twine around one another, rather than increasing the lateral spread of the plant. Cuscuta stems often twine around one another and achieve haustorial penetration on their own stems! Fig 11.3 shows that grass leaves can be completely penetrated by haustoria, but this cannot take place through more than one layer; shows that pressure of growth of the haustorium causes the stem to split length-wise for a short distance.

If seedlings fail to find a host they fall to soil level and continue elongating until they reach a length of 3-4 cm (Mirande, 1901, gives 7-8 cm). In the absence of host contact they become thinner and live for just over three weeks. The tip is swollen, raised slightly, and nutates, but the end withers away at this period.

FURTHER FIELD STUDIES ON CUSCUTA EUROPAEA

My observations are based on a survey of 13 Cuscuta sites along two small stretches of the River Avon at Staverton and Stoke Limpley. The river in these areas is slow flowing, holds a large volume of water which rises to near the top of the bank in winter and occasionally overflows, flooding low lying areas such as Staverton. There appears to be comparatively little bank erosion and the bank is stabilised by trees such as pollarded Willows, Alder, Hawthorn, Blackthorn, etc., along its length. The bank mostly rises vertically 1-2 m above water level. The soil is a rich brown alluvium very loose, friable and moist. Anglers occupy the bank about every 50 feet or so, and in such areas the vegetation, mainly nettles is beaten down.

Due to the run off of agricultural fertilisers, nettles form an almost continuous line along the top of the river bank, although they are absent in some areas. In the 13 sites studied the nettles were dominant and made up about 90% of the vegetation; the most frequent plants were *Glyceria fluitans*, *Impatiens glandulifera*, *Lamium album*, *Convolvulus arvensis*, *Epilobium hursutium*, *Carex sp.*, and *Arctium major*. 85% of the sites were at the extreme edge of the bank and only three at 0.5 m, 2.0 m, and 4.0 m, from the edge. Shade at the time of establishment comes from the nettle stand as well as adjacent tall herbs and trees, etc., and needs to be measured by

hemispherical photography to take into account the lateral light coming from the river direction, since they are on the edge of the bank. Estimates for the extent of areas of the colonies were, 25% 0.25 m², 31% 0.50 m², 25% 1.00 m², 6% 1.50 m², 6% 5.00 m², and 6% 100.00 m². The parasitised nettle shoots were smaller, yellow and with less inflorescences that the adjacent nettle shoots. Flower colours were either white or pink. 50% of the sites had abundant flowers, 33% a small number and 20% none.

The effect of Cuscuta on the nettle appears to be small, but needs more careful investigation.

The main factors having significant effects are those of man - farmers plough or mow their fields almost to the river edge, chop off nettle tops, and spray them with herbicides. The restriction of Cuscuta to the extreme bank edge could also be due to a requirement for high humidity or free water, e.g. I scattered large number of Cuscuta seeds in two nettle beds in my garden 4 years ago but the parasite has never appeared.

Further work should involve an investigation of Cuscuta seed banks. I collected some soil samples from Cuscuta sites and after separation of the seed found they fell into 4 categories: very large soft and green, large light-brown, and small, extremely hard brown or black. The size is determined by the number of seeds produced in the capsule, but are there ecological reasons, such as differences in dormancy, etc?

Cuscuta species are intermediate between hemi- and holo-parasites, with very low concentrations of chlorophyll and the thylakoids in the chloroplasts are greatly reduced. Cuscuta europaea lacks chlorophyll, the plastids do not contain thylakoids, and therefore it is a complete holoparasite. See also Stewart & Press (1990), and Graves and Graves (1995).

A FUNGAL PARASITE OF THE NETTLE

INTRODUCTION

The Nettle Rust (*Puccinia carcina* DC) was previously classified as *P. caricis* (Schum.) Rebent. This rust has two host plants (i.e. it is heteroecious) with pycnia and aecia on Urtica dioica and U. urens, and uredinia and telia on various sedges (Carex sp.). For details of the various varieties: - see, (Table 11.3 p 161) and Wilson & Henderson (1966).

Distribution: Europe, Siberia, Japan, America and Australia.

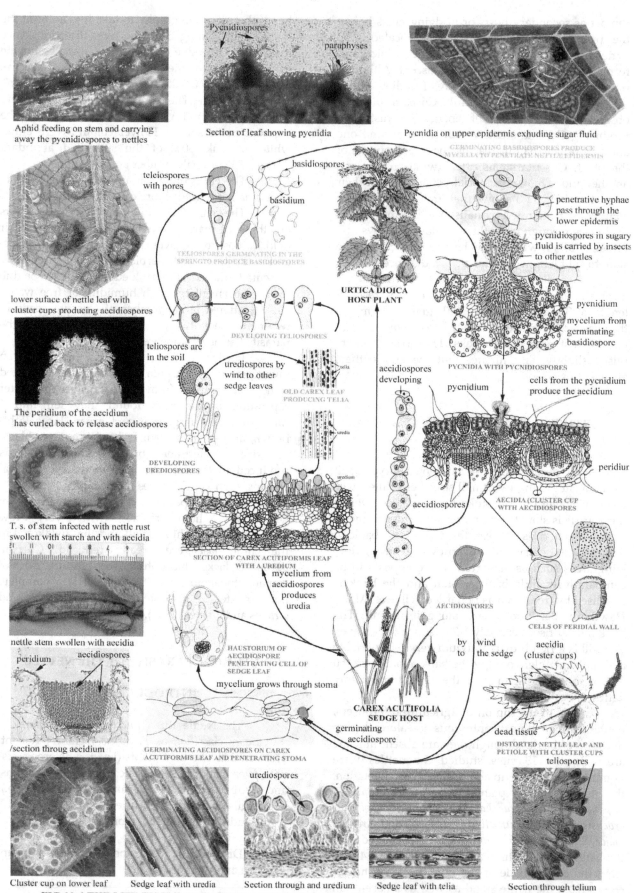

Aphid feeding on stem and carrying
away the pycnidiospores to nettles

Pycnidiospores
paraphyses

Section of leaf showing pycnidia

Pycnidia on upper epidermis exhuding sugar fluid

teleiospores
with pores

basidiospores

basidium

GERMINATING BASIDIOSPORES PRODUCE
MYCELIA TO PENETRATE NETTLE EPIDERMIS

penetrative hyphae
pass through the
lower epidermis

pycnidiospores in sugary
fluid is carried by insects
to other nettles

TELIOSPORES GERMINATING IN THE
SPRING TO PRODUCE BASIDIOSPORES

URTICA DIOICA
HOST PLANT

lower suface of nettle leaf with
cluster cups producing aecidiospores

DEVELOPING TELIOSPORES

teliospores are
in the soil

uredospores by
wind to other
sedge leaves

OLD CAREX LEAF
PRODUCING TELIA

telia

pycnidium

mycelium from
germinating
basidiospore

PYCNIDIA WITH PYCNIDIOSPORES

The peridium of the aecidium
has curled back to release aecidiospores

aecidiospores
developing

pycnidium

cells from the pycnidium
produce the aecidium

uredia

DEVELOPING
UREDIOSPORES

uredium

aecidiospores

peridiur

AECIDIA (CLUSTER CUP
WITH AECIDIOSPORES

T. s. of stem infected with nettle rust
swollen with starch and with aecidia

SECTION OF CAREX ACUTIFORMIS LEAF
WITH A UREDIUM

mycelium from
aecidiospores
produces
uredia

CELLS OF PERIDIAL WALL

AECIDIOSPORES

nettle stem swollen with aecidia

peridium
aecidiospores

HAUSTORIUM OF
AECIDIOSPORE
PENETRATING CELL OF
SEDGE LEAF

mycelium grows through stoma

CAREX ACUTIFOLIA
SEDGE HOST

germinating
aecidiospore

by wind
to the sedge

aecidia
(cluster cups)

dead tissue

/section throug aecidium

GERMINATING AECIDIOSPORES ON CAREX
ACUTIFORMIS LEAF AND PENETRATING STOMA

DISTORTED NETTLE LEAF AND
PETIOLE WITH CLUSTER CUPS

teliospores

uredospores

Cluster cup on lower leaf

Sedge leaf with uredia

Section through and uredium

Sedge leaf with telia

Section through telium

FIG 11.4 THE LIFE CYCLE OF PUCCINIA CARICIS ON URTICA DIOICA AND SEDGE (CAREX PALUDOSA)

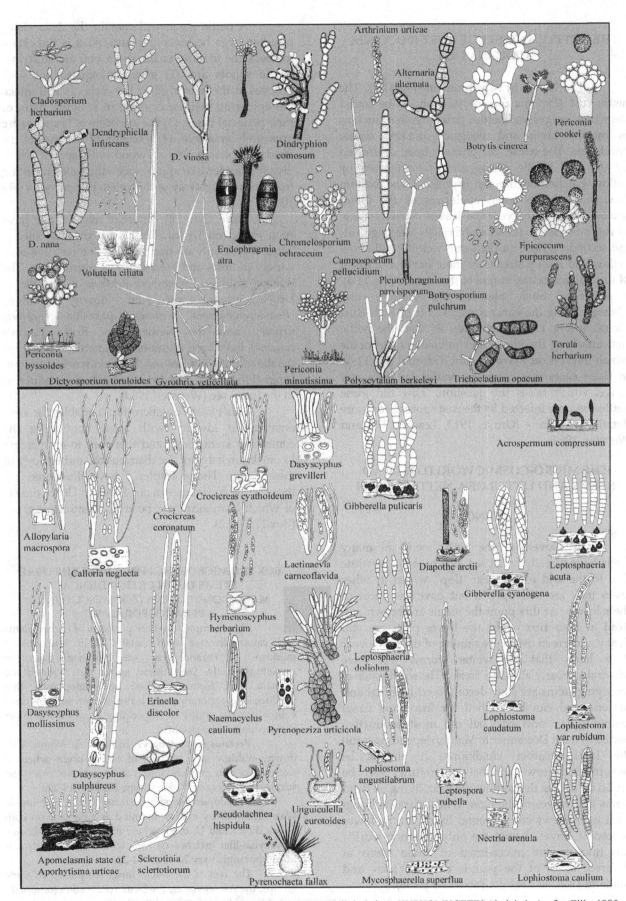

FIG 11.5 MICRO-FUNGI, ASCOMYCETES & COELOMYCETES(light baige), HYPHOMYCETES (dark baige), after Ellis, 1985.

157

THE NETTLE AND SEDGE RUST (PUCCINIA CARCINA DC.)

The life cycle is featured in (Fig 11.4). The nettle rust (*Puccinia carcina*) is likely to be found anywhere sedges and nettles grow together, such as in marshy areas and alongside ditches, rivers, ponds, etc. The nettle, the primary host, is affected by the rust in the spring and is manifested by yellow patches on the top (pycnidia) and bottom (aecidia – cluster cups) epidermis of the lower leaves. Later in the year the leaves of sedges, e.g. Lesser pond sedge (*Carex acutiformis*) – see page 161, the secondary host, in the same vicinity will show yellow and brown streaks on their leaves as a result of uredial and teleial stages of the fungus (Fig 11.4). I obtained much pleasure by viewing and photographing the various stages in the Nettle Rust life-cycle (Fig 11.4). Very often I found the nettle rust attacking the stems and petioles of the nettle which then become swollen and distorted (Fig 11.4). In these cases this occurs in nettles far from any sedge, which raises the question, 'how did these nettles become infected by the rust spores? For more details of Rusts: - (Grove, 1913, Leach, 1935, and Webster, 1980).

THE MICRO-COSMIC WORLD OF DEAD STEMS AND LITTER OF A NETTLE PATCH

1 FUNGI

By November the nettle stems in many areas have already collapsed and become prostrate due to the end of the year 'flop', whilst in other areas they are still upright but have lost most of their leaves. At this point the stems are brown and dead at their tips whilst the lower parts are still fleshy and green. At the beginning of the new - year it is likely that the winter storms will have prostrated nearly all nettle stems. The soft tissues of the dying stems are soon decomposed by fungi and bacteria and can be studied for incrusting fungi from October onwards, but the most productive period is from December to March, depending upon the local weather conditions. It should be remembered however, that micro-fungi can be found on nettles throughout the year, living on dead stems and leaves of the litter, whilst parasitic fungi such as mildews can be found living on the lower senescent leaves. About the only scientific work I can find on the micro-fungi of nettle stems at different times of the year is that of Yadav and Madelin 1968, (see results Table 11.4 p 156).

A nettle patch will contain the dead stems of other large herbaceous plants, so it is important to check the identity of the shoot you are studying. Nettle shoots are: (1) generally square but with grooves at the corner, (2) if the cortex is still intact, the epidermis will be covered in stinging hairs or their pedestal bases, (3) the leaf scars of branches are oppositely arranged, (4) a section of the base of the dead stem has a ring of wood with spaces which give it a ladder-like appearance - the holes resulting from the rotting away of the xylem parenchyma (Fig 10.1).

More than 50 different micro-fungi have been found on Urtica dioica with over 20 species being found only on this species. The rest live on a variety of hosts and are said to be plurivorous. The downy mildew *Peranospora debaryis* is specific to Urtica urens and the downy mildew, (*Pseudoperanospora urticae*), parasitic (*Septoria urticae*), and the Nettle/Sedge Rust (*Puccinia carcina*), have been found on both nettle species. For details of these species see the main work on micro-fungi (Ellis, 1985) and for an excellent introduction to the fungi see (Webster, 1980).

Ellis's work on micro-fungi enables the keen amateur to identify with some confidence the commoner stem fungi, and therefore to an increase in our knowledge of the distribution and ecology of these fungi. The examples I have illustrated are those of the commoner micro-fungi on Urtica dioica, of which I am sure of a positive identification, see (Box 11.1-11.2).

BOX 11.1. MICROFUNGI FOUND ON THE DEAD STEMS OF ON URTICA DIOICA MASTIGOMYCOTINA (ZOOSPORIC FUNGI) PERANOSPORALES

These simple fungi are parasites of higher plants and cause diseases such potato blight and downy mildews. In Peranospora, some hyphae, from the mycelium in the host tissue, grow out through the stomata and form branched sporangiophores that produce single sporangia. On leaves the top surface forms yellow patches whilst corresponding areas on the lower surface have white patches.

Peranospora debaryi Salmon & Ware. This downy mildew is a parasite of Urtica urens where it causes white to greyish-violet patches on the lower leaf surface. The sporangial size varies, 23-32μ X 19-25μ.

Pseudoperanospora urticae (Lib.) Salmon & Ware. This downy mildew is found as a parasite on both Urtica dioica and U. urens where it forms greyish-brown or greyish-lilac patches on yellow leaves, in Sept. and May. Sporangia vary 20-40μ X 14-22μ.

The rest of the micro-fungi are placed in three groups: the Ascomycetes, the Deuteromycotina (originally called Fungi Imperfecti) and the Basidiomycotina.

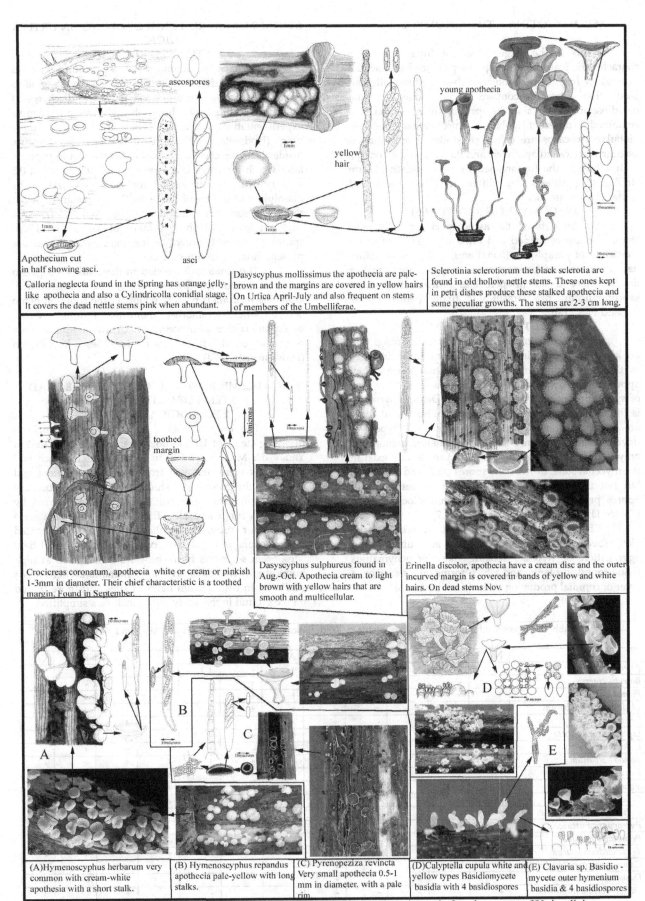

Apothecium cut in half showing asci.

Calloria neglecta found in the Spring has orange jelly-like apothecia and also a Cylindricolla conidial stage. It covers the dead nettle stems pink when abundant.

Dasyscyphus mollissimus the apothecia are pale-brown and the margins are covered in yellow hairs On Urtica April-July and also frequent on stems of members of the Umbelliferae.

Sclerotinia sclerotiorum the black sclerotia are found in old hollow nettle stems. These ones kept in petri dishes produce these stalked apothecia and some peculiar growths. The stems are 2-3 cm long.

Crocicreas coronatum, apothecia white or cream or pinkish 1-3mm in diameter. Their chief characteristic is a toothed margin. Found in September.

Dasyscyphus sulphureus found in Aug.-Oct. Apothecia cream to light brown with yellow hairs that are smooth and multicellular.

Erinella discolor, apothecia have a cream disc and the outer incurved margin is covered in bands of yellow and white hairs. On dead stems Nov.

(A)Hymenoscyphus herbarum very common with cream-white apothesia with a short stalk.

(B) Hymenoscyphus repandus apothecia pale-yellow with long stalks.

(C) Pyrenopeziza revincta Very small apothecia 0.5-1 mm in diameter. with a pale rim.

(D)Calyptella cupula white and yellow types Basidiomycete basidia with 4 basidiospores

(E) Clavaria sp. Basidio-mycete outer hymenium basidia & 4 basidiospores

FIG 11.6 Ascomycetes (Discomycetes=Cup fungi) and (D-E) Basidiomycetes commonly found on stems of Urtica dioica

This is the largest class of fungi and their characteristic feature is that spores produced in a sexual process are formed in a tubular/club-shaped sac called an ascus that generally contains 8 ascospores. Asexual conidiospores can also be produced. The asci are contained in different hyphal structures called ascocarps: globular ascocarps are called **cleistothecia**, cup-shaped ascocarps are called **apothecia** and flask-shaped ascocarps with a hole in the top are **perithecia**. **Pseudothecia** are similar to perithecia but differ in development and contain bitunicate asci.

DISCOMYCETES (CUP FUNGI)

In these fungi the ascocarp is generally cup-shaped or saucer-shaped and lined with the hymenium consisting of paraphyses (hairs) and asci. The asci either have a terminal lid for spore release (operculate forms) or do not have a lid (inoperculate forms). They grow saprophytically or parasitically upon plants (Table 11.5and Figs 11.6).

DEUTEROMYCOTINA

The Deuteromycotina group includes fungi that are known only in their mycelial state, or from their stages in their production of spores by asexual means; they appear to lack sexual processes in their life cycle. The type of spore, produced by members of the Deuteromycotina, is the conidiospore, produced on a conidium, and there are a great variety of these spores and types of development. There are 3 classes of Deuteromycotina, but only two need concern us here: - (1A) some only exist in the mycelial state, or in others spores produced variously, but not in pycnidia or acervuli. **Hypomycetes:** - (1B) Spores produced in pynidia or acervuli. **Coelomycetes** (Tables 11.6. 11.8 p 162, 164 and Figs 11.7).

The pycnidium has been dealt with in the Nettle/Sedge Rust life cycle. An acervulus is an aggregation of hyphae, looking like parenchymatous tissue found in plants, and which forms on its surface, a layer of conidial producing stalks (conidiophores).

STUDIES OF MICRO-FUNGI GROWING ON URTICA DIOICA
1 LEPTOSPHAERIA ACUTA

Perhaps the commonest fungus found on dead Urtica stems during the winter and a spring period is *Leptosphaeria acuta*. An article on the spore discharge of this fungus illustrates how observations and simple experimentation can increase our knowledge of these fungi (Hodgetts, 1917). Increase in the water pressure inside the ascus causes its outer cuticular coat to rupture, after which the inner coat elongates rapidly to about 0.3 mm beyond the orifice of the perithecium. On the dissolution of the tip of the ascus the spores are shot out rapidly in succession, this taking about 4-5 sec. They are shot out to a horizontal distance of 0.4-2.0 cm. These spores presumably infect young nettle shoots that are present throughout this period.

The amateur interested in these micro-fungi can make contributions by recording their distribution. *Leptosphaeria acuta* is present wherever the common nettle occurs whereas another parasitic fungus, *Nectria leptospharereia* that also occurs on Urtica dioica has only been collected from four localities in Britain (Hawksworth, 1974).

BOX 11.2 MICROFUNGI FOUND ON THE DEAD STEMS OF URTICA DIOICA
2 ECOLOGICAL STUDIES

The only ecological study of micro-fungi on decaying stems of Urtica dioica I am aware of is that of Yadav d& Madelin (1968). In October stems which had dried back were removed from two areas in Kent and placed on the ground in a study area (be careful, because when I tried this, my nettle pile was consumed by woodlice - fungi and all!). Each month 3-5 stems were removed for study. These collections were supplemented by collections at regular intervals from the original field sites. Stem segments from these were incubated at high humidity for two days prior to examination. There was a similarity in results from national sites and those placed on the ground in the study area. I include a simplified

Table 11.4 Species of fungin each month on stems of Urtica dioica (simplified from Yadav and Madelin 1968).												
	N	D	J	F	M	A	M	J	J	A	S	O
Alternaria tenuis	+	-	+	+	-	+	+	+	+	+	+	+
Botrytis cinerea	+	-	-	-	+	-	+	-	-	-	-	-
Phoma acuta	+	+	+	+	+	+	+	+	+	+	+	+
Cladosporium herbarum	+	-	+	+	-	+	+	+	+	-	+	+
Periconia cookeri	+	-	-	-	+	-	-	+	-	+	+	+
Leptospheraeria acuta	-	+	+	-	-	+	+	-	+	+	+	-
L. doliolum	-	+	-	-	-	-	-	+	-	+	+	+
Torula herbarium	-	+	-	-	+	-	+	+	-	+	+	-
Dendryphium comosum	-	+	-	-	-	-	+	+	+	+	+	+
Volutella ciliata	-	-	-	+	-	-	-	-	+	-	-	+
Calloria fusarioides	-	-	-	-	-	+	+	-	-	-	-	-
Ophiobolus erythrosporus	-	-	-	-	-	-	-	-	+	+	-	-
Pyrenopeziza urticicola	-	-	-	-	-	+	+	-	+	+	+	+
Periconia byssoides	-	-	-	-	-	-	-	-	-	-	-	-
Trichocladium opacum	-	-	-	-	-	-	-	-	+	-	+	-
Camposporium pellucidum	-	-	-	-	-	-	-	-	-	+	-	-
Dasyscypha sulphurea	-	-	-	-	-	-	-	-	-	+	-	+
Dictyosporium toruloides	-	-	-	-	-	-	-	-	-	+	-	+

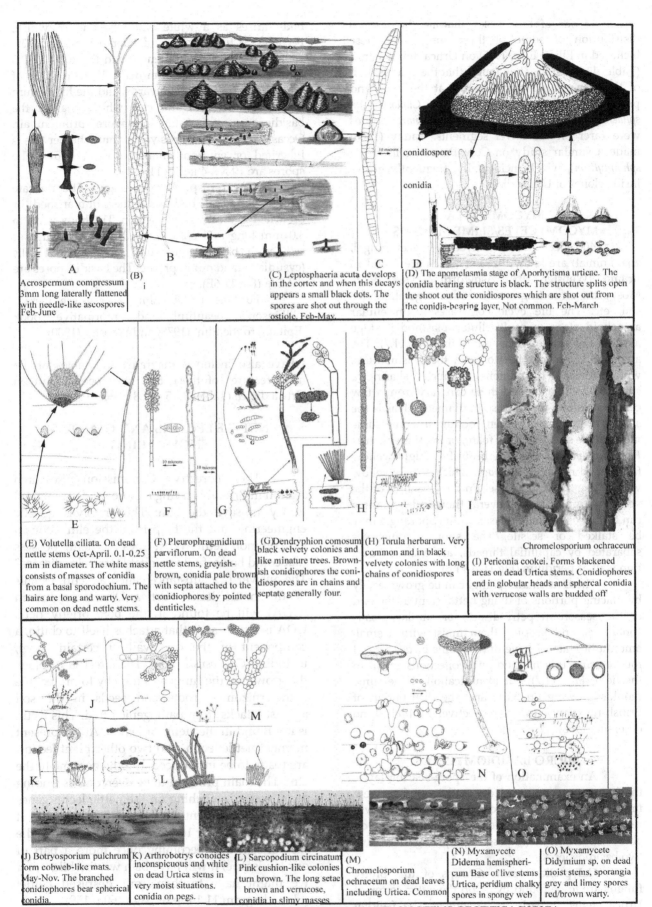

(A) Acrospermum compressum 3mm long laterally flattened with needle-like ascospores Feb-June

(B)
i

(C) Leptosphaeria acuta develops in the cortex and when this decays appears a small black dots. The spores are shot out through the ostiole. Feb-May.

(D) The apomelasmia stage of Aporhytisma urticae. The conidia bearing structure is black. The structure splits open the shoot out the conidiospores which are shot out from the conidia-bearing layer. Not common. Feb-March

conidiospore

conidia

(E) Volutella ciliata. On dead nettle stems Oct-April. 0.1-0.25 mm in diameter. The white mass consists of masses of conidia from a basal sporodochium. The hairs are long and warty. Very common on dead nettle stems.

(F) Pleurophragmidium parviflorum. On dead nettle stems, greyish-brown, conidia pale brown with septa attached to the conidiophores by pointed dentiticles.

(G)Dendryphion comosum black velvety colonies and like minature trees. Brown-ish conidiophores the coni-diospores are in chains and septate generally four.

(H) Torula herbarum. Very common and in black velvety colonies with long chains of conidiospores

Chromelosporium ochraceum

(I) Periconia cookei. Forms blackened areas on dead Urtica stems. Conidiophores end in globular heads and spherical conidia with verrucose walls are budded off

J) Botryosporium pulchrum form cobweb-like mats. May-Nov. The branched conidiophores bear spherical conidia.

K) Arthrobotrys conoides inconspicuous and white on dead Urtica stems in very moist situations. conidia on pegs.

L) Sarcopodium circinatum Pink cushion-like colonies turn brown. The long setae brown and verrucose, conidia in slimy masses

(M) Chromelosporium ochraceum on dead leaves including Urtica. Common

(N) Myxamycete Diderma hemispheri-cum Base of live stems Urtica, peridium chalky spores in spongy web

(O) Myxamycete Didymium sp. on dead moist stems, sporangia grey and limey spores red/brown warty.

FIG 11.7 HYPHOMYCETES AND MYXAMYCETES FOUND ON STEMS OF URTICA DIOICA

version of one of their tables showing the seasonal distribution of some of these fungi (i.e. those included in Ellis& Ellis, 1985) on Urtica dioica stems (Table 11.5 p 162). They found that the colonisation of these moribund stems begins at the apex and proceeds to lower segments, *Cladosporium sphaerospermium, C. herbarium* and *Alternaria tennuis* were rarer on the lower segments. Yadav (1966) made a similar study on Cow Parsnip (*Heracleum sphondylium*), which incidentally, frequently grows inside clones of Urtica dioica.

MYCOMYCOTA
MYCOMYCETES/SLIME MOULDS

400 species of Myxomycetes (mycet, fungal, zoa, animal) are known, 250 of which are found in Britain, (Webster, 1980; Ashworth & Dee, 1975). Most grow on rotting wood or other vegetation, dry soil, etc. The life cycle comprises a unicellular amoeboid stage, a multicellular plasmodial stage and a stage where spores are found (Fig 11.7). The amoebae come together to form the plasmodium, which consists of millions of nuclei sharing a common cytoplasm, and these can vary from a few centimetres to a metre or so in diameter. This is the stage most commonly seen, looking in some slime moulds like small blobs of foam, or in others such as *Physarum polycephalum*, a beautiful bright yellow fan-shaped reticulum through which radiate yellow veins – like the blood vessels in the mysentry of the vertebrate gut. One or several thousand sporangia can form from a single plasmodium. Sporangia may be stalked or sessile. The spores, sometimes separated by capillitial threads, are enclosed in a thin wall or peridium (Fig 11.7, 11.8).

These fascinating fungi can be grown easily by placing portions of dying nettle stem at the end of the season in petri dishes, or similar plastic containers, and keeping them moist with a small amount of water. I have drawn some of the types I found using this method and collections made in the field (Figs 11.7). For identification of the slime moulds growing on bark, and the distribution of British myxomycetes, see respectively, (Mitchell, no date; Ing, 1968).

MICRO BASIDIOMYCETES

An examination of the spore-bearing layer, the hymenium, mounted dry and in surface view under high power of a microscope (X 100-400), will reveal basidiospores borne, in groups of four, on club-shaped basidia (N.B. some jelly fungi only have two basidiospores).

Calyptella capula. Groups of this pretty fungus are to be found living on the outer cortex of Urtica stems as early as November The fruiting body arises as a white club, the end of which, becomes at first a disc and later bell-shaped. The stalks are 0.5-0.7 mm in length and the cups 1.0-2.5 mm in diameter and 2 mm deep. These clusters of white bells are face downwards, and the hymenium lines the inside of the cup which enables the basidiospores a free fall into more turbulent air. Occasionally the colour is yellow but whether this is inherited or environmental, I do not know. The spores are 10 X 3-4 μ (Fig 11.).

Clavaria sp. A rare fungus. The delicate white cylindrical body is either unbranched or branched in an irregular fashion. The body is up to 3.0 mm long and 0.2 mm in diameter. Groups of cells with basidiospores and large inflated cells (cystidia) stand out in profile. The basidiospores are 4 X 10μ (Fig 11.6E).

For the Dutch Elm Disease see Gerald Wilkinson's beautiful and informative book 'Epitaph to the Elm' (1978) and Webster (1980).

I have also included diagrams and tables of the main features of those that have been found on Urtica dioica (Tables 11.5 - 11.8 p 162-4).

NETTLE LECTINS AND GENETIC-ENGINEERING

The Forestry Commission Research Station in Britain is trying a more modern method to try to save the elm. This involves genetic engineering and the help from the elm's cousin the common nettle. What does the nettle possess that could be useful to combat Dutch elm disease? The answer is a substance called a lectin. Details of the nettle lectin, Urtica Dioica Agglutinin (UDA) will be found in the box. Briefly here, UDA is a substance that attaches itself to chitin, a component of the cell wall of certain fungi, including *Ceratosystis ulmi*. The effect is to block the growth of the fungi and thereby to protect the nettle rhizomes, roots and seeds in the soil against attacks from pathogenic fungi. This lectin is not found in the stems or leaves. At the present moment nettle lectin, and two other plant lectins, are ready to be introduced into the genome to the elm. The main problem to be overcome is finding some way of switching on the nettle lectin genes that will be present in the stem of the elm. It might take another 10 years, but if it results in the magnificent elm becoming once more a part of our landscape, it will have be n worthwhile – and we might have to thank our despised nettle! (Flow diagram 11.1 top of page 160 p 159).

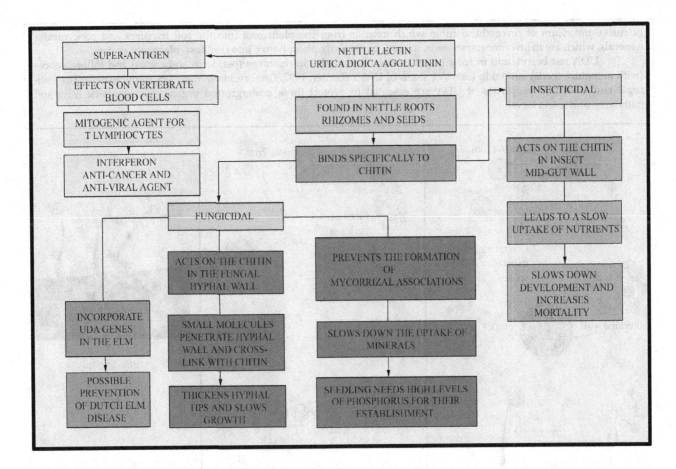

BOX 11.3. URTICA DIOICA AGGLUTININ (UDA)AND ITS ROLE IN NETTLE DEFENCE

Lectins have been known for nearly a century but have come into prominence in the last decade or two. Lectins are substances produced by plants that have physiological effects upon the blood cells of vertebrate animals. Lectin (from the Latin legere, to pick out, choose) was coined by Boyd & Shapleigh (1954) and refers to proteins of plant origin which agglutinate cells and bind specifically to certain sugars thereby showing antibody-like properties. For details of the biological properties, applications of lectins, and functions in plants, etc., see (ed. Bog-Hansen & van Driessche, 1986).

A lectin was isolated from the rhizome of Urtica dioica and named Urtica Dioica Agglutinin (UDA), (Peumans et. al., 1984). Chitin is the principle component of exoskeletons of insects and is also present on the cell walls of fungi and many algae and that UDA exhibits carbohydrate-binding specificity for chitin.

Types of white blood cells called T lymphocytes regulate the immune system by detecting changes in the cell surfaces produced by infection or other factors. Peumans et al. found that UDA, as an antigen, causes the T lymphocytes in the blood to produce interferon (IFN, in this case, HuIFN-γ) which is normally produced as an anti-viral and anti-cancer agent It was proposed that this lectin was classified as a superantigen, and is the first example of an organism having this ability, which is not related to infectious disease organisms and to a disease in mammals (Galelli & Truffa-Bachi, 1993, and Galelli et al., 1995).

It had long been suspected that lectins might act in plant defence and Huesing et al., (1991) showed that UDA possessed insectidal activity. UDA binds itself to chitin. It has been suggested that it slows - down insect development by binding with the chitin in the wall of the insects mid - gut. This binding could interfere with nutrient uptake.

In addition UDA has been shown to have strong anti-fungal properties but only against fungi which have chitin in their cell walls. It has been found that in relation to the fungus (Botrytis cinerea) UDA is effective at inhibiting growth (Broekaert et. al., 1989. These findings confirm the original hypothesis that chitin-binding lectins would protect seedlings against fungal attack. For lectins in plant defence see (Chrispeels & Raikhel, 1991).

Related to its anti-fungal activity is the fact that roots of Urtica dioica do not have any mycorrhizal fungal associations. This area was examined by Vierheilig et. al., (1996) who found no mycorrhizal structures on roots of the common stinging nettle collected around Basel (Switzerland). Experiments on mycorrhizal fungi showed an inhibition of fungal growth (i.e. tips of hyphae) shown by the application of extracts from stinging nettle roots and rhizomes. UDA inhibited fungal growth in a similar way (Broekaert et. al., 1989).

This is interesting because it might explain the need for high levels of phosphorus by seedlings in the establishment stage of the nettle. It is well known that the

163

extensive mycelium of mycorrhizal fungi which extends from the plant root into the soil transfers and concentrates minerals, which are in low concentrations in the soil, particularly phosphorus, into the 'host' plant root system.

UDA has been found in roots (outer periderm), and also in rhizomes (periderm and cortex) and inflorescences (with immature seeds) but not in leaves or stems of Urtica (Lerner, 1992, Lambrechts & Verbelen, unpublished). The antifugal and insectidal properties of UDA are essential to protect these underground organs against attack from soil pathogens and insect larvae.

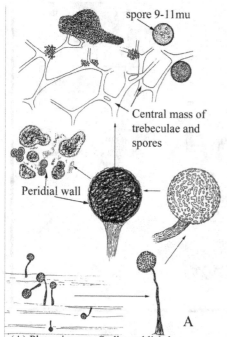

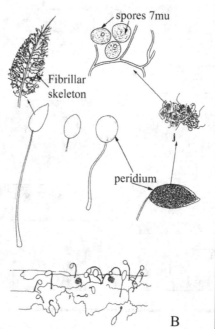

C
Physaria sp.

(A) Physarium sp. Stalks reddish-brown, 1-1.7mm, sporangia 0.3-0.6mm, whitish-brown with white patches, peridial wall with granular masses, spores light brown. Common on Urtica

Comatrricha sp. Stalks 1-2mm, blackish-brown sporangia which vary in shape, globose ones 0.5mm diameter. Peridium coco-brown and soft. On dead Urtica stems.

FIG 11.8 CORTICOLUS MYXOMYCETES

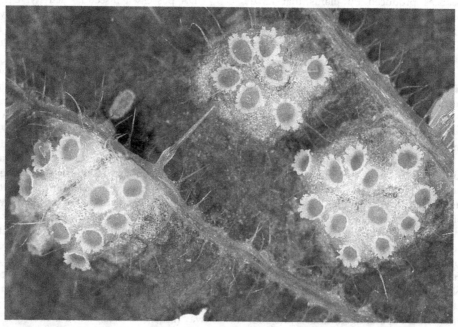

CLUSTER CUPS OF PUCCINIA CARCINA NETTLE RUST - FILL IN MOVE ON

TABLE 11.1. Eight habitat areas occupied by Cuscuta europaea in southern Britain (after Verdcourt, 1950).

AREA	COUNTY	HABITAT	NOTES	PRIMARY HOST	SECONDARY HOSTS
Leighton Buzzard	Beds.	Stream bordering fallow field.	Increasing in locality	Urtica dioica	Calystegia sepium, Glyceria maxima, Equisetum arvense.
Wargrave	Berks.	Banks of River Lodden	River dredged, confined to riparian community		Epilobium hirsutum, Cirsium sp., Urtica dioica.
Sonning	Oxon.	Banks of streamlet Nearby hedge	On banks. Hedge.	Urtica dioica	Heracleum Spondylium, Galium aparine, Humulus Lupulus, Urtica dioica, grasses
Harrold	Beds.	River Ouse	By river.	Urtica dioica	Angelica sylvestris, Cirsium vulgare, Solanum dulcamara, Achillea Ptarmica, Galium aparine
Milton Ernest	Beds.	River Ouse	By river.	Urtica dioica	Spreading to Cirsium arvense.
Stevington	Beds.	River Ouse	By river.	Urtica dioica	Conium maculatum colonised most together with, Brassica nigra, Eupatorium cannalinum, Urtica dioica, occasionally Cardamine flexuosa and Cornus sanguinea
Bath	Somerset	River Avon	By river.	Urtica dioica	Solanum dulcamara, Brassica nigra, Conium maculatum, Epilobium hirsutum, Cirsium arvense, Galium mollugo, Carduus crispus, Glechoma hederacea, Sparaganium erectum.
Bathford to Bristol		River Avon	Banks of river	Urtica dioica	

TABLE 11.2 Comparison of the life-cycles of Cuscuta europaea, an annual parasite growing principally on the Common Nettle (Urtica dioica) which dies back each year, and C. epithymum, which can be a perennial parasite in the form of hibernating tubercles on the established evergreen Gorse (Ulex europaeus), or an annual parasite on young Gorse plants or seedlings, or also on Callluna vulgaris and Erica sp. on moorland (after Shillito, 1952).

SPECIES	MONTHS (OVER A THREE YEAR PERIOD)
Cuscuta epithymum	J F M A M J J A S O N D / J F M A M J J A S O N D / J F M A M J J A S O N D — Seed Tubercles → Free-living Seedlings → Growing as parasite On young Gorse shoots → Hibernating tubercles → Spreading phase on old Gorse Flowering → Spreading & flowering → Hibernating tubercles on old Gorse → Free-living on young Gorse → Seeds

	MONTHS (OVER A ONE YEAR PERIOD)
Cuscuta europaea	J F M A M J J A S O N D — Tubercles → Seeds / Free-Living Seedlings → Growing as Parasite → Flowering and Fruiting → Seeds

Table 11.3. Varieties of Nettle/Sedge Rust, Puccinia caricina DC (based on Wilson & Henderson, 1966)

VARIETIES	COMMON NAME	SEDGE HOST	NETTLE HOSTS	HABITATS OF SEDGE HOST	FREQUENCY
urticae-acutae (Kleb) Henderson	Common Sedge	Carex nigra	Urtica dioica, U.urens	Marshes and flushes.	Common.
urticae-acutiformis (Kleb) Henderson	Lesser Pond Sedge	Carex acutiformis (paludosa)	Urtica dioica.	Marshes, wet meadow and swamps, ponds, streams.	Common.
urticae-flaccae (Hasler) Henderson	Glaucous Sedge	Carex flacca	Urtica dioica.	Wet and dry grassland on chalk and limestone, sand dunes, mountain flushes	Common.
urticae-hirtae (Kleb) Henderson	Hairy Sedge	Carex hirta	Urtica dioica, U.urens	Damp grassy places.	Common.
urticae-inflatae (Hasler) Henderson	Bottle Sedge	Carex rostrata	Urtica dioica.	Acid swamps, lake margins, reed beds.	Common.
urticae-ripariae (Hasler) Henderson	Greater Pond Sedge	Carex riparia	Urtica dioica, U piludifera.	Marshes, wet meadow and swamps, ponds, streams.	Common.
urticae-vesicariae (Kleb) Henderson	Bladder Sedge	Carex vesicaria	Urtica dioica.	Swamps, marshes, lake margins.	Frequent

	Diameter in mm.	Colour	Margins And Excipulum	Ascospores Size μ and Septa	Frequency	Season	Other details
1 Allophylaria macrospora	0.5	Pale buff/white disc	Ascus pore blue in I2	18-28X4-6	?	S-O	Mainly on dead stems of E. angustifolium
2 Calloria neglecta	→1	Pinkish-orange	-	8-14X3-3.5 1,3	VC	Mc-My	Cylindrocolla conidial stage, Ja-F. Paraphyses swollen at tip.
3 Crocicreas coronatum	→3	White/cream/pink	Toothed	16-20X4-4.5	C	S-N	Ascospores hyaline.Stalked.
4 C.cyathoideum	→2	Pale cream, pinkish	Curved when young	7-10X1.5-2.0	VC	Mc-O	Ascospores hyaline.Stalked.
5 Dasyscyphus grevillei	0.2-0.4	Straw	Incurved. H. granulate	20-35X3-4	VC	Ap-Ag	Ascospores hyaline.Paraphyses 2 thick
6 D. mollissimus	→2	Whitish, pale brown	Covered in yellow H's	10-15X1.5-2.0	C	Ap-Jy	. Ascospores hyaline
7 D. sulphureus	"	"	Sulphur-yellow H's	30-37X2-2.5, 0,3	C	Au-O	Ascospores hyaline.Similar to previous
8 Erinella discolour	1.0-1.5	Ochraceous	H's 500X4-5, septate	50-76x2-2.5, 6-10	C	Nov	Asci 100-120X8, Paraphyses tapered 2-3, thick, pore blued by iodine.
9 Hymenoscyphus herbarum	→3	Ivory white-cream		12-17X2.5-3, 1	C	S-D	Ascospores hyaline.Short thick stalks
10 Laetinaevia carneoflavida	→0.25	Pink, darker edge		10-15x3-3, 0-1	?	Ju-Jy	Ascospores hyaline. Paraphyses filiform and branched.
11 Naemacyclus caulium	→1	Greyish		40-50X1.5,7	R	Ap	Ascospores hyaline. Immersed, exposed when epiderm is split into 4 lobes
12 Pyrenopeziza urticicola	→0.5	Red-brown to Bl-br.	White fimbriate	6-7X1.1-1.5	C	Ap-Au	Ascospores hyaline. Discs pale greyish brown
13 Sclerotinia sclerotiorum	2-8	Golden brown		9-13X4-6	?	Ap-Ju	Ascospores hyaline.Stalks up to 2 cm. Arising from black sclerotia.
14 Unguiculellum hamulata	→0.2	Pale brown-whitish		5-6X2-2.5	?	My-S	Ascospores hyaline. Ap.covered, hooked hairs, 20-30. Paraphyses filiform.

Abbreviations, **H**, hairs, Bl, black, br, brown, Ap. apothesium, VC very common, C common. Shaded mainly confined to Urtica dioica.

Table 11.6. Coelomycetes found on Urtica dioica (after data from Ellis & Ellis 1985)

	Size mm	Description	Conidia	Frequency	Plant part	Season
Aporhytisma urticae Apomelasmia state	0.5	Conidiomata black and shining, immersed in black stroma.	Hyaline, 18-26X3-4.5	UC	D S	F-Mc
Pseudolachnea hispidula	?	Dark brown/black, dark brown setae. Subcuticular to erumpent, becoming cup-shaped.	Hyaline, 16-20X2-3	VC	D S	N-Mc
Pyrenochaeta fallax	0.1-0.18	Pycnidia immersed in grey areas dark brown, brown septate setae 100-200X5-7 around the ostiole	Hyaline, 4-6.5X1.5-2	?	D S	?
Septoria urticae	0.1	Pycinidia wpiphyllous, immersed.	Hyaline, curved, 30-50X1-2	?	LL	Ma-Au

Shaded mainly confined to Urtica dioica.

166

Table 11.7. Other Ascomycetes found on Urtica dioica (after data from Ellis, 1971)

	Fruiting body	Size mm.	Description	Ascospores Size µ / Septa	Asci	Conidiospores	Frequency	Plant part	Season	Additional
Acrospermum compressum	A	→3	Club-shaped, laterally compressed, apical pore. Blackish-brown	400X1		-	C	DS	F-Ju	
Diaporthe arctii	P	0.5	Extensive areas dark grey. Immersed, black protruding ostioles	12-15X3-4, 1	-	-	C	DS	Jy-N	Phomopsis state*
Erysiphe urticae	C		Appendages numerous and narrow.	3-5 sp.	6-10	Yes	?	LL	S-O	Powdery mildew
Gibberella cyanogena	P	0.25	P. black warted wall, purple with transmitted light.	20-30X5-7, 3	-		C	OS	O-My	Occasional on Urt.
G. pulicaris	P	0.2	Clusters dark brown, often appear warted	20-30X6-10, 3	-	See #	?	LP	Ja-Ap	. §Fusarial state.
Leptosphaeria acuta †	Ps	0.3-0.5	Superficial, conical and black.	40-60X5-7.5,8,10		*4.5X1.5-2	V	DS	F-My	*Phoma state
L. doliolum	Ps	0.4-0.5	Black with concentric rings, usually 2. (ascospores brown)	16-28X4-7, 3			Vc	DS	Ja-D	†
Leptospora rubella	Ps	0.2-0.3	First immersed, black red tip necks through epid. which is red.	120-180X1-1.5			Vc	S	Ap-Au	Asc. Straw col
Lophiostoma angustilabrum *	Ps	0.5	Immersed or semi-immersed, black. (ascosp. medium septum.)	24-30X4-5.5	-	-	Vc	DS	F-O	
L. caudatum *	Ps	?	Immersed black, with compressed necks showing.	26-30X7-8, 5-6.			Uc	DS	Ja-Ap	
L. caulium *	Ps	?	Immersed or semi-immersed,	20-30X5-6, 5			C	DS	Ja-D	
L. ortani var rubidum *	Ps	?	Immersed with necks protruding, host tissue red/magenta	25-30X4-5, 1-3			C	DS	?	
Mycosphaerella superflua	Ps	0.15	Immersed, crowded and black.	12-17X3-4.5, 1			C	DS	Mc	
Ramularia state of the above			White colonies 1-3 mm diam. on the lower side of living leaves			15-30X3-5.5 0-1	C	LL	Ap-S	‡
Nectria arenula	P	→0.25	Small groups, on thin subiculum, yellow/ochre-golcen/brown.	15-21X3-4, 1			FC	DS	Ja-D	
Ophiobolus erythrosporus	Ps	0.5	Immersed bec. superficial, black, often flattened cylind. necks.	140x3-4, Many			FC	DS	?	Ascospores, pink.
Plagiotheca immersa	P		Grey patches on epidermis, flattened with short (lateral)necks	50-60X2-3 #	AR		?	DS	My-Au	# parallel

† Nectria leptosphaeriae, and Pleurophragmium acutum are parasites of this fungus. ‡ Size of conidiophores emerging through stomata, 30-40X2-4. AR, Apical ring, † sometimes parasitised by Didymosphaeria conoidea with ascorspores 8-12X4-4µ. * Ps with laterally compressed, slotted necks and transversely septate ascospores. Shaded mainly confined to Urtica dioica. * With A-conidia fusiform, biguttulate, 7-9X2.5-3, and B-conidia filiform, curved , 16-22X0.5-1, on previous year's dead stems. OS, old cabbage stems. L L, live leaf, L S, live stem, D S dead stem. Uc, uncommon, Vc very common, Fc fairly common, C common. §Fusarium state has curved, fusiform, 2-5 septate macroconidia 35-55X4-5.5, with foot-cells. Parasitic on L. arboreus.

	Size mm	Description	Conidiophore	Conidiospore re Septa	Frequency	Plant part	Season
Alternaria alternata		Effuse grey, black of olivaceous black.	Brown up to 50X3-6,	Br. Chains, verruculose or smooth, muriform. 20-62X9-18	VC	A D	?
Arthrinium urticae	1	Pulvinate, small, round or elongated, bl.-brown-black.	Br. at septa, 40-75X1.5-2	Brown, 5-6X3-4	UC	D S	N
Botrytis cinerea	2	Effuse, grey of greyish-brown.	Br.Tree-like, 2 mmX16-30	V.pale brown ,smooth, 8-14X6-9	C	L P	?
Botryosporium pulchrum		Extensive, white, cobwebby.	Hyaline, brch. 12-15 thick	Minutely verrucose, hyaline, 6-9X3-4	?	L N	My-N
Camposporium pellucidum	-	Effuse, grey, brown, glistening.	Br. 80X6-7	Pale br. apical cell, long appendage, 140X12, 16.	-	o	Ja-D
Cladosporium herbarum	7/9		Nodose br, 250X3-6	Long, brch. mid-olivaceous brown, verruculose 0.1.	VC	D P	Jn-D
Dendryphiella infuscans		Effuse, brown.	Br. 500X4-6, nodes 7-9	Pale br., smooth or minutely verruculose, 0.2, 9-16X4-7	QC	D S	Ap-My
D vinosa		Effuse, velvety, rust to rusty-black	Br. 450X4-6, nodes 6-11	Verruculose pale to burnt sienna, 16-39X4-8	VC	D S	Ma-S
Dendryphion comosum		Grey-dark-reddish-br.-olive or black, velvety. 2-7 cm	Br.-bl. 100-500X9-14, 5-8	Chains, 10-50X5-8, pale-mid br. 1-7 (4)	VC	D S	Ja-D
D. nanum		Black, velvety, variable in size, up to 10 cm.	Bl. 80-300X10-12 (7-9 tip)	Solitary or chains, 5-11 (10-11) septa, Br, 45-90X10-12.5	C	D S	?
Dictyosporium toruloides	-	Colonies effuse, black, granular.	Conidia cheirtoid, 38-45X25-34, flattened.	Cells brown, terminal one hyaline.	C	D S	Ja-D
Endophragmia atra		Tufted, d. br. to bl., 6X1 cm.Synnemata bl.400x25-60	D. br. 4-5 thick.-10-15 at tip	Pale br. or hyaline, 28-43X15-23, bl. Bands at septa.	FC	D S	O-Ja
Epicoccum purpurascens	2	Sporodochia pulvinate, black, host tissue red-purple	Pale brown 5-15X3-6	Spherical or pyr. bl. or br., rough opaque, 15-20 diameter	F	D N	Ja-D
Gyrothrix verticillata	5	Effuse, thin, pale gtreyish brown. Setae pale brown.--	-300X3-4 wh. 3-4 hr. brch.	At base of setae, hyaline 10-15X1.5-2	UC	D S	S
Periconia. byssoides		Effuse, grey to black, hairy.	Br.-bl. 200-1400X10-20	Br. verrucose, 10-15 diameter, in short branched chains.	VC	D S	?
P. cookei		Effuse, grey to bladk, hairy.	As prv., no septa, tip 17-32	Br. verrucose,13-16 diameter.	FC	D S	?
P. minutissima		Effuse, grey to brown or black, hairy.	Brown up to 550X5-10	Straw to pale brown, verrucose, 4-6 in long brch chains.	C	D S	?
Pleurophragmium parvisporum		Effuse, thin, greyish brown, hairy.	Brown up to 400X4-6	Hyaline to p. br., smooth, 1-4 (3), att. by pointed denticles	VC	D S	Ja-D
Polyscytalum berkeleyi		Effuse pale grey or olivaceous grey, powdery.	80X3-5, br. to subhyaline	Dry long brch'd chains, hyaline to olive, 0-3, 10-30X2-3.5	C	D S	Mc-My
Torula herbarum		Up to several cm, olive when young to velvety black.	Br. Very short, see diagram	Brch'd chs, olive-br., verr.,3-10(4-5), 20-70X5-9 (30X7)	VC	D S	?
Trichocladium opacum	-			25-40X11-17,1-5	?	?	?
Volutella ciliata		White sporodochia, 0.1-0.25mm diam., white setae	Setae 250-500X8-9, verr.	Hyaline, smooth, 5-8X2, aggregated in slimy masses.	VC	D S	O-Ap

Abbreviations, Bl., black, br., brown, brch., branch or branched, d., dark, verr., verrucose, pyr., pyriforme, att., attached, VC very common, C common, FC fairly common, UC uncommon, QC quite common. Shaded mainly confined to Urtica dioica. o Generally on cupules of Beech

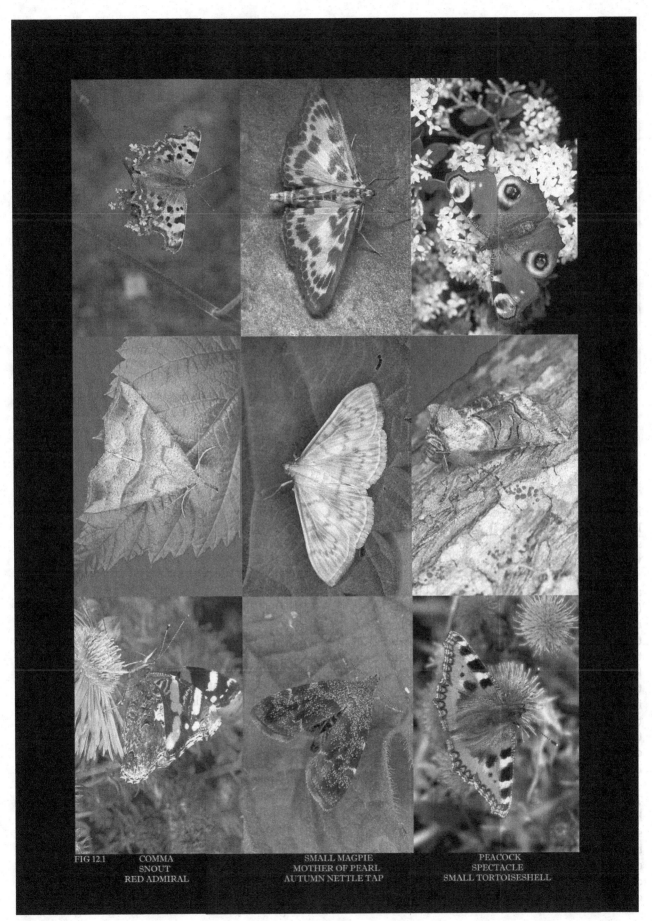

FIG 12.1   COMMA   SMALL MAGPIE   PEACOCK
SNOUT   MOTHER OF PEARL   SPECTACLE
RED ADMIRAL   AUTUMN NETTLE TAP   SMALL TORTOISESHELL

CHAPTER 12
INSECTS ON NETTLES 1
BUTTERFLIES AND MOTHS (LEPIDOPTERA)

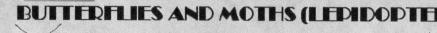

1 BUTTERFLIES

DENIZENS OF THE DAY

The butterfly farmer Hugh Newman wrote enthusiastically about his subject and inspired young readers like myself. He points out that some of our most beautiful Vanessid butterflies such as small tortoiseshells, peacocks and red admirals depend almost entirely on the stinging nettle in their caterpillar stage. Most people dislike this stinging plant and are prepared to get rid of it at any cost.

'When weed-killers are used, it is nearly always the nettle beds which are tackled first, and fewer breeding places mean fewer butterflies; in fact the more efficient we are in keeping things 'in order' the more we discourage the butterflies."

Hugh Newman 1967

INTRODUCTION

THE STINGING NETTLE AND INSECTS

Two chapters are required to cover the insects found on the stinging nettle. In the Introduction (Chapter 1) it was mentioned that 31 species of insect are restricted to the stinging nettle whilst 107 species rely on it to a certain extent. There are many guide books to the identification of insects and also the booklet 'Insects on Nettles', Davis (1983). My approach here is to consider briefly the insects that are specific to the nettle as well as those that have interested me during my field studies of the nettle. At this stage in the book sufficient knowledge of the nettle as a plant has been gained to enable a fuller understanding of why so many insects feed on this plant, as well as the strategies they use to avoid competing with one another for the food source. I hope my photographs and drawings will show the beauty of these often small insects and facilitate their identification.

'Why do so many insects feed on the nettle?' The answer to this lies in the fact that vertebrate herbivores are deterred from eating it due to its shield of stinging trichomes. Insects do not get stung because they are either too small or cannot generate enough force or are covered in armour or flexible cuticle and therefore cannot break the knob on the end of the stinging trichome. The nettle is common and widespread throughout the British Isles and therefore readily available to insects. Growth takes place most of the year with the exception of DecMarch when it is in the form of small evergreen shoots. Flowers also are produced over a long period and these are rich in nutrients. When eaten or cut down it has amazing powers of re-growth and young foliage is preferred by insects. It grows best on fertile soils and is high in nutrients (nitrogen, phosphorus, amino-acids, proteins, minerals, vitamins, etc.) which are essential for growth and therefore insects can complete their development in a short time. As a long-lived perennial, insects can over-winter on the evergreen shoots, or in the dead hollow stems, nettle litter, mosses etc., and in the underground rhizome system. Insects prefer to feed on nettles growing in open situations since these have thicker sun leaves, more nutrients and the higher temperature favours rapid growth (see also Chapter 13).

BRITISH BUTTERFLIES AND NETTLES

This part of the chapter deals with butterflies and of the 60 butterflies (excluding rare immigrants) which live in the British Isles, three (Small Tortoiseshell (*Aglais urticae*), Red Admiral (*Vanessa atlanta*) and Peacock (*Inachis io*) are largely dependent on the common nettle whilst another two Painted Lady (*V. cardui*), and Comma (*Polygonia c-album*) rely on it to a small extent. These five butterflies belong to the family Nymphalidae and are generally called Vanessids to distinguish them from the Fritillaries and Emperors which belong to the same family.

There can be few people in Britain who are not familiar with at least some of our beautiful Vanessid butterflies. These butterflies emerge early from hibernation and are the harbingers of spring, and associated with our hopes and aspirations that come with a New Year. Later in the season they are connected with the sun, summer days and as flashes of colour as they flutter between the massed flower heads of our gardens and the meadow flowers of our countryside. In autumn they are found sucking juices from our fallen fermenting fruits and from the late flowering ivy blossoms. The Vanessid butterflies, after their survival of our harsh and often drab winters, can be seen spreading out worn but still beautiful wings in the warm spring sunshine whilst resting on a bare patch near a nettle clone, or sucking nectar from the glistening yellow Celandines and gently swaying Bluebells. Who can

SMALL TORTOISESHELL *AGLAIS URTICAE L.*

Month	JAN.	FEB.	MAR.	APR	MAY	JUNE	JULY	AUG.	SEPT.	OCT.	NOV.	DEC.
Egg					oooooooooooo		ooooooooooo					
Caterpillar				ccccccccccccc		cccccccccccccc						
Chrysalis					ppppppppppp		pppppppppp					
Adult	hhhhhhhhhhhhhhhhhhhihiiiiiiiiiiiiiiiiiiiiiii					iiiiiiiiiiiiiiiiiiiiiiii i i iiiiiiiiiiiiiiiiiiihihihihihihhhhhhhhhhhhhh						

PEACOCK *INACHIS IO L.*

Month	JAN.	FEB.	MAR.	APR	MAY	JUNE	JULY	AUG.	SEPT.	OCT.	NOV.	DEC.
Egg					ooooooooooo							
Caterpillar				ccccccccccccccccccc								
Chrysalis						pppppppppppppp						
Adult	hhhhhhhhhhhhihihihihihihiiiiiiiiiiiiiiiiiiiiiiiiiiiiiiii					iiiiiiiiiiiiiiiiiiiiiiiiiiihihihhhhhhhhhhhhhhhhhhhhhhhhh						

COMMA *POLYGONIA C-ALBUM L.*

Month	JAN.	FEB.	MAR.	APR	MAY	JUNE	JULY	AUG.	SEPT.	OCT.	NOV.	DEC.
Egg				oooooooooooo			ooooooooooo					
Caterpillar				cccccccccccccc			ccccccccccccc					
Chrysalis					pppppppp		ppppppp					
Adult	hhhhhhhhhhhhhhhhihihihiiiiiiiiiiiiiiiiiiiiiiii				i iiiii i iiiiiiiiiiiiiiiiiiiiiiii i iiiihihihhihihihihihihhhhhhhhhhhhhhhhhh							

RED ADMIRAL *VANESSA ATLANTA L.*

Month	JAN.	FEB.	MAR.	APR	MAY	JUNE	JULY	AUG.	SEPT.	OCT.	NOV.	DEC.
Egg				ooooooooooooooooooooooooooooooooooooooooooooooooooo								
Caterpillar				cccccccccccccccccccccccccccccccccccccccccccccccccccccccccc								
Chrysalis							ppppppppppppppppppppppppppppppppppppppp					
Adult				iiiiiiiiiiiiiiiiiiiiii iiiiiiiiiiiiiiiiiiiiiiiiiiiiiiiiiiiiiiiiiiiiiiiiiiiiiiii i iiiiiiiii								

PAINTED LADY *CYNTHIA (VANESSA) CARDUI L.*

Month	JAN.	FEB.	MAR.	APR	MAY	JUNE	JULY	AUG.	SEPT.	OCT.	NOV.	DEC.
Egg				ooooooooooooooooooooooooooooooooooooooooooooooooooooooooo								
Caterpillar				cccccccccccccccccccccccccccccccccccccccccccccccccccccccccccccccc								
Chrysalis							ppppppppppppppppppppppppppppppppppppppppppppppp					
Adult		i i iiiiiiiiiiiiiiiiiiiiiiiiiiiiiiiiiiiiiiiiiiiii iiiiiiiiiiiiiiiiiiiiiiii iiii										

TABLE 12.1 THE LIFE CYCLES OF BRITISH BUTTERFLIES THAT DEPEND, PARTIALY OR ENTIRELY UPON URTICA DIOICA IN THEIR LARVAL STAGES

The coloured area for the egg, caterpillar, chrysalid and adult show the range of times of the year when these stages are likely to be found (after Thomas, 1991).

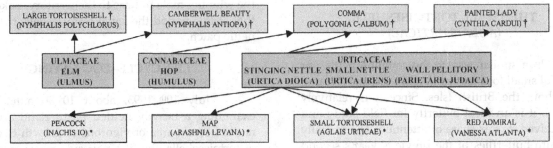

FLOW DIAGRAM 12.1. SHOWING THE MEMBERS OF THE URTICALES THAT PROVIDE FOOD FOR THE LARVAE OF THE BRITISH VANESSID BUTTERFLIES (NYMPHALIDAE).

The Vanessid larvae which are confined to the Urticales are marked with an asterisk and those that also feed on other Orders of plants are marked a sword sign. The larvae of Cynthia cardui (painted lady) feed largely on thistles (Cirium, Carduus) and to a smaller extent on mallows (Malva, Althaea), artichoke (Helianthus tuberosa); Nymphalis polychlorus (large tortoiseshell), sallows and willows (Salix), poplars (Populus), aspen (P. tremula), wild cherry (Prunus avium), pear (Pyrus communis); Polygonia c-album (comma) redcurrent (Ribes).

estimate the pleasure derived from the beauty of these insects, their fascinating often bizarre lifecycles, and the scientific uncovering of their ecology and secret-lives? Who can deny the need for their conservation?

Despite the greater interest in butterflies these days, I have found a lot of people are surprised to learn that the caterpillars of our Vanessid butterflies feed entirely or in part on the Stinging Nettle (see frontispiece p 165). So instead of hacking down the despised nettle in the interests of tidiness, why not leave the nettle alone with the possibility of increasing the number of our beautiful butterflies. Alternatively why not create a butterfly garden with a nettle patch and have the advantage of finding out more about many of the topics mentioned in this book which need further study, and all on your doorstep (see later).

There is now an increasing need to look at the relationships between butterflies *and their larval food-plants*, the latter being the most crucial factor governing their survival. Both butterflies and their food plants are affected by complex ecological factors, the most important of which are the influence of mankind on such things as pollution, destruction of habitat, intensive farming practices, global warming and climatic changes, over grazing, etc. Scientists, field naturalists and the general public can help by becoming involved in studies at different levels on the relationships between individual insects and plants or vice versa, such as in this nettle study. Only by understanding the lifecycle and the ecology of the Stinging Nettle (Urtica dioica) are we in a position to begin to appreciate its interaction with the insects associated with it. Because of lack of space I have considered those lepidoptera confined to nettles, briefly mentioned the others, and treated my favourites in a little more detail.

THE LIFE-CYCLES AND FOOD PREFERENCES OF BRITISH VANESSIDS

THE SMALL TORTOISESHELL (*AGLAIS URTICAE*)

In a similar way to the common nettle our beautiful small tortoiseshell (Aglais urticae) is found throughout the British Isles. Since it is relatively common it is an ideal butterfly for field study and has received its fair share of attention. The sexually immature butterflies of the previous year's second brood emerge from hibernation in March and feed on the nectar of the spring flowers. After a few days they become sexually active. In early April the males take up residence in the vicinity of well established nettle clones and the classical work on their territorial behaviour was pioneered by Baker (1972). After roosting, the males spend the morning basking, feeding in suitable areas in which nectar - producing flowers grow, and also migrating. In the afternoon they take up residence in areas containing well - established nettle clones where they defend their territory against other males. They tend to give up the first territory after 90 min. and move to another and therefore have two territories per day. In the territory they drive away rival males or leave to follow a prospective female. After courtship, which lasts 2-3 hours, the males follow the female into the nettle patch where copulation takes place.

Of the 20 territorial sites of the small tortoiseshell studied they had the following characteristics: 100% had full sunlight, approx. 80% contained the common nettle, 60% were by the side of a wall or hedge, approx. 20% were in an open field or in fields with nectar flowers and slightly less than 20% were by the edge of a wood or row of trees – very few were in corner areas. The presence of an edge area was quite important and could be used by migrating females as lines leading to possible oviposition sites. Nettles are probably recognised by the males visually by their shape due to their clonal growth habit, but more importantly I suspect, by their very strong 'cat urine' smell, particularly when in full growth. Since the males choose territorial sites that may only contain a few flowers, feeding must be carried out in other areas during the morning period.

Optimal sites by the end of the day could be occupied by up to 4 males. Territorial defence behaviour consists of the male who occupies a territory pursuing an intruder and results in the pair climbing vertically 7-10m in the air. A spiral path is seen which is due to each male trying to achieve a position slightly behind and above the other male. The subordinate male then tries to reverse his position by a series of dives, and climbs paralleling the other male, until one is driven away, after which the winning male returns to the territory. Baker says that at this period the small tortoiseshells roost in a nettle patch.

LIFE CYCLE--EGG LAYING

July 10th 1993, about 10 30 a.m., I was examining a heavily nettled pastureland area and noticed on an area of vigorous re-growth two pairs of tortoiseshells, the first pair side by side and the second pair with wings outspread and facing one another. Due to disturbance on getting out my photographic gear only one of each pair remaine

Freshy hatched small tortoiseshell of the first brood resting on the stinging nettle.

Hibernating A. urticae on a garage window with snow on the outside window-ledge.

This rather worn small tortoiseshell survived the winter in hibernation and is now soaking up the spring sunshine and seeking a mate

Aglais urticeae emerging from hibernation feeds on nectar from a bluebell.

Quite often as shown in this sequence two males compete for one female (light orange far right). In this case the male with the open wings managed to drive away the male with the closed wings (position shown with the pink arrows), after which the male moves up behind the female and resumes the courtship behaviour of vibrating his wing and tapping the female with his antennae. (Spring courtship)

Spring courtship with the male walking behind the female who at first has her wings closed. The gently vibrating wing of the male causes the female to open her wings showing acceptance of the male and courtship proceeds. This takes place in full sunlight, in the vicinity of nettle clones and nectar flower such as lesser celandines and bluebells. The female later walks into a nettle patch followed by the male and then copulation takes place.

Two male competing for a female the second male approaches from the side and then from the rear.

Courtship taking place on young nettle in the spring.

Summer courtship on re-growth nettles , notice the vibrant colours of these newly emerged adults.

FIG 12.2 HIBERNATION AND SPRING AND SUMMER COURTSHIP OF SMALL TORTOISESHELL BUTTERFLIES.

and on examination both were females laying eggs on the underside of young apical nettle leaves.

It is possible that both butterflies that flew off were females. Many observers have recorded females competing with other females whilst they are egg laying or laying eggs on the same leaf as other females so that occasionally leaves are found with over 1000 eggs in a big overlapping mass. Baker (1978) carried out the following experiment to find out whether sight or smell is involved in egg location. An egg - laying tortoiseshell was distracted and flew off a short distance, after which the nettle stalk with its eggs was removed and placed at a short distance away. The female flew back to the exact same spot on the nettle clone thereby showing that sight (topographical memory) was probably responsible for the location of the nettle rather than smell (pheromones).

BOX 12.1. DIARY 1996. COURTSHIP AND PAIRING

I had often seen courtship in the small tortoiseshell but failed to see the pairing. I wanted a photographic record of courtship so I walked over to one of a series of pastures grazed by cows and situated on the flood plain of the lower river Taw. These pastures support scattered but sizeable clones of the common nettle. This account is based on the entries to my diary of 1996: -

Feb. 21st. First small tortoiseshell seen in the garden.

April 12th. A sunny afternoon. Went to bridge lower pasture (B L P). This pasture supports 12-13 sizeable nettle clones and when approaching these I noticed a large number of tortoiseshells chasing one another and spiralling into the air. These were obviously males exhibiting territorial behaviour. Some were in good condition whilst others were tatty. One was minus a hind-wing and another minus half a hind-wing and yet this did not affect their flights. Each clone supported one or sometimes two males with outspread wings, sunning themselves. On my approach, they would fly at me and then career off and not always return to the same clone. Some were sunbathing on banks, others feeding on the nectar from lesser celandines and dandelions.

Courtship was taking place on grassy and bare areas as well as on the leaves of nettle clones. The female rests with her wings spread out and the male moves up behind her, spreads out his wings so that his front wings slightly overlap the hind wings of the female, and vibrates them up and down. At the same time he often nudges her with his head and beats her hind - wings with his antennae. The female responds by vibrating her wings gently. After a while, or if disturbed by another male, they take off in a low flight with the male flying parallel to the female but above her, and appearing to force her to land. Very often I noticed two males competing for the same female. In one case a male with closed wings was in-between the female and a male with outspread wings. The latter male opened and closed his wings in rapid succession whilst moving forwards, and after some time, the other male moved off to one side. After this, normal courtship proceeded between the other pair.

April 14-15th. Drizzle, no butterflies present in the pastures.

April 20th. A day when one of my ambitions was achieved. A sunny afternoon. I went to Waldron's lower pasture 2 (W L P 2). A line of nettles had grown up on the soil dredged from the drainage ditch. Many tortoiseshells were exhibiting territorial behaviour, spiralling into the air and diving after one another. A pair was undergoing courtship behaviour and just when I was about to photograph them, another male dived on them and all three went into a low flight over the ditch in to W L P 3 which also contains a number of nettle clones! After negotiating the ditch, I managed to locate them undergoing courtship behaviour. On my approach the male raised and lowered his wings in a warning reaction, whilst the female with vibrating wings appeared to take no notice. They took off and I pursued them several times and secured some photos. The pair landed near another nettle clone whilst being pestered by another male. As I watched, instead of the usual courtship the female walked into the nettle patch followed by the male. I gave them 10 minutes before I decided to look, which I solved by bending to the ground each nettle shoot until I found them. The female had climbed to just below the top of a shoot and the male had come up alongside her. Their abdomens were joined in copulation. The position was unusual since generally when butterflies pair they face in opposite directions. I managed to secure some photos. At 9.30 the next morning they were in the same position but their abdomens had parted.

April 23rd. A sunny afternoon so I visited B L P. Tortoiseshells were still undergoing courtship behaviour. I witnessed another pair disappearing into a nettle patch, and on looking, found them paired side by side in the same way as the previous pair. Time of copulation was 5.30 p.m., with the sun still out.

The eggs are laid on the underside of the leaf and because this is extremely hairy, anchorage of the eggs must be a problem. This might account for why after gluing down one egg layer the rest are often laid on top of these. Most batches number 80-100 eggs. Considering the majority of pastureland nettle clones range from 1.5-4.0 m^2 or more, there are generally enough shoots to feed the surviving full-grown larvae; for this reason laying large egg masses must be counterproductive.

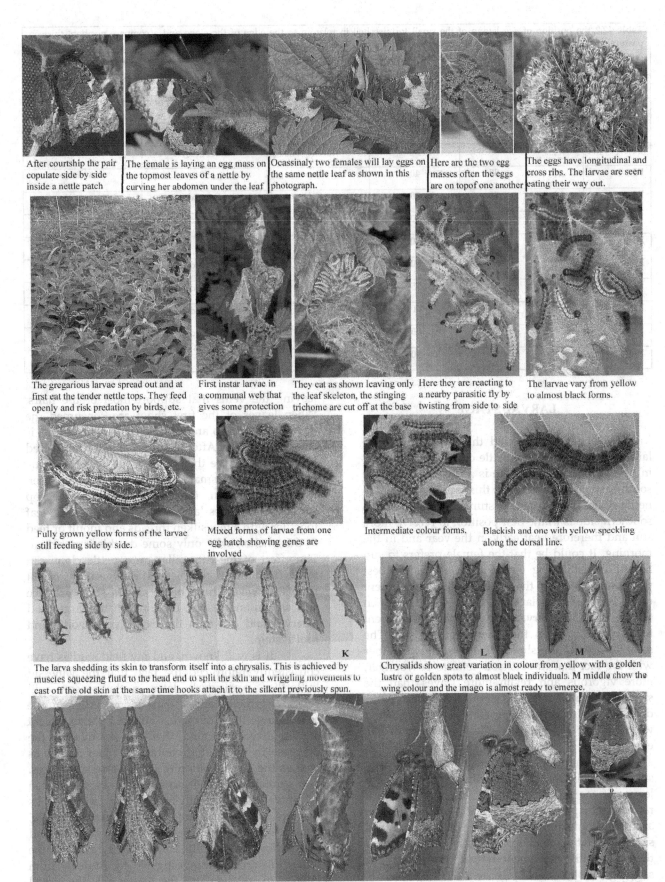

After courtship the pair copulate side by side inside a nettle patch

The female is laying an egg mass on the topmost leaves of a nettle by curving her abdomen under the leaf

Ocassinaly two females will lay eggs on the same nettle leaf as shown in this photograph.

Here are the two egg masses often the eggs are on topof one another

The eggs have longitudinal and cross ribs. The larvae are seen eating their way out.

The gregarious larvae spread out and at first eat the tender nettle tops. They feed openly and risk predation by birds, etc.

First instar larvae in a communal web that gives some protection

They eat as shown leaving only the leaf skeleton, the stinging trichome are cut off at the base

Here they are reacting to a nearby parasitic fly by twisting from side to side

The larvae vary from yellow to almost black forms.

Fully grown yellow forms of the larvae still feeding side by side.

Mixed forms of larvae from one egg batch showing genes are involved

Intermediate colour forms.

Blackish and one with yellow speckling along the dorsal line.

The larva shedding its skin to transform itself into a chrysalis. This is achieved by muscles squeezing fluid to the head end to split the skin and wriggling movements to cast off the old skin at the same time hooks attach it to the silkent previously spun.

Chrysalids show great variation in colour from yellow with a golden lustre or golden spots to almost black individuals. M middle show the wing colour and the imago is almost ready to emerge.

I never tire of waiting to see the miraculous happening of the emergence of the adult butterfy. Squeezing fluid to the head end caused the head piece to fall off followed by the antennae, legs and wing being withdrawn from the pupal case. Blood is pumped into the wings which expand and dry in the sun.

FIG 12.3 STAGES IN THE LIFE-CYCLE OF THE SMALL TORTOISESHELL (AGLAIS URTICAE)

Table 12.2 the position of egg laying of the small tortoiseshell in relation to the edge of the clone and a compass position, thirteen pastureland nettle clones were chosen. Compact nettle clone = *, Scattered nettle clone = †

Number of Clone	Symbol	Mean shoot Height cm	Height of shoot with eggs	Compass bearing	Centimetres from edge of clone.	Size of clone in metres
P1	*	90	82	S. E.	At the edge	2 X 1.4
P2	*	76	42	S.	40	2.4 X 1.2
P3	†	60	30	S.	At the edge	1.5 X 1.6
P4	†	20	20	S. E.	At the edge	-
P5	†	85	40	S.	50	4.5 X 3.4
P6	†	50	30	C.	Central	Large area
P7	*	85	70	S.	At the edge	2.3 X 1.0
P8	†	80	80	N.	50	-
P9	†	80	50	S. W.	At the edge	-
P10	*	85	75	S.	At the edge	0.7 X 1.4
P11	†	70	70	W.	At the edge	-
P12	*	80	80	S.	At the edge	-
P13	*	90	90	S .E.	50	-

LARVAL STAGE

Dennis (1984) found that eggs tend to be laid towards the edge of nettle clumps which grow in open situations and there is a preference for the south-east edge. I verified this by examining 13 nettle clones in 5 adjacent pastures (Table, 12.2). The southern side is in the best position to receive more sun and therefore heat early in the year and in the morning. It could be that the female prefers to sun herself whilst laying eggs, or this is in the best position to speed up the hatching and development of the larvae. Being black and gregarious it has been shown that the larvae are above the ambient temperature even in the absence of the sun. The same applies to the shoots near the edge, together with the fact that these shoots tend to be younger, more vigorous and retain more leaves than the shaded central shoots. The larvae hatch within 7-21 days depending on the temperature. They eat their way out but do not consume the whole of the eggshell.

The minute freshly hatched larvae produce silken threads that pull together and cover the leaves of the top of the shoot. The web acts as a retreat from predators, the effects of the weather and protection during moulting; since the larva is small in relation to the plant hairs, spinning over these facilitates movement across the surface. The stinging hairs offer no danger to insects (Chapters 8, 13) and the toxins in the leaf must be neutralised in the gut. The leaf area between the veins is eaten leaving the veins that support most of the hairs. When leaves of the first shoot are consumed the larvae move on to an adjacent shoot that in turn is covered in a web. After about 3-4 shoots are covered in webs the larvae then spread out over the nettle patch, firstly in smaller groups, and then when nearly full grown, they feed singly on the top surface. Sometimes larvae draw the top of the leaf together with a few silken threads and moult or feed in this shelter; why only some do this is not clear. The effect of the caterpillar on a nettle clone can result in almost complete skeletonisation of all shoots however these nettle clones soon produce side shoots and leaves, drawing on the large food reserves laid down in the extensive rhizome and root system.

It is well known, and my field studies have consistently reinforced the fact, that the vanessid butterflies, particularly later in the season, will select re-growth nettles (cut down earlier in the season) over those of mature adjacent plants. Recent studies have indicated that this is due to the decrease in nutritional content of older leaves as well as the accumulation of toxic waste substances. Few studies have been carried out on the nutritional advantage of re-growth foliage and looked at its nutrient content compared to that of mature foliage, and the effect of these on the growth and maturation of butterfly larvae. As a result of the latter, this area was investigated by Andrew Pullin (1987), in relation to the larvae of the small tortoiseshell (Aglais urticae) feeding on the common nettle (Urtica dioica). Leaf samples from

Peacock with wing up giving it the appearance of a dead leaf.

Showing the eye spots of the hind wings as a warning to predators or to direct birds away from the body

First instar larvae ready for ecdysis/moult, notice the absence of yellow spots

Larvae in large gregarious webs.

Two fully grown larvae on a nettle leaf notice the white spots and large spines.

Imago emerging from the pupal case.

pulling out the wings and legs notice the split proboscis.

The wings are blown up with blood and unfurl.

the wings expand and dry.

Wings fully expanded and dry.

Peacock larvae in various stages of pupation whilst hanging from the muslin of a breeding cage.

The variation in colour of the chrysalids enabling camouflage on various backgrounds.

A peacock variety artificially produced by exposing the pupa to low temperatures.

The larva feeds in a tent of leaves drawn together by silk.

The top view of a larva.
The colour ranges from brown-yellow.

The side view of a larva.

Pupation takes place within a tent of nettle leaves drawn together by silk threads.

The top and lower views of a chrysalid, and views of the adult feeding on nectar and rotting fruits in the autumn.

Various stages in the emergence of the adult butterfly from the pupal case and the unfolding and drying of the wings, an amazing event to witness.

FIG 12.4 STAGES IN THE LIFE-CYCLE OF THE PEACOCK (Rows 1-3) AND RED ADMIRAL (Row 4-5)

pastureland nettle clones, over 2 years, before and after re-growth (Aug. 1984 and July 1985) were analysed for their nitrogen content. Leaves were fed throughout the period to the larvae of the small tortoiseshell and their growth rates were measured by their increase in dry weight over time. Re-growth of U. dioica occurred in all patches. The high levels of nitrogen and protein in re-growth nettles resembled those found in spring nettle foliage. Total organic nitrogen was significantly higher in concentration, in the two weeks following pasture mowing, than it was in mature leaves (see also Growth, Chapter 14). Growth was more rapid in the larvae of Aglais urticae fed on re-growth leaves than those fed on leaves of mature nettle plants. The results therefore showed that re-growth leaves are better food for the small tortoiseshell larvae than those of mature plants. Pullin (1986) obtained similar results for larvae of the peacock (Inachis io) when fed on re-growth nettle leaves. The experiment does not match defoliation by caterpillars, since in this case only leaves are consumed, but it does follow complete removal or destruction of the above-ground part of the nettle clone by man in practices such as spraying and mowing (see later).

PUPATION

The occasional caterpillar pupates on the nettle, but the majority, when mature, move in a straight line up to 55m before pupating on a variety of suitable objects, usually at a height of about 1 metre. The instinctive behaviour of not pupating inside the nettle patch has undoubtedly been selected by evolution, due to the fact that it is teeming with insect predators and spiders, as well as high concentrations of parasitic flies and ichneumon wasps which could lead to high mortality. The chrysalids are generally well camouflaged but are often found by searching birds such as blue tits. I have found that certain batches of larvae produce chrysalids covered in gold metallic spots (Fig 12.3) and since these are likely to be conspicuous when lit by sunbeams this could be to their disadvantage. The pupal stage lasts from 2-4 weeks depending upon temperature.

The highest recorded breeding site in the British Isles is 330 m (1,100 feet). I have frequently found nests of small tortoiseshell larvae on the common nettle in the Austrian Alps between 1,900-2,000 m (2058-2167 feet).

PEACOCK (INACHIS IO)

The peacock and small tortoiseshell butterflies lay their eggs predominantly on the stinging nettle and in the spring they would be competing for nettle clones. However, it is very rare to find the larvae of these two butterflies on the same nettle clone, as well as to find more than one group of larvae on a single nettle clone; this is due to their territorial behaviour as well as small differences in their habitat preferences. The peacock is basically a woodland butterfly and it selects courtship territories which have the following characteristics: 100% are in sunlight and at the edge of a wood or row of trees, 50% in corners, and of lesser importance are 6% by the side of a wall or hedge, 20% contain nettles and none occur in open fields or contain flowers (Baker, 1972). The selection of different habitats for courtship by the two butterflies ensures that no confusion results from clashes between rival males of the two species; I have often witnessed small tortoiseshells driving off peacocks which have entered their territory. Interaction is further avoided by the fact that peacocks do not use nettle patches as roosting sites.

The male peacocks roost, bask and feed in the morning and occupy their territories in the afternoon. Each territory is occupied by a single male, who stays in his territory for the whole afternoon, generally about 4 hours. The male drives away other male intruders in a similar way to the small tortoiseshell, or is replaced by another male. When a female appears, he chases her and tries to remain with her for the whole afternoon. If he is successful, copulation takes place when she goes to roost amongst trees, bushes or ground - growing ivy (Baker 1972).

In Devon where dairy farming predominates I have found that the small tortoiseshell prefers to lay on nettle clones in open pasture which is to their detriment because these nettles are either cut down or sprayed just at the time the larvae are half-grown. This reduces the number of adults of the first brood; however, these butterflies can then use re-growth nettles abundant at this time and do not have to compete with peacock larvae since the peacock is single brooded.

The peacock larvae remain in gregarious webs until almost fully grown and are often heavily parasitised by ichneumon wasp and Phryxe flies. The adult larvae are black with conspicuous spots. The pupae tend to be of two types, green or brown, which increases their chances of being camouflaged in a variety of pupation sites away from the nettle. The adults are well camouflaged when their wings are closed and when disturbed they flash the eye-spots on their hind-wings to frighten off predators.

THE RED ADMIRAL (*VANESSA ATLANTA*)

The majority of eggs are laid on the common nettle. Competition with the peacock and small tortoiseshell butterflies for nettle sites is achieved by the laying of single eggs which enables (1) a greater distribution of eggs, (2) ovipositing females will lay in habitats favoured by Aglais and Inachis but also choose plants in more shaded situations, e.g. woodland edges and rides. Young re-growth plants are most frequently selected but larvae can also be found on older plants and in company with other vanessid larvae. Females can often be seen stopping briefly to deposit single eggs on the upper surfaces of the terminal leaves of nettle plants. The single egg strategy also enables the red admiral to lay on smaller more scattered nettle clones as well as individual plants of the small nettle and wall pellitory (*Parietaria judaica*) (See appendix Nettleworts).

The adult butterfly chooses the relatively delicate re-growth leaves and thinner leaves of nettles growing in partial shade. Added to this is the strategy of young caterpillars to bite about half way through the petiole near its base. This has two effects: (1) it causes the leaf blade to swing from a horizontal to a vertical position and hang by a thread-like petiole connection (2) it must cause the partial loss of turgor. The loss of turgor leads to slight wilting which brings the leaf margins closer together so that they can be fastened together more easily by silken threads. There seems to be little doubt that this protects the larva from predation by birds; unfortunately it does not protect against being 'stung' by ichneumon wasps which can either enter the tent or possibly sting the larva through the leaf. The fact that the larvae are spread out over a large area probably helps to compensate for easy detection by the ichneumon wasps. A final tent is spun between leaves and the chrysalis can be found suspended from the top of the tent. It hatches after about 17 days; the full time taken from egg to emergence is 49 days subject to changes in temperature.

COMMA (*POLYGONIA C-ALBUM*)

In the early spring the comma sunbathes alongside woodland margins being a woodland butterfly but, enters our gardens from July-late Oct. to seek nectar-rich flowers.

Diary entry 25th April 1996. *'A warm spring afternoon, the habitat being a wild narrow marshy pasture between a deciduous and a coniferous wood. The male comma in its territory is sunbathing on the path and suddenly flies directly at a peacock and they spiral to a great height before the comma dives down to return to the exact same spot. When disturbed during photography it flies to twigs in the nettle patch and vice versa. I witness several territorial spiral flights when other comma butterflies enter the territory of the resident male that returns to the exact same spot each time.'*

The female deposits her eggs singly on the upper surface of the leaves of the common nettle, the hop (*Humulus lupulus*) and elms (*Ulmus* spp.), although it has also been found on blackcurrent bushes (*Ribes* spp.). The older caterpillars are remarkable in that they are black with a white area covering the top hind part of the body, and appear like bird droppings from a distance. They feed on the underside of the leaf but the cryptic camouflage would help to protect when moving or during pupation. I have found the occasional comma caterpillar on nettles under buckthorn in my garden, and observed they pupate on the plant, generally attached to a leaf stalk. Thomas et al (1991) remarks that the hop is a favoured food plant, the vast majority feed on the nettle, and a few on currant bushes and elms. He has found that nettles in semi-shaded situations and sometimes in deeper shade beside woods are chosen, whilst those in open fields are avoided.

PAINTED LADY (*CYNTHIA CARDUI*)

This migrant butterfly prefers to lay its eggs on various thistles but in their absence will readily lay eggs on available stinging nettles.

Box 12.2. DIARY 1996. A YEAR OF PAINTED LADIES TO REMEMBER.

7th June. Visited Braunton Burrows Nature Reserve on the North Devon coast that comprises a three mile stretch made up of three lines of dunes and dune slacks. "Sea stock is a good show. A vast number of painted ladies are feeding on an area dotted with stork's bill (Erodium cicutarium). This must be a mass migration. 18 passed me in one direction over a 20 min period. They are in excellent condition, so probably migrated as soon as they hatched – possibly from N. Africa/Morocco. There are so many in the area that an area 3 m² contained 2-3 that were feeding. Most were flying rapidly in a northerly direction."

8th June. Went for run up Codden Hill, (a piece of moorland 629 feet [194 m]) in height. "Blue sky high cloud. 24 painted ladies seen over a four mile stretch together with 7 silver Y moths, both of which are migratory."

12th June. "Run up Codden Hill. Bright cloudy. Large number of painted ladies; some were laying eggs on nettles growing alongside a hedge near the top of the hill. Small plants were chosen and they only remained on the plants for a few seconds so it is likely only single eggs

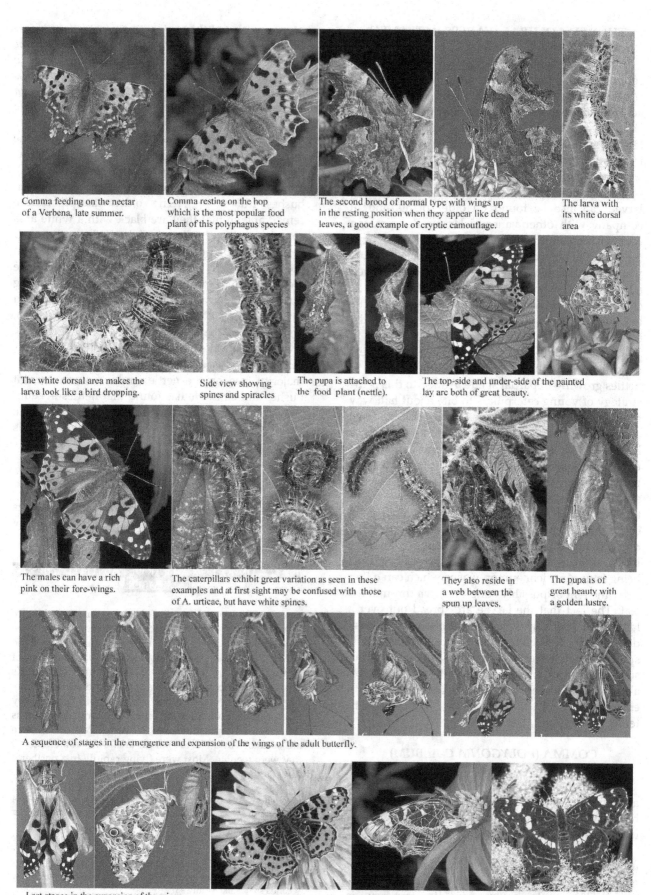

Comma feeding on the nectar of a Verbena, late summer.

Comma resting on the hop which is the most popular food plant of this polyphagus species

The second brood of normal type with wings up in the resting position when they appear like dead leaves, a good example of cryptic camouflage.

The larva with its white dorsal area

The white dorsal area makes the larva look like a bird dropping.

Side view showing spines and spiracles

The pupa is attached to the food plant (nettle).

The top-side and under-side of the painted lay are both of great beauty.

The males can have a rich pink on their fore-wings.

The caterpillars exhibit great variation as seen in these examples and at first sight may be confused with those of A. urticae, but have white spines.

They also reside in a web between the spun up leaves.

The pupa is of great beauty with a golden lustre.

A sequence of stages in the emergence and expansion of the wings of the adult butterfly.

Last stages in the expansion of the wings

The map butterfly once established a small colony in England.

FIG 12.5 STAGES IN THE LIFE CYCLE THE COMMA, PAINTED LADY AND THE MAP BUTTERFLY

were laid – to check later. More painted ladies and my first red admiral in perfect condition.

More silver Y's. Went to Chapleton. along the river Taw later in the morning. The ox-eyed daises (*Leucanthemum vulgare*) along the railway line were covered in masses of painted ladies – took photos. Went to Torrington in afternoon. Saw painted ladies laying eggs on nettles. Laid on top of nettle leaves, bluish-green ribbed, similar to those of the small tortoiseshell. 3 shoots examined with 2 eggs, 2 eggs and 1 egg."

15th June. "Went to Lee Bay. Lots of painted ladies on red valerian (*Centranthus ruber*)."

18th June. "Painted lady eggs have hatched. Egg shell eaten completely. Young caterpillars first eat the top palisade of the nettle leaf then retire to the base of the leaf where the edges of the cordate base are pulled in and a web spun, under which the larvae reside."

19th June. "Painted ladies were seen laying eggs on wilted and shrivelling nettle shoots and those of the creeping thistle (*Cirsium arvense*) after they had been sprayed with the herbicide Broadbent."

27th June. "Run up Codden Hill. Webs of painted lady larvae are found on the leaves of nettles along the boundary fence. The edges of larger leaves are pulled partially together and then the web is continued across the top. The black larvae have one yellow lateral stripe and about 1 cm long."

7th July. "Bishops Tawton lower pasture. Lots of painted lady caterpillars at different instar stages are on creeping thistle (*Cirsium arvense*) and a smaller number on the common nettle".

8th July. "Nettle Combe Area Codden Hill. Lots of fully grown painted lady larvae on nettles along field border. Two chrysalids were found within tents of spun-up nettle leaves, as per red admiral. These beautiful chrysalids are washed with coppery and golden reflections. A nettle area of 80 m² was covered in peacock and painted lady larvae. The latter were in leaves with a web over the top and with the larvae and frass inside – it is a messy larva. There were such a very large number of painted lady larvae that their webs covered about half of the area and most leaves were reduced to skeletons! Painted ladies when selecting plants for egg laying must compromise between thistles and nettles and when the former are not available then nettles are frequently used – but I have never seen such a large congregation of larvae as this!"

16th July. "Nettle Combe Area Codden Hill. Painted lady larvae fully grown, many chrysalids found on nettle plants."

18th July. "Bishops Tawton Pasture. This has been mown so vanessid larvae on nettles and thistles are likely to have been destroyed. Also a good nectar source for butterflies has also been removed."

22-27 July. "Painted ladies have hatched out. Some males have an extremely beautiful pink coloration on their wings."

13th Sept. "Codden Hill. Painted lady larvae are still on pastureland nettles."

It was a pleasure to be able to follow the life cycle of the painted lady and to have this beautiful butterfly gracing the flowers of our countryside and gardens. The nettle played its part in producing more of these beauties.

EUROPEAN MAP (*ARASHNIA LEVANA*)

This European butterfly which 50 years ago was found in southern Germany and Austria, Switzerland and northern and eastern France, has now spread to Spain, Sweden and Finland. It was introduced into England and temporarily established in 1912-14 in the Forest of Dean, Monmouthshire and Symond's Yat, Herefordshire. It may have died out normally but it is suspected an entomologist against introductions was largely responsible for its demise by catching as many adults as he could find (Maitland Emmett & Heath, 1990). Most butterfly breeders supply this butterfly or its larvae so perhaps further attempts will be made to introduce this beautiful butterfly into the British Isles. Its larva feeds on the common nettle and there are certainly enough of these to go around!

VANESSID BUTTERFLIES AND FARMING PRACTISES

Destruction of the habitat comes at the top of the list, and farming practises a close second, when considering the decline in species and number of British butterflies. This account is based on the effect of farming practises on vanessid butterflies over approximately 0.5 square miles of pasture adjacent to the River Taw, Devon. It is extracted from my diary for 1996, and from the point of view of a person interested in the fate of our butterflies, and therefore written in the passion of the moment.

Box 12.3. Diary 1966. FARMING PRACTICES AND SMALL TORTOISESHELLS, PEACOCKS AND PAINTED LADIES.

17th June. Pasture adjacent to Himalayan balsam area. This pasture is full of dock and with a small number of nettle clones. It appears to have been sprayed with a hormonal-type spray, 2-4 D? since the docks have over-grown into contorted shapes. The nettles are withered and the tops of their shoots are bowed over. Peacock, small tortoiseshell and painted lady larvae are languishing on these poisoned plants. I must come back and remove these to other nettles. Cows are grazing this sprayed area. There must be a possibility of the spray chemicals getting into the food chains and possibly to humans via diary and meat products.

19th June. Bishops Tawton Upper Pasture 1 (B.T.U.P.1). Vigorous grass growth with a lot of spear thistle suitable for painted lady larvae. There are about 10 nettle clones here with small tortoiseshell larvae from freshly hatched to nearly fully grown, so some adults could appear within a week or so. B.T.Bridge Pasture. Grass cropped by 33 cows/heifers but nettle clones intact. Tall nettles along the bank are negative for larvae. The 8 clones in this pasture each have small tortoiseshell larvae ranging from freshly hatched; second instar and a large number are nearly full grown.

In all lower pastures the nettles have been spot sprayed leaving the masses of creeping thistles fortunately for the painted lady.

I reach B.T.Lower P. 4. These nettle clones have just been sprayed, they are wilted and turning blackish and yet these clones are covered in masses of small tortoiseshell and peacock larvae. It is a distressing and depressing sight. I make a survey of the clones. Clone 1. Tortoiseshell webs, 2nd instar larvae and larger ones in rolled up leaves. Larvae not feeding so they must either be affected directly by the spray or from ingesting sprayed leaves. Clone 2. 2 lots of small tortoiseshell larvae wandering about looking for food, some fully grown. One chrysalid on nettle. Clone 3. Peacock larvae webs of 1st - 2nd instar. Clone 4. Freshly hatched egg masses of small tortoiseshell and peacock. Clone 5. Peacock webs. Clone 6. Freshly hatched peacock larvae and almost fully grown small tortoiseshell. Clone 7. Small tortoiseshell, two lots almost fully grown and younger peacock larvae. Clone 8. Groups of almost fully grown peacock larvae which could survive as only half of the nettle clone were sprayed. Clone 9. small tortoiseshell larvae. Clone 10. Two lots of small tortoiseshell larvae almost fully grown. Clone 11. 1st-2nd instars larvae of the small tortoiseshell. Clone 12. Peacock freshly hatched and small tortoiseshell larvae. Clone 13. Small tortoiseshell peacock larvae almost fully grown. Clone 14. Two lots small tortoiseshell fully and half grown. Clone 15. Small tortoiseshell eggs hatching.

I tried to remove some larvae to adjacent nettles in shaded hedge borders but I found these nettles covered in masses of the large nettle aphid and therefore unsuitable. I placed many of the freshly hatched larvae in my camera bag to transfer to other unsprayed nettle clones. Moving to B.T L.P. 5. The nettle clones here had been sprayed earlier and were dried black masses with no signs of larvae, but it is unlikely these would have survived because there were no nettles in the immediate vicinity.

The 40 odd nettle clones must occupy about 0.05% of pastures 4 and 5, so was it really necessary to spray these nettle clones? Did the farmer realise these nettle clones were covered in masses of larvae of some of our most beautiful butterflies? Would he/she have been prepared perhaps to cut down these nettles at a later date to save the potential butterflies? Since nettle clones almost always recover from spraying it seemed to me to be a waste of time, money and butterfly lives!

16th July. The Bishop Tawton pastures have now been mown, presumably to cut down thistles that rarely produce fertile seed but do provide a valuable nectar source for our butterflies. Many painted lady butterfly larvae will have made it to adult stage, but many more will have been destroyed. The nettles in B.T Bridge P. which were not sprayed earlier have now been mown which coincides with the 2nd brood of the small tortoiseshell which are just hatching out.

2nd Sept. 2nd brood of small tortoiseshells now out.

More detailed studies need to be carried out, followed up by programmes to educate farmers about butterfly food plants and life-cycles with a hope that they might consider changing the timing of their farming procedures.

IN THE INTERESTS OF TIDINESS

Tidiness is okay if in moderation, but taken to extremes, to the exclusion of everything else, it can destroy lives and also wildlife because strangely enough only a limited amount of wildlife can exist on the average mown bowling green! The following article summarises my feeling exactly and I make no excuse for quoting it in full. Taken from the Sunday Telegraph 24/4/1981. By DAVID BROWN the Agricultural correspondent.

"Butterfly stings a village"

VILLAGE SCENE

The title of 'Best Kept Village' might not go to the village of Nailsbourne, Taunton, Somerset because of the fondness of many villagers for butterflies. Patches of stinging nettles give rise to red admirals, small tortoiseshells and peacocks. With the picture-postcard village in mind the judges have made it clear that these nettles and those in the adjacent parish of Kingston St Mary must be cleared. This would mean fewer butterflies in the area as a result of the caterpillar's food plant being destroyed. The warden of the Somerset Trust for Nature Conservation Mr David Stewart has complained about the judges' lack of concern for wildlife.

'We all enjoy watching these colourful insects on a warm day but the increased use of chemical sprays on surrounding farms means that butterflies are on the way out in our villages,' he said.

THE BUTTERFLY/WILDLIFE GARDEN AREA

Hugh Newman was not only the second butterfly farmer, but also a superb storywriter who was able to infect young readers with his enthusiasm and love of butterflies, moths and insects. He was a prolific writer but his most famous book was the 'Butterfly Farmer' (1953). Later he published his famous book 'Create a Butterfly Garden' (1967). Since then many books have been written on this subject, notably Rothschild & Farrell (1983), Warren (1988).

I have a medium-sized garden, half of which is devoted to flowers, and the other two quarters to vegetables and a wildlife/garden area, which contains a pond, nectar plants and nettle patches. The object is to harbour and conserve some of our wild life in relatively undisturbed conditions and free from pollution, sprays, etc. and to provide an opportunity to examine wildlife on your own doorstep, at all seasons, and at night, without being arrested! The wildlife area gives me endless pleasure and more than the rest of the garden put together.

The courtship of small tortoiseshells and peacocks takes place in undisturbed countryside and the female butterflies lay eggs in these areas, and will not generally lay eggs on nettles in garden areas. This does not present any problem since in May and July-August caterpillars can be collected from wild nettles and transferred onto yours, or alternatively it is possible to buy them from butterfly dealers. Keeping conservation in mind, only remove as many as can be supported by the size of the nettle clones in your garden, unless spraying or cutting has taken place when you can transfer them to other clones.

In a similar way moth caterpillars which appear on your nettles can be followed through to the adult, and other smaller insect life-cycles can be followed (Chapter 13).

The comma, red admiral and painted lady, which lay their eggs singly on nettles, will lay eggs on garden nettles and I have found various stages of all of these butterflies on nettles in my garden. I'm sure your nettle patches will give you much pleasure but remember constant and close observation is necessary since many of these insects are very small and also some are only found at night.

MOTHS

DENIZENS OF THE NIGHT

MOTHS AND THE STINGING NETTLE

Most of my childhood in the 50's was spent collecting natural history specimens, chief amongst which were my favourite moths. There is only space for a synopsis of the moths recorded as being associated with Urtica as a larval foodplant. Forty three moths are associated with Urtica but only eight of these are mainly confined to it. **Lifecycles of the British moths whose larvae feed either almost entirely on Urtica (shaded), or those polyphagous species, which include Urtica occasionally in their diet. Included also are brief notes on their status, frequency, distribution, habitats and any other features which are of particular interest, [After, Newman & Leeds (1913), Heath & Maitland Emmett, ed's (1976...)]. The numbers refer to references relating to nettle/stinging nettle/Urtica, 1 = Newman & Leeds (1913), 2 = Bradley (1973), 3 = Ford (1949), 4 = Leach (1886), 5 = Stokoe & Stovin (1958), 6 = Beirne (1952), 7 = South (1907), 8 = Myerick (1927), 9 = Skinner (1984), 10 = Davis (1983), 11 = Carter (1986), 12 = Porter (1997), 13 = Heath Maitland Emmett , ed's (1976...).**

HEPIALIDAE SWIFTS

GHOST MOTH [*Hepialus humuli humuli (L)*].-- Common; resident; whole of Br. Is.; flies at dusk – 1 hour before sunset; grassland, downland, gardens, scrub and waste.-Herbaceous plants, the roots of grasses and Humulus, Arctium, Lamium, Urtica, etc; pupates in a gallery amongst the roots 8, 9, 12.

183

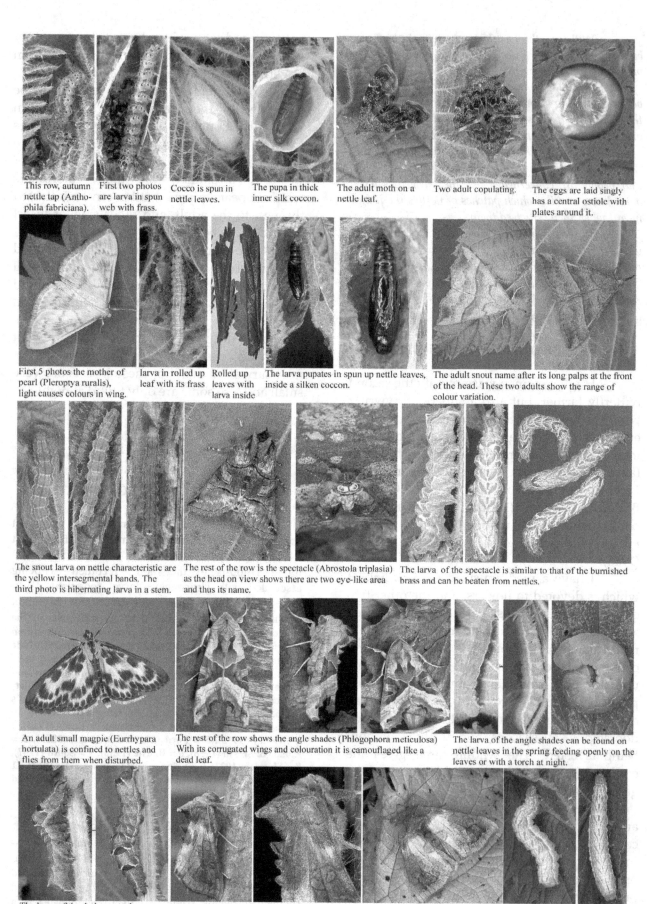

This row, autumn nettle tap (Anthophila fabriciana).

First two photos are larva in spun web with frass.

Cocco is spun in nettle leaves.

The pupa in thick inner silk coccon.

The adult moth on a nettle leaf.

Two adult copulating.

The eggs are laid singly has a central ostiole with plates around it.

First 5 photos the mother of pearl (Pleroptya ruralis), light causes colours in wing.

larva in rolled up leaf with its frass

Rolled up leaves with larva inside

The larva pupates in spun up nettle leaves, inside a silken coccon.

The adult snout name after its long palps at the front of the head. These two adults show the range of colour variation.

The snout larva on nettle characteristic are the yellow intersegmental bands. The third photo is hibernating larva in a stem.

The rest of the row is the spectacle (Abrostola triplasia) as the head on view shows there are two eye-like area and thus its name.

The larva of the spectacle is similar to that of the burnished brass and can he beaten from nettles.

An adult small magpie (Eurrhypara hortulata) is confined to nettles and flies from them when disturbed.

The rest of the row shows the angle shades (Phlogophora meticulosa) With its corrugated wings and colouration it is camouflaged like a dead leaf.

The larva of the angle shades can be found on nettle leaves in the spring feeding openly on the leaves or with a torch at night.

The larva of the dark spectacle.

The burnished brass (Diachrysia chrysitis) has a golden colour similar to a chrysalid, and the larva feed on the nettle.

FIG 12.6 THE NETTLE TAP, MOTHER OF PEARL, SNOUT, SPECTACLE, DARK SPECTACLE AND SMALL MAGPIE ARE CONFINED TO NETTLES

CHOREUTIDAE 'TAPS'

AUTUMN NETTLE TAP *[Anthophila fabriciana L.]*--Resident; throughout the Brit. Is.; habitats which support Urtica; flies during the daytime in the vicinity of the common nettle. -Restricted to Urtica and Parietaria (Wall Pellitory); leaves spun together by silk threads 3, 8, 10, 13.

TORTRICIIDAE TORTRIX'S/BELL MOTHS

(Pandemis dumetaria Treit.)--Resident; local; Britain except Scotland, Wales and West country; chalk downland; limestone, fen and marshes; flies at dusk. -Mainly on herbaceous plants including Urtica; in rolled up leaves 2, 8, 13. *Clepsis rurinana (L.)*-Resident; local; scattered throughout Britain and in south-western Ireland; woods and hedgerows.-Deciduous trees and bushes in the British Isles, but on Urtica on the Continent 2, 13. *Clepsis spectana (Treit.)*-Resident; common, throughout Brit. Is.; woods, fens, marshes, peat bogs, mosses; flies at dusk. -On herbaceous plants including Urtica, rarely on trees. 2, 10, 13. **APPLE MOTH** *(Epiphyas postrittana Walk.)*----Resident; distributed in the southern half of Britain; general occurrence; flies at dusk. -On trees, shrubs and herbaceous plants including Urtica. 2, 13. *Olethieutes lacunana(D &S)*--Resident; throughout the British Isles; general occurrence; flies at dusk. -Occasionally on trees and shrubs but mainly on herbaceous plants including Urtica 10, 13.

PYRALIDAE PYRALIDS

SMALL MAGPIE *(Eurrhypara hortulata L.)*-Resident; common; throughout the Brit. Is.; general occurrence; flies at dusk. -Urtica, but occasionally on other herbaceous plants; larva in rolled leaves or in leaves spun together 3, 4, 6, 8, 10, 13 . **DUSKY BRINDLED MOTH** *(Udea prunalis D. &S.)*--Resident; common; general occurrence; woods, hedgerows, gardens, scrub; adult nocturnal. -On bushes, trees and herbs, Urtica, Ulmus, Teucrium, Stachys etc; in slight web or turned down edge of leaf; pupa in cocoon 3,8,10,13. **WHITE BRINDLED MOTH** *(Udea olivalis D. & S.)*--Resident; common; throughout Brit. Is.; wood, hedgerows, gardens, scrub, waste ground; flies at dusk. -On herbs, Urtica, Stachys, Nepeta, Mercurialis, Rumex, Humulus, etc; web in spun leaf and turned down leaf; pupa in cocoon 3,4,6,10,13. *(Mecyna flavilis D. & S. spp. flavicularis Carad)* .Resident; local; southern England; chalk down-land, cliffs and under-cliffs; flies during the day and night. -Galium mollugo,

Artemesia campestris, Urtica urens. 4, 6, 13. **MOTHER OF PEARL** *(Pleuroptya ruralis Scop.)*-Resident; common; throughout Brit. Is.; general occurrence; flies at dusk and night. -Specific to Urtica dioica; larva in rolled up leaves; pupa in silk-lined chamber in rolled leaf. 3, 4, 6, 8, 10, 13.

ACTIIDAE TIGERS

GARDEN TIGER *(Arctia caja (L.)]*- -Resident; common; throughout Brit. Is.; general occurrence; flies at night. -Herbaceous plants, nettles, Urtica, Lamium spp., etc.; cocoon spun up anywhere 1, 7, 8, 10, 13. **CREAM SPOT TIGER** *(Arctia villica L.)*- -Resident; south, west and eastern counties of England; woods, hedgerows, chalk down-land, limestone, sand dunes, cliffs; flies at night.-Herbaceous plants, Urtica, Lamium spp., Teucrium, Stachys, etc.; earthern cocoon 5, 7, 10, 11, 13. **BUFF ERMINE** *[Spilosoma lutea Hufn)*--Resident; common; throughout Brit. Is.; general occurrence; flies at night. -Herbaceous plants, Rumex, Urtica, etc.; cocoon amongst litter; double brooded in hot years. 10, 13. **MUSLIN MOTH** *(Diaphora mendica Cl.)*--Resident; widely distributed throughout Brit. Is.; woods, hedgerows, chalk down-lands, limestone, gardens, parks; flies day and night.-Herbaceous plants, Rumex, Urtica, Plantago, etc.; cocoon near surface of earth or under moss on trees. 1, 5, 10, 13. **RUBY TIGER** *(Phagmatobia fuliginosa fuliginosa L)*--Resident; well distributed; England and Ireland; general occurrence; flies day and night.-Herbaceous plants, Rumex, Taraxacum, Urtica, Plantago, etc.; hibernates full fed; spins cocoon, in May in litter, or in twigs on moors 1,7,10,13. **JERSEY TIGER** *(Euplagia quadripunctaria Poda.)*--Resident and migrant; local; Devon, odd ones on south coast; woodland margins, hedgerows, garden, scrub, wastes and flies day & night. -Lonicera, Prunus & herbaceous plants, Urtica, Eupatorium cann., Plantago, Lamium, etc.; cocoon amongst litter or moss 1,7,8,9,12,13. **SCARLET TIGER** *(Callimorpha dominula L.)*--Resident; England; damp pastures, fens, marshes, river banks, ditches, cliffs; flies during the day. -Herbaceous plants, Urtica, Symphytum, Rubus fructicosa, etc.; cocoon amongst leaves on the ground 1, 5, 8, 9, 11, 13.

NOCTUIDAEN OCTUNINAE NOCTUIDS

THE FLAME *(Axylia putris L.)*-|-Resident; common; throughout Brit. Is.; general occurrence; flies at night.-Herbaceous plants, Galium sp., Cyanoglossus, Polygonum, Urtica etc.;; pupates in

185

Ruby tiger (Phagmatobia fuliginosa fulginosa) imago and larva, found sometimes on the nettle

The silver Y (Autographa gamma) named after the Y-shaped mark on the wings is a migrant and frequently the larva feeds on the nettle.

Silver Y larva notice only two prolegs

Silver y pupa in nettle leaves about to hatch.

Plain golden Y (Autographa bractea)

Beautiful golden Y (A. pulcrina) Larva similar to silver Y.

The dot (Melanchra persicariae) larva found occ. on Urtica

The hebrew character (Orthosia gothica) imago found early in the year and shows much variation.

Larvae of O. gothica is like that of the angle shades but has a has an unbroken white dorsal line

The ghost

Feathered ranunculus (Eumichtis lichenea)

Bright-line-brown-eye (Lacanobia leraceae)

White brindled moth (Udea olivalis)

Muslin moth (male) (Diahphora mendica)

Mottled rustic (Caradrina morpheus)

White ermine (Spilosoma lubricipeda)

The garden tiger (Arctia caja) with distinctive warning colouration. The imago shows remarkable variation in colour and patternation. Right a pair copulating.

The eggs laid in a mass

The eggs about to hatch (left) and the eggs hatching (right)

The first instar larvae (left) and second instar larvae (right).

A. caja pupa in the coccon (left) and the familiar wooly bear larva (right).

Buff ermine (Spilosoma lutea)

The scarlet tiger (Callimorpha dominula) with warning colouration it flies freely in daylight

C. dominula) larva on nettles

Jersey tiger ;arva(Euplagia quadripunctaria)

Large yellow underwing moth

The flame (Axylia putris)

FIG 12.7 MOTHS PARTIALLY DEPENDENT ON URTICA DIOICA FOR A FOOD PLANT

depuncta L.)--Resident; south west England, Midlands and Scotland; woodland margins and hedgerows; flies at night.-Herbaceous plants, Rumex acetosella, Primula verna, Urtica, etc.; pupates in earth. 12. **SETACEOUS HEBREW CHARACTER (Xestia c-nigrum L.)**--Resident; common; throughout Brit. Is.; general occurrence; flies at night.-Herbaceous plants, Rumex, Plantago, Stellaria, Urtica, etc.; pupates in earth. 12, 13.

NOCTUIDAE HADENINAE NOCTUIDS

DOT MOTH (Melanchra persicariae L.)--Resident; common; Brit. Is. except north Scotland; dry pastures, arable, gardens, waste ground; flies at night.-Herbaceous plants, Polygonum, Rumex, Urtica, etc.; pupates in earth. 10, 11, 12. **BRIGHT LINE BROWN EYE (Lacanobia leracea L.)**--Resident; common; throughout Brit. Is.; gardens, pastures, sand dunes; flies at night.-Herbaceous plants, Atriplex, Chenopodium, Rumex, Urtica, etc.; pupates in earth. 5, 8, 10, 11. **HEBREW CHARACTER (Orthosia gothica L.)**--Resident; common; throughout Brit. Is.; general occurrence; flies at night.-Deciduous trees and shrubs, Quercus, Salix, occasionally herbaceous plants, Rumex, Urtica, etc.; brittle cocoon in earth. 10, 12. **FEATHERED RANUNCULUS (Eumichtis lichenea Hb.)**-- Resident; England, Scotland except the north, southern Ireland; limestone, sand dunes, cliffs, maritime situations; flies at night.-Herbaceous plants, Senesio, Sedum, Armeria maritima, Centranthus ruber, Urtica, etc.; earthen cocoon. 13.

NOCTUIDAEA MPHIPYRINAE NOCTUIDS

MOUSE MOTH (Amphipyra tragopoginis Cl.)--Resident; common; throughout Brit. Is.; general occurrence; flies at night.-Deciduous shrubs, Salix, and herbaceous plants Rumex, Urtica, etc.; pupates in earth. 10. **ANGLE SHADES (Phlogophora meticulosa (L.)]**--Resident and migrant; common; throughout Brit. Is.; general occurrence; flies at night.-Herbaceous plants, Senesio, Primula, Urtica, etc.; pupates on surface of the ground. 9, 10, 11, 12. **FROSTED ORANGE [Gortyna flavago D.&S.)**--Resident; common; throughout Brit. Is.; woods, dry pastures, waste ground, salt marshes; flies at night.-Large stemmed herbaceous plants, Arctium, Carduus, Cirsium, Urtica, lives and pupates in stem above a fork. 13. **MOTTLED RUSTIC (Caradrina morpheus Hufn.)**-- Resident; common; throughout Brit. Is.; general occurrence; flies at night.-Herbaceous plants, Polygonum, Taraxacum, Urtica, etc.; cocoon in earth in Sept. turning to the pupa in May. 11, 13.

NOCTUIDAE PLUSIINAE NOCTUIDS/PLUSIDS

GOLDEN TWIN SPOT (Chrysodeixis chalcites Esp.)--Migrant; southern England, Wales and northern Scotland.-50 records since 1943-1990; accepts Urtica spp. in captivity. **BURNISHED BRASS (Diachrysia chrysitis L.)**--Resident and migrant; common; throughout Brit. Is.; acid grassland, garden, waste ground, fens and marshes; flies at night.-Herbaceous plants, Urtica, Arctium, etc.; cocoons on leaves of plant, sometimes 2 broods. 1, 5, 7, 8, 9, 10, 11, 12, 13. **DEWICK'S PLUSIA (Macdunnoughia confusa Steph.)**--Migrant; scattered over Britain; flies at night.-18 records; herbaceous plants, Urtica spp **SILVER Y (Autographa gamma L.)**-Breeding migrant; common; throughout Brit. Is.; general occurrence; flies at night.-Herbaceous plants, Urtica spp.etc.; cocoon amongst leaves of food plant; seldom survives winter frost. 1, 8, 10, 11, 12. **BEAUTIFUL GOLDEN Y (Autographa pulchrina L.)**--Resident and migrant; common; throughout Brit. Is.; woods, gardens, scrub; flies at dusk and night.-Herbaceous plants, especially Urtica spp. Lonicera etc.; silken cocoon on or near food plant. 1, 5, 7, 8, 9, 10, 12, 13. **PLAIN GOLDEN Y (Autographa bractea D.& S.)**-- Resident and migrant; common; throughout Brit. Is.; woods, gardens, scrub; flies at dusk and night.- Herbaceous plants, especially Urtica spp. Lonicera etc.; silken cocoon on or near food plant. 1, 5, 7, 8, 9, 10, 11, 12, 13. **GOLD SPANGLE (Autographa bractea D.&S.)**--Resident and migrant; common; throughout Brit. Is.; acid grassland, dry pastures, gardens, wastelands; flies at dusk and night.- Herbaceous plants, Urtica, Lamium spp., Glechoma, Eupatorium, etc.; cocoon amongst food plant; difficult to rear. 5, 7, 8, 9, 10,11, 12. **SCARCE SILVER Y (Syngrapha interrogationis L.)**--Resident and migrant; common; Brit. Is. except south east England; heaths, acid grassland; flies at day and night.-Calluna, Vaccinium myrtillus, Urtica. silken cocoon on food plant. 5, 8. **DARK SPECTACLE (Abrostrola trigemina Werneb.)**--Resident and migrant; common; woodlands, hedgerows, gardens, waste places, fens, marshes; flies at dusk and night.- Urtica dioica, Humulus lupulus; cocoon in or near food plant. 1, 5, 8, 9, 10, 11, 12, 13. **THE SPECTACLE (Abrostola triplasia L.)** Resident and migrant; common; woods, acid grassland, gardens, waste places, fens, marshes; flies at dusk and night.-Urtica dioica; pupates in slight web on litter or ground. 1, 5, 8, 9, 10, 11, 12, 13.

NOCTUIDAE HYPENINAE SNOUTS

THE SNOUT (Hypena proboscidalis L.)--Resident; common; throughout Brit. Is.; general occurrence; flies at dusk and night.-Specific to Urtica dioica; silken cocoon amongst leaves; double brooded in hot years. 1, 4, 5, 8, 9, 10, 11, 12, 13. **BLOXWORTH SNOUT (Hypena obsitalis Hb.)**--Migrant, temporary resident; Scilly Isles and south Devon; gardens, parks, waste ground, barns; flies at dusk and night.-Urtica dioica and Parietaria judaica; 11 records as migrant, 1884-1989; now temporary resident or resident; origin, Mediterranean. 7, 8,9,12, 13. **BUTTONED SNOUT** *(Hypena rostralis L.)*--Resident; south half of England; woodland margins, hedgerows, gardens, parks, scrub; flies at night.-Humulus lupulus and Urtica; silken cocoon amongst the leaves. 7, 8, 12. **SMALL FAN FOOT** *(Herminia grisealis D.& S. nemoralis Fabr.)*--Resident; common; throughout Brit. Is.; woods, hedgerows, gardens, parks, waste ground; flies at dusk and night.- Trees and shrubs Quercus spp., Alnus glutinosa, Betula sp., Tilia cordata, Corylus, Crateagus; herb,Urtica; narrow cocoon amongst leaves. 13.

For further details the reader should consult the many excellent books which are now available; for adults Skinner (1984), Brooke (1991), Heath & Maitland Emmett (1983-1991), for larvae, Carter & Hargreaves (1986), and Porter (1997).

THE TAP'S (CHOREUTIDAE)

THE AUTUMNAL NETTLE TA
(Anthophilia fabriciana L.)

If nettle patches are examined in late May-June and August-September, a small brown and white moth (11-13 mm) can often be seen flying about the nettles. When it lands on a nettle leaf it jerks its body and antennae up and down and this characteristic behaviour earns the group of moths to which it belongs the name 'taps'. The autumn nettle tap can be found at most times of the year under a web that partially draws leaves together. The full-grown larva is up to 12 mm, opaque cream with a bluish line along its back. Each segment in the region of the prolegs is covered in brownish-black spots, 12 per segment. The head is cream with black markings and the true legs are black. The autumn nettle tap can be found at most times of the year under a web that partially draws leaves together. The full-grown larva is up to 12 mm, opaque cream with a bluish line first studied the autumn nettle tap in 1973 and wrote about it, without any prior knowledge, in my notebook; this is quoted unaltered in Box 12.4 (please excuse the notebook phraseology)

Box 12.4. Notebook, April 1973. Notes on the Autumn Nettle Tap (Anthophila fabriciana L.)

"First observed about 16th February. It was noticed that certain nettle leaves were held together by silvery gossamers. Very often it was the cordate leaf base that was turned over on the top surface to make a tunnel. Only once have I seen the under-surface used. Also quite often the topmost leaves of the shoot are spun together so the caterpillar can feed on the young tender leaves. The caterpillar is extremely common and most nettle patches at this time of the year will be found to yield caterpillars on cursory observation. The web spun is quite extensive. The caterpillar spins a coarse outer net using stinging hairs as anchors, and these threads pull the leaf over to form a tunnel, any large stinging hairs are cut off and attached to the web. Next an inner firmer web is spun to form a silken tunnel in which the caterpillar resides. This inner web is open at both ends and from this stronghold the caterpillar crawls to various parts of the leaf and

feeds. Most often the feeding is in the main leaf area and as a result small holes are made ending at the main veins. The edges may also be eaten. During feeding the larger stinging hairs are avoided or cut off and placed on the web. This also applies to some of the non-stinging hairs. Examination of the faeces under a microscope reveals the presence of many fragments of the silicious walls of the smaller non-stinging hairs, glandular hairs, and also epidermis and quite often spongy and palisade mesophyll cells with chloroplasts which appear to have passed through undigested. Cystoliths remain unaffected.

The caterpillar stores its faeces in its web. Once the caterpillar forms its web, it stays in it until it is fully grown, so that the older caterpillars are found surrounded by a thick tunnel of faeces. I inadvertently kept some of these caterpillars on nettle leaves in a polythene bag for some considerable time without ventilation. Eventually the nettle leaves turned black and foetid and mould started growing on them. On observation I found the caterpillars still in their original tunnels under quite disgusting conditions but still appearing healthy – under similar conditions the majority of caterpillars would have been wandering around looking for food.

When kept in shallow petri dishes the caterpillars spin their webs between the top or bottom glass and the leaf. They do not seem to be at all perturbed by being exposed to light. Presumably they are satisfied so long as they have a surface on both sides, and the surfaces do not have to be opaque or lightproof. This fact can be taken advantage of when observing behaviour or photographing them. The caterpillars seem to have a certain territory since only so many will occupy a single leaf. One small leaf was placed in a petri dish plus 7 caterpillars 4 of these spun up on the inside of the leaf whilst the others wandered about for two days, although there was plenty of nettle leaf for all of them. It appears that the web must first be constructed before feeding commences and if this is not possible presumably the caterpillar would rather starve.

Evolutionary significance of leaf rolling – presumably hides the caterpillar from its predators, i.e. large predators such as birds which would find it more difficult to extricate the caterpillar from its tunnel. Smaller predators could find their way in after having located them by smell, movement, etc. The caterpillar is very sensitive to vibrations that cause it to freeze for long periods of time, a fact that is useful when carrying out drawings or photography. Contact elicits violent side to side contractions of the body and either forward or backward movement, so it shoots out of its tunnel and hangs suspended by a silken thread from the leaf – a good avoidance reaction. Ichneumon flies could gain entrance through the tunnel. I tried stinging a caterpillar with a stinging hair after which it was paralysed and died shortly afterwards. It is very unlikely this would take place normally. The hair tip has a rounded globule on it and it takes some pressure to break this. Also the caterpillar skin is very tough and flexible and can be indented to a high degree before the hair penetrates. The poison taken orally must presumably be neutralised. I haven't worked on the earlier part of the lifecycle yet – when and where are the eggs laid.

When first discovered in Feb. the caterpillars were just one mm or so in length. At maturity they are 10-11 mm. They are a creamy colour and an interesting feature for the physiologist is the dorsal heart that can be seen undergoing peristaltic type contractions. The speed of the contraction could be timed in relation to external factors. The heart appears green as the gut shows through it.

When the caterpillar is about to pupate it leaves its web and spins a cocoon on a fresh piece of leaf. This takes about 24 hours or longer to complete. The cocoon consists of a loose coarse outer web to hold the leaf together and a very fine thick inner web, similar to those of the Saturnidae, but in miniature. There is no outlet, the cocoon is closely woven at both ends and extremely tough, therefore, how does the moth escape? The answer is to be found in the pupa: the dorsal abdominal segments have rows of backwardly directed spines, also there are spinous hairs on the last segment. After emergence the pupa is seen sticking out of the end of the cocoon. It could be that the spines have a ratchet action against the cocoon wall and eventually force the pupa through the wall. There is no indication of the silk being dissolved as in some of the silk moths.

Emergence took place after about a fortnight. The adult is very irritable and flies on the slightest disturbance. It has a very long tongue, so, is it a nectar feeder? The male has long hairs along one side of the antennae. The second and third pair of legs have tibial and tarsal spines; for what purpose? The moth flies in sunshine and is dormant at night. A male and a female kept in a petri dish for two days mated, for it was noticed that the female had laid a number of green eggs, some on the nettle provided and some on the bottom of the petri dish. They were laid singly but close together. Throughout the egg laying the female appeared excited. The antennae were moved up and down to tap the leaves, the abdomen moved up and down and exhibited waves of contraction prior to laying – it was also extended and curved downwards to touch the food plant. The moth moved forwards inn short jerks during which the wings were moved up and down abruptly a few times but most of the jerky movements were due to the second and third pair of legs vibrating up and down – was this behaviour to test the food plant?"

BOX 12.7. BIRDS AND NETTLES

Birds do seem to show a preference for nettle stands. This could be connected with the fact they use these insect rich areas as a food source, or because dense growths of nettles afford shelter and are good hiding places for nests. I have occasionally found pheasants and ducks nesting in large nettle stands where they are very well hidden.

See chapter 4 Williamson also for birds and nettles. Blue tits normally build their nests in holes high above ground level so it is surprising to read of a blue tit (*Parus caeruleus*) that decorated its nest with leaves of Urtica dioica (Rheinwald, 1972). The use of nettle leaves may have been associated with their habit of searching nettle clumps for insects and their larvae. The tits are

intelligent insect hunters and interestingly enough, Royamata (1970), when investigating the selection of food by the great tit (*Parus major*), records the observation that they easily locate rolled-up nettle leaves containing larvae of the mother of pearl (*Pleuroptya ruralis*) and nip the leaf, which results in the larvae wriggling out of the end, after which it is ingested. It would be instructive to know whether this behaviour was learnt from another bird or as a result of trial and error when trying to extract these larvae from the rolled-up leaves.

Fuller and Poyer (1982), quote Bibby (1974), in saying that bearded tits (*Panurus biarmicus*), can use as habitats, a variety of rank vegetation such as beds of willowherbs and nettles, and that it might be conceivable that these birds, could live independently in these, rather than reed beds, in the winter. It is mentioned, (Ibis, 128 (4), 526, 1986) that the dunnock or hedge sparrow, (*Prunella modularis*) as well as eating insects, also eat seeds, and the main seeds eaten were those of Urtica dioica, so in both respects nettle patches are important feeding habitats.

Carrick (1936) conducted experiments on the effect of protective adaptations in insects. Larvae of the small tortoiseshell (Aglais urticae) in their later stages, with yellow and black markings and large spines, were placed near the sites of nesting birds and the number eaten over a period of time noted. Of 30 larvae, placed near a sedge warbler's nest, only one was eaten. When this experiment was repeated with young brown small tortoiseshell larvae with small spines, willow warblers ate all of them, so it is probable that spines rather than taste deter them.

CUCKOOS AND CATERPILLARS

Wyllie (1981) carried out a lot of personal observations on the feeding habits of cuckoos. Whereas almost all birds avoid distasteful caterpillars, with warning coloration, lots of long hairs and spines, these are just the types of caterpillars the cuckoo feeds upon; it has evolved a specialised gut to cope with these types of caterpillars. Cuckoos arrive about 24-30th April, and leave in the first to second week in July. There are about 5-10 cuckoos per 10 Km ^{2}. These can gorge themselves on hundreds of gregarious caterpillars at a time, so it is likely that they could be a significant factor in reducing small tortoiseshell and peacock caterpillars, according to Wyllie's observations: -"In June cuckoos may be seen systematically searching along hedges for the hairy, red, white and black caterpillars of the Gold-Tail moth. I once collected about 200 of these larvae and placed them on an isolated bush in a cuckoo breeding area. Within a few hours two cuckoos had located and eaten them all. Towards the end of the cuckoos' breeding season (late June and early July), the colonial larvae of the small tortoiseshell and peacock butterflies on nettle beds become common prey items. These may also be available to early fledgling young that later consume cinnabar moth caterpillars commonly found on ragwort. ......Conspicuous or gregarious insects of almost any kind are the preferred prey. .....The cuckoos main strategy when searching for food is to perch silent and motionless on a suitable vantage point from which it can scan the surrounding environment. It does not actively search for food but relies on keen eyesight and on the prey revealing itself by movement. Such a limiting method is only suited to the capture of quite large prey.   When food is widely dispersed and relatively small, frequent changes of position are necessary, a bird rarely spending more than a few minutes in one place. Longer survey periods from the same perch are rewarding when there are large or gregarious caterpillars to be found. The cuckoo perches upright, alert to any movements within a range of about 50m.   When a colony of caterpillars is found a cuckoo will scramble about rather clumsily gorging itself on the early captured prey. An individual's stomach can contain vast numbers of caterpillars."

CHAPTER 13

INSECTS ON NETTLES 2
FLIES, BUGS AND BEETLES

> *"Nor is it a presumptuous supposition, that a considerable proportion of these vegetables were created expressly for their entertainment and support. The common nettle is of little use either to mankind or the larger animals; but you will not doubt its importance to the class of insects, when told that at least 30 distinct species feed upon it;"*
>
> Kirby and Spence, 1858

> *"..., twenty-seven species may be considered more or less confined to nettle, plus a further nineteen oligophagous species and a few predators closely associated with it. The fauna has not been the subject of any intensive study, perhaps because the nettle is considered such a common-place plant. As a characteristic member of field margins and waysides, however, it makes a significant contribution to the faunal diversity and biomass of intensively farmed agricultural areas. The diversity of the fauna, moreover, raises questions of how and why there is such full exploitation of this host plant and its widespread occurrence makes it possible to study this in most parts of the country and to compare different habitats and soil types."*
>
> Davis B. N. K., 1973

INTRODUCTION

Richards, in the Biological Flora of the British Isles (Grieg-Smith, 1948), lists 27 species of insects in close association with Urtica dioica. The definitive study of insects on nettles is that of B. N. K. Davis, and his work will be reviewed later. The latter's book, 'Insects on Nettles;' is an invaluable guide to the identification and study of insects on Urtica dioica, and has helped greatly in my brief study in this area. I managed to sample nettles for insects over a short period and accumulate some photographs and tinted drawings, which I present here. This short study has given me great pleasure, enabling me to look at the diversity of insects found on Urtica dioica, their fascinating life-cycles, interactions with one another, and a glimpse at the unsurpassed beauty of some of these minute organisms when viewed under a powerful binocular microscope. Within the confines of this general book I include a summary, in table form, of those insects closely associated with nettles, their predators and parasites, and give more details of some I have been able to study more closely. The

reader is advised to consult Davis's work for identification, research ideas and methods for the further study of insects on nettles.

Most readers will be familiar with the characteristics of insects. The body is divided into head, thorax and abdomen, the head (6 segments) bears a pair of antennae and compound eyes, simple eyes or ocelli and biting (mandibles) or piercing, sucking mouthparts; the thorax (3 segments) bears 3 pairs of jointed legs and 2, 1 or 0 pairs of wings; the abdomen (usually 10 segments) bearing the genitalia, claspers and penis in the male, ovipositor or sting in the female.

FLIES (DIPTERA)

Flies have the following features: the adults feed on liquid food that is sucked up through a proboscis. They have one pair of wings and pair of balancing organs (halteres) which have replaced the second pair of wings. The larva, called a maggot, has no true legs and the head is generally reduced to mouthhooks, so that it feeds by sucking up juices. The larval skin may just harden to form the puparium.

The nettle gall midge fly (Dasineura urticae), notice the long ovipositor of a female.

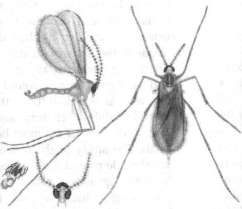

A male (left) with claspers on its abdomen, pectinate antennae, hairy feet and eyes that meet in the middle. The female (right) notice the long ovipositor, long legs and halteres for balance.

The single eggs laid on the nettle hatch into lavae which burrow into the plant and give out substances which cause galls. The latter can form on leaf bases, petioles and flowers.

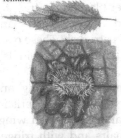

The gall above has formed on the midrib of a leaf. Cut open it shows a single chamber with one larva/maggot.

Diagrams of galls at the base of the leaf notice they form over the main veins. Each gall contains a single larva in a chamber which is open at the top by a slit.

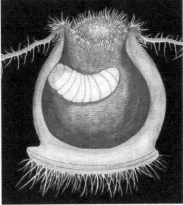

A diagram of a section of a gall on a midrib showing the maggot feeding on the inner tissue of the gall. The open top prabably allow the entry of air for respiration.

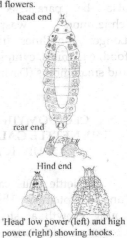

head end

rear end

Hind end

'Head' low power (left) and high power (right) showing hooks. Structure of the maggot.

The galls cut open here show that the chambers can coalesce and contain several different larvae, some are inquilines and others are hyper-parasites of the maggot.

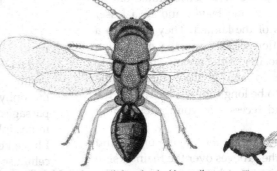

Pupae collected from these galls have hatched into gall wasps of the family Pteromalidae and have golden, ruby and green metallic patternation. Some of the most beautiful of insects.

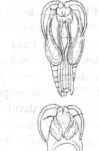

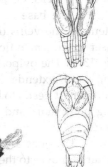

The cocoon and chrysalid of the nettle gall fly showing separate antennae and legs.

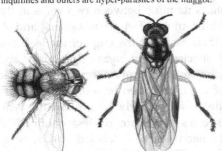

(L-R) Phyrxe nemaea (Tachinidae)/Berris vellata/ Dung fly, copulating, with fungus/ Hover flies the lavae feed on aphids on nettles/ Robber flies, female with gift.

FIG 13.1 LIFE-CYCLE OF THE NETTLE GNAT (DASINEURA) AND OTHER DIPTERA FOUND ON URTICA DIOICA

PLANT GALLS (CECIDIA)

Cecidia can be caused mainly by bacteria, fungi, roundworms, mites, bugs, green flies, jumping plant lice, scale insects, saw flies, gall wasps and gall midges. Substances given out by the parasite stimulate plant cell growth and this produces the characteristic gall shape which is determined by the host. The parasitic maggot sucks up the liquid from broken down cells. A community may develop inside galls of other predator parasites such as chalcid wasps, the larvae of which kill the original parasite; the latter predator parasites may also be parasitised by hyperparasites, e.g. ichneumon wasps and braconids. Lodgers/inquilines live as commensals sharing food, e.g. mites, cynipid wasps, certain flies, beetles and small moths (Darlington, 1968).

CECIDOMYIIDAE (GALL MIDGES) THE NETTLE GALL MIDGE (DASINEURA URTICAE [PERRIS])

Nettle galls can be found any time from June to September. These galls are concentrated on young growth at stem tips. Any nettles can be chosen; whole clones are sometimes galled, but I have often found them on scattered small single nettle shoots, by the sides of roads and paths and in built - up areas. Galls are most concentrated on the veins at the base of young leaves and to a lesser extent on the veins of the lamina. They occur to a lesser extent on inflorescences and the main stem (Fig 13.1). The ovipositor of the female is extremely long, and extends to almost the length of the abdomen. It needs to be long to reach inbetween the long plant hairs and recesses of young developing leaves.

The eggs are laid on the upper surface and the larva moves to the grooves over the main or side veins. Substances given out by the larva cause the leaf cells along the sides of it to grow up and then arch over it to enclose it within a chamber; however the margins do not join, and a narrow slit keeps it open at the top. The young galls are light green but as they become mature they turn crimson to purple. Isolated galls consist of a single cavity. However, where there are large numbers together at the base of a leaf the cavities are often confluent. Very often when dissected out the cavities are found to contain an average of 2-3 larvae of different sizes and types. A typical gall larva is opaque cream with a green line showing the position of the gut (Fig 13.1). Some

of these larvae are those of predator parasites. Galls I dissected also contained minute yellow Thrips urticae, and older blackened ones contained the pupae of the hyper-parasites of the Platygasteridae. These soon emerged as small wasps, whose thorax and abdomen are covered in a reticulum of depressions which diffract the light and produce metallic rainbow colours, and these insects must rank with some of the most beautiful insects on the earth. The study of the nettle gall community is a worthwhile project. Presumably when the gall larva is fully grown it stops producing growth - promoting substances and the gall tissue dies, becomes blackened and opens at the top to allow the larva to fall onto the soil below.

If nettle shoots with mature galls (Aug.- Sept.) are kept in a jar of water placed on a tray, the maggots can be collected at intervals and transferred to moist sand in a petri dish. These over- winter in the soil and the adults emerge in late April-May the following year.

The adults are very small (4-5 mm long) and similar to gnats. Their distinguishing characteristics are: The eyes join above the antennae; broad wings which are covered in black hairs and with fringed margins; long antennae which have bead-like segments with whorls of hairs at the base of the segments; the ovipositor is very long; the veins of the wings are very reduced (Colyer, 1951, Theobald, 1892, Richards & Davies, 1970).

LEAF MINERS (AGROMYZIDAE)

The members of this family are small to minute flies (wing 2-4 mm), the larvae of which are often leaf miners. The larvae have dark coloured mouth-parts and eat their way through the mesophyll of the leaves, leaving white squiggly passages. Nettles should be carefully examined for mines inbetween June- together with their parasites. I have kept these gall midges on nettles enclosed in cellulose acetate cylinders covered with a fine mesh cloth, so that pairing and egg laying can be observed, July & Sept.-Oct. The larva of Agromyza anthracina starts its mine between two veins in the leaf blade whilst those of A. pseudoreptans and A. reptans start their mines at the edge of the leaf. The other two species, Phytomyza flavicornis and Melanagromyza aenea, are stem miners and the larvae or puparia of these can often be found by splitting last year's dead stems early the following year. These five species are more or less confined to Urtica and need more detailed study; for identification see, (Davis, 1983, Spencer, 1972).

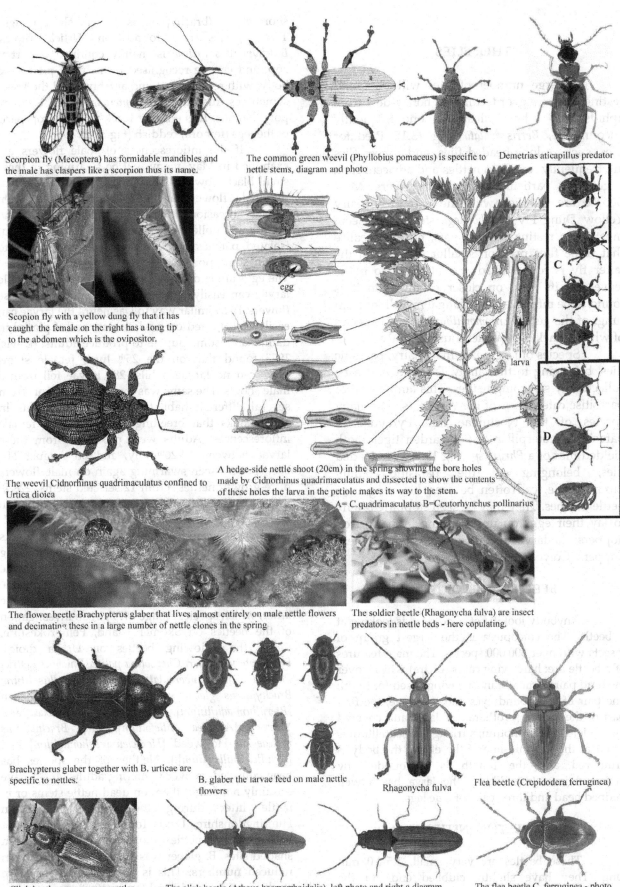

Scorpion fly (Mecoptera) has formidable mandibles and the male has claspers like a scorpion thus its name.

The common green weevil (Phyllobius pomaceus) is specific to nettle stems, diagram and photo

Demetrias aticapillus predator

Scopion fly with a yellow dung fly that it has caught the female on the right has a long tip to the abdomen which is the ovipositor.

egg

larva

The weevil Cidnorhinus quadrimaculatus confined to Urtica dioica

A hedge-side nettle shoot (20cm) in the spring showing the bore holes made by Cidnorhinus quadrimaculatus and dissected to show the contents of these holes the larva in the petiole makes its way to the stem.
A= C.quadrimaculatus B=Ceutorhynchus pollinarius

C

D

The flower beetle Brachypterus glaber that lives almost entirely on male nettle flowers and decimating these in a large number of nettle clones in the spring

The soldier beetle (Rhagonycha fulva) are insect predators in nettle beds - here copulating.

Brachypterus glaber together with B. urticae are specific to nettles.

B. glaber the larvae feed on male nettle flowers

Rhagonycha fulva

Flea beetle (Crepidodera ferruginea)

Click beetles are common nettles

The click beetle (Athous haemorrhoidalis), left photo and right a diagram

The flea beetle C. ferruginea - photo

FIG 13.2 THE BEETLES (COLEOPTERA) ASSOCIATED WITH OR CONFINED TO NETTLES

193

OTHER FLIES

A large number of flies will be found resting, sheltering, or feeding on honey-dew from aphids, and I have illustrated one frequently encountered, *Berris vallata* (Fig 13.1). Predator flies, such as long-headed flies, and robber flies are frequently found on nettles and adjacent rank vegetation, particularly bordering rivers. Most people are familiar with the extremely hairy Yellow Dung Fly *(Scathophaga stercoraria)*, seem most often resting on cow pats, but few realise that these flies prey on smaller flies. Often the latter fly is found dead and attached to nettle leaves by its legs; on closer examination it is found to be infiltrated by a fungal mycelium from fungi of the genus *Entomophthora*, several species of which attack flies (Waterhouse & Brady, 1982).

Species of large, extremely hairy, parasitic flies, belonging to the family Tachinidae, can be collected by sweeping nettles. This family of flies parasitise caterpillars of the vanessids, and many species of the Noctuidae and Pyralidae; a parasitised caterpillar of the garden tiger moth yielded flies of a *Phryxe sp.* (Fig 13.1). Big Headed flies, belonging to the parasitic family Pipunculidae, can often be seen hovering over nettle patches. They may be seen stopping briefly to lay their eggs on unsuspecting leaf and frog hoppers; the larvae feed inside the body of these hoppers (Colyer, 1951).

BEETLES (COLEOPTERA)

Anybody looking at a ladybird is looking at a beetle. The coleoptera is the largest group of insects with over 300,000 species. The main features of a beetle are: hard wing cases (elytra) which cover the hind pair of membraneous wings used for flight; one pair of compound eyes and antennae; the first part of the thorax (prothorax) is large and covered by a shield- the pronotum; a triangular scutelllum is fused at the top mid-line of the elytra; the body is armoured and the mouth is surrounded by powerful jaws (mandibles); the larva has a well defined head and three pairs of true legs.

FLOWER BEETLES (NITIDULIDAE)

These beetles are very small, 1.5-2.0 mm long. They have slightly clubbed ends to the antennae and the abdomen continues beyond the short elytra (brachypterous, Greek, short wings). Two species are found on Urtica dioica: *Brachypterous urticae* is mainly confined to Urtica spp. and can be recognised by its dark pitchy-red body, with reddish legs and antennae and the knees sometimes fuscous. *Brachypterous glaber* is more polyphagous. It is entirely black with the top parts of the legs (femora) reddish (Fig 13.2).

If the inflorescences of male flowers are examined in May, many will be swarming in these small black flower beetles, and it is noticeable that the male flowers are not liberating pollen. On certain occasions when I have wanted to photograph pollen liberation, I have had to seek out isolated patches of male nettles in hedgerows to obtain some not attacked by these flower beetles! The eggs are laid in the male flowers and the beetle larvae can easily be found by dissecting out these flowers. In a similar way to Dasineura the larvae can easily be collected on a white tray, and if placed in damp sand, some pupate to produce adults. (Davis, 1973),found that on the 25th June, female stems produced no larvae, whilst 281 larvae fell from 5 male shoots The same was found using shoots from several different habitats, disproving accounts in some books that breeding takes place on female inflorescences. Adults were produced from these larvae between 19-26th July, and on August 11th beetles were seen swarming again on male flowers of re-growth nettles. From 12 selected stems, 228 B. urticae, and 637 B. glaber were obtained. Although no larvae were found evidence, such as well-developed eggs in female beetles at this time, points to a 2nd generation of larvae and over-wintering pupae. The question is, do second generation larvae occur on re-growth nettles or inflorescences on side shoots of older nettles or on other plants, and if the latter, which species? (Sage 1977) in an investigation of the beetles on Skomer Island, Pembrokeshire, found the following beetles on Urtica dioica: *Brachypterus glaber, Chrysolina polita, Eniemus histrio, Phytobius quadrituberculatus,* and *Rhizobiellus litura; Brachypterus glaber* was also found on Bracken [*Pteridium aquilinum*], Ragwort [*Senecio jacobaea*] and Yarrow [*Achillea millefolium*], and *Brachypterus urticae* on Hogweed [*Heracleum sphondylium*] and [*Achillea millefolium*],). Neither of the species has been collected as over-wintering adults, and I have certainly not found them on dead nettle stems or in nettle litter during the winter period. In Huntingdonshire, Davis found equal numbers of both species on nettles in open situations, and from shaded sites, B. glaber was absent and B. urticae in reduced numbers. This is an ideal area for more study, see Chapter 15 and Davis (1983).

194

Table 13.1. The life-cycles of the hemipteran herbivores and their predators, associated with Urtica dioica. The shading represents the presence of **adults** and the dark shading that of new generations of adults (Based on Southwood & Leston, 1959, Davis, 1973, 1983).(Abbreviations h = hibernating adults. e = egg, e = egg & nymph, n = nymph, P = Predators, H = Herbivores)

HOMOPTERA FROG HOPPERS, LEAF HOPPERS, ETC.

APHROPHORIDAE FROG HOPPERS

	J	F	M	A	M	J	J	A	S	O	N	D		Notes
Javasella spp.	e	e	?	n									H	Feed on various trees as well as herbaceous plants. 1.
Cixius nervosus	e	?	n					e	e	e			H	Found locally in southern Eng., near woods and on willows in marshy ground; nymphs live on roots and pass winter. 1,3.
Cercopis vulnerata	e	e	?	n					e	e	e		H	On many kinds of trees,mainly alders and sallows, and shrubs. 1,3.
Aphrophora alni	e	e	?	n					e	e	e		H	
Philaenus spumarius	e	e	?	n						e			H	A wide range of woody and herbs; eggs laid on dead stems in the autumn; very variable in the dark pattern. 1,3.

CICADELLIDAE LEAF HOPPERS

	J	F	M	A	M	J	J	A	S	O	N	D		Notes
Aphrodes bicinctus	e	e	e	?	n					e	e	e	H	
Macustus grisescens	e	?	n								e	e	H	
Empoasca decipiens	h	h	h			n						h	H	Confined to Urtica. 1
Macropsis scutellata *	e	e	e	?	n			n	n		e	e	H	
Eupteryx urticae *	e	e	e	?	n			n	n		e	e	H	
Eupteryx cyclops *	e	e	e	?	n		n	n	n		e	e	H	Wide range of plants, including nettles and dead-nettles; attacks veg's, potatoes, etc., toxic saliva blemishes 1.
Eupteryx aurata	e	e	e	?	n						e	e	H	1
Macrosteles variatus	e	e	?	n							e	e	H	
Macrosteles sexnotatus	e	e	?	n							e	e	H	

HOMOPTERA PLANT LICE

	J	F	M	A	M	J	J	A	S	O	N	D		Notes
Trioza urticae *	e	e	e	?	n		n			n	h	h	H	Jumping plant lice. 1
Aphis urticata Small Nettle Aphid *	e	?	n	s	s	s	n		e	e	e		H	This has 2 forms, the spring (s) is black-dark green & in clusters, the summer (s) is yellow, in sparse colonies.
Aphis fabae Bean Aphid	e	?	n							e	e		H	The blackfly, black or olive green; spend winter on shrubs & the summer on veg's, beans & docks nettles etc. 1,3.
Rhopalosiphoninus latysiphon Potato Aph.	e	?	n							e	e		H	
Myzus ascalonicus													H	
Myzus cymbalariae													H	
Myzus persicae Peach Potato Aphid													H	1
Microlophium carnosum Large Nett. Aph. *	e	e	?	n							e	e	H	
Phorodon humuli Hop Aphid	e	e	e	?	n						e	e	H	

Books containing illustrations of adults, 1 Chinery, 1986, 2 Southwood and Leston, 1959, Bee et al, 1986.

HETEROPTERA PLANT BUGS

NAME	MONTHS JANUARY-DECEMBER												H/P	ADDITIONAL
	J	F	M	A	M	J	J	A	S	O	N	D		
NABIDAE DAMSEL BUGS														
Aptus mirmicoides Ant Damsel Bug	h	h	h	e	e	n	n	n					P	Comm. in the south of Br. Is.; hunts at night; usually brachypterous; larvae resemble ants, sometimes taken into ant nests
Dolichonabis limbatus Marsh Damsel Bug	e	e	e	e	n	n							P	Favours damp meadows; adults micropterous, very full winged forms occur, kills other hemipterans, flies, moths. 1,2,3.
Nabis rugosus Common Damsel Bug	h	h	h	h	n	n	n	n					P	Common throughout Br. Is.; usually brachypterous but frequently macropterous; hunts high on vegetation. 1,2.
CIMICIDAE FLOWER BUGS														
Orius spp.	h	h	h	e	n	n					h	h	P	
Anthocoris nemorum Common Flower Bug	h	h	h	e	e	n	n	n	n	h	h	h	P	Common throughout Br. Is.; could prod. 3 generations; feeds on aphids, red spider mites; mainly females in spring. 1,2,3.
Anthocoris nemoralis Common Flower Bug	h	h	h	e	e	n	n	n	n	h	h	h	P	Common throughout Br. Is.
LYGAEIDAE GROUND BUGS														
Heterogaster urticae Nettle Ground Bug *	h	h	h	h	e	e	n	n	n	h	h	h	H	Common throughout Brit. Is. but absent from Scotland and Ireland; 2,3.
Scolopostethus affinis	h	h	h	h	e	e	e	n	n	h	h	h	H	Common throughout Br. Is. less common in the north; usually brachypterous but macropterous ones are found.;2.
Scolopostethus thomsoni	h	h	h	h	e	e	n	n	n	h	h	h	H	Common, damp meadows, wastelands and woodland clearings; usually brachypterous; often with 3 segmented antennae.
MIRIDAE MIRID OR CAPSID BUGS														
Deraeocoris ruber	e	e	e	e	n	n			e	e	e	e	P	Comm. southern Eng. and Wales; scarce in North and Ireland; feeds on small insects and nettles; larvae dark purple. 2
Calocoris alpestris	e	e	e	e	n			e	e	e	e	e	H	--1
Calocoris norvegicus	e	e	e	n	n	n	e	e	e	e	e	e	H	Most parts of Brit. Is.; common in hedgerows, margins of woods and rivers; pest of vegetables; varies, evid. of clines. .2,3.
Lygocoris pabulinus Comm, Green Capsid	e	e	e	e	e	n	n	e	e	e	e	e	H	Throughout Brit. Is; eggs over-winters on woody host, summer hosts herbs; often pest of veg's. leaves holes etc. 1,2,3.
Lygocoris spinolai	e	e	e	e	n	n	e	e	e	e	e	e	H	Throughout Brit. Is; on various herbs and can cause damage to tops of shoots.
Lygocoris lucorum	e	e	e	e	e	n	n	e	e	e	e	e	H	Throughout Brit. Is; on herbaceous plants and fruits. 2.
Lygus rugulipennis	h	h	h	e	e	n	n	n	h	h	h	h	H	Throughout Brit. Is; on herbs but can be a pest of fruit and veg's; 2 generations; female can live for a long time. 2,3.
Lygus wagneri	h	h	h	e	e	n	n	n	h	h	h	h	H	Throughout Brit. Is; has a boreo-montane distribution, Exmoor, Lake district and Scotland.
Liocoris tripustulatus Com. Nettle Capsid *	h	h	h	e	e	n	n	n	h	h	h	h	H	Throughout Brit. Is. 1,2,3.
Calocoris fulvomaculatus	e	e	e	e	n			e	e	e	e	e	P/H	Throughout Brit. Is; hedgerows, thickets, and open woods, in moist situations; can be a pest of hops, feeds on tips. 2.
Calocoris sexguttatus	e	e	e	e	n	n	e	e	e	e	e	e	P/H	Widely dist. Brit. Is; woods and thickets; eggs over-winter on trees; larvae red-purple brown; feeds on Urtica & aphids. 2.
Heterotoma planicornis	e	e	e	e	e	n	n	e	e	e	e	e	P/H	Gen. dist. but rare in N. Eng., Scotland and N. Ire.; on herbs and unripe fruit; red larva; pred. of aphids and mites. 2.
Orthotylus ochrotrichus	e	e	e	e	n	n	e	e	e	e	e	e	H	Widely dist. Brit. Is; on herbs, esp. nettles in hedgerows and margins of woods; can pred. red spider mites & aphids
Orthonotus rufifrons *	e	e	e	e	n	n	e	e	e	e	e	e	H	Eng. up to Yorks, sparse in Wales, Ire.; feeds on flow. buds, unripe fruit of Urtica.; in damp woodlands; larvae bright red with white appendages; shows sexual dimorphism; males fully winged, females brachypterous. 2.
Plagiognathus chrysanthemi	e	e	e	e	n	n	e	e	e	e	e	e	H/P	Throughout Brit. Is; common in dry waste places, on herbs and nettles.
Plagiognathus arbustorum	e	e	e	e	n	n	e	e	e	e	e	e	H/P	One of the commonest and widespread capsids in Brit. Is.; on nettles; adults vary from red-brown to almost black. 2.

Books containing illustrations of adults, 1 Chinery, 1986, 2 Southwood and Leston, 1959, 3 Bee et al, 1986.

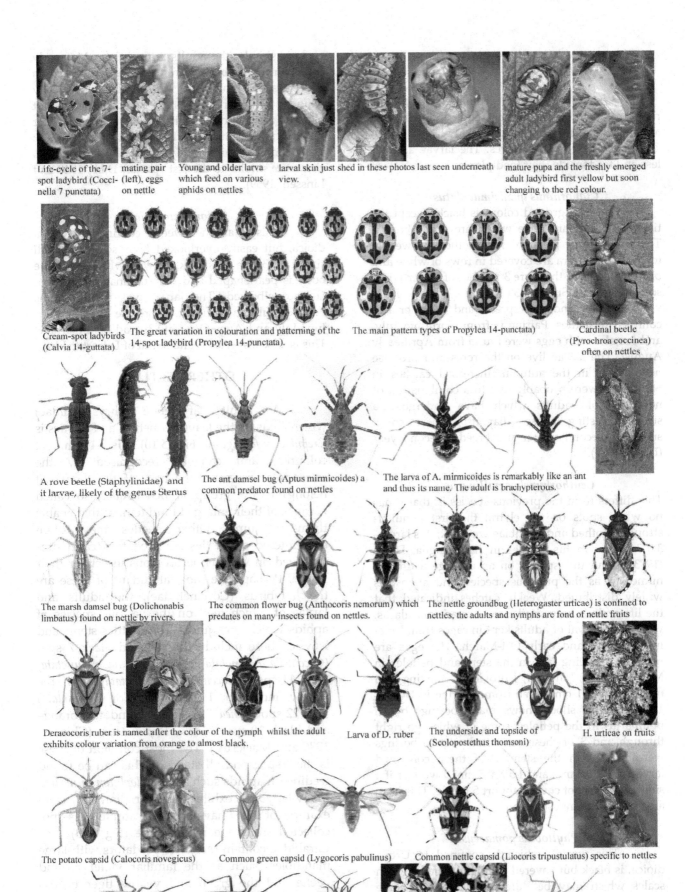

Life-cycle of the 7-spot ladybird (Coccinella 7 punctata)

mating pair (left), eggs on nettle

Young and older larva which feed on various aphids on nettles

larval skin just shed in these photos last seen underneath view.

mature pupa and the freshly emerged adult ladybird first yellow but soon changing to the red colour.

Cream-spot ladybirds (Calvia 14-guttata)

The great variation in colouration and patterning of the 14-spot ladybird (Propylea 14-punctata).

The main pattern types of Propylea 14-punctata)

Cardinal beetle (Pyrochroa coccinea) often on nettles

A rove beetle (Staphylinidae) and it larvae, likely of the genus Stenus

The ant damsel bug (Aptus mirmicoides) a common predator found on nettles

The larva of A. mirmicoides is remarkably like an ant and thus its name. The adult is brachypterous.

The marsh damsel bug (Dolichonabis limbatus) found on nettle by rivers.

The common flower bug (Anthocoris nemorum) which predates on many insects found on nettles.

The nettle groundbug (Heterogaster urticae) is confined to nettles, the adults and nymphs are fond of nettle fruits

Deraeocoris ruber is named after the colour of the nymph whilst the adult exhibits colour variation from orange to almost black.

Larva of D. ruber

The underside and topside of (Scolopostethus thomsoni)

H. urticae on fruits

The potato capsid (Calocoris novegicus)

Common green capsid (Lygocoris pabulinus)

Common nettle capsid (Liocoris tripustulatus) specific to nettles

The meadow plant bug (Leptoterna dolabrata) found on nettles by rivers - pairing.

Calocoris sexguttatus on hogweed and common on nettles

FIG 13.3 LADYBIRDS (COLEOPTERA) AND BUGS (HOMOPTERA) FOUND ON NETTLES

WEEVILS (CURCULIONIDAE)

Weevils all have a prominent snout (the rostrum) with jaws at the end and elbowed antennae that are normally attached half way down. Generally they are herbivores. The larvae are legless and feed inside their food plants.

Cidnorhinus quadrimaculatus

The background colour is black, except the tibia, tarsi and antennae which are reddy-brown. The front femur is either not toothed or weakly toothed. The elytra are covered in rows of white and brown scales but there are 3 patches of larger white scales (Fig 13.2). Size is 2-3 (-3.5) mm. This species is very common and widespread and more or less confined to nettles. Pairing is from April-mid July, and females with eggs were found from April-early August. The larvae live on the roots and produce new adults in the autumn. Increased catches in September were probably due to a combination of new and old adults which have undergone a summer resting phase (diapause); these could survive a second winter and breed a second year (Davis, 1973).

Ceuthorhynchus pollinarius

This differs from the previous species in that it has no white spots on the elytra; the first femur is strongly toothed and the tibiae are black; it is larger-3.0-3.7 mm. In his studies in East Anglia, Davis (1973) found this species on an average a fifth as numerous as the previous species, and almost as widely distributed. Weekly catches indicated that the life-cycle is very similar to C. quadrimaculatus, with the survival of adults kept in cages from June-mid October and early Oct-March. The eggs are recorded as being laid in the stem and petioles in May and June; however, I provide a drawing of a nettle shoot (31 cm) taken from a hedge in Devon, 12/3/95. This shoot shows many borings by C. pollinarius in the petioles, some of which go right through and 3 of these contained eggs. 6 borings were present in the stem, 2 of these contained larvae, 3.0 X 0.8 mm and 1.5 X 0.5 mm. I wonder if a single nettle shoot could support 5 larvae. This is an area for further investigation.

Phyllobius pomaceus

This weevil, which is confined to Urtica dioica, is black but covered in bright metallic green scales which may be differently coloured, some being golden green. The femora are toothed; the antennae are dark but rusty coloured at the base, and the legs are black. Length is 7.5-9.0 mm The life-cycle is simple: the adults appear from May-early July, pairing can be seen in June. The larvae feed on the roots and rhizomes. Widespread and locally abundant. (Other species are found on nettles but have no association with it are; P. pyri with copper scales and red antenna, P. parvullus; 2.5-3.5 mm; black abdomen with hardly any green scales and P. artemesiae similar to the last species, Dibb, 1948 and Linssen (1959).

Apion urticarium

This is another weevil confined to Urtica dioica, but easily overlooked because of its small size, 1.6-2.3 mm. It is dark red with white scales, the body is pear-shaped and the antennae are straight i.e. not elbowed. The larva lives in the stems between July and August. There are 2 generations June-July and Aug.–Oct., and the adults hibernate. This is a local species found south of Leicestershire.

OTHER BEETLES

An adult leaf beetle (Chrysomelidae) which feeds on the leaves of nettles and thistles is Crepidodera ferruginea (Fig 13.10). It is 3-4 mm, rust coloured, and can be recognised by the rectangular recess at the base of the thorax. It belongs to the group of flea beetles, so called because of their enlarged hind femora that enable them to jump. Other beetles most often encountered on nettles are predators/carnivores that feed on various herbivorous insects or their larvae. Perhaps the most abundant of these are the ladybirds (Coccinellidae), the adults and larvae of which feed on the various species of aphids which suck juices from nettles stems and leaves. These include the red and black 7 spot (Coccinella 7-punctata), 2-spot (Adalia bi-punctata) and 11-spot (Coccinella 11-punctata) and the yellow and black 14-spot (Propylea 14-punctata) and 22-spot (Thea 22-punctata), and the orange and black 10-spot (Adalia 10-punctata), (Chinery, 1986 and Maejerus,). The most common of these is the 7-spot, and all stages of this can be found feeding on aphids such as Microlophium carnosum. Many ladybirds exhibit great variation and, as an example of this, I have drawn a sample of 14-spot collected from one nettle clone (Fig 13.3). The Carabidae contain ferocious predators with large mandibles, such as the familiar violet ground beetle and the green and yellow tiger beetles found on moorlands. Another very common beetle belonging to this group is Demetrias (Risophilus) articapillus (4.5-5.5 mm) which is

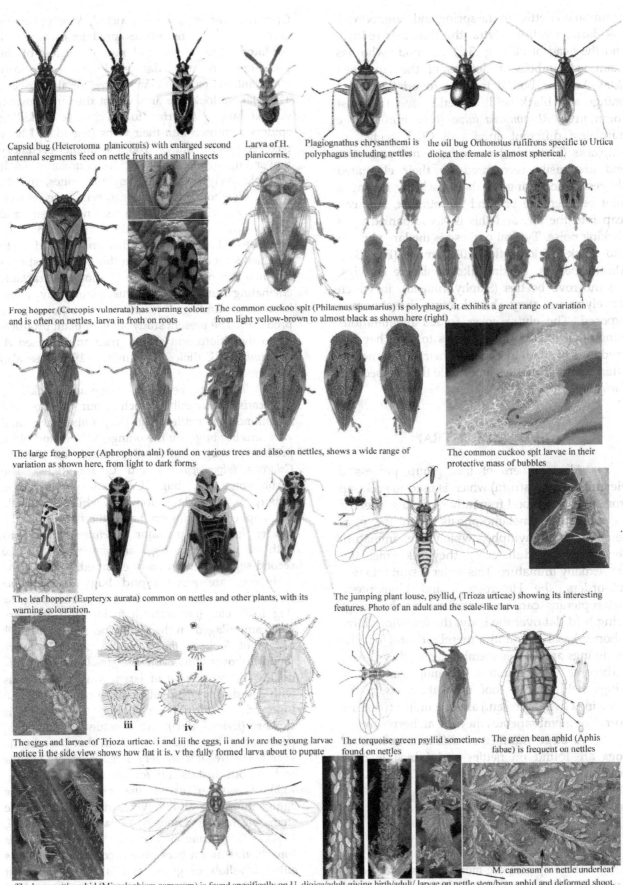

Capsid bug (Heterotoma planicornis) with enlarged second antennal segments feed on nettle fruits and small insects

Larva of H. planicornis.

Plagiognathus chrysanthemi is polyphagus including nettles

the oil bug Orthonotus rufifrons specific to Urtica dioica the female is almost spherical.

Frog hopper (Cercopis vulnerata) has warning colour and is often on nettles, larva in froth on roots

The common cuckoo spit (Philaenus spumarius) is polyphagus, it exhibits a great range of variation from light yellow-brown to almost black as shown here (right)

The large frog hopper (Aphrophora alni) found on various trees and also on nettles, shows a wide range of variation as shown here, from light to dark forms

The common cuckoo spit larvae in their protective mass of bubbles

The leaf hopper (Eupteryx aurata) common on nettles and other plants, with its warning colouration.

The jumping plant louse, psyllid, (Trioza urticae) showing its interesting features. Photo of an adult and the scale-like larva

The eggs and larvae of Trioza urticae. i and iii the eggs, ii and iv are the young larvae notice ii the side view shows how flat it is. v the fully formed larva about to pupate

The torquoise green psyllid sometimes found on nettles

The green bean aphid (Aphis fabae) is frequent on nettles

M. carnosum on nettle underleaf

The large nettle aphid (Microlophium carnosum) is found specifically on U. dioica/adult giving birth/adult/ larvae on nettle stem/bean aphid and deformed shoot.

FIG 13.4 MORE BUGS AND THE HOMOPTERA, FROG HOPPERS, PLANT LICE, PSYLLID AND APHIDS ON U. DIOICA

common on nettles in the spring and Aug.-Nov. It has darkish yellow elytra, the thorax is reddish and the head black (Fig 13.2). Anybody who has examined umbels of flowers of the Hogweed (May-Aug.) is bound to have found the bright orange and black soldier beetles, and the most common is *Rhagonycha fulva* (8-10 mm). Large numberof different species of Click beetles or Skipjacks (Elateridae) are to be found on nettles and are easily recognised by their elongated shapes. When lying on their back, by flexing a joint between the pro and mesothorax, they can leap into the air, and this is accompanied by a clicking noise. Typical of these is the large brown and black Click beetles (10-13 mm), (Fig 13.2). Minute beetles, looking like miniature earwigs, are the rove beetles (Staphylinidaed), in which the elytra are very short leaving the abdomen exposed. The elytra cover folded membranous wings that enable these beetles to fly. They are predators of small insects and their larvae and are often found on nettles and nettle litter, especially *Tachyporus* spp.

BUGS (HEMIPTERA)

All members of this group possess a piercing beak (rostrum) which is used to suck sap from plants or blood from other animals. There is an incomplete metamorphosis, with the eggs hatching into nymphs, which are immature versions of the adults except they lack wings and are sexually immature. This order is split into two sub-orders, the Heteroptera and Homoptera. Heteropterans can be recognised by the wings being held flat over the body; the forewings have a horny basal area and a membraneous top; the hindwings are always membraneous; they can be herbivores or predators. Homopterans have wings held like a roof over their body; the forewings (when present) are of a uniform texture horny, or membraneous; they are all herbivores.

A large number of different species of bugs are found on nettles and I include brief details of these and their lifecycles (Tab 13.1). For identification keys, see Davis (1983).

HETEROPTERA (BUGS)

Three species are more or less confined to Urtica. The nettle ground bug (*Heterogaster urticae*), common nettle capsid (*Liocoris tripustulatus*) and

Orthonotus rufifrons; the rest include 9 polyphagous herbivores, 5 herbivores/predators, and 7 predators. The largest and most ferocious of the predators are the damsel bugs, particularly abundant on nettles in marshy areas or along rivers. Their larvae look like ants whilst the larger marsh damsel bug is reported to be capable of killing spiders if thrown into their webs (Fig 13.3). I have received painful 'stings' from the smaller predatory flower bugs (*Anthocoris*). *Anthocoris nemorum* feeds non-selectively on aphids, psyllids, mites, mirids, thrips, leafhoppers, scale insects, etc. Over-wintering adults hibernate on dead nettle stems and willow bark. In spring adults switch from *Salix caprea* to U. dioica and this may be due to infochemicals emanating from this plant. Most eggs are then laid on the leaves of U. dioica. Attractants emanating directly from this plant may affect host/prey finding by insect parasitoids and predators. The present study showed plant products (from the chloroform soluble fraction) attracted *A. nemorum* to U. dioica (Dwumfour, 1992), see also (Anderson, 1962).

The large, beautiful orange and black bug, *Deraecoris ruber*, exhibits much colour variation and is common on nettles (Fig 13.3). Other large and very striking bugs are the orange, yellow and black predatory bugs commonly found on nettles, *Calocoris fulvomaculatus* and *C. sexguttatus*. The herbivorous oil bug *Orthonotus rufifrons* is dimorphic, the male is elongated whilst the female has a spherical abdomen, hence the name, and the bizarre herbivore/predator *Heterotoma planicornis* with its pale green legs, and antenna with the second segment enormously enlarged. Many of the herbivores are green capsid bugs *Plagiognathus chrysanthemi*, *Lygocoris pabulinus*, *Calocoris norvegicus* (Fig 13.3), etc., (are difficult to identify), they are well camouflaged on the nettle.The adults and 3-5th instars of *Scolopostethus thomsoni* (Fig 13.3) were found to over-winter on the dead stems of the nettle. The occurrence of larvae was synchronous with the development of nettle seed produced in June and maturing in August); the cycle *of S affinis* is similar (Eyles, 1963). The nettle ground bug (*Heterogaster urticae*) is unusual in that later in the year it congregates in very large numbers, adults and various instars, on female nettle plants (Fig 13.3). I wonder about the reasons for these aggregations; the adults over-winter in dead nettle stems, etc. for the various nymphal stages (Servadei, 1951). The common nettle capsid (*Liocoris tripustulatus*) has a background coloration which is either a yellow or green, and is one of the most frequent bugs found on nettles; it hibernates in dead nettle stems.

200

HOMOPTERA (FROG AND LEAF HOPPERS, PLANT LICE, APHIDS AND PSYLLIDS)

Anybody who has beaten insects from nettles onto a white sheet will know that most insects disappear within a very short space of time, particularly the frog hoppers. The most conspicuous frog hopper is the large *Cercopis vulnerata* which has black and red warning colours and appears early in the spring (Fig 13.4). Almost as impressive is the large yellow and brown *Aphrophora alni* that lives on trees such as the alder and then moves onto nettles. The common frog hopper *Philaenus spumarius*, which exhibits great variation in its patterns and coloration, is known more by gardeners as a pest of herbaceous plants, and for the protective bubble froth produced by the larvae, hence the common names spittle bugs and cuckoo-spit insects. Because of their small size, leafhoppers are not so well known. The larvae and adults of the three species of the genus *Eupteryx* can cause damage and curling to leaves. The three species *Eupteryx aurata* (Fig 30), *E. urticae* and *E. cyclops*, which live on nettles, have been studied (Le Quesne, 1972).

The study of Le Quesne is based around the theory that species which compete for the same resource, (nettle in this case) cannot co-exist unless they differ in some ecological factor. It was found that in populations of the three species (all have 2 generations per. year) although they overlap, their peaks are staggered. Competition is also reduced, by *E. aurata* favouring nettles in damp situations and being polyphagous, whereas the other two species are confined to nettles. The nymphs of these species are attacked by parasites of the *Dryinidae*, and all nymphs on nettles are heavily parasitised, whereas those of *E. aurata* living on other host species were not parasitised and therefore increased the chances of survival of this species. Further studies of *E. urticae* and *E. cyclops* may uncover different factors that enable their co-existence on Urtica dioica.

Perrin (1976) made studies of populations of the large nettle aphid *Microlophium carnosum* (Fig 13.4), that colonises U. dioica and U. urens. It is one of the most abundant weed-infesting aphids in this country and the numbers of this aphid on large nettle stands in many years reach epidemic proportions. Nettles infested with this aphid are covered in honey dew and festooned with the white cast skins of the nymphs. In his study Perrin chose three clones of nettles differing in the amount of shade received and investigated aphid populations, and their predators and parasites, over a 3 year period. *M. carnosum* populations on U. dioica increased rapidly during April-May and reached

their peaks in June, followed by a rapid decline. Below optimal temperatures and mortality due to natural enemies contributed to post peak development of aphid populations. Enemies included predators such as ladybirds and their larvae, the adults and nymphs of flower bugs *Anthocoris nemorum* and *A. nemoralis*, larvae of hover flies (*Syrphus spp.*) and lacewings (*Chrysopa spp.*), mirids, beetles of the *Carabidae*, *Staphylinidae* and *Phalangidae*, spiders, and parasites such as *Aphidius ervi* (Fig 13.5), and *Ephedrus lacertosus* and infection by fungi such as *Entomophthora aphidis* and *E. planchoniana*. Falls in populations were due to effects of: (1) host plant quality, (2) competition within aphid populations, (3) natural enemies. The food quality of the nettle clones was measured by the reproductive rate of caged aphids, and whilst high in May-June, it decreased rapidly in July-Aug. Reaction of the nettle to aphid infestations could have resulted in side-shooting and sparse flowering on stems, although these were not specifically measured. Mean growth rates of aphids did not correlate with nitrogen concentrations of stems and leaves, but amino acid composition of phloem sap is more likely to be important.

Aphid populations between different clones and within the same clones in different years showed great variation. Stems of some clones supported 500 or more aphids, in others the ceiling was 50 or less. With similar levels of parasites in 1972-1973 fluctuations in aphid populations could have been due to yearly variation in the nutritional quality of nettle clones which could be influenced by heavy aphid attacks the previous year; these could have reduced the accumulation of food in the rhizome system. It was noted however that nettle clones in high nitrogen areas, such as adjacent to dog-kennels, supported consistently high levels of aphids.

In my studies of nettle clones, grown in randomised blocks, I noticed that certain clones were susceptible to attack by *Aphis fabae*, whereas the majority were not affected. The life cycle of the jumping psyllid *Troiza urticae* which is the most abundant insect on nettles and has 3 generations, is shown in (Fig13.4), and the aphid *Microlophium carnosum* and its parasites. Davis concludes that the nettle must have a high degree of productivity because it seldom appears to be adversely affected by its insect populations (there is a need, however, for quantitative measurements on the effect of the insect load on nettle growth and seed production). The co-existence of this large number of insect species on one plant could only be achieved by minor differences in feeding habits and different seasonal population peaks of different species, as well as adaptations to different habitat conditions. All parts of the plant are utilised, and those competing for the same resource use different strategies such as weevils biting holes in leaves, as opposed to the bug *Scolopostethus*, which feeds on the margins of leaves. Davis (1975) also made a study on the colonisation of isolated patches of U. dioica by insects.

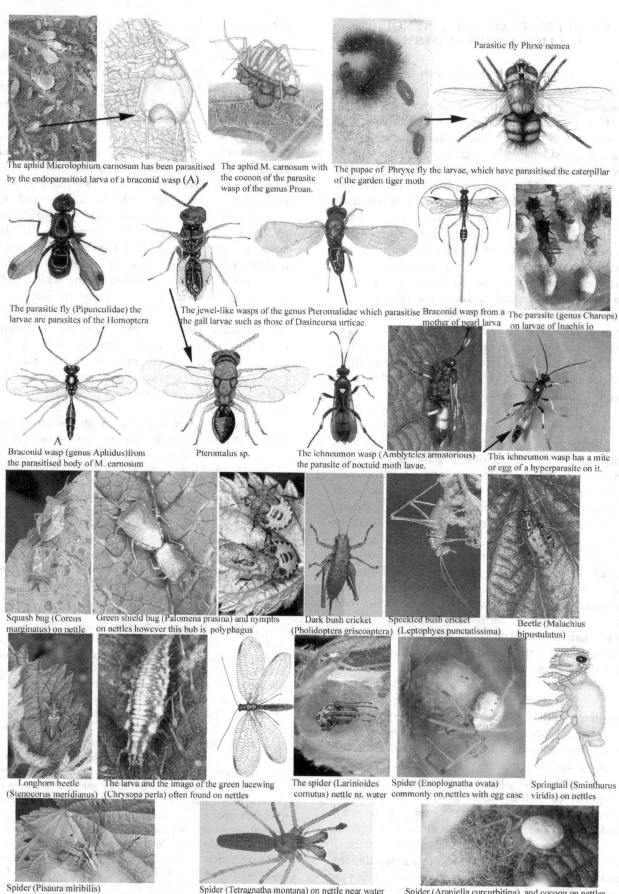

The aphid Microlophium carnosum has been parasitised by the endoparasitoid larva of a braconid wasp (A)

The aphid M. carnosum with the cocoon of the parasite wasp of the genus Proan.

The pupae of Phryxe fly the larvae, which have parasitised the caterpillar of the garden tiger moth

Parasitic fly Phrxe nemea

The parasitic fly (Pipunculidae) the larvae are parasites of the Homoptera

The jewel-like wasps of the genus Pteromalidae which parasitise the gall larvae such as those of Dasineursa urticae.

Braconid wasp from a mother of pearl larva

The parasite (genus Charops) on larvae of Inachis io

Braconid wasp (genus Aphidus)from the parasitised body of M. carnosum

A

Pteromalus sp.

The ichneumon wasp (Amblyteles armatorious) the parasite of noctuid moth lavae.

This ichneumon wasp has a mite or egg of a hyperparasite on it.

Squash bug (Coreus marginatus) on nettle

Green shield bug (Palomena prasina) and nymphs on nettles however this bub is polyphagus

Dark bush cricket (Pholidoptera griseoaptera)

Speckled bush cricket (Leptophyes punctatissima)

Beetle (Malachius bipustulatus)

Longhorn beetle (Stenocorus meridianus)

The larva and the imago of the green lacewing (Chrysopa perla) often found on nettles

The spider (Larinioides cornutus) nettle nr. water

Spider (Enoplognatha ovata) commonly on nettles with egg case

Springtail (Sminthurus viridis) on nettles

Spider (Pisaura miribilis)

Spider (Tetragnatha montana) on nettle near water

Spider (Araniella curcurbitina) and cocoon on nettles

FIG 13.5 PARASITIC FLIES, WASPS AND OTHER INSECTS AND ARACHNIDS ASSOCIATED WITH URTICA DIOICA

NETTLES AND CROP PESTS

One of the reasons given by farmers for spraying nettles is that they harbour pests. This is reasonable enough when they see large areas of nettles suffering aphid attacks. However, having looked at insects on nettles, it is apparent that the aphid attacks on nettles are largely caused by the large (*Microlophium carnosum*) and small (*Aphis urticata*) nettle aphids **and these aphids are confined to nettles in the U.K.** The bean aphid (*Aphis faba* (Fig 13.4)) only occurs to a small extent on nettles. Added to this is the fact that nettles occur in relatively small patches compared to the monoculture crops planted by mankind.

Perrin (1975) argues that Urtica dioica acts as a reservoir of natural enemies which are beneficial to plant crops. He lists the main natural enemies of aphids, psylllids and other predatory insects on Urtica dioica, as follows, *Coccinella 7-punctata*, *Adalia 2-punctata* (*Coccinellidae*, ladybirds), *Platycheirus albimanus* (*Syrphidae*, hoverflies) *Anthocoris nemorum*, *A. nemoralis* (Anthocoridae, flower bugs), *Heterotoma merioptera* (*Miridae*), *Aphidoletes sp.* (*Cecidomyiidae*, 'gall' midges), *Chrysopa carnea* (*Chrysopidae*, lacewings), *Aphidius ervi* (*Braconidae*), *Entomophthora aphidis*, *E. planchoniana* (Entomophthorales, fungi). Ladybirds were found to disperse from nettles in June, and the aphid parasitoids *Aphidius ervi and Ephedrus laceratus* in July, so these could then move to aphid infestations on crops.

Cutting nettles in May or early June had the worst effect on the species and numbers of ladybirds (*Coccinellidae*). Cutting nettles in mid-June, when there were maximum numbers of predatory adult ladybirds and flower bugs, was calculated as the best time to enable to maximum movement of natural enemies from nettles onto nearby crops, where they could reduce pest infestations.

In Czechoslovakia, Stary (1983) studied aphid parasitoids living on the aphids (*Aphis urticata* and *Microlophium carnosum*) in Czechoslovakia. He notes that Urtica dioica is widespread in various habitats and that the intensification of agricultural methods, although it has led to a decrease in species diversity, has resulted in an increase in certain species such as Urtica dioica. Parasitoids isolated on *Aphis urticata* were: *Ephedrus plagiator*, *Lipolexis gracilis*; *Lysiphlebus confuscus*, *L. fabarum* *; and *Trioxys acalephae* *; on Microlophium carnosum, parasitoids were; *Aphidius picipes*, *A. urticae* *(Fig 13.5),, *A. ervi* *; *Ephedrus lacertosus* *; *Praon grossum* *(Fig 13.38),, *P. volucre*; and *Trioxys centaurae* (* key members of the spectrum).

Nettle clones could act as reservoirs of parasitoids, prevalent about June, and coinciding with the occurrence of aphids on cereals. In this respect the exchange of parasitoids between Urtica and cereals could take place and Aphidius ervi could be the key species. However, in Czechoslovakia, Stary rates the semi-perennial leguminous plants, which cover a significant acreage, as more important as a source of parasitoids than Urtica.

I have obtained much pleasure from collecting, drawing and painting insects on nettles and although they are small in size (2-10 mm) average range, when magnified many are extremely beautiful, many are bizarre and have fascinating life cycles. They are well worth the studying in their own right, and I can thoroughly recommend the small book of B. N. K. Davis (1983) which enables the quick identification of most insect species associated with nettles; it is also thought - provoking and includes a section on collecting and methods for examination, as well as worthwhile projects that can be carried out at all levels. For the hymenoptera there is the excellent book 'The Hymenoptera' Gauld and Bolton (1988).

Also found on nettles are: -

(1) **(Thysanoptera)** - *Thrips urticae* which are minute (1-1.3 mm), yellow with a pair of small feathery wings – this species is confined to nettles.

(2) **(Orthoptera)** – Crickets, Dark bush cricket, *Pholidoptera griseoaptera* and Speckled bush cricket, *Leptophyes punctatissima.*

(3) **(Dermaptera)** - Earwigs, *Forficula auricularia.*

(4) **(Neuroptera)** – Lacewings, *Chrysopa spp.*

(5) **(Mecoptera)** – Scorpion flies, *Panorpa* spp.

(6) **(Hymenoptera)** - For the principle genera of parasites attacking insects on nettles see (Davis, 1983 and Gauld & Bolton, 1996).

(7) **(Arachnida)** on nettles Davis, 1983 gives a short list based on limited sampling, *Araneus cucurbitinus*, *Clubiona reclusa*, *Dictyna arundinacea*, *Enoplagnatha ovata*, *Linyphia clathrata*, *L. peltata*, *L. trangularis*, *Meta mengei*, *Philodromus spp. Tetragnatha montana*, *Theridion pictum*, *T. sisyphium*, *Xisticus cristatus.*

Bassett et al (1977) record the insects, fungi and angiosperm parasites associated with Urtica dioica ssp. gracilis in Canada. Lowman (1985) lists the insects associated with the giant stinging tree (Dendrocnide excelsa) in Australia. Davis (1989) carried out a survey of insects on Urtica dioica in central and southern Europe from 4-27th Sept., to compare the insect fauna with that of Britain. A large proportion of the British insects associated with U. dioica were recorded. Additions were *Arashnia levana* (Lepidoptera), *Phaneroptera nana* (Orthoptera), *Nabis pseudoferus* (Heteroptera) and *Scymnus interruptus* (Coleoptera).

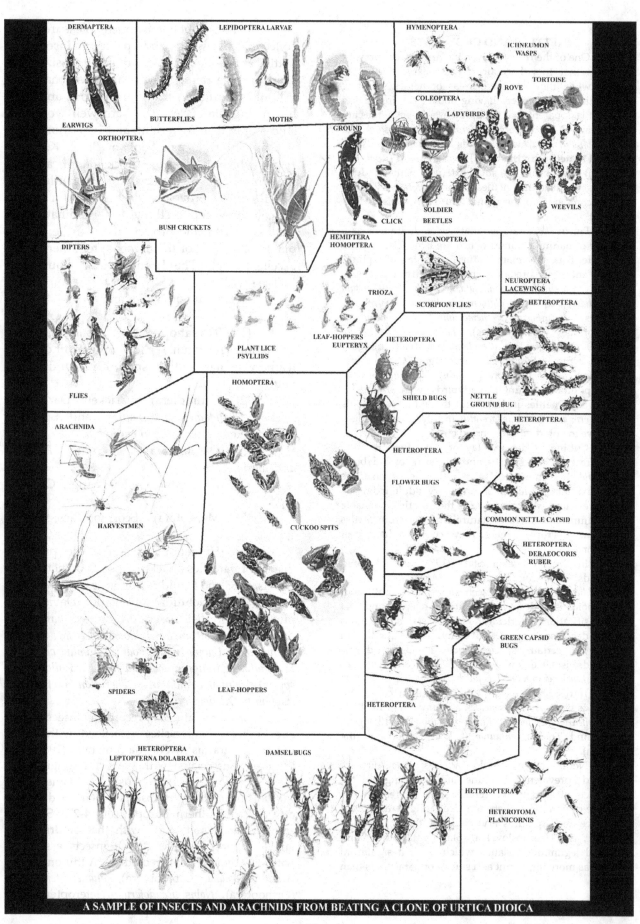

A SAMPLE OF INSECTS AND ARACHNIDS FROM BEATING A CLONE OF URTICA DIOICA

FIG 14 DIFFERENT HABITAT OF THE STINGING NETTLE (URTICA DIOICA)

WORLDWIDE AND ALTITUDINAL DISTRIBUTION

Urtica dioica is found throughout the British Isles (100% Vice Counties) and Europe (92% Territories) where it is undoubtedly native. It occurs throughout the Caucasus, W. Siberia; Far East and Central Asia (where it is largely adventive); Asia Minor, Armenia, Kurdistan and Iran (Komarov). Introduced by the agency of man, it is now found established in the temperate zones of both hemispheres. Probably dispersed as a contaminant of crop seed, it was carried to and is part of the alien flora in the following areas; New World where it has established itself mainly along the western coastal areas of Canada and the United States

temperate areas of India and China; also in Tibet (Grieg-Smith 1948). It is now a sub-cosmopolitan species.

In the British Isles Urtica dioica is found up to 338m (2750') on Ben Lawers in Scotland; 838m (2750') on Tal-y-Fan in North Wales and 670m (2200') on Mangerton, Kerry in Ireland. In Europe it grows at high altitudes in the Alps; 2615m (8578') on Arose Weisshorn in Switzerland and 2370m (7774') in the Austrian Tyrol (for more details see, Ascherson and Graebner 1918, Hegi 1910 and Grieg-Smith 1948). In India it occurs in the N.W. Himalayas from Kashmir to Simla at 2439-3048m (8-10,000') and in W.Tibet at 2439-3658m (8-12,000'), (Chopra). Therefore overall it has a very large altitudinal range.

Photo 14.1 Urtica dioica alongside a ridge in the Austrian Alps at 1,800m Alexander Enzinger Weg nr. Kaprun.

(Woodland 1982, Bassett 1974). In his' New-England's Rarities', Josselyn (1672) comments that the Common Nettle was 'the first plant taken notice of ' and includes it in his list of ' such Plants as have sprung up since the English planted and kept cattle in New England ' (Grigson, 1975). Also recorded from: South America where it is found in many Provinces of Chile which border the Andes - unfortunately no elevations are given, (Navas 1961); North Africa; the Union of South Africa, where it occurs together with a number of our common weeds (Phillips 1938); throughout Polynesia; New Zealand where it was first recorded in 1839 and now is distributed sparingly in waste places on both islands (Thompson 1922); Australia. Absent from the tropics, but found as an adventive in the N.W.Himalayas and the more mountainous

Although Urtica dioica is found at high altitudes, in such areas, it is sparsely distributed. At these elevations there is generally more rainfall and leaching out of minerals so that most of the soil is acidic and poor, and therefore unsuited for the establishment and growth of the Common Nettle. In such areas the Nettle is found associated with human disturbance, habitations, or cattle which eat nettle seeds which have fallen on grass and then disperse them in their droppings. The weathered dung releases high levels of phosphate and nitrate needed for seedling establishment of nettles. In the Austrian Tyrol the Common Nettle is found growing along rides, in clearings and along streams in the coniferous forests which extend to the tree line. Above the tree line their occurrence is always associated with man and nettle clones are found at the edges of fields or around cattle sheds, alongside footpaths, etc. I well remember a magnificent Austrian walk from the Alpincenter below the Kitzsteinhorn, along the Alexander Enzinger Weg to Kaprun. Having marvelled at the beautiful flora in the vicinity of the Alpincenter and the high hay meadows along the route, a ridge with near vertical sides was reached at about 1800m. It was interesting to find the Common Nettle growing amongst the alpine meadow flora alongside this very exposed pathway. Although the second week in August the nettles were about 150cm high, in full flower and with a small amount of seed (see Photo.). Did these nettles establish from seeds carried up on hiker's boots? To survive at this position the nettle must have a certain degree of climatic hardiness which enables it to grow at high wind exposure, low temperatures and a diminished growing season. No doubt its great adaptability allows it to mould its morphology to different environmental conditions including extremes of climatic conditions, and thus enabling it to grow in a large number of diverse habitats. Salisbury (1961) included Urtica in an analysis of species growing over 762m (2500'), and found these plants were unusual in that they all occurred throughout Britain.

HABITATS

HERBALS AND LOCAL FLORAS

Green in his Universal Herbal (1820) - containing accounts of all known plants in the world!- says of Urtica dioica, 'It is a formidable root weed on the sides of banks and ditches, in hedges, in uncultivated places in general and in pastures', and in relation to its use as a fibre plant, 'The growth of nettles is general throughout this country, particularly in strong fertile soils where on every bank, ditch and place which cannot be reduced to tillage they are produced in such abundance... The shady places in woods, parks and coppices are particularly favourable to their growth and they are accordingly found in such situations in the greatest perfection'.

In the last half of the 19th Century, the British Flora was reinforced by a large number of County Floras. Small advances were made by listing species variations, and specific locations together with recorders' names; however information on the habitats of common plants, such as Urtica dioica, is scant. Typical is the Flora of Dorsetshire, Manssel-Playdell (1874), Urtica dioica: 'Waste ground; native, common'. The impression is that, for common plants like Urtica either it was not worthwhile to give details of their various habitats because they were simply regarded as ubiquitous or the habitats had not been clearly defined at this point in time.

Towards the end of the 19th Century however this neglect of the importance of the habitat was to change with the crystallisation of the study of ecology, a word coined by Ernest Haekel in 1869. Ecology provided a driving force for naturalists and botanists alike at the beginning of the 20th Century, and led to the production of books on the British Flora with plants grouped in relation to their habitats, such as the beautifully produced pioneer series by A. R. Horwood 'A New British Flora - British Wild Flowers in their Natural Haunts' (1919). The author stated that it is the study of our native Flora by the method of Ecology which included for each species notes on pollination, seed-dispersal, fungal and insect pests, soil requirements.

THROUGHOUT THE BRITISH ISLES

In 1904 a committee of professional botanists was formed to survey and study the British vegetation. A.G.Tansley acted as editor for the work, which was published in 1911 and entitled 'Types of British Vegetation'. This work was later published in more detail in 1939 under the title 'The British Isles and their Vegetation'. The object was to survey the natural or semi-natural communities, which make up the vegetation of the British Isles, and as far as possible, *therefore, areas greatly affected by man were mostly excluded*. The carefully selected areas were sampled using quadrats placed in those parts of the community deemed to be typical. It is unlikely that the occasional patches of nettles would have been included, except in areas where they were generally distributed or abundant and regarded as 'natural' members of the community. For these reasons a complete picture of the habitats of the nettle at that time cannot be drawn from this work. Of the 14 main habitat areas (formations) U. dioica was recorded in 6 (see book for more details). These are as follows:-

(i) **Arctic Alpine**. (a) Cader Idris. Calciferous pillow larva at two altitudes 184-209m (1500-1700') and 221-295m (1800-2400'). Occasional (Evans, 1932). (b) Ben Lawers. On well-manured pasture, 'Lager-platz'.

(ii) **Clay and Loams. Pedunculate Oakwood** (a) Damp to wet heavy clay. Locally abundant. (b) Cambridgeshire, Buff Wood (Greig-Smith 1948).

(iii) **Sandy Soil. Grass Heath**. (a) Breckland, as a rabbit-resistant plant (Farrow 1917).

(iv) **Calcarious Soil. (a) Ashwood**. (a) Chilterns. Young wood, locally abundant. Mature wood, locally dominant (Watt, 1934). (b) Yorkshire, limestone ravine, Ling Ghyll, locally abundant (Harley). (c) Dolgelley, Merionethshire. On upland basic igneous rock, southern slopes of Craig-y-Benglog at an altitude of 270-380m (900-1250'). Locally abundant (Evans 1945).

FIG 14.2 (a) Dune-slack, under sallow, Braunton Burrrows, N. Devon.

(c) On grey dunes with Clematis vitabilis Pembroke, South Wales.

(e) Pasture with cattle, near Porthleven, Cornwall.

(g) Acidic pasture near coast along granite wall, Zennor, Cornwall.

(b) Behind shingle bar, on shingle at head of valley, Solva, S. Wales.

(d) On shingle bank River Taw, North Devon.

(f) Permanent acidic pasture with horses, Allerford, Somerset.

(h) Acidic pemanent pasture on flood plain of R. Taw, Chapleton, Devon.

208

(b) Chalk Grassland. (a) Cambridgeshire, Fleam dyke. Grassland on chalky boulder clay. Local.

(c) Chalk Scrub (a) Cambridge. Hawthorn scrub, chalky boulder clay (Ross).

(d) **Limestone Pavement** (a) Yorkshire, Colt Park. Clefts in mountain limestone (Harley).

(v) **Marsh. Alder-Willow Wood** (a) Norfolk carrs. Most abundant plant.

(vi) **Fen. Fen Carr (Alder Wood)** (a) Norfolk. Wheat Fen broad. Abundant. (b) Shropshire. Sweat Mere. Locally abundant to abundant. (c) Suffolk. Valley Wood Fen. (d) East Anglia. Esthwaite Fens. Occasional. (e) Wicken Fen. Frequent.

It is also recorded in several habitats on Ailsa Craig, a rocky island adjacent to the Firth of Clyde (i) growing in soil, rich in guano, at the foot of bird cliffs (ii) boulders under scree slopes, (iii) foot of cliffs, talus slopes (Vevers 1936). Ireland, Galway. Boulder beaches.

ON FARMS

The Agricultural Adviser to Norfolk County Council, G.H.Bates (1933) wrote an article on the Stinging Nettle, which was published in the Journal of the Ministry of Agriculture. This article contained some good observations of the nettle habitats in the vicinity of farms, giving the following habitats:-

(i) **Arable Land.** Not a common weed of arable land because the shallow rhizomes are buried by ploughing, unlike those of the Creeping Thistle (Cirsium arvense).

(ii) **Pasture.** It may be troublesome when present in grass where it may range from small patches to larger more dominant areas.

(iii) **Hedgerows**. Most prevalent at the base and in the hedge itself they may become dominant. He observes that a loose surface covering of road sweepings, leaves, twigs, etc. can provide cover for the rhizomes as well as nitrogen for their growth. He noted that they spread out from the hedge base and that of 50 patches observed 41 resulted from heaps of hedge cuttings or grass mowings from the bank whilst the others were probably due to stone, gravel, sand heaps, tree trunks, drain pipes, etc.

(iv) **Ditches**. Nettles tended to establish on ditch - clearings, which were thrown on the edge of the bank.

(v) **Woods**. These are colonised to a greater or lesser extent, quite often coming up through piles of brushwood.

(vi) **Buildings**. At the base of walls of rural areas. Lairages of live stock where urine seeps through the walls, also walls of barns, cartsheds and other buildings. He attributes this to loose soil near the wall, which allows early growth of rhizomes and surface litter.

(vii) **Ruderal** habitats. Observations showed that heaps of stones, sand or gravel left near the edges of roads often become colonised with nettles with time or after their removal.

(viii) **Rabbit Burrows**. The nettle patches in the vicinity of burrows he says are due to light sand thrown out in the areas studied and not due to high nitrogen since rabbits do not foul their burrows.

This study is important because it is the only survey at this period which focuses directly on the nettle habitat. Bates's ideas or reasons for nettle establishment will be mentioned later.

BIOLOGICAL FLORA OF THE BRITISH ISLES

After the formation of the British Ecological Society, the renowned series on the ecology of individual plants (Autecology) the 'Biological Flora of the British Isles' was published in its famous Journal of Ecology starting in 1913.

The Biological Flora of Urtica species (U. dioica and urens) appeared in 1948 and was compiled by Greig-Smith There is three habitats of Urtica dioica given by Grieg-Smith, which are not included in those of Tansley or Bates. These are:

(i) **On Trees**. Occasional epiphyte on willow, ash, hornbeam, oak and poplar (Hegi). Epiphyte on pollard willows near Cambridge, where it occurred on 306 out of 3951 trees (Willis and Burkill,1893).

(ii) **Lias Clay. Larch Plantation**. (a) Warwickshire, Newnham, (Greig-Smith,1948).

(iii) **Riverbank** (a) Berkshire, Newbury. Growing at water level, (Greig-Smith 1948).

Perhaps he omitted hedgerows because they are regarded by some to be extensions of the woodland type habitat; this is the first mention of the river bank as a habitat, as far as I can ascertain. Next, a county flora which included a vegetation survey of plants in relation to their habitats deserves special consideration.

FIG 14.3 (a) Pasture with sheep, bank along a feeding stream into the River Taw, North Devon (b) Bottom and sides of a small moist valley grazed by cattle, E. Codden Hill, North Devon.
(c) flood plain area un - grazed meadow of the River Taw, Newbridge, North Devon.
(d) Moist acidic valley with adjacent pasture grazed by cattle, near Simonsbath, Exmoor, Devon
(e) Old derelict cow-shed Urtica dioica and Elder (Sambucus niger), Norfolk.
(f) Around abandoned farm machinery, pasture with sheep, Exmoor, Devon.
(g) Old greenhouse with luxuriant growth of Urtica dioica on the fertile soil.
(h) On the ruins of a farmhouse high up in the Wicklow mountains, Ireland.

FLORA OF WILTSHIRE

Donald Grose published the Flora of Wiltshire in 1957, after 16 years of hard work. There is no flora which can compare with the second part of this work, which deals with the 'Vegetation of Wiltshire'. The survey carried out for the vegetation analysis involved looking at 26 different habitats (divided between calcareous and non-calcareous) and compiling 30 habitat lists for each five kilometre square; the total lists were then adjusted, for calculations sake, to 5000.

Stands of approximately 250-350 square yards were sampled for occurrence, which is the presence of a particular species in a stand, and given a value of 1. Frequency of a species in a stand was classified as either abundant=10, frequent=6, occasional=3, and rare=1. In assessing frequency, equal measure is given to numbers and size. A small species may be ranked as abundant by its numbers, whilst a larger species may be assessed by its size although less in number. The summation of degrees of frequency is used to asses the frequency of a species in one or more types of habitat and is calculated by multiplying occurrence by frequency for each stand, thus giving a quantitative estimate. For example, if 10 stands are sampled in a particular habitat and the plant is found in all stands it has an occurrence value of 10, whereas if it is abundant in 5 of these stands and rare in the other 5 stands, its overall frequency is therefore 50+5=55. For this scheme to work it must be non-selective, i.e. areas with rare flowers or large areas of species must not be consciously chosen. This is why it works so well and gives a better indication of the habitats of the nettle, with a few reservations, which will be mentioned later.

The European plant communities were first crystallised by Warming in his 'Oecology of Plants' ( ). The vast number of ecological plant studies undertaken in Europe during the 20th Century are, outlined in the monumental, yet readily readable work, of Heinz Ellenberg in his 'Vegetation Ecology of Central Europe' 1986. I give below a brief

Table 3.1. Occurrence of the Common Nettle (Urtica dioica) in Wiltshire. From the 'Vegetation of Wiltshire', the second part of the 'Flora of Wiltshire' by D. Grose, (1957). Table of the summary habitat lists in relation to the Common Nettle Urtica. dioica. (Symbols, + = non-calcareous soils), * = calcareous soils. ♣Occurrence = presence in a stand or list. ♦Frequency = related to its abundance - see text.)

Habitat	No. of Lists within each habitat type	Occurrence of U. dioica ♣	Frequency of U. dioica ♦	Rank Order, for all species, i.e. 1 is the most frequent.
A Woodland +	229	155	421	8
B Woodland *	78	61	229	2
C Beechwood	37	26	60	12
D Scrub +	37	24	82	4
E Scrub *	55	40	130	3
F Hedges +	91	70	160	10
G Hedges *	30	21	65	10
Summary A-G	557	397	1147	6
H Heath +	85	Very rare, below 30 on lists.		
I Grassland +	1054	Negative		
J Grassland *	1054	Negative		
K Roadsides +	30	23	65	6
L Roadsides *	12	9	18	19
M Railway Banks	24	9	27	18
N Tracks +	30	Negative		
O Tracks *	18	Negative		
Summary H-O	2367	Negative		
P Bogs	3	Negative		
Q Marsh	90	Negative		
R Rivers, Canals and ponds +	60	Negative		
S Rivers, Canals and ponds *	12	Negative		
Summary P-S	165	Negative		
T Cultivated +	903	204	249	27
U Cultivated *	903	Negative		
V Waste Ground +	54	34	133	1
W Waste Ground *	54	39	158	2
X Gravel and Sand Pits	9	Negative		
Y Chalk and Limestone Quarries	30	17	65	3
Z Walls and Stony Places	18	12	16	18
Summary T-Z	1971	444	777	21
Grand Summary of habitats	5000	1272	2653	7

summary of his references to natural and man-made plant communities in Europe which include Urtica dioica and the reader needs to consult this excellent book for greater details.

EUROPEAN PLANT COMMUNITIES WHICH INCLUDE URTICA DIOICA

NATURAL COMMUNITIES

A BROAD-LEAVED WOODLAND MAIN ECOLOGICAL GROUPS

(a) **Oak-Hornbeam Wood**. Amongst, and classified as a species of the late flowering herbaceous field layer.

(b) **Wild Garlic-Beechwood**. Damper higher fertility soil than limestone beechwoods, thus favouring U. dioica.

(c) **Moist-soil mixed Beech woods**. U. dioica is listed amongst moisture indicators

(d) **Woodrush (Luzula)-Beechwood**. On weathered sandstone, U. dioica developed 10-13 years after fertiliser application (see later).

(e) **Maple and Ashwoods**. Four types: (i) On slopes and ravines (ii) Bottom of shaded steep-sided valleys (iii) Colluvial deep soils at the foot of slopes (iv) Alongside narrow brook channels usually dominated by Ash. Soils have good water supply and are rich in nutrients especially nitrate. U. dioica is found on all four types and classified as a hygromorphic and nitrophilous herb.

(f) **Slope-foot Sycamore-Ashwoods and Brook-channel Ashwoods**. Wet soil and high nitrogen favours nitrophilous perennials such as Urtica.

(g) **Lime and Oak-Hornbeam Woods**. On loam with a high water table and with U. dioica in the herb group of moisture indicators (see later).

B FLOOD PLAINS

This includes the vegetation in the river valley, which may be flooded even if for a short period. Although subjected to fluctuating conditions all plants in this area grow in exceptionally fertile conditions. The debris of the drift-line breaks down to produce high levels of nitrate ideal for light - loving nitrate plants.

(a) **Amphibious River Bank**. Often flooded, but sometimes dry, and found in the middle and lower reaches of the river. These areas include gravel and sand banks, which Urtica colonises at later stages in the succession.

(b) **Virgin Forest of White Willow**. Here Urtica dioica grows together with Reed Grass (Phalaris arundinacea) and Tall Brome (Festuca gigantea) under White Willow, the first tree colonist.

(c) **Flood Plain Woods**. There are four main types of these woods where U. dioica is found very frequently:

(i) **Poplar-Willow Flood Plain Wood**. Relatively often flooded.

(ii) **Poplar Flood Plain Wood**. Flooded less often.

(iii) **Elm Flood Plain Wood** With some other trees including White Willow or Ash.

(iv) **Flood Plain Elm-Oakwood**. This area is seldom flooded.

(d) **Grey Alder Woods in Mountain Valleys and Foothills**. Here the decomposition of nitrogen-fixing Alder root-nodules probably helps to increase the soil nitrate content and favours nitrophilous plants such as Urtica.

(e) **Alder-Swamp Woods**. Urtica is abundant in all of the following communities:-

(i) **Typical Alder (Alnus glutinosa) Swamp Wood**. On peat.

(ii) **Alder-Ash Wood**. On mud or muddy peat.

(iii) **Oak-Ash Wood**. Mud-covered loamy sand on the edge of the wet plain.

C SUB- ALPINE

Pasture resting-places for Cattle or Game. These are heavily dunged resting places, cowsheds and milking places which have become extremely fertile with up to 250kg N/ha per annum. U. dioica occurs together with Great Alpine Dock (*Rumex alpinus*).

D HABITAT AREAS CREATED AND MAINTAINED BY MAN'S ACTIVITIES

(a) **Planted Broad-Leaved Forests**
(i) **Poplar and Robina Stands**. *Robinia* being a member of the Leguminoseae enriches the N content of the soil by the N-fixation of its root nodules and dead leaves. This enables ruderal plants such as Urtica dioica to establish.

FIG 14.4 (a)Nettles growing alongside a railway line, Devon.
(c) At its luxurious best under poplar on the alluvial bank of the River Taw, Devon.
(e) River bank with Impatiens glandulifera, Phalaris arundinacea, Oenanthe crocata, etc.
(g) Alongside a freshwater lake with Phragmites communis, Looe Pool, Cornwall .

(b) In a Cornish hedgebank with a variety of plants, wall pellitory (Parietaria judaica) and pink campion
(d) Nettles and umbellifers growing alongside a secondary road, Devon
(f) Continuous stands on a bank alongside a drainage canal, Kings Lynn, Norfolk.
(h) Dominant on the bank-edge with Impatiens glandulifera of a slow river Otter, South Devon

213

(ii) **Spruce Forest with Fertiliser Addition**. Lime or nitrogen fertilisers can increase the productivity of Pine and Spruce Forests and encourage nitrogen indicators such as U. dioica.

(b) **Woodland Edges, Bushes, Hedges and their Herbaceuos Margins**.

(i) **Scrub and Hedge Communities**. Blackthorn Hornbeam Association. Grouped as species requiring high nitrogen, including U. dioica.

(bi) **Herbaceous Edging to Woodlands and Scrub Communities**.

(i) **Fringing Communities requiring Nitrate and High Humidity**. Found on the shaded side of the woodland stand. U. dioica and other plants of waste places occur.

(ii) **Stinging Nettle-Ground Elder Association**. This is by far the most frequent community in Central Europe and corresponds to the shaded fringing communities.

(iii) **Stinging Nettle-Crosswort Association**. These communities require more light. An example of this association is found in the Leine-Werra mountains (Dierschke 1974).

(c) **River and Meadow Bank Plants**. U. dioica is grouped in the highest (5) nitrogen plant indicator group and in the summary by Meyer 1957 it grows in plots of the highest recorded nitrogen values and has the greatest degree of cover.

(d) **Ruderal Communities of Drier Sites**. Summer, Winter Annual Ruderal Communities.

These communities are found amongst buildings, rubble, rubbish tips as well as roadsides and railway embankments. Three main types of communities are identified:-

(i) **Shortlived Pioneer Species**.

(ii) **More Permanent Annual Communities**.

(iii) **Perennial Hemicryptophyte Communities**.

U. dioica occurs in all three communities as a 'companion' type not confined to any particular type.

Urtica dioica is included in the list of native ruderal plants belonging to Central Europe before it felt any influence of man (Scholz 1960).

(e) **Perennial Ruderal Communities**.

(i) **Alongside Village Streets and Walls**. U. dioica grows together with Broadleaved Dock and White Dead Nettle. In similar situations it also occurs as part of the Mugwort Shrub and Burdock Communities. Because of the heat reflected by house walls, this area is regarded as a xerophyte habitat and this is mirrored in the structure of the plants which have a high density of stomata and corresponding transpiration patterns (Grosse- Brauckmann 1953).

AUTECOLOGICAL ACCOUNTS OF THE COMMONER BRITISH PLANT SPECIES

In England, the Natural Environmental Research Council's Unit of Comparative Plant Ecology (NERC) was set up in 1962. Two extensive vegetative studies have been brought together and published in a book 'Comparative Plant Ecology' (Grime, Hodgson and Hunt 1987) which is an Autecological Account of the common British species. The aims were not only to bring together facts about species, plant biology and distribution but also to identify measurable characteristics which can be used to interpret the ecology of species, their present abundance, and possible responses to changes in land use and vegetation management. These accounts supplement or add to the autecological accounts, so far published as the 'Biological Flora of the British Isles', as well as providing autecological information on species where no 'Biological Flora' accounts exist. The work of Grime and his co-workers on the autecology of plants was based on vegetative structures, other field observations, published sources, and laboratory screening techniques.

The vegetation surveys were carried out within an area of 3000 km2 surrounding Sheffield. The work is mainly based on Survey II (1967) where sampling was carried out subjectively within selected vegetation, and involved 2748 permanent 1m² quadrats, placed within 32 'terminal' categories, which covered most habitat types. For each Quadrat, measurements included altitude, slope, aspect, soil, pH, floristic diversity, hydrology and bare soil. There were detailed investigations on shoot phenology and seed banks and screening experiments including nuclear DNA amount, germination characteristics and relative growth rate. The plants were then categorised according to the three main regenerative strategies, competitors, stress-tolerators and ruderals, the C-S-R model (Grime, 1979).

Habitat analysis is what we are concerned with here, although it is important to keep in mind

Table .3.2. Results based on the Survey 2 of the Natural Research Council's Unit of Comparative Plant Ecology (NERC), of vegetation within an area of 3000 km² surrounding Sheffield, England, (1967). The analysis of vegetation involved measurements within 2748 1m² permanent quadrats
Frequency, Abundant = 100%, Frequent = 60%, Occasional = 30% and Rare = 10%. Shaded habitat

Primary Habitat	Intermediate Habitat	Terminal Habitat	Frequency ÷ Number Quadrats	% Occurrence in each Habitat	Frequency
	Aquatic Mire	Still	1/156	0.64	R
	Aquatic	Running	0	0	-
WETLAND	*Mire*	Unshaded	14/142	9.9	R
	Mire	Shaded	33/78	42.3	F
ARABLE		Arable	16/122	13.1	O
		Meadows	3/38	7.9	R
GRASSLAND	*Permanent Pastures*	Enclosed	1/42	2.4	R
	Permanent Pastures	Unenclosed Limestone	2/53	3.8	R
	Permanent Pastures	Unenclosed Acidic	0	0	-
		River Bank	41/49	83.7	A
		Verges	3/70	44.3	F
WASTELAND		Paths	8/51	15.7	O
	Wasteland and Heath	Limestone	8/98	8.2	R
	Wasteland and Heath	Acidic	4/151	2.7	R
		Rocks	0	0	-
		Scree	9/36	25.0	O
SKELETAL		Cliffs	3/117	2.6	R
		Walls	14/137	10.2	O
		Manure and Sewage	42/46	91.0	A
		Soil	53/59	89.0	A
		Bricks and Mortar	16/40	40.0	F
		Cinders	7/66	10.6	O
SPOIL		Lead Mine	5/50	10.0	O
		Coal Mine	0	0	-
	Quarries	Limestone	3/93	4.3	R
	Quarries	Acidic	0	0	-
		Hedgerow	42/53	79.2	A
	Plantation	Broad-leaved	9/111	8.1	R
	Plantation	Coniferous	8/100	8.0	R
WOODLANDS	*Woodland*	Limestone	18/111	16.2	O
	Woodland	Acidic	11/240	4.6	R
		Scrub	13/128	10.2	R

that (i) the area sampled was selective (ii) that no maritime or montane habitats are included.

In the Sheffield area U. dioica is abundant in habitats rich in manure or sewage, on the loose disturbed soil of spoil heaps, along river banks and in hedgerows. It is frequent along roadside verges, in shaded mires and in ruderal habitats such as brick and mortar spoil. It is occasional on arable land, alongside pathways, scree and walls, on cinders and lead mine spoil, and in limestone woodland. In the remaining habitats it is rare but of these it is generally absent from areas where water is free-standing throughout the year, heathland, and meadows, arable and in habitats not included in this study such as coastal dunes and montane habitats.

In the British Isles the common stinging nettle although widespread is certainly not ubiquitous. *In the absence of disturbance by man or his animals* Urtica dioica is not found growing in natural or semi-natural areas of the following habitats: primary dunes; moorland and heathland; montane habitats above the tree-line; salt marsh; aquatic habitats; floodplain where flooding is frequent throughout the year; woodland areas where light levels are below 8% such as young conifer plantations, under beech stands, and ancient deciduous woodland; and upland grasslands. It does occur in a lot of these habitat areas now, albeit often in small pockets, due to disturbance by man and his animals, together with their

resulting sewage and dung. There is evidence to show that U. dioica has increased in abundance as a result of high fertiliser applications that started in earnest in 1939. Urtica dioica can only establish and grow successfully as a competitor plant in soils with high levels of phosphate and nitrate, and it also needs disturbance to produce bare soil for its establishment by seed (Chapter 15).

Photos Nettle (U. dioica) habitats in Fig 14. (1) Alongside walls of farm buildings, (2) Alluvial soil by river and under willow medium shade height 2-3m , (3) Edge of bluebell wood with bluebells, yellow archangel and pink campion, (4) Alongside a ride in a larch plantation, (5) Cliff side near the sea Cornwall, (6) By a fence on the edge of a pasture grazed by sheep, (7) Whipsnade zoo on limestone with guinea fowl, they like bird dropping rich in nitrogen and phosphate, (8) Alongside a wall, (9) River bank with Himalayan balsam, (11) In the autumn when the nettles have flopped and grown up from side-shoots, (11) Growing up through bramble in the spring, (12) Regrowth from the base of sprayed nettles, (13), A clone growing on burnt ground, (14) River bank nettles coming up in the spring with seedling plants of Himalayan balsam over-topping them, (15) At the bottom of a hedge bank (16) Similar area to (14) but later with the Himalayan balsam over-topping the nettles.

CHAPTER 15

THE COMPETITOR PLANT

1 THE GROWTH REQUIREMENTS OF THE COMMON NETTLE

> "The growth of nettles in general throughout this country particularly in strong fertile soils where on every bank, ditch and place which cannot be reduced to tillage **they are produced in such abundance that the quantity if collected would be of great magnitude**.....The shady places in woods, parks and coppices are particularly favourable to their growth and they are accordingly found in such situations in the greatest perfection.....In shaded valleys where the soil has been a blue clay or strong loam.....the **plant will sometimes attain the height of 12 feet and upwards to 2 inches in circumference in general they are 5-9 feet in height** and those growing in patches on a good soil standing thick and in a favourable aspect will average about $5\frac{1}{2}$ feet ... "
>
> Thomas Green, 1816

NUTRITIONAL REQUIREMENTS

IS THE NETTLE A NITROPHYTE/NITROPHILE?

The classic work on the ecology of Urtica dioica was carried out by Carsten Olsen (1921), whose object was to find out the factors that determine the occurrence of Urtica stands in the woods of Denmark. He found that nettles grow in large close communities particularly on peaty soil in alder bogs in woods, and around inhabited places on sand and clay, close to human habitations where sewage is discharged. In certain locations, nettle plants and other species within the clone had high nitrate tissue levels, whereas plants outside the clone, such as *Deschampsia caespitose*, had low values. Soil samples from 20 woodland localities were measured for their nitrification power after 25 days' incubation. There was a direct positive relationship between nettle height and the nitrifying power of the soil, with the tallest plants growing on soil of intense nitrification. The smallest amount of phosphoric acid found in a nettle area was 2.6 mg per L, and below this value, even in areas of good nitrification, Urtica did not occur. In a sand culture experiment using Urtica rhizome cuttings growth was positively related to the amount of nitrate but ammonium was toxic. Olsen concluded that Urtica is found in areas of high nitrogen supply (nitrification), and therefore, this could be the factor governing its distribution.

Plants that require high nitrate levels for maximum growth are called nitrophytes and Ellenberg (1979), on a scale of 0 – 9, gave Urtica dioica a rating of 8 (range 7-9). As a competitor plant it can compete well with other nitrogen loving - plants and Rosnitschek-Schimmel (1985) showed that the roots and rhizomes of Urtica built up a store of nitrogen (i.e. amino acids) during the summer and autumn and in the spring these amino acids were passed to the shoots where they were used to make proteins for rapid growth. Nitrate appears to become important later in the spring when the capability for its reduction (by nitrate reductase) has been developed. Gebauer et al, 1988, investigated 48 plant species from 7 different families in 14 natural habitats in Central Europe in relation to their nitrate requirements and confirmed the classification by Ellenberg of a value of 8 for Urtica dioica as a plant only found in soils rich in mineral nitrogen.

Many studies have been carried out to establish a scientific explanation for Shakespear's observations. Olsen's study showed that soil within

> "The strawberry grows underneath the nettle,
>
> And wholesome berries thrive and ripen best
>
> Neighbour'd by fruit of baser quality:"
>
> Shakespeare

216

nettle clones has a high level of nitrification and high phosphate level so these nutrients could become available to plants growing in the vicinity. Nettles are rich in minerals (Chapters 5, 9) and these are returned to the soil when the shoots die back and are decomposed. It may be that these well known facts were the basis for the use for a long time in Sweden of nettle water, an aqueous extract of shoots of Urtica dioica, to fertilise and stimulate growth of horticultural plants. (To prepare nettle water: 1.0 kg of fresh nettle or 183 g of dried nettles are mixed with 10 litres of water and allowed to decompose over a period of 14 days after which the

nettle water resulted in about 20% higher weight of the fresh shoot. Spring nettle water gave greater growth than that made from mid-summer nettles. Other effects of nettle water are to give plants dark green leaves (due to high chlorophyll levels) and resistance to parasites such as aphids (it is well known also that nettle water can be used as an insecticide spray).

2 THE MINERAL REQUIREMENTS OF URTICA DIOICA

The classic paper that resolved the problem and to a large extent explained the main factor governing the distribution of Urtica is that of Pigott and Taylor (1964). They studied an area of woodland where nettle patches occurred alongside areas of dog's mercury (*Mercurialis perennis*). Samples of soil taken inside nettle patches and inside dog's mercury areas showed that total organic nitrogen, ammonia and nitrate for the two areas were similar; however could the distribution be explained by some other soil factor acting at the germination/seedling stage? They tested this by sowing seed on fresh soil in pots and also on small areas of soil in natural woodlands. When sown on soil where nettle seedlings were naturally found, the seedlings grew vigorously, but when sown on soil from sites supporting Mercurialis, the seedlings remained very small with cotyledons and 1-2 pairs of unexpanded foliage leaves. The seedlings then turned dark bluish-green with deep crimson-purple undersides. The addition of nitrate to the soil made no difference to the seedlings and they eventually died.

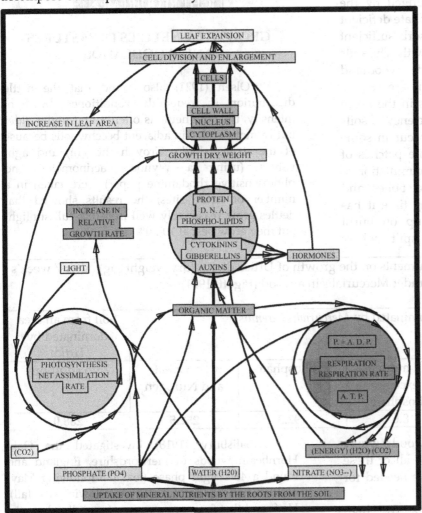

FLOW DIAGRAM 15.1 Relationship between nitrogen and phosphate and their role in the growth of Urtica dioica

water is filtered off. It can be stored for a long time.

Peterson & Jensen (1985, 1988) have carried out investigations to establish whether there is a scientific basis behind the effects of nettle water on plant growth. Plants of barley and tomato were grown in sand and peat-sand mixture supplied with dilute nettle water (10X dilution) or a nutrient solution with the same mineral composition. The

Next Urtica seedlings were grown on soil known to be deficient in phosphorus. They became stunted and no further growth took place even if other mineral elements were added. However, the addition of phosphorus in the form of orthophosphoric acid or phosphate (20 mg per litre) caused immediate vigorous growth. The seedlings

217

of Mercurialis grew well on soils low in phosphate and the addition of phosphate made no difference to their growth.

Soils taken from a large number of different British woodlands would not support the growth of nettle seedlings, indicating that the levels of phosphate in these soils were limiting; however these soils did allow normal growth of Mercurialis. It appears that Urtica cannot absorb sufficient phosphate for its growth if the phosphate level is below 1 mg of phosphate per litre. The interesting fact is that almost all British soils under 'natural' vegetation, judged by the performance of the nettle, are phosphate deficient and yet most other plants can absorb sufficient phosphate from this for normal growth. The soils where Urtica is native, alongside woodland streams, alder woods and fen carr, are rich in soluble phosphate. In upland areas in the north and west of Britain, phosphate deficiency of soils is prevalent. However nettles do occur in some areas where there are isolated fertile patches of phosphorus and nitrogen, due to accumulation of urine and faeces, in lairages, and bones and tissues of dead animals. For a long time it has been known that nettles spring up on burnt ground, where blood has been spilt, where

The results showed that the addition of phosphate over the first three weeks increased the relative growth rate of Urtica by a factor of 2.5X. This was due to an increase in the diameter of the leaf cells and the number of palisade cells. The resulting increase in photosynthesis leads to an increase in leaf production and dry mass (Flow diagram 15.1). The growth effect is increased by increases in both phosphate and nitrogen (Table 15.1) which enable Urtica to out - compete neighbouring plant growth.

LIGHT REQUIREMENTS

GROWTH OF NETTLES IN PASTURES AND WOODLANDS

Olsen (1921) also found that the nettle distribution is frequently conditioned by light intensity, thus the nettle is often found under alder but cannot survive in adjacent beechwoods because of the strong shade. Growth (ht. cm) and light values (using a Wynne's actinometer and photosensitive rhodamine paper) were taken in a number of nettle sites; the results showed that nettles grow reasonably well in 5-10% full sunlight but they grow best at 10-20% full sunlight.

Table 15.1 the effect of various treatments on the growth of Urtica dioica (dry weight mg), after 7 week's growth, on a woodland soil taken under Mercurialis in a wood (Pigott, 1971).

Soil from a site dominated by *Mercurialis perennis*					Soil from an area dominated by *Urtica*
No addition	+ Nitrogen	+ All nutrients except phosphate	+ Phosphate	+ Phosphate and Nitrogen	No addition
5.8	3.9	8.6	192.3	252.5	288.0

animals have died, under brushwood, where there are faeces, etc. This is because all of these areas are rich in phosphate, which is needed for nettle seedling establishment.

The requirement of Urtica for high phosphate levels could be accounted for as follows: Urtica has no mycorrhizal fungi associated with its roots because they produce lectins (Chapter 11) which destroy fungi and therefore has difficulty in absorbing phosphate as effectively as plants with mycorrhizal fungi.

Further studies by Pigott (1971) verified the earlier results by growing Urtica seedlings under standard conditions in a growth cabinet in soils with and without phosphate (Table 15.1).

Salisbury (1918) investigated the Oak-Hornbeam woods of Hertfordshire, England and found a 48% light phase (leaf fall-following May) and 0.8-1.4% shade phase (May-following leaf fall). He found that for many species of woodland plants, survival was related to the light received in the light phase combined with the time factor. The earlier the plant developed leaves the greater the shade it was able to survive in during the summer. Urtica was absent from paths, rare in coppiced areas and rare-frequent in margins of woods and rides. It was listed as a medium shade plant. Related to the shade phase he found that British woodland plants, in general, flower one month earlier than non-woodland plants.

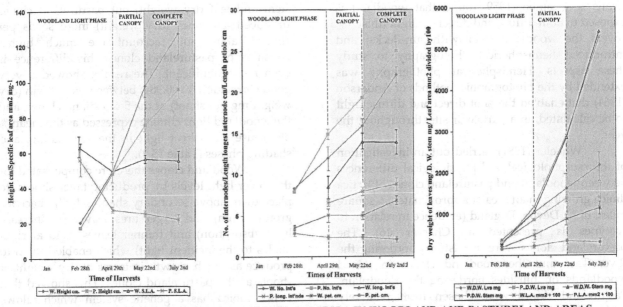

FIG 15.2a THE GROWTH OF SELECTED CLONES OF U. DIOICA IN WOODLAND AND PASTURELAND AREAS
Three to six shoots per nettle clone were removed at different times of the year as indicated on the graphs, to enable growth, particularly in woodland clones to be compared during the pre-shading and shading phases (Wheeler K. 1981).

CLONE 13   CLONE 17   CLONE 12   CLONE8   CLONE7   CLONE6(View sideways)

CLONE 16   CLONE 11   CLONE10   CLONE 1&2

CLONE 6   CLONE 14   CLONE 9   CLONE 4

FIG 15.2b PHOTOGRAPHS OF THE WOODLAND AND PASTURELAND CLONES OF URTICA IN THE FIELD GROWTH STUDIES, THE RESULTS OF WHICH ARE GIVEN IN FIG 15.2a.

Evans & Coombe (1959) found that woodland is exposed to both diffuse and direct sunlight (this covers the woodland floor with sun-flecks) and introduced hemispherical photography to study these aspects. Hemispherical photography was extended by the photographic methods of Anderson (1964) that enabled the % of direct and diffuse light to be calculated, in a particular site, throughout the year.

Wheeler (1981) carried out an investigation of the morphological and physiological differences between woodland and pastureland clones of Urtica dioica growing in an area of approximately 6 square miles, of N. Devon, England (evidence in relation to ecotypes is presented in Chapter 16). The pastureland clones were in pastures bordering the River Taw and the woodland clones in mixed woodlands on hillsides bordering the floodplain. Pastureland clones were chosen from relatively undisturbed open areas, or slightly-shaded areas

stem and leaf dry weight, but pastureland clones produced 4.6 times (dry weight) more seeds per shoot. Taking into account the much higher densities of pastureland clones this difference is even more significant. The results showed a very good correlation (r = 0.984) between the growth (dry weight mg per shoot) of the 5 woodland clones, and the woodland light climate expressed as the mean % of diffuse and direct light in the pre-shading and shading phases (Table 15.2).

Woodland clones therefore compensated for the lower light levels by producing taller shoots (to place them above secondary shading by herbaceous ground flora) and larger area leaves (to increase light absorption) and thinner leaves (held at right angles to the incident light) which enabled them to produce as much growth in terms of dry weight of shoots as the pastureland clones. This showed that Urtica dioica has a genetic system which allows plastic growth changes in relation to environmental

Table 15.2 correlation between light climate, using hemispherical photography, and mean dry weight mg of woodland clone shoots.					
Woodland clones	(1) Mean dry weight shoot mg	(2) Pre-shading phase Mean of diffuse & direct light	(3) Shading phase Mean of diffuse & direct light	(4) Mean value of (2) + (3)	
7	13,303	60.6	33.1	46.7	Corre-lation coefficient (1):(4) r = 0.984
12	9,298	38.7	34.0	36.6	
17	8,602	45.9	20.2	32.9	
8	7,013	51.4	14.8	33.1	
13	6,660	37.7	24.2	30.9	

bordering woodlands. Since fifteen shoots per clone needed to be removed during the four harvests, only large woodland clones could be sampled, and these occurred in more open areas. In both habitats eight clones were studied and included approximately equal male and female.

The results (Fig 15.2) showed that in the pre-shading phase there were no significant differences (with the exception of longer petioles in woodland clones) between all woodland and all pastureland clones. In the shading phase all the woodland clones were significantly taller, had longer internodes and petioles, the leaf areas were 3-4 times higher and specific female clones. The light climate was measured by hemispherical photography. Harvests were taken in the light phase (28th Feb.), near the end of the partial tree canopy (29th April), and in the shade phase (22nd May & 2nd July). The limitations were inability to include changes in weight of the rhizomes and roots, and the matching of woodland shoots due to large shoot variability in this habitat. Leaf areas were 2-5 times higher than those of all pastureland clones. There were no significant differences between all woodland and all pastureland clones in relation to

differences. The woodland clones however were less successful in terms of seed production (fitness) and survival. Rhizome studies also showed that woodland clones have thin relatively unbranched rhizomes compared to the massive underground mats of pastureland clones (see later).

The reaction of established plants of Urtica dioica to shading is also paralleled in the seedling growth stages (Wheeler, 1981). Growth analysis studies of seedling plants from woodland and pastureland clones, under various shadings for 6 weeks in an open garden situation, showed that they grow just as successfully (in terms of final dry weight at similar stages in ontogeny) at 25-67% relative light as those at 100% light. The maximum growth was at 67% light. Compensation for the low light levels was brought about by the same plastic growth changes in morphology and anatomy as were found in the field studies. At 8% relative light the strategy of increasing the specific leaf area did not compensate for their low food production and therefore growth was poor and no flowers were produced.

In a similar experiment carried out under greenhouse conditions, at very low light levels (10-

20 W m-2), priority was given to maximum hypocotyl (stem) elongation to enable higher light levels to be reached. This strategy results in there being insufficient food for the expansion of the cotyledons, and unless higher light levels are reached the seedling eventually dies (for more details see later, under seedling establishment). These results explain why nettles are not found in very deep shade i.e. below 8% relative light, such as in Beech woods or dense conifer plantations. They are often found in deep shade, as a result of successional changes in woodland growth, but their growth is much reduced and they do not flower.

MOISTURE/WATER REQUIREMENTS

Urtica dioica grows best in areas which are moist, and many of its habitats are near water, e.g. alongside streams and rivers, in willow and alder woods, fen carr, in marshy areas in valley bottoms, flood plains, alongside streams or in moist areas in woods, alongside irrigation canals and ditches, around ponds and lakes, etc.

Ellenberg (1988) classifies the common nettle as a moisture indicator, and in his study of oak-hornbeam woods places it in group IV, damp to fairly wet, less - acid soil. As an indicator of moist or wet soils Urtica dioica occurs with Lady Fern (Athyrium filix femina), Touch-me-not (Impatiens noli tangere), Enchanter's Nightshade (Circea lutetiana) and Hedge Woundwort (Stachys sylvatica). Measurements of the suction tension (negative water potential, in bar) in these woods in the soil around the roots of herbaceous plants showed that Urtica dioica, as a moisture indicator, was wilting at soil values of -1 to -6 bar, whereas plants of dry soils such as Lungwort (Pulmonaria obscura) was normal at -25 bar.

A study of 11 mixed broad-leaved woods in north-west Germany showed that Urtica dioica was more frequent and very flourishing in those with low bar values, i.e. -2 - 6. In Beech and mixed Beech woods, lists of moisture indicators include Touch-me-not (Impatiens noli tangere), Enchanter's Nightshade (Circea lutetiana), Hedge Woundwort (Stachys sylvatica), Urtica dioica, Festuca gigantea, Wood Stichwort (Stellaria nemorum), Wood Speedwell (Veronica montana) and Carex remota. In mixed Maple and Ash woodlands, the more or less hygromorphic and nitrophilous, quick growing and large-leaved herbs were Urtica dioica, Ground Elder (Aegopidium podograria), Pink Campion (Silene dioica) and Touch-me-not (Impatiens noli tangere). Ellenberg points out that these herbs only grow with the same luxuriance in sub-alpine tall herb communities and in riverside woods which are fertilised by mud containing organic material and left behind after flooding.

In the vegetation of the floodplain, a 'virgin forest' of White Willow was dominated by Festuca gigantea and Urtica dioica with a background of Phalaris arundinacea. Urtica is included as a pioneer of the amphibious new gravel of the river bank area, together with tall herbs such as Mugwort (Artemesia vulgaris), Melilot (Melilotus officinalis) and Tansy (Tanacetum vulgare). In floodplain woods dominated by Willow, Poplar, Elm and Oak in the Czechoslovakian lowland, Urtica dioica has a high constancy of 5 and is dominant in Poplar-Willow and Poplar floodplain woods. Urtica dioica is found in the herb layer of woods rich in Alder and Ash in the upper Spreewald where it has a higher constancy in the lower moisture values in these areas (8.0-6.0, mF).

It is well known that Urtica dioica cannot survive immersion of its rhizomes and root system in water for long periods and this is backed up by the observations of Srutek (1993). High moisture and nutrient content of the soils in river floodplains causes the formation of large stands of Urtica dioica in central Europe. This is especially so in floodplain meadows which have been abandoned, such as in the vicinity of the Luznice river, Trebon, Czech Republic. These areas are covered in stands of Urtica dioica that occupy elevated or shallow depressions with Phalaris arundinacea, Carex gracilis and Glyceria maxima in the deeper and moister depressions. *Urtica is found only in places where the water table does not stay above the soil surface for long periods of time.*

Boot et al. (1986), simulated drought by transfer of root systems between nutrient solutions and air to examine the effects of desiccation on the flowering of Urtica dioica and U. urens. Under temporary drought (1-3hr day-1) the yield by U. dioica was greater than that of U. urens, which is explained by the latter diverting photosynthate into flowers and fruits. After prolonged drought (5hr and 7hr day –1) U. dioica prevented wilting by stomatal closure (drought hardening), slowing down yield, number of nodes and inflorescences, whilst U. urens continued to wilt but with a more sustained production of nodes and flowers. The strategy of U. dioica safeguarded its survival and eventual reproduction as a long-lived perennial of relatively undisturbed habitat. This contrasted with the strategy of U. urens where growth and reproduction ensured seed production, even at the risk of drought mortality, which was more important for this annual of temporary disturbed arable habitat.

1 REGULATION OF CLONAL DENSITY

From Dawn Macleod, 'A Book of Herbs' (1968), about the **Wergula**, the Saxon name for nettle.

> *"When last winter had passed and spring renewed the face of the earth, when the days grew longer and milder, when flowers and herbs were stirred by the west wind, when green leaves clothed the trees, then my little plot was overgrown with nettles. What was I to do? Deep down the roots were matted and linked and rivetted like basket-work or the wattled hurdles of a fold......"*
> **Walafred Strabo** (Horticultural monk, 1000 years ago)

For a general understanding of the morphology and anatomy of the underground stolons (stems), rhizomes and roots of the common nettle consult Chapter 2. For a general account of ecology and growth of U. dioica see Šrûteck and Teckelmann, 1998. Each year the nettle produces stolons that grow a certain length and then turn up at the tip to produce a telescoped shoot in the autumn. This evergreen shoot over-winters and grows into next year's shoot, and the process is repeated yearly. Each dead shoot leaves a stump or scar, so by tracing these scars back along the rhizome system it is possible to estimate its age. In practice it is not so easy because often the rhizomes branch, and shoots can sometimes be produced on older parts of the rhizome system; however the method is accurate over the last 4-5 years of the nettle's growth. If a clone is dug up, the dating method enables the mean density of shoots of a developing clone, and the mean length of rhizome produced per year, to be calculated over a number of years and differences between clones growing in different habitats to be taken into account. Clones in three habitat areas were dug up and measured (Table 15.3 p 220 and Fig 15.3a).

Habitat 1 (Fig 15.3a and Table 15.3) A female clone in an open area of a silted-up riverbank open to flooding, had a mean height 1.88m, the rhizomes grew predominantly in one direction, and over 5 years the mean rhizome increase per year was 17 cm and the mean density 39 shoots m². At the end of 1994 the clone had 498 potential stolons per m²; however, since most neighbouring nettles had a mean density of 97 shoots m²; it was obvious that most of the potential stolons at the beginning of 1995 would fail to develop into shoots (see later). Analysis of the rhizome system showed that at least two other adjacent clones were invading the area of this clone. This clone had a total of 44.27 m of rhizome plus stolon per m², and this together with the extensive root system (not measured) would be capable of storing considerable amounts of food such as starch, etc. This would explain the nettle's phenomenal power of rapid growth in the spring and re-growth after cutting. The dense rhizome mat could also deter the growth of other invading plants.

Habitat 2 (Table 15.3) is a Nettle/Garlic/Himalayan Balsam community (for a description see **Area 1** under floristic diversity). The density of nettle shoot in the area is related to the density of *Impatiens glandulifera*: (a) pure nettle area, height 2.3 m, density 40-48 shoots m², (b) nettle with some Impatiens, height 2.3 m, density 30-34 shoots m²; (c) nettle with a lot of Impatiens, height 2.3 m, density 20-37 shoots m² In the area studied the mean nettle height is 2.3 m, the mean yearly rhizome increase in length 39.9 cm and the mean density 20 shoots per m2. The long rhizome length in this area could be due to nutrient depletion by competing *Impatiens glandulifera* and trees which increase the shading level. Šrûtek (1995) found that a sparse nettle clone establishing itself within a dense stand of Purple Small-Reed (*Calamagrostis canescens*) growing in wet meadows spreads relatively fast with numerous long rhizomes, so that its scattered shoots avoid competition.

Habitat 3 (Table 15.3) In a woodland area where there are small scattered nettle clones thin rhizomes grow predominantly in one direction, rarely branch and show a low yearly increase of 11.9 cm and a very low density of 1.3 shoots per m². In this case it is likely that unfavourable growth conditions such as nutrient depletion and quite heavy shade, due to successional changes, are responsible. This small study shows the importance of relating clonal growth to different habitat conditions.

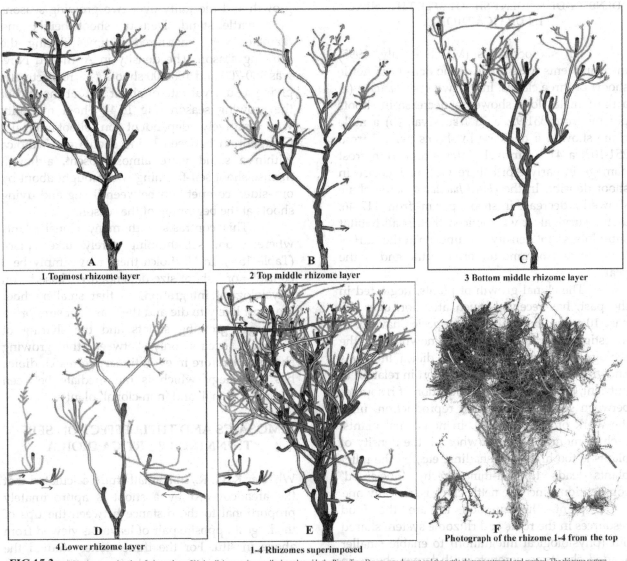

1 Topmost rhizome layer (A)

2 Top middle rhizome layer (B)

3 Bottom middle rhizome layer (C)

4 Lower rhizome layer (D)

1-4 Rhizomes superimposed (E)

Photograph of the rhizome 1-4 from the top (F)

FIG 15.3a A 0.56 m2 area, on the edge of a large clone of Urtica dioica growing on alluvium alongside the River Taw, Devon, was dug out and the nettle rhizome extracted and washed. The rhizome system was divided into four portions according to depth and each was drawn onto a sheet of cellulose acetate (A-D). The four sheets were then super-imposed to give the original rhizome system in space (E-H). See Fig 14.4 for the analysis of the results. (Legend leaves ▓ and stolons ▓ 1995 shoots & rhizomes▓1994 rhizomes▓1993 rhizomes▓1992 rhizomes▓1991). (Wheeler K. 1995 unpublished).

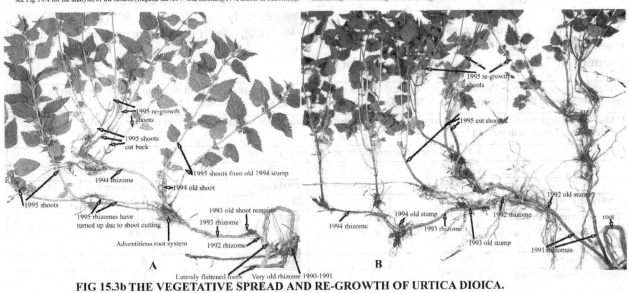

FIG 15.3b THE VEGETATIVE SPREAD AND RE-GROWTH OF URTICA DIOICA.

(A-B) These nettle plants had been cut down in May and had started to produce regrowth from the cut stems at the expense of producing stolons for next year's growth. The stolons will appear later in the year when the re-growth has sufficient reserves to the rhizome system. The portion of the rhizome system of (A) is 5-6 year's old whilst that of (B) is five year's old (Wheeler K. 1995. unpublished)

223

DENSITY-DEPENDENT SHOOT SELF-THINNING IN URTICA DIOICA

On six occasions (March – July, 1995) measurements were made of the density of nettle shoots of three clones. In the two *open habitats*, (a) a the female clone showed a decrease in shoots per m² from 331-93, a 28% survival, (b) a male clone showed a decrease in shoots per m² from 251-102, a 41% survival. After stress from frost damage in early April there was an increase in shoot density. In the *closed habitat* a nettle clone showed a decrease in shoots per m² from 117-46, a 39% survival. It was noticed that in all habitat sub-plots, shoot density was uneven at the start of the year and became uniform by the end of the year.

The clonal growth of plants, neglected in the past, has received much attention over the past 10 years, but only a few species have been investigated. Although a lot is known about the ecology and physiology of Urtica dioica, little was known about the reproductive effort in relation to nutrient, light, etc., and the allocation of resources between sexual and asexual reproduction, until the work of Šrůtek (1995). In non-clonal plants, such as mono-cultures of wheat, if the density of plants is too high then shading, etc., by the taller plants leads to self-thinning by 'one-sided' competition. Since the nettle clone is basically one plant, the question is, are the food resources in the roots and rhizome system shared out (physiological integration) to enable smaller shaded shoots to compete with larger shoots in the clone, resulting in a delay or absence of shoot self-thinning?

To answer such questions, Hara and Šrůtek (1995) focused on the seasonal shoot dynamics of Urtica dioica by measuring shoot growth and mortality over two growing seasons in a nettle stand. Density, shoot height and diameter were measured 5 times during the growing season. The density in April and Nov. was 400-700 and 100-200 shoots /m² respectively, giving a survival rate of about 30% at the end of the growing season (Fig 15.4). Shoot mortality was positively dependent on shoot density. Competition between living shoots of U. dioica within a stand were almost absent, although intense shoot self-thinning was brought about by one-sided competition between living and dying shoots at the beginning of the season.

This contrasts with many clonal plants where shoot self-thinning rarely takes place (Table 15.4). In U. dioica there may simply be a control of shoot-size-dependence based on physiological integration, so that smaller shoot are most likely to die and these are not supported by larger growing shoots and the sharing of resources occurs only between the growing shoots. Therefore in evolutionary terms U. dioica has a strategy which is intermediate between accepted 'clonal' and 'non-clonal' plants.

MOSAICS AND THEIR EFFECT ON SELF-THINNING IN URTICA DIOICA

Wheeler K. G. R., in a small study calculated that the area covered by a shoot is approximately proportional to the distance between the tips of the largest opposite pair of leaves as viewed from above in situ. For the three clones studied the mean density/ m² and (mean distance/cm between the tips of the largest leaf pair) were respectively as follows, 93/(10.4), 102/(9.9), 46/(14.0), which gives a correlation coefficient of 0.99.

Table 15.3 clonal growth in Urtica dioica showing differences in density and the length and age of different parts of the rhizome system per square metre in three different habitats in North Devon, England. (Wheeler K G R. unpublished 1981)

HABITAT 1. Large nettle bed, alluvial area on bank of R. Taw, with flooding. Open unshaded. Area 0.56 m². Female clone, 52 stems m². Height 1.88 m. Rhizome depth 10-13 cm. 21/11/94

	Year of clonal rhizome of stolon (Age in years from present i.e. 1994)					
	1994-95 (0)	1993-94 (1)	1992-93 (2)	1991-92 (3)	1990-91 (4)	1989-90 (5)
	Potential Stolons	1st rhizome	2nd rhizome	3rd rhizome	4th rhizome	5th rhizome
Density shoots per 0.56 m ²	289	30	27	6	3	1
Rhiz/stolon mean length cm	11.5 *	17.04	17.17	17.0	24.3	
Rhiz/stolon standard deviations.	11.3	10.31	9.59	12.43	12.89	
Density shoots m²	498	52	46	11	5	1
Rhiz/stolon mean length cm, m ²	3150 *	664	515	187	121	-
Mean grand total length of main stolons plus rhizomes 46.37 metres per square metre						

HABITAT 2. Large nettle bed on alluvial soil on the bank of the River Taw. Flooding frequent. Medium shade from willows. Area sampled 1.0 m² Sex? Height 2.3 m Stem density 20-30. Rhizome depth 2.5-22.5 cm. 24/11/94.

	Year of clonal rhizome of stolon (Age in years from present i.e. 1994)					
	1994-95 (0)	1993-94 (1)	1992-93 (2)	1991-92 (3)	1990-91 (4)	1989-90 (5)
	Stolons	1st rhizome	2nd rhizome	3rd rhizome	4th rhizome	5th rhizome
Rhiz/stolon mean length cm	42.8	48.8	35.5	46.5	26	
Rhiz/stolon standard deviations.	14.8	31.4	25.1	10.2	-	
Density shoots m²	28	20	7	2	1	
Rhiz/stolon mean length cm, m²	1198	780	247	93	26	

Mean grand total length of main stolons/rhizomes 23.44 metres per square metre

HABITAT 3 Very small, scattered nettle clones on clayey loam in mixed woodland of medium shade. 3 areas of 1.0 m² sampled. Sex? Height? Rhizome depth 10-15 cm. 2/3/95.

	Year of clonal rhizome of stolon (Age in years from present i.e. 1994)					
	1994-95 (0)	1993-9 (1)	1992-93 (2)	1991-92 (3)	1990-91 (4)	1989-90 (5)
	Stolons	1st rhizome	2nd rhizome	3rd rhizome	4th rhizome	5th rhizome
Rhiz/stolon mean length cm	12.4	15.5	14.3	10.3	7	
Rhiz/stolon standard deviations.	8.41	3.31	5.5	9.5	-	
Density shoots m²	2.3	1.3	1.3	1.0	1.0	
Rhiz/stolon mean length cm, m²	28.5	20.2	18.5	10.3	7	

Mean grand total length of main stolons plus rhizomes 0.85 metres per square metre

Table 15.4 mortality and competition patterns of clonal plants in comparison with those of non-clonal plants in crowed mono-specific stands (After Hara and Šrůtek 1995).
* De Kroon and Kwant (1991) and De Kroon, Hara and Kwant (1992); † Suzuki (1994a); this study; § De Kroon (1993) and De Kroon and Kalliola (1995).

Plants	Density-dependent shoot self-thinning	Competition between living shoots
Many clonals	absent, almost absent or brief only in later stage of a growing season	absent or almost absent
Brachypodium pinnatum*	absent	asymmetric
Carex flacca*	almost absent	asymmetric
Polygonum cuspidatum†	absent	symmetric
Urtica dioica‡	from, the early growing stage each year	symmetric but very weak (nearly absent)
Gynerium sagittatum§	occurs over years	asymmetric
Non-cloonals	from the early growing stage	mostly asymmetric

If self-thinning is related to shading this would account for the close relationship between leaf size and shoot density in a mature clone. It follows that since nettles in closed situations have larger leaves and longer petioles than nettles in open situations the former will have lower shoot densities than the latter.

2 AGE OF NETTLE CLONES

Rackman (1994) mentions the deserted village of Little Gidding (Huntingdonshire), forgotten by 1640, but still marked by an elm grove full of tall nettles, and moated houses of 1150-1330 and 1550 generally to mark social status. These moats were used for sewage and fish, and very often, lines of nettles today mark their former position. Woods are generally low in phosphate, so nettle patches in this habitat may indicate places of past human habitations.

Annual shoot scars on a nettle rhizome system (see previous) can be found up to 5 years after which the picture becomes blurred. Cross sections of the mid-points of 1st, 2nd, 3rd, 4th and 5th year rhizome portions (n=3) were taken and a good linear relationship between age and the ratio of rhizome diameter ÷ pith diameter was found, (this ratio for a one year - old stem was 1.0, and for a five year - old stem 4.0) giving a correlation coefficient r = 0.897. However, rhizome portions of known ages up to 10 years ago would be needed to calculate whether the linear relationship between rhizome diameter/pith diameter of rhizome still holds and if so extrapolation to older thicker rhizomes (5-

Re-growth nettle in late June on verge cut earlier

Re-growth nettles on the edge of a field where grass was earlier cut for silage.

Re-growth of nettles as a result of attack by Cuscuta europaea growing on the top of a river bank.

Regrowth nettles after spraying with Roundup herbicide which was not very effective.

After spraying, in a moist area roots are formed at the nodes

Defoliation of nettle clones (left) and the resulting re-growth from axillary shoots (right).

Destruction of a large nettle clone by the sleeping of cattle at night.

Re-growth nettles showing the over-reaction in some cases when even non-stinging trichomes grow abnormally producing pedestal bases.

FIG 15.4 THE POWER OF RE-GROWTH IN U. DIOICA IN RELATION TO HERBIVORES, MOWING AND SPRAYING.

8 cm) would be possible. It would be expected that the annual increase in diameter of rhizomes would fall with age or contraction of rhizomes to occur. This area needs more investigation.

3 RE-GROWTH POWERS OF URTICA DIOICA

Urtica dioica has basically two survival strategies in relation to disturbance (i.e. removal of plant biomass), (1) defensive stinging trichomes are effective against most vertebrate herbivores, (2) rapid re-growth in relation to insect herbivore defoliation, vertebrate trampling and cutting and spraying by man (Flow diagram 1.1 and Fig 15.4), see also (Meijden et al, 1988).

The effect of cutting and nutrient level on stinging trichome density of Urtica dioica and Wigandia urens (Pullin, 1989, Cano-Santana & Oyama, 1992) have been reviewed (Chapter 8). Such studies show that on re-growth, Urtica dioica and other stinging plants divert more resources to the production of greater stinging trichome densities on leaves and stems compared to the original growth. Re-growth plants are therefore better equipped to deter grazing by vertebrate herbivores. The higher nutritional quality of re-growth nettles compared to older mature nettle plants (which accumulate insecticides such as phenols and other secondary metabolites) causes many butterflies and other insects to preferentially select re-growth nettles for feeding and egg-laying (Pullin, 1987, Chapter 12).

3 RESOURCE ALLOCATION STRATEGY NETTLE GROWTH AND DEFENCE

Mutikainen, et al, (1994, 1995) used rhizome material of Urtica dioica grown under greenhouse conditions with supplementary lighting to investigate simulated herbivory. Of the 7 treatments, 1 control: 2 (early small damage) and 3 (early large damage) *before* anthesis (flower opening): 4 (late small damage) and 5 (late large damage) *after* anthesis:, 6 and 7 *before* anthesis, treatments, 6 removal of the terminal bud plus 1st two leaf pairs and 7 removal of the terminal bud. Small damage was the removal of half the leaf blades from the four topmost leaves and large damage the same but involved all leaves.

(1) Large damage before anthesis resulted in a decrease in the inflorescence dry weight in both sexes. (2) On small damage, before anthesis both sexes of the nettle compensated or over compensated for inflorescence dry weight. (3) Apex damage decreased branching in the male plants, but in the female plants there was an increase in branching by clipping damage as well as the removal of apical tips and buds but the inflorescence mass decreased and this was probably due to the increased cost of producing branches. In both sexes the stinging trichome density increased slightly as a result of clipping (simulated herbivory). Both sexes compensated for the loss of the shoot apex by producing inflorescence masses similar to those of the control plants; they did this by an increase in the mass of inflorescences on the side branches. (Refer to paper for more details).

BOX 14.1 RESPONSES TO HERBIVORY, MODIFICATION BY COMPETITION AND FERTILISATION

The second paper of Mutikainen and Walls (1995) concentrates on how the nettles compensate for damage by herbivores. It looks at compensation in relation to inherent factors in different Urtica species and environmental factors. The compensatory continuum hypothesis of Maschinski and Whithanm (1989) in short, states that in favourable environmental conditions the effects of herbivory on plant fitness (ability to reproduce) are expected to be less detrimental than when resources are limited and competition is high. If resources are limiting, the sources allocated to defence are not available for other functions such as growth and reproduction.

The effects of herbivory are expected to be influenced by the life strategy of the plant, with annual plants allocating a greater proportion of resources to reproductive structures regardless of the environmental stress, whilst perennials under these conditions allocate more to survival, see previous Boot et al (1986). For this reason the authors chose Urtica dioica (perennial), and U. urens (annual) as experimental plants; the northern European species U. sondenii (previously U. dioica sub species gracilis) was also chosen because it appears to be subjected to less insect and vertebrate herbivore damage (mainly reindeer) than the more southern U. dioica, and therefore has a lower density of stinging trichomes.

The experiment was similar to that of the previous experiment and involved, (1) seed material of U. dioica and U. urens, and rhizome material of U. sondenii, (2) simulated herbivory consisted of heavy clipping before anthesis, and removal of the apical tip, (3) environmental factors such as density (1 or 3 ramets per pot), and fertilisation at two levels.

In accordance with the continuum hypothesis, in terms of height growth the negative effects of apical tip removal were more detrimental at the low fertilisation

level. In the case of U. urens the high fertilisation level counteracted the detrimental effects of the removal of the apical tip, suggesting that the increased resource availability can counteract the negative effect of herbivore damage. However the other results did not support the continuum hypothesis since there was a stronger decrease in inflorescence dry mass of plants growing at low density and high fertilization application, compared to those plants grown at low density and low fertilisation, as a result of apical tip removal. In the perennial species the removal of the apical tip led to a reduction in branching regardless of fertilisation and density, and the reproductive output of the plants decreased (see previous).

The three species also differed in their response to simulated herbivory and trichome density. The defensive responses of the perennial species were stronger than that of the annual U. urens. The differences between the two perennial species, in changes in trichome density in relation to herbivory, could reflect the differences in levels of herbivory which the species experience in their natural habitats. There were negative correlations between trichome density and other life history traits that suggested the existence of trade-offs between defence, and functions such as growth and increase in biomass. Other authors have found that other plants which have structural defences, e.g. hairs, thorns, spines and prickles, produce these in higher levels in stressful environments and in juvenile tissue, which also appears to be true of nettles. The results support the idea that the negative correlation of defence with other traits was stronger in plants grown at lower resource levels. In U. dioica there was no trade off between defence and reproductive output, probably due to the high herbivore pressure it is normally subjected to. This was less so in U. sondenii (trichome density, no./cm² in U. dioica = 66.1 and U. sondenii = 3.2) which under natural conditions is subjected to less herbivore damage. The main conclusion is that the costs of structural defence may be costly but are not universal and their expression depends on the environments where they are measured.

4 SEEDLING STRATEGY OF URTICA DIOICA

1 SEED CHARACTERISTICS AND GERMINATION

The nettle fruit is an achene (Fig 15.5 a-b). The achenes are very small and the mean values are 0.8mm wide by 1.2mm long and each weighs 0.2mg i.e. 5000 weigh one gram. The embryo is surrounded by an endosperm (food reserve) and the achene is enclosed within the 4 persistent perianth segments. The germination is epigeal with the hypocotyl elongating to bring the pericarp and the enclosed cotyledons above soil level. After the endosperm is absorbed by the cotyledons the pericarp falls off

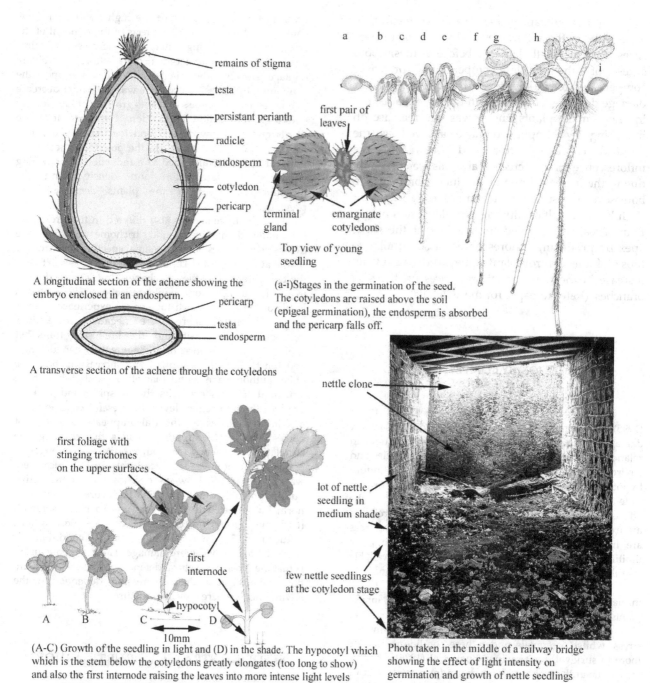

remains of stigma

testa

persistant perianth

radicle

endosperm

cotyledon

pericarp

A longitudinal section of the achene showing the embryo enclosed in an endosperm.

pericarp

testa

endosperm

A transverse section of the achene through the cotyledons

first pair of leaves

terminal gland

emarginate cotyledons

Top view of young seedling

(a-i)Stages in the germination of the seed. The cotyledons are raised above the soil (epigeal germination), the endosperm is absorbed and the pericarp falls off.

first foliage with stinging trichomes on the upper surfaces

first internode

hypocotyl

A   B   C   D

10mm

(A-C) Growth of the seedling in light and (D) in the shade. The hypocotyl which which is the stem below the cotyledons greatly elongates (too long to show) and also the first internode raising the leaves into more intense light levels

nettle clone

lot of nettle seedling in medium shade

few nettle seedlings at the cotyledon stage

Photo taken in the middle of a railway bridge showing the effect of light intensity on germination and growth of nettle seedlings

FIG 15.5 THE FRUIT STRUCTURE AND GERMINATION IN URTICA DIOICA.

and the cotyledons expand (Fig 15.5 c-e). The bright green cotyledons are broadly round with an emarginate tip. At this stage there are no stinging trichomes because it is hardly a mouthful for the average-sized cow; however, these do appear in small numbers on the first foliage leaves. The cotyledons fall off after a few weeks and any injury to the shoot is counteracted by the development of lateral shoots (Fig 15.5).

GERMINATION AND ESTABLISHMENT IN WOODLAND AND PASTURELAND CLONES OF URTICA DIOICA

1 LABORATORY STUDIES

The production of seed and seed dispersal in U. dioica are dealt with in chapter 16, but suffice it to say here that a large nettle clone can produce millions of seeds, most of which fall within a few metres of the clone whilst a small percentage is dispersed by various other methods.

Grieg-Smith (1948) found that seeds of U. dioica need light to germinate and that full sunlight and variable temperatures gave the best germination. Wheeler (1981) verified these results using seeds from woodland and pastureland clones of U. dioica. The requirement of light stimulus for germination is favoured by 2 ecological pressures: (1) weed seeds such Urtica sp. are characteristic of disturbed ground and more likely to be buried by cultivation, burrowing animals, washing into the soil etc., but germinate when brought back to the surface, (2) these species build up seed banks in the soil. In both cases the seeds of this group are very small. Germination in light-sensitive seeds is mediated by the photosensitive pigment phytochrome, with its reversible red/far red system; seeds germinate when exposed to red light but this is erased when followed by far red light.

This was verified under field conditions by Pigott (1971) who investigated the germination of seeds of Urtica dioica under woodland conditions in relation to light and phosphate. His results showed that: (1) the highest germination occurred at high light intensities in a glade, (2) 40-50% germination took place under lower light intensities under a sparse canopy of *Betula verrucosa*, (3) no germination occurred under a dense canopy of *Acer pseudoplatanus* or a single leaf of *Rheum*, both of which had a high irradiance of far red light, but otherwise sufficient light transmission for germination to take place, (4) phosphate had no significant effect in stimulating germination.

Leaves, which are basically green filters, remove a certain degree of red light (R) for photosynthesis and transmit far red light (FR). In open woodland situations, or under light leaf canopies, the R/FR ratio is high and germination of U. dioica seeds is relatively high. Under dense leaf canopies or areas of high leaf area index which have a low R/FR ratio, there is and inhibition of the germination of Urtica seeds. It follows from this that any germination of Urtica seeds in woodland must take place, either in relatively open situations, or in the pre-shading phase from leaf fall in the autumn to leaf expansion in the spring.

Wheeler (1981) investigated the germination and establishment of U. dioica in woodland and pastureland areas using permanent quadrats of 0.09 m². There were 15 sampling dates between June 25th and 8th August, 1981.

WOODLAND AREAS (AUTUMN)

In woodlands in the autumn in the majority of areas studied there was no germination except in areas with clearings and areas with gaps in the canopy. Before leaf fall, low light levels and unfavourable spectral light quality are unsuitable for germination, whereas after leaf fall from trees and herbs, most seed is covered. In addition to the former facts, the seed is enclosed within the persistent perianth, which remains green in woodland situations and therefore transmits a high proportion of far red light that inhibits germination of Urtica seedlings.

WOODLAND AREAS (SPRING)

In the majority of woodland quadrats germination started in the second week of March and continued up to tree leaf expansion in mid-May which is much later than that of pastureland nettles (Fig 15.6 & 15.7). The later germination in woodland areas is related to the period of breakdown of the leaf litter which is necessary to allow in light for germination. This is backed up by the work of Al-Mufti et al (1978) who show that a heavily shaded woodland site that included U. dioica showed a dramatic change in leaf litter dry weight from 200 g m^{-2} in Nov - 30 g m^{-2} in mid-March which coincides with the germination of woodland seed.). In quadrats 17 & 18 in a spruce plantation, Urtica seedlings were present on Jan 18th and this could have been due to the open nature of the pine needles which led to high light penetration early in the year (Fig 15.7, 1-3). Also the density of seedlings was very low even at the peak germination period, 3 per m² (range 1-8). Bryophytes growing on leaf litter reached their peak in March to April and could have a negative effect on Urtica germination.

Brief studies were carried out on seedling growth of Urtica seedlings in relation to the litter microhabitat. In a deciduous larch/oak/ash area the seeds appear to cement (they have a mucilaginous layer on the outside of the pericarp when wet) onto litter twigs, etc, at different levels in the litter. The seedlings germinating lower down at low light levels respond with a tremendous extension of the hypocotyl which is capable of raising the cotyledons into much higher light levels, in this pre-shading woodland phase (Fig 15.7 B). All seedlings died before 8th August apart from two at the 2-3 leaf-pair stage and the latter were in an open canopy area and these could have survived after the last observations. Field observations indicated that high mortality of seedlings is caused by shading from tree, shrub and herb layers, mollusc attacks, fungal attack, trampling and limiting factors such as water, minerals, etc.

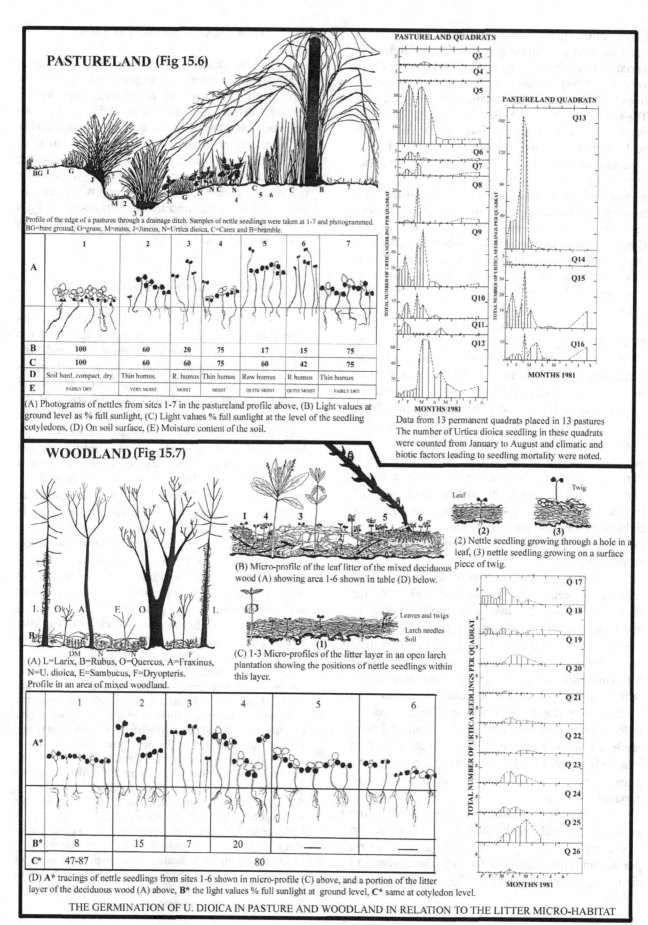

PASTURELAND (Fig 15.6)

Profile of the edge of a pasturee through a drainage ditch. Samples of nettle seedlings were taken at 1-7 and photogrammed.
BG=bare ground, G=grass, M=moss, J=Juncus, N=Urtica dioica, C=Carex and B=bramble.

	1	2	3	4	5	6	7
A							
B	100	60	20	75	17	15	75
C	100	60	60	75	60	42	75
D	Soil hard, compact, dry.	Thin humus.	R. humus	Thin humus	Raw humus	R humus	Thin humus
E	FAIRLY DRY	VERY MOIST	MOIST	MOIST	QUITE MOIST	QUITE MOIST	FAIRLY DRY

(A) Photograms of nettles from sites 1-7 in the pastureland profile above, (B) Light values at ground level as % full sunlight, (C) Light values % full sunlight at the level of the seedling cotyledons, (D) On soil surface, (E) Moisture content of the soil.

PASTURELAND QUADRATS

Q3, Q4, Q5, Q6, Q7, Q8, Q9, Q10, Q11, Q12

MONTHS 1981

PASTURELAND QUADRATS

Q13, Q14, Q15, Q16

MONTHS 1981

Data from 13 permanent quadrats placed in 13 pastures
The number of Urtica dioica seedling in these quadrats were counted from January to August and climatic and biotic factors leading to seedling mortality were noted.

WOODLAND (Fig 15.7)

(A) L=Larix, B=Rubus, O=Quercus, A=Fraxinus, N=U. dioica, E=Sambucus, F=Dryopteris.
Profile in an area of mixed woodland.

(B) Micro-profile of the leaf litter of the mixed deciduous wood (A) showing area 1-6 shown in table (D) below.

(C) 1-3 Micro-profiles of the litter layer in an open larch plantation showing the positions of nettle seedlings within this layer.

Leaves and twigs
Larch needles
Soil

(2) Nettle seedling growing through a hole in a leaf, (3) nettle seedling growing on a surface piece of twig.

Leaf   Twig

(2)   (3)

	1	2	3	4	5	6
A*						
B*	8	15	7	20	—	—
C*	47-87	80				

(D) A* tracings of nettle seedlings from sites 1-6 shown in micro-profile (C) above, and a portion of the litter layer of the deciduous wood (A) above, B* the light values % full sunlight at ground level, C* same at cotyledon level.

TOTAL NUMBER OF URTICA SEEDLINGS PER QUADRAT

Q 17, Q 18, Q 19, Q 20, Q 21, Q 22, Q 23, Q 24, Q 25, Q 26

MONTHS 1981

THE GERMINATION OF U. DIOICA IN PASTURE AND WOODLAND IN RELATION TO THE LITTER MICRO-HABITAT

PASTURELAND AREAS (AUTUMNAL)

A preliminary study involved placing 11 permanent quadrats (30 cm X 37.5 cm) in two pastureland areas (2/9/75 – 27/10/74), one above and one on the floodplain of the R. Taw. At this time of the year bare soil areas are created by trampling, cutting, grazing, cow dung areas, urine areas where grass is killed, mole hills, slowing down of grass growth, etc. High rainfall and suitable temperatures and light levels favour germination of uncovered seed. Maximum germination occurred at the end of August to the beginning of September, but by the end of October, only two well developed seedlings remained in the 11 quadrats, and even these were thought unlikely to survive the winter. Shorter days, lower temperatures and light levels are unfavourable for seedling growth and high mortality is caused by abundant mollusc predation, fungal attack such as damping off, trampling, low levels of nutrients, etc. (Fig 15.6).

PASTURELAND AREAS (SPRING)

The fate of seedlings was followed over a six-month period (29/4/79, 1/6/79, 29/9/79), in 5 different pastureland areas (Fig 15.6). In two areas all seedlings died whereas in the other three areas 16% of the seedlings were still alive, 6 months later. At the end of six months the quadrat on a steep bank had 2 seedlings at the 5 leaf-pair stage and one at the 6 leaf-pair stage which could have survived to the following year. Banks of various kinds are a favourite habitat of U.dioica, and this could be explained by the increased chance of seedling establishment in this type of habitat. One area, across a ditch boundary, was chosen to do a more detailed study of the growth strategy of Urtica seedlings in relation to the micro-habitat (Fig 15.6). The growth strategy of Urtica seedlings, i.e. extending the hypocotyl at the expense of cotyledon expansion, is shown to work in three areas of this habitat. The sketch profiles show that the cotyledons are raised from low light levels to levels at which cotyledon expansion takes place which enables the growth rate to be high enough for the seedling to survive; however, later shading by herbaceous vegetation is likely to shade out the majority of seedlings.

This study shows that establishment of a nettle seedling in a pasture must be a very rare event due to (1) competition for light, nutrients, water, space, etc., from vigorously growing perennial plants, (2) under bramble light levels are too low, (3) biotic factors such as predation by slugs, snails, rabbits, voles and cattle trampling or eating seedlings, which at this stage have only a few stinging hairs, (4) in the area studied the Nettle/Sedge rust (*Puccinia caricis*) (Chapter 11) attacks nettle seedlings and the pycnia and aecia produce orange spots on the leaves and premature leaf fall.

Major disturbance events, which leave large bare areas of soil containing nettle seed or rhizome, and which take a long time to be colonised by surrounding perennials, are the most likely areas for seedlings to establish in pastures. These disturbances are mainly due to farming practices in pastures such as (1) leaving soil from dredgings alongside drainage canals or ditches, (2) leaving hedge clippings, or tree trunks, etc., (3) burning hedge clippings, (4) disturbance and natural manuring by pigs, (5) use of organic fertiliser such as chicken manure which carries nettle seeds and if not scattered uniformly can quickly produce nettles, (6) shallow ploughing and re-seeding which scatters nettle rhizome, (7) filling hollows with soil containing nettle material, etc., (see Chapter 14).

FIELD GERMINATION OF URTICA DIOICA IN RELATION TO TEMPERATURE AND LIGHT

In the study area the maximum germination of seed took place from Feb – March when the mean temperature was 10° with a temperature fluctuation in the region of 5°C and this is in line with laboratory findings (see also, Thompson, et al. 1978). No doubt maximum germination occurs in full sunlight. However, more important in relation to the microhabitat is that germination will also take place low down in the litter layer in conditions of relative low diffuse light, although the possibility of the occasional sun fleck cannot be ruled out. In this respect, in open situations all surface seed germinates but it is likely to be replaced at the end of the year. In more closed situations only a proportion of the surface seed germinates and this conserves the seed bank in areas where the production of seed is much lower.

SEED BANKS

Wheeler (1981) investigated seed banks of U. dioica in woodland and pastureland areas (Fig 15.6-7). The significance of the seed bank is that seeds remain dormant in the soil after the present destruction of vegetation by man or successional changes, only to give rise to plants when conditions once more become favourable (Salisbury, 1961). Thompson (1978) found that buried seed density is correlated positively with disturbance (i.e. partial destruction of vegetation) and negatively with stress. This is in line with the study of Wheeler (1981) who found that female woodland nettle shoots under shade stress (20–35% diffuse sunlight) produced approximately 80% less seed than pastureland nettle shoots. The seeds from seed banks (collected and separated under dim-light with a dark green filter in place) were germinated in a greenhouse. Urtica seed from pastureland and woodland seed banks showed (1) no germination in the dark, (2) at a shading equivalent to maximum 2,400 Lux, and mean maximum temperature 24.1° C and temperature fluctuation of 11.3°C, 70.06 ±14.0% of all woodland seed and 49.6 ± 12.3% of pastureland seed germinated by the end of 9 days Pastureland seed banks on the average contained 7.5 times more seed than woodland seed banks. Pastureland seed banks varied from 4156-7986 m² inside clones, to 1754-1798 m² outside clones. Woodland areas compared to pastureland areas had a higher percentage of the total seed bank in the 0-2 cm litter layer. In woodland and pastureland areas a reasonable correlation was found between size of seed bank and % diffuse light in the area. At 40% relative light seed banks contained 1664 viable seeds per m² and at 9% relative light 88 viable seeds m². Viable seeds in the seed bank decrease from deciduous-dominated areas to coniferous-dominated areas. There was also a good correlations between seed rain in the area and the light climate (r = 0.966) and between seed rain and the seed bank (r = 0.8038). Shading stress caused a reduction in Urtica seed banks in woodland habitats.

5 THE COMMON NETTLE AS A COMPETITOR PLANT

Urtica dioica is classified as a competitor plant and as such has a rapid maximum potential relative growth rate (Grime 1977 & 1978).

RELATIVE GROWTH RATE

Estimates of the maximum relative growth rate (R_{max}) and mean relative growth rate P, of 132 flowering plants in the Sheffield area were determined from the growth of seedlings 2-5 weeks after germination, (Grime and Hunt, 1975). In several disturbed and/or productive habitats, fast growing species were predominant

whereas species of low (R_{max}) were virtually absent. The reverse was true of stable unproductive habitats. Urtica dioica had the second highest (R_{max}) 2.35 ± 0.06, and the highest P. U. dioica has a small seed weight and exceptionally high R_{max} and inhabits fertile fields or manure heaps. At one extreme high R_{max}, is associated with tall stature, the capacity for extensive lateral spread above and below ground and the capacity to deposit a dense layer of litter. This combination of characteristics is conducive to effective capture of light, water, mineral nutrients and space. This accounts for why U. dioica frequently occupies extensive areas of productive, relatively undisturbed vegetation, apparently excluding the majority of plants by its superior competitive ability above and below ground.

THE RELATIONSHIP BETWEEN LITTER, STANDING CROP AND COMPETITIVE/DOMINANCE IN PLANTS

Al-Mufti et al, (1977) investigated 13 sites at 5 week intervals (from April-October) and removed above ground living material (standing crop) and dead plant material (litter) over randomly placed 0.25 m² quadrat areas. The study included two sites (1&6) where Urtica dioica was the dominant competitor and another site (7) where it failed to be a dominant competitor.

SITE 1. The site was a bed of U. dioica on derelict land of a dale floor on the site of a disused sheep pen adjacent to the River Lathkill. The area was dominated by U. dioica, but also included Galium aparine and mosses growing on the leaf litter. Litter consisted mainly of Urtica stems and remained more or less constant (approx. 500 g m²) and standing crop reached a plateau of 550-650 g m². The growth (dry weight) of Urtica was most rapid from April to mid-June and then more slowly to reach a peak in September (approx. 450 g m⁻²). Mosses reached a peak in July and a rapid decline in August to September, to recover in November.

SITE 6. The area consisted of a stand of U. dioica in a small clearing (25 m) in mixed deciduous wood and scrub 50 m from a small stream. There was no overhead shade. Litter consisted mainly of Urtica stems and remained above 500 g m⁻² with a maximum in October and the standing crop reached a plateau of 750 g m⁻².

The growth of Urtica was rapid in the pre-shading phase but continued to rise to a peak in August (approx. 390 g m^{-2}) followed by a rapid decline. The frequency of mosses, mainly attached to the stems of Urtica, was the highest in the study at a maximum high level in April and from then declining to a low in Nov.

SITE 7. The area was in Totley Wood, adjacent to a clearing with a sparse tree canopy, under which the relative light value was 11%. There were 9 plant species present none of which were dominant, and included *Poa trivialis, Ranunculus ficaria, U. dioica, Circea lutiana, Veronica montana, Festuca gigantea, Anemone nemorosa, Galium aparine and Mercurialis perennis.* The peak of the standing crop in August was 250 g m^{-2}, only 20% of that of Site 6, and there was a scarcity of herbaceous litter 30-100 g m^{-2}. Tree litter was higher 200 g m^{-2} but fell to a minimum in early spring to 10 g m^{-2}. U. dioica showed low vegetative vigour and many shoots failed to produce flowers. The peaks of growth were similar to Site 6 but the peak was only 50 g m^{-2}. Urtica was the dominant herb at sites 1 & 6 due to its dominant height, dense leaf canopy (max. in June-August where light and temperature were conducive to high productivity) and later spread by rhizomes which also provide reserve photosynthate to enable rapid shoot expansion in the spring. The low species density is greatly influenced by the shading and nutrient depletion by Urtica, but could be due to the presence of the higher density of herbaceous litter that could exclude vernal or evergreen plants. In Urtica stands the presence of abundant mosses in the litter could shade or act as a barrier to the extension of the shoots of certain plants. Without doubt in site 7 the high level of shade reduced the competitive ability of Urtica to

that of a debilitated competitor, and results in a greater floral diversity in the area. The results of all 14 sites suggests that high species densities are characteristic of areas where standing crop plus litter values fall between 350-750 g m^{-2}; above this competitive exclusion occurs (see Fig 15.8 and Box 15.2).

MOSSES AND NETTLE LITTER

The importance of mosses in the ecology of the nettle patch has already been mentioned (Al-Mufti, 1977). The two commonest mosses growing on the nettle litter are the robust bright green *Brachythecium rutabulum* and the more delicate feathery *Eurhynchium praelongum*. The gametophyte and sporophyte plants of these mosses are structures of great beauty (Fig 15.9). The influence of the moss layer on the germination of nettle seeds has been mentioned. The classical work on Brachythecium rutabulum (Furness & Grime, 1982) showed that it maintained exponential growth and attained a relative growth rate of 0.071 day ^{1}, a value exceeding that of the seedlings of 10 vascular plants. Maximum growth occurred at 19°C (lower than that of Urtica which is 30°C) but at 5°C the reduction in relative growth rate was less than 40% (Fig 14.8). The moss grows better on the nettle litter, which could be due to its water holding capacity or the release of nutrients as a result of decomposition by microbes. Its capacity to grow at low temperatures may be related to the tendency of this moss species to exploit the cool conditions of spring and autumn and explain the ability of the species to live on the litter microhabitat of the nettle patch.

RRincon (1990) investigated the colonisation by B. rutabulum of dead nettle stems placed at different

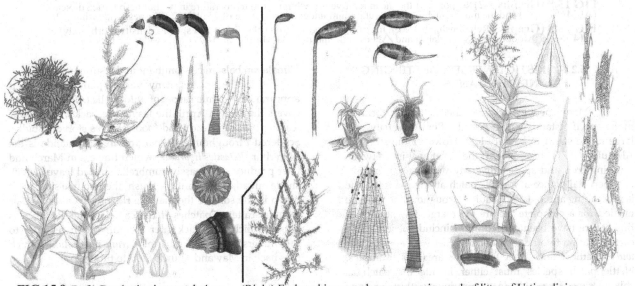

FIG 15.9 (Left) Brachythecium rutabulum   (Right) Eurhynchium praelongum growing on leaf litter of Urtica dioica.

inclinations. The results showed that the steeper the inclination the more rhizoids ('roots') are produced, and that this might provide a mechanism to enable this moss to emerge through litter deposits. The greater growth of nettle stems, compared with artificial stems plus nutrients, indicates B. rutabulum is intercepting and using nutrients from the decaying nettle stems.

The moss layer, as well as the nettle litter, produces a micro-habitat for various plants and animals, e.g. insects, other arthropods, molluscs, protozoans, algae, fungi, worms, rotifers, etc.(Chapters 11,12,13) and this food web in likely to have implications for both the mosses and the nettle. The study would be a worthwhile project for a keen naturalist.

and survive (1) as short-lived annuals and ephemerals, (2) as vigorous competitors capable of equalling or outgrowing the nettle, (3) or vernal plants completing their cycle before they are shaded out by herb and tree canopy expansion. To avoid competition for nutrients, storage organs and root systems must occupy different areas of soil, or have uptake nutrient at different points in time.

AREA 1 HIMALAYAN BALSAM (IMPATIENS GLANDILIFERA) AND URTICA DIOICA (see Fig 14)

Floodplain adjacent to the River Taw, North Devon, frequent flooding; fertile alluvium; medium to quite heavy shade, shaded by woods to the south and west and scattered elsewhere; little interference by man; nettle area approx. 200 m², mean height 2.50 m, litter largely washed away and some debris deposited large areas of mud in the spring; garlic dominant in spring and nettle and

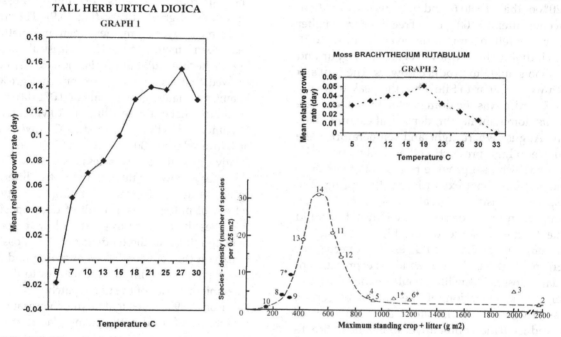

FIG 15.8 (Graphs 1-2) Response of the mean relative growth rate R to temperature in the tall herb Urtica dioica (Al-Mufti 1978) and the moss Brachythecium rutabulum under an irradiance of 25 W m-2 (Furness and Grime,1982).
FIG 15.8 (Graph 3) Relationship between maximum standing crop (plus litter) and species density (herbs only) at at 14 sites, ● woodlands, ○ grasslands and △ herb communities (Al-Mufti et al, 1977). Sites with * are Urtica sites.

BOX 15.2 FLORISTIC DIVERSITY OF STINGING NETTLE STANDS.

Many people describe the nettle as forming mono-specific stands and expect the floral diversity of a large nettle stand to be very low. However the study of Al-Mufti (1977) has shown the relationship between standing crop and species diversity within nettle stands. A superficial glance at a nettle patch at one point in time is misleading and detailed studies throughout the year are needed for a complete picture to emerge; few studies of this nature have been carried out. I include observations carried out on two nettle areas, together with species lists *within* nettle clones in a few other areas as examples. Nettle patch species must either invade the patch as rhizomes etc., from outside, or germinate within the clone

Himalayan balsam co-dominant in the summer.

In the spring many **vernal plants** make their appearance. A white carpet of wild garlic (*Allium ursinum*) covers the area in April; the leaves die back in May-June leaving the seed heads and food reserves stored in bulbs. Scattered throughout the area and in local stands is the Butterbur (*Petasites hybridus*) which flowers in March and later produces the massive umbrella-shaped leaves which shade out adjacent plants or 'push' them to one side, deep down in the soil are the massive rhizomes. Other vernals include scattered patches of Lesser Celandine (*Ranunculus ficaria*) which dies back later to return food reserves to root tubers, and Cuckoo Pint (*Arum maculatum*) which dies back in May and returns food to tubers.

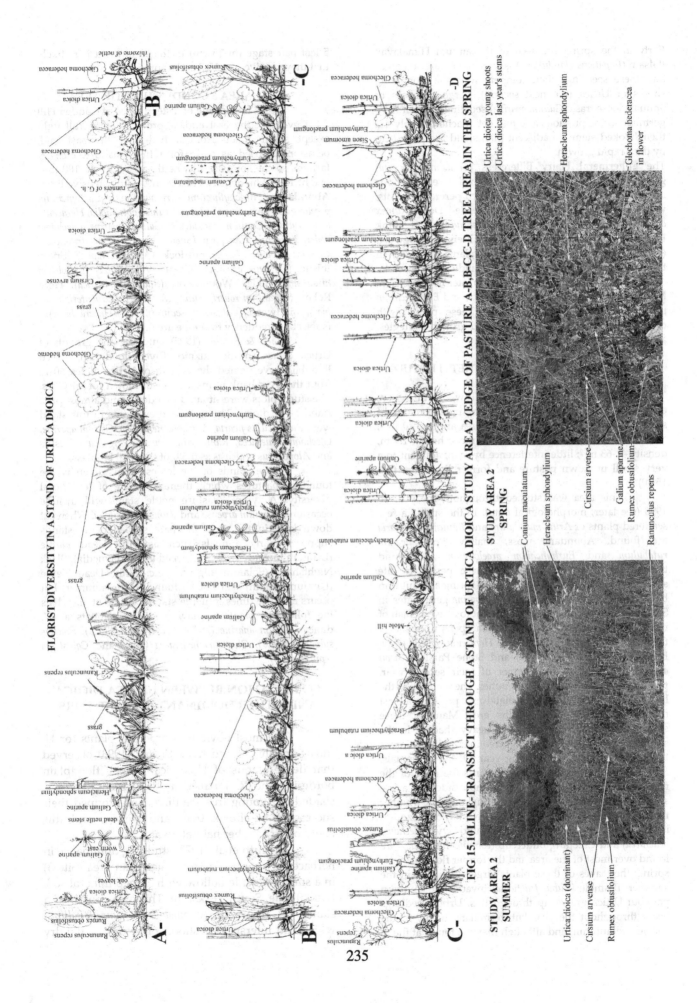

FLORIST DIVERSITY IN A STAND OF URTICA DIOICA

A-
Ranunculus repens
Rumex obtusifolius
Urtica dioica
oak leaves
worm cast
dead nettle stems
Galium aparine
Heracleum sphondylium
grass
Ranunculus repens
grass
Cirsium arvense
grass
Urtica dioica
Glechoma hederacea
Galium aparine
runners of G. h.
Urtica dioica
Glechoma hederacea
Glechoma hederacea
Urtica dioica
Rumex obtusifolius
thizome of nettle
-B

B-
Urtica dioica
Rumex obtusifolius
Glechoma hederacea
Brachythecium rutabulum
Glechoma hederacea
Galium aparine
Heracleum sphondylium
Brachythecium rutabulum
Galium aparine
Urtica dioica
Galium aparine
Glechoma hederacea
Galium aparine
Brachythecium rutabulum
Euthynchium praelongum
Urtica dioica
Galium aparine
Euthynchium praelongum
Conium maculatum
Euthynchium praelongum
Glechoma hederacea
Rumex obtusifolius
-C

C-
Ranunculus repens
Urtica dioica
Glechoma hederacea
Urtica dioica
Rumex obtusifolius
Euthynchium praelongum
Galium aparine
Urtica dioica
Brachythecium rutabulum
Mole hill
Galium aparine
Urtica dioica
Galium aparine
Glechoma hederacea
Urtica dioica
Galium aparine
Euthynchium praelongum
Glechoma hederacea
Urtica dioica
Euthynchium praelongum
Sison amomum
Glechoma hederacea
Urtica dioica
-D

FIG 15.10 LINE-TRANSECT THROUGH A STAND OF URTICA DIOICA STUDY AREA 2 (EDGE OF PASTURE A-B,B-C,C-D TREE AREA) IN THE SPRING

**STUDY AREA 2
SPRING**

Conium maculatum
Heracleum sphondylium
Cirsium arvense
Galium aparine
Rumex obtusifolium
Ranunculus repens

Urtica dioica young shoots
Urtica dioica last year's stems
Heracleum sphondylium
Glechoma hederacea
in flower

**STUDY AREA 2
SUMMER**

Urtica dioica (dominant)
Cirsium arvense
Rumex obtusifolium

235

Early in the spring the seed of the **annual** Himalayan Balsam (*Impatiens glandulifera*) germinate in bare soil areas and these seedlings then compete with the elongating shoots of Urtica (see next section). Large numbers of annual Goosegrass (*Galium aparine*) seedlings, which have germinated the previous autumn, get attached loosely via their hooked stems to adjacent plants and are pulled up by their rapid growth.

The **ephermeral** Hairy Bittercress (*Cardamine hirsuta*) grows throughout the year and its explosive seed pods assist by scattering its seeds. . Scattered **perennial** plants, which develop later, are the Broad-leaved Dock (*Rumex obtusifolia*), Bindweed (*Calystegia sepium*) and Pink Purslane (*Claytonia sibirica*), and the **biennial** Hogweed (*Heracleum sphondylium*). Nettle plants covered in tangled masses of goosegrass and bindweed cause the 'crash' that opens up more open areas later in the season. **Mosses** such as *Brachythecium rutabulum* and *Eurhynchium praelongum* cover the nettle litter. These plants with different life forms and life cycles, and growth strategies, are able to live within this nettle stand.

AREA 2 NEWBRIDGE LIME KILN NETTLE STUDY AREA

Edge of floodplain of River Taw, North Devon, occasional flooding; friable alluvium; open but slight shade from trees to the west; nettle area approx. 10 m ^{2}, abundant litter from nettle and trees, mean height 1.9 m, density 41-63 m ^{2}; little interference by man; adjacent to a very small unmown pasture and former lime kiln, (Fig 15.10).

This area was studied throughout the year in 1996 (see later, morphological data). In the spring a few scattered plants of *Arum maculatum* and *Ranunculus ficaria* are found. Abundant moss, mainly *Brachythecium rutabulum* and *Eurhynchium praelongum* are found throughout the year but decline for a period in late summer. Micro-fungi are abundant in spring and autumn but decline in the summer. *Galium aparine* germinates in September and is sufficiently abundant to cause a crash of nettles from late July onwards which opens up some of the area to light. The biennials, *Heraceum sphondylium*, Hemlock (*Conium maculatum*) and Stone Parsley (*Sison amomum*) flower in the summer of their second year, produce seed, then die in late summer. The seeds from the latter plants germinate immediately to produce a vast number of seedlings within the area. Many of these survive to the spring, but due to heavy shading in the summer, only a few of these survive mainly in gap areas to produce adults the following year. Of the perennials, *Rumex obtusifolia* occurs mainly towards the edge of the nettle area, but seedlings are also found inside, and a few scattered Cirsium arvense occur throughout, but whether the latter establish from seed or by invasion by rhizomes is not known. The stolons of Ground Ivy (*Glechoma hederacea*) and Creeping Buttercup (*Ranunculus repens*) are found over most of the area and the former flowers in the spring; the leaves of these plants largely die back in the summer. Bramble (*Rubus fructicosa*) invades the southern part but Urtica grows up through this. Urtica seedlings occur throughout the year but germinate mainly in the spring and autumn, and although they are found at the 4-

5 leaf-pair stage (ht 15 cm) in the summer, it is unlikely that they survive (Fig 15.7 and Photo 15.10).

AREA 3 CODDEN HILL TIP AREA

North facing side of a steep slope of Codden Hill (N. Devon) at the east end, approx. 300 feet; full light except slight shade from a hedge at the east end; occasionally used as a tip for refuse, manure, etc., by farmers so the soil is fertile; nettle area approx. 100 m ^{2}, height 1.9-2.0 m, density 116-128 m ^{2}, with extensive litter. **Abundant**, *Brachythecium rutabulum*, *Eurhynchium praelongum*. **Occasional** plants, *Rumex obtusifolia*, *Heraceum sphondylium*, *Conium maculatum*, *Galium aparine*, *Glechoma hederacea*, Pink Campion (*Silene dioica*), *Rubus fructicosa*, *Cirsium arvense*. **Rare**, Burdock (*Arctium lappa*), Spear thistle (*Cirsium arvense*), Great Willowherb (*Epilobium hirsutum*), Hedge Woundwort (*Stachys sylvatica*), Herb Robert (*Geranium robertianum*), Male fern (*Dryopteris felix-mas*), Bindweed (*Calystegia sepium*), Ivy (*Hedera helix*) - (subjective frequency for nettle area).

Hara & Šrutek (1995) studying the growth of Urtica dioica in the Luznice River floodplain, Czech Republic, investigated the growth of Urtica dioica 30 m from the river bank in meadows not mown for 40 years. The study plots were situated in a dense and almost pure stand of U. dioica. The under-storey plants in this stand were *Ranunculus ficaria*, *Anemone nemorosa*, *Galium aparine*, *Glechoma hederacea*, *Ranunculus repens*, *Angelica sylvestris* and *Alopecurus pratensis* as 0-5% of the total biomass.

Nettle stands of the lowest floral diversity are found in pastures which themselves are of low floral diversity. A typical pasture nettle stand will include occasional *Cirsium arvense* and *Rumex obtusifolia*. When cut down later in the year, the bare soil in nettle stands supports many annuals such as Pink Dead Nettle (*Lamium purpureum*), Chickweed (*Stellaria media*), Black Nightshade (*Solanum nigrum*), etc. White Dead Nettle (*Lamium album*) will not be found in the summer, but occurs at other times in nettle stands. Grime et al, lists the following plants as having similar habitats as U. dioica: *Galium aparine* (78%), *Poa trivialis* (74%), *Stachys sylvatica* (73%), *Glechoma hederacea* (70%) and *Calystegia sepium* (61%).

COMPETITION BETWEEN URTICA DIOICA AND OTHER DOMINANT COMPETITORS

The most obvious competitor plants for U. dioica are shrubs and trees. Šrutek (1993) observed that dense stands of U. dioica, on the floodplain bordering the R. Luznice in the Czech Republic, shaded out young tree seedlings and stopped their succession to climax trees and shrubs, and this could occur in other habitat areas.

Al Mufti et al, (1977) studying dominance in herbaceous vegetation, investigated an area (Site 3) in a small roadside hollow with a deep mineral soil, Lathkilldale, South Yorkshire. This area contained a stand of fireweed (*Chamaenerion angustifolium*) which had interspersed shoots of U. dioica, the dry matter of which exceeded that of C. angustifolium in the spring. By the beginning of July, however, most of the Urtica was submerged by the canopy of C. angustifolium and caused a premature decline in dry matter of Urtica compared to the other sites (see previous study). On Exmoor Devon and in Scotland C. angustifolium very often occupies habitats, such as roadside verges, normally filled by U. dioica and this could be due to lack of nutrients or differences in climate which reduce its competitive ability.

Ellenberg (1988) mentions garden escapes of the genera *Aster, Solidago, Helianthus* and *Rudbeckia*. Growing 1-2 m height, they first invaded ruderal places and now colonise river valleys not persistently flooded. They managed to gain a footing along water edges of clearings in Willow and Alder stands smothering out

there was a very wet spring and summer and Impatiens dominated the area. The quadrat supported Urtica 47m^2 (ht. 1.8m, largest leaf area 153,000mm^2) and Impatiens 10m^2 (ht. 2.0m, largest leaf area 201,000mm^2): the heavier shading for Urtica by I. glandulifera was reflected in its thinner than normal stems.

The climbing plants *Galium aparine* and *Calystegia sepium*, when present in high densities, can have a weakening effect on Urtica some years, causing it to crash and shading out much of the light which has more effect when it is growing in shaded areas.

6 THE GROWTH STRATEGIES OF THE COMMON NETTLE

Rash of nettles that is spreading nation-wide?

'A rash of giant stinging nettles is breaking out over England, claim botanist. The weeds, which once skulked around the edges of meadows and in graveyards, are now sweeping across wide tracts of countryside and choking riverbanks. The nettle thrives on phosphates in farm fertilisers and sewage effluent in rivers.'

New Scientist, 29/10/1994.

perennials such as Urtica dioica and *Senesio fluviatilis*. Also mentioned in this group are the Japanese Knotgrass (*Reynoutria japonica*) from Asia and Himalayan Balsam (*Impatiens glandulifera*) from the East Indies.

COMPETITION WITH HIMALAYAN BALSAM (IMPATIENS GLANDULIFERA)

When Impatiens colonised Habitat Area 1 (see floristic diversity) Urtica dioica grew to 3m and Impatiens to 3-4m. Since then the vigour and density of U. dioica has diminished. A permanent 1m^2 quadrat was placed in the area in 1995. Impatiens seeds germinated in Feb. and by April increased to 650m^2, after which the number of plants declined to 2m^2 (mean ht. 2.25m) by July. Urtica shoot density started at 128m^2 in March and dropped to 46m^2 (mean ht. 1.9m) in July. Impatiens has buttress roots and although lignified at the base it is mainly supported by hydrostatic pressure (it seems incredible that this annual can outgrow and partially shade out the perennial Urtica with its underground storage reserves). In 1999

IS THE NETTLE INCREASING IN ABUNDANCE? CIRCUMSTANTIAL EVIDENCE

Stories involving nettles generally make headlines but is there any hard evidence available to support this statement? For the establishment of Urtica dioica the seedling plants need (1) high levels of soil phosphate, (2) bare soil resulting from disturbance. For vigorous and continued growth, high levels of nitrogen are needed by this competitor plant.

INORGANIC FERTILISERS: NITROGEN AND PHOSPHORUS

A good account of crop nutrition is given in Archer (1993). In the mid-19th century phosphate deficiency was prevalent in upland soils and widespread in the lowlands also, except those supplied with appreciable quantities of farmyard manure. The greatest increase in nitrogen use took place in World War II and in the 1970's. Phosphate usage doubled in World War II but has remained constant since.

Table 15.6 United Kingdom Fertiliser use (1000's tonnes of nutrient), after Archer (1993).			
	Nitrogen (N)	Phosphorus (P_2O_5)	Potassium (K_2O)
1874	34	90	3
1939	60	170	75
1945	172	346	115
1969	790	476	458
1986	1,572	434	510

NITROGEN

Nitrate is very soluble and is lost from the soil by leaching.

PHOSPHORUS

Phosphorus is taken up in smaller amounts than nitrogen. Urtica dioica produces lectins (Chapter 11) to inhibit the attack of roots and rhizomes by fungi and bacteria. For the latter reason Urtica has no mycorrhizal associations, which probably accounts for why its phosphorus uptake is slow and why high phosphate levels are needed in order to prevent phosphorus deficiency.

It follows from these facts that before the mid-19th century Urtica dioica would probably have been distributed in smallish patches where there were high concentrations of phosphorus and nitrogen. Phosphorus also occurs in organic form in detergents that are increasingly used and discharged into rivers with wastewater. There has also been increasing pollution of streams and rivers by slurry and human sewage, both rich in nitrogen and phosphorus. Woodlands which were deficient in phosphorus now have phosphate fertilisers added to improve the growth of trees (Binns, 1975).

SOIL DISTURBANCE BY MANKIND

Disturbance by mankind and domesticated animals has greatly increased during the 21st century due to the availability of energy from fossil fuels, leading to increased mechanisation characteristic of intensive farming methods, and the ever increasing human population which exploits the natural environment for food production. Disturbance scatters rhizomes and provides opportunities for the establishment of nettles by seed.

BOGS

Management practices or pollution are resulting in increased productivity in infertile wetlands and therefore a consequent reduction in species richness (Grime, 1979). Changes in vegetation and environment at Askhan Bog, small valley mire near York, U.K., have been followed over 13 years using permanent quadrats (Hogg et al., 1995). Numerous species have declined whilst a few species such as the nitrophilous Urtica dioica, Sphagnum fimbriatum and Molinia caerula have increased in abundance. As well as increased acidity it is thought that aerial pollution is also responsible. There have been large increases in the concentration of nitrate and ammonia in the air and rain in recent decades. Burning, cropping and grazing and topsoil removal can be used to reduce fertility but cannot stop atmospheric nitrogen input.

RIVERBANKS

Recently research has been carried out on the distribution of Urtica dioica along the Luznice River on the border between Austria and Czechoslovakia (Srutek, 1993). On the Austrian part of the floodplain small farms have been preserved with diverse species meadows and pastures and there is an absence of over fertilisation. In the Czech part of the floodplain over the last 30-40 years there has been intensive farming leading to permanent grass stands with artificially sown grasses, whilst the wetter parts are not used at all, leading to wet ruderal stands of Phalaris arudinacea and Urtica dioica. Less competitive herbaceous species such as grasses, and shrubs and trees, are retarded by dense stands of Urtica and Phalaris. Trees can only succeed by greater disturbance in these areas by floodwater.

The man-induced spreading of U. dioica is common in Central Europe at present (Ellenberg, 1988). It is concentrated in ruderal sites (e.g. rubbish heaps, construction sites, areas around mountain cottages, along roads, etc.) and river floodplain. The expansion of U. dioica is most progressive, particularly along rivers and streams and/or in other types of wetlands (Hlavacek and Pysek 1988, (Srutek, et al. 1988, Prach et al. 1990). Many of the autecological features of Urtica dioica support the rapid spreading of this species (Grime et al. 1988, Wheeler 1981). On the other hand it is very sensitive to regular and frequent cutting which affects it considerably (van der Maarel, 1980).

Where meadows are regularly mowed, U. dioica is limited to the riverbank. The species-richest stands with Urtica were found in Austrian regions with mowed floodplain meadows. A lot of species from rich meadows have been found even in riverbank stands of Urtica and Phalaris. (Other invasive species spreading along the river were *Epilobium adenocaulon, Impatiens glandulifera, Rudbekia laciniata* and *Spiraea salicifolia*).

ROADSIDES

Increase in nettles alongside roads has been due to disturbances where the movement of soil disperses seed or rhizomes. In the past disturbances included macademisation of roads, ditch cleaning and hedging etc., and more recently the creation of motorways and road management processes. Roadsides adjacent to farmland, which could receive windblown or leached fertilisers, will allow more vigorous and competitive growth of established nettles or their seedlings. The distribution of nettles on road verges is also affected by mowing since they are absent from the mown part of roadside verges whilst concentrated in areas of unmown grass such as areas fringing hedges, hedgebanks and ditches. The following survey is related to the roadside habitat.

BOX 14.3 EVIDENCE FOR THE INCREASE IN ABUNDANCE OF URTICA DIOICA IN WILTSHIRE OVER THE LAST 50 YEARS

The Vegetation of Wiltshire, in The Flora of Wiltshire, D. Grose (1957), was surveyed approximately 50 years ago (Chapter 3). The paper by J. Oliver, 'The Common Stinging Nettle (Urtica dioica L.) in Wiltshire' (1994), followed the same method used by Grose but centred on one species, Urtica dioica. The aims were to obtain a semi-quantitative estimate of the occurrence and frequency of U. dioica and other commoner plants within the 26 habitat types with a view to finding any difference in abundance (frequency) or ubiquity (occurrence in the habitat) of U. dioica over the last 50 years. Oliver found that many results agreed with those found by Grose, but that the frequency of the nettle had increased to a large extent in the following habitats, (first letter = frequency, Grose, 1957 / second letter = frequency, Oliver, 1994; [A = abundant, F = frequent, O = occasional, R = rare]), Recently coppiced non-calcareous oakwood (R/O), Disturbed chalk grassland (O/F), Limestone grassland (R/O-F), Roadside on neutral soil (R/A), Roadside on calcareous soil (R/O-A), Railway bank (R/O), Footpath (R/A), Cart track (R/A), Track in chalky soil (R/F-A), Rivers and Riversides (R/A), Lake in non-calcareous soil (R/F). In the summary lists of habitat types U. dioica moved as follows (first figure is the order from the top, Grose, 1957 / second figure is the order from the top, Oliver, 1994), Hedges (9/2), Roadside non-calcareous soils (6/2), Roadside calcareous soils (19/2), Tracks (below 30/1).

STUDY 1. The area chosen was a 9 X 1 km square centred on Lockeridge, Wiltshire. Every path, track, road and river bank was walked (July, 1994) and nettle counts were made per 100 m and graded from 1000 or more stems (indicating a more or less continuous band of nettles 2 m wide) to 1 nettle or seedling. On this basis, 86.8% of the 53 km measured, had some degree of nettle density.

STUDY 2. Oliver carried out a 250 mile (10% of the total Wiltshire road mileage) roadside nettle survey. 66% of the total road length showed nettles to a greater or lesser extent.

STUDY 3. In 1994 the Wiltshire River Monitoring Scheme recorded U. dioica in 31 out of the 32 sites sampled (97%).

STUDY 4. Marginal and bank-side vegetation of the Kennet and Avon Canal (65 km) was investigated and it was found that 163 out of 173 sub-sites (94%) had nettles (36% abundant and 38% frequent).

Also mentioned in the surveys is the vigorous growth of nettles in riverside/riverbank, ditch and woodland habitats, often over 2m in height.

The main conclusions are: -

(1) 'The findings show countywide **networks** of nettles, and therefore represent more than **patchy** abundance. Such networks are most continuous in agricultural areas but thin out and can almost disappear in unproductive habitats. Wiltshire is, however, mostly heavily farmed.'

(2) 'nettles are now found in virtually all of the 65 Wiltshire habitats described by Grose (1957), even if mainly confined to margins such as track-sides, around cattle troughs or cart-parking areas.'

(3) The Perennial Rye Grass is placed at the top of the list for the commonest plant, in 1994, and Urtica dioica is placed second, compared with seventh in 1957.

Vegetation development in a former orchard (after removal of trees) with a loamy moist soil was subjected to different treatments and then analysed over 9 years (van der Maarel, 1980). (1) Mown plots changed from a tall herb and grass vegetation with dominant U. dioica, to grass vegetation dominated by *Arrhenatherum elatius*. (2) Establishment and/or rapid spread of Urtica can be brought about in Arrthenatherum dominated sites by (re) introduction of nitrogen fertiliser.

WOODLANDS

The following work is given in Ellenberg (1988). Species that prefer relatively damp soil and which serve as nitrate indicators, found in Wild Garlic–Beech woods, are *Stachys sylvatica, Impatiens nolitangere, Circaea luteiana*, or Urtica dioica. One of the most informative long-term trials on the effect of one fertiliser application on the acid-soil Beech woods (*Querco-Carpinetum luzuletosum*) in the urban forest of Hannoverian München was analysed by

Grabherr (1942). Plots were fertilised respectively with KP, CaK, CAP and CaKP (K=potassium, P=phosphorus, Ca=calcium. After 13 years there was an increase in the abundance of Urtica dioica which would have been related to increases in nitrification as a result of fertiliser treatments, as well as the effect of phosphorus, making it possible for the establishment of Urtica plants from seed.

COMMONEST AND RARITY IN THE BRITISH FLORA

This account is based on the two papers of Hodgson (1987) on the commonness and rarity in plants, and is based on the vegetation studies carried out by the National Ecological Research Council (NERC), within the Sheffield area, Grime et al (1988). The land use in this area is: **lowland**, 67% agricultural, and 18% urban, 15% other; **upland**, 79% agricultural, 11% urban and 10% other.

Since 1939 with the development of intensive agriculture, very little of the existing vegetation is unaltered, whilst there is a range of fertile and/or frequently disturbed habitats. The vegetation was analysed under 6 main habitats: aquatics, mire, arable, open habitats, grassland and woodland. The 723 native species were classified as 21% common, 39% frequent, 23% common and 17% rare. A greater proportion of common than of rare species is associated with productive conditions and indicates an association between rarity and habitat infertility.

Common species are particularly associated with habitats such as intensely managed agricultural land, gardens and urban wasteland, all of which are disturbed and vice versa, for rare species. Commonly occurring vegetation has less species richness per m² and vice versa for rare species. There is a suggestion that common species, e.g. *Agrostris stolonifera*, *Poa trivialis* and *Urtica dioica*, are found under a wide range of environmental conditions and vice versa for rare species.

Species have changed in abundance as a consequence of marked changes in land use within historical time. The species that exploit recently made habitats (e.g. arable land, demolition sites, river-banks, and paths) are likely to be increasing whilst those associated with older habitats (e.g. scree, unenclosed pasture, broad-leaved plantations) have declined. About half of the rare native species are confined to 'pre-1840' habitats. A disproportionately large number of species are restricted to less fertile habitats. The low proportion of species associated with fertile habitats may be accounted by widespread occurrence of dominant species in fertile habitats and the wide ecological range of many commoner species. The consistent presence of alien species of man-made environments throughout the world may also be a result of global scarcity of species adapted to more fertile conditions. The abundance in today's flora is related to the effects of modern land use which produces habitats that have been colonised by plants such as Urtica dioica which have wide ecological amplitude. The reasons why so few plants, such as U. dioica, exploit productive habitats are considered in the next chapter.

LEAF HOPPER (EUPTERYX AURATA) - HOP ON

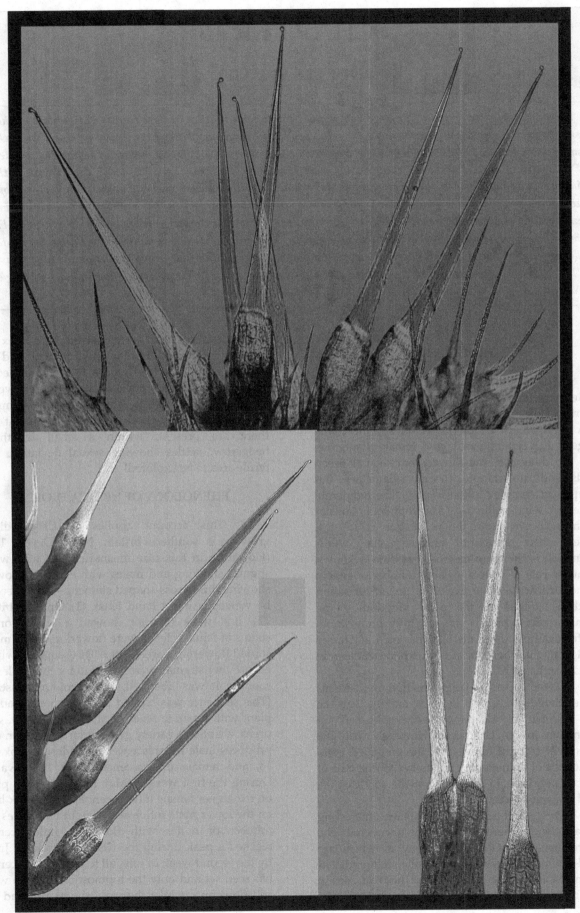

241

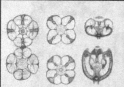

CHAPTER 16

NETTLE SEX LIFE

"There is ample provision in the open countryside for the pollination of pure female individuals of the stinging nettle (Urtica dioica) by male ones. In view of the large quantity of the pollen produced by each male, even female plants standing some way from the male ones are not in danger of remaining sterile. For a strong male individual that carried 4 inflorescence branches at each node, each shoot with inflorescences at 6 nodes, the count gave no less than 45 million pollen grains. Each anther enclosed on the average 1,500 pollen grains, the 4 stamens thus altogether give 6,000. The number of flowers in the inflorescences decreased from below upwards in the sequential tiers, as an average one could accept 1,247 for the number of male flowers per node in question. Therefore, 1,247 X 6 X 6,000 = 44,892,000. For male hemp plants I found 12,500,000, for Mercurialis annua I found 36,000,000 pollen grains on average, thus, Urtica dioica surpasses, with its almost 45 million pollen grains, that of strong individuals of Dog's Mercury.'

INTRODUCTION

The classification of plants is based on the stable characteristics of their flowers and the flowers of Urtica dioica have been introduced in Chapters 1-3. A brief recap: U. dioica as its specific name suggests has separate male and female plants, i.e. they are dioecious, the flowers have small green tepals and are minute (1-4mm diameter), but grouped in complex inflorescences. The temperate nettles are wind-pollinated (Anemophilous) but not much is known about the pollination of tropical nettles; their structure suggests that wind-pollination is the main method, but little is known about the role of insects. A large number of genera of the Urticaceae have explosive pollen liberation which is unique to the plant kingdom – the mechanism of which is still not fully understood. See for example other mechanisms such as Harley (1971) for a different type of explosive mechanism in a Brazilian Labiate.

More papers on the pollination mechanisms in the Orchidacea appear in a few months than the total number of all papers ever published on pollination in the Urticaceae. However, with the clearing of tropical forests and the predicted mass extinctions of animals and plants in the first half of this century, I would rather be a nettle – at least the wind is always there!

Yes, wind-pollinated plants are interesting and a lot is out there waiting to be uncovered. The controversy over GM crops, many of which are wind-pollinated, has shown the pollen fall predicted by the leptokurtic curve does not hold in certain circumstances because wind can carry pollen over larger distances than previously thought. Sex can also be influenced by the environment and the change from male to female is not confined to certain fish but takes place in the nettle relative the hemp (*Cannabis sativa*). The sex of the common nettle is also influenced by the environment and there are present, within a small length of hedgerow, nettles showing sexual deviations – a fertile area to be explored!

PHENOLOGY OF URTICA DIOICA

This account applies to Urtica dioica growing in southern Britain, North Devon, 1999. (Flowering in this case means females with white stigmas showing and males with exploded flowers showing the 4 cross-shaped stamens – these need to be viewed using a hand lens). (1) **Open habitats**. The first week of May showed a proportion of shoots of female clones were flowering whilst males started flowering a week later. This sequence would ensure that stigmas were ready to receive pollen as soon as it was liberated, thus avoiding wastage. (This sequence was backed up by a monoecious (a plant with separate sexes on the same plant e. g U. urens, chapter 3) variety growing in my garden that produces male inflorescences on nodes, approx. 15-18, and female inflorescences from 19 upwards. During the first week of May flowering took place on the higher female inflorescences and a week later on the lower male inflorescences). In both sexes the number of nodes with flowering inflorescences reached a peak during the first two weeks of June. By the second week in July, all female inflorescences has seed set and only the topmost one or two were still flowering, whilst the male shoots still had 6-8 nodes with flowering inflorescences. At this time there was an abundance of side branches on both male and female shoots and many of these had flowering inflorescences on several nodes. The flowering on side shoots continues into September. Clones cut down in May were 60 cm high by the beginning of August and flowering at most nodes, and this continues until early October. (2) **Closed/Shaded habitats**. At the beginning of the year flowering starts one to several weeks later than nettles in open situations. By the end of July flowering is still taking place on the main shoots and seed set is low. The long flowering period in U. dioica, which varies within and between clones, under different environmental conditions as a result of re-growth, etc., maximises seed production. Seed dispersal begins from late July onwards.

THE MALE FLOWERS OF URTICA DIOICA

The male flowers vary from yellow-green to dark crimson and are borne on the top surface of cymosely-branched inflorescences, four at each node. The flowers are minute (1-2mm) in diameter and their structure is shown (Fig 16.1). As the flower opens it expands to 3mm after the reflexed filaments push back the four tepals, exposing the eight swollen anther sacs around the central transparent urn-shaped pistillode. At the moment of explosion the four reflexed stamens flick backwards either together or one at a time, the two anther sacs of each stamen throwing out two arcs of pollen through the open slit in each side of the anther. The exploding stamen was based on a superb synchro-flash photograph taken by Saroshi Kuribayashi (Fig 16.2) which shows the two arcs, with the pollen thrown 1-2cm from the plant into the turbulent air currents where it is carried away. After discharge the flower withers and falls off and is replaced by another which grows up from below, so flowering even within a single inflorescence takes place over a longer period of time. As growth on the main shoot produces more nodes with inflorescences, and eventually inflorescences on side shoots, flowering can continue until September.

THE EXPLOSIVE/CATAPULT MECHANISM FOR POLLEN LIBERATION IN THE FLOWERS OF THE NETTLES AND OTHER MEMBERS OF THE URTICACEAE.

HISTORICAL

Andrea Caesalpino, an Italian physician, philosopher and botanist, in the first textbook of botany (1583), recognised, in dogs'-mercury (*Mercurialis*), nettle (*Urtica*) and hemp (*Cannabis*), the existence of sterile as well as fertile flowers, and says that these sterile flowers are male. In Oliver's translation (1894-95) of the Pflanzenleben, Kerner writes: -

"In some species at the very moment when the anthers burst open the pollen is ejected violently into the air and ascends obliquely in the form of a little cloud of dust. In this country the Nettles afford a good example of this phenomenon. Anyone standing in front of a bed of Stinging Nettles on a bright summer morning, and waiting until the first rays of sunshine fall on the flowers will be surprised to see small pale-coloured clouds of dust ascending here and there from amidst the dark foliage. At first the clouds are solitary, and are given off at measurable intervals; by degrees they become more frequent, and at times one may see five or six or more arising at the same moment and at no great distance from one another. But gradually the little explosions become less frequent again, and in another half-hour there is an entire cessation of the phenomenon. On inspection one easily discovers that it depends on the fact that the filaments bearing the anthers are coiled in the bud, and suddenly spring up at the same moment that the dehiscence of the anthers takes place. (Speaking of Pilea microphylla now known as the artillery plant) ..... One only has to sprinkle the plant with water at a time when it is covered with flower-buds and then take it out of the shade into the sunshine, and the phenomenon is immediately exhibited. All over the plant the flower-buds explode, and a whitish kind of pollen is discharged into the air in the form of a little cloud."

Spontaneous explosive pollen release is unique in the plant kingdom and confined to members of the Urticales: (1) it occurs in all 48 genera of the Urticaceae, e.g. *Urtica* *, *Pellonia* *, *Pilea* *, *Parietaria* *, and *Laportea* *, (2) the majority of the 37 genera of the Moraceae, e.g. the mulberry (*Morus*) and the paper mulberry (*Broussonetia* *), (3) in the Ulmaceae it is found in the hackberries (Celtis), (4) it is absent in the 2 genera of the Cannabaceae, (5) it is absent from the 6 genera of the Cecropiaceae, although in the genus *Poikilospermum*, which have inflexed stamens, these straighten gradually when the flower opens (Berg, 1977, 1989). It is clear from this that there are 3 main types of pollen liberation in the Urticales (1) from straight stamens, (2) from reflexed non-explosive stamens and (3) from reflexed explosive stamens. Bauhin G. (1600) knew of pollen explosion liberation in the Urticaceae in the genera marked *.

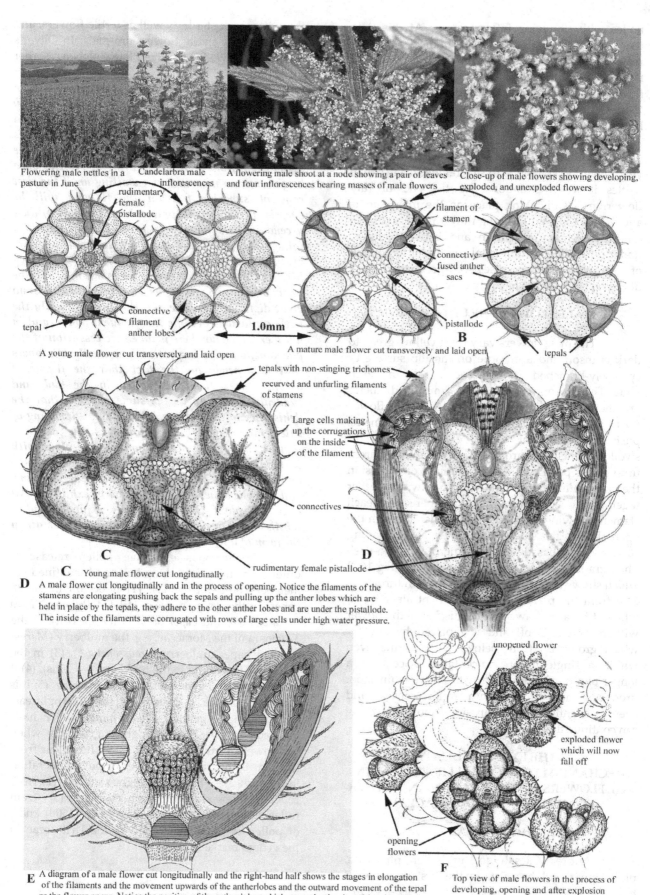

Flowering male nettles in a pasture in June

Candelarbra male inflorescences

A flowering male shoot at a node showing a pair of leaves and four inflorescences bearing masses of male flowers

Close-up of male flowers showing developing, exploded, and unexploded flowers

rudimentary female pistallode

filament of stamen

connective fused anther sacs

tepal

connective filament anther lobes

pistallode

tepals

A A young male flower cut transversely and laid open

1.0mm

B A mature male flower cut transversely and laid open

tepals with non-stinging trichomes

recurved and unfurling filaments of stamens

Large cells making up the corrugations on the inside of the filament

connectives

rudimentary female pistallode

C Young male flower cut longitudinally

D A male flower cut longitudinally and in the process of opening. Notice the filaments of the stamens are elongating pushing back the sepals and pulling up the anther lobes which are held in place by the tepals, they adhere to the other anther lobes and are under the pistallode. The inside of the filaments are corrugated with rows of large cells under high water pressure.

unopened flower

exploded flower which will now fall off

opening flowers

E A diagram of a male flower cut longitudinally and the right-hand half shows the stages in elongation of the filaments and the movement upwards of the antherlobes and the outward movement of the tepal as the flower opens. Notice the position of the anther lobes which are under the rim of the pistallode.

F Top view of male flowers in the process of developing, opening and after explosion

FIG 16.1 THE STRUCTURE, DEVELOPMENT AND OPENING OF THE MALE FLOWERS OF URTICA DIOICA

Taking into consideration explosive liberation of pollen in the Urticales is the most unique mechanism in the plant kingdom it seems incredible that only three papers [Askenasy (1880), Goebel (1915, 1924), Mosebach (1932)] appeared up to 1932 and just another descriptive one in 1967: the exact mechanism is still not clear.

Josis gives an account of the study of Askenasy on explosive pollen liberation in Parietaria. The concave side of the reflexed stamen is in a state of compression but is prevented from straightening by obstacles such as the perianth on the outer side and the rudimentary ovary (pistillode) on the inner side, and inbetween these two, the anthers are pinched. The main constraint was the anther that was glued to the filament, and only when this resistance was overcome did the filament straighten in a sudden jerk ejecting the pollen. The removal of a stamen did not necessarily result in it straightening because the osmotic pressure had to reach a critical level first, but small stimuli such as vibration or heat could trigger the process. Placing the stamen in strong solutions plasmolysed the cells, but a certain resistance to straightening was shown due to the fact that the convex surface of the filament was longer than the concave side, therefore the releasing movement must overcome the resistance offered by the greater length of the convex side.

Goebel and Mosebach studied various species of the following genera: *Laportea*, *Pilea* and *Pellonia*, but Goebel (1924) also includes *Urtica*, *Parietaria* and *Broussonetia*. To avoid repetition this account is mainly based on the more recent findings of Mosebach. In *Laportea moroides* (Fig 16.2 d-f) the filament consists of three parts: (1) the basal part is straight and roughly cylindrical, (2) the middle part called the hinge/lever is flat, bent into a U-shape, the inner surface is covered in transverse corrugations and it forms the catapult apparatus, (3) the top piece leads to the connective that unites the anther lobes. The filament contains a central strand of vascular tissue otherwise the tissue is mainly parenchyma whose walls consist of cellulose, hemi-cellulose and pectin, although the tissue of the outer side consists partly of collenchyma. These tissues are thought to give the extensible and elastic properties needed for the explosive recoil/backlash of the filament. Mosebach thought that the inner corrugations result from the inner surface, trying to keep pace with the growth of the outer surface, and since the inner surface is shorter, then folding must occur. The cells of the filament must undergo rapid changes in their shape and size during the explosion, to enable the backlash bending of the filament. *The exact mechanism is still not known.*

At the time of flowering large amounts of starch are present in the filament (Fig 16.2 b-c) and when this is converted into sugar (glucose) results in the formation of a high osmotic pressure in the cells. The osmotic pressure was 10 atmospheres in *Pilea spruceana* and 13 atmospheres in Laportea moroides, equal to the highest osmotic values in other tissues of these plants, whilst that of *Pellonia daveanana* was 21 atmospheres and exceeded that of the inner surface must exceed that of the cells on the outer surface of researchers agree with Askenasy that the mechanism is restrained by the perianth, pistillode and the gluing of the anther wall to the filament base, but that explosion takes place once these forces are exceeded. Goebel believed that an irritating effect (stimulus) triggered the explosion, such as dry air, rise in temperature, warm water, cut inflorescence, turpentine, and alcohol applied to the filament. Mosebach explains these stimuli, especially paraffin oil, bone oil, xylol, ether, and alcohol, as acting by dissolving the glue that holds the anthers down. However, it is questionable whether either the glue or fragile anther wall could resist the high atmospheric forces operating within the filament in the absence of other constraining forces, and the nature of this glue was not found. (I found whilst observing pollen liberation in Soleirolia soleirolii cases where the filaments had sprung back, but broken off below the anther which was stuck in place under the pistillode. This meant that the cells of the filament must have been torn apart by the tensions set up!

Goebel places the explosive stamens of the Urticaceae together with the stimulus-responsive stamens such as Berberis, Opuntia and others. Mosebach disagrees with Goebel and believes that the explosive mechanism of the Urticacean stamens occurs when a critical difference in pressure occurs between the two sides of the filament, *and is independent of external stimuli.* External stimuli such as dryness, warmth, vibration, etc., can however accelerate the explosion, and he quotes *Pilea serpyllifolia* as an example.

Celtis belongs to the family Ulmaceae of the nettle order Urticales, see Box 1.3 Introduction. The flowers of the Ulmaceae are generally unisexual of bisexual with a perianth of five of six tepals with the introse anthers opposite each tepal. The pistil consists of two fused carpels with a bifid stigma (Heywood, 1978). Although the stamens are slightly reflexed the pollen is normally shaken out by the wind. The first account of explosive pollen liberation in the Ulmaceae is given by Cuellar (1967) who describes this for *Celtis laevigata* (Mexican hackberry tree). In the male flowers the six reflexed stamens are considerably flattened because they are pressed on one side by the tepals and on the other by the anthers (a rudimentary pistil (pistillode) of hairs is in the middle of the flower).

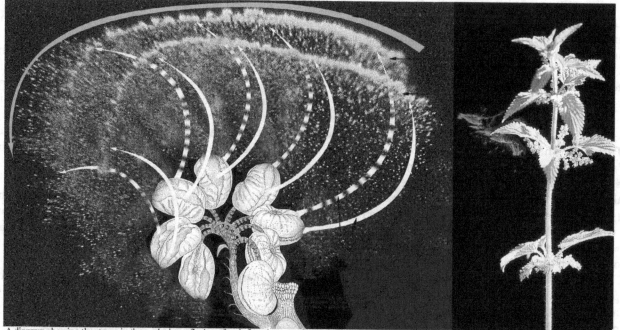

A diagram showing the stages in the explosive reflexing of an inflexed stamen filament, throwing out two pollen masses from splits in the two anther sacs, into two arcs several centimeters into the turbulent air layer outside the plant space.

A male nettle shoot kept in the dark, then exposed to sunlight, a flower exploded

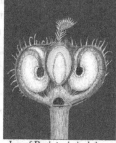

L.s.of Parietaria judaica with hermaphrodite flowers (Urticaceae).

Top view of a male inflorescence branch showing flowers in different stages, two old and two newly exploded flowers with the cross -shaped stamens. Discharged flowers fall off.

Stamens sometimes explode two at a time, the other two are just about to do the same

Male flower was cut and placed on a black card, it exploded and as a back-lash jumped several cms into the air

Below a stamen that has just exploded, showing the reflexed filament with its ridges of large cells, the two pollen sacs blown open and the scattered pollen grains.

Below the stamen is about to explode, above it has exploded

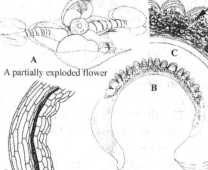

starch grains in large cells

A A partially exploded flower

B

C

D longitudinal section of a reflexed stamen showing cells on both sides

Exploded stamen showing ridges on the filament

E

F

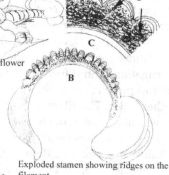

5   1
6   2
7   3
8   G   4

G Shapes of filaments placed in various solutions see book text

middle part of the stamen filament showing the large top cells and the narrow elongated lower cells

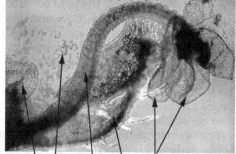

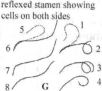

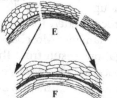

Pistallode, pollen, filament, tepal, split anther sacs

FIG 16.2 STAGES IN THE EXPLOSION OF THE STAMENS OF URTICA DIOICA.

Cuellar makes the observation that the filaments are reflexed (looped) and the anthers are cemented to the base of the receptacle. In a similar way to Urtica the filaments increase in diameter and length and reach state of high turgidity. One minute (approximately) before explosive liberation the anthers change colour from green to yellow (the colour of the pollen) and a lateral line of dehiscence proceeds from the top to the base of the anther on both anther sacs. At this point the tissue holding the base of the anther to the receptacle splits allowing the resistance to the straightening of the anther to lessen and enabling the reflexed stamens to spring back and straighten. The pollen is catapulted, through the slits in the anthers, into the air to a distance of six centimeters. Cuellar mentioned the change in colour of the anther prior to pollen liberation and I have noticed the same changes in the anthers of Urtica dioica prior to explosion. This change seems to be due to the absorption of water in the anther; the resulting powdery pollen can be seen along the dehiscence line of the two anther sacs. This appears to be very similar to the explosive pollen release in the Moraceae and Urticaceae. More investigation on pollen release in the Urticales is needed.

I found that in the case of Urtica pilulifera the reflexed stamens slowly bend back and pollen is released by the wind in a similar way to grass pollen release. Corner (1962), in his classification of the Moraceae, noticed that the genera with straight stamens rarely had a pistillode. He concludes (1) the

inflexed stamen has evolved in parallel in different Moraceous and, even Urticaeous and Ulmaceous groups or genera, (2) the introrse stamens in inflexed flowers makes for a more effective wide-spread explosive stamen mechanism.

The significance of explosive pollen release in the Urticales has been described by Berg (1989).

Although there is air movements in the understory of an evergreen forest these are normally too weak to shake out pollen so the evolution of a mechanism of explosive pollen release could have enabled these plants to move into this habitat. A large number of the Moraceae and the Urticaceae living in the forest understory occur near streams where there is more air movement which would faciliatate pollen movement after explosion. It is also possible that plants with explosive pollen release living in more seasonally open vegetation could have moved into these from the original forest habitats. Even *Broussonetia* and *Morus* have made the transition into more or less temperate regions.

POLLEN

Strasberger's work in the pollen production in Urtica dioica (frontispiece) was rather conservative if we take into account that male inflorescences on a single shoot can occur on 10 nodes and also on large numbers of side branches. Considering that the average density of male shoots = 100 m^2, then the pollen production per m^2 = 4,500,000,000, which means that 2 m^2 of a male nettle clone would produce more pollen grains than the present human population. Since the pollen finds its way to the stigma of the female flowers entirely by chance this enormous pollen release is necessary.

POLLEN STRUCTURE

The most comprehensive study on the

Table 16.1, the pollen characteristics of the British members of the Urticaceae, (simplified and modified from Sorsa & Huttunen, 1975). Operculum = lid, Annulus = ring, Tectal processes = processes on the surface of the pollen grain. LM = light microscope, SEM = scanning electron microscope. All sizes are in μm.

	Number of pores	Size	Pore size - diameter		Pore characters Operculum Annulus		Tectal processes		Special characters
			LM	SEM			LM	SEM	
Urtica dioica	3	15 x15	1.5	1.4	-	+	5	0.3	Spinules sharply tapered, broad at base
U. pilulifera	Many	25	2.0	1.3	-	+	5	0.2	-
U. urens	3	15 x17	1.3	1.9	-	(+)	4-5	0.2	Spinules narrow ± regularly distributed; grains goniotreme
Parietaria judaica	3	14 x16	1.0	1.4	-	-	4	0.4	Short spicules
Soleirolia solerolii	3	12 x13	0.8	1.1	+	-	4	-	Processes in rows or small groups

pollen morphology of the Urticaceae is that of Sorsa & Huttunen (1975). A summary of the pollen characteristics of the 6 British species (Tab 16.1) shows that most grains are roughly spherical, most have 3 pores and small spicules on the surface. The pollen of insect-pollinated plants, are fewer, larger and with prominent sculpturing and spicules on the surface which are more likely to get caught on the hairs/bristles of insects.

BOX 15.1 NETTLE POLLINOSIS

Hay fever/pollinosis is caused by pollen mainly from wind-pollinated flowers such as tree pollen early in the year, and that of grasses, sedges, rushes and nettles etc., later on. The widespread abundance and continuous flowering of nettles make them important contributors to air-borne pollen. Air sampling in America (William, et al, 1970), revealed the prominence of urticaceous ('nettle type') pollen in several mid-western states from July-Sept. The level of 200 grains m³ annually exceeded that of other weeds, excluding the Ragweed (*Ambrosia artemesiifolia*), which is a chief cause of pollinosis in North America. The main nettle contribution in Michigan came from *Urtica gracilis, Laportea canadensis* and species of *Pilea, Parietaria* and *Boehmeria*. The testing of 420 patients sensitive to antigens in pollen was carried out using epidermaly-administered pollen extracts (1:20). Two plus reactions to *U. gracilis* and to *L. canadensis* occurred in 20% and 21.4 % respectively. Supplementary cutaneous tests, with 1: 500 pollen extracts of U. gracilis, produced 62%, two plus reaction, in the 108 patients. Nasal provocative tests of 16 patients with late summer hay fever gave 11 positive responses to U. gracilis pollen and two of these exceeded skin and mucosal responses of short ragweed pollen. It is concluded that exposure to nettle pollen may 'prime' the allergic reaction of pollinosis sufferers to subsequent ragweed pollinosis to bring about increased severity.

FEMALE INFLORESCENCE AND FLOWERS OF URTICA DIOICA

The single cavity of the ovary contains a single straight (orthotropous) ovule, with the micropyle at the stigmatic end. The pollen tube grows down the stigma, penetrates the micropyle and the embryo sac. One of the male gametes fuses with the ovum/egg (chapters 1-2). The perianth consists of four tepals, two small ones at the edges, and two large ones closely pressed to the sides of the lens-shaped ovary. The tepals are covered in large non-stinging hairs but the flower stalks are covered in stinging trichomes. The penicillate stigma caps the ovary and is above the perianth. The stigma presents a large volume and surface area for the capture of pollen grains. One stigma on a young flower, dimensions 0.5 mm, consisted of 136 cylindrical multicellular filaments (460μ X 18μ) with

a surface area of 4.08 mm ² covering a volume of space 0.95 mm ³ (Fig 16.4).

It is of historical importance that the great cytologist Eduard Strasburger uncovered the details of double fertilisation in Angiosperms (seed plants), using none other than the humble stinging nettle (Strasburger, 1910).

ADAPTATION OF THE URTICALES AND OF URTICA DIOICA TO WIND-POLLINATION.

The primitive angiosperms are thought to have been insect-pollinated (entomophily) and wind-pollination (anemophily) is thought to be a derived condition suited to *open* situations occupied now by grasses, rushes, sedges, nettles, etc. In northern *deciduous* forests it is the dominant method of pollination, it is also characteristic of island floras. Anemophily is unsuited to jungles where there is little wind and dense vegetation (Whitehead, 1968). To avoid self-pollination, the direction of development via dicliny towards dioecy (see chapter 16) in anemophilous plants has often taken place. Adaptations to anemophily, found in female plants (Faegri,), are feathery stigmas with a large surface area and frequently sticky for catching pollen grains, reduction of the perianth, exposure of the flowers above the leaf mass on aerodynamically favourable inflorescences, a reduction in the number of ovules since few pollen grains are caught, and these all occur in U. dioica and the members of the Urticales (Whitehead, 1968).

Many groups within the Urticales are anemophilous, most of the Ulmaceae, the Cannabaceae, the Urticaceae, many Moraceae and Cecropia. Assuming that the ancestral members of the Urticales occupied humid tropical vegetation and were entomophilous, moves towards anemophily could have resulted (1) in the development of slender filaments and large anthers, or (2) the development of explosive pollen release or anther detachment (*Cecropia*). In both cases movement into more open habitats and temperate areas could have followed. In the case of explosive pollen release individuals could have been able to survive and pollinate in relatively closed (forest) habitats (Berg, 1989).

The following developments for anemophily in male plants would have followed: (1) production of vast numbers of pollen grains, (2) pollen grains of size (20-40μ) for the best capture by the stigmas, (3) grains with a thin and smooth extine, (4) because of the large fall off (over a few metres) in pollen from its source, individuals of the species should be reasonably large and not too widely spaced, (5) flowering should take place and

Female clone with exposed white stigmas /Single female shoot with flowers full out Two female inflorescence branches closer up Pink female type Close-up with white penicillate stigmas Female shoots with candelabra-like masse of fruits

penicillate stigmas

multicellular stigma filaments

achene

small tepal
large tepal of perianth

Stages in deveopment from the young fertilised pistil to the fruit which conists of perianth enclosing the fruit/achene

Micrographs showing pistil with stigmatic filaments and pollen Achenes enclosed in perianths

fruits masses

Young pistils with developing embryos

FIG 16.4 FEMALE FLOWERS AND THE DEVELOPMENT OF THE FRUIT IN URTICA DIOICA

pollen should be released at the time of the year to coincide with low precipitation and adequate wind. Most of these characteristics are now present in anemophilous males of the Urticales including U. dioica.

SEXUAL TYPES IN URTICA DIOICA

A casual glance at clones of Urtica dioica in the main flowering season gives the impression that they are either male or female (dioecious). This is because the flowers are so small (1-2 mm). However when stinging nettle inflorescences are examined with a hand lens it becomes evident that deviations from the dioecious condition are very common. Strasburger (1910) discovered the latter fact, and to give the credit to him, and to get the flavour of the time, I quote the pieces below: -

"I had available to me Urtica dioica in different sexual combinations from the Botanical Garden in Bonn and from the immediate neighbourhood of Bonn. In the Urtica dioica group of our system in the Botanical Garden a few stood out from among the vigorous examples, with hermaphrodite and female flowers in the lower inflorescences, but only female ones in the upper inflorescences.

In another rather shady place on the garden lawn, we found a female stem with very isolated hermaphrodite flowers, finally, on the side of the paths in the neighbourhood also plants of which the lower inflorescences had only male flowers, or male, hermaphrodite and female flowers, whereby the latter appeared at the top of the inflorescences. Higher up the inflorescences in these flowers were initially predominantly hermaphrodite and at the end mostly female. In short, we succeeded to bring together all possible sexual combinations for our dioecian stinging nettle.

Individual dioica stinging nettles that are exclusively sexually separated are with all that, very rare in this area. This I found out during numerous excursions, when I carefully studied every example of this stinging nettle that I encountered".

Strasburger goes on to account for many sexual abnormalities in relation to monoecious and hermaphrodite flowers of U. dioica which I have also studied in Devon, so it is easier to give my illustrated account.

249

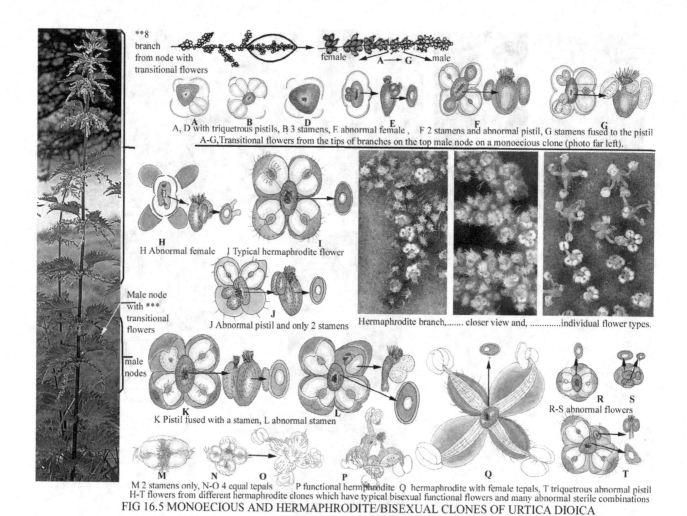

**8 branch from node with transitional flowers

female ← A → G → male

A, D with triquetrous pistils, B 3 stamens, D abnormal female, F 2 stamens and abnormal pistil, G stamens fused to the pistil
A-G, Transitional flowers from the tips of branches on the top male node on a monoecious clone (photo far left).

H Abnormal female   I Typical hermaphrodite flower

J Abnormal pistil and only 2 stamens

Male node with *** transitional flowers

male nodes

Hermaphrodite branch,....... closer view and, ...individual flower types.

K Pistil fused with a stamen, L abnormal stamen

R-S abnormal flowers

M 2 stamens only, N-O 4 equal tepals   P functional hermphrodite Q hermaphrodite with female tepals, T triquetrous abnormal pistil
H-T flowers from different hermaphrodite clones which have typical bisexual functional flowers and many abnormal sterile combinations

FIG 16.5 MONOECIOUS AND HERMAPHRODITE/BISEXUAL CLONES OF URTICA DIOICA

MONOECIOUS CLONES

Monoecious clones have separate male and female flowers on the same plant. No doubt a thorough study would uncover all types of clones, from males with a few female flowers, to females with a few male flowers. My limited studies identified 3 types.

Type 1. This is the most obvious type to identify and I have grown a piece of this clone, found alongside a railway embankment, in my garden. In the shoots of this clone the bottom-most three (mean) inflorescence nodes are male, followed by transitional node four and above this the rest of the nodes on the shoot are female. The inflorescence on the transition node four has side-branches which are female at the bottom and male at the top, with a middle zone of transitional flower types (Fig 16.5) Re-growth, from earlier cutting, shows the same pattern. The female flowers at the top of the shoot flower about a week before the male flowers, thus favouring cross-pollination; however, some self-pollination

is bound to take place. The switch from genes, for the suppression of femaleness (giving male) on the lower nodes, to genes for the suppression of maleness (giving female) above this zone, appears to be related either to differences in the ontogeny of the shoot or to differences in a chemical/hormonal influence at the transition point. For the influence of the environment on the floral sex and sex change in plants see Freeman et al (1980, 1981).

Type 2. In this clone most nodes have inflorescences containing mixed male and female flowers except the topmost ones which are mainly female. A small proportion of hermaphrodite and abnormal sterile hermaphrodite flowers also occur in the inflorescences.

Type 3. In this clone, the plant appears at first sight to be a normal female, but on closer inspection, male flower are seen to be concentrated at the tips of the inflorescence branches, with hermaphrodite and abnormal sterile hermaphrodite flowers inbetween.

250

HERMAPHRODITE/BISEXUAL CLONES

In hermaphrodite individuals of Urtica dioica, the majority of the flowers have 4 functional explosive stamens, and a central fertile pistil containing an ovule, which is capped with a penicillate stigma. Hermaphrodite clones at a distance appear like females but are more yellow due to the presence of stamens. They can be found occasionally after careful searching but appear to be less frequent than monoecious types.

In pastures I have found hermaphrodite clones, adjacent to clones that were predominantly female with a few hermaphrodite flowers, and ones that had female, hermaphrodite or mixtures of both on different parts of the shoot. Results showed that the most abundant flowers were hermaphrodite with 4 stamens, whilst other

Urtica dioica stores massive amounts of starch and other food substances in rhizomes and roots during the winter. As a result of rapid growth in April-May, the meristems, developing leaves and buds which act as sinks for food substances translocated from the underground storage system. Hormones (cytokinins) which are root-born, and mediate the flow of photosynthate from leaves to various sinks control the root/shoot ratio in U. dioica. Different levels of nitrogen supply, and their effect on cytokinins, also bring about changes in the root/shoot ratio (Beck, 1996). In U. dioica, extensive herbivory has a negative effect on sexual reproduction, whilst only slight herbivory is compensated for. The production of greater stinging

Table 16.2, hermaphrodite type of Urtica dioica showing the % of different sexual types per quarter of a nodal inflorescence

Node number	F	F 1 M	F 2 M	F 3 M	Hermaphro-dite	Others	Totals per ¼ node
12	34	7	18	25	24	23	132
13	0	3	1	7	54	136	201
14	0	0	3	10	131	240	365
15	1	1	8	11	181	284	486
%excl.others	6.8	2.2	5.8	10.2	75.0		

hermaphrodite flowers had 3, 2, and 1 stamen in order of abundance, with some female flowers on lower nodes. The greatest number of flowers, however, could not be classified because they were too small (less than 0.5 mm) or abnormal. It could be that there is not sufficient space on the inflorescence for hermaphrodite flowers to develop which might also account for the reduction in the number of stamens. Sexual variation of abnormalities show flowers with filaments and anthers fused with the ovary wall, 2 fused carpels, and 6 stamens next to 6 equal tepals (Fig 16.5 and Table 16.2).

In some flowers the stamens are functional and explosive, whilst in others the stamens are small and non-functional and the pollen just falls out. The hermaphrodite flowers appeared to be of two types: (1) Male type hermaphrodite flowers, in which the pistil has a stigma, 4 equal tepals, but in which the flowers fall off after staminal explosion, indicating that the pistil is sterile. (2) Normal hermaphrodite flowers, which have 2 small and 2 large tepals and a persistent carpel. Flowers with triquetrous ovaries were also found.

There is a need to quantify the extent of monoecious, hermaphrodite and dioecious clones in different areas, and to ascertain the significance of the various types in nettle reproduction. There is a need to determine the genetic systems that are operational and their interaction with the internal and external environment, along the lines of studies carried out on Hemp (*Cannabis sativa*), see chapter 16.

ACTORS AFFECTING THE REPRODUCTIVE EFFORT IN URTICA DIOICA

trichome densities leads to less biomass allocation to sexual reproduction in females. Further experiments also showed that density and fertiliser treatment also affect inflorescence dry mass significantly (Mutikainen, et al, 1994, 1995). Šrůtek (1995) studying the growth responses of U. dioica to nutrient supply, found that high nutrient supply increased the allocation of biomass to reproductive organs and to vegetative organs. Stresses of various kinds lead to less allocation of photosynthate to seeds; for example, shade dramatically reduces seed production in U. dioica, compared to that of open situations (Wheeler, 1982, chapter 14). The growing inflorescences and developing seeds cause them to become strong sinks for photosynthate from leaves. The female perianth and green ovary can also carry out photosynthesis and pass over photosynthate to the seeds (Maun, 1974). Later in the year, towards the end of seed production, photosynthate is translocated to the underground sinks such as the developing stolons, and stored in the rhizomes and roots for next year's growth.

SEED PRODUCTION, DISPERSAL AND SPREAD IN URTICA DIOICA

Urtica dioica is an opportunist, growth competitor plant and has been spread from its native northern temperate zone to most countries throughout the world which it has successfully colonised to become a sub-cosmopolitan plant, but it cannot grow in the tropics. The spread has been aided by man distributing contaminated seed and nettle seed used for medicinal purposes, etc. (chapter 5, 14).

Prior to the 19th century, in Britain its distribution has been patchy and related to its natural habitat of fen carr, fertile woodland areas and local fertile areas resulting from dung and urine from cattle or wild animals and areas disturbed by man or animals. The use of fertilisers in the mid-19th century and modern farming techniques has favoured its spread (chapter 15).

A large proportion of the British flora is now alien species spread by man and some with great powers of vegetative reproduction have spread entirely by this method, e.g. *Elodea canadensis* and *Reynoultria japonica* (Japanese knotweed). The latter plant was introduced in 1886 as a female plant and has now spread throughout Britain and established large clones. It is likely that much of the spread on U. dioica has been by vegetative means but the amount must largely be guesswork.

In line with other weed spread U. dioica has a high reproductive capacity and produces from a single shoot 20-40,000 seeds. With a density of 100-200 shoots per m2 it follows that small clones are producing millions of seeds whilst in large clones the number must be billions. It must however be kept in mind that half of the clones are unproductive males.

The fruits are mainly dispersed by the wind which is aided by the persistent perianth. Verkaar, et al, (1983) point out that in chalk grassland species wind is the most important factor in dispersal in seeds with no specialised structures (barochorous). The experimenter's field observations for the dispersal of short lived species in Dutch chalk grasslands were in agreement with a model and indicated limited dispersal of seeds (0.3-3.5 m). The distance of dispersal depends on the height of shoots, which vary from 1-3 m (mean 1.5 m). Wheeler showed, from seed bank evidence, that most seed falls within large clones and the seed bank declines rapidly one metre or more from the clone. In the event of destruction of the clone, wind dispersed seed (plus that of the seed bank) in the immediate vicinity will provide the opportunity for seedling establishment when conditions once more become favourable.

A large number of habitats of U. dioica are in the vicinity of water (chapter 14) and most gravel banks along side streams and rivers in Devon are colonised by the nettle and other pioneer species. The perianth around the fruit should take some time to wet, delaying sinking and thus aiding dispersal.

In a study of the Luznice river, Cechoslovakia, Šrutek (1993) states that the high seed production and seed spreading by regular floods enables Urtica dioica to occupy most places in the abandoned non-managed parts of the flood plain.

It has been found that animals such as cattle can ingest nettle seed stuck to grass and deer eat nettle seed masses for antler growth and lactation, whilst many birds also eat the seeds. The seeds will be dispersed in the dung which is high in nitrogen and phosphates thus giving the seedling ample opportunity to establish. In Devon the cattle are often allowed into woodland in the winter and I have found nettle clones within their dung areas. Heinitz ( ), in relation to the food of animals in Sweden, gives a large list of plants, including U. dioica, disseminated by cattle, the seeds being passed through them in their excreta; Salisbury (1961) mentions similar for cattle, horses, pigs and goats.

The basic work on seed dispersal is that of Ridley (1930), and he attributes the widespread distribution of U. dioica throughout the world to animal dispersal by animals, on fur, feathers of cloth. He spent some time walking through nettles at Kew Gardens and founf six single fruits and clusters on stalks adhering to his clothes. The achene is enclosed in a perianth of four lobes with non-stinging hairs on the outside. These hairs catch onto clothing and the fruit will eventually fall off and with drying release its achene.

It is a well known fact that the bare soil in the vicinity of rabbit burrows and badger setts is colonised by stinging nettle clones. Since these animals do not urinate or defaecate in the regions of their burrows it must be concluded that the seeds of U. dioica were carried there on the fur on the bodies or feet of these animals. In a similar way stinging nettles growing on walls and pollarded willows are likely to have been carried there by animals. Ridley studying an enclosed area at Kew under a tree explained the appearance of U. dioica as due to the excreta of birds, and the habits of some birds, e.g. hedge sparrows, magpies, etc., of eating nettle seeds which has already been mentioned. Urtica dioica has been found on cliffs under gull colonies, and in South Africa, Urtica has been found growing in areas of mixed gull and cormorant colonies (Gillham, in Perring, 1974).

A very good account of dispersal and distribution in the Urticales is given by Berg (1983). The majority of 'amentiferous' families are associated with the northern hemispheres and have dry diaspores (achenes) which are often wind dispersed. The production of small seeds (microspermy) is related to the herbaceous habit, and the ability to grow more or less in the open, as pioneer plants. Autochory (i.e. self dispersal) is found in some urticaceous genera (*Elatostema* and *Pilea*), the achenes being ejected by inflexed staminoids, and since this is closely related to the mechanism of male explosive pollen release, will be considered next.

Establishment of the nettle from seed is a rare event with its limited food reserves but is aided by its initial high relative growth rate. On establishment its rapid and tall growth can shade out competitor plants whilst its production of a vast number of underground rhizomes and lateral stolons mean that most of its success is due to purely vegetative means.

EXPLOSIVE FRUIT DISPERSAL IN THE URTICACEAE (PILEA AND ELATOSTEMMA)

This type of fruit dispersal occurs in all genera of the Elatostemeae and is mentioned here because of its relationship to the explosive pollen liberation found in the Urticaceae. In *Elatostemma*, *Lecanthus*, and *Pilea*, the staminodes (the filament part only of previously functional stamens) have inflexed filaments that eject ripe fruit from the flower. The first studies, dealing with the morphology, were those of Goebel (1915) which were followed later by the anatomical and physiological studies of Mosebach (1932). In *Pilea stipulosa* the broad fleshy staminodia are bent inwardly under the fruit just like functional stamens (Fig 16.6). During ripening there is an increase in turgor pressure in the cells which attempts to straighten the staminode. Once a critical value is reached, the force on the fruit is sufficient to eject it, resulting in the straightening of the staminodes. The top part of the staminode is stuck to the fruit and the inward bending is caused by one-sided (i.e. the outer side) growth during development. The epidermis of the staminode consists of long cells on the outer surface and small cells on the inside. Further in centrally, there are giant cells (560µ) which run alongside strands of vascular tissue.

The tension appears to be developed in the giant cells, which in the reflexed state are extremely deformed. In a similar way to the filaments of explosive stamens the cells show high elastic extensibility. Again the explosion is spontaneous and not due to a stimulus. Ether causes explosion by dissolving the adhesive that sticks the filaments to the fruit. It would be interesting to apply modern techniques, to compare the changes in the staminodes on fruit liberation, with those taking place in filaments on explosive discharge of pollen. Berg (1989) considers that this method of fruit release may have originated from ancestors that had hermaphrodite flowers.

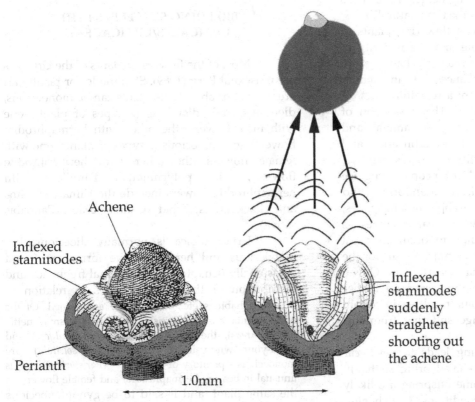

Achene

Inflexed staminodes

Perianth

Inflexed staminodes suddenly straighten shooting out the achene

1.0mm

Fig 16.6 Explosive fruit liberation in Pilea stipulosa (after Goebel 1915).

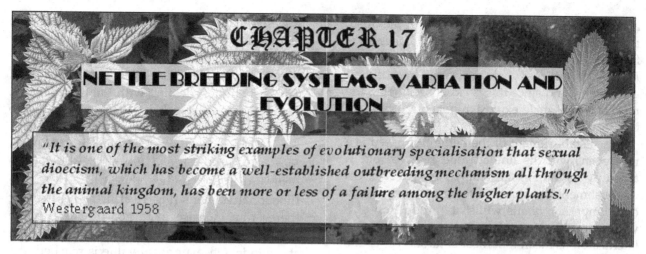

"It is one of the most striking examples of evolutionary specialisation that sexual dioecism, which has become a well-established outbreeding mechanism all through the animal kingdom, has been more or less of a failure among the higher plants."
Westergaard 1958

BREEDING SYSTEMS

INTRODUCTION

Breeding systems in plants have been dealt with extensively in two recent books, 'The Natural History of Pollination' (Proctor, Yeo and Lack, 1996), and 'Plant Breeding Systems' (Richards, 1997). Although a lot is known about breeding systems much still remains to be uncovered, such as, the significance of dioecy in plants. The latter subject alone includes many topics where field studies and simple breeding experiments with common plants like the stinging nettle, are likely to be particularly rewarding for the keen naturalist.

Approximately 80% of flowering plants of the world are hermaphrodite and the majority of these have evolved elaborate mechanisms to prevent or lessen the chances of inbreeding resulting from self-pollination; a remaining 10% of the world's flora is dioecious. The possession of separate sexes, in the majority of animal and dioecious plants, results in cross-fertilisation and cross-pollination/cross fertilisation respectively, and ensures out-breeding. Most people recognise that in humans, inbreeding leads to uniformity and the accumulation of undesirable mutant genes, which is why breeding with near relatives is discouraged. Inbreeding tends to occur in royal families, and it is thought that a mutant gene for the blood disorder haemophilia occurred in Queen Victoria and was subsequently passed on to her descendants via her daughters, resulting in certain male members of the lineage suffering from this disease.

In plants out-breeding leads to new *gene combinations* and variation in the offspring, so that in a changing environment, some offspring are likely to be adapted to the new conditions. The changes being wrought on Earth by mankind, as a result of the energy derived from fossil fuels, have enabled intensive agriculture, produced extensive pollution and climatic changes; for plants to survive these rapid changes, genetic variability of offspring which results from cross-breeding is vital. Variation is also needed to ensure plant survival in the constant fight against the continually evolving disease organisms and predators such as fungi, bacteria, viruses and herbivores respectively. Plants containing beneficial *mutations*, resulting from sexual reproduction, that give an advantage in the changing environment will be selected, whilst plants with detrimental mutations will die, leading to changes which result in further evolution.

BREEDING SYSTEMS IN THE URTICALES/URTICACEAE

Most of the flowers of plants of the Urticales are unisexual Berg (1989). Staminodes or pistillodes are present or absent; the plants can be monoecious, dioecious, androdioecious (2 types of plants, one with male flowers, the other with hermaphrodite flowers), gynodioecious (2 types of plants, one with female flowers, the other with hermaphrodite flowers), or polygamous. Families with hermaphrodite flowers include the Ulmaceae (elms and hackberries), and Cannabaceae (Cannabis sativa).

Urtica dioica is normally dioecious, but monoecious and hermaphrodite forms are found occasionally (Chapter 16). The actual frequency and distribution of these sexual types in relation to different habitats etc., needs to be ascertained. Of the other members of the British Urticaceae the small nettle (*Urtica urens*), the roman nettle (*Urtica pilulifera*) and mind-your-own-business ** (*Soleirolia soleirolii*) are monoecious - pellitory-of-the-wall ** (*Parietaria judaica*) is unusual in bearing hermaphrodite and female flowers on the same plant, and is said to be gynomonoecious (for these see later and ** the appendix p 266-83).

DIOECY IN THE URTICALES AND OTHER PLANTS - DISTRIBUTION

The comment of Westergaard is probably related to the assumptions that the low estimates of the incidence of dioecy at that time were true, and that since the population consists of 50% females there is a reduction in seed production. Dioecy has received much attention recently, due to advances in the area of plant breeding and ecological studies, as well as it being the main breeding system in animals.

Kay and Stevens (1986) reviewed the

Berg (1978) describes the five genera of the **Cecropiaceae** as being strictly dioecious. The **Cannabaceae**, including the hemp and hops, are dioecious.

ORIGIN

Floral anatomical studies by Bechtel (1921) showed that flowers in the Urticales were derived from hermaphrodite flowers made up of two whorls of perianth parts, at least 2 whorls of stamens and a pistil formed of 2 or more carpels forming a bilocular ovary and several carpels. The original

---

BOX 17.1. BRITISH DIOECIOUS SPECIES, TOGETHER WITH A FEW EXAMPLES FROM EACH.

Caryophyllaceae, Red campion (*Silene dioica*), **Aquifoliaceae**, Holly (*Ilex aquifolium*), **Rhamnaceae**, Buckthorn (*Rhamnus catharticus*), **Rosaceae**, Cloudberry (*Rubus chamaemorus*), **Crassulaceae**, Roseroot (*Sedum rosea*), **Grossulariaceae**, Mountain currant (*Ribes alpinum*), **Eleagnaceae**, Sea buckthorn (*Hippophae rhamnoides*), **Loranthaceae** Mistletoe (*Viscum album*), **Apiaceae**, Honewort (*Trinia glauca*), **Cucurbitaceae**, White bryony (*Bryonia dioica*), **Euphorbiaceae**, Dog's mercury (*Mercurialis perennis*), **Polygonaceae**, Common sorrel (*Rumex acetosa*), **Urticaceae**, Stinging nettle (*Urtica dioica*), **Myricaceae**, Bog-myrtle (*Myrica gale*), **Salicaceae**, Black-poplar (*Populus nigra*), Goat Willow (*Salix caprea*), **Empetraceae**, Crowberry (*Empetrum nigrum*), **Oleaceae**, Ash (*Fraxinus excelsior*), **Valerianaceae**, Marsh valerian (*Valeriana dioica*), **Asteraceae**, Butterbur (*Petasites hybridus*), **Hydrocharitacea**, Frogbit (*Hydrocharis morsus-ranae*), **Najadaceae**, Holly-leaved Naiad (*Najas marina*), **Liliaceae**, Butcher's-broom (*Ruscus aculeatus*), **Dioscoraceae**, Black bryony (*Tamus communis*), and **Cyperaceae**, Dioecious sedge (*Carex dioica*).

---

frequency, distribution and reproductive biology of the dioecious species in the native flora of Britain and Ireland. In their analysis they state that hermaphrodite and monoecious individuals have been found in nearly all individuals examined, but particularly in *Potentilla fructicosa* (Shrubby cinquefoil) and Urtica dioica, with dioecious populations in parts of the range of species and monoecious or hermaphrodite populations in other parts of the range (see later). Of the 1377 species in the native angiosperm flora of the British Isles, 59 species are dioecious (Box 17.1).

Renner and Ricklefs (1995) scored all flowering plants of the world for the presence or absence of monoecy or dioecy. 7% of Angiosperm (flowering plants) genera contain at least some dioecious species, and about 6% of species (14,620 of 240,000) are dioecious. The greatest concentration of dioecious genera were found in Thorne's superorder, the **Malvanae** (including the orders *Malvales, Urticales, Rhamnales* and *Euphorbiales*) with most found in the families **Euphorbiaceae**, **Moraceae** and **Urticaceae**, the latter two containing 62% and 52%, respectively. Monoecious families have a parallel distribution to dioecious families.

hermaphrodite ancestors have evolved into dioecious species via intermediate forms such as gynodioecy and monoecy. These changes involve mutant genes that produce male or female sterility. Evidence for the hermaphrodite ancestry in the Urticales is also found by the possession of pistillodes in male flowers and occasional staminodes in female flowers. Considering dioecious plants generally, because of their scattered distribution through many families (polyphyletic), it is generally believed that they are of recent origin and are evolutionary unstable. The dioecious condition is reversible or frequently becomes extinct.

Dioecy is at its highest on oceanic islands such as Hawaii (27.7%) and New Zealand (14.4%), Bawa (1981). Early in their evolutionary history these islands would have been largely bare and with a large number of available ecological niches to be filled, a situation favouring out-breeding plants capable of rapid evolution. There is some evidence to support the idea that islands would first be colonised by individual plants that were hermaphrodite and self-fertile in-breeders. Mutations producing unisexual flowers and favouring out-breeding would have been selected, as these plants would produce off-spring with a high level of variation, some of which would be capable of filling the large numbers of diverse niches.

ADVANTAGES AND DISADVANTAGES OF DIOECY.

The main disadvantage of dioecy is that only 50% or so of the plants are female which reduces seed production and therefore reproductive fitness. Hermaphrodites can achieve out-breeding by such mechanisms as self-incompatibility, or preventing self-pollination by having stamens and pistils arranged differently in space, or maturing at different points in time. It has been maintained that the main advantage of dioecy is that it is a complete out-breeding system, and therefore best suited to produce the variety of offspring for rapid evolution of the species. Other advantages would include no stigma clogging or ovule wastage as in hermaphrodites. In the wind and insect pollinated, dioecious species of the Urticales, the uncertainty of pollination has resulted in changes resulting in the following advantages: (1) a reduction of ovule number to one to cut down wastage, (2) reduction in the size of females resulting in an increase in number of females on the inflorescences, (3) the absence of stamens in female flowers reduces the obstacles removing pollen, (4) seed production of individual female plants is greater than that of individual female hermaphrodite plants.

DIOECY IN RELATION TO TROPICAL FOREST TREES

Berg (1977, 1983 and 1989) and Friis (1989) have produced some excellent articles on the systematics, seed types and dispersal in the Urticales, but the fact remains that very little is known about the ecology of the large number of dioecious species which inhabit tropical rainforest areas. Renewed interest in dioecious plants has resulted from studies of dioecy in tropical forest trees, Bawa (1975, 1980 and 1981). Dioecy may have originated in relation to selection pressures such as adverse or changing habitats, conditions that favour an out-breeding system; however, Bawa maintains that other selective pressures are likely to be involved, such as resources to male and female functions, sexual selection, seed dispersal, pollination and predation.

Analysis of the dioecious species in the floras of 12 areas showed a high incidence in tropical forests and a figure of 9% dioecious species for tropical forest in Panama could be representative of other tropical forests. In relation to growth form, trees in tropical areas have an incidence of 22% dioecious species and up to 38% individuals in forest areas were found. Bawa (1980) has argued that dioecious trees that produce large seeds, the food resources of which enable the resulting seedlings to survive long periods in low light levels on the forest floor until a gap opens in the canopy are more likely to selected. The production of large seeds enclosed in fleshy edible fruit masses that are attractively coloured are more likely to be eaten and dispersed by birds, bats and monkeys in their droppings. The separate females found in dioecious plants should enable heavy investment of resources in the production of fleshy fruits as they are freed from having to use resources for stamen production. Bawa obtained a good correlation between dioecy and animal dispersal of seeds in tropical forests of Costa Rica. As a result of the lack of wind in tropical forests, principally animals carry out pollination of plants in these areas. Flowers in dioecious plants were found to be small and white, yellow or pale green and grouped into conspicuous masses to attract to animals/insects. As rewards for insects, nectar is produced by females, and nectar and sticky pollen is available from males. Bawa found that in dioecious trees in the Costa Rica dry deciduous forest, 'trap-lining' solitary bees mainly carry out pollination of dioecious trees. Because of the large distances between trees of the same species in tropical forests, pollination in dioecious species is going to be less than in self-compatible hermaphrodites; however, the progeny of the former are going to be of a superior quality.

SEX DETERMINATION IN PLANTS AND IN THE URTICALES

Sex determination in plants has been reviewed by Westergaard (1958) and by Richards (1997). In a similar way to animals, in plants sex is determined by a pair of sex chromosomes, and in most cases, females contain two similar chromosomes denoted XX (homogametic sex) and the males two dissimilar chromosomes denoted XY (heterogametic sex). All eggs produced by females contain an X chromosome whilst male gametes contain either an X or a Y chromosome and these occur in a 50:50 ratio, so that theoretically, on fertilisation females (XX) and males (XY) are produced in equal numbers. The X chromosome carries *recessive* male sterility genes, and the Y chromosome carries *dominant* female sterility genes. Females (XX) have at least two male sterility genes which suppress maleness, whilst males (XY), although they posses a male sterility gene on the X chromosome, this is counteracted by a dominant female sterility gene carried on the Y chromosome.

In hemp (*Cannabis sativa*), hop (*Humulus lupulus*) and stinging nettle (*Urtica dioica*) the heterogametic sex is the male. Sex in plants is determined also by a quantitative system involving a balance between esc-deciding genes on the sex chromosomes interacting with sex genes on the other chromosomes (autosomes).

Sex expression, in some species of plants, is more easily affected by the environment than in most animals. This is particularly true in the case of *Cannabis sativa*, which is one of the few plants where in the vegetative state, male plants, can be distinguished from female plants. Wild hemp is dioecious; however, since males mature before females, for fibre production monoecious plants or 'uniformly ripening' varieties have been bred. Sex changes in diecious types of hemp have been achieved by treatment with hormones (auxins, gibberellins, and cytokinins), carbon monoxide, high boron, manure, photoperiod (long of short day) and trauma such as the removal of parts of the plant, Freeman et al (1980). Sex in *Humulus lupulus* can also be altered by day length and temperature. There is a need for similar experiments to be carried out on Urtica dioica.

SECONDARY SEXUAL CHARACTERISTICS IN URTICA DIOICA

A good account of secondary sexual characteristics in plants is found in Richards (1997). Reproductive differences affect flower size, number and reward (nectar and pollen): vegetative differences generally result from the heavier reproductive load in females and involve different patterns of growth, recourse allocation, timing or longevity. These differences may be genetically or environmentally determined, see also Lloyd and Webb, (1977).

VEGETATIVE

With a few exceptions, e.g. hemp, the differences between the vegetative characteristics of males and females of dioecious plants are so small that recognition of the sexes is not possible at this stage (Lloyd and Webb, 1977). This applies to Urtica dioica where any small sexual differences at this stage have to be considered against the great variability both within and between clones of this plant. Pollard and Briggs *(1982) and Wheeler †(1981) grew rhizome portions from various clones of U. dioica under field conditions for the measurement of genetic differences. In relation to sexual differences, females were significantly larger than males in the following respects: height (0.04,* 0.001†), internode length (0.001,* 0.05†), diameter of base of the stem, (0.05†), width and length of leaf at node 13 (at the level of the lower part of the inflorescence (0.001†); the specific leaf area was less than in males, i.e. females had thicker leaves. Sruteck (1995) analysing the growth of plants from seed, found that, statistically, plant height and branching is not affected by sex. For phenological differences see Chapter 16.

Mutikainen, et al, (1994) investigated sexual differences in U. dioica in relation to simulated herbivory. In females, both leaf clipping and apex damage increased branching. In males, apex damage, branching was decreased. Stinging trichome density on new leaves (e. g. these emerged after herbivore damage) of females was higher than in males, which could be explained by the increased demand for defence in females due to their higher and longer allocation to reproduction.

There is a need to study differences in density between male and female shoots in isolation and competition with one another, and in relation to different habitat areas.

SEXUAL DIFFERENCES

I must admit this is one area I neglected, and no data as far as I know is available on the sexual differences in relation to flower size, number and rewards. From my drawings of male and female flowers (Chapter 16) I have found that the average lens-shaped female flowers are about 0.5 mm at the time of stigma protrusion whereas male flowers at anthesis are 2-3 mm in diameter. The latter reflects the large anther size and pollen load necessary in this out-breeding and wind-pollinated plant.

GENDER RATIOS IN URTICA DIOICA

Little information is available on the ratios of male and female populations of the stinging nettle. In his preliminary studies of U. dioica in relation to sampling of insects on nettles (e.g. different insects feed preferentially on different sexes) Davis (1973) mapped out, using $0.25m^2$ quadrats, the density of male and female shoots in a large stinging nettle bed 3 x 2.5 m at Holm Fen. There was clearly an intimate mix of both sexes in the patch with an over proportion of male to female stems of 1: 1.1. The patchy nature reflected the growth centres for individual plants. The only other study is a M.Sc. study, Kitchingham (1979) that was unobtainable, but was reported in Kay and Stevens (1986). It was found that female shoots predominated in 11 populations of Urtica dioica sampled in southern Britain. In the overall total of 3627 shoots it was found that female shoots predominated and samples varied from 53.5% female (n=114, n.s.) to 89.9% females (n=287), with 68.5% being the mean. More studies are needed to confirm the female predominance ratio in U. dioica. Different clones/genets of U. dioica can often be distinguished in the vegetative state by their appearance. In the reproductive, there are differences in the inflorescences, for example in males the colour varies from light crimson to yellow-green and loose to compact inflorescences, and in females, from pink to white stigmas and compact to more lax pendulous inflorescence branches. Richards (1997) states that the gender ratio of genets (clones) in plants will be the accidental by-product of male and female competition and depends on: - (1) Competition between X and Y containing pollen grains, (2) differential survival of male and female genets at the establishment stage, (3) the efficiency of pollen flow from male to female flowers.

ECOTYPES/PHYSIOLOGICAL RACES/GENCOLOGICAL DIFFERENTIATION IN RELATION TO URTICA DIOICA.

NTRODUCTION

The stinging nettle is a plant that is found in a wide variety of habitats (Chapter 14). When U. dioica is collected from its various habitats, the plants vary greatly in their morphological and anatomical structure, and many of these varieties have been named by taxonomists/systematists. These differences, together with the physiological differences they produce, enable them to survive in habitats with different edaphic (soil), climatic and biotic (animals and plants) factors. The question remains 'To what extent are these observed differences in the plants (phenotypes) due to modifications in relation to the environment, or the possession of genes (genotype), selected at the seedling stage, that enable their survival in the different habitats?' The appearance of an individual (Phenotype) is determined by its genes (Genotype) interacting with the environment, (i.e. Phenotype = Genotype X Environment).

Many plants have genotypes that are hardly affected by the environment, whereas others like the stinging nettle have genotypes that allow great modification (plasticity) in relation to environmental conditions. At the beginning of this century, no doubt stimulated by evolution and such areas as Darwin's finches, botanists found that when plants of the same species from widely different habitats are grown under uniform conditions in a 'standard' garden soil, the differences they originally exhibited either disappear or remain. In the former case it is apparent that the original differences must have been produced by the different environments that they were found in (as a result of a genetical system that allows plastic changes in relation to the environment), whereas in the latter, these differences must be due to inherited genes.

By using this garden technique on species of plants that grow in a wide range of habitats involving differences in climate, it was found that many species had become adapted to differences in climate as a result of changes in their genotype that produce distinct climatic races or ecotypes. The classical case is the study of the comparative physiological ecology of arctic and alpine populations of Oxyria digyna, Mooney and Billings (1961) that showed the existence of distinct climatic races/ecotypes in this species. It was found later that ecotypes/physiological races could exist over much smaller distances when selection pressures are high, as in the vicinity of waste tips containing toxic metals, Bradshaw (1952d) and Mc Neily (1968). Turesson (1936) defined the ecotype as genetically distinct forms, each confined to a different habitat, these distinct habitats having originated 'through the sorting and controlling effects of the habitat factors upon the heterogeneous species-population.'

DO DIFFERENT ECOTYPES OF URTICA DIOICA EXIST IN RELATION TO WOODLAND AND PASTURELAND HABITATS?

Ecotypes have been found in Solidago vigaurea from exposed and shaded habitats, Björkman and Holmgren (1963, 1966), and since then in a wide variety of plants. The morphological differences between populations of Urtica dioica growing under pastureland and woodland conditions have been shown by shading experiments in this species to be largely due to the different levels of light operating in the two habitats (Chapter 15). Wheeler (1981) collected rhizome and seed from woodland and pastureland clones of U. dioica growing within a 6 square mile area of floodplain and wooded hillsides alongside the River Taw, Devon, England. These clones were then grown under standard greenhouse/environmental chamber/garden conditions, in replicated and randomly arranged experiments, to ascertain whether there was any evidence for the existence of ecotypes/physiological races in U. dioica, in relation to the two habitats. The growth of clones were tested in relation to: (1) light (67%, 45%, 25%, 8% and full sunlight), (2) standard garden conditions, (3) chlorophyll content of leaves, (4) different mineral combination, nitrogen, phosphorus and calcium, (5) germination, (6) differential shading. Although statistically differences were found in the growth between different woodland and pastureland clones (interspecific), and between different woodland or different pastureland clones (intraspecific), there were no overall differences between *all* woodland and *all* pastureland clones in relation to the factors tested.

The study indicated that the differences observed between woodland and pastureland clones of U. dioica in their natural habitats are due to a genetic system that allows plastic growth change in morphology and anatomy (many of which bring about changes in the photosynthetic system), that enable U. dioica to grow with different degrees of success in the two habitats. This study showed that there was no evidence for the existence of ecotypes in woodland and pastureland clones of U. dioica over a relatively small area. This does not preclude the existence of ecotypes in U. dioica in relation to other habitats, or different soils, climatic or biotic factors, or over more widely separated areas, shown by the following study.

THE 'STINGLESS' ECOTYPE OF WICKEN FEN

A preliminary study, Pollard and Briggs (1982), was made of the intraspecific variation in U. dioica from clones collected from various habitats (fen, woodland, grazed and ruderal). Rhizome material (30 cm long) from each clone was divided into six, potted up and the pots sunk into soil in two plots in randomised blocks, one in the open and the other shaded (for the shading results see Chapter 15). Populations (defined as topdemes, a term referring to local populations) differed significantly in stinging hairs, leaf shape and height. The Wicken population was significantly different from the rest of the populations in relation to stinging hairs and leaf shape. Whereas all other populations increased in hairiness when moved from shade to the open, the Wicken Fen population remained stinging in both treatments. The Wicken Fen population also had significantly later flowering and was taller with narrower leaves.

As a continuance of their genecological studies of U. dioica, Pollard and Briggs (1984), considered the patterns of variation of the stingless variant population of U. dioica at Wicken Fen. This was accomplished by taking samples of rhizome and seed from 24 nettle clones in a line (transect) across the fen, and then growing the parents (rhizome) and progeny (seed) under garden conditions. The parents and progeny were scored in relation to the characteristics of the variant stingless form. The results, analysis and discussion are complex but extremely interesting. The variant form was confined to the centre of the fen whilst the ordinary type was at the two ends. Gene flow by pollen and seed could not be ruled out, and in the absence of evidence for the continued selection of this variant, its future is debatable. The frontispiece to this chapter alludes to a well known fact, which this book has tried to emphasise, that the existence of a nettle clone can very often be traced back to 'man's' activities in the past, in providing this opportunist plant the ideal conditions for its establishment by seed, or by rhizome when soil is disturbed.

The author's main conclusions are that: (1) seed and movement of pollen allow significant gene flow into the sedge fen, (2) this pollen flow has significant within-population effects that act to even out the variability in the adult generation, (3) the patterns of variability in the adults do not suggest that the range of variability in the seed population is being limited by natural selection, (4) in the case of this long-lived perennial selection is more likely to be related to historical factors rather than current ones. This fen nettle is considered next under varieties, and it relation to herbivore has already been considered (Chapter 8).

VARIATION IN URTICA DIOICA

The general morphology of a typical plant of Urtica dioica is illustrated in Chapter 2. Considering shoots from one nettle plant/clone, various structures of the stem vary as the shoot develops and becomes older, i.e. during its ontogeny. Fig 2.1, show that the leaves change in shape, size, hair type and density, margin type, etc., according to their age, a condition called heterophylly. Generally the lower part of the stem has high densities of stinging hairs and less stinging trichomes, whereas this is reversed on the upper reproductive part of the stem. It is important first to become familiar with the appearance/morphology/structure, at different stages in ontogeny, of a 'typical' plant of U. dioica. Whole shoots from a clone should be pressed at different times of the year to study variation with time. Next, plants should be collected from a wide variety of habitats which differ in climate, soil and biotic factors including man-made, to provide a wide range of environmental/non-inheritable variation. Plant from various habitats can also be grown under standard garden conditions to record genetic/inheritable variation (Chapters 15 and 16).

Weddell (1854) in his monograph on the Urticaceae, gives 14 varieties of U. dioica and many of these are included, together with others, in Ascherson and Graebner's (1908-1918) Central European Flora, and these are now reviewed. (Unfortunately no recent work on the varieties and species of the Urticeae has been published).

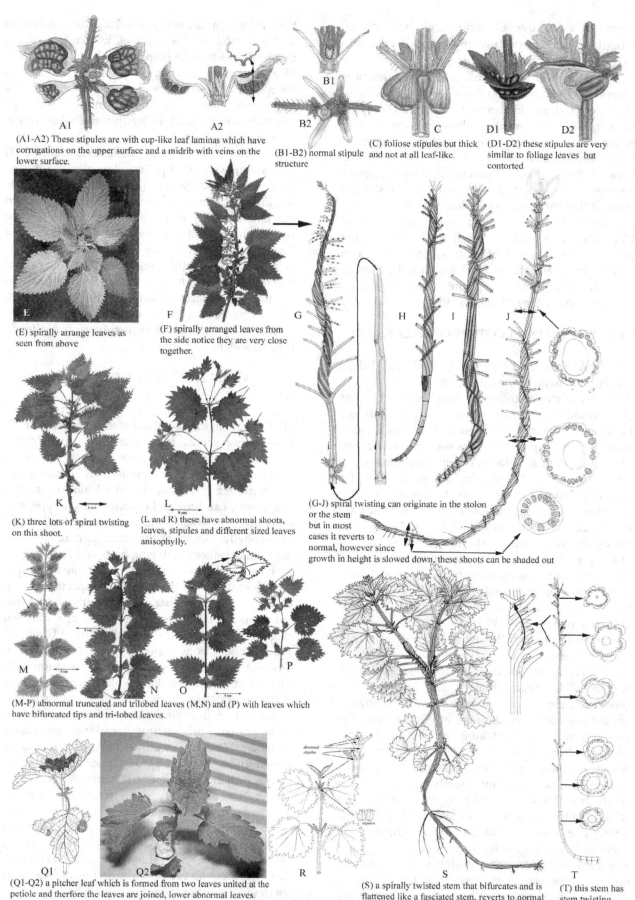

(A1-A2) These stipules are with cup-like leaf laminas which have corrugations on the upper surface and a midrib with veins on the lower surface.

(B1-B2) normal stipule structure

(C) foliose stipules but thick and not at all leaf-like.

(D1-D2) these stipules are very similar to foliage leaves but contorted

(E) spirally arrange leaves as seen from above

(F) spirally arranged leaves from the side notice they are very close together.

(G-J) spiral twisting can originate in the stolon or the stem but in most cases it reverts to normal, however since growth in height is slowed down, these shoots can be shaded out

(K) three lots of spiral twisting on this shoot.

(L and R) these have abnormal shoots, leaves, stipules and different sized leaves anisophylly.

(M-P) abnormal truncated and trilobed leaves (M,N) and (P) with leaves which have bifurcated tips and tri-lobed leaves.

(Q1-Q2) a pitcher leaf which is formed from two leaves united at the petiole and therfore the leaves are joined, lower abnormal leaves.

(S) a spirally twisted stem that bifurcates and is flattened like a fasciated stem, reverts to normal

(T) this stem has stem twisting.

FIG 17.1 VEGETATIVE VARIATION, SPIRAL TWISTING, FASCIATION , PITCHER AND LEAF ABNORMALITIES IN URTICA DIOICA

260

The British material (Natural History Museum, London), of varieties of U. dioica, contains the following: microphylla, hispida, umbrosa, subinermis and angustifolia. It is time for a more serious collection of British and European material of U. dioica to categorise the variations more clearly in relation to the plant's characteristics, to include plants from habitats, climates, soils and biotic factors, and to grow portions of the clones under garden conditions.

Ascherson and Graebner (1908-1918) describe a possible hybrid U. urens x U dioica. Plant 1-1.2 m high, sparsely covered in stinging hairs, much branched. Leaves thin (7 cm long x 3 cm wide) roughly notched-serrated, elliptic-ovoid-rounded. Flower clumps only female, dense and di-based, spiked, 1.5 cm long, stalk 3 cm.

BOX 17.2. EUROPEAN VARIETIES OF URTICA DIOICA, AFTER ASCHERSON AND GRAEBNER (1908-1918)

U. dioica var. **kioviensis** (Wedd. 1857) has been raised to specific level. This plant is characterised by a creeping rootstock, i.e. the stalk is thick, soft and limp, mostly lying low down and rooting, therefore giving the plant a scattered creeping habit. Inflorescences are loose, the lower ones staminate and the upper pistillate. The stipules are large, the lower free and the upper united: Wet osier beds and ravines. Varieties of kioviensis in northern areas include **radicans**, which has broad, thin and limp leaves (Hungary), and **pilosa**, where particularly the young leaves are densely grey-haired. The latter is found on the moors and reed banks of rivers and lakes in N. E. Germany; in places where mowing several times of the year, causing the limp low-lying stalks of the plant to cover large areas.

Several monoecious varieties occur, (1) **monoeca** in which the plants are mostly large and firm with the lower inflorescence nodes mostly female and upper ones usually male and female (rarely hermaphrodite), (2) **androgyna**, lower flower clumps male, middle mixed, and upper female (lower Austria and Galicia), (3) **mirabilis**, stem dainty (up to 85 cm) covered in bristles, higher up more densely-haired, with sparse stinging hairs; leaves medium sized; flower clumps partly female and partly hermaphrodite – the latter with a fruit nodule (Galicia). Monoecious varieties are occasional and widespread (Chapter 14).

Dioecious plants with leaves smaller than typical, on small plants, have been split into four varieties. The main variety is **microphylla**, small plants with a woody base and mostly with branches; leaves mostly $\frac{1}{2}$ - $\frac{1}{3}$ a long as typical, lanceate with reduced cordate base. Found on slopes, sunny hills, scree or on rocks. Mainly found in the south-east areas of Europe. The plant remains the same when grown in a garden area. Other similar varieties without such uniform reduction of leaves are, (1) **montana**, 25-30 cm high; branches at the base; leaves on the lower branches are very small, rounded at the base, egg-shaped and tapered – rocks and walls in Transylvania, (2) **parvifolia**, 30-35 cm high; branched at the base; stalk not branched; leaves up to 6 cm long, (3) **Czarnohoiensis**, to 45 cm high; scarcely bristly and very sparse stinging hairs; leaves 47-7 cm long and rather broad, uppermost narrower, more deeply incised with serrations/dentations rather normal (Galicia about 1, 700 m).

There are two varieties of dioecious plants with medium to long leaves and covered with dense grey hairs. Galeopsifolia is so densely covered in hairs it is like a felt; leaves egg-shaped to lanceolate, hairy on the upper-side but felt-like below; almost without stinging hairs; flower clumps spicate with felt-like hairy stalks (seed later, Fen or 'Stingless' Nettle). U. dioica var. **pubescens** is raised to specific level (Komarov, 1970) Monoecious perennial; stem, 30-100 cm, with a dense woolly coating of simple hairs interspersed with numerous stinging hairs; the lower surfaces of leaves and petioles densely woolly-pubescent; inflorescence and perianth densely woolly. Coppices, riverside deciduous woods and weed infested places: Balkan Peninsula, southern Russia, Caucasus and Asia Minor.

Urtica dioica is largely un-branched when growing in a clump but a bush-like variety has been named **ramosissima**; plant big and strong, 1.5-2.0 m; the stem has a woody base and is very branched giving it a shrub-like appearance. (This is a characteristic of individual plants when they first establish on bare ground).

Many nettle varieties are named after the characteristics of their leaves. **Duplicati-serrata**; the cordate leaves are doubly serrated with the leaves and stalk with an abundance of stinging hairs. **Trilobescens**; some of the middle teeth of the leaf have dentations with side dentations making them three lobed; found in alder swamps and in humid shady places. (This is also characteristic of the leaves of nettle plants in the spring). **Macrodonta**; the individual dentations are strongly predominant or in abundance. **Lamiifolia**; plant large; lowest leaves kidney-shaped, middle cordate but long and tapered, roughly cut in by serrations with bristly hairs on the veins; pastures and mountains 2000 m, after mowing. (This is characteristic of young plants). **Curvidens**; leaves barer, very long tapered with the serrated-dentated teeth curved forwards. **Xiphodon**; the end tooth of the leaf is considerably lengthened; Asia and similar forms are found in Europe.

Forms with large leaves. **Carpatica**; plant 1, 5 dm (?m) tall; leaves 20 cm long by 12 cm broad, lower ones cordate; probably all areas; not very densely grouped stinging hairs. **Sarmatica**; plant large and firm; leaves cordate, 15 cm long X 10 cm wide, upper ones cordate, elongated, but smaller up to 4 cm broad; roughly broadly serrated (up to 11 mm); more or less airy veins; Galicia.

Forms with medium to large leaves. **Hispida**; dark green and greatly covered in stinging hairs; leaves heart –shaped – egg-shaped – lance-shaped, with short points; southern areas Mediterranean and east Asia up to 1,500 m. Horrida; the stem leaves and flower perianths covered in rough bristles (stinging hairs?). Hispidula; male plant with light coloured whitish inflorescences; female plant dark-green with blackish inflorescences in fruit (a doubtful plant). Typica; plant densely covered with short (stinging?) hairs in-between which are non-stinging hairs; this is the most frequent form. Glabrata; stalk and leaves almost bare except for sparse stinging hairs; in southern and south east Europe, up to the Himalayas.

Forms with narrower leaves. Angustifolia; leaves rounded at the base, long lanceolate to narrow egg-shaped – lanceolate; east Asia, Siberia, southern Russia but not rare in Europe. Subinermis; almost without stinging hairs which occur on occasions mostly in ones; these should not be confused with older plants where the hairs have been rubbed off. Umbrosa; the stalks and leaves are thinly haired and almost without stinging hairs; a form found frequently in forests.

Spicata; in this plant the leaves in the region of the inflorescence disappear; plant large; lower leaves large.

(A-A1) a nettle with a large fused leaf, abnormal branching and the original stem ends in a fasciated piece crowned by a row of small leaves.

(B-D) these shoots were found in a shaded area and are the late upturning of stolons with abnormal juvenile-type leaves.

(E) damage to the top of the shoot leads to truncation and 4 leaves in this example, shoots appear from petioles (stems)

(F-H) shoot tip damage (F) single leaf at the first node on the apical shoots, (G) three apical leaves with three shoots, (H) four apical leaves and four shoots due to cessation of growth in the top two internodes.

(I-J) single leaves produced on what look like petioles but in fact are shoots

(J-K) spirally twisted shoots and abnormal leaf arrangement

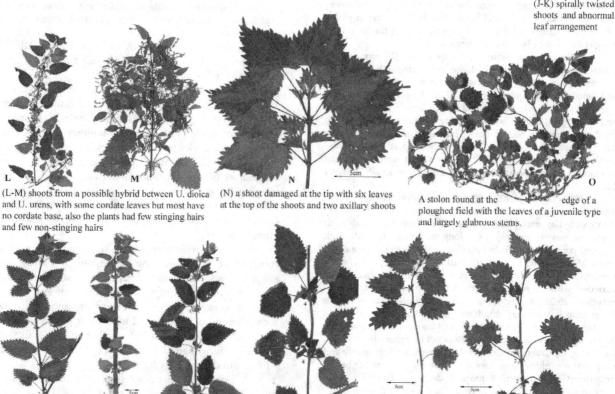

(L-M) shoots from a possible hybrid between U. dioica and U. urens, with some cordate leaves but most have no cordate base, also the plants had few stinging hairs and few non-stinging hairs

(N) a shoot damaged at the tip with six leaves at the top of the shoots and two axillary shoots

A stolon found at the   edge of a ploughed field with the leaves of a juvenile type and largely glabrous stems.

(P-R2) three leaved varieties with (R1-R2) having four leaves per node at the base.

(S-T) these have some alternate leaves and normal types also.

FIG 17.2 LEAF ABNORMALITIES, SHOOT DAMAGE, THREEE LEAVED TYPES AND HYBRIDS.

PLANT FREAKS/TERATOLOGY IN URTICA DIOICA

Teratology is the study of 'monstrous forms' (Greek, teras-atos = monster) which results from abnormalities of development and growth. These abnormal growth forms are particularly common in plants that exhibit a wide range of variation such as Urtica dioica. Various authors have sorted these forms into form, number and size, of; root, stem leaf and flower, or, due to pathogenic organisms, hormonal activity, genetic causes.

During the course of my fieldwork on the stinging nettle I have found many examples of growth abnormalities that have been drawn, photographed and pressed. Most of the growth variations are found in relation to sudden growth, i.e. most common in the spring, or re-growth after cutting. I have subsequently read about these growth forms of U. dioica in the German work, Pflanzen Teratology (Penzig, 1922); however, since they are only given a brief mention I will describe them in more detail here.

PATHOGENIC

The growth caused by the Nettle and Sedge Rust (Puccinia Caricis) and galls caused by the Nettle Gall Midge (Dasineura urticae) have been dealt with in Chapters 11 & 13 respectively.

STIPULES

Stipule varieties are shown in Fig 17.1. The stipules are generally small and inconspicuous (B1-B2). However, occasionally particularly on re-growth nettles they become enlarged. In (C) the enlarged stipules have a leaf-like character. In (A1-A2) the stipules are cup-shaped with the bottom leaf-like lamella thrown into corrugations; the underside has a mid-rib with side veins all covered with non-stinging hairs. In (D1-D2) the stipules are large and leaf-like, the lamella thrown into folds, and there are veins and a definite leaf apex. Pressed specimens; (1) a stem with enlarged stipules on node 7 & 8, at node 9 there is a small deformed leaf on one side and from this node upwards

the enlarged pair of stipules on each side are joined (connate) but with a bifid tip.

STEM SPIRALLING/TORSION

Spiral twisting of the stem, (Fig 17.1) occurs, almost entirely, in the spring. The stems are shorter than normal and look different from above due to the spiral arrangement of the leaves. These shoots can produce inflorescences but most will be shaded out. The spirals mainly pass in an anti-clockwise direction, but are sometimes clockwise. The leaves produced by these shoots are normal. The most likely places to find them are along the sides of pastures and steep hedge-banks alongside roads. The torsion can originate in the stolon (Fig 17.1, I-J) or in the lower part of the shoot (Fig 17.1, G, and H). In most cases intermediate stem portions are almost straight (Fig 17.1, I), in others several portions are straight (Fig 17.1, J). The spirals are generally tight lower down the stem but looser higher up. One of the most incredible spirals (Fig 17.1, G) shows the lower part of the stem has buds on the same side, on nodes 1 and 2, slightly staggered node 3 and the signs of a spiral node 4, but the main spiral is just over a single spiral pulled out along the whole length of the stem. Another impressive plant (Fig 17.1, S) begins spiralling on the primary rhizome but this straightens out to produce a shoot with 4 leaves per node. It bifurcates at one point, undergoes a slight spiral on both stems before straightening out, after which the right-hand shoot becomes normal.

STEM FASCIATION

Fasciation is rare in U. dioica, but is shown (Fig 17.2, A1). What attracted me to this shoot was the very large leaves, the largest of which is bifurcated and appears to be two leaves fused, the opposite leaf is normal and torn. At this point the original stem apex appears as a flattened fasciated stem crowned with a row of leaves, from very small to small, subtended by a row of stipules. The stem is continued with the first leaf being alternate, and although there is a pair of leaves at the next node, one leaf has a stipule high up on the petiole.

(A-B) (A)Three-leaved variety marked with tie, (B) normal and 3-leaved variety top view, (C-D) coloured varieties, (C) yellow variety and crimson variety could be due to due to lack of nutrients and high sugar levels respectively during rapid spring growth, (D-E) purple and red due to high sugarlevels due to rapid growth.

(F-G) Yellow varieties are common in the spring and most of these are due to rapid growth and lack of minerals needed for chlorophyll production.

(H-I) Sectoring and speckling are likely to be genetical in nature and if so would probably persist or grow out, so examination and growing under garden conditions would be necessary to establish whether it is environment &/or genetical.

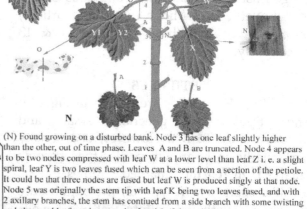

(N) Found growing on a disturbed bank. Node 3 has one leaf slightly higher than the other, out of time phase. Leaves A and B are truncated. Node 4 appears to be two nodes compressed with leaf W at a lower level than leaf Z i. e. a slight spiral, leaf Y is two leaves fused which can be seen from a section of the petiole. It could be that three nodes are fused but leaf W is produced singly at that node. Node 5 was originally the stem tip with leaf K being two leaves fused, and with 2 axillary branches, the stem has contiued from a side branch with some twisting and abnormal leaf number at nodes 5 and 6 (3-leaved), then normal growth.

(J-L) yellow varieties indicating nutients reach tissue near veins first for chlorophyll production, (M) spraying affects tips.

FIG 17.3 FURTHER GROWTH ABNORMALITIES AND COLOURED VARIETIES IN URTICA DIOICA

THREE-LEAVED AND VARIABLE-LEAVED SHOOTS

Once I had discovered a nettle stem with whorls of 3 leaves at nodes, instead of two, further searching proved this variant occurred generally throughout the United Kingdom (Fig 17.2, F-R2). Small pastures yielded from 6-10 three-leaved shoots on the average. This characteristic tends to run in certain clones, some of which have 2-3 of these variant shoots. The condition occurs in the stolon and continues as these turn up for the next year's shoots, and this is why this variety is found mainly in the spring. It could be due to the larger size of the apical meristem of these variant stolons, but although many 3- leaved shoots are large and vigorously growing, this is not always the case. The shoots affected are on clones with scattered shoots and on the outside of larger clones. The condition is confined to the apical meristem only, and the side shoots are of the normal type.

Shoots with a variable number of leaves at different nodes are quite frequent, on careful searching. The sequence of leaf numbers per node; is from the bottom of the stem (left) to the top (next line (right), of three pressed specimens is given below: -

1-2-1-2-2.	2-2-1-1-2.	2-2-2-2-3-3-3-3-2.	2-2-2-3-2.	2-2-2-2-2-1-2-1-1-2

2-2-2-2-2-1-1-2-2.	2-2-1-3-4-2-2-2.	2-2-2-3-2-2.	1-4-4-4-3-3-3-2-2-2.

1-2-1-2-3-1-2.	2-2-4-3-3-3-2.	2-2-4-3-(above this point the shoot is normal and bifurcates.)

In these stems the leaf primordia are slightly out of phase, so that single leaves on two successive occasions would be alternate. Single leaves can alternate with nodes with 3 leaves whereas 4 leaves per node indicate a breakdown in the time sequence separating primordial; however, there appear to be no hard or fast rules. These shoots invariably revert to the normal type higher up.

TERMINAL INJURY VARIANTS

This type of injury is most likely to be due to insect damage, although vertebrates cannot be ruled out. It occurs at an early stage of development. Generally it results in a whorl of 4-6 leaves at the apex of the stem, and a varying number of shoots originating from the leaf primordia in the axils of these leaves. Pressed specimens include, at the apex of the stem: (1) 6 leaves and 3 shoots, (2) 3 leaves and 3 shoots, (3) 2 leaves and 2 shoots, (4) 4 leaves and 3 shoots, (5) 4 leaves and 2 shoots, (6) 4 leaves and 4 shoots.

A normal shoot produced as a result of terminal injury (Fig 17.2, G-H), differs from that of another injured shoot (Fig 17.2, I). The latter shoot gives the impression that a shoot is growing out of the petiole; however, examination of a later stage (Fig 17.2, F, J), shows that the correct explanation is that *a shoot* has only produced one leaf at its first node

THE SYSTEMATICS/CLASSIFICATION/TAXONOMY OF THE NETTLE FAMILY (URTICACEAE).

INTRODUCTION

I have a great admiration for the taxonomist who is essential to bring order out of chaos and responsible for establishing the phylogenetical relationships between plants. I remember talking to a Dr Melderis at the herbarium in the Botany Department of the Natural History Museum in London. When I claimed an interest in nettles he said 'I have recently been chopping down some eight feet high nettles in my back garden' and then added' I suppose you wouldn't be interested in looking at our collection of British and European specimens of Urtica dioeca, but I'm afraid they have been much neglected,' and no doubt hoping that I would be the person to take them under my wing! Looking at the specimens and varieties of U. dioica I would agree with Pollard that many varieties of Urtica (in his case U. dioica var. galeopsifolia) are based on poor inadequate descriptions in past works, or based on small fragments of a herbarium specimen in one state of development thus making comparisons and decisions as to its varietal status of a field collected plant difficult.

THE TRIBE URTICEAE

The classification of plants leading up to the Tribe Urticaceae has been dealt with (Introduction, Chapter1) and the reader is advised to read this first: the nettle sub-class Hamamelidae (p 6-7), the nettle order Urticales (p7-8), nettle family Urticaceae (p9-10) and the tribe Urticeae (p10). The 48 genera and 900 species of the Urticaceae were the result of the work of Weddell (1856-7) and his classification has remained largely unchanged. The *tropical members* of the Urticaceae have received much attention with the publication of several important floras, Robinson (1910-11) on Philippine Urticaceae, Rendle (1917) on the African Urticaceae, Killip (1960) on the Urticaceae of Panama, Liu & Huang (1967) the Taiwan Urticaceae and the monumental revision of Weddells classification by Chew: Laportea (1969), Discocnide (1969), Dendrocnide (1969-71). Friis has revised Girardinia (1981), Obetia (1983), Forsskaoleae (1988) and is working on Pilea. .

TEMPORATE MEMBERS OF THE GENUS URTICA

There are 45 species of Urtica distributed throughout the temperate areas of the two hemispheres but with the majority of species in the northern hemisphere and with the species of the Old World tropics found in the temperate climate of middle and upper mountain elevations, Miller (1971) and Friis (1989). It is ironic that whereas the tropical genera of the Urticaceae have largely been revised by Chew and Friis there is still not a revised monograph on the genus Urtica.

THE BIOSYSTEMATICS OF THE PERENNIAL SPECIES OF URTICA IN NORTH AMERICA

Miller (1971) points out that the genus Urtica is in need of a monographic study especially in North America. Ten species are recognized north of Mexico, **seven perennials** Urtica *californica, U. holosericea, U. Lyallii,* in the west; *U. serrra* in the south west; *U. dioica, U. procera* and *U. viridis* northern species and restricted to central and eastern sections; and *U. gracilis* northern and transcontinental. Urtica dioica seems to be a circumpolar species complex. **Two annuals** are *U. urens* naturalized in Florida and S. Carolina and the native *U. chamaedryoides* from Central Florida west to Texas and Mexico. A third annual *U. gracilenta* is found iin Arizona, New Mexico and Texas. Bade chromosome numbers for the species are x=11, 12 and 13. Woodland et al (1974) revising the Urticaceae in Canada gives chromosome numbers of 2n=26 and 2n=52 for U. ssp gracilis and 2n=52 for U. ssp dioica.

Woodland et al (1977) writes a monograph on U. dioica which is split into two subspecies, U. dioica ssp. dioica (European stinging nettle) and U dioica ssp. gracilis (American stinging nettle). The American stinging nettle is widespread throughout Canada and extends northwards through the Boreal Forest to the edge of the sub arctic (also in central Alaska). It grows on nutrient rich soils and areas disturbed by man as well as in open woodland and in these respects is similar to the European stinging nettle. The authors give an interesting account of the two

sub species in relation to Names, Morphology and variation, Economic importance, Geographical distribution, Habitat, Hybrids, Population dynamics, Hybrids, Human manipulation and response to parasites. U. dioica ssp gracilis differs from U. dioica ssp dioica by being predominantly monoecious (pistillate plants occasional, staminate ones rare) stems are rigid, and the plants have an upright habit; Leaf blades and stems are glabrous (without hairs) but with stinging trichomes on the lower leaf surfaces only. U. dioica ssp dioica described in the key appears to differ from the British stinging nettle which rarely is sprawling (except in the autumn where tall nettles may flop over) and branching is only vigorous in establishing plants whilst large clones may have a small amount of side branches at the top of the shoots towards the end of the year. Woodland et al (1976) gives an account of **annual species** of Urtica, *U. gracilenta, U. urens, U. chamaedryoides* and *Hesperocnide tenella.* Chromosome counts for U. urens, 2n=26 with x=13 (in Europe counts of 2n=52 have been found).

Most of the characters used to separate the perennial taxa of Urtica are the variable vegetative ones and Herman (1946) stated that 'identification appeared to depend upon the idiosyncrasies of the taxonomist'. He concluded that the perennial taxa of eastern North America should be considered as a single element of the Eurasian North American species. Selander (1947) noted the similar morphology of species of Urtica growing in North America and Fennoscandinavia. These considerations lead to the papers of Woodland et al (1982) to examine the chromosome number, hybridization and palynology of the seven species of North American taxa of Urtica mentioned above.

Chromosome counts showed that the Urtica species had two ploidy levels; U. breweri, U. holosericea, and U. procera are all diploid (n=13), and U. californica, U. dioica, U. lyallii are tetraploid (n=26). Both n=13 and n=26 were found in U. gracilis. Individuals from thirty populations representing the seven species were used in crossing experiments. Crosses between U. lyallii (n=26) x procera (n=13), U. californica (n=26) x holosericea (n=13) U. californica (n=26) x procera (n=13) produced F1 hybrids that were sterile. All diploid x tetraploid crosses were infertile. Urtica gracilis (n=13) x procera, x holosericea, x breweri (all n=13) produced fertile offspring. (Details of morphological characters of the hybrids see the full paper).

With U. holosericea and U. breweri to the west of the Rocky Mountains and U. procera to the east although separated geographically, normal pairing of chromosomes during meiosis of the F1 plants indicated that reproductive barriers do not exist between these three species which form a semi-discrete unit. All pairing of tetraploid taxa produced fertile hybrids. The three western tetraploid taxa U. californica, U. lyallii and some populations of U. gracilis have variable vegetative morphology but are best considered as components of one plastic taxon. U. dioica native to the Old World, diecious with weak stems, when crossed with native tetraploids which are monoecious and with erect stems, produced fertile offspring, dioecious and weak stemmed, this indicates close genetic relationship despite their geographical isolation. (Map 17.2)

The results supported the following taxa, (1)

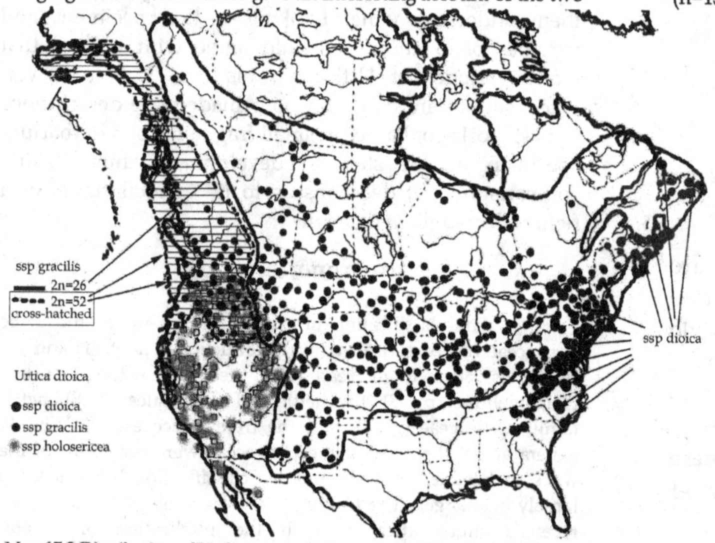

Map 17.2 Distribution of U. dioica ssp dioica, ssp gracilis and ssp holosericea (Woodland 1982)

KEY TO NORTH AMERICAN PERENNIAL *URTICA* SPECIES

Inflorescence a panicle of either staminate or pistillate flowers; perennial plants, strongly rhizomatous.

Plants dioecious; stems usually weak, sprawling, branched; stems and leaf blades on both surfaces usually strongly hispid with stinging hairs ....1 *U. dioica* L. subsp. *dioica*

Plants usually monoecious (pistillate plants occasional, staminate ones rare); stems upright; stinging hairs usually on lower leaf faces only; stems glabrous to woolly.

Lower face of leaves glabrous to puberulous; stems glabrous to strigose, green...2 *U. dioica* L. subsp. *gracilis* (Ait) Selander

Lower face of leaves villous, tormentose to woolly; stems villous to woolly, canescent ...3 *U. dioica* L. subsp. *holosericea* (Nutt) Thorne

266

Introduced U. dioica, **U. dioica spp. dioica;** (2) U. californica, U. gracilis, U.lyallii, and the U. procera complex, **U. dioica spp. gracilis;** (3) U. holosericea and U. breweri complex, **U. dioica ssp. holosericea.**

THE ORIGIN OF URTICA DIOICA: THE FEN ORSTINGLESS NETTLE,
URTICA DIOICA VAR. GALEOPSIFOLIA, OR URTICA GALEOPSIFOLIA (WIERZB. EX OPIZ.)

Geltman (1992) considers that U. dioica var. galeopsifolia of Wicken Fen should be raised to specific level. This nettle occurs in damp mesotrophic fen communities in particular, at the margins of shrubby areas with other shade tolerant herbs. Similar plants are found nearby at Chippenham Fen. Geltman (1986, 1992 in Russian) in his studies on cytotaxonomical and ecological-geographic studies of the genus Urtica in the U.S.S.R. makes the assumption that the Wicken Fen variety would appear to belong to a separate species U. galeopsifolia Wierzb. ex. Opiz., that he had recognised for Western and Central Europe or some intermediate form between this species and U. dioica.

U. galeopsifolia was described from Hungary by Opix (1825) and differs from U. dioica by: leaf blades almost completely lack stinging hairs but possess a felt of non-stinging hairs; the inflorescence is found (nodes 13-22) and is related to later flowering than U. dioica. Unlike U. dioica which is tetraploid (2n=52, 2n=48), U. galeopsifolia is presumably diploid (2n =26). U. galeopsifolia has the distinct habitat of damp woodlands, riverbanks and valleys and eutrophic fens. In Central Ukraine, U. galeopsifolia is found in *Phragmites* fen and *Alnus glutinosa* woodland in steep valleys. It is also found in Hungary, Czechoslovakia and Netherlands.

Geltman considers that originally U. dioica could have originated as a hybrid between U. galeopsifolia (2n=26) and U. sondenii (2n=26). U. sondenii occurs in Siberia and Northern Europe and the leaves are hairless (glabrous) but hairs of both types are found on the stem nodes and inflorescences. Geltman considers that U. galeopsifolia was likely to have been present in the Pliocene period and to have penetrated to Britain at the time of the land bridge. He postulates that the original 'primary' U. dioica hybrid could have occupied 'Wicken Fen' area after the last glaciation and that the 'secondary' U. dioica was derived from these two. Selection pressures at the time could have been grazing animals, including domesticated ones. *So the possible origin of U. dioica was apparently connected with human activity.* Response to the disturbance of habitats by the human settlements is indicated by its seeds found as early as the time of the Mesolithic culture (Godwin, 1975). It is probable that because of drainage in Britain most populations of U. galeopsifolia became extinct but some are preserved in protected wetlands like Wicken Fen. Geltman also considers that U. dioica var. pubescens which also occurs in wetlands should be regarded as a separate species related to U. galeopsifolia.

THE FUTURE FOR URTICA DIOICA

Hodgson (1986) reviews the commonness and rarity of plants (in relation to an area of 3000km2 of the Sheffield, Britain) and the reasons for both commonness and rarity. The lowland area is predominantly arable and the upland mainly grassland. The flora of the British Isles (Sheffield) dates from the Pleistocene (c. 1000000 BP) and is marked by ice ages (ending c. 10300 BP) see Introduction (Chapter 1). The land bridge between Britain and Europe was broken C. 7000 BP. Apart from other factors the influence of man has been predominant in the transition from hunting to a pastoral economy in C. 5000 BP. Deforestration was well advanced in Anglo-Saxon times –c. 1100 BP. This was followed by the Industrial Revolution 18th Century, resulting in industrial pollution and then afforestation replacing deciduous woodland by conifer plantations. Much land was ploughed up because of WWII (1939) so little of the existing vegetation can be considered unaltered and fertile and frequently disturbed habitats now predominate.

Estimates of maximum potential growth rate (R max) indicates many species in fertile habitats have the potential to grow rapidly, whilst those for unproductive areas have low R max. The greater proportion of common than rare species is associated with productive conditons. Any factor (whether mechanical or environmental) that results in destroying part of a plant (i.e. its biomass) is regarded as disturbance. More common species are associated with intensely managed agricultural land, garden and urban wasteland, all of which are disturbed and fertile. Rare species occur in undisturbed and disturbed areas of low fertility. Rare species are associated with areas of intermediate environmental stress and/or disturbance. The analysis of the extent to which species occur in several habitats showed that certain species (e.g. Agrostris stolonifera, Poa trivialis and Urtica dioica) are found in a wider range of environmental conditions. Rare species are restricted to less common environmental conditions. Thirteen species are ahead of U. dioica in commonness but U. dioica has third place in the number of habitats where species are common. Species which can exploit man-made habitats, produce large amounts of viable seeds and have species mobility will find suitable sites for seedling/or vegetative establishment.

One of the anomalies of the survey is that there is only a low proportion of species associated with fertile habitats but this might be explained by the dominance of these species and their widespread occurence. The commonness and rarity are most affected now by changing patterns of land use. The greater level of fertility and disturbance is resulting in the replacement of stress tolerant species by those with competitive and ruderal strategies. The fate of many plant species was probably determined a long time ago before man's impact on the planet became substantial.

Hodgson (1987) carried out a study of polyploidy in the Sheffield flora to answer the question 'Why do so few plants species exploit productive habitats'? It has been assumed that plants with a base number less than thirteen are usuallyll diploid whilst those above this are likely to be associated with a genus of polyploid origin. *Urtica dioica* is a tetraploid with a base number n=13 and with extant (still living) diploid relatives e.g. perennial European species, *U. atrovirens* 2n=26, *U. kioviensis* 2n=22. It is assumed that polyploids from genera with extant diploids will be at a more recent stage of polyploid evolution. According to Geltman (1992) the progenitors of U. dioica, *U. galeopsifolia* and *U. sondenii* existed in similar areas towards the end of the last glaciation (See Chapter 1) and had the opportunity for hybridization to produce the tetraploid 'primary' U. dioica. The plants could have exhibited variations in leaf shape and hair types and probably had no stinging hairs on the leaves. These may have appeared in Wicken Fen. From these the 'secondary' typical U. dioica with stinging hairs on the leaves developed. The presence of grazing animals would have resulted in the selection of variants with high densites of stinging hairs.

The results of the Sheffield study showed that polyploidy is higher in polycarp perennials and is correlated with both abundance and plant strategy. It was found that polyploids from genera with extant diploids (such as Urtica) tend to have a higher percentage of common species in the Sheffield area than diploids or relictual (survivors from an earlier period) polyploids; although they constitute a small proportion in the stress-tolerant category they reach their highest percentage amongst competitor plants. Chapter 1 has considered the likely response of Urtica to vertebrate herbivores and mans attempt at forest clearance and the domestication of animals during the prehistory period. Its increase in abundance after WWII with the application of fertilizers and modern agricultural practices has

267

also been considered in Chapter 15. In Britain there are still many 'under exploited niches' in the abundance of disturbed habitats and this could be due to (1) maladaption amongst polyploids and diploids, (2) the British flora is recent with few species, (3) Britain's geographic isolation. These niches are likely to be filled by evolution involving diploids and by the continued invasion of alien species. Other diploid species of Urtica could hybridise, but could it mean the demise of the `U. dioica?

POSSIBLE EVOLUTIONARY STAGES OF THE COMMON STINGING NETTLE (URTICA DIOICA L.)

The most important variation in the history of nettle success was undoubtedly the modification of the ordinary stinging hair into the stinging trichome thus ensuring its protection against vertebrate herbivores and it is likely that this happened relatively early on in the evolution of the Hamamelidae. Botanists are in agreement that the most primitive habit is the tree habit so the nettle trees are the most primitive members of the tribe Urticeae. At the present day they are centred in the tropics of the Indonesia-Malay area see Map 18.1 (Appendix). Their seedlings are abundant in the understorey in gap areas of the tropical forest but little has beeen written about their germination and survival in relation to vertebrate herbivores present in these areas. The young trees have greater densities of stinging trichomes than the parts of the adult trees and this is likely to be due to more browsing pressure during the establishment stage but no studies are available as yet! Botanists agree that the more primitive state of the flower is bisexual so the reduced state of unisexual flowers of most members of the present day Urticaceae is secondary and has resulted in the present high level of dicliny in this family. It is likely that the flowers were originally insect pollinated and the reduction in the flower size was compensated for by them being amassed in complex inflorescence arrangements to make them conspicuous to insects which were attracted to their pollen and nectar. Another important evolutionary innovation was the development of inflexed stamens capable of reflexing suddenly to throw pollen out of the already split anther sacs. Explosive pollen release would have enabled pollen to be carried away in the weak air currents present in tropical areas and enabled some of these plants to change eventually to wind pollination. Some lines would have developed the herbaceous habit and eventual radiation of these plants to the more temperate areas of the northern and southern hemispheres took place. The seasonal nature of these areas resulted in more effective transport of pollen by the wind thereby increasing the number of viable seeds. With the advent of man and his eventual domestication of animals nettles were protected against these vertebrate herbivores and thrived in the highly fertile areas and disturbed areas which resulted. The rest of the story has been revealed in the pages of this book, but what about the future of the common stinging nettle which has spread to most countries of the world. Will its demise predicated by Hodgson take place?

WILL THERE BE A DEMISE OF THE COMMON STINGING NETTLE?

Without doubt U. dioica is almost ubiquitous in the U K and there is evidence at the present that it is spreading, so what factors could lead to its demise? No doubt the answer lies in its spread in the various countries where it has been introduced and relating this to the various factors in these countries that favour its increase or lack of spread. However, no such study exists so any ideas are in the province of a certain amount of speculation but based on the growth requirements of this plant.

Global warming is likely to have an effect because it is known U. dioica prefers a temperate climate and has not done well in the hotter countries where it was introduced, e. g. Southern Africa. This could be related to its vegetative spread by rather delicate stolons which penetrate best a moist friable soil. Although introduced into North America in about 1672 it is regarded as rare by Woodland and is confined to the western coastal area of Canada and the United States. As pointed out by Woodland this could be due to lack of sufficient density by this dioecious plant to effect efficient set of viable seeds but it could be due to the fact that U. dioica subsp. gracilis occupies very similar habitats. The fact that U. dioica subsp. dioica is a tetraploid and the American subsp. gracilis is a diploid means that hybridization is not possible. The fact it is confined mainly to the coast could mean the moister more temperate climate suits it best. It also appears to differ radically in its growth pattern which is sprawling and may be related to lack of stolon penetration. In any event it would be a worthwhile project to find out why it has not spread well in North America.

The most likely reason for its decline would be competition with other competitor plants from Europe or other countries, coupled with global warming. It has been mentioned that in Europe garden escapes such as *Aster, Solidago, Helianthus* and *Rudbeckia* growing to a height of 1-2m have moved into ruderal area and then to river valleys where they have smothered out Urtica. In the U K the Japanese Knotgweed (*Reynoutia japonica*) introduced in 1888 has colonized most of Great Britain and is now becoming a pest plant. Most of it is from a female plant and its spread is entirely vegetative and brought about by man especially by road transport witnessed by the number of clones found on roadside verges. It has also colonized river banks and moist valley areas where large clones have replaced Urtica and other native plants. It grows 1-2m in height, forms dense monospecific stands and has deep seated roots and rhizome system so is difficult to eradicate. The fireweed or rose-bay willow herb (*Chamaerion angustifolium*) although native is mixed with a sterile cultivar and a century ago was on rocky slopes and scree but now has spread to ruderal areas, roadsides, woods, etc., throughout the country. Urtica can grow with it but never at its usual vigour. The Himalyan balsam (*Impatiens glandulifera*) has been treated in detail (Chapter 15) but is replacing Urtica in damp valley areas and alongside river banks.

However the ubiquitous U. dioica is common, widespread and occupies many different habitats, its large clones have existed from time immemorial and are self renewing from seed and persistant seed banks. Farmers with their modern application of vast amounts of chemical fertilizer which leach into surrounding areas provide the highly fertile areas needed for maximum growth of U. dioica, and there is little sign of the return of organic farming. It has existed since the last glacial period and all that can be predicted about the fate of mankind when the oil runs out means it is likely to outlive mankind.

The common stinging nettle may be a much maligned plant on account of its stinging properties and its unattractive appearance but I hope the reader or browser of this book will have found a lot of interest because after all the story is based on the relationship between this plant and man throughout his short existence on this planet. It has taken a lot of courage to produce this book and although it is not expected to be a best seller and has been much maligned by the conventional book publishers I hope it will make its presence felt, as does the common stinging nettle. I have certainly got a lot of pleasure from entering the world of the nettle patch and its ecological relationships and bringing together the information from many famous scientists in the first book every published on the world of Urtica dioica and this most notorious group of tormenting plants, the nettles and their relatives. I hope the book will stimulate more work on this fascinating plant and its relatives and give pleasure to other researchers but they must be prepared to be stung!!!

FIG 18.1 THE HABITATS OF THE PELLITORY-OF-THE-WALL (PARIETARIA DIFFUSA)

(A) in a crevice in a sandstone wall, notice the shoots are spreading out in a fan-shape in the plane of the wall, which mimimises the effect of the wind in this exposed position. (B) this herringbone style wall composed of shale, in north Devon provides an ideal habitat because of the spaces between each slate. (C) human habitations, such as cracks in the base of walls and pavements, are favoured in this seaside resort in south Devon and even been trapped in a mini-greenhouse! (D) on a sloping cliff face, Baggy Point, north Devon. (E) a limestone cliff-face, Berry Head, south Devon. (F) old churches with un-pointed walls are a favourite habitat. (G) it has to compete with other wall plants on this wall, such as, wallflower, dandelion, Soleirolia (base), ivy-leaved toadflax, and the most competitive wall daisy. (H) a wall crevice in an old habitation.

INTRODUCTION

Most people are amazed to learn that, in the British Isles there are also two other members of the Nettle Family and these belong to the Tribe Parietarieae, called generally, by Lindley, the Nettleworts. These include the Pellitories, the Wall Pellitory (*Parietaria judaica*), and a garden escape the Mother-of-Thousands or Mind-Your-Own-Business (*Soleirolia soleirolii*). Although the nettleworts do not sting and do not remotely resemble nettles at a glance, if their minute flowers are looked at through a hand lens they are nearly identical to those of the nettles.

PELLITORY-OF-THE-WALL (PARIETARIA JUDAICA L.)

"Owls and ravens haunt the buildings,
Sending gloomy dread to all;
Yellow moss the summit yielding,
Pellitory decks the wall."
G. Crabbe.

INTRODUCTION

The majority of the general public is no doubt unaware of the existence of the humble Pellitory-of-the-Wall (I will use Pellitory, for this plant, throughout this account). A review of the literature reveals that the Pellitory is a plant which has been sadly neglected by writers and botanists alike; it has little folklore, it is not mentioned by Tansley in his 'Vegetation of the British Isles', as yet it has not appeared in the 'Biological Flora of the British Isles' or in detail in the NERC 'Comparative Plant Ecology' and little is known about its ecology, physiology or biochemistry. There is also a need for a comprehensive review of the Tribe Parietarieae to which it belongs. Our immediate and remote ancestors probably knew this plant better as a useful medicinal plant. A study of its secret life is likely to reward the attentions of field naturalists, plant ecologists and physiologists alike.

French, Parietaire. German Ausgebreitetes Glaskraut.

The generic name Parietaria comes from the Latin paries, a wall, which refers to one of its main habitats. Parietaria plants, collected in Palestine by Linnaeus's student Hasselquist, were described by Linnaeus in his 'Flora of Palestine' (1756) and the plant described and named as *Parietaria judaica* L. has been shown to agree in main features with our British species (Townsend). This means that the specific synonyms, diffusa and ramiflora, and wrongly applied officinalis, have now been replaced by the correct judaica.

The name Pellitory is not found before the sixteenth century; previously the name of the plant was Parietary which is thought to have changed over time into Perritory and then into Pellitory by changing r's for l's (Horwood), or to come from the Old French, Paratorie or Parritory (Grigson). Our Pellitory must not however be confused with the Algerian Pellitory (*Anacyclus pyrethrum*), Persian Pellitory (*Chrysanthemum roseum*), or Dalmation Pellitory (*Chrysanthemum cinerariaefolium*), all of which belong to the Daisy Family (Compositeae) and are important medicinal herbs (Grieve).

Pellitory is also called by several common names: Billie Beatie (Ireland), Wall Sage (Warwickshire), Hammerwort, Lichwort, Wallwort, Peletir, and Peniterry. Wallwort and Lichwort are appropriate because 'it grows neere to old wals in the miost corners of churches and stone buildings' (Gerarde). The local word Peniterry was used by frightened schoolboys who would run to a wall where Pellitory was growing and grasping a plant would repeat the 'Words of Power'
"Peniterry, Peniterry that grows by the wall.
Save me from a whipping,
or I pull you roots and all." (Horwood 1919)
Anne Pratt says it used to be called Perdiceum, (presumably derived from the Systemic name of the Partridge, *Perdix perdix perdix)*, because Partridges are said to feed upon it, and that in old times housewives called it Vitraria because it served to scour glasses, pipkins, etc. Vitr, as first part of a word, pertains to glass and the scientific basis for the scouring properties of Pellitory are due to a high density of cystoliths, containing silica and calcium carbonate which are present in the leaves.

Parietaria judaica is found in S. and W. Europe to Switzerland and W. Germany; Channel Islands and British Isles; Central Asia, east to Tian Shan and Pakistan; N. W. Africa, Egypt, Palestine and Iraq.

Paratieria judaica is native to the British Isles. It is widely distributed, local in England, Wales and Ireland, but rare in Scotland and absent in the north- Dumfries, Kirkcudbright, Roxburgh, Linlithgow, Eastern Highlands, Fife, S. Perth, Forfar, W. and N.Highlands.

It is also absent from the Isle of Man.

In Asia its habitats are rock crevices in mountains, caves and near springs (Jarmolenko). In Europe and Britain it grows in cracks in walls, hedge-banks and stony places on well-drained soils (Grey-Wilson).

In Britain the habitats of the Pellitory are split between natural and man-made. John Gilmour states, in his book 'Wild Flowers' (N/N Series), that Pellitory grows in abundance on sea cliffs and regards this as its natural haunt. This is in line with its distribution in Devon, shown in the 'Atlas of Devon Flora' (Ivimey-Cook), where the Pellitory is concentrated along the coast and shortly inland.

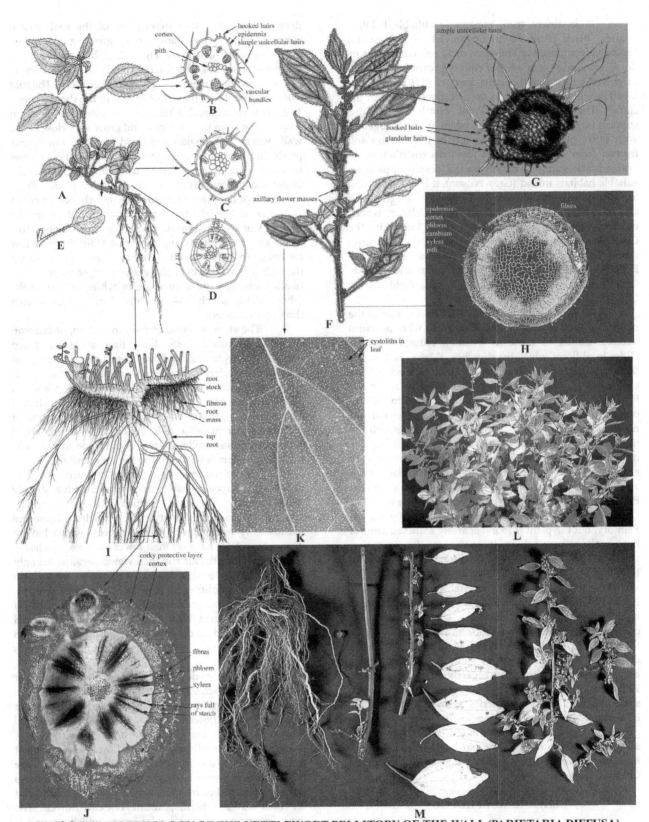

FIG18.2 THE MORPHOLOGY OF THE NETTLEWORT PELLITORY-OF-THE-WALL (PARIETARIA DIFFUSA)

(A-E) a greenhouse pellitory seedling, height 5.5 cm, showing early formation of side shoots and the fibrous root system. (A-C) plan diagrams of transverse sections of the stem at points, A, B, C, on the diagram, (A) the primary plant body and (B-C) the beginning of secondary thickening, (D)a greater magnification of one seedleaf/cotyledon. (F) young shoot of pellitory in early June. The plant surface is glossy but the dense covering of hairs give it a matte appearance. Clusters of female and hermaphrodite flowers are housed in bracteate cups in the axils of the leaves. The young flowers at the top of the shoot have their stigmas protruding, the stamens of the flowers at the middle of the shoot are exploding and liberating clouds of pollen for wind pollination. The older flowers at the bottom of the shoot are producing elongated pink tubular perianths surrounding the developing fruits. (G) a transvers section of stem showing the long simple unicellular, hooked and glandular trichomes on the epidermis. (H) transverse section of the middle of the stem with secondary thickening showing the main tissues. The young stem is made up of a large amount of parenchyma in the cortex and pith and lacks collenchyma and has only a few fibres and therefore is brittle and easily snaps which might faciliatate vegetative spread in some habitats. (I) the root system is very extensive and the tap root quite often persists and is large there are also large lateral branches and these all penetrate into rock fissures in its main rocky habitat. There is also a root stock and the extensive root system is important in storing water and nutrients, (J) the t. s. stained with iodine, shows that the stores large amounts of starch in the xylem parenchyma. (K) a leaf in glycerol viewed with transmitted light shows the dot-like cystoliths. (L) grown in open situations shoots appear on all sides. (M) a mature plant shows the extensive root system and although most of the fruits have been blown off or dispersed by contact, the tip is still producing flowers, so flowering takes place over a long period of time.

271

It is absent from apparently suitable habitats inland. Berry Head, South Devon, which is a coastal headland, composed of limestone rock, and famous for its flora, is one such area where Pellitory grows in profusion in crevices in the cliff, at the base of cliff ledges and together with other plants on the soil covered parts of the cliffs. The cliffs at Baggy Point, North Devon, also support large stands of Pellitory, where it grows together with other plants, towards the top of the cliff on soil formed from the eroding cliff face. Its distribution, in Wales, is also said to be mainly coastal, despite apparently suitable habitats inland (Grey-Wilson); it is also recorded as widespread near the sea in Cornwall (Margelts and David). The other natural habitat area of Pellitory is rock outcrops such as the limestone areas found in the Cheddar Gorge in Somerset, and the magnesium limestone cliffs at Knaresborough, to the east of the Pennines, where it is found in association with Bloody Cranesbill (*Geranium Sanguineum*), and Field Garlic (*Allium oleraceum*), (Lousley).

Its distribution inland shows that it is akin to the nettle, in that it is a follower of man who provides habitats similar to those in which it naturally grows. Older local floras which list churches, abbeys, castles, old farm buildings and walls where the Pellitory used to grow enable the naturalist to revisit these sites to see if the Pellitory still exists. Absence might be due to natural causes, or modern practices such as the occasional but necessary pointing up of old buildings, together with the tidy mania regimes such as spraying, regular mowing and more importantly the use of the dreaded strimmer to eliminate 'weeds' from the most inaccessible places such as the edges of walls. In his connection, the village Bishop's Tawton, North Devon, where I live, the local 14th Century church, recently repointed and very tidy, has no Pellitory, but the plant is found sparsely scattered around the small village where it grows in the following situations: bases of buildings, cracks between walls, buildings and the pavement or road, old crumbling walls and dry stone walls. In the coastal area of Mortehoe, North Devon, for example, Pellitory grows in abundance in the crevices of dry stone walls, some of which are completely covered in the plants, as well as growing at the base and lower sides of the steep roadside banks, many of which started off as stone walls before they became covered in soil and vegetation. In the Flora of Wiltshire, Grose records Pellitory as growing amongst the stone debris in limestone quarries, as well as growing on limestone walls, where it is frequent. It is also recorded as growing on sandy soils. I have found it on sandy soil in the vicinity of the ruins of the old lighthouse, Braunton Burrows, and it is also found on sandstone outcrops in Cheshire (Newton).

GENERAL MORPHOLOGY

The growth form of the Pellitory depends upon its habitat, environment, season, age in years and inherited characteristics, and for these reasons I am going to describe a single plant growing out from a wall crevice, a few feet above a country road, in late May. The main branches of the plant spring from a substantial rootstock deep in a crevice. (My description of the root system refers to that of a one-year-old plant growing underneath my greenhouse bench-see Fig 18.2 It has an extensive fibrous root system with a large number of roots 2-3mm. in thickness and a mass of slightly thinner roots. The root system is about half the extent of that of the shoot system. The main branches, 2-3 mm in diameter and 30-40 cm long, spring from the rootstock and grow very close to the wall where the majority spread out in one plane producing a fan-like arrangement. A few shoots grow horizontally or downwards at various angles. Some of the larger shoots have produced large side branches. From the centre of the plant numerous smaller shoots (10 cm or so.) grow out in all directions, either directly from the rootstock or are side branches from the main shoots. Most of the shoots are producing flowering side- shoots, a few cm long. The whole plant is slightly glossy when viewed through a lens; however the general appearance is dull (matte), due to a thick covering of white hairs over the whole plant, which feels slightly 'furry' when drawn through the fingers.

The stem is round (terete) in section, of crimson colour interspersed with long thin strips of green photosynthetic tissue, and with a dense covering of simple unicellular trichomes of various lengths. It is woody at the base but snaps when subjected to a slight bending force. The top portion of the shoot is translucent due to a large proportion of ground tissue consisting of very large parenchyma cells, whilst the sub-epidermal supporting tissue (collenchyma) is only one to two cells thick, so the stem is brittle and snaps very easily.

The leaves are entire, roundly to narrowly ovate to lanceolate, apex obtuse to accuminate, with a slightly wavy margin. The upper surface and leaf margin is covered with a high density of short hairs. There are usually only two pairs of lateral nerves, which have a dense covering of hairs on their lower surfaces. If a leaf is boiled to remove the air and then viewed against the light with a hand lens, a high density of refractive, punctiform (dot-shaped) cystoliths will be seen. The petiole, which is much shorter than the blade, is crimson with strips of green, covered in a high density of white hairs, and narrowly grooved at the top. It is very narrow (1 mm width) and has an arc of three vascular bundles. Stipules are absent.

At each node there are two axillary flower clusters, one on each side of the axillary bud or shoot. The flower clusters are polygamous i.e. bisexual, or either male or female flowers. [The possession of bisexual flowers is rare in the Urticaceae and is regarded as a primitive feature (Berg)]. The flower arrangement (inflorescence) is a compound, cymose dichasium. The typical flower cluster is shown (Fig 18.3), which follows its developmental course. The female flower is central and on either side is a hermaphrodite/bisexual flower. The three flowers are surrounded by bracts, which are united at their bases to form three shallow cups each containing one flower. The central (terminal) female flower is made up of a pistil surrounded by a green, hairy perianth. The pistil is composed of a glossy, green, ovately spherical ovary, from the top of which grows a long, slender, crimson style, capped with crimson, penicillate stigma

Labels within the figure:

female flower with stigma protruded

old hermaphrodite flower with stamens about to explode

young hermaphrodite flowers with stigmas protruded

old fertilised flower with the tepals elongated into a pink tube with the fruit enclosed at the base

old hermaphrodite flower with exploded flowers

fertilised carpel with withered stigmas

C

D female flowers

A

B

E

G1

stigma

carpel

tepals

bracts

H

I

F

J3

J1

J2

K3

K1

K2

G2

FIG 18.3 THE STRUCTURE OF THE FLOWERS OF PARIETARIA DIFFUSA

(A-B) show the cluster of axillary flower on shoots of pellitory notice that the topmost flowers are young and the female and hermaphrodite flower have some of their flowers with protruded stigmas. Further down the shoot the tepals of the hermaphrodite have been pushed back by the expansion of the filaments of the stamens and some flowers have exploded stamens. The anthers fall off leaving the thick filaments which later wither. Notice at this level the stamens are exploding near flowers with protruded stigmas so there is a chance of self-pollination taking place. Once the egg in the ovule has been fertilised the tepals grow out around the fruit to form a pink tube that is covered in hairs. (C-D) show the flower groups in more detail. (E) shows a half-section of a young hermaphrodite flower with the stigmas protruded, at this stage the stamens are immature. At this stage they can only be pollinated by pollen from another flower, shoot or different plant.(F) the same flower once pollination and fertilisation have taken place, now the stamens expand and eventually explode (G1-G2) and the pollen cannot pass onto the stigmas of the same flower. (H-I) amongst the hermaphrodite flowers are small female flowers with outer bracts and with the ovary surrounded by four tepals. These tepals will grow into the same tubular pink structure as in the hermaphrodite flowers. The flowers can be arranged in two main types of clusters, (J1-J3) in groups of seven and (K1-K3) in groups of three. (J2&K2) show the bracts on the under-surface and (J1&K1) show the top view showing the male and hermaphrodite flowers each with their four tepals. (J3&K3) show the floral diagram of the flower clusters with their stamens and carpels.

273

from which long stigmatic hairs radiate like pins in a pincushion. The four free tepals of the perianth enclose the ovary and their crimson tips come together around the base of the style.

After development a glossy, dark olive-black fruit called an achene (1.5 x 1.0 mm) is formed enclosed within the enlarged, dead and hairy perianth. The perianth, together with its enclosed achene, falls off at an early stage as a dispersal unit.

The hermaphrodite flower is made up of a central pistil whose development is synchronous with, and the same as, that of the female flower. The four stamens are enclosed within the four tepals of the perianth. The green and purple blotched, hairy tepals are united at the base but are free at the top where each one curves over to enclose a stamen. The stamens, like those of Urtica, are reflexed but differ from the latter by having thicker elastic filaments with more pronounced cellular ridges. Prior to explosive pollen liberation, the filaments under tension push the tepals back then suddenly straighten, catapulting the pollen from the two split anther lobes several centimetres into the air.. Unlike Urtica, the anthers fall off and the fat filaments persist for some time in the flower before they eventually wither. The remarkable feature of Parietaria is that after pollen liberation, the united part of the perianth elongates to about twice its original length, then turns pink and eventually purple to resemble the corolla found in insect pollinated flowers. These changes cause the developing pink and purple fruit clusters to look like flower clusters and make the plant more attractive. The olive-black achene is enclosed within the cylindrical perianth which contracts at the bottom and the top end to keep it in place. As in the case of the female flower the perianth with its enclosed achene is dispersed as a unit, after constriction at the perianth base causes it to fall off. The two hermaphodite 'fruits' (perianth plus achene) fall off more easily than the female 'fruit' which on occasions is likely to be liberated together with the bracteate base when this falls off.

REPRODUCTION AND LIFE CYCLE

The Pellitory does not produce any structures for asexual reproduction and considering the nature of its habitat, (e.g. crevices in rock faces and walls), it is unlikely that organs of vegetative reproduction such as rhizomes, runners, etc., would be to its advantage. It reproduces sexually by producing female and hermaphrodite flowers on the same plant. The flower clusters on the main stem show considerable variation. I would define a normal flower cluster as consisting of a central female flower, flanked on either side by a hermaphrodite flower. In most stems, the clusters at the base of the stem are normal, or occasionally consist of single female flowers; however, the ones produced towards the top of the stem show all variations of from three to seven hermaphrodite flowers, surrounding a central female flower. The majority of top flower clusters consist of one female and six hermaphrodite flowers (Fig 18.3). The side shoot clusters are always of the normal type. The developmental stages of the normal clusters (Fig 18.3) show that the female and

hermaphrodite flowers produce a style capped by a penicillate stigma at a very early stage. The mass of unicellular hairs radiating from the stigma present a large surface area to the wind-borne pollen and once pollination has taken place they soon wither. Only after pollination do the perianth segments of the hermaphrodite flowers open, allowing the elastic filaments of the stamens to spring back, catapulting the pollen from the two anther sacs into the air to produce minute powder-puff explosions. The puffs of pollen, which are shot into the air several centimetres from the plant, are then wafted away on air currents or more forcibly whisked away by the wind. The stigmas mature first in the flowers at the top of the main shoot, and after they have withered, the same flowers which are now lower down the stem, produce pollen. Because of this sequence, it has been stated that self-pollination cannot take place. Admittedly this arrangement certainly increases the chances of cross-pollination; however, self-pollination must also take place because, (a) the pollen puffs can be carried by air currents or the wind from the lower flowers to the stigmas of the upper flowers (b) the flower clusters on the side shoots are at the stigma stage at the same time as the adjacent older flower clusters, on the main shoot, are liberating their pollen. In Britain, Pellitory is scattered in its distribution, and in the regions where it does occur it is often found as isolated plants spread out over a large area; pollen is therefore likely to be at a low density and under these circumstances self-pollination is an essential strategy for its survival.

(Fig 18.4) shows that the fruits of hermaphrodite flowers are tightly enclosed within the enlarged perianth and the two are dispersed as a unit. The fruits of the female flowers are also tightly enclosed within the perianth and liberated together with the bracteate cup when this dehisces. In both flower types the fruit is also held in place by intermeshed, fine 'cobwebby' hairs inside the perianth. Wind is the principle method of fruit dispersal. The fruit is relatively heavy in relation to the smaller feathery seeds characteristic of most wall plants, e g., Dandelion (*Taraxacum*), Willow Herb (*Epilobium*), Pink Valerian (*Centranthus*), Ragwort (*Senesio*), etc., The hairy perianth, or bracteate base, increases the surface area and acts as a wing enabling the fruit to be carried upwards by the winds gusting against a cliff or wall face. It is thought that Pellitory plants growing high up on church towers might gain this considerable height by simply dropping their topmost fruits into higher wall crevices and these developing into plants which continue the upward course (Ridley). Pellitory plants are also found growing on harbour walls and the walls bordering rivers, streams, estuaries, etc. In these situations it is possible that fruits could have been deposited there at high water levels, established themselves, and then worked their way up the wall later. The fruits contain air and are covered on the outside with a glossy, waxy layer; they are said to be able to float for three days (Praeger). The flattened end of the fruit, which was attached to the cup (receptacle), consists of a thin layer of oil-containing cells called an Elaiosome (Sernander). The latter author found that ants collect seeds which have elaiosomes and take them back to their nesting chambers where the oily material is eaten. The

274

seeds are normally collected where they have fallen to the ground but in rare cases may be gathered from the plant. Many seeds are buried in the nest but others are dropped off on the way. Ant runs can often be seen on banks and on ruins, etc., so Pellitory seeds could find suitable germination places. One thing these authors omit in the case of Pellitory is the fact that the fruit is inside the perianth, so presumably the ants must cut it free before they can carry it off. The perianth, and cupule in the case of female fruits, is covered with long hairs and smaller hooked hairs which readily stick to most objects and therefore are capable of being dispersed by larger animals. Since the plants grow on walls bordering streets and buildings, they are likely to become attached to the clothing of passers-by. All these methods should enable the fruits of Pellitory to be dispersed quite effectively over relatively short distances.

The most important phase in the life cycle of any plant is the establishment phase when conditions for germination and growth must be suitable. No data is available on the conditions for the latter two processes. Pellitory plants, which grow in the soil under my greenhouse bench, produce fruits which germinate freely. By removing the surface soil together with the germinating seedlings I have established that the fruits from hermaphrodite flowers germinate within the perianth, and since this comes to lie horizontally, the young root (radicle) and shoot (hypocotyl) initially grow horizontally before they grow down and up respectively (Fig 18.5). I have found cupules with female flowers still containing fruits which are fertile but ungerminated, so it might be that the persistent perianth needs to rot away before germination can take place. The germination is epigeal, with the cotyledons (first seed leaves) coming above the ground, and the stages are shown in (Fig 18.5). Side shoots are produced at an early stage and flowering and fruit formation occur within the first year. An established plant, in Devon, starts flowering on mid-May, with the main flowering period in June, and then extending through to September. The root system is fibrous, with several large roots growing 20 cm or more and a mass of smaller surface roots which bind the soil, so the root system is well adapted to removing water and minerals stored in the deeper rock recesses, as well as absorbing surface run-off, and atmospheric dew and humidity under drier conditions. The bases of the main stem and roots swell up with storage food and persist after the aerial shoots die down in the autumn; the buds persist at soil level, and therefore the plant is a Hemicryptophyte.

Data is needed for the time and conditions for germination and growth under field conditions. Moss states that it prefers calcareous soils, and exists in non-calcareous regions mainly in man-made habitats which provide calcium, such as the mortar in walls and buildings. This could explain why it tends to be confined to farms and villages, but fails to grow on adjacent dry stone walls in more outlying areas. Its distribution shows that it favours areas where humidity and rainfall are high, and this might explain its rarity in drier areas such as eastern England. Frequently plants growing high on walls, die back under drought conditions, but very often they appear again in years when conditions are more favourable.

PLANT RELATIONSHIPS

Plants and animals (biotic factors) also affect Pellitory. In its natural habitat of cliffs and walls it often grows in isolation and therefore faces no direct plant competition. The Wall Daisy or Mexican Fleabane (*Erigeron karvinskianus*), which has become naturalised and is increasing particularly in the Southwest of England, occupies a similar ecological niche and could be competing with Pellitory for wall sites. In the case of near vertical dry-stone walls, which in time fill in with soil and become banks, the Pellitory still forms stands, because under these conditions, even competitive plants associated with it [Ivy (*Hedera helix*), Cow Parsley (*Anthriscus sylvestris*), Cleavers (*Galium aparine*), Alexanders (*Smyrnium olusatrum*), Nettle (*Urtica dioica*), Pink Campion (*Silene dioica*), Bramble (*Rubus fructicosa*), cannot grow sufficiently vigorously to shade it out. On less steep banks, where competition with other plants becomes stiffer, it often survives low down on the bank, adjacent to the road. It occurs at the base of shaded walls with other rank weeds [Cow Parsley (*Anthriscus sylvestris*), Pink Campion (*Silene dioica*), Nettle (*Urtica dioica*), Bramble (*Rubus fructicosa*), Black Bryony (*Tamus communis*), Alexanders (*Smyrnium olusatrum*), Cleavers (*Galium aparine*), Creeping Thistle (*Cirsium arvense*), Dock (*Rumex obtusifolia*)], where it can still hold its own by growing a metre or so in height; the same is also true where it grows in its most favourable habitat on the limestone cliffs of Berry Head (Devon) where I have found it growing to over a meter in height through bramble, etc. However outside its natural habitat it would not be able to survive against more competitive plants which would completely outgrow and overshadow it.

ANIMAL RELATIONSHIPS

Larger animals (quadrupeds) feeding on Pellitory include goats, particularly in the Orient, and, in his Flora Britannica, Mabey quotes a Cornish farmer who noticed his horses were fond of eating Pellitory which grows in profusion on the walls of old buildings on his farm. There is very little information on animal relationships with Pellitory, which is not surprising, because in this country this plant is relatively uncommon, grows in awkward or inaccessible places, and very often near to human habitations where such activities as fiddling with plants on walls or in gutters is likely to be viewed as suspicious behaviour and difficult even for the dedicated field naturalist to explain away. The Pellitory is fragile because of its succulent and brittle nature, so the following procedures are recommended for collecting insects: observation for larger animals; gently shake the plant and collect insects on a white tray or sheet held underneath; for larger plants it is permissible to remove a few shoots for closer observation at home; alternatively grow Pellitory in the garden and await colonisation.

The stem of the Pellitory consists of a cortex of soft, succulent tissue, therefore mechanical barriers have evolved to protect it against insects and smaller animals; these consist of a dense covering of straight hairs underneath which is a layer of short hooked hairs, and the leaves also have a high density of cystoliths. Pellitory plants in my garden are grazed by slugs and snails as evidenced by mucous trails overlaying damaged leaves; mollusc activity is best viewed by torchlight at night. These molluscs do not seriously affect adult plants but it is a different matter for seedlings. There is a dry stone wall in my garden which is a home to a large concentration of slugs and snails so I was not surprised when, after planting young Pellitory plants in the crevices I discovered their meagre remains covered in molluscan mucous the next morning.

FIG 18.4 CHANGES FROM FLOWER TO SEED DISPERSAL IN PARIETARIA DIFFUSA

(A-K) typical flower cluster showing early flowering stages through to fruit formation. (a-b)pollination stage with stigmas protruded, (c-d) with fertilisaation completed the stamens explode to liberate their pollen, (e-f) the perianth of the hermaphrodite flowers elongate to twice their length and become pink to purplish, taking on the appearance of the corolla of wind-pollinate flowers, (h) the perianth of the female flower turns brown and hard to tightly enclose the achene. The fruit is attached to the bracteate base and the two are dispersed as a unit. The wings of the bracts aid wind-dispersal, whilst their hooked hairs aid animal dispersal. (j-k) the hermaphrodite flowers dehisce and the achene is dispersed inside the hairy perianth, in a similar way to the fruit of the female flower.

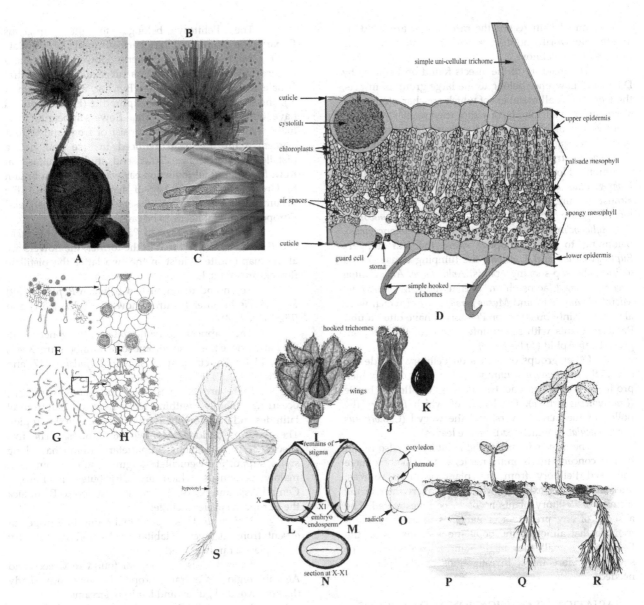

FIG 18.5 ADDITIONAL ANATOMY, FRUIT DISPERSAL AND STRUCTURE, GERMINATION IN PARIETARIA DIFFUSA

(A-C) micrographs of the carpel with details of the stigma which reveals the large number of stigmatic hairs which are simple and uni-cellular. They present a large surface area to the capture of diluted pollen grains in the air. (D) a transverse section of a portion of pellitory leaf showing the main tissues, with details of the cystoliths, trichomes and the mesophyll. (E-H) the epidermis of a leaf, (E-F) the upper epidermis and (G-H) the lower epidermis. The upper epidermis is covered in simple hairs, long straight and shorter hooked hairs, spherical cystoliths are formed inside enlarged cells. In a similar way the lower epidermis is covered in the same type of trichomes as the upper epidermis but the cells are slightly tesselated and full of stomata together with their guard cells. (I-J) the fruits are dispersed in two parts, the female flowers are dispersed together with their bracts and the hermaphrodite flower are dispersed in their perianths. Dispersal in both cases is either (1) by the wind catching the wing-like structures on the perianth or the bracts, or (2) by contact with animals due to the hooked hairs on the perianths and bracts, (L-O) show the structure of the fruit, which is quite large and contains a substantial endosperm thereby giving the young seedling a good chance of establishing itself in rocky habitats. (P-R) shows that the seed in some cases germinates inside the perianth and germination is epigeal with considerable enlargement of the cotyledons taking place under suitable light conditions. these are covered in hooked hairs, even so they are readily eaten by molluscs. They form an extensive and persistant tap-root system when this is possible. (S)

Considering the nature of the file-like rasping radulas of molluscs, each made up of sharp chitinous teeth; this was likely to happen. How far this prevents establishment in the wild state would be a difficult but worthwhile project. The role of ants and larger animals in bringing about seed dispersal has been considered. Man creates the habitat for the Pellitory on the one hand but is also responsible on the other hand for their destruction, by spraying the base of walls with herbicides, tidy mania, repointing and demolishing walls and buildings.

The insects associated with the Pellitory in Huntingdonshire have been studied by Davis and Lawrence, who sampled nine churchyards and other sites over a two-year period. They used a Dietrick vacuum net with a one-foot sampling head, which works by sucking the insects off the plant; however the main drawback is the noise generated which hardly makes the operator unobtrusive! The insects they collected from the Pellitory are also found on the nettle and since these are dealt with in detail later the reader is advised to read this paper first.

The immigrant butterfly, the Red Admiral (*Vanessa atlanta*), lays the occasional single egg on Pellitory and the caterpillar can easily be found because it lives in a tent of leaves which are drawn together by silken threads. In a similar way, the brown and white micro moth Autumn Nettle Tap (*Anthophila fabriciana*), occasionally lays eggs on the Pellitory and the presence of the caterpillar is indicated by a fine silk web over the top leaves, or individual leaves, within which it feeds.

Emmett and Heath record the rare, temporary resident, and the Bloxworth Snout (*Hypena obsitalis*) moth, as laying its eggs on the Pellitory.

The majority of the insects found on Pellitory by Davis and Lawrence belong to the large group of insects, the Hemiptera, all members of which are characterised by a piercing and sucking beak, either used to suck plant sap (herbivores), or blood and body juices (carnivores). The bugs (Heteropterans) recorded are the Nettle Ground Bug (*Heterogaster urticae*), Nettle Capsid (*Liocoris tripustulatus*), Common Flower Bug (*Anthocoris nemorum*) and *Plagiognathus arbustorum*, with the last three of these almost certainly breeding on the Pellitory, (Single site recordings are *Scolopostephus affinis*, *Heterotoma planicornis*, *Orthotylus ochrotrichus* and larvae of *Calocoris norwegicus*). Belonging to the Homoptera were the leaf hoppers *Eupteryx aurata* and *E. collina*, the Jumping Louse (*Trioza urticae*), the sap-sucking aphids, *Aphis fabae*, *Aulacorthum circumflexum*, *Macrosiphum avenae* and *M. funestum*, *Microlophium evansi* and *Myzus persicae*; all of which were almost certainly breeding on Pellitory. I have often found Pellitory plants with severe infestations of the blackish-green Bean Aphid (*Aphis fabae*).

Other groups of insects on Pellitory include the small fly (*Agromyza anthracina*), the larvae of which produces leaf mines and two beetles, the flower beetle (*Brachypterus urticae*), the larvae of which feed on the pollen of the male flowers, and the weevil (*Cidnorhinus quadrimaculatus*) which feeds on the leaves.

The insects found on the Pellitory are also found in high concentrations on the nettle, and are likely to have colonised Pellitory from this plant or other sources; alternatively, the extent to which they overwinter in the vicinity of Pellitory plants needs to be investigated. The absence of any predators or parasites in this list might indicate that although the populations of insects on the Pellitory are small, they might stand a greater chance of survival. More insect investigations on this plant are needed!

VARIATION, CLASSIFICATION AND GENETICS

British floras give a height range of 15-50 cm for Pellitory but in the Flora Europaea the height is given as no more than 40 cm (Ball). In Devon and Cornwall it varies from 7 cm on high walls, to 100 cm when emerging through bramble and growing in shaded places such as the base of hedge-banks and walls. The range of leaf length is given as 2.5-7.5 cm (Syme), and as not more than 5 cm (Ball). Leaf shape varies from orbiculate-ovate to ovate-elongate but otherwise there is little variation in the margin or venation. Growth habit ranges from spreading and decumbent to erect, and there is variation, within and between plants, in relation to stem branching.

The Pellitory belongs to the sub-genus Euparietaria Kom., and has hermaphrodite or pistillate flowers, but no staminate flowers. Flowers of Parietaria judaica have been described as unisexual, i.e. a central female with two lateral males (Butcher, and Clapham et al), and male, female and hermaphrodite (Hutchinson). I have found that smaller abnormal flowers appearing to be male occur rarely and these consist of from one to four stamens with the pistil reduced in size and like a pistalloid in appearance. Townsend, studying material at Kew, found gradual reduction eastwards, i.e. from Britain to Greece, in the number of female flowers of the decumbent Parietaria. A closer study of British and European material needs to be carried out.

Jarmolenko separated *P. judaica* from *P. officinalis* and *P. erecta* by the fact that in the former, the flowers are all hermaphrodite, whilst in the two latter the pistillate flowers are on the lower part of the shoots.

Townsend distinguished between *P. judaica* and *P. officinalis* in other features shown in Table (18.1) and (Fig 18.3& 18.4).

There appears to be no data on the genetics. In the Parietarieae the basic chromosome numbers are, X = 7, 8, 11, 13 for Parietaria species, with *P. judaica* x=7, and x=10 for *Soleirolia* (Friis).

There are 20 species of the genus Parietaria, occurring mainly within temperate or subtropical latitudes and occasionally in montane areas in the tropics. The genus is divided into two sub-groups. The five species of the sub-genus (Euparietaria Kom.) have long styles supporting penicillate stigmas, and it comprises mainly perennials which are distributed in Europe, Central Asia and N. W. Africa. In addition to P. judaica the European species include: -

P. officinalis L. is a perennial found in Europe but absent from the west. Habitat, rocks and fissures dry stony places, rarely a weed.

P. erecta L. is a perennial found in Greece and Aegean region, Central Europe. Habitats are shady thickets, wooded gullies and banks of streams.

P. mauritanica Durien. Annual. South half of the Iberian Peninsula and N. W. Africa. The fifteen species of the sub-genus Freira (Gaud) Kom, have a sessile stigma or a very short style, are mainly annuals, some are weeds, and are represented in both New and Old Worlds. European species include - *P. lusitanica* L., *P. debilis* Forster and *P. cretia* L., see (Burges et al). For further information on species see: -Weddell, Jarmolenko 1936, 1941, Townsend, Miller, Bassett et al, Woodland 1989.

HERBAL MEDICINAL PROPERTIES

In his Materia Medica, produced at the

Table 18.1 Comparison of fruit characters of Parietaria officinalis L. and P. judaica L. (After Townsend).		
	Parietaria officinalis	Parietaria judaia
Perianth of fruit from the female flower	Length 2.75-3 mm. Longer than bracts. Conspicuous. Segments broadly lanceolate, margins uniting only at the tip.	Length 2-2.25 mm. Only slightly longer than bracts. Inconspicuous. Segments mainly lanceolate. Gradually uniting at the tip.
Perianth of fruit from the hermaphrodite flower.	Up to 3 mm. Long. Bell-shaped.	3-3.5 mm. long. Tubular and compressed.
Fruit (Achene)/	1.5-1.8 mm. long. Asymmetrical.	1-1.2 mm. long. Symmetrical.

beginning of the first century A.D., Dioscorides prescribed Pellitory for the ' suppression of wine '. From the Middle Ages it was known to be effective ' for dispersing obstructions and aiding the flow of liquors '.

John Gerard in his Herball 1597 describes several uses for the Pellitory:

It " helpeth such as are troubled with old cough....the decoction with a little honey is good to gargle a sore throat '. 'The juice held awhile in the mouth easeth pain in the teeth.... With sugar... cleanseth the skin from spots, freckles, pimples, wheals, sunburn, etc. He says it was used in the Middle Ages in plasters for broken limbs and tightness of the chest, and in the form of an ointment it is good for piles and a remedy for gout and fistulas. The leaves can be applied as poultices for bathing slow-healing wounds, burns and skin infections."

Nicholas Culpeper in his Herbal 1652, was influenced by the ' Doctrine of Signatures ' (e.g. giving Pellitory for stones in the bladder because it grew on stones) and astrology where it was placed under the influence of Mercury. Culpeper gives a whole list of diseases to be cured using Pellitory, many of which are questionable. However he ends with its most important use....' The juice boiled to a syrup with honey and a spoonful drunk every morning is good for dropsy' The latter use by herbalists and peasants still exists to the present day, whilst herbal medicine prescribes it for use as a diuret and a laxative. As a diuret it acts through the high levels of nitre or saltpetre and flavones found in the plant. Its diuretic action of stimulating the products and flow of water/urine from the kidneys makes it effective in conditions such as dropsy (accumulation of serous fluid in the tissues), it also stimulates the passing of stones accumulating in the bladder or kidneys, and the washing away of germs which cause inflammation of different parts of the urinary system e.g. pyelitis (cavity of the kidney), nephritis (kidney), cystitis (bladder), and urethritis (urethra). For this purpose 1 onz.of the plant is added to 1 pint, or 30-40 gm to 1 litre of boiling water and this is taken in wineglass doses four times a day. The fresh plant is better than the dried. It can be used together with Wild Carrot or Parsley Piert, or together with Birch (Betula), Juniper (Juniperus), Rupturewort (Herniaria), and Restharrow (Ononis) all of which are for the infection of the urinary tract.

Other constituents include: sulphur, tannic acid, bitter principles, calcium salts and mucilage.

An additional non-medical use - It used to be laid in corn granaries to drive away weevils.

PELLITORY AND POLLINOSIS

In the areas of Spain, the Mediterranean, Athens and Greece, P. officinalis and P. judaica are the main cause of pollinosis in Europe. There has been an increase in this problem over the years 1987-1993 and the seriousness can be judged by the fact that in excess of 38 published medical papers appeared in 1996 alone. The allergens in the pollen lead to allergic diseases, pollinosis, rhinitis and conjuctivitis (inflammation of the nose and eye respectively), and possibly hypersensitivity pneumonitis.

MIND-YOUR-OWN-BUSINESS (SOLEIROLIA SOLEIROLII ([REW] DANDY})

INTRODUCTION

A French round-the-world voyage of discovery took place from 1817-1820. The ship (a 350 ton corvette with 20 cannons) Uranie, named in honour of the muse of astronomy and geometry, was captained by Louis Claude-Desaulses de Freycinet and had on board the pharmacist and botanist, Charles Gaudichard-Beaupre . The Uranie left Toulon on September 17, 1817 and for about a month sailed the Mediterranean during which time the islands of Corsica and Sardinia were visited. Gaudichard-Beaupre and his plant collectors discovered a small prostrate plant whose mass of delicate entwining stems were covered with minute bright green leaves to form large mats which filled crevices in the rocks and cliffs. In the mountainous areas the plant grew luxuriantly forming yellow-green carpets in shaded, humid conditions and was especially abundant alongside waterfalls and streams. The pressed plant was eventually deposited in the Herbarium of the Achives du Museum d'Histoire Naturelle. Gaudichard-Beaupre finished writing up the ' Botany of the voyage of the L'Uranie' in 1826 and in his account published in 1830 he named this plant Soleirolia, Gaudich.

Earlier the French botanist Requien described the characteristics of the genus and the description of the species of the same plant collected from Corsica by a Mr. Soleirol, captain of the military engineers, who travelled through all Corsica and assembled a considerable herbarium of the plants of the island. Soleirol found this pretty plant at Cervione in a shaded place against a high defensive wall where it formed a thick carpet or lawn; he also found it grew on the Corsican cape or headland. Requien named this plant in 1825 as Helxine Soleirolia. Possibly from the ancient Greek name for Pellitory or from the generic name Helxine after the ivy, Hedera helix, from the Latin helix, a coil, and in this case refers to the entwining nature of the stem of this plant, whilst the specific name was in honour of its collector, Soleirol.

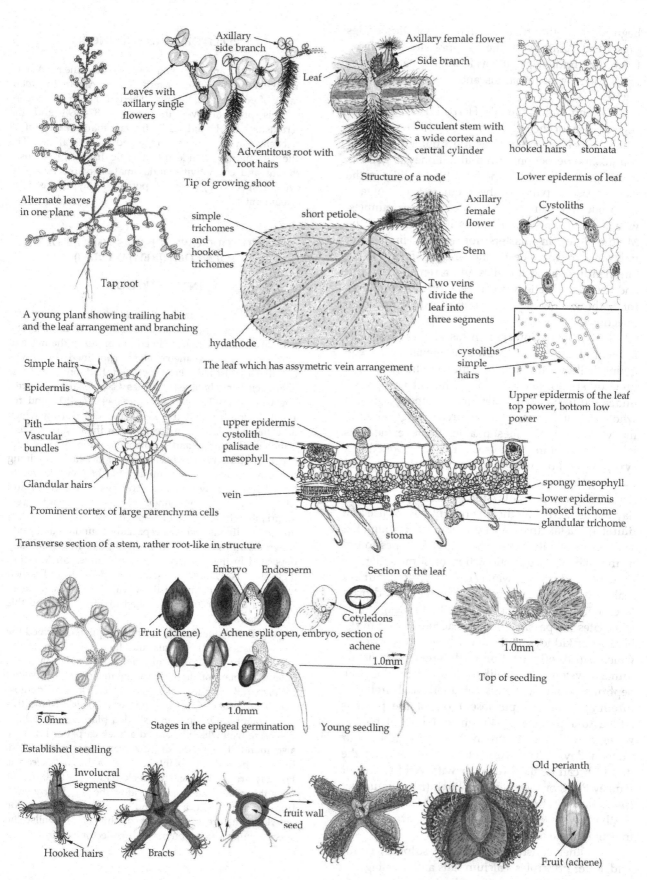

Axillary side branch

Leaves with axillary single flowers

Leaf

Axillary female flower

Side branch

hooked hairs   stomata

Lower epidermis of leaf

Adventitous root with root hairs

Succulent stem with a wide cortex and central cylinder

Tip of growing shoot

Structure of a node

Alternate leaves in one plane

simple trichomes and hooked trichomes

short petiole

Axillary female flower

Cystoliths

Stem

Two veins divide the leaf into three segments

Tap root

hydathode

cystoliths simple hairs

A young plant showing trailing habit and the leaf arrangement and branching

The leaf which has assymetric vein arrangement

Upper epidermis of the leaf top power, bottom low power

Simple hairs

Epidermis

Pith
Vascular bundles

Glandular hairs

Prominent cortex of large parenchyma cells

Transverse section of a stem, rather root-like in structure

upper epidermis
cystolith
palisade
mesophyll

vein

stoma

spongy mesophyll
lower epidermis
hooked trichome
glandular trichome

Embryo   Endosperm

Section of the leaf

Fruit (achene)

Cotyledons

Achene split open, embryo, section of achene

1.0mm

1.0mm

Top of seedling

5.0mm

1.0mm

Stages in the epigeal germination

Young seedling

Established seedling

Involucral segments

Old perianth

fruit wall
seed

Hooked hairs   Bracts

Fruit (achene)

Stages in the development of the fruit which is covered in hooked hairs for fruit dispersal by animals

FIG 18.6 THE STRUCTURE OF SOLEIROLIA SOLEIROLII (MIND-YOUR-OWN-BUSINESS), FRUIT AND GERMINATION

Sprengel in 1827 changed the generic name from Helxine to Parietaria because Linneus had already used Helxine in 1758 as a substitute for *Fagopyrum*. The name *Parietaria soleirolii* (Req.) Sprengel, was used as late as 1941 in the Index Londiensis. However, because of the great differences between soleirolii and the genus Parietaria, most botanists rejected Sprengel's classification.

Gaudichard-Beaupre accompanied another short voyage of the ship Bonite under Captain Nicholas Vaillant (1836-1837), and in his writeup of the plants collected; he renamed *Soleirolia* as *Soleirolia Corsica* Gaud. Weddell in his Monograghie des Urticees, in 1865, retains Requien's name of *Helxine soleirolii* and keeps it in the separate genus Helxine. The name was retained until 1964 when Dandy changed it to *Soleirolia soleirolii* (Req.) Dandy (see Heywood). Although I can see the logic of using the first name given to a plant, (provided it has not been allocated previously to another plant!), it is unfortunate that this unique plant ends up with a double name both based on its collector Soleirol, whereas a specific name, more descriptive of some characteristics of the actual plant or its ecology, would be more appropriate.

DISTRIBUTION

Soleirolia is indigenous to the islands of Elba, Corsica and Sardinia but has become naturalised in Europe, particularly in the west and Southwest; Balearic Islands, Azores, France, Belgium and Holland. In Ireland it occurs mainly in the coastal areas. In Great Britain it is found mainly in the coastal areas of southern England and is abundant particularly in the counties of Devon and Cornwall in the Southwest; it is also found on the outlying islands of Man, Wight, Scilly and the Orkneys (Jalas and Suominey, Ivimey-Cook and Perring).

During the Victorian era it was grown as a potted plant in cool greenhouses and eventually as a garden plant which escaped. In the Flora of Cornwall 1972 (Thurstone), it is recorded as an alien on a churchyard wall at St Just, Roseland in 1917 and is reputed to have escaped from a rectory garden. In 1920 it was recorded on a wall of a cottage garden Trewidden, Penzance. Since then it has spread but is never found far from human habitation.

In Devon and Cornwall it is commonest around habitations in damp and shaded combes which lead down to the sea. In Lee Bay for example it is found in the following situations: (a) It is fond of dry stone walls in damp shaded places, where it roots in the crevices and spreads out over the stones to form continuous mats, (b) In the form of tall cushion-like carpets it grows underneath Butterbur adjacent to a steep road which directs water into this area, (c) In gardens, (i) alongside streams, (ii) as a cover plant around potted plants and objects to mellow harsh outlines and also as a potted plant forming a yellow-green hemispherical cushion cascading over the rim, (iii) creeping up walls, around ponds, and in moist shaded corners where competition from other plants is low, (iv) a favourite place is sunken steps bordered by walls leading up to a garden situated on a steep slope, where, in the shaded moist conditions, it grows along the step borders of walls and creeps up the walls, (v) on lawns in the shade of trees near the sea it can replace grass to form a Soleirolia lawn, (d) on artificial cliffs alongside gouged out roads, in the moist areas of water runoff, it competes with other plants including members of its own family Pellitory and the nettle (Fig 18.7).

GENERAL MORPHOLOGY

Soleirolia is a perennial herb which in milder sheltered areas in southern England survives the winter as a dense evergreen mat. Since buds remain above the soil/rock surface in the winter, it is classified as a chamaephyte (Raunkier). All features of Soleirolia are small so they need to be viewed with a x10-x20 hand lens or better still in 3D, through a binocular microscope, where they are revealed as objects of interest and beauty.

The following description applies to a mat of Soleirolia in my garden, which developed naturally in a corner recess formed by the concrete drive to my garage meeting a small abutting brick wall (Fig 18.6). Water, carrying dust and debris, drains from a higher concrete area into this corner. The brickwork soaks up the water to keep the environment moist, whilst the shade cast by the house, means that the plant only gets direct sunlight in the morning. I removed an end piece of the plant mat; however it offered some resistance because its root mass penetrated small fissures in the concrete and brickwork. Turning the plant mat over it was found to consist of a thin layer of soil and debris, enclosed in a mass of adventitious roots and intertwining branching stems. After carefully washing away the enclosed debris the mat can be separated into a number of stem systems which unite with deeper brown and then blackened stems which appear to be dead. However, on closer examination these stems are giving off healthy roots and shoots. I was amazed to find, after taking a section of the black stem, that the epidermal and cortical cells are dead, with thick brown walls akin to those of cork, however, the central vascular core is alive with cytoplasmic cell contents and abundant starch grains (see Anatomy Fig 18.6). Further investigation is needed to find out how many years these stems remain alive and their importance as organs of food storage and perennation. The whole plant/mat consists of old stems which have produced side branches which in the following year have produced side branches, and so on; in this way the mat builds up. The prostrate stems increase growth within and at the periphery of the mat, whilst the side branches they give off grow towards the sun, and increase the depth of the mat, converting it into more of a cushion.

End of a shoot showing male and female axillary flowers

Piece of a clone showing many male flowers, some exploded

Piece of a clone showing pre--dominatly female flowers

The anthers are still stuck and the turgor has resulted filament rupture

Male flower with 4 tepal segments

pistallode anther and inflexed filament

tepal pistallode reflexed filament after explosion

Stem showing one exploded flower and another in bud

An open male flower ready to explode

A male flower just opening

penicillate stigma
perianth
tepals

ovary
ovule

involucre
bracts
tepals

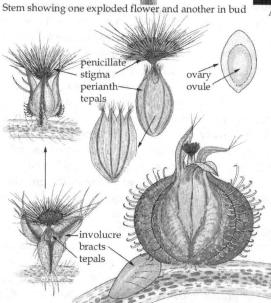

Young fruit with hooked hairs for dispersal by animals

As a typical feature of a damp/wet garden area, here on the wall & in pots

A favourite place for Soleirolia on a wall above a stream with lower liverworts and campanula.

A shaded moist part of the garden, Soleiroilia on a wall at the side of steep shaded garden steps, also with wall daisy

FIG 18.7 THE FLOWER STRUCTURE, REPRODUCTION AND FRUIT DEVELOPMENT IN SOLEIROLIA SOLEIROLII

Looking at the end of a shoot of the present year, it consists of a prostrate stem with alternate leaves and short side branches, (produced from buds in the axils of these leaves) which grow outwards and upwards to form a mosaic of side branches and leaves. Under damp conditions the majority of nodes on the stem produce a single adventitious root and these roots unite up to form the very extensive fibrous root system mat. The stems vary from 0.75-1.00mm, they are light crimson in appearance but when viewed under a lens, they are seen to have a common central cylinder and a crimson stippled surface. The stem is round and like a root in structure with the vascular tissue confined to the centre. There is quite a dense covering of four different hair types, short and long straight hairs, short hooked hairs and glandular capitate hairs.

The leaf is rectangular but with rounded corners (suborbicular) and varies from 3-6 mm long to 2-4 mm wide (Diagram 18.6). A very short petiole (1 mm) is attached asymmetrically to the leaf, and this design appears to minimise the overlap of leaves as well as leaving the male and female flowers exposed to collect pollen during wind pollination. The ends of the larger veins terminate in water glands/hydathodes, which remove surplus water from the plant. Viewed against the light, the thin yellow-green leaf is broken up by a high density of irregularly shaped, clear, translucent areas, the cystoliths. The upper epidermis has a scattering of glandular and large unicellular hairs, whilst the lower epidermis is covered in all four hair types.

On the lower part of the stem adjacent to each node is a conical protuberance, the root primordium, which remains as such if the plant is growing on a dry wall, but if the plant is growing under moist conditions, it rapidly (within 24 hrs.) develops into an adventitious root (Fig 18.6).

Single female flowers develop in most leaf axils. The youngest flower are found at the tips of the shoot, and following it backwards, all stages up to the mature fruit and eventually dehisced fruit heads can be seen. The ends of the shoots are festooned with pink and white plumes which are the protruding stigmas of the female flowers; these are remarkably large compared with the small size of the female flowers and are designed to provide a large surface area for picking up the pollen grains during wind pollination.

Although the female flowers are abundant, the male flowers, which occur mainly at the tips of the branches, are few and far between. Male flowers can be more easily be found on plants growing high up on walls under adverse conditions, than on plants growing more luxuriantly in the shade where they are more hidden; however careful searching of debris under these plants will often reveal the dehisced male flowers.

Unexploded male flowers (2 mm across) and exploded flowers were drawn (Fig 18.7). The four, equal, free, crimson spotted perianth segments are incurved at their upper ends to enclose and hold the four inflexed stamens in place, they are fringed with woolly hairs which are also found lower down around the ovary and anther lobes making the latter difficult to observe in the partially opened male flower. The filaments of the stamens are wide but thin, fleshy and elastic, similar to the Parietaria type, with numerous and pronounced folds of cells on their upper surfaces. The connective is green and lies adjacent to the sides of the small rudimentary central ovary/pistilloid. It is notable that this ovary would appear to offer only partial resistance to hold the stamens in place so, the lidded perianth segments, woolly hairs and frictional resistance of the flattened anther sides, are more important in this respect. As in all members of the Urticacae, when the pressure in the cells of the filaments overcomes the restraining forces holding the stamens in place, the elastic filaments spring back causing an explosion which throws pollen from the two open anther sacs into the air (see nettle). The water pressure /turgidity in the cells of the filaments are so high that I observed one filament to break off at the tip and recoil leaving the anther in place (presumably in this case the forces holding the anthers in place are greater than the forces holding the filament cells together).

The female flower is minute, just 0.5 mm high and broad. The superior ovary is surrounded by four fused pink perianth segments which are free at their tips, where the four dentate ends are covered in long hairs which surround the base of the short style. The penicillate stigma is large, 1mm across, forming a hemispherical head, and is made up of long radiating unicellular filaments which may be white or pink in different plants; they present a large surface area for the capture of pollen grains. Three green bracts surround the flower. The base of the perianth is surrounded by 3-6 (average 4) bract-like structures which are green with crimson ridges and are in close contact (connate), the midribs form raised ridges covered with large hooked hairs; these make up what is called the involucre.

REPRODUCTION AND LIFE CYCLE

Soleirolia has a great capacity for spreading asexually by vegetative reproduction which has earned it one of its commonest names, ' Mother of Thousands '. Each node contains a root primordium, so that the smallest piece broken off will, under moist/wet and shaded conditions, quickly take root and spread in area. In nature, foraging birds and small mammals, hedgehogs, voles, mice, etc., break off pieces of the plant which, helped by the hooked hairs, stick to the feet, beaks, etc., and get dispersed. In the hands of a nurseryman, thousands of cloned individuals could be produced from a small plant. Introduced into a small, shaded, moist back garden, as a plant to add colour and fill in the cracks between paving stones and dry stone walls, it can quickly overrun surrounding areas. Attempts to eliminate it by grubbing out are difficult and counterproductive, because the scattering of minute fragments which quickly form whole plants, leads to even more plants; for this reason many gardeners have called it the ' Curse of Corsica '.

No data is available relating to the sexual reproduction of Soleirolia. As pointed out under morphology, single female flowers develop in most leaf axils. However solitary male flowers are found in leaf axils towards the end of shoots, but they seem to occur abundantly early in the spring but infrequently later in the year (After flowering the male flowers fall off, so looking for dehisced male flowers in the debris under plants, would add to the evidence that male flowering is perhaps more frequent than it appears). When male flowers explode liberating their pollen several centimetres into the air, a proportion is likely to fall onto adjacent female flowers and result in self-pollination. In areas where Soleirolia is abundant pollen could be carried to adjacent plants of different clones where cross-pollination will occur. However, in most areas, due to the apparently low frequency of male flowers and the relative sparse distribution of Soleirolia plants, the chances of cross-pollination are likely to be low. A cursory examination of fruits indicates that seed set is quite high showing that pollination is successful. This area needs more research.

The fruit, an achene, is on the average 0.7 mm long by 0.5 mm wide and is enclosed in an involucre with an average of four hooked ridges (range 3-6). The average width of the fruit including the surrounding involucre is 1.5 mm (range 1.3-1.8 mm). The fruit is dispersed enclosed within the persistent involucre, which with its hooked hairs is ideally suited for animal dispersal (see also asexual reproduction). The fruits being small and light are easily blown around by the wind (the involucral ridges acting as wings) and are likely to lodge in small crevices. One of the favourite habitations of Soleirolia is a vertical bank or wall alongside a stream, where it occurs in long stretches, probably as a result of colonisation by water dispersal; the fruits fall directly into the water where they float and are carried downstream.

The structure of the fruit is similar to that of other members of the Urticaceae: the embryo has the radical pointed towards the original stigma end and it is enclosed in a thin endosperm (food supply). The achene wall is dark brown mottled with light brown and hard and glossy/waterproof (Fig 18.6). No data is available for germination. The fruit is tightly enclosed within the involucre; so does it naturally germinate as such, or when the involucre breaks down? I collected 33 fruits from several different plants, removed their involucres, and placed in a petri dish on filter paper covered with a shallow water layer. They were exposed to diffuse sunlight near a window and the temperature was an average 21° C. day and 11° C. night temperature. Germination was slow to begin with but increased with time, perhaps indicating that inhibitors in the fruit wall are gradually diffusing out. After 25 days 42.4% of the seeds had germinated. For stages in germination see Fig 18.6. The seedling produces a long primary root, which at an early stage develops side roots. There are small microscopic simple hairs on the hypocotyl. Germination is hypogeal with the cotyledons coming above the surface of the soil. The cotyledons are emarginate and covered on the top surface with long simple unicellular hairs and a smaller number of glandular hairs. The first node is covered in hooked and glandular hairs and the first leaves are opposite. Axillary buds soon develop in the axils of the cotyledons.

REPRODUCTION AND LIFE CYCLE

In most situations Soleirolia grows in isolation in shaded moist habitats which other plants find difficult to colonise; vertical dry stone walls, between paving stones, alongside pathways and vertical walls, banks bordering streams. In some habitats Soleirolia forms a ground cover mat below stories of other plants, generally in border areas e. g. adjacent to roads, buildings, etc., where due to shallow soil, deep shade, etc., other plants can only grow sparsely and poorly and therefore cannot shade Soleirolia out. In very shaded lawns Soleirolia can compete successfully with grass and become dominant. In vertical habitats where plants can only grow in one plane it is able to survive with other urticaceus plants, nettles, Parietaria, etc., because they cannot shade it out. Its smallness enables it to colonise small habitats, cracks between rocks and paving stones and then spread out over roads or concrete areas holding on with its adventitious roots and growing into mats which trap dust and organic material to build up a soil which further supports it.

Small animals such as spiders and woodlice use Soleirolia for shelter but I have not as yet found any animal feeding on it except small thrips.

VARIATION, CLASSIFICATION AND GENETICS

Where it grows high up on walls exposed to the sun, it forms a thin prostrate mat 5-7.5 cm thick, with small leaves 3-4 mm long and 2-2.5 mm wide, the stems are crimson and the leaves are yellow-green tinged with pink and with crimson veins, internodes have a mean length of 1.3 mm.

In damp shaded conditions the plant forms a thick cushion with a thickness of 15-20 cm, large leaves 5-6 mm long and 3.3-4.5 mm wide, the stems are light-yellow tinged with pink and the leaves are light to mid-green, internodes are 4-13 mm long.

Stigma colour varies from white to pink and the involucre has from 3-6 ridges (mean 4), the achenes range from 0.6-0.9 mm long (mean 0.7 mm) by 0.4-0.6 mm wide (mean 0.5 mm) and from light to dark brown, (See also garden varieties, Chapter 1, Introduction).

The Tribe Parietarieae includes five genera, two of which are considered here, Parietaria and Soleirolia. Soleirolia contains just one species and differs from the genus Parietaria in having solitary axillary flowers, with male and female on the same plant, the fruits are enclosed within an involucre.

The half chromosome number (haploid) is, $x=10$.

AS A GARDEN PLANT

Gardeners have bestowed on Soleirolia several different names: Mother-of-Thousands and the Curse of Corsica (see previous). Mind-Your-Own-Business is recorded as a local name used in Barnstaple and recorded in the Flora of Devon, 1939, (Martin and Fraser), and probably refers to the plant's ability, under suitable conditions, to spread rapidly and for the stems ('noses') to creep (poke) into places in the garden where they are not wanted. Baby's Tears may apply to the tear-shaped leaves, which cascade down over a wall, like tears running down a baby's cheeks.

Areas on the garden which are suitable for its growth have been considered previously. It is a good garden cover plant and can be used to soften harsh edges such as staging and pots and in hanging baskets for conservatories. To soften the areas of concrete it likes nothing better than dark corner spaces in courtyards and gaps under walls and alongside steps etc. It would make a small lawn in dark damp places but is too delicate for traffic and therefore unsuitable for large areas. It is a good pot plant for patios, conservatories or cold greenhouses. A potting compost of 1 part leaf mould and 1 part loam is recommended, with a moderate watering regime.

There are two main varieties: Golden Queen, syn. Aurea, has gold-green leaves and Silver Queen, syn Variegata, has variegated silver leaves.

Where temperatures fall below -5 degrees C it quickly blackens; however it generally grows back in the spring (alternatively protect with a layer of straw or garden felt).

URTICACEAE
TREE NETTLES

The genus *Dendrocnide* (Greek, *Dendro* = tree, *cnide* = nettle), was created by Miquel (1851) and includes small to large softwood trees with very painful stinging hairs. The structure and poisonous principles of the stinging hairs/trichomes have been dealt with (Chapters, 6-8). This short account is extracted largely from the monograph of Dendrocnide by Chew Wee-Lek (1969), a work produced for the Botanic Gardens of Singapore. The thirty-six species of nettle trees are distributed essentially as lowland trees in Southeast Asia and the Pacific, but they are abundant species-wise in the Philippines and New Guinea (Map 18.1).

Most of the nettle trees are soft-wooded and not more than 15 m (48ft) high but the largest is the Giant Nettle Tree (*Dendrocnide excelsa*) of Australia 35 m (113') high with buttresses at the base 2 m (6.5') high. The leaves are unlike those of true nettles, and more similar to those of the popular house plant, the Indian Rubber Tree (*Ficus elastica*), thick, leathery, ovate-elliptical in shape and with smooth margins. The flowers are a few millimetres in diameter, unisexual, and carried on branched inflorescences where they are variously arranged, some in fan-like masses and others in small bundles or tufts. The stigmas of the female flowers are strap-shaped. The fruits are achenes, 2-5 mm, and some like D. excelsa have a fleshy crimson fruit developed from the perianth and are dispersed by animals. The habitat is mostly lowland primary forest that is slightly shady and moist. Some species in New Guinea can tolerate more exposed habitats of secondary forests or abandoned gardens.

The seedlings colonise forest clearings or areas that have been disturbed. At the seedling and young plant stage they are covered in dense stinging trichomes to deter vertebrate herbivores but at the tree stage the density of these hairs is much less because vertebrate herbivores pose less of a threat. In common with U. dioica they are fed on by numerous insects because these small

creatures do not generate sufficient force to break off the terminal knob of the stinging trichome. Nettle trees are the most primitive members of the Urticaceae and herbaceous relatives could have developed from these. At present little to nothing has been written about the ecology of these plants, such as establishment, relationship with forest vertebrate herbivore and insects, fruit dispersal, pollination biology, etc.; perhaps the virulent stings of these tropical tormentors are to blame!

Map 18.1 Distribution of nettle trees (Dendrocnide sp..) after Chew

HOUSE PLANTS

Most of the ornamental plants belonging to the Urticaceae are from the genus Pilea, which contains 250 spp. found in warm-tropical rain forests in the Old and New World. They are prone to frost so need to be kept in a warm greenhouse or as houseplants. The most famous of these plants is the Artillery Plant, Gunpowder Plant or Pistol Plant (*Pilea microphylla*, formerly *P. mucosa* Lindl.) which used to be and were grown in the ferneries of Victorian greenhouses. This annual to short-lived perennial has intricately branched stems (6", 15 cm) with minute leaves, more or less in one plane, giving it a fern-like appearance. This dwarf-like appearance makes it a popular edging plant for greenhouse borders or in mixed houseplant arrangements. The minute clusters of mature male flowers, when handled or sprayed with water, cause the inflexed stamens to straighten in succession, catapulting pollen into the air in little clouds, thereby simulating the effect of puffs of smoke from distant guns. Native to USA, Mexico, West Indies and South America, and has become naturalised in the Balkans of Europe.

The beautiful Friendship Plant (*Pilea involuctrata*, syn. *P. mollis*) is a creeping perennial. It is named after the dark green leaf blades that are thrown into folds at right angles to one another producing a quilted effect. Variegation results from the lighter

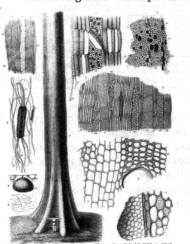

Fig 18a A plate of Laportea gigas (D. excelsa), Weddell H. A. 1865

Table 18.1 The thirty-five species of nettle trees in the Indio-Malay area.
D = dioecious, M = monoecious. F = few, F F = few confined to the flowers. Date = of first herbarium specimen. St. =stinging.(After Chew 1969)

Chronological * Species of Dendrocnide	Date	D or M	Ht. m	St. hairs	Distribution, habitat, fibre uses, etc.
1 Stimulans	1781	D	7	Yes	Wide-ranging. Primary forests up to 1200 m.
24 Oblanceolata	1922	D	10	Yes	Borneo, **endemic**. At 1500 m. Long purple female inflorescences.
30 Elliptica	1954	?	10	Yes	Borneo and Philippines. Primary and secondary forests to 400 m.
19 Crassifolia	1911	D	6	Yes	Philippine Island
5 Meyeniana	1837	D	5-7	Yes	Formosa and Philippines
19 Densifolia	1911	D	6	Yes	Philippine **endemic**.
19 Rigidifolia	1911	D	3	Yes	Philippine **endemic**.
19 Subclausa	1911	D	3	Yes	Philippine **endemic**. Wide ecological tolerance, roadside 500m – mossy forest 1000 m.
18 Venosa	1910	D	10	Yes	Philippine **endemic**.
29 Urentissima	1928	D	4	Yes	China and Vietnam. Riverine trees in lower montane forests 500 m.
31 Basirotunda	1957	D	15	F F	China, Burma, Thailand. Shade trees in dense primary forest, near streams. 500-1000 m.
2 Sinuata	1825	?	10	Yes	Southeast Asia, Malay Peninsula.
10 Luzonensis	1856	D	?	F F	Philippine **endemic**. Forested valleys near streams. 2000 m.
8 Peltata	1851	D	30	Yes	Java, Bali, New Guinea. Up to 1300 m, common at 500 m. Primary and Secondary forest. Bark used as loin cloths by the Papuans.
32 Carriana	1969	D	27	F	Philippines, Lesser Sunda Islands, Molucas and New Guinea.
14 Ternatensis	1869	D	10	F	. Molucas, Tanimbar Islands, New Guinea.
16 Torricellensis	1905	D	15	Yes	New Guinea. **Endemic**. Sub-canopy tree in rain forests, 100-500 m.
16 Corallodeshe	1905	D	6	Yes	New Guinea. **Endemic**. Small tree along rivers in primary forests below 500 m.
4 Moroides	1834	M	10	Yes	Southern Moluccas, North-eastern Australia. The most vicious of all stinging trees.
24 Cordata	1922	M	10	Yes	Timor, Tanimbar Islands, New Guinea, New Britain, Australia (Queensland).
7 Photinophylla	1847	D	20	F F	Australia, **endemic**, in dense rainforest.
12 Vitiensis	1868	?	10	F F	Samoa, Fiji, and New Caledonia. Shade tree along rives in primary forest, below 1000 m.
9 Excelsa	1854	D	35	Yes	Australian, **endemic**. The tallest of all nettle trees.
32 Morobensis	1969	D	25	F F	New Guinea, **endemic**. Highlands above 2000 m.
29 Nervosa	1922	D	12	F F	New Guinea and Solomon Islands. Prim. and Secon. forests. Abandoned gdns. To 1300 m.
6 Latifolia	1844	D	12	F F	Pacific Islands (Micronesia & Melanisia) Has been cult. under name, Laportea Schomburgii var. veriscolor
24 Rechingeri	1922	D	14	Yes	New Guinea, Bismarck Archipelago, Solomon Islands. Common at 500 m.
24 Schlechteri	1922	D	10	-	New Guinea, Bismarck Archipel. Slender trees shrubby, nr. streams in prim. for. to 1200 m.
15 Longifolia	1898	D	8-10	Yes	Celebbes, Molluccas, New Guinea, Bismarck Archipelago and Solomon Islands.
10 Microstigma	1856	D	10	Yes	Lesser Sunda Islands, Celebes and Moluccas.
2 Amplissima	1825	D	8	Yes	Celebes and Moluccas.
32 Kjellbergii	1969	D	7	Yes	Celebes.
12 Harveyi	1868	D	10	F F	Fiji, Tonga, Samoa and Cook Islands. Dominant tree in canyons in prim. for. below 800 m.
23 Mirabilis	1914	?	4	Yes	New Guinea and Solomon Islands. Cultivation by villagers as an ornamental.
32 Celebica	1969	D	2	Yes	Celebes, **endemic**.
32 Kajewskii	1969	D	5-6	Yes	Solomon Islands, **endemic**.

green margins and centres of the quilts, and the coppery-red colorations on exposure to strong light. The minute rosy-red flowers are found clustered in the leaf axils. Native to Central and South-America. The variety 'Moon Valley' is more upright with deep purple sunken veins.

The most popular houseplant in this group is the perennial Aluminium Plant (*Pilea cadierei*) so named because of the silvery-white surface of the leaf which is divided by the deep green main and side veins. It grows to about 10" (25 cm) in height and has inconspicuous

brownish-green flowers. Indo-China (Annam). Creeping Charlie (*Pilea nummulariifolia*) is a creeping perennial with rounded deeply quilted leaves up to 2 cm long. West Indies and tropical South America.

A handsome perennial houseplant that has become available in Britain recently is *Pilea peperomioides*. This plant produces a thick brown succulent stem covered in persistent stipules and has spirally arranged leaves at the top. The leaves are thick, succulent and peltate i.e. supported by a long stalk attached to the underneath of

286

which veins radiate in all directions. If kept in strong light and dry conditions it produces a number of branched inflorescences supporting minute flowers; the smaller are female and the larger male. Native of China (Yunnan).

Members of the genus Elatostema are evergreen perennials and are widely distributed in tropical and subtropical Asia where they are found in forest clearings. They are cultivated for their decorative leaves that are in two ranks and heavily marked with silver and bronze. The trailing types can be grown in hanging baskets or used as a ground cover. *Elatostema repens* (syn. *Pellonia daveanana, P. repens*) is a trailer from Malaya, Burma and Indo-China. The bronze-green leaves with a tinge of violet have a central band of bright green in var. repens, or white blotches in var. viridis. Another trailer is *Elatostema pulchra* (syn. *Pellonia pulchra*) has dark green leaves with even darker veins and is purple underneath. The stems are greenish-pink. Found in Vietnam.

OTHERS

Cow-itch (*Urera baccifera*) is a stinging shrub up to 6.25 m (21 '), which is used as a cattle hedge in tropical America. The effects of the sting are likened to an electric shock and are followed by hours of intense pain. It has panicles of pink-red flowers followed by white, waxy fruits.

General books on the members of the Urticaceae and other nettle groups include: - Everard, and Morley 1970, Heywood, ed., 1978, Milne L, and M, 1967, and Brickell, ed., 1996.

George Forrest, the famous plant collector had discovered specimens of *Pilea peperomioides* in 1906 and 1910 in the Tsangshan range, which rises to 14,000 ft (4,250m) close to the ancient city of Dali (Tali) in western Yunnan. *Pilea peperomioides* Diels. has been in cultivation as a houseplant for many years In 1978 leaves and an inflorescence were sent to Kew and it then became apparent that the plant belonged to the Nettle family, the *Urticaceae* and the plant was a *Pilea*. A family in Cornwall had acquired a plant about 20 years previous when their daughter was on holiday with a Norwegian au pair who the family had previously employed It transpired that a Norwegian missionary, Agnar Espegren brought the plant to Norway from China in 1946 As he did so he gave away pieces of the plant and so it is now a widespread windowsill plant and where it is known as 'the missionary plant'. The big question then needing an answer was, how had the plant travelled from the mountains of western Yunnan to the windowsills of Britain. It transpired that a Norwegian missionary, Agnar Espegren brought the plant to Norway from China in 1946. I have three plants at home which have survived for 27 years and flower.

(Note Erratum on the CD-ROM since these were sent to Canada before the correction of some errors these are still on the figures of the first 200 CD-ROM'S i.e. Fig 13.3 Rove beetle does not belong to the genus *Tachyporus* and in Fig 18.11 the plant is *Pilea peperomioides*.

This new two column format necessitated a few minor changes in text size on some pages to keep the book content per page match the old single column format. It should make reading more restful to the eye- update 2005)

FIG 18.11 *Pilea peperomioides* the ideal house plant you can neglect and it thrives

Fig 18.10 The alumunium plant (Pilea cadierei)

the blade towards the upper end of the leaf and from

287

BIBLIOGRAPHY

Author index: the number/s in brackets at the end of each reference is/are the page/s where the reference occurs.

ABDELHAFID TAHRI, SABAH YAMANI, ABDELKHALEQ LEGSSYER, MOHAMMED AZIZ, HASSANE MEKHFI, MOHAMMED BNOUHAM & ABDERRAHIM ZIYYAT, 2000. Acute diuretic natriuretic and hypotensive effects of a continuous perfusion of aqueous extract of *Urtica dioica* in the rat. J Ethopharmacology, Vol 73:(1-2): 95-100. (147)

ALLAN, M., 1977. Darwin and his flowers. Faber and Faber.London. (51)

ALLEN, E. A., 1976. The Naturalist in Britain. Penguin Books. (33)

AL-MUFTI, M. M., 1978. A quantitative and phenological study of the herbaceous vegetation in three deciduous woodlands at Totley (South Yorkshire). PhD. Thesis, University of Sheffield, (229, 232-3, 234, 236)

AL-MUFTI, M. M., C. L. SYDES, S. B. FURNESS, J. P. GRIME and S. R. BAND, 1977. A quantitative analysis of shoot phenology and dominance in herbaceous vegetation. Journal of Ecology 65, 759-791. (229, 232-3, 234, 236)

ANDERSON S., J K.WOLD, 1978. Phytochemistry 17, 1885-1887. (126)

ANDERSON, M. C., 1962. Bionomics of six species of *Anthocoris* (Heteroptera: Anthocoridae) in England. Transactions Royal Entomological Society London 14, 62-95. (200)

ANDERSON, M. C., 1964. Studies of the woodland light climate. II Seasonal variation in the light climate. J. Ecol. 52, 643-663. (220)

ANDERTON, R. BRIDGES, P. H. LEEDER, M. R. AND SELLWOOD, B. W., 1979. A Dynamic Stratigraphy of the British Isles (16)

ARBER, A., 1938. Herbals, their Origin and Evolution. 2nd edition. Cambridge University Press. , (30, 33)

ARCHER, J., 1993. Crop Nutrition and Fertiliser Use. Farming Press Ltd. Ipswich. (237, 238)

ASCHERSON, P. and P. GRAEBNER., (1908-1918) Mittle europäischer flora. Vol. 4, 607-616. Leipzig. (40, 206, 261)

ASKENASY, E., 1880. Über explodierende staubgefäße. Verh. Nat. –med. Ver. Heidelberg 2. (245)

ASTON,, 1923. in HURST, E. 1942. The poison plants of New South Wales. Poison Plants Committee. Sydney. (84)

AUSTIN, J., 1818. Persuasion. (51)

BABINGTON, C. C., 1881. Manual of British Botany. (32)

BAHRDT, H., 1849. De pilis plantarum. Dissertation. Bonn. (71, 88)

BAKER, R. R., 1972. Territorial behaviour of the nymphalid butterflies, *Aglais urticae* (L.) and *Inachis io* (L.). Journal Animal Ecology 41, 453-469., (178, 172)

BAKER, R. R., 1978. The evolutionary ecology of animal migration. London. (174)

BALL., 1964. Urticaceae. In HEYWOOD, V. H. and T. G. TUTIN (eds.) 1964. Vol. 1 BURGES, N. A., D. H. VALENTINE, S. M. WALTERS and S. A. WEBB. Flora Europaea. Cambridge University Press., (35, 278)

BANCROFT, T. L., 1889. On the materia medica and pharmacology of Queensland plants. Transaction Intercolonial Medical Congress, Australia p. 927. (82)

BARTON, CASTLE, 1877. British Flora Medica p. 297. (63)

BASSETT, I. J., C. W. CROMPTON and D. W. WOODLAND, 1974. The family Urticaceae in Canada. Canadian Journal of Botany 52, 503-516. (206, 279)

BASSETT, I. J., C. W. CROMPTON and D. W. WOODLAND, 1977. The biology of Canadian weeds. 21. *Urtica dioica* L. Canadian Journal Plant Science 57, 491-498. (40, 204)

BASSETT, J., C. CROMPTON and S. FORGET (D. W. WOODLAND), 1982. Biosystematics of the perennial North American Taxa of *Urtica*. I. Chromosome number, hybridization, and palynology. Systematic Botany 7 (3) 269-281. (266).

BATES, G. H., 1933. The great stinging nettle. Journal Ministry of Agriculture 39, 912-922. (17, 209)

BAWA, K. S., 1980. Evolution of dioecy in flowering plants. Annual Review of Ecological Systematics 11, 15-39. (256)

BAWA, K. S., 1981. Modes of pollination, sexual systems and community structure in a tropical lowland rainforest. Abstracts, XIII International Botanical Congress, Sydney. (255, 256)

BAWA, K. S., P. A. OPLER, 1975. Dioecism in tropical forest trees. Evolution 29, 167-179. (256)

BEAGLEHOLE, J. C., 1969. The Voyage of the Resolution and Adventure 1772-1775. Hakluyt Society. Cambridge University Press. (80, 117-18)

BECHTEL, A. R., 1921. The floral anatomy of the Urticales. American Journal of Botany 8, 386-410. (255)

BECK, E. H, .1996. Regulation of shoot/root ratio by cytokinins from roots in *Urtica dioica*: Opinion. Plant and Soil 185, 3-12. (252)

BEINTEMA, J. J., W. J. PEUMANS, 1992. The primary structure of stinging nettle (*Urtica dioica*) agglutinin. FEBS 10798, 299, (2), 131-134. (163)

BEIRNE, B. P. 1952. British Pyralid and Plume Moths. London. (183)

BENTHAM, G., HOOKER J. D., 1930. Handbook of the British flora. Kent. Reeve & Co. Ltd. (32)

BERG, C. C. 1977. Urticales, their differentiation and systematic position. Plant Systematics and Evolution, Supplement 1, 349-374. (7, 8, 243, 256)

BERG, C. C., 1983. Dispersal and distribution in the Urticales–An outline. Sonderband der naturwissenswchaftlichen Vereinung Hamburg 7, 219-229. (253, 256)

BERG, C. C., 1989. 11. Systematics and phylogeny of the Urticales. In, CRANE, P. R. and S. BLACKMORE (eds.), Evolution, Systematics, and Fossil History of the Hamamelidae, Vol. 2: 'Higher' Hamamelidae. Systematics Association Special Vol. No. 40B, pp. 193-220. Clarendon Press. Oxford. , (78, 243, 247, 249, 253, 254, 256, 272)

BERGMANN, E. 1882. Untersuchungen über das Vorkommen der Ameisensäure und Essigsäure in den Pflanzen und über die physiologische Bedeutung derselben im Stoffwechsel. Bot. Zeit. 39, 730-754. (89)

BESECKE, W., 1909. Entwicklungsgeschichtliche Untersuchungen über den anatomischen. Aufbau pflanzlicher Stacheln. Dissertation. Berlin., (73)

BETJEMAN, J., 1958. John Betjeman's Collected Poems. John Murray London. (53)

BINNS, W. O., 1975. Fertilisers in the forest: a guide to materials. Forestry Commission. Leaflet, 63. (247)

BJÖRKMAN, O., P. HOLMGREN., 1963. Adaptability of the photosynthetic apparatus to light intensity in ecotypes from exposed and shaded habitats. Physiologia Pl. 16. 889-913. (258)

BLUNT, W., 1971. The Compleat Naturalist. Collins. London. (80)

BOG-HANSEN, T. C., and E. van DRIESSCHE (Eds.) 1986. Lectins, Biology, Biochemistry and Clinical Biochemistry. Berlin de Gruyter. (163)

BOORDE, A., 1542. A Dyetary of Helth. (Ed. FURNIVALL, F. J. 1870. Early Text Society. London). (62)

BOOT, R., D. J. RAYNAL., J. P. GRIME., 1986. A comparative study of the influence of drought stress on flowering in Urtica dioica and U. urens. Journal of Ecology 74, 485-495. (35,221)

BOOTH, V. H., M. P. BRADFORD., 1963. Tocopherol contents of vegetables and fruits. British Journal of Nutrition 17, 575-581. (117)

BRADLEY, J. D., W. G. TREMEWAN., 1973, 1979. British Tortricid Moths. Ray Society. London. (183)

BRADSHAW, A. D., 1952. Populations of Agrostis tenuis resistant to lead and zinc poisoning. Nature (London) 169, 1098. (258)

BREDEMANN, G. (DERSELBE G.), 1940. Fasergehalt und Faserausbeute bei Fasernesseln in ver-schiedener Stengelhöhe.Faserforsch., Leipzig 14, 148-155. (141)

BREDEMANN, G. (DERSELBE G.), 1942. Nährstiffaufnahme und Nährstoffbedarf der Fasernesseln. Bödenkunde U. Pflanzen. Berlin. 30 (pant H2/3), 95-137. (141)

BREDEMANN, G. (DERSELBE G.), 1952. Untersuchungen über die Beeinflussung des Fasergehalts der Pfropfreiser bei wechselseitiger Pfropfung faserarmer und faserreicher Nesseln (Urtica dioica L.). Ber. Deutsch. Bot. Ges. 65, 145-154. (141)

BREDEMANN, G., 1959: Die Grosse Brennessel Urtica dioica L., Forschungen uber ihren Anbau zur Fasergewinnung. Mit einem Anhang uber ihre Nutzung fur Arznei-und Futtermittel sowie technische Zwecke von Dr. K. Garber. Akademie Verlag Berlin (144)

BREDEMANN, G., 1938. Die Nessel als Faserpflanze. Forschungsdienst 5, 148-161. (138-9)

BRENCHLEY, W. E., 1919-1920. The uses of weeds and wild plants. Science Progress 14, 121-133. (136)

BRICKELL C 1996. The Royal Horticultural Society A-Z Encyclopaedia of Garden Plants. Dorling Kindersley London. (287)

BRENCHLEY, W. E., 1920. Weeds of farmland. Longmans. (136)

BROEKART, W. F., J. van PARIJS, F. LEWNS, H. JOOS and W. J. PEUMANS, 1989. Science 245, 1100-1102. (126)

BROEKERT, W., J. V. PARIJS, J. LEYMNS, H. JOOS and W. J. PEUMANS, 1989. A chitin-binding lectin from stinging nettle rhizomes with anti-fungal properties. Science 245, 1100-1102., (163)

BROER, J, BEHNKE B. 2002. Immunosuppressant effect of IDS 30, a stinging nettle leaf extract, on myeloid dendritic cells in vitro. J Rheumatol.29(4): 656-8. (147)

BROMFIELD, Flora Vectensis, Phytologist 1860. (33)

BROOKS, M., 1991. A Complete Guide to British Moths. Jonathan Cape Londona. (188)

BROSSE, J., 1983. Great Voyages of Discovery. Translated S. HOCHMAN, Oxford. England. (80)

BRUGGEMANN, H., 1937. Biedermanns Zentralbl., (B) Tiererährung, 9, 37. (122)

BURTON, J., 1976. Field and moor. p. 81-88. Kinsmead Press. (4, 101, 115)

BUTCHER, R. W. 1961. A New Illustrated British Flora. Leonard Hill, London. (279)

CAMDEN, W., 1586. Brittania. (33)

CAMPBELL, T., 1777-1844. Letters from the south. (50, 129)

CANNING, A. J., J. H. S. GREEN., 1986. Nepalese 'allo' (Girardinia): improved processing and dyeing. Tropical Science 26, 79-82. (129)

CANO-SANTANA, Z., 1987. Ecologia de la relación entre Wigandia urens (Hydrophyllaceae) y sus herbivoros en el Pedregal de San Angel. D. F. (México). Tesis Profesional, Facultad de Ciencias,UNAM. México. (112)

CANO-SANTANA, Z., and K. OYAMA 1992. Variation in leaf trichomes and nutrients of Wigandia urens (Hydrophyllaceae) and its implications for herbivory. Oecologia 92, 405-409. (112, 226)

CAPPA, V., 1965. Sul valore alimentare della Urtica dioica L. Atti. Sella Soc. Italians Delle Scienze Veterinarie, Vol. 19, 261-264. (123)

CARRICK, R., 1936. Experiments to test the efficiency of protective adaptation in insects. Transactions Royal Entomological Society London 85, 131-140. (189)

CARTER, D. J, B. HARGREAVES 1986. A Field Guide to Caterpillars of Butterflies and Moths of Britain and Europe. Collins. London. (192, 183)

CHAUCER, 1382-1386. Troilus and Criseyde. (48)

CHAURASIA, N., 1957. Inaugural-Dissertation zur Erlangung der Doctorwürde. Pachbereichs Pharmazie und Lebensmittelchemie der Philipps-Universitat. Maeburg/Lahn. (126)

CHEW, W. L., 1965. Laportea and Allied Genera. Gardens Bulletin Singapore XXI, 195-208. (81, 265)

CHEW, W. L., 1969-1971. A monograph of Dendrocnide Urticaceae p. 1-104. A monograph of Laportea Urticaceae p. 111-178. Gardens Bulletin Singapore 25, 1-104, 111-178. (81, 83, 84, 85, 283-86)

CHINERY, M., 1986. Insects of Britain and Western Europe. Collins London. (198)

CHOPRA, R. N., R. L. BADHWAR and S. GHOSH, 1949. Poisonous plants of India. Gov. Ind. Press. Calcuta. (44, 81, 206)

CHRISPEELS, M. J., N. V. RAIKHEL., 1991. Lectins, lectin genes, and their role in plant defence. The Plant Cell 3, 1-9. (163)

CLAPHAM, A. R., TUTIN, T. G. and WARBURG E. F., 1960. Flora of the British Isles. Cambridge University Press. (32, 35, 279)

CLARE, J., 1793-1864. : ROBINSON, E. and D. POWELL Ed. John Clare. Oxford University Press. (51)

COCKAYNE, L. 1919. New Zealand Plants. Wellington, Marks, Government Publ. pp 28, 171, 193, 198. (80)

COLLIER, H., G. B. CHESHER, 1956. Identification of 5-hydroxytryptamine in the sting of the nettle (URTICA DIOICA). British Journal Pharmacology 11, 186-189. (93)

COLLINSON, M., 1989. The fossil history of the Moraceae, Urticaceae (including Cecropiaceae), and Cannabaceae. In Evolution, Systematics, and Fossil History of the Hamamelidae, Vol. 2: Higher Hamamelidae. Editors P. R. Crane and S. Blackmore. Clarendon Press, Oxford, 1989. (16)

COLYER, C. N., C. O. HAMMOND, 1951. Flies of the British Isles. Warne. London. (192, 194)

CORNER, E. J. H., 1962. The classification of Moraceae. Gardens' Bulletin Singapore 19, 187-252. (247)

CORRENS, C., 1909. Vererbungsversuche mit blass (gelb) grunen und buntblattriigen Sippen bei Mirabilis jalap, Urtica pilulifera, und Lunularia annua, Z. Vererblehre, 1, 291-329. (31)

CORSI, G., 1992. The stinging hair of Urtica membranacea POIRET (Urticaceae). II Histochemistry. Phyton (Horn Austria) 32 (2), 247-253. (71, 92)

CORSI, G., F. GARBARI, 1990. The stinging hair of URTICA MEMBRANACEA POIRET (URTICACEAE). I. Morphology and ontogeny. (71, 73)

COTT, H. B., 1936. The effectiveness of protective adaptations in the Hive-Bee, illustrated experiments on feeding reactions, habit formation and memory of the Common Toad (Bufo bufo). Proceedings Zoological Society London 1936, 111-133. (64)

CRONQUIST A., The Evolution and Classification of Flowering Plants. 1968. (1981, 1988). (6, 7)

CUELLAR, H. S., 1967. Description of a pollen release mechanism in the flower of the Mexican Hackberry, Celtis laevigata. Southwestern Naturalist 12, 471-474. (241)

CULPEPPER, N., 1805. English Physician and Complete Herbal. (Various editions). (2, 58-63, 114, 279)

CZARNETZKI, B. M., T. THIELE and T. ROSENBACH 1990. Int. Arch. Allergy Appl. Immunol. 91, 43-46. (92, 126)

DARLINGTON, A., M. J. D. HIRONS, 1968. Plant Galls. Blandford Press. London. (192)

DARWIN, C., 1854. A naturalist's voyage round the world. John Murray. London. (51)

DARWIN, E., 1791. The Botanic Garden. Johnson. London. (150)

DAVIS B. N. K., 1989. The European distribution of insects on stinging nettles, Urtica dioica L.: a field survey. Boll. Zool. 56, 321-326. (204)

DAVIS, B. N. K., 1973. The Hemiptera and Coleoptera of Stinging nettle (*Urtica dioica* L.) in East Anglia. Journal of Applied Ecology 10, 213-237. (192, 194, 195-96, 198, 257)

DAVIS, B. N. K., 1975. The colonisation of isolated patches of nettles (*Urtica dioica* L.) by insects. Journal of Applied Ecology. 12, 1-14. (203)

DAVIS, B. N. K., 1983. Insects on nettles. Cambridge University Press. (15, 170, 183, 192, 194, 200, 203, 204).

DAVIS, B. N. K., C. E. LAWRENCE. 1974. Insects collected from (PARIETARIA DIFFUSA Mert. and Koch and URTICA URENS L.) in Huntingdonshire. Entomologists Monthly Magazine 109, 252-254. (38, 277-8)

DAVIS, D., 1958. Modern veterinary practise. 39 (7), 60. (87)

DE CANDOLLE, A. P., 1832. Cours de Botanique. II. Physiologie Vegetale. Paris, Lib. Fac. Med. (30, 32)

DE GUBERNATIS, A., 1878-1882. La Mythologie des Plantes, ou les Légendes du Régne Végétal. (122)

De KROON, H., 1993. Competition between shoots in stands of clonal plants. Plant Species Biology 8, 85-94. (225)

De KROON, H., R. KALLIOLA, 1995. Shoot dynamics of the giant grass *Gynerium sagittatum* in Peruvian Amazon floodplains. A clonal plant that does show self-thinning. Oecologia 101, 124-131. (225)

De KROON, H., R. KWANT, 1991. Density-dependent growth responses in two clonal herbs. 1. Regulation of shoot density. Oecologia 86, 298-304. (225)

De KROON, H., T. HARA and R. KWANT, 1992. Size hierarchies of shoots and clones in clonal herb monocultures: do clonal and non-clonal plants compete differently? Oikos 63: 410-419. (225)

DENNIS, R. L. H., 1984. The edge effect in butterfly oviposition: batch siting in *Aglais urticae* (L.) (Lepidoptera: Nymphalidae). Entomologist's Gazette 35, 157-173. (176)

DIBB, J. R., 1948. Field Book of Beetles. Brown & Sons. Hull. (148)

DILLON, P. M., S. LOWRIE and MCKEY, 1983. Disarming the "Evil Woman": Petiole constriction by a sphingid larva circumvents mechanical defences of its host plant, *Cnidoscolus urens* (Euphorbiaceae). Biotropica 15, 112-116. (111)

DIOSCORIDES, P., De Materia Medica. Ed. R. T. Gunther. 1933. (31, 57-62, 114, 279)

DOBREFF, M., 1924. Ueber ein neues Sekretin in der Brennessel (*Urtica dioica* L.) Munchener Medizinische Wochenschrift. 24, 773-774. (58, 122)

DRAGENDORF, J. G., 1905. Heilpflanzen. In F. Czapek, Biochemie der Pflanzen. Vol. 1, p. 1-828. Jena, G. Fischer. (88, 89)

DREYER, J. G., DREYLING, et al. 1996. Cultivation of stinging nettle (Urtica dioica L.) with high fibre content as a raw material for production of fibre and cellulose: Qualitative and quantitative differentiation of ancient clones. Journal of Applied Botany 70(1-2): 28-39. Inst. Angewandte Botanik, Abtlg. Nutzpflanzenbiologie, MarseillerStrasse 7, D-20355 Hamburg, Germany (143). ((144-45)

DREYER, J., DREYLING, G. FELDMANN, F., 1998: Fibre Nettle (*Urtica dioica* L.) as Industrial Fibre Crop for Composites (PMCS)? Tagungsband Carmen e. V., "Biomass for Energy and Industry", 10th European Conference and Technology Exhibition. 8-11 Juni, Wuerzburg. S. 516-519. (144)

DRUCE, G. C., 1928. British Plant List. Arbroath. Bundle & Co. (40)

DRUCE, G. C., 1930 Flora of Northamptonshire. p. 207-208. Arbroath. (40)

DRURY, S. M., 1984. In VICKERY, R. (Ed.) Plant-Lore studies. Folklore Society. Mistletoe Series. (114)

DUVAL-JOUVE, M. J, 1867. Etude sur les stimulus d'ortie. Bull. Soc. Bot. Fr. 14, 36-48. (71, 74, 76)

DWUMFOUR, E., 1992. Volatile substances evoking orientation in the predatory flower-bug *Anthocoris nemorum* (Heteroptera: Anthocoridae). Bulletin Entomological Research 82, 465-469. (200)

DYSON, S. L., 1909. Children's flowers. Religious Tract Society. London. (4-5)

ELLENBERG H., 1979. Zeigerwerte der Geläßpflanzen Mitteleuropa. Scripta Geobotanica, Bd. 9 Goltze, Göttingen. (216)

ELLENBERG, H., 1988. Vegetational Ecology o f Central Europe. Cambridge University Press. (37, 221, 211-14, 240, 237)

ELLIS, M. B. and J. P. ELLIS, 1985. Microfungi on Land Plants. An Identification Handbook. Croom Helm. London & Sydney. (158, 160)

ELLIS, M. B., 1971. Dermatiaceous Hyphomycetes. Commonwealth Mycological Institute. Kew. England. (158)

ELLIS, S. B., S. WEISS, 1932. Journal Pharmacology 44, 235. (94)

ELLNAIN-WOJTASZEK M., W. BYLKA and Z. KOWALEWSKI, 1986. Herba Pol. , 32, 131-137. (126)

EMMELIN, N., W. FELDBERG, 1947. The mechanism of the sting of the common nettle (URTICA URENS). Journal Physiology 106, 440-455. (90-91)

EMMELIN, N., W. FELDBERG, 1950. Watsonia, 1 (V). (90)

ERSTIC-PAVLOVIX, N. and R. DZAMIC, 1985. Agrohemija 3, 191-198. (126)

EVANS, G. C., D. E. COOMBE, 1959. Hemispherical and woodland canopy photography and the light climate. Journal Ecology 47, 103-113. (218)

EVERIST, S. L. 1964. A Review of the Poisonous Plants of Queensland. Proc. Roy. Soc. Queensland. Vol. 74 (1): pp 1-20. (83)

EYLES, A. C., 1963. Life Histories of some Phyparochrominae (Heteroptera: Lygaeidae) Trans. Soc. Brit. Entom. Vol 15 Pt 8 p 136-166. (200)

EVERARD B AND MORLEY B D 1970. Wild Flowers of the World. Ebury Press and Michael Joseph London. (287)

FAEGRI, K., L. PIJL, 1971. The principles of pollination ecology. pp. 43, 46, 100. (248).

FELDBERG, W. ,C. H. KELLAWAY, 1937. Liberation of histamine from the perfused lung of the guinea-pig by bee venom. Proceedings Physiological Society. (90)

FELDBERG, W., 1950. The mechanism of the sting of the common nettle. British Science News 3, 75-771. (90)

FERNIE, W. T., 1914. Herbal Simples p. 351-355. Bristol John Wright & Sons. (64, 116)

FISCHER, 1932. (Names of Plants) (11, 42)

FLURY, F., 1927. Z. ges. exp. Med., 56, 402. (88,89)

FORD, L. T., 1949. A guide to the smaller British Lepidoptera. London. (185)

FOURNIER, P., 1948. Le livie des plantes medicinales et Veneneuses de France. Vol. III p. 138-145. (58, 59, 63, 65, 116, 122)

FOX-DAVIES, A. C. A., 1969. A compleat guide to heraldry. Nelson. (43)

FRANCIS, W. D, 1951. Australian Rain-Forest Trees. Forestry and Timber Bureau. Commonwealth of Australia. (84)

FRANCIS, W. D., 1955. Australian Stinging Trees. (C. J. White Memorial Lecture). (84, 86)

FRANCKEN-WELZ, H., M. SCHERR-TRIEBEL, AND J. LÉON. 1999. Ertragsund Qualitätsbildung von Lein, Hanf und Fasernessel in Abhängigkeit von Bestandesdiche und N-Dungung. Mitteilungen der Gesellschaft für Pflanzen bauwissenschaften 12: 177-178. (144)

FRANZ, CH., 1982. Arzneidrogen. Qualitätssicherung durch Anbau und Züchtung. Deutsche Apoth. Zeitg. 122; 1413-1416. (147)

FREEMAN, D. C., E. D. McARTHUR, K. T. HARPER and A. C. BLAUER, 1981. Influence of environment on the floral sex ratio of monoecious plants. Evolution 35, 194-197. (251)

FREEMAN, D. C., K. T. HARPER and E. L. CHARNOV, 1980. Sex change in plants: old and new observations and new hypotheses. Oecologia 47, 222-232. (257)

FRIEND, H., 1883. Flowers and flower lore. George Allen and Co. Ltd. London. (42, 45)

FRIIS, I., 1981. A synopsis of *Girardinia* (*Urticaceae*). Kew Bulletin Vol. 36 (1), p. 143-157. (82, 265)

FRIIS I. 1982. A synopsis of *Obetia* (*Urticaceae*). Kew Bull. Vol. 38 (2): pp 221-228. (265)

FRIIS, I., 1989. 11. The Urticaceae: a systematic review. In, CRANE, P. R. and S. BLACKMORE (eds.), Evolution, Systematics, and Fossil History of the Hamamelidae, Vol. 2: 'Higher' Hamamelidae. Systematics Association Special Vol. No. 40B, pp. 193-220. Clarendon Press. Oxford., (9, 256, 278)

FULLER, R. J., T. POYER, and A. D. POYER, 1982. Bird Habitats in Britain. Calton. British Trust Ornithology & N. C. C. (189)

FURNESS, S. B., J. P. GRIME, 1982. Growth rate and temperature responses inn Bryophytes. 1. An investigation of *Brachythecium rutabulum*. Journal of Ecology 70, 513-523. (233)

FUSSWEDER, A., B. WAGNER and E. BECK, 1988. Bot. Acta 101, 211-219. (126)

FYLES, F., 1920. Principle and poisonous plants of Canada. Department Agriculture Canada Bulletin 39. (87)

GALELLI A., P. TRUFFA-BACHI, 1993. *URTICA DIOICA* AGGLUTININ A super-antigenic lectin from stinging nettle rhizome. Journal of Immunology 151, 1821-1831. (163)

GALELLI, A., M. DELCOURT, M. –C. WAGNER, W. PEUMANS and P. TRUFFA-BACHI, 1995. Selective expansion followed by profound deletion of mature Vβ8.3[+] T cells in vivo after exposure to the superantigenic lectin *Urtica dioica* agglutinin. American Association Immunologists. 154, 2600-2611. (163)

GANßER, D. and G. SPITELLER, 1995. Aromatase inhibitors from *Urtica dioica* roots. Planta Med. 61, 138-140. (62)

GAUDICHARD B., 1826. Botan. Du Voyage de l'Uranie. 504 Voy. Bonite. T. 114. (279)

GAULD, I, and B. BOLTON, 1988. The Hymenoptera. Oxford University Press. (203)

GEBAUER, G., H. REHDER and B. WOLLENWEBER, 1988. Nitrate, nitrate reduction and organic nitrogen in plants from different ecological and taxonomic groups of Central Europe. Oecologia (Berlin) 75, 371-385. (225)

GELTMAN, D. V., 1986. Systematic and ecological-geographic characteristics of the species from the affinity of *Urtica dioica* (Urticaceae) in the flora of the USSR Bot. Zhurn. 71, 1480-1489. [In Russian]. (263)

GELTMAN, D. V., 1992. *Urtica galeosifolia* Wierzb. Ex. Opiz (Urticaceae) in Wicken Fen (E. England). Watsonia 19, 127-129. (263, 267)

GERARDE, J., 1633. The Herball. Ed. T. Johnson. (Minerva Press, London 1974). (30, 32, 34, 56, 60, 63, 270, 279)

GILMOUR, J. 1954. Wild Flowers. N/N Collins. London. (270)

GODWIN, H., 1975. History of the British flora. Cambridge University Press. (263)

GOEBEL, K., 1915. Schleuderfrüchte bei Urticifloren. Flora N. F. 108. (245, 253)

GOEBEL, K., 1924. Die Entfaltungsbewegungen der Pflanzen und deren teleologische deutung. usw., 2. Aufl. Jena, 224, 406-407. (245)

GÓMEX, F., L. QUIJANO, JS. CALDERÓN and T. RIOS, 1980. Terpenoids isolated from *Wigandia kunthii*. Phytochemistry 19, 2202-2203. (112)

GOODSPEED, T. H., 1961. Plant hunters in the Andes. Univ. California Press. (117)

GORUP-BESANEZ, E. F., 1849. Notiz über das vorkommen der Ameisensäure in den Brennesseln. Jour. Prakt. Chemie 48, 191-192. (89)

GRABHERR,, 1942. see ELLENBERG (240)

GRANT WATSON, G., 1943. Walking with Fancy. Country Life Ltd. London. (3-4)

GRAVES, J. D. and M. C. GRAVES, 1995. Parasitic Plants. Chapman & Hall. London. (156)

GRAVIS, A., 1886. Recherches anatomiques sur les organs vegétatives de l'*Urtica dioica*. Mem. Acad. Roy. Sci., lett. beaux-arts. Belg. 47, 1-257. (21, 26.)

GREEN, T., 1816. Universal Herbal. (32, 34, 57, 61, 81, 133-34, 207, 216)

GREENOAK, F., 1985. God's acre, the flowers and animals of the parish churchyard p. 43. Orbis. London. (114)

GREINERT, M., 1886. Beiträge zur Kenntnis der morphologischen und anatomischen Ver-hältnisse der Loasaceen mit besonderer Berutcksichtigung der Behaarung. Diss. Freiburg i. Br. (190, 206, 208, 229.)

GREY-WILSON C.,& M. BLAMEY1989. The Illustrated Flora of Britain and Northern Europe. Hodder & Stroughton, London. (272)

GRIEG-SMITH, P., 1948. Biological flora of the British Isles: URTICA DIOICA L. Journal of Ecology. 36, 343-351. (35, 190, 206, 229.)

GRIEVE, M., 1931. A modern herbal. Vol. II p. 575-576. Jonathan Cape. (60, 65, 121, 124, 135, 137, 157, 270)

GRIGSON, G., 1975. The Englishman's flora p. 255-258 Phoenix House Ltd. London. (34, 42, 206, 268)

GRIME, J. P. and B. C. JARVIS, 1976. Shade avoidance and shade tolerance in flowering plants. 2: effects of light on the germination of species by contrasted ecology. In: Light as and ecological factor. 2L Symposium of the British Ecological Society No. 16, G. C. Evans, R. Bainbridge and O. Rackham (eds), 525-532. Oxford: Blackwell Scientific. (37)

GRIME, J. P. and R. HUNT, 1975. Relative growth-rate; its range and adaptive significance in a local flora. Journal of Ecology 63, 393-422. (232)

GRIME, J. P., 1977. Evidence for the existence of three primary strategies in plants and its relevance to ecological and evolutionary theory. American Naturalist 111, 1169-1194. (232)

GRIME, J. P., 1978. Interpretation of small scale patterns in the distribution of plant species in space and time. In: Structure and functioning of plant populations, A. H. J. Freysen and J. E. Woldendorp (eds), 101-121. Amsterdam: North-Holland. (232)

GRIME, J. P., 1979. Plant strategies and vegetation processes. Chichester: Wiley. (238)

GRIME, J. P., HODGSON J. G. and HUNT T. R., 1988. Comparative plant ecology: A functional approach to common British species. Unwin Hyman. London. (9, 35, 37, 214-15, 238, 240).

GRIME, J. P., S. F. MACPHERSON-STEWART and R. S. DEARMAN, 1968. An investigation of leaf palatability using the snail *Cepaea nemoralis* L. Journal Ecology 56, 405-420. , (112.)

GROSE, D. G., 1957. The flora of Wiltshire.and The vegetation of Wiltshire. Reprinted EP Publishing Ltd. 1979. (152, 211, 239, 272)

GROSSE-BRAUCKMANN, 1953. See Ellenberg 1988. (214)

GROVE, W. B., 1913. The British Rust Fungi, their biology and classification p.1. (158)

HABERLANDT, G., 1886. Zur Anatomie und Physiologie der pflanzlichen Brennhaare. Sitz-ber. Akad. Wien 93, 122-145. (71, 74, 75, 88, 89, 102, 179).

HALD, M., 1942. The nettle as a culture plant. Folk-Liv 1942, 28-49. (130-31)

HALLIDAY, G. and M. BEADLE, 1983. Flora Europaea. Cambridge University Press. (150).

HAMMERTON, J. A, 1935? (Ed.) Outline of nature in the British Isles. Amalgated Press Ltd. London. (5.)

HANCZAKOWSKI, P. and B. SZYMCZYK, 1992. The nutritive value of protein of juice extracted from green parts of various plants. Animal feed Science and Technology 38, 81-87. (124.)

HARA, T. and M. ŠRUTEK, 1995. Shoot growth and mortality patterns of *Urtica dioica*, a clonal forb. Annals of Botany 76, 235-243. (224, 236)

HARDY, T., 1880. The Trumpet Major. (51)

HARINGTON, J, 1607. Regimen Sanitatis Salernitanum. (48)

HARLEY, R. M., 1971. An explosive mechanism in *Eriope crassipes*, a Brazilian labiate. Biological Journal of the Linnean Society 3, 159-164. (242)

HATFIELD, A. W, 1975. How to enjoy your weeds p. 93-99. Frederick Muller Ltd. (63, 121).

HAWKSWORTH, D. L. (Ed.) 1974. The changing flora and fauna of Britain p. 89. Academic Press. London. (160).

HEATH, J., A. M. EMMET, and others., 1976- ?. The Moths and Butterflies of Great Britain and Ireland, Vols. 1, 2, 7, 8, 9, and 10. Harley Books. Essex. (188, 183, 277)

HEGI, G., 1910. Illustrierte flora von mittle Europa. Vol. 3, 139-141. München. (206).

HEINITZ, Dispersal, see RIDLEY., (252).

HERRICK, R., 1648. Hesperides. , (50).

HEYWOOD, V. H. and T. G. TUTIN (eds.) 1964. Vol. 1 BURGES, N. A., D. H. VALENTINE, S. M. WALTERS and S. A. WEBB., Flora Europaea. Cambridge University Press. (241)

HEYWOOD, V. H. 1964. Flora Europaea. Notulae Systematicae as Floram Europaeam spectantes. 4-6. (277, 281)

HEYWOOD V H ED. 1978. Flowering Plants of the World. OUP London. (287)

HLAVACEK, R. and P. PYSEK, 1988. Herb communities of plouznice river floodplain between Mimon and Borecek (district Ceska Lipa). Seceroc es. Prir. 21, 31-66. [in Czech] (238).

HODGSON, J. G., 1986. Commonness and rarity in plants with special reference to the Sheffield flora. Parts I-IV. Biological Conservation 36, 199-314. (240, 267).

HODGSON, J. G., 1987. Why do so few plant species exploit fertile habitats?. An investigation into cytology, plant strategies and abundance within a local flora. Functional Ecology 1. 243-251. (240, 267).

HOGG, P., P. SQUIRES and A. H. FITTER, 1995. Acidification, nitrogen deposition and rapid vegetational change in a small valley mire in Yorkshire. Biological Conservation 71, 143-153. (238).

HOOKE, R., 1665. Micrographia: or some physiological descriptions of minute bodies made by magnifying glasses with observations and inquiries thereupon. John Martyn James Allestry, Printers to the Royal Society. Dover facsimile of the first edition, Dover Pub. Co., New York. (66-68).

HOOKER, J. D, 1891. Himalayan Journals p. 126-127. Ward Lock, Bowden & Co. (81-82).

HORWOOD, A. R., 1919. A new British flora-British wild flowers –their natural haunts. Vol. 3 p 230-233. Gresham Publishing Co. Ltd. London. (6, 207, 300).

HOUSMAN, A. E., 1940. A Shropshire Lad. p. 28 George Harrup Co. Ltd. (52).

HRYB, D.J., M. S. KHAN, N. A. ROMAS and W. ROSNER, 1995. The effect of extracts of the roots of the stinging nettle (*Urtica dioica*) on the interaction of SHBG with its receptor on human prostatic membranes. Planta Med. 61, 31-32. (62).

HUESING, J. E., L. L. MURDOCK and R. E. SHADE, 1991. Rice and stinging nettle lectins: Insecticidal activity similar to wheat germ agglutinin. Phytochemistry 30 (11), 3565-3568. (163).

HUGHES, R. E., P. ELLERY, T. HARRY, V. JENKINS and E. JONES, 1980. The dietary potential of the common nettle. Journal of Science Food Agriculture 31, 1297-1286. (123).

HUGHES, R. E. 1975. James Lind and the cure of scurvy. An experimental approach. Medical History 19, 342-351. (117).

HUTCHINSON J. 1969. British Wild Flowers Penguin Books. London. (278)

HUTTON, J. H. 1923. Some Economic Plants of the Naga Hills. Agricultural Journal India 18, 567-571 (129).

IIDA, M., Y. ASAMI, T. TANAKA, G. HONDA, M. TABATA, E. SEZIK and E. YESILADA, 1994. Studies on genus *Urtica* in Turkey (1) Identification of *Urtica* in Turkey by internal structure of axis and petiole Natural medicines 48, 237-243. (59).

İLHAMI GÜLÇIN, İRFAN KÜFREVIOĞLU, MÜNIR OKTAY & MEHMET EMIN BÜYÜKOKUROĞLU, 2004. Antioxidant, antimicrobial, antiulcer and analgesic activities of nettle (*Urtica dioica* L.). J. Ethnopharmacology. Vol. 90 (2-3):205-215. (147)

ING, B., 1968. A census catalogue of British myxomycetes. The Foray Committee. The British Mycological Society. (162).

INGROUILLE M., 1995. Historical Ecology of the British Flora. Chapman & Hall, London. (16).

IVIMEY-COOK R. B.1984. Atlas of the Devon flora. Exeter. Devonshire Association. (270, 281)

JACQUES-FÉLIX, and H. RABÉCHAULT 1948. Recherches sur les Fibres de quelques Urticacées Africaines. Agron. Trop. 3, 339-384, 451-488. (129).

JANZEN, D. H, 1966. Coevolution of mutualism between ants and *Acacia* in Central America. Evolution 20, 249-275. (112).

JANZEN, D. H., 1967. Interaction of the Bull's-Horn acacia (*Acacia cornigera* L.) with an ant inhabitant (*Pseudomyrmex ferruginea* F. Smith) in eastern Mexico. Kansas University Science Bulletin, 47, 315-558. (112).

JARMOLENKO, A. V. 1956. Urticaceae, in Komarov, V. L. (ed), Flora URSS, 5, 399-401. Leningrad. (278)

JAQUES, R., and M. SCHACHTER, 1954. Brit. J. Pharmacol. 9: 53. (93).

JENNINGS, T. J and J. P. BARKHAM, 1995. Food of slugs in mixed deciduous woodland. Oikos 26, 211-221. (113).

JOUAD, H., M. HALOUI, H. RHIOUANI, J. EL HILALY & M. EDDOUKS, 2001. Ethnobotanical survey of medicinal plants used for the treatment of diabetes, cardiac and renal diseases in the North centre region of Morocco (Fez-Boulemane). J. Ethnopharmacology. Vol.77 (2-3): 175-182. (147)

KAY, Q. O. N. and D. P. STEVENS, 1986. The frequency, distribution and reproductive biology of dioecious species in the native flora of Britain and Ireland. Botany Journal of the Linnaean Society 92, 39-64. (256, 257).

KERNER VON MARILAUN, A, 1894. Pflanzenleben. Translated by F. W. OLIVER. The Natural History of Plants. Gresham Pub. Co. London. (6, 157, 243).

KILLIP, L. P. 1960.Flora of Panama. Annals of Miss. Bot. Gds. Vol. 47: pp 179-198. (265)

KIRBY, R. H., 1963. Vegetable Fibres. Leonard Hill. London. (129)

KIRBY, W. and W. SPENSE, 1858. Introduction to entomology p. 216. Longman, Brown, Green, Longmans & Roberts. London. (15, 98, 190).

KNOLL, F., 1905. Die Brennhaare der Euphorbiaceen-Gattungen *Dalechampia* und *Tragia*. Sitz. –Ber. d. kais. Akad. d. Wiss. Wien, Math. –Nat. Kl. 114, 1. Abt., 29-48. (88, 104-5).

KÖHLER, K., K. SCHMIDTKE, AND R. RAUBER. 1999. Eignung verschiedener Pflanzenarten zur Untersaat in Fasernesseln (*Urtica dioica* L.). In H. Hoffmann, and S. Müller (eds.). Beiträge zur 5. Wissenschaftstagung zum Ökologischen Llandbau. Köster Verlag, Berlin, Germany. p. 496-500. (144-45)

KOMAROV, V.L. ed., 1970. Flora of the U S S R, Vol. 5. Translated H. Landau. Keter Press. Jerusalem. (30, 31, 32, 35, 129, 277).

KORCHAGINA, L. N., V. F. RUDYUK and V. T. CHERNOBAI, 1973. Rast. Resur. 9, 577-581. (126).

KRZESKI, T., M. KAZON, A. BORKOWSKI, A. WITESKA and J. KUCZERA, 1993. Combined extracts of *Urtica dioica* and *Pygeum africanum* in the treatment of benign prostatic hyperplasia: Double-blind comparison of two doses. Clinical Therapeutics Vol. 15, No. 6, 1011-1020. (61).

KUDRITSKAYA, S. E., G. M. FISHMAN, L. M. ZAGORODSKAYA and D. M. CHIKOVANI 1986. Khim. Prir. Soedin. 5, 640-641. (126).

KUESTER, 1916. In Zimmermann editor. Encyclopaedia of Plant Anatomy, Uphof. Plant Hairs. (78).

KUIJT, J., 1969. The biology of parasitic flowering plants. University California Press. Berkeley & Los Angeles. (150).

LAFONTE, A. M., 1984. Devon Print Group. Exeter. (47).

LANCASTER, R., 1983. Plant Hunting in Nepal p. 137. Croom Helm. London. (82).

LARGE, E. C., 1940. The advance of the fungi. Jonathan Cape. London. (82).

LAUDERMILK, J., 1952. Natural History (66, 74).

LAWSON, P., 1852. Synopsis of the vegetable products of Scotland. Div. IV. Section I p. 11. (51).

LE QUESNE, W.J., 1972, Studies on the coexistence of three species of *Eupteryx* (Hemiptera: Cicadellidae) on nettle. Journal Entomology A 47, 37-44. (201).

LEACH, M. (Ed.), 1950. The standard dictionary of folklore mythology and legend Vol. II p. 788. Funk and Wagnall. New York. (43, 59, 62, 129).

LEACH, W., 1935. A Textbook of Practical Botany p.79-82. (158).

LEECH, J. H., 1886. British Pyralides. London, (183).

LEEUWENHOEK, A. Van, 1687. (67-68).

LEHNE, P., K. SCHMIDTKE AND U. RAUBER. 2001. Ertrag von Fasernesseln im ökologischen Landbau bei unterschiedlicher Nährstoffversorgung. In Mitteilungen der Gesellschaft für Pflanzenbauwissenschaften 13:158-159. (145)

LENGGENHAGER, K, 1974. Neues uber den mechanismus der nesselstiche. Ber. Schweiz. Bot. Ges. 84, 73-80. (78).

LEO, P. , A. MICELI, C. ANTONACI and G. VIGNA., 1993. Characterisation and enzymatic hydrolysis of nettle (*Urtica dioica* L.) Deproteinated biomass. Journal Science Food Agriculture 63, 391-395. (125).

LERNER, D. R. and N. V. RAIKHEL., 1992. The gene for stinging nettle lectin (*Urtica dioica* Agglutinin) encodes both a lectin and a chitinase. Journal Biological Chemistry 267 (16), 11085-11019. (164).

LESCHENAULT, ?. Mem. Mus. 6 362. (81).

LEUNG, T-W. C., D. H. WILLIAMS, J. C. J. BARNA, S. FOTI, and P. B. OELRICHS, 1986. Structural studies on the peptide moroidin from *Laportea moroides*. Tetrahedron 42, No. 12, 3333-3348. (92, 95-6).

LEVIN D. A., 1973. The role of trichomes in plant defence. Quarterly Review Biology 48, 3-15. (112.)

LEWIS, T., 1927. Blood vessels of human skin and their responses. Shaw & Sons, Ltd. London. (93).

LINDLEY, J., 1853. The Vegetable Kingdom p. 260-261. (p. 157). (81).

LINNAEUS, 1759. Systema Naturae. (31).

LINNAEUS., 1753. Species Plantarum. (34).

LINNAEUS, C. 1756. Flora Palaestina sustit B. J. Strand. Upssala. (269)

LINSSEN, E.F., 1959. Beetles of the British Isles. Warne. London. (198).

LLOYD, D. G. and C. J. WEBB, 1977. Secondary sex characters in plants. Botanical Review 43, 177-216. (257).

LOTTI, G., C. PARADOSSI and F. MARCHINI., 1985. Riv. Soc. Ital. Sci. Aliment. 14 , 263-270. (123).

LOUSLEY J. E. 1950. Wild Flowers of Chalk & Limestone. N/N. Collins. London. (270)

LOVE, A. and D. LOVE, 1961. Chromosome numbers of central and north-west European species. p. 125. (40).

LOWMAN, M. D., 1985. Temporal and spatial variability in insect grazing of the canopies of five Australian rainforest tree species. Australian Journal Ecology 10, 7-24. (204).

LUBBOCK, J, 1892. Seedings Vol. I p. 43. (228).

LUCAS, R., 1959. Common and uncommon uses of herbs for healthful living. Arc Books. New York. (58, 60).

LIU, T. S., and W. D. HUANG. 1976. Urticaceae. In H. L. Li, T. S. Lui., T. C. Huang, T. Koyama, and C. E. DeVol (eds), Flora of Taiwan, Vol. 2, Epoch Publ. Co., Taipei, pp 162-229. (265)

LUTZ, D., 1914. The poisonous nature of the stinging hairs of *Jatropha urens*. Science 40, 609-610. (105).

LYTE., 1578. Nievve Herball , (28).

MAAREL, E. VAN DER., 1980. Towards an ecological theory of nature management. In W. Haber (ed.), Verh. Gesellschaft fur Okologie 9, Gottingen, pp. 13-24. (237, 239).

MABEY, R., 1996. Flora Brittanica. Sinclair-Stevenson. (114, 120, 276).

MAC CLINTOCK., 1957. The Countryman., (34).

MACFARLANE, W. V., 1963. The pain-producing properties of the stinging tree *Laportea* p. 31-37. In, 'Venomous and Poisonous Animals and Noxious Plants of the Pacific Region' ed H. L. KEEGAN. Pergamon Press. Oxford. (84).

MACFARLANE, W. V., 1963. The stinging properties of *Laportea*. Economic Botany 17, 303-311. (84).

MACLEOD, D., 1968. A book of herbs. Gerald Duckworth. London. (48, 222).

MAITAI, C. K., S. TALAKAJ, D. TAKALAJ and D, NJOROGE 1981. Smooth muscle stimulating substances in the stinging nettle tree *Obetia pinnatifida*. Toxicon 19, 186-188. (92).

MAITAI, C. K., S. TALALAJ., D. NJOROGE and R. WAMUGUNDA., 1980. Effect of extract of hairs from the herb *Urtica massaica* on the smooth muscle. Toxicon 18, 225. (92).

MAITLAND EMMET, A. and J. HEATH, (Eds.), 1990. The Butterflies of Great Britain and Ireland. Harley Books. England. (181).

MAJERUS, M. E. N., 1994. N/N Series. Harper-Collins, London. (198).

MARGETTS & DAVID., 1980.Revision of Cornish Flora. (272)

MARTIN, W. K, G. T. FRASER., 1939. Flora of Devon. P 579-80. (284).

MARTY. F., 1968. Infrastructures des organs secreteuses de la fueille *d'Urtica urens*. Comptes, Rendues Acad. Sci. Paris D. 266, 1712-1714. (71, 73).

MASIAS, M. A. and R. G. POSITANO, 1990. Urticaceae Poisoning. Journal American Podiatric Medical Association 11, 613-616. (87).

MAUDUIT, VICOMTE DE –, 1940. They Can't Ration These. Michael Joseph. London. (142).

MEIJDEN, E., M. WIJN and H. J. VERKAAR, 1988. Defence and re-growth, alternative strategies in the struggle against herbivores. Oikos 51, 355-363. (226).

METCALFE, C. R. and L. CHALK, 1950. Anatomy of the Dicotyledons Vol. II p. 1244-1254. Oxford. Clarendon Press. (143).

METCALFE, C. R., 1942. Economic value of the common stinging nettle. Nature 3794, 83. (137, 141)

MEYEN, F. J. F., 1837. Ueber Die Secretionsorgane der Pflanzen. Berlin, (71, 102).

MEYRICK, E., 1970. A Revised Handbook of British Lepidoptera. Reprint E. W. Classey. Middlesex, England. (183).

MILLER, N. G., 1971. The genera of the URTICACEAE in the South-eastern United States. Journal of the Arnold Arboretum. 52, 40-68. (261-2, 277)

MILLER, P., 1741. Gardener's Dictionary. (34).

MILLER, P., 1790. Garden Kalendar. (56).

MILNE L, AND MILNE M 1967. Living Plants of the World. Nelson London. (287)

MILNE, R. and L. HASTINGS, 1998. Home-spun solutions. Kew Spring, 10-11. (14).

MITCHELL, D. W., (no date). A key to the corticolous myxomycetes. The British Mycological Society. (162).

MOAL LE A. M. and P. TRUFFA-BACHI, 1988. Cell. Immunol. 115, 24-35. (126).

MOLLO, A., 1922. Observations on the use of nettle in feeding poultry. Staz. Sper. Agr. Ital., 55, No. 10-12, p. 490-496. (123).

MOONEY, H. A. and W. D. BILLINGS, 1961. Comparative physiological ecology of arctic and alpine populations of *Oxyria digyna*. Ecological Monographs. 31, 1-28. (258).

MORRIS, M. G., F. H. PERRING, 1974. The British Oak. E.W. Classey Ltd. Berkshire. (9).

293

MOSEBACH, G., 1932. Über die schleuderbewegung der explodierenden staubgefäße und staminodien bei einigen Urticaceen. Planta 16, 70-115. (245).

MOSS C. E.1914. Cambridge British Flora. Cambridge. (274)

MUTIKAINEN, P. and M. WALLS, 1995. Growth, reproduction and defence in nettles: response to herbivory modified by competition and fertilisation. Oecologia (Berlin) 104 (4), 487-495. (226, 227, 252).

MUTIKAINEN, P., M. WALLS and A. OJALA, 1994. Sexual differences in responses to simulated herbivory in Urtica dioica. Oikos 63, 397-404., (226, 257, 252).

NAVAS, B. E., 1961. El genero Urtica en Chile. Bol Soc Argent Bot Roma 9, 395-413. (35, 206).

NESTLER, A., 1925. Zur Kenntnis der Wirkung der Brennhaare unserer Urtica-Arten. Ber. Deutsch. Bot. Ges. 43, 497-504. (88, 89).

NEWELL-ARBER, E. A., 1910. Plant life in alpine Switzerland. 119. John Murray. London., (35, 37).

NEWMAN, L. H., 1954. Butterfly Farmer. Country Book Club. London. (183).

NEWMAN, L. H., 1967. Create a butterfly garden. Worlds Work Ltd. (170).

NEWMAN, L. W. and H. A. LEEDS, 1913. Textbook of British Butterflies and Moths. Gibbs & Bamforth, Ltd. (183).

NEWTON, A., 1971. Flora of Cheshire. Cheshire Community Council. Chester. (272)

OLIVER, J., 1994. Wiltshire Archaeological Society. (239).

OLSEN, C., 1921. The ecology of Urtica dioica. Journal Ecology 9, 1-17. (216, 218).

OSSADCHA-JANATA, N., 1952. Herbs used in Ukrainian folk medicine. p. 69-71. (57, 60, 115).

PALAISEUL, J., 1972. Grandmother's secrets. p. 222-225. Penguin Books. (59, 62, 78).

PANK, F., 1991. Qualitätsbestimmende Merkmale der Arznei- und Gewürzpflanzen und ihre Abhängigkeit von Sorten, Anbautechnik, Ernte und Nacherntebehandlung. Kurzfassung der Vorträge auf dem 103. VDLUFA-Kongreß vom 16, bis 21, Sept.: 135 (147)

PARIJS, J. V., H. M. JOOSEN, W. J. PEUMANS, J. M. GEUNS and A. J. Van LAERE, 1992. Affect of the Urtica dioica agglutinin on germination and cell wall formation of Phycomyces bladesleeanus Burgeff. Archives Microbiology 158, 19-25. (163).

PARKINSON, 1640. Theatrum Botanicum. (32).

PATTEN, G., 1993: Urtica. Medicinal plant review. Aust. J. Med. Herbalism 5 (1, 147)

PENZIG, O., 1922. Pflanzen teratology pp 220-221. (263).

PEPYS, S., 1660-1669. The diary of Samuel Pepys. (50).

PERRIN, R. M., 1976. The population dynamics of the Stinging nettle aphid, Microlophium carnosum (Bukt.). Ecological Entomology 1, 31-40. (203, 201).

PERRING, F. (Ed.), 1974. The flora of changing Britain. E. W. Classey. London. (281)

PERRING, F. (ed.) 1974. GILLHAM, M. E., 'Seed dispersal by birds', In, The flora of changing Britain. Classey. London. (253).

PETERSON, R. and P. JENSÉN, 1985. Effects of nettle water on growth and mineral nutrition of plants. I. Composition and properties of nettle water. Biol. Agric. Hortic. 2, 303-314. (217).

PETERSON, R. and P. JENSÉN, 1986. Effects of nettle water on growth and mineral nutrition of plants. II. Pot – and water culture experiments. Biol. Agric. Hortic.4, 7-18. (217).

PETERSON, R. and P. JENSÉN, 1988. Uptake and transport of N, P and K in tomato supplied with nettle water and nutrient solution. Plant and Soil 107, 189-196. (217).

PETLEVSKI, R., M. HADŽIJA, M. SLIJEPČEVIČ & D. JURETIČ, 2001. Effect of 'antidiabetis' herbal preparation on serum glucose and fructosamine in NOD mice. J. Ethnopharmacology. Vol. 75 (2-3):181-184. (147)

PETRIE, J. M., 1906. The stinging property of the giant nettle tree (LAPORTEA GIGAS WEDD.D) Proceedings Linnean Society New South Wales 31, 530-545. (44, 83, 88.)

PEUMANS, W.J., M. DE LEY and W. F. BROEKART, 1984. FEBS. Lett. 177, 99-103. (126, 163).

PIEDALLES, A., 1921. Wild vegetables. (p. 111) (115).

PIGOTT, C. D. and K. TAYLOR., 1964. The distribution of some woodland herbs in relation to the supply of nitrogen and phosphorus in the soil. Journal Ecology 52, 175-185. (217).

PIGOTT, C. D., 1964. Nettles as indicators of soil conditions. New Scientist 21, 230-232. (218).

PIGOTT, C. D., 1971. Analysis of the response of URTICA DIOICA to phosphate. New Phytologist 70, 953-966. (218).

PILGRIM, R. L. C., 1959. Some properties of the sting of the New Zealand nettle URTICA FEROX. Proceedings Royal Society London B. 151, 48-56., (256).

POLLARD, A. J and D BRIGGS, 1982. Genecological Studies of Urtica dioica L. I. The nature of intraspecific variation in U. dioica. The New Phytologist 92, 453-470. (256).

POLLARD, A. J., 1981. Genecological Studies of Urtica dioica L. Ph. D. Dissertation, University of Cambridge. (257).

POLLARD, A. J., 1986. Variation in CNIDOSCOLUS TEXANUS in relation to herbivory. Oecologia (Berlind) 70, 411-413. (99, 100, 101).

POLLARD, A. J.and D BRIGGS, 1984. Genecological Studies of Urtica dioica L. II. Patterns of variation at Wicken Fen. The New Phytologist 96, 483-499. (15, 259).

POLLARD, A. J.and D BRIGGS, 1984. Genecological Studies of Urtica dioica L. III. Stinging hairs and plant herbivore interactions. New Phytologist 97, 507-522. (100).

PORTER, J., 1997. Caterpillars of the British Isles. Viking. (183, 188).

POTTER,, 1907. Potter's Cyclopaedia of botanical drugs and preparations p. 247-248. (65).

POWER, H., 1664. Experimental Philosophy. (66).

PRACH, K., S. KUCERA and J. KLIMESOVA, 1990. Vegetation and land use in the Luznice River floodplain and valley in Austria and Czechoslovakia. In: WHIGHAM, D. R., R. E. GOOD and J. KVET (eds.), Wetland ecology and management: case studies, p. 117-125. Kluwer Acad. Publ.,Dordrecht. (238).

PRAEGER, R. Lt. 1934. The Botanist in Ireland. Dublin Hodges, Figgis & Co, Ltd. (274)

PRATT, A., 1899-1905. Flowering plants of Great Britain Vol. 5 p. 20-31. Frederick Warne & Co. (6, 120, 121, 143, 270).

PRIOR, R. L. A., 1863. On the popular names of British plants. Williams and Norgate. London. (11).

PROCTOR M. C. F., P. YEO, 1973. The Pollination of Flowers. Collins N/N London (5,254)

PROCTOR, M. C. F., P. YEO and L. LACK, 1996. The Natural History of Pollination. Harper/Collins. London. (5, 254).

PROKOP, E, 1994. The control of nettles on Little Wittenham Nature Reserve, Oxfordshire. (viii)

PULLIN, A. S. and J. E. GILBERT 1989. The stinging nettle (URTICA DIOICA L.) increases trichome density after herbivore and mechanical damage. Oikos 54, 275-280. (15, 100, 226).

PULLIN, A. S., 1986. Effect of photoperiod and temperature on the life cycle of different populations of the peacock butterfly Inachis io. Entomology Experimental Applied 41, 237-242. (178)

PULLIN, A. S., 1987. Change in leaf quality following clipping and re-growth of Urtica dioica and consequences for a specialist insect herbivore Aglais urticae.. Oikos 49, 39-45. (176, 226).

PULLIN, A. S., 1988. Environmental cues and variable voltinism patterns in Aglais urticae (L.). Entomological Gazette 39 (2), 101-112. (176).

QUELCH, M. T. 1945, Herbal Remedies and recipes and some others. Faber and Faber. London., (65, 120, 128).

QUELCH, M. T., 1946. Herbs and how to know them. Faber and Faber. London. (65, 120,128).

RACKHAM, O., 1994. History of the Countryside. BCA. London. (17, 64).

RADUNZ, A., Z. Naturforsch. , C: Biosci. 31C, 589-593. (126).

RANSON, F., 1949. British Herbs. Penguin. (156).

RAY, J., 1660. Ray's flora of Cambridgeshire. (translated by EWEN, A. H. and C. T. PRIME. 1975. p. 126. (30, 32, 64, 132).

REANBEY, P. H., 1958. Dictionary of British surnames. Routledge Kegan Paul. London. (43)

REGULA, I. and Z. DIVIDE, 1980. The presence of serotonin in some species of the Genus Urtica. Acta. Bot. Croat. 39, 47-50. (92, 93, 94).

REGULA, I., 1970. 5-Hidroksitriptamin u ljutoj koprivi (Urtica pilulifera). Acta Bot. Croat. 29, 69-74. (93).

REGULA, I., 1970. Kromatografska identifilacija serotonina u koprivi (Urtica pilulifera var. Dodartii (L.) ASCHERS. Acta Bot. Croat. 33, 89-91. (92, 126).

REGULA, I., 1972. Kromatografska identifilacija alkaloida bufotenina u ljutoj koprivi (Urtica pilulifera L.). Acta Bot. Croat. 31, 109-112. (92).

RENDLE, A. B. 1917. Flora of Africa. Urticaceae: pp 241-306. (265)

RENNER, S. S. and R. E. RICKLEFS, 1995. Dioecy and its correlates in the flowering plants. American Journal of Botany 82 (5), 596-606. (255).

REQUIEN, M. 1825. Ann. Sci. Nat. 5: 384. (279)

RHEINWALD, G., 1972. Ornithol. Mitt. 24 (3), 47. (189).

RHODE, E. S., 1935. Shakespeare's wild flowers. Medici Society Ltd. London. (49).

RICHARDS, A. J., 1997. Plant Breeding Systems. Chapman & Hall. London. (254, 257).

RICHENS, R. H., 1983. Elm. Cambridge Univ Press. (9).

RIDLEY, H. N., 1930. The dispersal of plants throughout the world. Reeves & Co. Kent. (253, 274).

RINCOM, E., 1990. Growth responses of Brachythecium rutabulum to different litter arrangements. Journal of Bryology. 16, 120-122. (233).

ROBERTS, H. A. and P. M. FEAST., 1972. Fate of seeds of some annual weeds in different depths of cultivated and undisturbed soil. Weed Research 12, 316-324. (38).

ROBERTSON, P. A. and W. V. MACFARLANE, 1957. Pain-producing substances from the stinging bush Laportea moroides. Australian Journal Experimental Biology & Medical Science 35, 381-394. (84-86, 92).

ROBINSON, C. B. 1910. Philippine Urticaceae. Philippine Jnl. Sc. V, 6: pp 465-593. (265)

ROSNITSCHEK-SCHIMMEL, I., 1985. Seasonal dynamics of nitrogenous compounds in a nitrophilic weed. I. Changes in inorganic and organic nitrogen fractions of the different plant parts of Urtica dioica. Plant Cell Physiol 26:169-176. (21, 147).

ROTHSCHILD, M. and C. FARRELL, 1983. The Butterfly Gardener. Michael Joseph/Rainbird. (183).

ROUPPERT, K., 1914. Beiträge zur Kenntnis der pflanzlichen Brennhaare. Anzeiger Akad. Wiss. Cracovie, Ser. B, 887-896. (71, 73).

ROUPPERT, K., 1916. Weitere Beiträge zur Kenntnis der Pflanzlichen Brennhaare. Bull. Acad. Polon. Sci. Lett. Ser. B, 161-168. (71, 73).

ROUSSEAU, J. T., 1794. Letters on the elements of botany. p. 447. Translated T. MARTYN. , (3).

ROWAN, K., 1889. A flower hunter in Queensland and New Zealand. (45, 83).

ROYAMA, T., 1970. Factors governing the hunting behaviour and selection of food by the Great Tit (Parus major L.). Journal Animal Ecology 39, 619-659. (189).

ROYLE, F., 1855. The fibrous plants of India. (129).

SAEED, A., W. EI-ERAQY and Y. AHMED, 1995. Flavonoids of Urtica urens L. and biological evaluation Egyptian Journal of Pharmaceutical Science 36, 415-427. (40).

RUCKENBAUER, P., H. BÜRSTMAYR, AND A. STÜRTZ, 2002. The stinging nettle: Its reintroduction for fibre production IENICA Newsletter No. 15. (145-46)

SAGE, B., 1977. The Coleoptera of Skomer Island, Pembrokeshire, and their Ecology. Nature in Wales, Vol. 15., September p 184-208. (194).

SAKHARAM, J. and D. D. SUNDARARAJ, 1950. Stinging hairs of Tragia Cannabina L. F. Journal Indian Botanical Society 30, 88-91. (106).

SALISBURY, E. J., 1918. The oak-hornbeam woods of Hertfordshire, parts III and IV. Journal Ecology 6, 14. , (218).

SALISBURY, E., 1961. Weeds and Aliens. N/N Collins. London. (31, 32, 33, 206, 232).

SAXENA, P. R., K. K. TANGRI, and K. P. BHARGAVA, 1966. Identification of acetylcholine, histamine, and 5-hydroxytryptamine in GIRARDINIA HETEROPHYLLA (DECNE.). Canadian Journal Physiology and Pharmacology, Vol. 44, 621-627. (92).

SAXENA, R. R., M. C. KISHOR, and K. P. BHARGAVA, 1965. Identification of pharmacologically active substances in the Indian stinging nettle URTICA PARVIFLORA (ROXB.). Canadian Journal Physiological Pharmacology 43, 869-876. (92).

SCHACHT, H., 1856. Lehrbuch der Anatomie und Physiologie der Gewachse. Berlin, G. W. F. Muller. (75).

SCHALLER, G. B. 1963. The Mountain Gorilla. University Chicago Press. Chicago. (15).

SCHILLER, I., 1849. Principles of scientific botany. Translated E. Lankester. Longman, Brown, Green, & Longman. London. (131).

SCHLEIDEN, J. M., 1915? The solving of the problem of the stinging nettle. (110).

SCHMIDT, J. O., 1982. Biochemistry of insect venoms. Annual Review Entomology 27, 111-178. (95).

SCHMIDTKE, K., R. RAUBER AND K. KÖHLER. 1998. ertragsbildung von Fasernesseln (Urtica dioica L.). Mitteilungen der Gesellschaft für Pflanzenbauwissenschaften 1 : 107-108. (144-45)

SCHRANK, F. P., 1794. Von den nebengefässen der Pflanzen und inrem Nutzen. Halle. (Original not available). (71).

SCHULZE-TANZIL, G, DE SP, BEHNKE B, KLINGELHOEFER S, SCHEID A, SHAKIBAEI M. 2002. Effects of the antirheuatic remedy hox alpha–a new stinging nettle leaf extract–on matrix metalloproteinases in human chondrycytes in vitro. 1:Histol Histopathol. 17(2):477-85. (147)

SCOTT, W., 1771-1844. Rob Roy. (50)

SELANDER, S. 1947. URTICA GRACILIS AIT. IN FENNOSCANDIA. Svensk Botanisk Tidskrift, Bd. 41, H. 2: 264-282. (266)

SERVADEI, A., 1951. Nota sull' Heterogaster urticae F. e sul genere Heterogaster Schill. Redia 36, 171-220. (200).

SHAKESPEARE, W., 1595. (49-50, 216).

SHILLITO, J. F., 1952?. Dodders-Notes for Teachers. School Science Review, 372-381 (192).

SINGH, V, 1994. Herbal remedies for worm infestation in Kashmir Himalaya. Fitaterapia LXV (4), 354-356. (59).

SKINNER, B., 1984. Colour Identification Guide to Moths of the British Isles. Viking Books. London. (183).

SMITH, 1951. p. 106. (64).

SORSA, P. and P. HUTTUNEN, 1975. On the pollen morphology of the Urticaceae. Annales botanici fennici 12, 165-182. (247).

SOUTH, R., 1961. The Moths of the British Isles, 2 Vols. Warne London. (183).

SOUTHWOOD, R., 1986. Plant surfaces and insects - an overview. In JUNIPER, B. and R. SOUTHWOOD (Ed's), 'Insects and the Plant Surface.' Edward Arnold. London. (112).

SOUTHWOOD, T. R. E. and D. LESTON, 1959. Land and Water Bugs of the British Isles. Warne. London. (195-196).

295

SOWERBY, J. E., and Smith J.E., edited by J. G. B. Syme., 1863-1879. English Botany. 3rd edition. R. Hardwicke. London. (31, 32, 278).

SOWERS, A. E. and E. L. THURSTON, 1975. Silica incorporation in the cell wall of the stinging nettle URTICA DIOICA. Proceeding Electron Microscopic Society America 33, 584-585. (71, 72).

SOWERS, A. E. and E. L. THURSTON, 1976. The regulation of silica incorporation into the stinging cell wall of URTICA PILLULIFERA. Proceeding Electron Microscopic Society America 34, 38-39. (72).

SPENCER, K. A., 1972. Diptera, Agromyzidae. Handbooks for the Identification of British Insects 10, 5 (g). (192).

ŠRUTEK M., 1995. Growth responses of Urtica dioica to nutrient supply. Canadian Journal of Botany 73, 843-851. (224, 252, 247).

ŠRUTEK, M., 1993. Distribution of the stands with Urtica dioica L. Along the Luznice river floodplain on the border between Austria and Czechoslovakia and land management. Vegetatio 106, 73-87. (221, 236, 252).

ŠRUTEK, M., V. BAUER, L. KLIME◉ and J. PINOSOVA, 1988. Ecology of plants important in agriculture practice in Luznice River floodplain. Collection Sci. Papers Agron. Agr. Univ. in Ceské Budejovice 5, 105-118. (238).

ŠRUTEK, M., M., TECKELMANN, 1998. Review of biology and ecology of Urtica dioica. Preslia, Praha 70:1-19, (222).

STARÝ P., 1983. The perennial stinging nettle (Urtica dioica) as a reservoir of aphid parasitoids (Hymenoptera, Aphidiidae). Acta ent. bohemoslov. 80, 81-86. (201).

STELLA, M. DANTAS MD, 1999. Menopausal symptoms and alternative medicine. Primary Care Update, for OB/GYNS Vol. 6 (6):212-220.(147)

STEWART, G. R. and M.C. PRESS, 1990. The physiology and biochemistry of parasitic Angiosperms. Annual Review Plant Physiology Plant Molecular Biology 41, 127-151. (155).

STOKOE, W. J. 1958. The Caterpillars of the British Moths, 2 Vols. Warne. London. (185).

STRASBURGER, E., 1910. Sexuelle und apogame fortpflanzung bei urticaceen. Jb. Wiss. Bot. 47, 245. (71, 242, 250).

TANSLEY, A. G., 1953. The British Islands and their vegetation. Cambridge Univ. Press. (207).

TECKELMANN, M., 1987. Kohlenstoff-, Wasser- und Stickstoffhaushalt von Urtica dioica L. an natürlichen Standorten. Dissertation, Bayreuth. (147)

THEOBALD, F. V., 1892. British Flies. Elliot Stock. London. (188).

THISELTON-DYER, T. F., 1889. The Folklore of Plants. Chatto & Windus. Piccadily. (43).

THOMAS, E., (1878-1917) p. 85. (53).

THOMAS, J. and R. LEWINGTON, 1991. The Butterflies of Britain and Ireland. Dorling Kindersley. London. (171).

THOMPSON, G. M., 1922. The naturalisation of animals and plants in New Zealand. Cambridge University Press. (35, 206).

THOMPSON, K. and J. P. GRIME, 1979. Seasonal variation in the seed banks of herbaceous species in ten contrasting habitats. Journal of Ecology 67, 893-921. (231, 232).

THURSTON, E. L., 1969. An anatomical and fine structure study of stinging hairs in some members of the Urticaceae, Euphorbiaceae and Loasaceae. Ph. D. dissertation, Iowa State Univ. (71, 72, 102).

THURSTON, E. L., 1974. Morphology, fine structure, and ontogeny of the stinging emergence of Urtica dioica. American Journal Botany 61, 809-817. (69, 71, 72).

THURSTON, E. L., and LERSTEN N, R., 1969. The morphology and toxicology of plant stinging hairs. Botanical Review 35, 393-412. (71, 72, 88, 98, 103).

THURSTON, E. L., and N, R. LERSTEN, 1969. Plant stinging hairs. Botanical Review 35 (A), 393-412. (71, 72).

THURSTON, E.L., 1976. Morphology, fine structure and ontogeny of the stinging emergence of Tragia ramosa and Tragia

saxicola (Euphorbiaceae). American Journal Botany 63 (6), 710-718. (103, 104, 105).

TORTORA, G. R., and N. P. ANAGNOSTAKOS, 1990. Principles of Anatomy and Physiology. Harper Collins. New York., (94).

TOWNSEND, C. C., 1968. Parietaria officinalis & P. judaica. Watsonia 6(6), 365-370. (270, 278).

TUBERVILLE, T. D., P. G. DUDLEY and A. J. POLLARD, 1996. Responses of invertebrate herbivores to stinging trichomes of Urtica dioica and Laportea canadensis. Oikos 75, 83-88. Copenhagen. (110).

TURNER, W. S., 1961. The Phoney War on the home front. Michael Joseph. London. (142).

UNTERMEYER, L. 1920. Modern British Poetry (53)

UPHOF, J. C. T., 1968. Dictionary of Economic Plants. Lehie. Verlag von J. Cramer. Wheldon & Wesley. (129),

VERDCOURT, B., 1948. CUSCUTA EUROPAEA L. In biological flora of the British Isles. Journal Ecology 36, 358-365. (150, 152, 165).

VERDCOURT, B., 1950. The habit of CUSCUTA EUROPAEA L. in Britain. Watsonia 1. Pt. V, 291-295. (150, 152, 165).

VERKAAR, H. J., A.J. SCHENKEVELD and M. P. van de KLASHORST, 1983. Th ecology of short-lived forbs in chalk grasslands: Dispersal of seeds. New Phytologist 95, 335-344. (252).

VETTER, A., WIESER, AND G. WURL. 1996. Untersuchungen zum Anbau der Großen Brennessel (Urtica dioica L.) und deren Eignung als Verstärkungsfaser für Kunststroffe. Final report 2/1996 of the project Plants for Energy and Industry. No. 11.10.430. Thüringer Landesanstalt für Landwirtschaft, Dornburg, Germany. (145)

VICKERY, R., 1995. A dictionary of plant-lore. Oxford University Press. (62, 47, 114, 115, 156).

VIERHEILIG, H., B. ISELI, M. ALT, N. RAIKHEL, A. WIEMKEN and T. BOLLER, 1996. M Resistance of Urtica dioica to mycorrhizal colonization: a possible involvement of Urtica dioica agglutinin. Plant and Soil 183, 131-136. (163).

VISHNEVSKII, O. V. and D. V. PROSHUNINA, 1989. Farm. Zh. 2, 50-53. (126).

VOGL, C. R., HARTL, A. (2002): Dry matter and fibre yields, and the fibre characteristics of five nettle clones (Urtica dioica L.) organically grown in Austria for potential textile use. American Journal for Alternative Agriculture (17) 4: 195-200. (144-146)

VOGL, C. R., HARTL, A. (2003): Production and processing of organically grown fibre nettle (Urtica dioica L.) and its potential use in the natural textiles industry. American Journal for Alternative Agriculture 18 (3): 119-128.(144-146)

WAGNER, H., J. WILLER and B. KREHER, 1989. Planta Med. 55, 452-454. (126).

WARREN, E. J. M., 1988. Creating a Butterfly Garden. Webb & Bower. Michael Joseph. (183).

WATERHOUSE, G. M., & B. L. BRADY, 1982. Key to the species of Entomophthora sensu lato. The British Mycological Society. (194).

WATSON, H. C., 1850. Cybele Brittanica. (31).

WATT, J. M., BREYER-BRANDWISK, and G. MARIA, 1962. The medicinal and poisonous plants of southern Africa. p. 1042-1046. Livingstone. Edinburgh. (59, 63).

WEBSTER, J., 1970. Introduction to the Fungi p. 274-278. Cambridge University Press. (162, 159).

WEDDELL, H. A., 1854. Revue de la famille des Urticées. Annales des Sciences Naturelles Botanique Paris 1, ?-212. (261, 277).

WEDDELL, H. A., 1865. Monographie des Urticées. Archives du museum d'histoire naturelle IX. (9, 31).

WEDECK, H. E., 1973. Dictionary of gypsy life and lore. p. 321. Peter Owen. London. (43).

WEDEL, L.M., 1792-1796. Samlinger om Agerdyrkning og Landvaesen p. 11-15. Copenhagen. (131).

WEIß, F., 1993. Effects of varied nitrogen fertilization and cutting treatments on the development and yield components of cultivated stinging nettles. Acta Horticulturae, 331

WESTERGAARD, M., 1958. The mechanism of sex determination in dioecious flowering plants. Advances in Genetics 9, 217-281. (254, 255, 256),(146-7)

WETHERILT, H., 1992. Evaluation of *Urtica* species as potential sources of important nutrients. In CHARALAMBOUS, G. (Ed) Food science and human nutrition. Elsevier Science Publishers B. V. (40, 62, 115, 116, 117, 124).

WHEELER, K. G. W., 1981. A study of morphological and physiological differences between woodland and pastureland clones of the great stinging nettle, *Urtica dioica* L. Unpublished PhD. Dissertation Exeter University, England. (219, 220, 231-8, 225-6, 228-32, 238, 252, 257, 258).

WHITEHEAD, D. R., 1969. Wind pollination in the Angiosperms: Evolutionary and environmental considerations. Evolution 23, 28-35. (248-9).

WILKINSON, G., 1987. Epitaph for the Elm. Arrow Books. Great Britain. (9).

WILKINSON, Lady. 1858. Weeds and wild flowers. John Van Voorst. London. (4, 122).

WILLIAM, R., M. D. SOLOMON and B. S. JERRY CATHEY, 1970. Pollen of the nettles: A potential determinant of intractability in ragweed pollenosis. American Academy of Allergy 45 (2), 99. (248).

WILLIAMSON, H. A, 1951..... Chronicle of Ancient Sunlight. Volumes 1-15. Sutton Publishing. reprint 1999. (53).

WILLIS, C. L., 1969. Toxic constituents of the stinging nettle. M. S. Dissertation, Iowa State University. (103).

WILSON, M. and D. M. HENDERSON, 1966. British rust fungi. Cambridge University Press. (155).

WILSON, W. KING, 1941. Feeding dried nettles to livestock. Nature 3739, June 28, 796-798. (122).

WINKELMANN-KÜSTER, G. 1914. Das Haarkleid der Loasaceen. Diss. Erlangen. Bonn. (71, 108).

WINTERITZ, R., 1907. Einige Bemerkungen uber Urticaria arteticialis. Arch. Syphilis und Dermatol. 85, 263-270. (88).

WOODLAND, D. W., 1974. The family Urticaceae in Canada. Canadian Journal of Botany. 52, 503-516. (35, 277).

WOODLAND, D. W., J. BASSETT, C. CROMPTON 1977. The Biology of the Canadian Weeds; 21, Urtica dioica L. Can. Jnl. Of Pl. Sc. 57: pp 491-498. (266)

WOODLAND, D. W., 1982. Biosystematics of the perennial North American Taxa of *Urtica*. II Taxonomy. Systematic Botany 7 (3) 282-290. (35, 206)

WOODLAND, D. W., 1989. 17. Biology of temperate Urticaceae (nettle) family. In, CRANE, P. R. and S. BLACKMORE (eds.), Systematics Association Special Volume No. 40B, pp 309-318. Clarendon Press, Oxford. (9, 279).

WOODLAND, D. W., J. BASSETT, C. CROMPTON & S. FORGE. 1982. Biosystematics of the Perennial North American Taxa of Urtica, 1. Chromosome Number, Hybridisation, and Palynology. Syst. Bot. 7 (3): pp 269-281. (266).

WYLLIE, I., 1981. The Cuckoo. Batsford. London. (185).

YADAV, A. S. 1966. The ecology of microfungi on decaying stems of *Heracleum sphondylium*. Transactions British Mycological Society 49, 471-485. (162).

YADAV, A. S. and M. F. MADELIN, 1968. The ecology of microfungi on decaying stems of URTICA DIOICA. Transactions British Mycological Society 51 (2), 249-259. (158).

YUNCKER, T. G., 1921. Revision of the N. American and West Indian species of Cuscuta. Illinois Biological Monograph 6, pts. 2 and 3. (152).

298

Small tortoiseshells dependent on the nettle, what a joy to behold, - Hope you enjoyed the book!

Printed in the United States
by Bookmasters

Printed in the United States
By Bookmasters